Anonymous

The Connecticut quarterly

Vol. 2

Anonymous

The Connecticut quarterly
Vol. 2

ISBN/EAN: 9783337713171

Printed in Europe, USA, Canada, Australia, Japan

Cover: Foto ©ninafisch / pixelio.de

More available books at **www.hansebooks.com**

The Connecticut Quarterly.

"Leave not your native land behind." —*Thoreau.*

FIRST QUARTER.

VOL. IV. JANUARY, FEBRUARY, MARCH, 1898. NO. 1.

THE WRECK OF THE FLEET-WING.

BY HERBERT RANDALL.

Illustrated by E. T. Sherman.

THE sinuous ripples blithely sang,
  Light as the heart of May;
Soft blew the breeze from off the shore,
  The rainbows in the spray.
The shining cliffs, the dimpled sky,
  The laughing face of day,
Exultant life,—all rallied when
  The "Fleet-Wing" sailed away.

On sped the ship o'er plangent waves,
  Her pennons flying free;
Past bar and bell-buoy, rock and shoal,
  To deep and open sea;
A gallant captain ruled her helm,
  And merry lads had she;
Guitar and voices rendered night
  A mingling melody.

The swift white birds soared
   numberless;
The silver track lay wide!
So smooth it was the fishers
   cast
Their sun-browned seines
   beside.
And all that night was gossa-
   mer,
The moonshine and the tide
A-sparkle led the "Fleet-Wing"
   on;
A queenly spirit-bride.

But lo! A stormy petrel came,
   Complaining on the light;
His burnished wings thrice struck the ropes
   In his encircling flight;
And all the sea grew purple-dark,
   The sailors stood afright,
Their pallid lips averred the touch
   Had left a fateful blight.

A salt-mist settled like a pall,
   The halyards creaked, the snow
Mixed with the murky, sobbing sounds,
   The ropes flapped to and fro;
And incantative spirits seemed
   To urge the winds to blow;
The "Fleet-Wing" like an elfin rode
   The great waves, high and low.

But lurked within the rigging, wet,
The stormy-petrel's blight,
And drearer, darker, closed around
The reeling, rattling night.
The click-clack, swift-sharp-arrowed hail
Fell, mocking the dim light,
And sterner grew the challenge for
Supremacy of right.

Still upon that ridge of darkness
Rode the ship each trembling crest,
Resolute did every sailor
Bare his weather-hardened breast;
More determined, stay and tackle,
More defiant, gust and sleet,
Fiercer, louder, more chaotic
Did the thundering waters meet.

Present, past and future
hate
Centered into one great
force;
Surf and sea and tide and
fate
Grasped the "Fleet-Wing"
in her course;
Sleet and rain and gathered
winds
Of the centuries com-
bined;
Bolt on bolt the lightning
fell
Like the venging fires of
hell.

Flash and crash and cant and boom!
Roar and rush and plunge and fume!
Rockets bursting on the gloom!
　Curses! Clanging chains! "Make fast!"
"Starboard!" "Aft!" A sinking mast!
　Calls to God upon the blast!
Frenzy and a void for sleep,
　For a hymn the boiling deep.

When the ragged morning dawned
  Of the "Fleet-Wing" not a trace;
Not a scar the ocean wore
  On its wrinkled face.
Rotting in the slimy ooze
  Lies the "Fleet-Wing's" grave.
Hedged by unknown creeping things
  Is her burial place.

. . . . . .

On the beach the curlews whistle;
  Near, the fishers cast their seines;
Murmuring the breeze-kissed ripples
  Circle as the summer wanes.
Sad eyes fill with deepest meaning
  When the moaning surf complains—
Strain to catch some shadowy phantom
  On the night-wind's sobbing rains.

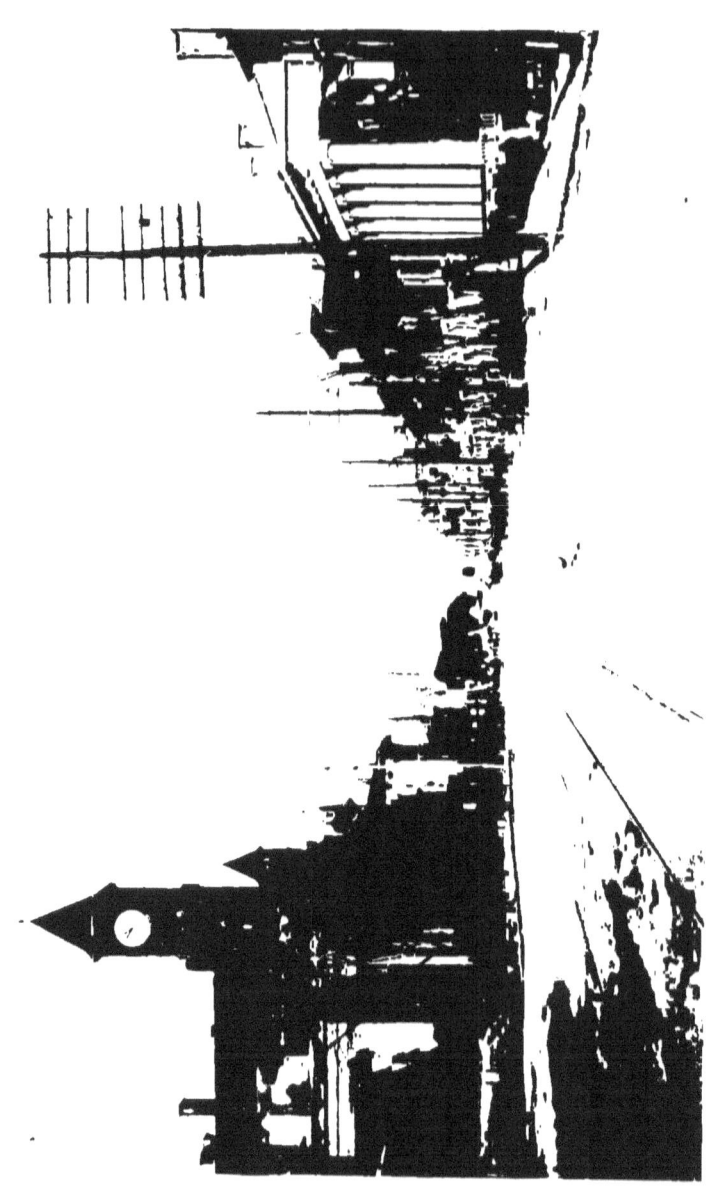

MIDDLETOWN

BY GRACE IRENE CHAFFEE.

Middletown, or Mattabesett, the Indian name by which the town was first called, was not settled for some time after the Pequot war in 1637, although there were many settlements along the sound and further up on the river. One of the causes which concurred to prevent an early settlement here was the fact that a large Indian tribe, very hostile to the English, existed at the point where Middletown now stands. Their wigwams stood thick at all places desirable for settlement. Their great sachem, Sowheag, had his stronghold on the high ground, back from the river, and his warriors were clustered thickly about him. The English were, therefore, naturally unwilling to come and settle in the vicinity of so formidable a neighbor.

But on Oct. 30, 1646, the General Court appointed a Mr. Phelps to join a committee for the contemplation of a settlement in Mattabesett. We are not expressly informed how soon and thoroughly the ground was examined, or the site for settlement fixed. The first few pages of the town records are lost, and others are nearly obliterated; consequently the names of persons, enrolled, who were preparing to occupy the land and put up dwellings, are not known. However, rapid progress was not made, and it was not until the year 1650 that actual settlement was begun. On March

THE GAYLORD PLACE.
The Oldest House now Standing in Middletown.

20, of that year, the addition was made of "Samuel Smith, senior, to the committee about the lands at Mattabeseck, in the roome of James Boosy." This committee reported that these lands might support fifteen families, but a greater number than that were soon here. These were settled north and south from Little River.

In 1651 the records state: "It is ordered, sentenced and decreed that Mattabeseck shall bee a Towne, and that they shall make choyce of one of theire inhabitants according to order in that state, that so hee may take the oath of a Constable, the next convenient season."

"It is ordered that Mattabeseck and Norwaulk shall be rated this present year in theire proporcon, according to the rule of rating in the country, for

THE JEHOSAPHAT STARR PLACE.

theire cattle and other visible estate, and that Norwaulk shall present to Mr. Ludlow, and Mattabeseck to Mr. Wells, in each Towne one inhabitant, to bee sworn by them Constables in theire several Townes."

In the autumn of 1652 the town was represented in the General Court, and in November, 1653, the name Middletown was given to "the plantation commonly called Mattabeseck." It is probable that the name of Middletown was given to the township on account of its central location, because it lay between the towns up the river and Saybrook at its mouth. In 1654 the number of taxable persons was thirty-one.

Before the commencement of the settlement, a large tract of land comprising most of the township, was given to Mr. Haynes, the Governor of Connecticut, by Sowheag, for which a small consideration was given in return. But the Indian title was not wholly extinguished until about twelve years after. Then, Sowheag having died probably, a tract of land extending from Wethersfield (then including Glastonbury, to Haddam, was, for a further and

RUSSELL LIBRARY.

full consideration, given to Samuel Wyllys and others acting in behalf of the town. The original deed was written the 24th of January, 1672, in which the Indian proprietors of the territory gave "the tract of land within the bounds of Wethersfield on the north, Haddam on the south, and to run from the great river the whole breadth toward the east six miles, and from the great river toward the west so far as the General Court of Connecticut hath granted the bounds of Middletown shall extend, with all the meadows, pastures, woods, underwood, stones, quarries, brooks, ponds, rivers, profits, commodities and appurtenances whatsoever belonging thereunto, unto the said Mr. Samuel Wyllys, Capt. John Talcott, Mr. James Richards and John Allyn, in behalf of and for the use of the inhabitants of the town of Middletown, their heirs and

THE ALSOP PLACE.

assigns forever." A small tract of land was reserved to remain the possession of the heirs of Sowheag. The original deed with thirteen Indian signatures affixed is entered in the old Court Book of records, folio 70, April 5, 1673, by John Allyn, secretary.

In the district north of the city, now known as Newfield, the Indians held lands until 1713; and the reservation laid out on Indian Hill, they retained until 1767, when, having become reduced to a a small number, they sold their right and united with the Farmington Indians.

The records of the town are so deficient, it is not known who were the first settlers. The earliest remaining entry on the town books is Feb. 2, 1652, and that is a vote for building a meeting house. From this building as a centre was laid out, in 1663, the bounds of Middletown, four miles south, five miles west and three miles east. About this meeting house clustered the dwellings of most of the settlers, at the upper end of Main street a little above Washington. A few others settled further south, at the southern end of Main street, and a portion settled in what is now Cromwell, then called the "Upper Houses," or North Society. In 1670 there were only fifty-two householders in the town, but thirty-five surnames, those being generally relatives. With two or three exceptions, these were of English extraction, coming directly from the British Isle, from towns in the eastern part of Massachusetts, or from earlier settled towns in Connecticut.

The increase of population in Middletown was very slow. There was nothing to invite a rapid immigration here at first. The country was rough,

BROAD STREET.

and the labor of cultivating even small portions of the soil was great. Markets for that which was produced were distant and difficult to reach. Imports were small, and were mostly limited to articles of necessity. The colonists suffered more from privations and hardships than we can calculate. They had little property and everything to begin anew. At first their dwellings were wretched, being hardly a shelter from the wind and rain. They had little furniture, and that of the plainest only. Their clothing was all of rude home manufacture. They were inexperienced in subduing a forest, deficient in implements for cultivating the ground, had scarcely any teams, horses, cattle or sheep. There were but few mechanics among them. An hundred pound lot was reserved to tempt a blacksmith to come among them, and it was not until Sept. 1661, that one appeared who pledged himself "to inhabit upon the land and to do the Townes worck of smithing during the term of four years, before he shall make sale of it to any other." Examination of the town records also discovers the fact that "at a towne meeting Feb. 9th, 1658, theer was granted to the shoomecker eagellston a peas of meddow that was

MAIN STREET, SHOWING POST OFFICE AND OLD COURT HOUSE.

intended for a shoomecker formerly, leying from creack to creack buting on the bogey meddow, as allso a howse lot beyond goodman meller in case not by and if by then to give him upland answerable to a howse lot and he ingaging to inhabit it seven year upon it as also doth ingag to indeevour to sut the towne in his trade for making and mending shoes." They looked to their clearings and forests for support. From the former they obtained their food and a few articles for barter; from the latter, materials for boards, staves and hoops, which were also bartered for groceries and articles of clothing.

For the next hundred years settlements were made in Westfield, Middlefield, Portland, then called East Middletown, Middle Haddam, Haddam Neck, East Hampton and other places.

In 1679 the population was increased sufficiently for the building of a new meeting house, and on the 11th of November of that year "the town by vote

THE BENJAMIN DOUGLASS PLACE.

agreed to build a new meeting house, thirty-two feet square, and fifteen feet between joints." It was erected on Main street, on the east side, about opposite what is now called Liberty street. In this all the inhabitants worshipped at least twenty-three years, and the greater part of them more than thirty-five. By 1750 there were five local parishes formed in the township, all of them Congregational, and a church was organized by the inhabitants of the first parish of Middletown and Westfield, called a "strict Congregational Church."

The early settlers were a very religious people. All attended public worship, and before they had a meeting house they worshipped God under the boughs of a tree. Their first sanctuaries were humble structures, but they were grateful for the accommodations they afforded. Not long after the settlement commenced, the people employed Mr. Samuel Stow, a native of Concord, Mass., and a graduate of Harvard College, as candidate for minister of the gospel. He preached to them for some time, but some difficulties arising in the town respecting him, a vote was passed to discontinue his ministry and look elsewhere. The difficulties came before the General Court, and a Mr. Nathaniel Collins was appointed to succeed, and was ordained Nov. 4th, 1668.

In the early settlements of Connecticut, people were assembled for public worship by the beat of a drum, and the place was guarded by armed men as a security from attacks by the Indians. The beat of the drum was necessary to collect the soldiers who acted as guard, and it also collected the congregation. Mr. Giles Hamlin gave a drum to the town, and never did a chime of bells sound sweeter. The people did not need it, that they might know the Sabbath

WASHINGTON STREET.

had come. It was on their minds through the week, and before the sun sank in the west on Saturday, worldly concerns were laid aside that their minds might be free to keep the day in a holy manner. But this told them when the time arrived for them to start for the sanctuary, and while there was danger from the Indians, when they might go in safety. A drum was used in the Upper Houses more than sixty years after the settlement began.

After the people in Upper and East Middletown had become distinct parishes, they undertook to build a new meeting house much larger than either of two houses that existed. In this church a choir was introduced. It was large and well trained. The elder President Adams, who attended worship here in 1771, says of the singing: "I heard the finest singing I ever heard in my life. The front and side galleries were crowded with rows of lads and lasses, who performed all their parts in the utmost perfection — a row of women all standing up and playing their parts with perfect skill and judgment, added a sweetness and a sprightliness to the whole, which absolutely charmed me."

It has been said that the early ministers were superior men, men of talents and learning. Mr. Collins, the first pastor, was an excellent character, whose brilliancy illuminated the whole colony. Cotton Mather wrote an elegy on him. He died in 1684, and was succeeded by the Rev. Noadiah Russell, one of the founders and trustees of Yale College. His son, Rev. William Russell succeeded him. The fourth pastor of the first church in Middletown, the Rev. Enoch Huntington, was a member of Yale College and distinguished for high scholarship. Beside the duties of his ministry, he engaged in teaching young men, preparing them for college or business. Many from abroad as well as from home vicinity, were under his tuition, and among the names of his pupils can be found those of many literary, distinguished and useful men.

COMMODORE THOMAS McDONOUGH.

Only one mode of worship, Congregational, was observed in Middletown for about a century after the settlement was commenced. The various other denominations now represented all arose after 1750.

Before leaving this period, however, mention must be made of a few eminent and influential citizens. Mr. Nathaniel White, who resided in the Upper Houses, was a man of high religious character and sound judgment. He was one of the first magistrates of the town, and held military commissions. Another whom the people delighted to honor was Mr. Giles Hamlin, as, also, his son John Hamlin, and his grandson Jabez Hamlin. Mr. Giles Hamlin was elected representative to the General Court twenty-two times. Mr. John Hamlin was a member for seven sessions, and then an assistant for twenty-six years. The excellence of Giles Hamlin may have contributed to bring forward his son John Hamlin; and his excellence combined with that of his father may have had more influence in bringing forward Jabez Hamlin. John Hamlin besides being advanced in military life to the rank of Colonel, was put into the commission of the peace as early as 1733 or 4; was a justice of the quorum for Hartford County, from 1745 to 1754, and then judge of that court thirty years. He was elected a representative to the General Assembly forty-three times, and was repeatedly Speaker of the Lower House. He was also for a time a member of the Council of Safety. He was judge of probate from the formation of Middletown district in 1752 till 1789, and mayor of this city from its incorporation in 1784 until his death. Jabez Hamlin was publicly educated and possessed a well formed and well balanced mind, unusual sweetness and uniformity of temper, and courtliness of manner. He descended to his grave, rich in the esteem of men, and beloved of his God. He is buried in the old graveyard of Middletown, lying on the banks of the Connecticut river, which is one of the oldest in the United States. His inscription reads thus: —

"In memory of the Hon. Jabez Hamlin, Esq., son of the late John Hamlin, who deceased æt. 82, April 25th, 1791, having been honored by the public confidence from youth to advanced years and employed in various grades of office until he was called to higher duties of Magistracy. After a life of great usefulness in Church and State, he died in a good old age, respected, beloved, lamented."

Ship building flourished in East Middletown about 1767, but quarrying became of more importance. The place was subsequently named Portland from Portland in England, whence freestone is transported in immense quantities

* GOLD MEDAL PRESENTED TO COMMODORE MCDONOUGH BY CONGRESS IN RECOGNITION OF HIS VICTORY ON LAKE CHAMPLAIN. OBVERSE AND REVERSE SIDES. ACTUAL SIZE.

to London and other parts of the country, as the freestone from our Portland is carried to New York and other places in the United States. As early as October 11, 1669, an entry on the town records states that "It was at ye towne meeting granted unto Mr. Adams, shipwright, for building a vessel or vessels this winter liberty to get timber upon the commons and liberty of building place so that they doe not cumber ye passage of carts to ye landing place." In 1680 but one vessel was owned, and that was only 70 tons. There was only one other on the river, a vessel of 90 tons at Hartford. The trade was carried on in these two vessels. In 1730 only two vessels were owned here; both united rated at 105 tons. There were, also, but two merchants. One of these was James Brown, an excellent Scotchman from Edinburgh, who used to cross

* "The Medallic History of the United States of America," 1776-1876, by J. F. Loubat, LL. D has an engraving of this medal. There is one also in "Lossing's Field Book of the Revolution," but the reverse side is different. We incline to think that Loubat's book is correct and give it as he has.

the country to Boston on horseback, once or more in the year, to make his contracts. Some years later there were still but three or four merchants.

But in the latter half of the seventeen hundreds, a very profitable trade was opened with the West Indies. Middletown offered great advantages for

GENERAL J. K. T. MANSFIELD.

carrying on this commerce, being situated on the largest river in New England, having a fine harbor to which vessels could ascend drawing ten feet of water, with rich towns on its banks where articles suitable for the West Indian market could be easily procured. The most successful in this trade was Richard Alsop, who had been educated a merchant in the store of Philip Livingstone in New York. He knew well how to avail himself of these advantages. He came to this town and commenced business about 1750. He had his stores in the lower rooms of the old town house, standing on Main street, a little above Washington. He engaged in commerce and prospered so much that he sometimes insured vessels for others on his private responsibility. He was a man of integrity, generosity and public spirit. His fellow citizens repeatedly elected him a representative to the Legislature. He died early in the Revolution. George Phillips, Col. Mathew Talcot and others were likewise engaged in the trade at this time.

This trade stimulated agriculture; and by this time the best lands in all the parishes were brought under cultivation, and yielded abundant crops of wheat, rye,[1] barley, oats, flax, maize, and English grasses. Great quantities of provisions, and great numbers of cattle and horses were sent to the West Indies; and great quantities of rum, sugar, molasses and salt were imported. Provisions in large quantities were sent from the river to New York, to be consumed there, or re-shipped for foreign markets, and thence various articles of merchandise were brought back in return.

THE GENERAL MANSFIELD PLACE.

The West India trade, and almost all other trade, the Revolutionary War deranged, or rather suspended, but it was resumed after the war was over.

For fifty years previous to the breaking out of the war, Middletown had become gradually more and more prosperous. The increase in agriculture, domestic manufactures and other industries which the West India trade conduced to, had the effect of rapidly increasing the population. Shipbuilding was an outcome of the growth of commerce and was carried on at many points along the river. Carpenters, blacksmiths, wheelwrights, shoemakers, etc., had multiplied to meet the requirements of the enlarged population ; and for many years the industry and frugality of the people was rewarded by prosperity. Some of the principal trad-

GUN POINT.

ers at this time were Elijah and Nehemiah Hubbard, Col. Lemuel Storrs, George and Thompson Phillips, sons of the George Phillips before mentioned, and General Comfort Sage ; Joseph W. Alsop, a younger man, also succeeded in it.

To enter into the details of the effects the war had upon Middletown, and the history of the many lives influenced thereby, would require much time. Suffice to say that Middletown took its due share in the derangement of commerce, suffering and disorder that the war carried in its wake for the next few years. Alarm and indignation was first excited by the passage of the Boston Port Bill, and the arrival of Gen. Gage in May, 1774 to enforce it by stopping the trade of that important town, and with it to a great extent, the trade of Massachusetts and New England. The House of Representatives, then in session at Hartford, passed strong resolutions against the unrighteous act, many towns did the same, and pledged their co-operation in defence of the rights of the people. On the 15th of June in this year, more than five hundred inhabitants of this town assembled and gave such a pledge.

THE OLD COURT HOUSE.

One measure, which was the subject of much consideration about this time was the breaking off from all trade with the mother country, so long as she should continue her arbitrary proceedings. How the people felt on this point is clear from an incident which occurred, when the delegates from Massachusetts were on their way to the first Continental Congress. Stopping in Middletown, Dr. Eliot Rawson, Mr. Alsop, Mr. Mortimer and others, the committee of correspondence Matthew Talcott and Titus Hosmer, Mr. Henshaw and many other gentlemen called upon them to pay their respects, and to assure them that they would abide by whatever was decided upon, even to a total stoppage of trade to Europe, and the West Indies. This assurance is the more noticable, because the wealth of the town at that time, was mainly derived from foreign commerce, and some of the gentlemen present were principals in carrying it on. Congress assembled, and formed an association for non-importation, non-exportation and non-consumption "of British goods." This measure, thus pursued here and elsewhere, was designed to show Great Britain that the Americans were determined not to submit to oppression, and that if they could not live peaceably with her, they would endeavor to live without her. Trade, therefore, was rudely interrupted, and all prosperity and progress was for the time at an end.

THE RIGHT REV. JOHN WILLIAMS

After the Revolution had come to a successful issue, commerce began to revive, althought it never afterward reached the prosperity it had enjoyed before the war. In order that commerce might be pursued to a greater advantage, a petition was signed and presented to the Legislature in 1784, that a part of Middletown, where commerce had been principally and almost wholly carried on before the war, might be invested with city privileges. The signers alleged that "many inconveniences were felt by them, as well as by strangers, for want of due regulations of the police of the town;" and that keeping the high ways in good repair, removing the ob-

RESIDENCE OF BISHOP WILLIAMS.

structions from the channel of the river and many other regulations for commercial convenience, were impossible to be accomplished without a separate and special jurisdiction. The petition was granted in May of the same year. At the same time Hartford, New Haven, New London and Norwich were constituted cities.

In 1815 there were in the city two hundred and nineteen dwelling houses, and three hundred and fifty-three families. In 1850 there were six hundred and three dwelling houses, and seven hundred and eighteen families. There were also seven Churches, four Banks, a Court-house, Gaol and Alms-house, the University buildings and a High School.

In connection with the war of 1812, one illustrious name must be mentioned, that of Commodore Thomas McDonough. He was the distinguished hero of

THE RUSSELL PLACE.

Lake Champlain. Although born in Delaware, his long residence in Middletown, and his alliance in the family of Mr. N. Shaler of Middletown, give us a claim to his memory. He received during his life numberless honors, medals and gifts from different states and towns. He was in the naval service till near the time of his death, and it was upon the sea that his death occurred, November 10, 1825. On the arrival of his remains at New York, the authorities of the city, in sympathy with the feelings of the nation, deeply mourned the loss to their country; the vessels in the harbor displayed their colors at half mast, and a detachment from the militia accompanied the hearse through the city. He is buried in the old "Riverside Cemetery" in Middletown, and his inscription reads:—

"Sacred to the memory of Thos. McDonough of the U. S. Navy. He was born in the State of Delaware, December, 1783, and died at sea of pulmonary consumption, while on his return from Command of the American Squadron in the Mediterranean on the 10th of November, 1825."

In 1861 the Civil War broke out. The news of the bombardment of Fort Sumter was the cause of great excitement in Middletown, and called forth demonstrations of loyalty and patriotism from all classes. One illustrious name, of which Middletown feels justly proud, must be mentioned in connection with this period, that of General J. K. F. Mansfield. He was one of the State's most highly esteemed citizens. His whole life was one of military ser-

ON HIGH STREET

vice. He was killed at the battle of Antietam, on the 17th of September, 1862. A special meeting of the common council was called to take action in relation to his death, and it was voted that a committee proceed to New York to escort the remains to this city; and another committee was appointed to make all necessary and proper arrangements for the funeral, which took place on the 24th of September following. He was buried with the military honors to which his rank was entitled, and the solemn occasion attracted a large gathering of people from all parts of the country.

The city is replete with historical legend. The illustration showing what is known as Gun Point is a spot up Little River with a story of Revolutionary times attached to it. The British were advancing up the Connecticut river and had arrived at Essex. The citizens of Middletown, in expectation of having their stores and ammunition pilfered, carried their guns to this point on Little River and there sunk them in order that they might not fall into the hands of the British. Hence the place derives its name of Gun Point.

The old house on Washington street, immediately behind the Stueck block, is believed to be the oldest house now standing in the city. It was known as the Gaylord house, and was erected about 1722 by Samuel Gaylord. The initials of himself and wife, S. & M., are still to be seen cut in a stone on the side of a fireplace therein.

On South Main street is the old Kilbourn house, believed to be the second oldest house in existence in Middletown. It was known formerly as the Hub-

WESLEYAN CAMPUS.

bard mansion. The land with the unfurnished house was bought by John Kent in February, 1733. He occupied it until his death in 1775. It then became the property of his daughter, wife of Elijah Hubbard, and afterward of their son, the Hon. Samuel D. Hubbard, of whom Mr. Kilbourn purchased it in 1854. There are many other old houses in town.

The manufacture of woolen cloths and fire-arms was carried on early in the century in Middletown. In 1810 the Middletown Woolen Company built a mill on Washington street and did a successful business for a number of years. It was one of the first factories in this country that used steam as a motive power. In 1814 a woolen factory on Pamecha River was started by John R. Watkinson, and continued for over twenty years. Colonel Simeon North started a pistol factory at Staddle Hill about 1810. He is said to have been the first manufacturer of pistols in this country. He had a large government contract for many years, from 1812. Oliver Bidwell commenced about 1810 on the upper Pamecha to make guns, and had a government contract. Colonel

Nathan Starr, Jr., erected a factory at Staddle Hill in 1812 and manufactured government swords, and later, muskets and rifles.

In 1850 Middletown already possessed numerous manufactories, many of them now being immense concerns. It would be impossible in this article to enter into detail, but mention must be made of some of the more important ones then existing. In Pameacha there existed the factories of H. L. Baldwin and F. Baldwin, the first making bank and store locks, the last, closet locks. Another concern making locks was the William Wilcox & Co manufactory. I. W. Baldwin had an extensive and profitable business in a sash and blind, flooring and planing mill. The Pameacha Manufacturing Company had the tweed or jean mill and a business of $20,000. Machinery, castings, iron dirt scrapers, corn shellers, plows, etc., were made at the works of William Stroud.

THE HIGH SCHOOL.

In the South Farms, the Russell Manufacturing Company, with an invested capital of $100,000, employed about two hundred operatives in the manufacture of India rubber suspenders, cotton and worsted webbing. In the city itself the establishment of W. & B. Douglas employed eighty workmen at their large pump manufactory. Jesse G. Baldwin was engaged in the silver-plating business, with thirty workmen employed. There were, besides these, many minor concerns of which none now remain. These were as follows: H. H. Graves & Co., britannia coffee and tea urns; Nathaniel Bacon, bank and safe locks; H. E. Boardman, gaiter boots; J. K. Penfield, patent grummets; Penfield & Camp, medicated liquid cuticle, a substitute for sticking plasters in surgical operations; H. Salisbury & Co., making of gold spectacles; C. F. Smith, manufacture of sand paper. There were also manufactories in Cromwell, Westfield and Middlefield. Those here catalogued which remain at the present day are much enlarged and improved, and there are numerous concerns now existing then unknown.

Middletown of to-day, as a place of residence and natural beauty, has few equals. Its wide streets, numerous trees, general healthfulness and charming location render it delightful. Picturesquely situated in the bend where the river makes its graceful turn eastward, about twenty-seven miles from its mouth, the city stands on a gentle slope, gradually stretching up west from the banks of the river to an elevation of 155 feet. It is surrounded on all sides by charming scenery, the character of the country being strikingly and pleasantly diversified. Perhaps no place in Connecticut enjoys a more lovely site, or

SOUTH GREEN, SHOWING SOLDIERS' MONUMENT AND M. E. CHURCH.

abounds more in the picturesque. It is impossible for an observing student of nature to acquaint himself with its variety of scene without being enchanted at the ravishing little picture spots that meet him everywhere. The river itself, with its windings in and out, contributes no small share to the beauty of Middletown's environment.

As a whole, perhaps the city may be best viewed from the grounds of the last new building at the State Institution for the Insane, which, standing on an eminence around which the river sweeps, commands a magnificent prospect of the whole scene in all its details to its utmost boundaries. The view of the surrrounding country, with the long line of blue hills in the far distance and the winding river immediately beneath, the city in the middle distance nestling in the bend of the river, its spires and towers peeping through a thick growth of trees, is like a panorama.

The insane asylum itself is a collection of splendid buildings and attractive grounds. In 1866 the town of Middletown granted to the state, for the purposes of a hospital, 158 acres of land, and the cornerstone of the original building was laid June 20, 1867. The institution has been enlarged from time

CONNECTICUT HOSPITAL FOR THE INSANE.
Main Hospital.

to time, so that 400 acres of land are now occupied. It is one of the largest institutions of its kind in the world.

Wesleyan University is located in Middletown. It was chartered in 1831. Although it is under the patronage of the Methodist church, it is not a sectarian school. It is well situated at the highest part of the city and occupies extensive grounds. The five principal buildings— North College, South College, Chapel, Library, and Orange Judd Hall, all of stone and of fine architecture, stand in a line on the front campus facing High street and extending from

CONNECTICUT HOSPITAL FOR THE INSANE.
Middle Hospital.

College street beyond William. Beside these buildings are others in the rear; an observatory and its transit house, the physical and electrical laboratories, a large and elegant gymnasium erected in 1894, beside the residence of the president of the college in one corner of the campus, and Webb Hall, the ladies' dormitory, opposite. There are also many elegant society club-houses in connection with the college, which in beauty of architecture contribute largely to the adornment of the city. The illustration showing High street gives a small view of Webb Hall, the Psi U and the D. K. E. club-houses.

Berkeley Divinity school occupies a large area at the corner of Main and Washington streets. Beside the school proper, chapel and library, there is also the residence of the Rt. Rev. John Williams, bishop of Connecticut and senior bishop of the Episcopal church in the United States.

In the southwestern portion of the town stands the Connecticut Industrial School for Girls. It is a private institution under the patronage of the state. It was among the first institutions of its kind organized in the United States. It was incorporated in 1868, received its first inmates January, 1870, and was formally opened the 30th of June following.

Middletown has improved rapidly within the last few years. The old court house, built in 1832, has been torn down and a handsome new municipal building erected in its place. A large and elaborate new high school has been built on the corner of Pearl and Court streets, in which the city feels a just pride. Many other improvements are noticeable. Middletown is undoubtedly awakening from the lethargy which has characterized it for so many years. It has been termed, and perhaps not inappropriately, "the graveyard of Connecticut." But the name will apply no longer. Our quiet but beautiful little town has awakened to a tardy recognition of its advantages, and an activity heretofore unknown now marks it.

A REVOLUTIONARY THANKSGIVING.

A True Story of Olden Time.

BY DANIEL DOANE BIDWELL.

Winter had settled in early. It had come with a rush, chasing away unceremoniously the dreary, effeminate, Indian summer days, and substituting a sharp, crisp cold which sent the blood coursing through the veins with a vigor leading old Gran'ther Aaron Olmsted to announce that he felt "fit to fight the Britishers." The cider had been stored in a dozen barrels in the shadows of the north cellar, the corn was husked and was sleeping in its crib, and the big pumpkins lay in yellow waves on the barn floor.

The old Olmsted homestead stood on the west side of the wide village street, in East Hartford, a highway now over-arched by three rows of leafy elms—noble centennarians whose aged boughs, interlocking, form two grand Gothic arches. It was a scanty half-mile from the Great River. Its upper windows commanded one of the fairest views in Connecticut Colony. A narrow fringe of wooded upland reached westward to a rich meadow bordered by a sweeping curve of the Great River. Beyond, a second meadow stretched to the stores of outlying farm-houses of Hartford. Islanded against the cold blue of the November sky and the russet and gold of the late autumnal foliage, rose the steeple of the First Church of Christ in the colony's northern capital.

It was a hospitable mansion in which the Olmsted family were to collect. Lengthwise it stood to the street and two good stories high with the gambrel roof—changed later to a gable. A ponderous brass knocker, polished till it gleamed, hung on the mammoth front door, which was divided horizontally. A gigantic chimney permitted fireplaces in the lower story rooms and in two of the chambers. In the rear was a long ell, over whose roof rose a long well-sweep. It may be said, parenthetically, that the first piano in East Hartford was consumed when the house burned, in 1876. For a week or more the children in the Olmsted household had been pounding cinnamon and cloves in a gigantic lignum-vitæ mortar, and chopping suet and meat for mince pies, and stoning raisins and slicing citron, and making the rafters of the old colonial homestead echo with the busy preparation for that apostle of festivals—Thanksgiving.

Those sturdy days were still half a century or so earlier than the introduction of prepared spices. It was almost in the crude state that the material used for seasoning came to the kitchen. Its reduction from raw material to culinary ammunition was assigned to the army of children as their natural obligation. On those youngsters who had been "froward" was laid the penalty of preparing a salt, evolving it by the ascending steps of washing, drying and pounding, from primitive rock-salt. For a week the main business of mankind in the little Puritan theocracy had been the secular duty of making pies. By dozens and scores these had come forth daily from the kitchen and been consigned to the icy cavern of "the north room." Seemingly, they were made of anything vegetable or animal that is on the earth or in the waters under the earth.

Early on Thanksgiving morning all sorts and conditions of Olmsteds, even to the third and fourth generation, began to arrive. The homestead was the rallying point of Gran'ther Aaron from all over the colony. It was hoped that two score would sit down to the dinner which would be awaiting the family on their return from "meetin." Of the six sons of the white-haired grandsire all were to be on hand at the hospitable board saving Captain Gideon, who was a prisoner to the red-coats in the West Indies, unless perchance he was in Davy Jones' locker. Of the six daughters, all with their families were to attend. Of the third generation no fewer than twenty-seven were to pay their tribute to the turkeys and pies, and of the fourth there were two, little Mehitable Burnham, just a twelvemonth old, and Pardon Olmsted, three months younger. With the early morning began to arrive other individuals also—individuals not so desirable. Various loafers from the quiet country-side straggled 'round the skirts of the rambling colonial mansion, and stopped in the lean-to and the wood-shed which led off from the savory kitchen. As the morning wore on they departed, laden with jugs and brimming pitchers of cider, given to them by Gran'ther Aaron's ungodly grandson, Nehemiah, or with turkey drumsticks and pies of divers kinds, the gifts of stout Mistress Olmsted. Among the beneficiaries were some of the few remaining Indians of the neighborhood, miserable, squalid, half-drunken creatures, stigmatized by that most withering of Puritan adjectives, "shiftless." There was also a visitor whom the children and even their parents regarded with curiosity, mingled in some measure with apprehension. This was a youth of swarthy complexion and foreign and mysterious appearance, who had come with a party of horse traders that had pitched their tents on Bidwell's Lane some days previously, announcing that they were trading and buying horses to deliver to General Washington at Morristown, to recruit the continental cavalry. There were not lacking those who "suspicioned them 'ar traders were as like to wring the necks of gobblers as to buy horses."

When the bell of the village meeting-house began to remind the people of duties spiritual the army under the Olmsted roof-tree was ready to respond to its invitation. Nehemiah Olmsted and Ozias Bidwell, two of the third generation, were left in charge of the homestead when the reunited family filed soberly down to the meeting-house. The two young clansmen were placed on this detail not so much because they were the most reliable for that duty, but the more because well-grounded apprehensions were entertained regarding their froward conduct in the temple and consequent rebukes from Levi Goodwin, the tithing-man. They were fit predecessors of the Comstock Cavalry of a later day. When good, old, logical Parson Williams had reached his seventhly and had consequently become well started on his sermon, the two young harem scarems left in charge of the family fort had wearied of their labors as an investigating committee. They had examined the yawning depths of the brick oven, raided the buttery and pantry, hidden Gran'ther Aaron's gold-headed walking stick, loosened the king-bolts on five of the family chaises in which the Olmsted progeny had journeyed to the mansion, introduced unnecessary pepper into the star chicken-pie, doubled in half-sections the lower sheet in each bed, and employed their mischievous ingenuity in every fertile prank and trick which their active boyish minds could devise.

As they sat in the low-ceiled kitchen, sighing for new worlds of deviltry, two figures darkened the passageway leading in from the lean-to. Looking up they saw first the swarthy horse-trader who had left in the early morning freighted with a pitcher of cider, drawn by Nehemiah's own grimy hands, and with two of Mistress Olmsted's famous pies. Behind the trader was one of his companions from the camp on Bidwell's Lane.

"Is it hungry ye are again?" was Nehemiah's salutation. "It is, young sir," was the reply, in a foreign accent.

"Sit down then, if ye be so minded, and we will feed you."

Nehemiah motioned with a wave of his hand towards a settle. He produced a plate and heaped it with steaming potatoes and turnips, and dexterously whipped off two drumsticks from one of the six turkeys which were to feed the convened clans, saying as he layed the edibles before his visitors: "Begin on them two scalps."

Presently a felicitous idea occurred to Ozi, who had cut a big wedge from the erring chicken-pie, in which the boys had inserted a double allowance of pepper. This he carefully chose from the section which the youngsters had spiced. Laying it on one of Mistress Olmsted's choicest plates he presented it to the second of his callers, and then deemed it seemly to withdraw to the seclusion of the pantry. Thither Nehemiah discreetly followed him. In a few seconds the lads were rewarded for their industry by the sound of violent sneezing mingled with strange foreign oaths. Looking out they discerned their victim gesticulating fiercely. In a short time they saw him approaching their hiding place. Seeing that he would be discovered, Ozi made a virtue of necessity, and emerged from his retreat to enquire solicitously, "Be ye ill?"

With a threatening sweep of his hand the man demanded milk or cider to wash down the pepper. "Give him both together," advised Nehemiah, under his breath, but Ozi was content with proffering a mug of cider. At that moment was heard the sound of wheels approaching on the road. Hastily gulping down the liquid, the boys' visitor rushed with a valedictory sneeze from the kitchen and out of the lean-to. The lads followed him and then turned with cheerful faces to welcome Gran'ther Aaron, who was depositing a load from the family chaise.

A few seconds later startled exclamations summoned them to the dining room. Mistress Aaron and a half-score of female Olmsteds were pointing to the table, where crumpled linen and missing knives and forks betrayed the operations of an invader.

"Look yonder," cried the good old lady: "What did I tell you!" she continued in prophetic frenzy. "They've let in some thief, who has stolen our silver. 'Twould have been better to have disgraced our family before the tithing man than have let this come to pass!"

Explanations were given in short order, and the male Olmsteds repaired as a sort of committee of the whole to the camp on Bidwell's Lane.

The gypsies were on the point of striking their tent, but a few minutes of salutary persuasion by Gran'ther Aaron and constable Timothy Bryant, supported by the evidence of the two boys, resulted in the recovery of the articles which had been stolen by the confederate of the victim of the medicated chicken-pie.

As for Nehemiah and Ozias, it is said that they have transmitted their deviltry to their descendants, but it may be nothing more than the fact "that boys do not seem to change as much as men."

THE HOME OF TIMOTHY AND JONATHAN EDWARDS.

BY MARY SEABURY STARR.

As one strolls through the heavily shaded streets of South Windsor, an appreciation of comfortable thriftiness overspreads him. Even the great elms, knarled and weather-beaten by the forces of a hundred years, breathe from their swaying branches a suggestion of sturdy resistance, crowned by the dignified bearing of proud old age. From the hollow trunks and mutilated limbs of these landmarks of history we can weave the story of the Hessian soldiery, prisoners of the Revolution. A merry lot of young fighters they must have been, for the streets of the quiet town echoed with the sounds of horse-racing, and the bright coins of the gambling table glistened before the eyes of our Puritanical forefathers. At Lafayette's command these naughty disturbers of the peace were set to work planting three rows of tiny elms to line the thoroughfare, unconsciously setting up for themselves rugged monuments to a defeated cause.

On either side of the roadway, broad fields of waving vegetation form a restful variety of changing color. Long stretches of tobacco, stiff and tropical in form and deep in tone, contrast with the easy swaying of a field of grain, bright from the rays of the summer sun and intensified by the background of heavy woods. Over yonder lie the flat stretches of meadow land, quiet and motionless, save for the occasional glimpse of a group of hay cutters or the

STREET VIEW, EAST WINDSOR HILL.

lazy movement of a herd of cattle. This picture of peaceful prosperity is framed by the purple mass of the Farmington hills. The faint lines in the distance are dimmed by the August haze, sometimes losing themselves in the blue of the heavens which seem to entice the fading forms into the uncertainty of space. It is a dreamy, restful picture, and if one cares to call up suggestions of a buried past, the silent "God's acre" at East Windsor Hill will transmit to the busy mind the strange charm of its atmosphere laden with the mysterious stillness of its unwritten history. The sinking stones are moss-covered and cracked, sometimes leaning against one another for support, sometimes wholly covered by the persistent weeds or the clinging blackberry vines.

HOUSE OF TIMOTHY EDWARDS.

Near the center of this crumbling spot is a long stone tablet bearing the following inscription:

In memory of Rev. Timothy Edwards
Paftor of 2nd society in Windsor
(whofe fingular Gifts and piety rendered
him an excellent, and in the judgment of
Charity by the bleffing of heaven, a
fuccefsful minifter of the Gofpel)
who died January ye 27th Ad 1758
in the 89th year of his age and 64th of
his miniftry—and his remains
bury'd under this stone

AN EPITAPH:

The man of God who nobly pled
His Mafter's Cause alafs! is dead
His Voice no more!—but awful Urn
Still speaks to Men their great Concern
His Praise on Souls by Heaven impreft
This mouldering Stone will long but laft
When Grace completes the Work begun
Bright Saints will fhine his living Crown.

HOME OF TIMOTHY AND JONATHAN EDWARDS. 35

The name of Timothy Edwards stands out strong and clear in the annals of early Connecticut. The little colony of settlers broke ground at Windsor in 1635. We all know something of their struggle for life. The banks of " Ye Great River" were a favorite hunting ground for the Indians, and although the new comers found favor in the sight of the red-skinned warriors, nevertheless that treacherous twist of the Indian character caused the pale-faced colonist to be ever on the alert for the war whoop. Despite the hardships and dangers the brave little band struggled on, building its church and making its laws.

The town of Windsor included a tract of land some ten or twelve miles in

SITE OF TIMOTHY EDWARDS' HOME.

area, divided by the Quonetakut River into equal parts. The first settlement was on the west side, at what is now Windsor, but the meadows across the bright water furnished tempting pasture land for the cattle, and before many years had passed a few of the more adventurous members broke loose from the mother settlement and cast their lot among the Podunks and Scantics.

For some twenty-five years the old settlement was considered as home When the blasts of "ye trumpet" echoed beyond the waters, the few offspring colonists would brave the drifting ice cakes of winter or battle with the rising freshets of summer, their light canoes making dangerous marks for the arrow- heads of the tawny foe, as they obeyed the distant summons, whether for prayer or battle.

Rude houses sprang up along the bank of the hill which overlooked the fertile meadows, and the new life was passing outside the narrow limits of childhood, when the advancement was stopped by the battle cries of King Philip's War (1675).

Cut off from the mother colony and surrounded on all sides by infuriated savages, the doom of the pale-faces seemed sealed. Many of them removed to the protection across the river, leaving the more daring of their comrades to build a fort as a meagre refuge against the ravages of the Scantics.

Distant echoes of this troublesome past have come down to us on the wings of tradition, weaving for our imagination hasty sketches of that far-off struggle. The war was a short one, and better days were in store for the colonists of the Windsor Farmes.

In 1680 a petition was made to the assembly for the privilege of supporting a separate minister and of building a new church. For fourteen years the petition was refused, as the rich land of the meadows formed a paying supplement to the little town of Windsor. However, the fifty families of the Farmes were persistent in their clamorings, and the mother town at last ceded the request.

DOORWAY TO GRANT HOUSE, EAST WINDSOR HILL.

In 1694, "It was granted that all those on the west side of the river that have estate in land or otherwise on the east side, their estate shall be rated to the ministry of the west side, and this order to take no place till they of the east side have a minister settled among them, and to continue no longer than they do keep a minister there."

In 1697, "It was voated also that Mr. Edwards should be called to offise as soon as conveniently may be, and those that are male church members do treat with him respectin' that matter."

About this struggling community Timothy Edwards cast the influence of his power, drawing many an unruly nature unconsciously within the radius of his wonderful personality.

Wales was the original home of the Edwards family, but history confuses the distant line of their descent. The father of Timothy Edwards was one Richard Edwards of Hartford, "a respectable merchant and an exemplary Christian." In the Connecticut Historical Society's rooms at Hartford may be seen a curious yellow manuscript. The cover is torn and the neatly written pages are defaced in places, but the precise old-fashioned writing is easily discernable, giving us a living picture of this same thriving merchant in the language of his son. It is entitled, "Some things concerning my dear and honored father, Mr. Richard Edwards, late of Hartford, deceased, who departed this life in the comfortable hopes of a glorious resurrection to life again April 20, 1718, on a Sabbath day, about singing time in the forenoon, aged, according to his own statement, within about a fortnight or three weeks of 71, or within a very little of it at least."

It then goes on to describe his personal appearance as follows : "He was of middle height, rather taller than shorter than men of ordinary pitch, of a straight, well-shaped body, not corpulent but rather sparse and slender with a good proportion and symmetry in its parts. He had, especially in his younger years, a very good head of hair and comely countenance. Since I can remember, he was, at least in my eyes, as pleasant a man to look upon as most I have seen, and he had a smile that made him (upon occasion) appear with a still more graceful and amiable aspect, for it had a pleasantry in it beyond what I have seen in many—yea, most others."

Timothy Edwards was born May 14, 1669. He was given all the advantages which the new country offered. Harvard was then the only college in New England, and from there he received on the same day his two degrees of bachelor and master of arts, "which was an uncommon mark of respect paid to his proficiency in learning." Long hours were spent in the study of theology, and the young minister had laid a substantial foundation for the hard task of his life work. Despite the stern conditions of his surroundings he had already succumbed to Cupid's arrow and his Psyche was realized in the beautiful Esther Stoddard, daughter of the Rev. Solomon Stoddard of Northampton. Perhaps this student of young Harvard had sought relaxation from the society of classic poets or early theologians with the merry girls of the Boston boarding school, amongst whom was Esther Stoddard. Probably these college days were interwoven with Timothy Edwards' courtship. In November, 1694, he was married, and a few days later the substantial two-story house, the gift of Richard Edwards, opened its doors to the bonny bride. Work on the meeting-house was pushed forward, and by 1696 a rough building was completed in the corner of what is now the old burying ground. Close at hand was the fort, and, while the pilgrims offered up their silent prayers, one ear was kept open for the yell of the savages. Timothy Edwards' house was a little distance towards the south, across the street. Even now the old well from which little Jonathan quenched his thirst may be seen, although the house was torn down during the early days of this century. It was a well-made building of more than ordinary size, long and narrow and low. Off toward the west were the waving meadows and glistening Connecticut. On the other side the land sloped gently away toward a noisy little brook at the edge of the dense forest which stretched away toward the east in black uncertainy.

We are inclined to picture these forefathers of ours as treading a moral path of painful straightness, looking neither to the right nor to the left for relaxation from the stern calls of rigid discipline. If we glance in fancy for a few moments through the diamond-shaped panes of the Edwards house on the night of the "ordination ball," we will find

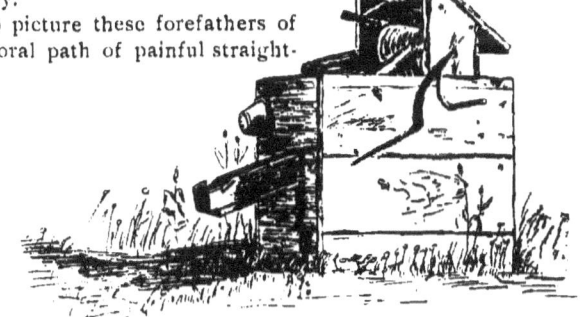

THE OLD WELL.

our mouths watering for the good things to eat, sent by the neighbors, and our feet beating time to the music. We will long to catch an echo of the thrilling tales of the weather beaten group about the great fire-place, or to join in the more quiet gossip of the women, grouped together on the broad bench about the wall and watching the movements of the young host and his pretty

38   HOME OF TIMOTHY AND JONATHAN EDWARDS.

bride in their quaint dress of long ago. It is a pleasant suggestion of good comradeship on the outskirts of the howling wilderness, a bright little spot peering out of the dreary background.

The early years of missionary work were trying ones. The Indians were tireless in their attacks, and there were trifling dissensions among the colonists, many of whom were rough adventurers, daring in spirit and wholly uncouth in manner. The seating of the meeting-house was a source of miserable contention. At last the following rules were made and peace was partly restored to the rural atmosphere, May 27, 1724: "There being a general dissatisfaction with the seating of the meeting-house, it was ordered to be reseated and the rules adopted by vote were:

" 1. That shall be 1 head to a man and age and estate, to take it from the building of the meeting-house until now.

" 2nd. That the men shall sit on the men's side and the women on the women's side and it shall be counted disorder to do otherwise.

" 3rd. That the seaters shall fill up all the seats with young persons viz, where the married are not seated."

THE CONGREGATIONAL CHURCH, SOUTH WINDSOR.

Roger Wolcott, the future governor, heads the list on the new seating roll.

The path of the young preacher was not strewn with roses. His natural sympathies were far away from the agricultural life, and the primitive civilization about him grated upon his sensitiveness. It was hard for the struggling parish to eke out even the small salary demanded of them, and the family beneath the sloping roof of the pastor's house was a large one. Amongst the

HOME OF TIMOTHY AND JONATHAN EDWARDS. 39

eleven children, Jonathan, the fifth child, was the only son. The father of this little flock was wont to say "that his sixty feet of daughters must be clothed," and sometimes it was difficult to find the wherewithal. A little school was started at the parsonage and it soon became famous throughout the land, and no examination for college was considered necessary if the candidate came from under Mr. Edwards' care. As the daughters finished their education in Boston, where they were all sent, each one found their place on the staff of teachers.

In 1711, when the little Jonathan was eight years old, the distant war cry resounded throughout the land, and Timothy Edwards went as chaplain on an expedition designed for Canada. The fleet of about twenty men-of-war

STREET VIEW, SOUTH WINDSOR.
Showing elms planted by the Hessians.

reached Albany August 15, 1711, after a tedious voyage. The following letter has come down to us, written at a discouraging time, but filled with words of tenderness which gave new enthusiasm to the anxious family at the East Windsor home.

" *To Mrs. Esther Edwards, on the East side of the Conn. river in Windsor:*

" . . . Whether I shall have any time to write to you after this, I know not ; but however that may be, I would not have you discouraged or overanxious concerning me, for I am not so myself. I have still strong hopes of seeing thee and our dear children once again. I cannot but hope that I have had the gracious presence of God with me, since I left home, encouraging and strengthening my soul, as well as preserving my life. I have been much cheered and refreshed respecting this great undertaking, in which I verily expect to proceed and that I shall before many weeks are at an end see Canada.

"Remember my love to each of the children—to Esther, Elizabeth and Mary, Jonathan, Eunice and Abigail. The Lord have mercy on them and save them all—with our dear little Jerusha. The Lord bind up their souls with thine and mine in the bundle of life.

"Though for a while we must be absent from each other, yet I desire that we may often meet at the throne of grace in our earnest prayers for one another, and have great hopes that God will hear and answer our prayers.

"The grace of God be with you.
"I am thy loving husband,
"TIMOTHY EDWARDS."

Scraps from another letter show us that the weeds were not suffered to grow in the path to knowledge trodden by the boy Jonathan.

August, 1711. "I would have Jonathan keep what he hath learnt in his Grammar and I would have none of them forget their writing." Again: "I desire thee to take care that Jonathan don't lose what he hath learnt but that as he hath got the accident and about two sides of 'Propria quæ maribus' by heart so that he keep what he hath got I would therefore have him say pretty often to the girls. I would also have the girls keep what they have learnt of the Grammar and get by heart as far as Jonathan hath learnt, he can keep them as far as he had learnt—and would have both him and them keep their writing, and therefore write much oftener than they did when I was at home. I have left paper enough for them which they may use to that end."

JONATHAN EDWARDS.

The expedition failed in its attempt, and, after two years, Timothy Edwards returned home sick and exhausted. Again he gathered up the reins of discord and again by the pure words of his teaching he sought to instill new hope into the hearts of his tired flock.

His sermons are full of vital force, well rounded by the breadth of learning. He preached the story of a substantial hell and of a perfect peace.

Amidst these strange conditions of circumstance the character of Jonathan Edwards was moulded. His home life was carefully guarded by the refined influences of his mother and of his little army of sisters, while the strong hand of his father was ever stretched out to help him. Beyond the high sill of the parsonage were only crude beginnings, and yet, from the very center of these primitive surroundings, came the boy who was to become one of the greatest conquerors of human thought. He was a poetical, dreamy lad, easily moved by the sights and sounds of that world of uncultivated nature about him. He loved to wander along the brook by the edge of the forest and he was subject to strange religious impressions. When a mere child he and a couple of comrades erected a booth in a swamp close by and retired to it each day for prayer. The two little comrades were willing enough to drive the nails, but when the next chapter of the episode was disclosed, we can hardly believe that their boyish fancies would allow them to leave the butterflies and dancing sunbeams for quiet meditation. I suspect that the little Jonathan was left to solitary reflection.

When scarcely beyond the age of babyhood the originality of his thoughts is very impressive, and the letter which he wrote when only twelve years old

THE OLD CEMETERY AT EAST WINDSOR HILL.

is strikingly unnatural in its deep suggestions. Someone had stated that the soul was material and dwelt in the body until the resurrection. The idea impressed the thoughtful little listener as ridiculous. His reply is full of a hidden humor:

"I am informed y^t you have advanced a notion y^t the soul is material & keeps wth ye body till ye resurrection, as I am aprofest lover of novelty you must alow me to be much entertained by this discovery. 1st I w^d know whether this material soul keeps wth in ye Coffin and if so whether it might not be convenient to build a repository for it in order wch I w^d know w^t shape it is of whether round, triangular or foresquare or whether it is a number of Long fine strings reaching from y^r head to y^r foot and whether it dus not Live a very discontented life. I am afraid when y^r coffin Gives way ye earth will fall in and crush it but if it should chuse to Live above Ground and hover about ye Grave how big it is whether it covers all ye body or is assined to y^r head or breast we it dus when another body is Laid upon y^t. Souls are not so big but y^t 10 or a dozen of you may be about one body, whether yy will not quarril for ye highest place."

The paper on spiders, also written at the age of twelve, has become famous as a bit of childish literature. The following small selection from the long article will serve as an illustration of the logical reasoning and observance of the boy:

"Especially late in the afternoon may these webs that are between the eye and that part of the horizon that is under the sun be seen very plainly, being advantageously posited to reflect the rays and the spiders themselves may be very often seen travelling in the air, from one stage to another, amongst the trees, in a very unaccountable manner. But I have often seen that which is much more astonishing. In very calm and serene days in the fore mentioned time of year, standing at some distance behind the end of a house or some other opaque body so as just to hide the disk of the sun and keep off his dazzling rays and looking along close by the side of it, I have seen a vast number of little shining webs and glistening strings brightly reflecting the sun-

GRAVESTONE OF TIMOTHY EDWARDS.

beams, and some of them of great length and of such a height that one would think they were tacked to the vault of the heavens and would be burnt like tow in the sun, and make a very beautiful pleasing as well as surpassing appearance. It is wonderful at what distance these webs may plainly be seen. Some that are at a great distance appear several times as big as they ought so great doth brightness increase the apparent bigness of bodies at a distance as is observed of the fixed stars."

Yale, at this time, was just springing into notice. The infancy of the college was an uneasy one. During this uncertain period our dignified Institution of Learning was tossed from pillar to post, resting at New Haven, Wethersfield or Hartford, as the case might be.

It was to this unsettled school that Jonathan Edwards was sent at the age of thirteen. Here, as his path lengthens beyond the narrow limits of his first home, we will leave him, with his future still dim before him, merely pausing to roughly sketch the outline of his maturer life.

The years which followed were a stormy contrast to the protected surroundings of childhood. His disposition was not an enviable one, although from his own concise definition of his character, self-esteem can scarcely be numbered among his faults:

"I possessed a constitution in many respects peculiarly unhappy, attended with flaccid solids, vapid, sizy and scarce fluids and a low tide of spirits, often occasioning a kind of childish weakness and contemptibleness of speech, presence and demeanor."

His long ministry at Northampton ended in unfortunate controversy and he was forced to resign his charge, removing to Stockbridge, Mass., where he labored for eight years among the Housatonnuck Indians. Here he wrote his famous articles on "The Freedom of the Will." From the reputation which this work brought to him he was offered the presidency of Princeton College. He lived long enough to merely enter upon his duties there, dying March 28, 1758.

Only two months before Timothy Edwards was laid to rest in the little cemetery at East Windsor, close by the church to which he had willingly devoted the busy years of his long life.

The record of his tireless activity forms one of the purest pages in the history of those days.

During his last years his work was somewhat lightened by the help of an assistant, so that he was able with a greater degree of comfort to enjoy that home life which was ever so dear to him.

The solid doors of the parsonage were always open to the little flock of grandchildren.

The blazing logs on the fire-place offered a crackling accompaniment to the tales of pioneer life. About the bent figure of the white-haired old man was often clustered an eager band of small listeners.

The neglected cemetery, the theatre of these scenes of long ago, is now surrounded by a white picket fence which seems to serve as a barrier between the past and the present, separating the cloudy atmosphere of far-off beginnings from the highly cultivated sphere of our reality.

SORROW.

BY SALLY PORTER LAW.

When Sorrow spreads her sable cloak
About our shoulders bowed and bent,
And bids us follow where she leads,
Until our strength is well nigh spent,
'Tis then we turn to Thee, oh God,
And heav'nward lift our streaming eyes
In mute appeal, with aching hearts,
And beg Thee listen, ere Hope dies.

SABRINA'S TEA CUPS.

BY SARAH L. L. CASE.

"Say, dear, you don't really dislike the name of Sabriny, do ye? Cousin Hiram, he used to quote something from one of the poets about some 'Sabrenah,' he called it, 'sitting knittin' lilies in her hair,' an' I used to think it sounded pretty. I always meant you should have something for your name, an' I mean to. I'll settle it right away."

Thus said old Miss Elder as she struggled out of a 'bad turn,' looking up into the anxious face of Sabrina the younger, bent over her.

It was out Litchfield way in a lonely hillside farmhouse, the loneliest of them all, the home for seventy years and more of the old lady who was nearing to the "end of the road, however long it be."

The late sunshine of an October day streamed in through the few flickering leaves of the yellowed maple outside, through the blindless window, glanced at the dying fire and seemed to linger on Miss Elder's wasted hands as she sat propped up against the pillows.

"All a-dying, ain't we, Sabriny?" she panted to the plump little matron, "the day an' the fire an' the beauty o' the year an' I sure enough—there now, you needn't mend the fire, I ain't chilly—less you be."

Sabrina Morse settled back in the rocker comfortably. She had fixed up the room till it shone with the neatness of the old days when Miss Elder was in her prime "and kept things goin' wonderful," according to the neighbors, "with no man about 'cept Alec, an' he did'nt amount to no more'n a pasley patch."

Alec was the only relative she had in the world, and "shif'less," to be sure; after his marriage to French Canadian Leonie he had departed, but for some months of his aunt's wasting illness was at the old homestead again, on the farm of many acres which he knew was to be his own when its present owner should enter upon the better inheritance.

The quieting potion and the gruel had been administered and still the patient would talk.

The sunset rays fell across the trembling hands stretched out on the bright patchwork quilt, and feebly rubbing them together, "There shall I bathe my weary soul in seas of heavenly rest—so, only more so," she said, as she basked in the yellow light and listened to the tap tap of the leaves softly blown against the window. "No pantin' an' fightin' for breath pretty soon for me." Then looking at the knotted homeliness of her poor hands, from which the idleness of a few months had not effaced the marks of years of heavy work, she rambled on: "To think I am going to have hands belongin' to me young an' limber an' ready for playin' on harps an' viols—if that is goin' to be the next duty, an' plenty o' voice for singin', don't seem like it, does it? I've had to fight for a bare livin'—but there! thank the Lord, I ain't beholden to nobody, never was, never will be. I never did lop down on anybody's help but my own—only you're so good, Sabriny, a nussin' me up. An' Sabriny Morse, while I have what I have, an' a mite o' breath, I want it settled right sure 'bout my chiny teacups. Doctor'll be comin' round this evenin'—it's his day, an' he ain't been in sence last week, an' he'll be on hand to see 'em signed an' sealed an' delivered—yes, he's here now," she laughed. Her quick ears had caught the rattle of the doctor's gig coming over Gully Brook down the highway.

"Now, Sabriny, be sure and call the children in—Alec an' Linnie, 'fore the doctor goes, 'cause I want to say something."

Almost as broad and smiling as the sun-bath about them—as doctors should be—entered the doctor, blithe in manner and face most comforting to the two women. The professional greeting and inquiry and advice over, after a while he seconded his patient's wish that Alec and his wife come in.

Now, with a solemn air, Aunt Sabrina said: "I ain't never made any will, I haint much to leave anyway, but you all know just how 'tis. I've just come to this old place, you know how I've labored early and late to keep it as Granther left it, and now the mortgage is riz, paid up every cent on it, an' it'll go in the natural way to Alec, my nephew—yes, to you, Alec, and your heirs.

"But I want to say just now an' here that them cups in the corner cupboard, them Davenport cups, yaller an' gilt, an' the sarcers an' plates, I want Sabriny Morse to have for her name, that her ma who was my best friend when we was young, named her for my sake.

"'T don't seem so very long either, Sabriny, 't we was young girls together —an' not long neither since she was a-settin' in that very chair where you're a-settin' now, with you a teenty little mite of a red-haired baby in her lap, an' a-tellin' me your new name. A pretty baby you was, too—I never liked red hair before, but I always liked your'n. But about the namin', I thought I'd do something for you, never realizing what a sight o' things you'd be doin' for me —and you have been such a comfort, Sabriny!

"That's all I'm p'ticklar about, 'cept Alec—I want to be buried in the n'theast corner o' our lot in the old ber'rin' ground an' next Pa, 'tween him an' Cousin Hiram, an' I want a stun like Hiram's, don't forget, within six months after my goin'; an' Alec, you an' Linnie must remember 'bout them cups; the milk cup an' the sugar cup an' the teapot you may have, Linnie, if you will prize them, for the children. Well, Sabriny, I shan't use the cups no more, let the doctor take them home for ye to-night."

"No," protested Sabrina the younger, "they brighten up that corner, they mustn't be moved yet a while, you'd miss the sight of them after all these years."

"P'raps I would. Wall, do as you think best, they're yourn," assented the weary woman, dropping off into a sleep of exhaustion.

Alec and his wife slipped from the room, she with a little shrug of dislike as she passed the watcher, for the pretty cups were the things she most coveted of all her aunt's possessions.

Dr. Walter mended the fire and pulled down the shade, and advised the nurse as he lighted the lamp for her to sleep when she could and stay herself with some good gruel, and then went out into the moonlighted October evening.

Sabrina dozed until her charge stirred, then the invalid seemed very wide awake, and in spite of gentle warnings, very talkative.

"I'm glad you hev them cups," she said, "I wouldn't hev parted with 'em for gold while I was a livin', breathin' human bein,' so to to speak, to anybody. I've had people tryin' to purchase 'em, an' you know I've been pretty poverty pinched by times—an' never did I give 'em up. I always supposed they were my Davenport cups 'cause I got 'em of the old Jesse Davenport estate at the vandoo in 1849, but of late years I heerd tell it was the name o' a kind o' chiny ware. I'll tell you how I got 'em after I've had my cup o' broth."

Sabrina heated the broth, and going to the cupboard took down one of the dainty cups of buff and yellow gold decoration, and carefully wiping it, she filled and brought it to the sick woman, sitting on the side of the bed to feed her after tucking a towel under the sharp chin and wasted cheeks. A pleased smile came over Miss Elder's face as she said: "Jest like I did for poor Hiram when he came home from Californy. And the way I got them cups, Sabriny. Wall, you know, I ain't never, an' couldn't never be extravagant if I wanted to be, but when I was a getting ready to be married—you didn't know I ever expected to be? wall, folks didn't then, but I did, an' that was enough. Hiram Coles an' I had it all settled between ourselves—nobody else knew—and when the Californy fever broke out, the gold seekin,' you know, in '49, we weren't so very young, then, but we'd been o' that mind for a good many years, an' I knew if ever he got settled he'd be glad to have me to take care o' him—he was a sort of rover, by nature, Hiram was, always plannin' and dreamin' an' I was jest the steady one for him if I do say it, but he was so conscientious I wan't a bit afraid o' his falling into temptation, but I felt a awful sinkin' o' fear when he said he was a-going off with the rest o' them, the gold hunters. My! how fur off that Californy seemed to me them days—now they say you can get there in less'n a week.

"I'd a begged to be let go, too, I dare say, for I had stren'th for any kind o' pioneering, for anythin' he'd be called on to bear an' to do, but you know when your pa and ma are gettin' oldish and need you near 'em, you can't, if you are oldest gal at home, jest strike out for yourself.

"He said he was sure to come inside a year, or two at the furthest, then he'd have enough to buy and furnish the little farm he wanted, he was sure on't. I most felt so, too, he was so certain on't.

"I fixed him up some things for his long journey; he was going overland but I didn't know what bleaching bones that meant for many a poor fellow.,

"An' we said good-bye — harder for me to say to my one tall slim chap than 'twill be for me to say good-bye to the whole living world pretty soon. Oh, but it was wringin' hard! You'll never know, my Lord, yes.

"Wall, next day after he'd gone was old Col. Davenport's vandoo sale. I wasn't goin' mopin' about, which wouldn't a helped nothin', so I went with the others about here to see what the young Davenports were goin' to let go of the old Colonel's belongin's—most everything, it seemed. The old Colonel had been such a fast liver, he'd used up all his cash, about. When I see 'em, I thought them bright cups, your teacups now, would be the very nicest thing fur the money I'd laid out to spend, if I could get 'em for that, an' I did, an' had enough to bid off the plates, too; but when I asked about them, an' the sugar cup an' the creamer an' the teapot, they said them had been sold for special price an' favor, an' was to be took to a young lady in the country. Now I never dreamed it was me, but it was, an' Hiram he'd done it for a good-bye present for me.

"You may guess I prized 'em more than ever, an' I'a made me that corner cupboard with his own hands, an' I was busy—wall, I always was, but some o' my sewin' them days was for the little home that was to be, an' I pictured having your pa and ma—they was married about that time, to take tea with me an' the minister, an' all of us drinkin' tea out o' them cups in my own house, an' my Hiram at the head o' his own table.

"Yes, he'd gone an' I waited, an' I didn't get any word from him, an' then what I heard was discouragin'—only pitiful news o' sickness an' bad luck an' such. And I waited one, two, three, four years, a little bit o' hope one while that he was doin' well an' he hoped to get home.

"Then I heard that he could never come, no, never—'at he was dead—an' I went into the deepest kind o' black for him in my soul, an' still nobody knew 'at we'd been more than friends an' cousins.

"I never did favor folks a-gossipin'—congratulations or pity, till all things was set and settled.

"I give him up—I had to, an' I had to work harder'n ever after pa died and Brother Joe leavin' Alec here scarce fifteen, an' never real handy, an' Joe's widder warn't smart nor poor mamma neither, so I got used to runnin' the farm an' could do it as well as any man; but pa, he'd never paid off the mortgage, 'n I wanted to for Alec's sake. I guess folks thought me awful stingy, for its close an' plain we lived, an' after Alec married an' went off, I did live awful poor.

"But the sixth year Hiram had been gone—I was thirty-four then—he was a year or two younger'n me, one night some one was rappin' on that door yonder—it was an October night like this, but chillier. I opened the door an' there was that poor Hiram, a shadder of himself, all a-worn out with his hardships an' fever an' travelin'. 'Oh, you blessed livin' ghost, come in, come in !' says I, jest so. Course I got him in, an' into a good warm bed, an' brought him gruel in a bowl an' a cup o' chicken broth, soon's ever I could make it, in one o' our cups, so I told him, an' he looked as pleased as such a shadder could. Poor dear, poor dear, he had suffered so, all them years ! an' I in good old Connecticut in comparative ease an' comfort.

"Wall, Sabriny, he had next day what old Dr. Walter called a congestive chill, an' he didn't get over it; 'fore he went out o' his head he talked o' wantin' to be married 'fore he died. I was willing,' but he got worse awful fast; he seemed to come to himself a little, an' at the last he was a-whisperin' he hoped one o' the Lord's own many mansions, jest a little one, would be a place for us somehow, together.

"Then he dropped away—he was a lyin' there, my Hiram, with me a-holdin' him by the hand, but I couldn't hold him. 'N more'n forty year I've been goin' on toward that house an' home—you're comin', too, in due season, Sabriny. Now, a little more gruel, an' I'll rest."

Sabrina Morse was still a watcher by the old friend's bedside when a few days later the feeble life spark went out. A word of trust, a gleam of joy that the long journey was so nearly over—then the dark.

It was perhaps a week after the simple funeral that the doctor's gig rolled to Mrs. Morse's door and the doctor, son of the old doctor, came bringing the legacy from Miss Elder's corner cupboard.

"Here are the twelve plates and the twelve cups with saucers, none cracked or chipped, which I heard Miss Elder say were to be yours, Mrs. Morse, but Alec's wife declares she gave her the rest of the set; I don't remember that I heard her say anything about them, but I'm sure she must have meant you to have it all as a sort of birthright," said the doctor.

"But the rest are hers," explained the widow. "I hope she'll really prize the pretty things, they're so pretty, aren't they, doctor? For mine, I shall have a corner cupboard made straightway. Advise me how and where."

The year went on and still another year since Miss Elder was laid away next to Hiram in the northeast corner lot in the old cemetery, and yet grasses and daisies ran riot there and Alec was urged in vain to heed his aunt's request about the headstone, "one like Hiram's," small and plain, and still he and Linnie "didn't feel to afford it."

"I could get one for her myself," said the troubled name-child, Sabrina, "but she'd most rise and walk if a charity stone, as she'd call it, was set at her grave, she who would not in her most pinched days take a cent's worth of help. She meant it paid for out of that hundred dollars she left in the bank, and she did all her life so slave to lift the mortgage off the farm to leave it clear for that couple. They ought to respect her wishes. It's a shame!"

About this time Dr. Walter developed a great passion for collecting old china and other "olds," and Mrs. Morse concluded after a wakeful night that dear old Miss Elder's independent spirit should be respected. She should in a manner buy her own gravestones, for she, Sabrina Morse, would sell to the doctor her beloved Davenport cups and the stone should be set. And Dr. Walter was glad to purchase the treasures for a sum that would pay for the memory tablet to be placed in the old lot beside Hiram's. "But I can't let the plates go," affirmed the little widow, "I'll have these for a keepsake of my mother's old friend."

And during the weeks following *his* wakeful night, no doubt, the doctor himself affirmed on his next call to her: "Sabrina Morse, I've bought for a good price from Linnie and Alec Elder—she wants to get a melodeon for her oldest girl—the old Col. Davenport teapot and sugar bowl and creamer for my collection, and now Sabrina Morse if you only would let me have your plates, why—well, I'd like to say that I'll give you all of my cups and things—in fact, with all of my worldly goods and my clumsy old self, I'll gladly thee endow— if you'll only say I may have you."

And the rosy widow did not say a word for the surprise of it, but someway the doctor knew.

And "Sabrina's teacups" and the rest of the glittering array, shining and with a new lease of unbroken pleasure-giving, adorn the old-fashioned sideboard or table of the good doctor and his cheery little helper to this day.

MEMORIES OF MERIDEN.

BY FRANCES A. BRECKENRIDGE.

The steep declivities of nearly all the mountainous elevations of Connecticut face in a southerly direction. Between these hanging hills the land undulates from east to west, forming sheltered depressions, in which many, indeed most of the early colonists located their farms, often choosing the lowest and least sunny spot for their dwelling house and outbuildings.

Occasionally though, and nearly always by a family of known English origin, a large and roomy house, with some pretension to architectural symmetry and ornament, would be built upon the summit of a hill. Such is the position of the old "Johnson house," plainly to be seen from many of the city streets.

The original Johnson made a sensation by entering town with his family, in

THE JOHNSON HOUSE.

what an old resident called "an equipage." This equipage was a vehicle with a canvass top. Its prototype was exhibited at the State Fair of 1892. This vehicle was considered elegant, and gave a certain social position to the new-comers. The Johnson farm included part of the west mountain and quite all of the cliff known as West Peak. This purchase was not by other thrifty farmers considered an especial evidence of good judgment. The mountainous forest was, most of it, hemlock, and no self-respecting housekeeper of that era would buy hemlock wood for any purpose, unless cheated into it, a feat only accomplished by slyly inserting a log or two of the objectionable timber into an honest looking load of hickory and maple. For many years the mountain was considered a nearly worthless adjunct of the property, but within the last few years it has acquired a value other than its forests. The men of the

Johnson family were just the silent, grave, stern men of that day. The mother, slightly paralytic, equally serious and formal, and the two daughters, called by the children of that formal time " Miss Amanda " and Miss Huldah," might have stepped bodily out of Mrs. Gaskell's "Cranford." The writer has just one memory of one of these ancient sisters. She sat stiffly upright, her withered hands crossed, as she gave out that "she considered red flannel extremely conducive to health." Besides the equipage aforesaid, the family brought with them good store of china and Wedgewood ware. Cut glass decanters and wine glasses adorned the mahogany sideboard. China and pewter cider mugs had their own place. The pewter cups and platters had a commixture of silver, rather more than one of silver to sixteen of pewter. There are still extant certain pieces of old china and glass, once their property. An old pitcher with the parting of the to-be bride of "Old Robin Gray" and her Jamie depicted on one side, and the ship with white sails flaming, and the tossing waves beneath which bore Jamie away from her, on the other, had been in some long gone

THE ALLEN PLACE

time broken into many pieces, carefully replaced and joined together with putty now dried by time into a hardness equal to the pottery itself. An old stoneware flip mug, with a surface as smooth and fine as china, is hooped with metal bands.

The cut glass on the sideboard was not kept solely for show. Callers were always refreshed by a small modicum of cherry brandy or foreign wine from the decanters, dispensed in the tiny wine glasses. Their loaf-cake, rye bread, cream biscuits and honey were famous in all the region round about.

The formalities of a tea-party were once described by a lady who assisted at the function. Upon the arrival of the guests, they were met at the door by both sisters, and by them helped in the arranging of best caps and lace collars.

They were then escorted sedately to one of their chairs by one of the sisters, and "negus" was mixed with much precision and with distinguished solemnity by the other. The delectable tipple was then dispensed by both, and was partaken of with serious appreciation by all, including the minister and his wife, who were always the guests of honor at such solemn divertisements. The family coat of arms was, and perhaps still remains, cut into the panelling of what was the best parlor.

THE COE PLACE.

The old, old white rose, single to be sure, but fragrant, and with buds when half opened of absolutely perfect loveliness, can still be found on the premises, as can also the almost extinct red and white striped York and Lancaster rose. The family is extinct, and the old house is to this generation a landmark—nothing more.

THE RICE HOUSE.

In this section of the town are also the farms owned respectively by members of the Allen and Coe families. Commodious and handsome dwellings have been built on both of these estates, which have descended from father to son. The old farmhouses are still standing, but are in no way distinctive. Nearer the city is another farmhouse which antedates its centennial by many years. Low in its elevation, it is large upon the ground. Substantially built, its wide low hall with its staircase rising directly from it, gives an air of roominess not usual in dwellings of that period. This hall now furnished with "things new and old" gives access to the cosy rooms on each side, with their cupboards and corner fireplaces. This is and has been for more than a hundred years the "Rice Farm." There, many a year agone, Deacon Ezekiel Rice, a widower with seven children, brought home as his bride the sometime widow of Dr. Hall of Wallingford. Into the family of seven girls and boys the new wife brought her three daughters. From that time, all the young people lived in the peace of a singularly harmonious home. Somebody, with more truth than elegance, said of them that "they were stirred together with a long stick and never afterward did anyone know to which side of the house did they belong." To these ten, six more were added, and the sixteen grew up and all but one married. From the shelter of its broad roof have gone out into the world those who are known in pretty nearly every state in the Union. Among

its later inmates are those who have been and are in close relationship and friendship with men and women known beyond the limits of our own country for their important station in the political world, and for the wealth of their intellectual resources.

The house and land surrounding is still owned and occupied by members of the family name. Before the present dwelling was built, more than a century ago, there was another, of which only the door stones and an old well were discoverable some years since. At the southwest corner of the low dooryard terrace, there stands a vigorous, and although distorted, very beautiful maple. This tree was a good size when the present house was built, and is at least a hundred and fifty years old. A tall and vigorous pine tree has a pretty bit of family history connected with it. One of the daughters, then a little girl, went to Middletown with her big brother, she riding behind him on a pillion. Going over the mountain she saw the tiny tree, only a few inches high, and she transplanted it in the home door yard. Some years ago it seemed to be dying. It is a landmark, and would be missed, but it has taken a new start and bids fair to live through another generation. Besides these, visibly striving to renew its youth, is an ancient stump of a "golden sweeting" apple-tree, the parent of which was brought to Wallingford from England. It is, itself, the parent of all that especial fruit in these parts.

From the first this home was the center of good cheer and of an intelligent, social culture.

In the northern section of the town is standing another quaint dwelling. Its long, low, picturesque roof once sheltered one of the large families of the olden time. It is still occupied by a member of the family, and, like the three

BLACK POND.

before mentioned, is still held in the family name. This was not exactly a farmhouse. Years ago, its owner, Squire Patrick Clark, conducted a thriving tin business that with its numerous surrounding low workshops gave that corner of the town the name of "Clarksville." Tinware making was then the most important Meriden industry, antedating that of ivory comb making, which afterward outgrew its predecessor, but of which no trace is left except the pretty artificial lake known as "Prattsville Pond." In its day the tin business quite held the town. Not only were the shops at Clarksville kept busy, but there were those of "Squire" Noah Pomeroy at the "East Side," and two separate concerns belonging to members of the Yale family in the center of the town, and another, quite as thriving as any of the others, carried on by "Goodrich and Rutty." Of those old workshops not a vestige can now be found. Streets with sidewalks and electric lights now traverse the precincts where the "apprentices" soldered the pots and pans, doing their evening "stint" by the obscure radiance given out by tin lamps filled with whale oil, or by tallow candles.

The Pomeroy shops are gone. Even "Black Pond," the adjacent east side natural lake, the only natural lake in the town limits, has lost its weird notoriety as a fathomless water. Since the trees from the overhanging mountain side have been cut away, the sunlight falls as brightly there as anywhere, and it is now known to be no deeper than any mountain side lake is apt to be.

As the tinware and ivory comb business declined, the present industries which give Meriden the title of "Silver City" grew naturally out of the small but very well paying trade in britannia metal. This was at first confined to the manufacture of spoons and tea and coffee pots of homely and inelegant pattern, and except perhaps a simple beading, of a perfectly plain finish.

The leading Connecticut industry, rivaling for many years that of clock-making, was that of tinware. Northern tin-peddlers pervaded the Southern States, and what were then known as fortunes were thus accumulated, of which Meriden had its generous share. Since then other business ventures have started, developed into more or less importance in their own time, have declined and passed out of the needs of this newer day.

THE PATRICK CLARK HOMESTEAD.

But the great factories of this later dispensation, growing still more and more extensive in their operations and varied in their merchandise, have grown up from and have been evolved out of, more or less directly or indirectly, those low, unpretentious, nearly forgotten workshops of seventy years ago. The men who conducted the enterprises of those years were all of them economical, thrifty and painstaking. Besides these qualities, they were both, farmers and manufacturers, eminently God-fearing, Sunday-keeping men. They strove,—even if they sometimes, being but human, failed—to have "a conscience void of offence."

NERVA.

A Story of Pastoral Connecticut.

BY MILO LEON NORTON.

PART I.—DESOLATION.

Fortunes are made and lost in a day, is a common allusion to the fluctuations of Wall street, but yet to one who has little knowledge of the feverish excitement, the anxieties, the depressions and exhilarations peculiar to speculation, this expression is as meaningless as the terms of a quadratic equation to one who has never progressed beyond the simple calculations of arithmetic. There is a fascination about speculation, like all forms of gambling, that is almost irresistible ; and the fact that some succeed allures others on to almost certain ruin.

George Smith had been a successful operator on Wall street. Whatever he touched turned to gold. His great ambition was to become a millionaire, but, having attained this, he was just as ambitious to add another and still another million to his pile. How few learn the lesson of moderation. How few ever succeed in curbing the insatiate craving for more, that becomes a passion, a mania, robbing men of much of the real enjoyment of, and relish for the good things of life.

George Smith became interested in a new, gigantic railway project in the West. This was to be the master financial stroke of his career. The bonds were issued, the scheme duly lauded by the well-paid metropolitan press, the bonds were being taken by investors ; indeed, success seemed assured. But a rival operator saw a chance to steal a march on his fortunate rival. A syndicate was formed. Legislation hostile to the Smith system was secured by a process best known to those familiar with the lobbies of legislative bodies. False reports were circulated. The stocks depreciated. In short, George Smith, triple millionaire that he was, found himself out-generaled, and ruined. The bubble had burst.

Gathering up a few scattering securities he realized what he could upon them, cast into the pool again, and lost. Luck had turned. There was no use. Prematurely aged at fifty, when he should have been in the prime of life ; hopeless and nerveless, what could he do ? He still possessed some real estate, but this under forced sale did not realize its full worth, a few thousands, and depositing this, he cast about for some business opening, for he had abandoned speculation forever. He was soon astounded to learn that the bank which held this remnant of his fortune had failed. The very roof above his head must now be sold and he must seek inexpensive quarters elsewhere.

Misfortunes never come singly. They came upon him and overwhelmed him like an avalanche.

It is not surprising that this run of ill-luck that had swept from him in a few months what had taken him so many years to accumulate, should completely prostrate him. Many a man has ended his life by suicide at such a crisis in his affairs. But he was too utterly crushed by his misfortunes to even think of suicide. He lapsed into a sort of stupor, from which nothing could arouse him. He took little interest in anything. He ate and slept and conversed aimlessly, nervelessly.

Mr. Smith's family consisted of a wife and two daughters. One of the latter, the older, was with her mother in Europe, the other was with her father. The two sisters were as unlike as two persons could well be. The elder one was proud, haughty, calculating, like her mother, her horizon bounded by her own desires and ambitions. Her mother had married for money, not love. Born of an old, aristocratic family, she inherited the blue blood of her ancestors. Fortunately for her, her husband had settled upon her an immense sum, the income of which, coupled with her own private fortune, placed her above the possibility of want. The news of her husband's failure, which would have excited wifely sympathy and compassion in most women, only deepened her alienation from her husband. To her, financial misfortunes were criminal. Henceforth their paths would be divergent.

She wrote at once to her youngest daughter to join them in Paris, where they could live at their ease, and leave the man who had brought all this disgrace upon them to shift for himself. To this proposition the youngest daughter made a prompt and indignant refusal. What! Leave her father to bear his burden of disaster alone? Not she. Her father had done too much for her to be recompensed with such ingratitude.

The stately family mansion was sold. Some of the most useful furniture, and some precious souvenirs were reserved, rooms were secured in a quiet locality, and a talent for management was developed in this girl of twenty, that surprised herself: she who had never been required to give an anxious thought for the morrow.

A few months after taking up their abode in their new quarters, Nerva—for I must now introduce her by name—was reading aloud to her father, who listened, half heeding, in his listless way, when her eyes rested upon an illustration of an old farm-house, its windows broken, its weather-boards fallen off in places, its chimney of hewn stone still defying wind and weather, its doors unhinged, and tangled vines and shrubbery growing wild and luxuriant about the stone door-steps of the old deserted habitation. It was one of those abandoned houses so common in New England. There was something about it in keeping with the dilapidation into which their fortune had fallen ; something about the old ruin that seemed consonant with the ruin and desolation that had come to her heart. Not only had she lost her position in society as a belle and heiress, petted and admired and envied, but the young fortune-hunting lawyer to whom she had been betrothed, when she had promptly released him from the engagement, had as promptly accepted the release, not without a show of regret, to be sure, but as she well knew, without a particle of sincerity about it. Hollow and insincere as she then knew her affianced to have been, yet the sudden rending of ties so sacred, the sudden blasting of the hope that, perhaps, after all he would be true to her despite her loss of fortune, the dashing to earth of all the hopes and dreams that had taken possession of her young life, almost crushed her beneath their accumulated weight. But the sight of her poor father, sitting day after day, helpless almost as a child, yet trustful and gentle and kind as he always had been since her earliest recollection, nerved her to struggle bravely against the overwhelming disasters that had befallen them. Her eyes followed the descriptive text, and she read, with languid interest, paragraph after paragraph.

All at once a sudden inspiration came to her. How nice it would be to live in the seclusion, the solitude, of such an old home. How sweet to bury one's self in such an old tomb. The close companionship with nature, the gentle murmur of the brooks, the perfume of the new mown hay, the beauty of the wild flowers, the shadows of the leafy wood, and the grandeur of the hills ; how all these things would inspire her very soul, and soothe and heal her wounded heart.

She laid down the magazine at last, and sat and thought, and thought, and thought.

* * * * * * * *

It was a perfect day. May, the lovely bridal month of the year, had decked herself with apple blossoms, the loveliest of all fruit blossoms. All nature was gay with bud and bloom, and brilliant with vernal sunshine. A New England train wound in and out among the hills of Litchfield County. It labored up a steep grade through a wild gorge, a canyon they would call it in the wild West, through which a stream of water dashed over gray rocks, spread out into miniature lakes, or glided along underneath drooping willows or black stemmed alders. Farther along a deep cut in the solid rock of the gorge, worn away by untold ages of falling water, afforded an ideal site for a mill-dam. One had time only to catch a glimpse of a deep, dark chasm, into which plunged the waters from the weir above, when the train gave a lurch, as it rounded a curve, and then traversed the border of a placid mill pond, upon which was reflected the deep blue of the sky, and the cloud-fleets that sail on aimless voyages along the uncharted currents of the upper air. A little island, a continent in miniature, with a cape here, a gulf there, beetling crags a cubit high, rocky promontories, bold headlands—what one could imagine Australia to be, could he view it from the moon—seemed to float upon the lakelet, to nestle there as an emerald might nestle upon the bosom of a sleeping maiden.

Farther along the train emerged upon a plain. A stream wound through it in serpentine spirals, fringed with water-loving alders and mottled maples. The plain itself, like a great river, stretched away to the north, skirting the frayed edges of the bordering hills, or yielding to the encroachments of huge masses of metamorphic rock. Scores of cattle grazed in the pastures. Farm houses, surrounded by cherry trees in full bloom, partially revealed their white-painted gables and weather-beaten roofs in the distance.

Another lurch of the train, another sharp curve, and the train rushed into a narrow defile in the mountain. Huge boulders and angular masses detached from the heights above, lay scattered about. Through the very hearts of many huge rocks the engineers had blasted the way for the locomotive. There were pools, shaded by sombre hemlocks ; there were cascades dashing over the rocks, or tumbling down the mountain side ; there were wooded slopes, and gray, bald crags of rock, towering high above the tree tops.

Still farther on the spire of a village church, and clusters of snow-white houses were seen, and the train came to a halt at a little station,—"deepo," the villagers persisted in calling it. At the station two passengers alighted. They were Nerva and her father.

They were quickly approached by the local Jehu of the village livery stable, who proffered his services.

"Can you take us out to the Weston farm?" asked Nerva.

"Certainly, ma'am. But there's nobody living there," replied Jehu.

"I know it. We wish to go out there, and have you come for us at six o'clock," said Nerva, motioning toward a lunch basket, which Jehu quickly stowed away, with his passengers, into his carryall.

With Yankee inquisitiveness Jehu plied his passengers with questions on the way, eliciting very little information, however. Nerva desired very much to be left to her own reflections, and to closely observe the country through which they were driving. She soon turned the tables on the questioner, who could not have been more inquisitive had he been conducting the cross-questioning of a witness, by asking the names of owners of houses and farms which they passed, and listening to their biographies as glibly told by her informant.

Three miles from the station a small rural hamlet was reached. The road descended to it from a lofty ridge, at the foot of which it nestled. Ledges of mossy rocks cropped out here and there, barely admitting the passage of the wagon. Little streams of water trickled down the rocks, and off through the meadows. Great, spreading elms and symmetrical maples lined the roadway upon either side. Half a dozen farm-houses, some of them very old, with great chimneys protruding from their roofs, stood behind the rows of shade trees. The first settlers had found many relics of the aborigines in the shape of arrow heads, stone axes and other implements, and so they named the place Indian Hollow, and "Injun Holler" it had ever since been called. Only one descendant of the original settlers remained. The rest had died, or drifted away to livelier and more congenial scenes. The throb of the great world's pulse came to the few families in the hamlet but faintly through the medium of the press. They plowed and sowed, and reaped and mowed, in the summer, and cut their year's supply of fuel in the winter, as their fathers had done, and were content, with one exception, and he, still a young man, had worked his way through an agricultgral college and come back full of new-fangled ideas, strange and new to his neighbors, to whom the good old ways were all sufficient. All these facts and much more Nerva learned as they drove on.

A turn in the road brought them to a grassy lane. The bushes on each side had not been cut; the fences were out of repair; white birches, the vanguard of the hosts of the wilderness, had taken possession of once cultivated fields; tangled vines and brambles were everywhere, illustrating the fact that nature abhors a vacuum.

Up this lane, over a hill, across a rude bridge in the hollow beyond, Jehu guided his team and drew up at a solitary, deserted farm-house. Nerva did not need to be told that it was the place they had come to see, for she recognized it instantly by the picture she had seen in the magazine.

Dismissing the carriage, father and daughter proceeded to explore the old dwelling. Thanks to the durable, hand-rived shingles, the rain had penetrated but little through the roof, and most of the ceilings were intact. The windows were broken, the doors unhinged, and the floors warped by sun and storm. They climbed up into the great empty attic, where the wasps built their nests of clay, and the spiders spread their nets for the unwary fly. They walked through the tenantless rooms, descended into the capacious cellar, looked up from the cavernous fire-place to the blue sky above through the chimney flue, and looked out of the unglazed windows. Then they went out and sat on the velvety grass beneath a spreading cherry tree, white with its mass of bloom, and ate their noontide lunch.

The old house stood on a terrace upon the hillside. To the south was a mountainous region densely wooded. To the north were sloping hillsides, where were long rows of apple trees in picturesque stages of decay and death. Broken down stone fences divided the land into fields where once the yellow grain had fallen before the reaper's cradle, and the tall corn had waved its tassels in the autumn sunlight. To the west lay open fields and pastures overgrown with brush and brier. To the east were meadows, and beyond them pasture lots. A good-sized brook flowed through the meadows, cool and sparkling, singing in an undertone the songs it had learned of the rustling leaves in the woodlands, where it had its birth, and where the song birds warbled over its cradle.

A path led across the meadow out into the wood-lot beyond, crossing the brook over a bridge of rude construction. Just beyond the bridge was a cliff of gray rock, towering a hundred feet into the air, its precipitous sides covered with stunted trees and laurels, while lichens and ferns clung to the rocks, softening their hard surfaces with velvety greens and silvery grays.

Leaving her father sleeping peacefully on the grass, Nerva followed the path till she came to the bridge. A trout shot like an arrow through the shallow water when her foot touched the planking. She paused a moment, listening to the music of the stream, and then passed on to the foot of the cliff. Following a foot-path, she scrambled from rock to rock, clinging to the trunks of trees, until she reached the summit, where a view of exquisite beauty rewarded her for the effort.

The hills of Litchfield County appear much more enchanting to the distant observer than they do to the weary traveler who descends one hill and crosses a narrow valley, only to be compelled to climb another hill, and to repeat the process for many a long mile. But viewed from a distance there is a pastoral beauty in these long, sloping ridges, running north and south, unexcelled by any landscape in the world. A superb view of these hills, checkered by dividing fences, and dotted with white farm-houses, was spread out before Nerva as she stood there.

After a long time she retraced her steps, and regaining the wood-path soon came to the ruins of a mill-dam. The pond, which covered several acres, was empty, but the old water-line could be seen upon the shores. In some places the meadow sloped down to what had been the water's edge; at other places the shore was precipitous and rocky. Nerva saw that the dam could be easily repaired, and instead of the repulsive marsh a lake of rare beauty could be formed.

A few steps below the dam she found the rotting segments of an overshot wheel. This suggested to her mind that the pond could not only be made ornamental, but useful.

Returning to the farm-house by another route she rejoined her father, and with him visited the orchard, the fields and the woodlands adjoining. The father, somewhat aroused from his listlessness, took considerable interest in his surroundings. Reared on a New England farm he instinctively knew the adaptability of different soils to different crops. This evidence of returning intelligence was very gratifying to Nerva, and confirmed her in the opinion that with the quiet and change that this secluded spot would give, her father might be greatly benefitted if not restored to his former self.

On the day following, in consideration of the payment of a few hundred dollars, the old Weston farm that had lain idle for a quarter century, changed owners, and Nerva found herself possessed of landed estate.

[To be Concluded.]

INSPIRATION.

BY DELIA B. WARD.

"Look, then, into thy heart and write!"—*Longfellow*.

So many tuneful bards have sung
So many rhymes in every tongue,
Can any thoughts have gone astray
To charm the poet's soul to-day?
Have all our loves and joys been told?
Are all the rain-drops set in gold?
The glamour of the woods doth thrill
Each quickened sense, delighted, still,
Eolian strains of wind-swept trees;
The zephyrs' gentler harmonies,
A subtle rapture thus uplifts
The heart, in gratitude for gifts.
So we will sing as they have sung:—
For poesy is ever young;—
The human soul's beatitudes,
And Nature's sympathetic moods.

EARLY TEXT BOOKS IN CONNECTICUT

BY ELLEN BRAINERD PECK.

There is a charm which ever hallows an old book—the charm of antiquity. As we peruse the pages we are transported in thought from our present surroundings to a contemplation of the customs and environments that belonged to its time. Something of the atmosphere that emanated from the impulse and the action of the period of its making seems to be still lingering about it. There is a particular interest which is attached to the methods of instruction that bore a part in the education of our colonial ancestors; but a more especial interest belongs to the early American text-books studied by those who lived in the stirring times of our early independence. In considering these early text-books, we naturally think of what sort and manner of book they were, when was the period of their greatest usefulness, and by whom, and under what circumstances they were compiled; and, in doing this, the people of Connecticut are, haply, led to their own state. Before we begin to examine these interesting books, it is perhaps best to survey briefly the condition of the educational affairs as they were prior to the Revolutionary War and to note how great was the lack of school-books in those days.

The colonist of Connecticut, who was imbued with the spirit which prevailed in all New England (the keen desire for knowledge), felt the necessity of providing, as quickly as might be, a means of educating the children of the colony. For, upon the growing generation, the New Englander well knew depended the continuance toward the success of the nation which he had striven to found. Moreover, men realized that the one way to rise in the eyes of their fellow-citizens lay along the path of education. So, in this way, came about the importance of the school in New England.

In Connecticut, "as early as 1648 the assembly passed a law providing for common education, every town containing fifty families was required to sustain a good school, where reading and writing should be well taught." It is not to be wondered at, that books at this time were a luxury, since so few of them were in the colonies and when the financial condition of affairs was such that the expense of printing them could not be undertaken.

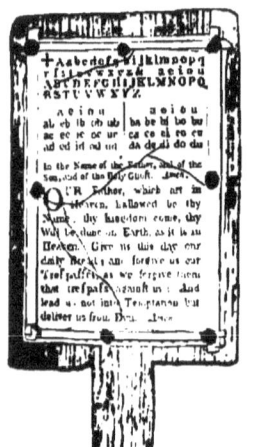

THE HORN BOOK.

One of the present generation can hardly understand the feeling of the forefathers for a book of learning, and they guarded it with the care of a treasure, that it might be handed down from the oldest to the youngest in a family.

The New England Primer, which revealed so strongly and clearly the character of the Puritans, was called the little bible of New England, and it is described as having stiff oak covers, unbeautiful prose, rough and stern poetry and crude pictures.

Such was the book wherefrom many a child studied lessons and doubtless knew by rote its oddly religious and laughably instructive rhymes. It must have been an uninteresting little book in its day, but now it is interesting because of its quaint character and puritanic primness.

Beside this little book the children had lessons from the Bible and the Psalter, and these were about the only books that were in use in those days of the colonies. The teaching under this order of things, was compelled to be for the most part oral, and the teacher often possessed only a manuscript copy of any subject he taught.

The advancement in such schools as this must have been slow and difficult. The youngest pupils were sometimes supplied with a very curious contrivance, which took the place of the regulation book and which was called by the name of the "Horn Book." This was made of a thin board, with a handle, and to this board was fastened a leaflet, upon which was inscribed the alphabet, the Lord's Prayer, and some sentences. This remarkable and unique device was oftentimes suspended from the girdle of the young pupil for convenience. Over the leaflet, very frequently, was fastened a thin pane of horn, that the page might be kept fair. This Horn Book had long been in use in old England, and it antedated the art of printing. This device continued to be in use till about the middle of the eighteenth century.

The poet Cowper describes the Horn Book in the following verse:

> "Neatly secured from being soiled or torn,
> Beneath a pane of thin translucent horn,
> A book (to please us at a tender age),
> 'Tis called a book, though but a single page.
> Presents the prayer the Saviour deigned to teach,
> Which children use, and parsons when they preach."

Later along in the schools, the three R's—reading, writing and arithmetic —were required to be taught, and a pupil of average ability was supposed to become proficient through the rule of three, as proportion was then called. Rev. Heman Humphrey, D.D., president of Amherst College, wrote in a letter to the Hon. Henry Barnard concerning schools between the years 1790 and 1800, and the books that were then studied: "Our school books were the Bible, Webster's Spelling Book (third part mainly), one or two others were found in some schools for the reading classes—grammar was hardly taught at all in any of them, and that little was confined almost entirely to committing and reciting the rules. Parsing was one of the occult sciences in my day ; we had some few lessons in geography by questions and answers, but no maps, no globes, and as for blackboards, such a thing was not thought of till long after. Children's reading and picture-books we had none, the fables in Webster's Spelling Book came nearest to it. Arithmetic was hardly taught at all in the day schools; as a substitute, there were some evening schools in most of the districts. Spelling was one of the daily exercises in all of the classes." This testimony coincides with that of others who have written on the subject concerning the instructional appliances of that period, and shows how poorly equipped the schools were, and how limited the scope of an education to those dependent on the common school.

But the mention of Webster's Spelling Book in this extract from President Humphrey's letter reveals the first bright spot in the means of acquiring instruction in those days, the glow of the dawn in the world of text-books. Up to this time in the history of the educational affairs of our country, there had been no idea of a text-book as a distinctive type of book, which was to be rendered interesting as well as instructive, and no allurements toward the path of learning, evidently, were regarded as needful. It was the general opinion that people should be impelled personally toward an education by the love of knowledge and through a sense of duty which ought to induce them to make the most of their opportunities and of themselves. This is, of course, the feeling which should animate all people, the personal obligation to make the most of themselves, though unfortunately it has never been sufficient to lead the masses. But it was natural that amid toil and great hardship, little thought could be given to the making of the ways of education pleasurable either by books or otherwise. The children were sent to school to learn their lessons in the plain, hum-drum way provided for them. Our feeling is somewhat curious and quizzical, yet withal reverent when we examine a dingy, unpretentious little volume printed in the year 1790 or thereabout. " Books think for me," wrote Charles Lamb from his world of them; but in this country, in its young days, the small and scanty volumes filled but slightly the longings in the hungry minds of our ancestors. If the subject of the text-book were to be treated in

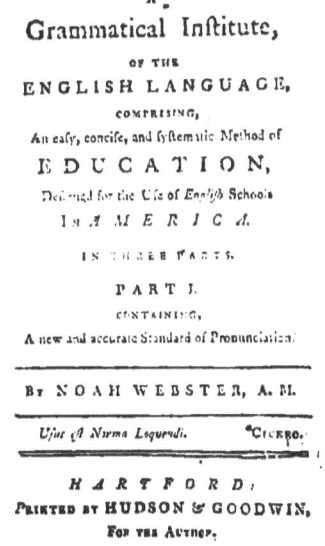

TITLE PAGE OF WEBSTER'S GRAMMATICAL INSTITUTE.

strict detail up to those in use by the present generation of pupils and the textbooks taken one by one through the series of advancements it would be almost inexhaustible.

S. G. Goodrich, better known perhaps as Peter Parley, who was a native of Ridgefield, Conn., in describing a school of his town as it existed between the years 1803 and 1806, gives the following list of books as those used there: "The catechism, which was probably the New England Primer, and Webster's Spelling Book, the Bible, and Daboll's Arithmetic (which held its place in the schools for nearly thirty-five years), Webster's Grammar, which even the master did not understand, and Dwight's Geography, which had neither maps nor illustrations, and was merely an expanded table of contents of Morse's Universal Geography."

Furthermore, William Woodbridge writes concerning another one of these early schools: "As for geography, some few schools studied Morse's and a few others used as a sort of reading book Nathaniel Dwight's System of Geography;" and Mrs. Emma Willard wrote of a school which she attended when she was a young girl, "Saturday morning I went and received my lesson in Webster's Grammar and Morse's Geography."

In reading the names of the books mentioned in these extracts, we find that they were all written by Connecticut men. And we draw the conclusion from such references as to what extent the text-books of Connecticut men prevailed in these early schools, and it is evident that they were the only ones of American authorship then in the country. This was at the crucial and formative period of the nation when things were either to make or to mar its prosperity, and we learn from further study that among these books was one which pre-eminently served as the base whence the character of the text-book in general was builded. The witnessing of both history and biography goes to show conclusively that to Connecticut belongs the honor of first instituting the distinctive class-book. A noted Frenchman, who visited this country about forty years ago, wrote of Connecticut that from its small area went forth teachers, law-givers, and clock-makers; and, if we may so use the word, Connecticut has been a creative state—a state whence impulses strong and powerful have gone forth toward the betterment of the country.

It is to this energy of its inhabitants that we can attribute its success in educational affairs, and this honor of being the state that gave the first impetus to the evolution of the text-book. As soon as circumstances so framed themselves in the course of the construction of this commonwealth and the finances of the country were in a better condition, then the text-book began to be thought of. When the time is ripe, a thought that is running as a thread through a period finds an exponent for its expression. When the right hour came in the growth of our history then a new method and theory of teaching were developed and given to the people. Since that time school books have rapidly increased and advanced for all branches of study. This period came after the close of the Revolutionary War, for during that struggle, education and schools suffered with and like everything else in the country. When the war was finished, in the calm that followed, men might turn their attention to those advancements which would make toward the progress of the United States.

It was during this time that Noah Webster, who in the year 1758 was born in the town of West Hartford, Connecticut, had published in the year 1783 the first part of his Grammatical Institute. This Grammatical Institute was composed of a speller, a grammar and a reader; and in the two succeeding years after the speller was published, the grammar and reader appeared.

Previous to Webster's speller the Dilworth speller had been in use, and it can be remembered even now by some of the oldest inhabitants of New England. In a measure, the Dilworth book served as a model for Webster's speller, although it differed materially, as Mr. Dilworth was an Englishman with all the national prejudice of his nation at that time, and his book savored altogether of English form and custom, for it contained long lists of the abreviations of honorary English titles, which although they might be needful in England were hardly so necessary here; moreover, it dealt with words more current in England than in America, for each country has its own preferences and shades of meaning in its vernacular, and Mr. Dilworth omitted in his book American linguistical additions.

Noah Webster wished to break away from all this, and to gain a new footing; he desired to lay aside this English spirit of ceremonial, the forms and the very evident spirit of subserviency toward the aristocracy which seemed to pervade the Dilworth speller, and, in short, in contradistinction to the English work, to establish in all American schools a pure national spelling-book. So, although the Dilworth speller may have aided Webster in his ideas in regard to forming a speller, yet between the two works lay the distance of the ocean, for one had to do with England, the other with America. This is a favorite remark of Webster's: "In the year 1782, while the American army was lying on the banks of the Hudson, I kept a classical school in Goshen, Orange county, State of New York. I there compiled two small elementary books for teaching the English language. The country was impoverished, intercourse with Great Britain was interrupted, school-books were scarce and hardly obtainable, and there was no certain prospect of peace." This work, which was undertaken by Webster at this time, was "The Grammatical Institute of the English Language, comprising an easy and systematic method of education, designed for the use of schools in America." This work had a large and imposing title, but the famous speller part became best known as Webster's spelling-book. Perhaps Webster builded even wiser than he knew when he penned in the following paragraph the aims of his indefatigable labors: "I spared no pains to make the orthography correspond to the analogies of our language and the usages of the country, banishing the French spelling and the harsh Indian pronunciation." And in very truth he performed well this task which he set for himself. Webster other-where made this statement: "That the spelling book did more for the language of a nation than any other book." How far he realized the great truth that was in these words, we cannot now know, but from our coigne of vantage (the lapse of time) we can look backward, conscious of the changes that time with its fulfilling touch has wrought, and of the great stride in the progress of affairs and of education, and we can realize in its fullness Webster's statement. It has been cogently written,—"The peasant of the Apennines drives his goats home at evening over hills that look down on six provinces, none of whose dialects he can speak." What a contrast this is to affairs in America, whose great area extends three thousand miles, and where we speak a uniform language! This gift of a uniform speech we owe to Noah Webster, whose dictionary and spelling book were the two great influences in keeping the language in this country pure. This spelling book attained speedily to a marvelous success and widespread popularity, and as it was used in all parts of the country, it exerted a far-reaching influence, and probably a greater one than that of any other single book of study ever published. Webster bestowed much attention in his speller upon orthography and analogy, as he tells us, and the fables, which were one of the features of the book, became household words wherever the speller went; and they were beneficial in every way, beside interesting the child who read them, for they taught morality, legality, and patriotism. To-day, all over the United States, we are free from marked differences of pronunciation which result from dialects, and we are exceptionally free from provincialisms. This happy state of our speech we trace rightly to the harmony of spelling and pronunciation produced by the wide use of Webster's spelling book. The sales of this work were enormous, and it passed through various editions and revisions. By the year 1847 it had reached the sale of no less than twenty-four million copies, and by 1870 of over forty million. This book has held its own nearly to the present time, but it is now superseded by more modern and improved methods.

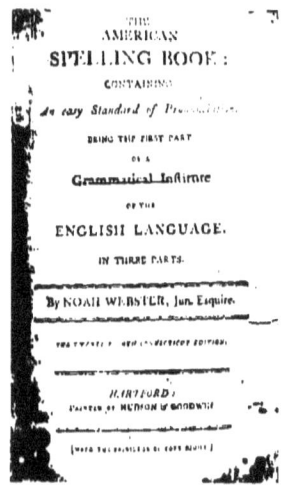

TITLE PAGE OF WEBSTER'S SPELLING BOOK.

Fortunately, the speller preceded the dictionary, as by the ample proceeds which its sales brought, Webster found the wherewithal to allow him the leisure to mature the plan of his dictionary. This speller was also the means of a most important movement in the laws of the country, as it gave the impulse to the earliest action of the States and Congress in regard to the laws of copyright. Before this work was published Webster took the manuscript and rode on horseback to visit the influential men of the different States, and showed to them his projected work. In this way he succeeded in gaining their active co-operation in the matter of the copyright law, for which Webster petitioned the legislatures of the States, and saw his efforts achieve success.

The reader which he compiled, although a popular book, did not gain for itself such a popularity as the speller, which could not be hoped for. It was composed of selections for reading taken from the masters of English prose, and is interesting, although it has not been in use in schools for some years.

The grammar division of the Institute was by far too radical in theory to establish itself, but it was nevertheless a work of merit. Mr. Chauncey Goodrich (who was the son-in-law of Noah Webster) says of this grammar: "It was a highly original work, the result of many years of diligent investigation." Webster disapproved earnestly of English grammar being conformed in its plan to the grammars of the Latin and Greek languages in the nomenclature and classification. However, it was impossible to carry out this plan, for there existed in the minds of the people too great a prejudice against such an entire change in nomenclature, and this hindered the grammar securing wide acknowledgement. In the year 1807, Webster, who had profited by his former experience and who saw wherein he had failed, issued a "Philosophical and Practical Grammar of the English Language," and this work was more satisfactory in its result.

Webster, in some ways, was a man of radical views, and even at the early date in which he lived, favored the since much discussed phonetic spelling, but he did not think that his time was ready to adopt it with success and advantage. Few of our day think of the great debt to Noah Webster which is owing him from all of his countrymen, or realize how potent was his work and his life in this nation.

Contemporaneous with Webster, Caleb Bingham lived, acquiring celebrity as a teacher in Boston, whom I briefly shall mention, as he was originally from

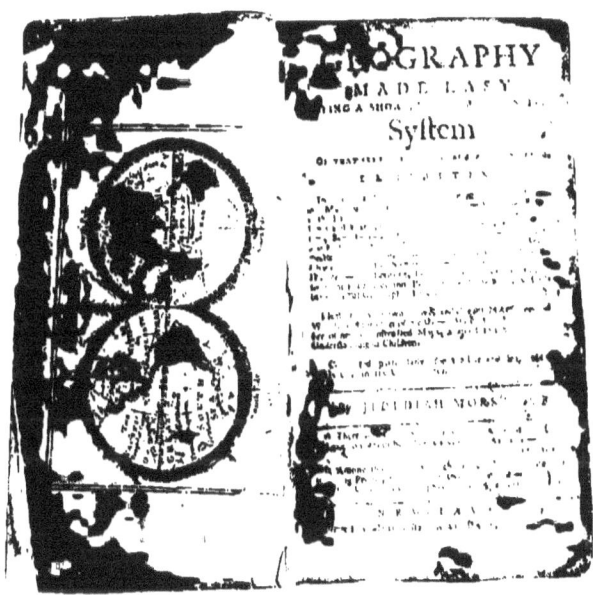

TITLE PAGES OF MORSE'S GEOGRAPHY.

Connecticut, although he is closely allied to the educational history of Massachusetts.

Caleb Bingham wrote school books, some of them dealing with the same subjects as those which employed Webster's attention, and some of Mr. Bingham's admirers have claimed a somewhat rival fame for his books with the books of Webster. This claim cannot be sustained. In the case of the readers there may have been justice in it; but as for spellers, Bingham's was completely lost sight of in the fame of the Webster Spelling Book. There was no question of rivalry in them, for the Webster book stood in conspicuous pre-eminence.

In the lists of books studied in the early schools, Morse's Geography frequently meets the eye. This book was written by Jedidiah Morse, a learned and talented man, whose birthplace was Woodstock, Connecticut. The first geographical work that he issued, called "Geography Made Easy," was adapted from some of the larger English works on the subject.

Dr. Morse had used this system of geography written in manuscript in teaching his pupils before he issued it in book form to the public, and his students so much liked it that they frequently made copies of it for their own purposes. This induced Dr. Morse to have the work published for general use, and the first edition appeared in the year 1784 as the first work of the kind published in the United States. This fact brought the geography into prominence as being first in the field, and the great excellence of the work gained for it the favor of the public. These remarks are in the preface: "Geography made easy, being a compendious system of that very useful and agreeable science." And farther on we read: "To the young gentlemen and ladies throughout the United States this compendious system of geography, a science no longer esteemed as a polite and agreeable accomplishment only, but a very necessary and important part of education, is with the most ardent wishes for their improvement, dedicated and devoted by their very humble servant, the author."

Some time after this geography was published, Dr. Morse brought out The American Geography, in the year 1789. This book passed through many editions, and was deservedly popular. In the year 1812 we find it issued in two bulky volumes, between whose leathern covers lay a very encyclopedia of knowledge. The American Review and Literary Journal for the year 1802 gives a long, comprehensive and critical article to this work which was just then issued, in one of its editions, and in an improved style. The Review makes the statement that " The blunders of European geographers are many, and sometimes ridiculous, and that Americans who wish to gain a knowledge of the geography of their own country would find this work of Dr. Morse's authentic, and they would do well to study it." This geography gives in its introduction an account of all geographical theories in a concise manner, from the time of Thales, the philosopher. The American Review closes its article with this paragraph: " The public has been so long acquainted with the merit of Dr. Morse as an author that we need not here enter into a particular examination." As Dr. Morse wrote so early among text-book makers of our country, and with but poor material, it cannot be expected to find in his work the advanced ideas and methods which came later on as the geographical science was developed, but it was a wonderful book for its time, and contains for a reader of the present day even much valuable information. These geographies had a large circulation, and gained for Dr. Morse the title of the father of American geography.

I wish to speak now of perhaps a less famous and less widely known geography, but of one deserving great commendation, which was the joint work of Mrs. Emma Willard, of honored memory, and of William C. Woodbridge, who lived from his infancy almost his entire life in Connecticut. He was born in Massachusetts, but when he was an infant his parents moved their family to Middletown, Connecticut. In regard to the subject of geography, Mrs. Willard wrote: " The books of geography, being closely confined to the order of place, and those of history to that of time, by which much repetition was made necessary, and comprehensive views of topics by comparison and classification were debarred." She also goes on to write in detail of the faults in the geographies

EARLY TEXT BOOKS IN CONNECTICUT.

of her time, and points out how these errors may be remedied, and also to tell the way in which she formulated her own geography. Her methods of teaching she had for some time previous to publication used in her seminary at Troy, New York, and the young ladies under her instruction had so greatly benefited therefrom that Mrs. Willard concluded to have the geography published, setting forth her views of that science.

At the same time that Mrs. Willard was preparing for the publication of her work, William C. Woodbridge was similarly engaged in regard to the same study. It so happened that Mrs. Willard was persuaded to mingle her ideas on the subject with Mr. Woodbridge's, and the result of this happy conjunction of thought was the Willard-Woodbridge geography. As Mrs. Willard was a Connecticut woman, her class-books are of educational interest to this state; these works were all of a high grade of excellence and the results of the

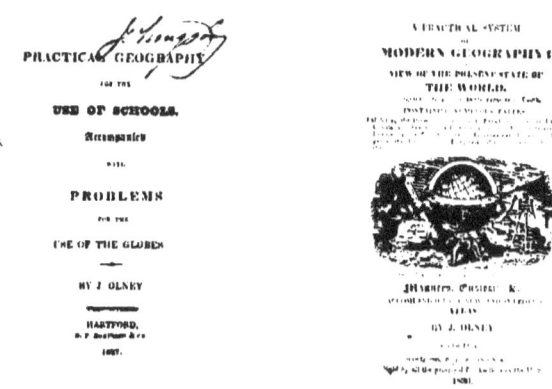

TITLE PAGE OF OLNEY'S GEOGRAPHY. (FIRST EDITION.)

TITLE PAGE OF A LATER EDITION OF OLNEY'S GEOGRAPHY.

thought of a woman who was in advance of her time. Such books, as in their individuality make a marked step forward in the methods of study, and are truly imperishable stones in the structure of education. I will not here enumerate all of Mrs. Willard's educational works, but they were many, both geographies and histories, modern and ancient.

In continuing the subject of geographies we come to the most noteworthy and famous of all the early geographies, that of Jesse Olney.

In the year of 1827, when Mr. Olney was thirty years of age, he issued to the public a geography and atlas, a work that proved a most wonderful success, and attained immediate popularity. It was, at once, introduced into nearly all schools and was regarded as a standard work. For as many as thirty years both public and private schools, in the United States, adopted Olney's geography. It was improved and enlarged very many times, and went through ninety-eight editions, which ran as high as eighty thousand copies. The popularity of this geography was second to Webster's Spelling Book. Olney's geography marked an epoch in the theory of this science and in the method of its instruction. It was a decided and revolutionary advance, when new and different theories were developed and made practicable, when the old ways of teaching were put aside by the vigorous ideas of a practical instructor. Olney keenly felt the lack in geographical class books then in vogue, and his dissatisfaction brought about the fortunate result of the new system, and the entire change in geographies. For Olney utterly discarded the old plan of teaching this study, which was long and roundabout, and which started with the solar system, and then worked its way through a labyrinth of explanation until, at last, it came to the earth. Olney abandoned all this and began with the concrete whence he worked to the abstract—with the near at hand, and from there he went to the distant. By this method the pupil became familiar with the earth's surface, and with the geographical terms, as applied to home objects, and thus he could the more easily comprehend the subject when he came to study the distant countries. That this plan of teaching should immediately overthrow the old method is not at all astonishing, nor that it should establish itself in the place of the former method. Since the introduction of Olney's geography into schools there has been, materially, almost no change in the method, and there is little reason to suppose that a better theory could be adopted. This author, who so thoroughly revolutionized this science of geography, to its great advance, and for a better understanding and comprehensive view of the study, was born in Union, Tolland County, Connecticut, in 1798.

VIEW OF MAIN STREET, HARTFORD.
From an Olney Geography, edition of 1830.

At this point I shall make brief mention of two books that are valuable historically, though not well-known now. Frederick Butler, A. M. had published in the year 1817, a catechetical compend of general history, sacred and profane, from the creation of the world to the year 1817 of the Christian era, which book was in three parts. This seems an extensive design, and Mr. Butler in his preface remarks: "The school establishments in America are upon the most wise and liberal plans ever devised by man. They are the basis upon which all our civil and religious liberties rest. They are in general well supplied with useful and valuable school books in the different branches of science." We can gather from this remark in praise of the schools in America, and in the commendatory words about the numerous school books, how greatly the schools must have advanced in every way, which was due to the increasing prosperity of the nation. Mr. Butler goes on to say that he presents this book to the public, as previous to its publication there had been no such compend of general history published in the United States for the use of schools. The preface of the book which is dated at Wethersfield, Connecticut, October 15, 1817, is particularly interesting because it so clearly states the condition of educational affairs in the United States, and also because it is the first book of its character to be issued from the press in this country.

Let us return in thought now to the end of the eighteenth century, and consider the science of arithmetic and its growth. In the year 1796 there was printed and sold by one Thomas Hubbard, an introduction to arithmetic, for the use of common schools. This work was published in Norwich, Connecticut, and it was written by Erastus Root, A. B.

I deem worthy of attention this remark in the preface of this work as particularly demonstrating the trend of feeling and thought at the time ; " Transatlantic authors will no longer do for free and independent America— we have coins and denominations of money peculiar to ourselves; in these our youths ought to be instructed and familiarized." Further on in the preface we come upon this paragraph: " Here too the tree of liberty first put forth its blossoms after having been eaten for ages by the canker worm of feudal gothicism." The following statement of Mr. Root cannot fail to be amusing, and all young students of the arithmetic must have deeply admired his judgement. Mr. Root says " I have omitted fractions not because I think them useless, but because they are not absolutely necessary." The date of this preface was Hebron, Connecticut, June 8, 1795. It is worth while examining this crude method of arithmetical science, and to contrast the book with the elaborate treatises on the subject in use at the present time.

In naming Daboll's arithmetic, we speak of a book which enjoyed an enviable popularity, and of which S. G. Goodrich spoke in the passage already quoted from him (that this arithmetic had been used for nearly thirty-five years in schools), and it was undoubtedly the most widely used and popular arithmetic of its day, and its day was a long period. The following words introduced one edition of Daboll's arithmetic to its public: " The schoolmaster's assistant, improved and enlarged, being a plain, practical system of arithmetic adapted to the United States, by Nathan Daboll, with the addition of the practical accountant for farmers and mechanics, best methods of bookkeeping, for the easy instruction of youth, designed as a companion to Daboll's arithmetic." This book appeared in the year 1833. Daboll himself studied Cocker's arithmetic, an English work of exceeding difficulty, whose definitions were extremely long and most complicated and hard to understand. The study of such a verbose and difficult work must have impressed Daboll so that he felt the urgent need of a simpler book for the American schools. " The Schoolmaster's Assistant " was published in the year 1799, and Daboll met with difficulties and obtacles in the way of its publication. The publisher was doubtful as to whether the book would prove a success, or not and pecuniarily reward him for undertaking the printing of it, after allowing Daboll the royalty of but one cent a copy. Noah Webster, Prof. Meigs of Yale, Prof. Messer of Brown University, with other noted men gave the arithmetic their hearty endorsement

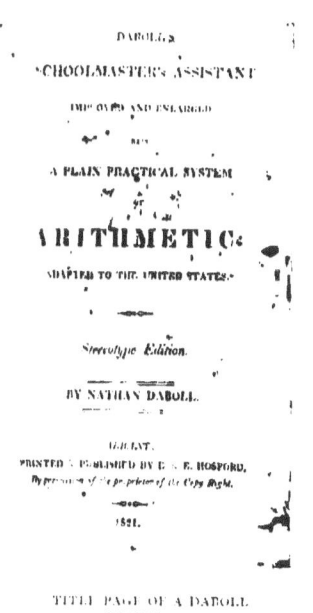

TITLE PAGE OF A DABOLL ARITHMETIC.

and approval, so that the first edition was issued under favorable auspices
The eminent success of the arithmetic removed all doubts of its financial value
from the mind of the publisher, and this fact was most fully attested, as the
first edition appeared when the publisher was in his prime, and though he lived
to the ripe age of ninety-eight years, he died when the arithmetic was still in
the tide of popularity. This arithmetic held its own against all newer arithmetics, as we have seen, for many years, and stood side by side with Webster's
Spelling Book almost, in popular favor. Daboll's arithmetic was by no means
an easy book, but there was no book to even approach it in excellence of
method through these many years of its use. The master who taught it possessed a sort of key to all the problems which it contained, in the form of a
manuscript book. To this book the pupils referred when they found it impossible
to solve an example. This sum-book stood in the stead of the table of answers
placed in the back of our mathematical text-book of to-day. Nathan Daboll
was born in Centre Groton, Connecticut, in the year 1750. As his career was
that of a teacher, he had ample opportunity to observe how great a need there
was for a good arithmetic in the school work, and as all his impulses were
those of a great educator, he felt the inspiration to help to supply the want.
He went to work to remedy this state of things, by devoting all the
leisure which he could gain in his life of teaching to compile his arithmetic.

We are now a nation whose schools and text-books rank well with those of
the nations of highest educational standard in the world; we should be generous in our gratitude to these men who rose up among their people as benefactors, and whose good sowing we are harvesting to-day; whose books were the
outcome of excellent foresight and persevering work.

When we read on the fly-page of some well thumbed school book of long
ago, a signature written in a childish hand, the name and the age of the young
student who conned its pages, something which we term association brings
an imagery about it:—

> " Even while I look, I can but heed
> The restless sands incessant fall,
> Importunate hours, that hours succeed,
> Each clamorous with its own sharp need,
> And duty keeping pace with all."

THE ANCIENT BURYING GROUND OF HARTFORD.

Opportunities for Descendants of Old Connecticut Families to Join in Memorials.

BY EMILY S. G. HOLCOMBE.

As the CONNECTICUT QUARTERLY deals with subjects of peculiar interest to the descendants of the old families of Connecticut whose ancestral lines converge to that little band of English pioneers who settled in Hartford in 1636, and who later were interred in the ancient cemetery of that place, I can but feel that the redemption of that cemetery has for them more than a passing interest. How familiar in Connecticut family traditions are the names of Hooker, Haynes, Wyllys, Talcott, Whiting, Webster, Lord, Denison, Goodwin, Wadsworth, Stanley, Stanton, Steele and others, most of whom are among the illustrious dead gathered together in that silent company. As early as 1640 the cemetery was established, and until 1803 was the only place of burial, so it contains the dust of all who died in Hartford during that period of 163 years. Rich and poor, high and low, all were there laid to their final rest.

Gradually as time wore on and high buildings were erected around this burial place, it disappeared from public view to become a thing of the past almost forgotten by the later generations. Few of the hurrying footsteps passing along the busy thoroughfare ever turned aside to enter that historic spot where slept a company of great men, fathers of the city, the state and the nation. Very few of the residents of Hartford, even those descended from its early citizens, ever visited that obscure ground. Hidden from sight, protected by a locked gate at the terminus of an inconspicuous alley, it truly was not an inviting spot nor an easy one to find. An occasional stranger having made a pilgrimage hither to visit the graves of his ancestors where sentiment might revel as at a sacred shrine, zealously hunted up the key and entered the cemetery, only to gaze with horror at its neglected condition and the tottering ancient headstones fast crumbling into dust. Large trees undisturbed had grown to such a size as to create a dense shade, and these with the shut-in situation of the ground produced great dampness and singular decay in the stones. Where monuments of like age in open country grounds only become covered with moss, suffering the obliteration of epitaphs, perhaps, the stones in the old Hartford burying ground owing to the dampness mentioned have desintegrated and many have fallen to pieces. When the Ruth Wyllys Chapter, D. A. R., undertook the task of redemption a year ago they had no reason to hope for such results as have since been accomplished, as they were told by those experienced in such matters that nothing could save those stones already far advanced in decay. But the Catfal process has wrought wonders, and to-day many stones which were apparently doomed to destruction now stand erect and so restored that they are almost a true image of their fresh and perfect youth. Although Hartford ground holds the ashes of that noble company of men and women, not to her alone belongs the honor of descent from those illustrious forefathers. Scattered all over Connecticut are families from that fine old stock and to a great extent over the entire country. For Connecticut blood has been a colonizing influence for many generations. To reach the descendants of those persons buried in the old burying ground hundreds of letters have been written and circulars distributed, and the responses have been most generous and spontaneous. The fund for the restoration of any monument is open to all the

GOLD STREET.

descendants of the ancestor whose memory is being thus honored and preserved. The persons engaged upon this work earnestly hope that this opportunity for co-operation may become very generally known in all parts of the country where reside descendants of Hartford's "founders" and early citizens. A full record will be made and preserved of all the work done in the cemetery under the auspices of the Ruth Wyllys Chapter, D. A. R., and these lists of descendants joining in a mutual work of honoring a common ancestor and caring for his burial place as well as preserving his monument will make a most interesting record for future generations to read. It is hard to realize, but nevertheless true, that we are making a history which generations yet unborn will contemplate and study. The summer has been a season of busy work in the old cemetery and ninety stones have been restored, but as there are five hundred memorials in the yard needing treatment, it will be seen that but a beginning has been made and there is still ample opportunity for the assistance of those who are interested.

Just where the great Hooker, the "Father of the Constitution," was buried is not known, but his monument stands near the entrance in near company to others of that illustrious band. Many descendants have been happy to join in the honor of restoring and preserving the stone erected to his memory. Those having already contributed are: Mr. John Hooker, Mrs. John C. Day, the Misses Day, Mr. Edward W. Hooker, Miss Rosile Hooker, Dr. Edward B. Hooker and family, Mrs. Martha W. Hooker, Mr. Thomas W. Hooker, Mrs. Sarah A. Talcott, Mr. Charles Hooker Talcott, of Hartford; Mr. William Gillette of New York, Mr. Henry G. Newton of New Haven, Mrs. S. M. Hotchkiss of New Haven, Mr. W. E. Downs of New Haven, Mr. Charles E. Mitchell of Nyack, N. Y., Mr. George S. Talcott of New Britain; Mrs. William (Nancy Hooker) Hill, Mrs. George R. (Adeline F. Hill) Bowman and Miss Clara Lee Bowman, of Bristol ; Miss Ellen Francis Hooker and Mr. Joseph Hooker Woodward, Hartford; Miss Mary Cheney and Miss Alice Cheney, South Manchester; Mrs. C. D. Bramble, New London. Any descendants of the Rev. Thomas Hooker who have not already identified themselves with his memorial can do so by communicating with Mr. John Hooker, 16 Marshall street, Hartford.

The next table stone to the north of Thomas Hooker's is that of Governor John Haynes, one of the most conspicuous figures in early Connecticut colonial life, and the first governor of the colony, being elected in 1639 and re-elected governor every second year and deputy-governor every alternate year until his death in 1654. His wife, Mabel Harlakenden, that representative of English royalty, does not lie by his side, for she later married Samuel Eaton and removed to New Haven. The descendants of Governor Haynes have been prompt and generous in their contributions, and those already on the list are : Colonel Frank Cheney and family, Mrs. Edward Hooker, Miss Rosalie Hooker, Miss Caroline Day, Miss Mabel H. Perkins, Miss White, Mr. John C. Day, Miss Catherine S. Day, Miss Alice H. Day, Miss Mary K. Talcott, Mr. James P. Taylor, Henry A. Perkins, Mr. Edward Perkins, from Hartford; Mr. John T. Terry and family, New York; Mrs. Charles P. Turner, Philadelphia; General Charles Darling of Utica; Mrs. John F. Maynard of Utica; Mrs. Walter Ferguson, Stamford; Miss E. Gertrude Taylor, Sandusky; Mrs. J. A. Woolworth, Sandusky; Mr. Anson Phelps Stokes, New York; Miss Olivia Stokes, New York; Miss Caroline Phelps Stokes, New York; Mr. John Bliss, Brooklyn, N. Y.;

Prof. Thomas Day Seymour, New Haven; Miss Emily Seymour, Hartford; Miss Caroline Day Bissell, Hartford; Col. Louis R. Cheney, Hartford; Miss Eliza Trumbull Cheney, Hartford. Any other desiring to be identified in this work can please send their names and contributions to Miss Mary K. Talcott, 815 Asylum avenue, Hartford.

During the next summer a most beautiful monument will be erected to the Wyllys family; it will be an exact reproduction of one of the finest types of early colonial work and be placed near the center of the grounds where it is known the Wyllysses were buried. This will be a memorial of one of the most illustrious families ever living in Hartford; three of whose members occupied the position of Secretary of the Colony and State consecutively from 1712 to 1809. Hezekiah Wyllys from 1712 to his death in 1734; his son George from 1734 to his death in 1796; Samuel, son of George, 1796 to 1809.

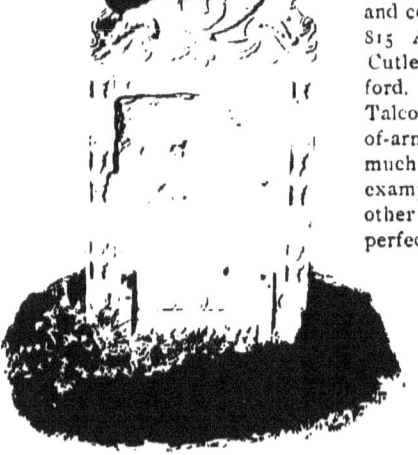

BEFORE RESTORATION.

Many descendants have already contributed, but any one a Wyllys descendant can join in this family circle by sending name and contribution to Miss Mary K. Talcott, 815 Asylum avenue, or Mr. Ralph W. Cutler, Hartford Trust Company, Hartford. The monument to Governor Joseph Talcott, one of beauty and bearing a coat-of-arms, had fallen into a condition of much decay but now stands a beautiful example of the power of redemption. Another governor whose memorial has been perfectly restored by his descendants is that of Governor Leete. The most extraordinary restoration of any stone is that of Mabel Wyllys Talcott, because from a mere wreck it has undergone complete transformation. Although still standing upright, it having suffered great desintegration and seemed but a shadow, the front and back surfaces had long ago flaked off until in the center of the stone but one-half inch of firm texture remained. There was nothing to indicate the identity, except an instinct of Miss Talcott's, which was verified by an examination of Dr. Hoadley's list of stones where we procured the exact original inscription. A border of carved leaves on the top of the stone and a fragment of carving at the bottom alone remained of the original beautiful design, but it was a valuable index, and with such clues we have restored the stone from that spectre of a monument which seemed ready to fall at the slightest touch, to its original character, and now it stands perfect in every detail and as fitting a memorial of Mabel Wyllys Talcott as could be desired. It seems almost unnecessary to state that there has been absolutely no modernizing, such a thing would be looked upon as desecration by the committee of the Ruth Wyllys Chapter. The necessary cleaning gives of course a fresh appearance, and it needs hardly an argument, it seems to me, to prove that the inscriptions when effaced should be recut, for a gravestone with no record has lost its value and is of no more service than a lump of field granite. When a choice piece of antique colonial furniture is brought forth to be given the place of honor in the household and a broken foot is repaired that the revered article may stand firm and safe, and some accumulations of dust scraped off to make this household god clean and attractive, I have never heard the process stigmatized as that of "modernizing." There are practical details of restoration which must be accomplished, and when an old stone which stands at a ridiculously unsteady angle of 45 degrees and has lost every word of its record is cleaned, straightened and the inscription recut exactly like the original with no change in any respect from its colonial characteristics, can any restoration be more true or free from the criticism of "being modernized?" In cases where the inscriptions have disappeared, as has frequently been the case, the exact originals have been found in Dr. Hoadley's priceless list of epitaphs copied by him in 1870. To his foresight and to the patient work of twenty-seven years ago, as well as to his present courtesy, all who are interested in this work of redemption in the cemetery are greatly indebted, and I feel that the value of this list can hardly be overestimated. A one dollar subscription has been started for one of the founders of Hartford whose descendants are legion, Ozias Goodwin, the father of all of that name in this part of the country. It seems singular that with so many Goodwins born in Hartford, who lived, died here and were buried in the old cemetery, there should be so few stones of that name now existing — only ten.

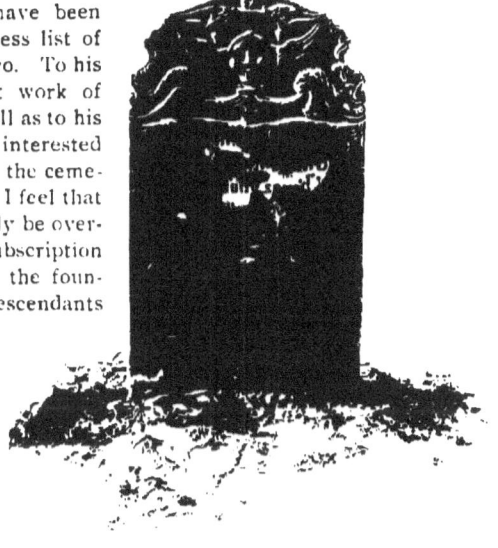

AFTER RESTORATION.

I am told that the Goodwins were buried where the Waverly now stands, possibly also under the church or chapel or even the sidewalk. Contributions may be sent to Mrs. W. N. Pelton, 792 Asylum avenue, or Mrs. John M. Holcombe, 79 Spring street. Thirty dollars have already been subscribed.

Descendants of the Rev. Timothy Woodbridge may send to Miss Mary K. Talcott, 815 Asylum avenue. Samuel Stone's descendants may send to Mrs. W. N. Pelton, 792 Asylum avenue, Hartford. The Rev. Samuel Stone left no descendants in the male line, so there are no representatives of his name, but there are numerous direct descendants from his daughters — one the wife of Thomas Butler, has many representatives; his daughter Elizabeth married first William Sedgwick, second John Roberts; Rebecca married Timothy Nash; Mary married Joseph Fitch.

In case sums donated exceed the amount required for the stone in question, the balance will be used on the improvement of the cemetery, and this work is almost as important as the care of the stones. There are several fine table stones not yet arranged for, and I give them as follows, hoping thus

ROW OF STONES BEFORE RESTORATION.

to find persons interested in their preservation: Mrs. Eunice Wadsworth, 1736; Thomas Wadsworth, 1716; Lieut. Col. John Allyn, 1696; Mr. John Ellery, no date; Daniel Lord, 1762; Elisha Lord, 1725; James Richards, 1680, coat-of-arms carved on stone; John Ledyard, 1771; William Ellery, 1812; Dr. Eliakim Fish, 1804 (the daughter of Dr. Eliakim Fish married John Morgan, one of the founders of Christ Church and for whom Morgan street was named. Are there any descendants?); Deacon Solomon Smith, 1786. The table monuments of the pastors of the First (or Center) Church will be restored by their descendants, except the one erected to the memory of the Rev. Edward Dorr. As he left no children the First Church has put his tomb in perfect order. McLean, 1741; William Stanley, 1786 (Mr. Stanley left all his property to the South Church); Rev. Benjamin Boardman, Pastor South Church, 1802; Anna Smith Strong, 1784, wife of Dr. Nathan Strong, dau. Dea. Solomon Smith, gr. dau. George Talcott.

What seemed a very necessary improvement to this sacred God's Acre was to convert the neighboring alley, called Gold street, whose tenements overhung this sacred spot and whose filth often desecrated it, into a broad, fine avenue by removing the old rookeries and thus place the ancient cemetery upon a spacious and beautiful thoroughfare, where, in a position public and honorable in the center of the business portion of the city, the throngs who daily pass could read the historic names of those so long since buried there and meditate upon the deeds that live in the nation's life and the veneration of a grateful people. Eighty thousand dollars it would cost to buy these buildings, and to aid in this matter the Ruth Wyllys Chapter offered to raise by public subscription the sum of ten thousand dollars to be used in any way determined by the Street Board. The Chapter issued a public appeal asking for $15,000—$10,000 to devote to the city to aid in the widening of Gold street, the balance for the improvement of the cemetery. In two weeks from the publication of the appeal $10,000 had been pledged, and after that figure was reached the contributions were for the cemetery work. Our "Fund" had reached the sum of $13,000 in June. The old First Church had a fund of its own to raise, and very soon the voluntary subscriptions amounted to $10,000; so with the $13,000 contributed to the "Ruth Wyllys Chapter Fund" it will be seen that the citizens of Hartford have contributed nearly $23,000 to redeem her ancient cemetery from neglect and give it a proper setting. In compliance with the requirements of the law, the matter of widening Gold street has twice come before the Common Council, and this body has *unanimously* directed the necessary steps to be taken. The matter is still in the hands of the Street Board.

During the last summer much interest has been aroused all over the country. Sympathetic chords have been touched and responses have come from a wide extent of territory, even as far west as California. We seem entering upon a period of renewed patriotism when the very atmosphere is teeming with the spirit of loyalty and reverence for the "Founders" of this, "our country," and I am sure when the old cemetery is brought to public view adornments will be added and memorials of various kinds created. There may

A ROW OF RESTORED STONES.

Connecticut preserve some of her traditions in beautiful design and enduring stones and honor the sacred dust of those whose "ability, valor, sufferings and achievements are beyond all praise." May their descendants not enjoy a justifiable pride that they are linked to that historic past and those early patriots through the long chain of lineal descent?

In the center of the cemetery is a venerable monument erected sixty-two years ago to the memory of the "Founders of Hartford," and bearing the following names:

NAMES ON THE CENTRAL MONUMENT.

John Haynes,	William Andrews,	Joseph Easton,
Thomas Hooker,	Samuel Wakeman,	Richard Olmsted,
George Wyllys,	Jeremy Adams,	Richard Risley,
Edward Hopkins,	Richard Lyman,	Robert Bartlett,
Matthew Allyn,	William Butler,	Thomas Root,
Thomas Welles,	Thomas Lord,	John Wilcox,
John Webster,	Matthew Marvin,	Richard Seymour,
William Whiting,	Gregory Wolterton,	Benjamin Burr,
John Talcott,	Andrew Bacon,	John Bidwell,
Andrew Warner,	John Barnard,	Nathaniel Ely,
William Pantrey,	Richard Goodman,	Thomas Judd,
William Westwood,	Nathaniel Richards,	Richard Lord,
James Olmsted,	John Pratt,	William Kelsey,
Thomas Hosmer,	Thomas Birchwood,	Richard Butler,
Nathaniel Ward,	George Graves,	Robert Day,
William Wadsworth,	William Gibbons,	Seth Grant
John White,	Edward Stebbing,	Thomas Spencer,
John Steele,	George Steele,	John Baysey,
Thomas Scott,	George Stocking,	William Pratt,
William Goodwin,	Joseph Mygatt,	Thomas Bull,
Thomas Stanley,	William Bloomfield,	William Holton,
Samuel Stone,	William Hill,	Francis Andrews,
John Clark,	William Hyde,	James Cole,
John Crow,	John Arnold,	John Skinner,
James Ensign,	Arthur Smith,	Thomas Hale,
Stephen Post,	John Maynard,	Samuel Hale,
Stephen Hart,	William Hayden,	Thomas Olcott,
William Spencer,	Thomas Stanton,	Thomas Selden,
John Moody,	John Hopkins,	William Parker,
William Lewis,	Nicholas Clark,	Samuel Greenhill,
William Rusco,	John Marsh,	Ozias Goodwin,
Timothy Stanley,	Edward Elmer,	Thomas Bunce,
Richard Webb,	Richard Church,	Clement Chaplin.
	Zachariah Field,	

These names represent the fountain-head of most of the pure streams which have carried American national principles to the furthermost regions of this country.

I append the list made in 1835 of gravestones standing in the old cemetery now in the possession of Dr. Chas. J. Hoadly, State Librarian, and president of the Connecticut Historical Society. The Hartford *Courant* says: "It should be carefully read so that those who have relatives buried in the Ancient Hartford Cemetery may know the fact. They can then find a reason for helping to put that sacred spot in order."

Dr. Hoadly has also a list of burials called the "Sexton's List," from 1749 to 1806, including two thousand names. This has been copied and prepared for print by Miss M. K. Talcott, registrar Ruth Wyllys Chapter, and will be published in the four numbers of the CONNECTICUT QUARTERLY beginning in

THE ANCIENT BURYING GROUND OF HARTFORD.

the issue of April next. All these lists give but a fraction of the number buried in the old cemetery, which, be it remembered, was Hartford's only burial place from 1640 to 1803, and where Dr. Walker estimates there were nearly six thousand interments.

NAMES ON THE GRAVESTONES STANDING IN 1835.

Name	Died.	Age.
Aggnis, Margaret	1781	20
Austin, Mary, wife of John	1753	76
Adams, Frederick	1798	1
Arnold, Jonathan	1710	39
Arnold, Hannah, wife of Jonathan	1714	35
Allyn, Hon. Col. John, Secretary Colony 34 years	1696	
Burr, Sarah	1750	69
Burnham, Elisha	1770	53
Children of Elisha and Sarah Burnham.		
Burnham, Sarah	1770	25
Burnham, Abigail	1770	13
Burnham, Ephraim	1770	20
Burnham, Richard	1766	18
Bunce, John	1794	44
Bunce, Thomas	1711	36
Bunce, John	1794	6
Bunce, Elizabeth, wife of Thos.	1741	65
Bunce, Joseph	1750	72
Bunce, Susanna	1780	25
Children of Caleb and Martha Bull.		
Bull, Martha	1759	9
Bull, George	1759	3
Bull, Susannah, wife of Capt. Thomas	1680	70
Bull, Rebecca, wife of Caleb, Jr.	1775	27
Bull, Caleb, son of Caleb, Jr.	1775	6
Bull, Jefferson		2
Bull, James, son of Frederick	1778	18m
Bull, Epaphras, son of Aaron	1747	15m
Bull, Esther, wife of Joseph	1783	42
Bull, Abigail, wife of Aaron	1758	40
Bull, Daniel Deacon	1776	68
Bull, Mary, wife of Daniel	1760	86
Bull, Elizabeth, wife of Daniel	1775	55
Bull, Catherine, wife of George	1800	32
Bull, Mary, wife of David	1763	42
Bull, Ruth, wife of Thomas	1805	40
Bull, Thomas Parkin, son of Amos	1794	3
Bacon, Elizabeth, wife of Andrew, formerly of Timothy Stanley	1678	76
Bigelow, Jonathan	1710	62
Bigelow, Timothy	1747	45
Bigelow, John	1780	41
Bigelow, Jonathan	1749	75
Bigelow, Rebecca	1754	44
Bigelow, Jonathan	1779	55
Bigelow, Thomas	1767	31
Bigelow, Jonas	1756	4
Bigelow, Levina	1756	10
Bigelow, Abigail, wife of Daniel	1757	32
Bigelow, Timothy	1761	31
Bigelow, Hannah, wife of Timothy	1763	25
Balch, Sarah, wife of Ebenezer	1756	20
Bidwell, James	1718	26
Bidwell, Martha, wife of Jon'an	1735	46
Bassett, Elsey, wife of John	1778	80
Bassett, Willimytje, daughter of Frederick	1777	12
Barnard, Thomas	1724	43
Barnard, Ebenezer	1799	73
Barnard, Sarah, wife of Samuel	1776	30
Butler, Jerusha	1777	61
Butler, Patty, wife of Norman	1806	43
Butler, Moses	1801	86
Butler, Sarah, wife of Moses	1813	84
Boardman, Daniel, son of Oliver	1799	8
Boardman, Daniel E., " "	1803	1
Boardman, Benjamin (Rev.), pastor Second Church	1802	71
Boardman, Anna, wife Rev. Benjamin	1809	92
Bow, Rosanna	1780	24
Benton, John, Jr.,	1790	38
Benton, Andrew	1683	63
Bliss, David	1791	33
Bliss, Wealthy, daughter of Isaac	1799	5
Beauchamp, John	1740	88
Beauchamp, Margaret, wife of John	1727	59
Brown, William	1803	39
Brown, Phebe	1798	25
Brainard, Hezekiah	1727	46
Benjamin, Charles	1792	7m
Bolles, John	1799	11
Bolles, John	1783	4m
Bolles, Harris	1782	2
Breck, Helena, wife of Rev. Mr. Breck, formerly of Rev. Mr. Dorr	1797	78
Brewster, Alithea, wife of Prince	1802	58
Beckwith, Elizabeth, wife of Samuel	1793	33
Beckwith, Hart	1790	1
Bradley, Aaron	1802	61
Burr, Mary, wife of Timothy	1785	34
Burr, William	1800	53
Burr, Mittie, wife of William	1773	
Burr, William	1792	20
Burr, Thomas	1777	50
Burr, Sarah, wife of Thomas	1799	73
Burr, Timothy	1799	50
Burr, Samuel	1792	47
Burr, Moses	1792	77
Burr, Elizabeth, wife of Moses	1796	74
Burr, Mary, wife of Joseph	1796	36
Burr, Rebecca	1778	3
Burr, Rebecca	1775	2
Burr, Sidney	1795	2m
Burr, William H., son of Timothy	1800	9m
Branthwaite, Robert	1790	64
Branthwaite, Ruth, wife of Robert	1799	61
Babcock, John	1706	65
Babcock, Andrew	1790	17
Barlett, Isaac	1794	35
Beach, Sally, daughter of Miles	1800	16
Barrett, Rebecca, wife of Capt. Jos.	1770	47
Bradley, John, son of Aaron	1802	19
Caleb Bull's family tomb:		
Bull, Esther, wife of Joseph	1783	41

82 THE ANCIENT BURYING GROUND OF HARTFORD.

Name	Died	Age
Bull, James J.	1821	48
Bull, Joseph	1797	63
Bull, Caleb	1789	72
Bull, Martha	1786	62
Cadwell, Matthew	1719	51
Cadwell, Deborah, wife of Edward	1772	85
Cadwell, Edward	1751	71
Cadwell, John	1751	29
Coleman, Deborah, wife of John	1757	27
Cooke, Aaron	1725	61
Cooke, Martha, wife of Aaron	1732	65
Cooke, Moses	1738	38
Cooke, Joseph	1747	67
Cooke, Mabel, wife of James	1800	38
Cooke, Jeremiah, son of James	1790	17
Collier, Jennett, wife of Hezekiah	1806	75
Collier, Hepzibah, wife of Hezekiah	1770	57
Collier, Grove	1768	29
Collier, Hezekiah	1763	56
Collier, Thomas Capt.	1763	54
Collyer, Ann		
Collyer, Joseph	1738	61
Collyer, John	1740	6
Collyer, Thankful, wife of Daniel	1792	85
Coomes, Miriah	1794	9m
Crocker, Lucy, wife of Freeman	1796	46
Conkling, May, wife of Benjn.	1789	36
Clark, Eunice	1774	10
Clark, Daniel	1679	16d
Currie, James	1763	36
Cowles, Hannah, wife of John of Hatfield	1683	70
Cole, Lidiah	1683	28
Cable, John	1798	58
Colt, John, son of Peter	1785	8
Church, Elizabeth, wife of Joseph	1751	26
Caldwell, John, father of Major John	1758	29
Caldwell, Mary, daughter of John and Hannah	1736	2
Caldwell, Margaret	1775	1
Caldwell, John	1777	18m
Caldwell, Samuel	1782	3
Chapman, Robert	1711	63
Cotton, Elizabeth, wife of Daniel	1701	49
Chenevard, Margaret, wife of John M.	1783	76
Chenevard, Jane, daughter of John M.	1788	63
Chenevard, John Capt.	1805	72
Chenevard, Hepzibah, wife of John	1774	33
Chenevard, Michael	1801	30
Chenevard, John Michael	1735	56
Chenevard, Mary	1774	9m
Chenevard, William	1778	1
Chenevard, Henry	1781	10d
Caldwell, Margaret, wife of John	1708	40
Caldwell, James	1801	3
Caldwell, James Church	1795	1
Caldwell, Hepzebah	1795	4
Deming, Lemuel	1724	23
Dennison, George	1694	74
Doolittle, Enos	1806	56
Doolittle, Asenath, wife of Enos	1804	45
Duplessy, Francis	1731	38
Davenport, Elizabeth, wife of William	1697	27
Dorr, Edward, pastor First Church	1772	50
Day, Samuel C.	1804	31
Day, Mary	1804	3
Day, Mary	1798	1
Deming, Pownal	1795	46
Deming, Elizabeth	1793	2
Danforth, John	1805	10m
Danforth, Lucinda	1803	4
Dwight, Charles	1799	6w
Deane, Barnabas	1794	51
Ellery, Experience, wife of William	1773	26
Ellery, Mary, daughter of William	1781	19
Ellery, William	1812	72
Ellery, John (buried April 16, 1764)		
Ellery, Eunice, wife of John	1800	60
Eddy, Susannah, wife of Charles	1734	27
Edwards, Mary, wife of Richard	1723	62
Edwards, Richard	1718	71
Edwards, Samuel	1732	30
Eggleston, Elihu	1803	59
Ensign, Lucretia, wife of Thomas	1701	21
Ensign, Thomas, Jr.	1752	59
Ensign, Thomas	1759	16m
Ensign, Moses	1751	45
Flagg, Samuel	1757	53
Flagg, Sarah, wife of Samuel	1769	64
Flagg, Mary	1750	18
Flagg, Ruth, wife of Jonathan	1787	42
Fowler, Melzar	1797	20
Fish, Eliakim (Dr.)	1804	63
Fish, Sarah, wife of Eliakim	1803	66
Fish, Huldah, wife of Miller	1806	41
Farnsworth, Joseph	1741	48
Farnsworth, Mary	1741	43
Foster, Isaac (Rev.), pastor First Church	1682	
Foote, John	1803	40
Gardiner, David, of Gardiner's Island	1689	54
Gross, Rebecca, wife of Jonah	1718	32
Goodwin, Daniel	1772	67
Goodwin, Samuel	1776	66
Goodwin, Mary, daughter of Samuel and Lodema	1786	15
Goodwin, Sarah, wife of Nathaniel	1676	29
Goodwin, Abigail, wife of Samuel	1748	32
Goodwin, Abigail, widow of Captain Daniel	1776	73
Goodwin, Daniel	1700	44
Goodwin, Dorothy, wife of Lieut. Daniel	1746	79
Goodwin, Sarah, wife of Nathaniel	1740	60
Goodwin, Nathaniel	1746	79
Goodwin, Daniel	1790	44
Goodwin, Hannah	1805	48
Goodman, Abigail	1708	29
Goodman, Richard	1730	76
Goodman, Richard	1763	58
Goodrich, Abigail, wife of Lieut. Gov. Chauncey	1778	24
Gardiner, William	1766	24
Grimes, James	1794	17
Gilbert, Jonathan, Jr.	1741	40
Gilbert, Mary, wife of Jonathan	1700	74
Gilbert, Jonathan Cornet	1682	64

THE ANCIENT BURYING GROUND OF HARTFORD.   83

Name	Died	Age
Hyde, Sarah, wife of Ezra	1799	56
Holtom, Joseph	1770	77
Hamlin, Giles	1712	21
Hosmer, Sabra, wife of Joseph	1789	62
Hosmer, Susanna, wife of Stephen, Jr.,	1738	27
Hosmer, Joseph	1777	72
Hosmer, Thomas	1732	57
Hosmer, Stephen, son of Stephen	1673	5d
Hosmer, Mary, dau. of Stephen	1684	13
Hosmer, Sarah, dau. of Stephen	1685	4
Hosmer, Stephen (Dea.)	1693	49
Hosmer, Frances, wife of Thomas	1675	75
Hosmer, Thomas	1687	83
Hooker, Thomas (Rev.), pastor First Church	1647	61
Hooker, Thomas (Doct.)	1756	64
Hooker, Roger	1698	30
Hooker, Nathaniel	1711	40
Hooker, Nathaniel	1763	53
Hooker, Mary	1765	65
Hooker, Mary	1763	20
Hopkins, Betsy, wife of Jesse	1799	26
Hopkins, Daniel, three infant children of		
Hopkins, Sally, wife of Daniel	1796	29
Hopkins, Rebecca, wife of Asa	1791	29
Hopkins, Asa	1805	48
Hopkins, Lemuel (Doct.)	1801	50
Hart, Alcis Evelyn	1805	22
Hansom, Joseph	1804	33
Hinsdale, Magdalen, wife of Barnabas	1782	42
Hinsdale, Barnabas	1725	58
Hinsdale, Experience, wife of Amos	1781	61
Hudson, Maria, wife of Henry	1805	21
Haynes, John (Hon.), first Governor of Connecticut	1654	
Haynes, Joseph (Rev.), pastor of First Church	1679	38
Haynes, Sarah, wife of Rev. Joseph	1705	67
Haynes, John	1713	44
Haynes, Mary, wife of John	1726	54
Haynes, Sarah, daughter of John	1724	27
Hubbard, Cornelia, wife of Nehemiah	1781	28
Hall, Alley, daughter of William	1772	2
Hall, Jerusha, wife of Henry	1804	24
Hastings, Jonathan son of Lieut. Josiah, of Chesterfield, N. H.	1798	30
Howard, John	1804	35
Hancock, Patty, wife of Jonathan	1803	20
Hempsted, Anna, daughter of Doctor Hempsted	1799	32
Hempsted, Anna, wife of Doctor Hempsted	1797	66
Hempsted, Benjamin	1793	1
Jepson, Mrs. Susanna	1772	32
Jones, Pantry	1796	81
Jones, Amasa	1785	57
Jones, Hope, wife of Amasa	1798	63
Jones, Nathaniel	1773	92
Jones, Rebecca, wife of Nathaniel	1776	84
Jones, Levi, blown up in school house	1766	50
Jones, Daniel	1802	46
Jones, Olive, wife of Daniel	1788	27
Joy, Sarah, wife of John	1764	34
Keith, William	1745	31
Keith, Marianne, wife of William	1784	83
Knox, William	1787	55
Knowles, John	1754	64
Knowles, Rachel, wife of John	1739	38
Kilbourn, Abigail, wife of Nathaniel	1798	71
Kilbourn, Samuel	1789	17
Kennedy, Leonard, Jr.,	1796	17m
Lyman, Thomas	1727	49
Lyman, Martha, wife of Justin	1798	35
Lyman, Lorinda	1794	7
Ledlie, Mary, wife of Hugh	1809	79
Ledyard, Nathaniel, blown up in school house	1766	26
Ledyard, Austin	1766	25
Ledyard, John	1771	71
Lawrence, John, treasurer of Connecticut	1802	84
Lawrence, Margaret, wife of John	1775	49
Lawrence, Roderick	1783	27
Lawrence, John, Jr.,	1774	26
Lawrence, Mary Ann	1790	25
Lawrence, William Henry	1792	3
Lord, Abagail, ch. of Richard	1698	3m
Lord, Richard, ch. of Richard	1699	4
Lord, Abigail, ch. of Richard	1694	2m
Lord, Richard	1712	42
Lord, Mary (Alias Hooker)	1702	58
Lord, Elisha	1725	24
Lord, Mary, dau of John H.	1748	15m
Lord, Epaphras	1738	7
Lord, Daniel	1762	1
Lord, Daniel Edwards	1763	
Lord, John Haynes	1796	72
Lord, Rachel, wife of John H.	1803	77
Lord, Elizabeth, wife of Elisha	1786	32
Langrell, Thomas (Doct.)	1757	29
Law, Lydia	1799	42
Lette, William, Gov. of Conn.	1683	
Marsh, Katy, dau. of Capt. Saml.	1768	4
Merrills, Hannah	1730	49
Merrils, Mary, wife of Gideon	1750	29
Merrils, Christian, wife of Chas.	1778	23
Merrils, Martha Smith, wife of George	1793	37
Morrison, Ann, wife of Normand and formerly of John Smith	1766	64
Morrison, Roderick	1755	30
Marshall, Josiah	1712	47
Marsh, John	1744	76
Marsh, Elizabeth, wife of John	1742	72
Marsh, Samuel	1802	72
Marsh, Catherine, wife of Capt. Samuel	1797	67
Morgan, Elizabeth, wife of Dwell	1793	23
Morgan, Lavinia ⎱ Wives of	1792	18
Morgan, Sally ⎰ Elias,	1795	29
McCracken, Rebecca, wife of John	1803	21
Mather, Elizabeth, daughter of Rev. Allyn	1785	7
McLean, Susan, wife of Allen	1741	30
Mills, Caroline	1802	2
Messenger, Rachael, daughter of Daniel	1737	17
Messenger, Lydia, daughter of Daniel	1725	18
Muir, William	1806	52

	Died.	Age.
McLean, Allen, son of Neal	1741	3
Moore, George Smith	1788	2
Moore, Ebenezer, Jr.,	1793	17m
Moore, Anna	1802	3
Moore, David	1807	4
Moore, James Grant	1807	6
Moore, Mary Smith	1808	18
Moore, Mary Smith		26
Moore, Robert	1814	30
Nevins, Robert	1764	50
Nevins, Samuel	1705	2
Nevins, Marion	1770	17
Nevins, Robert	1780	21
Nichols, Cyprian	1756	84
Nichols, Cyprian, son of William	1749	6m
Nichols, Abigail, dau. of William	1750	5
Nichols, Rachel, wife of James	1789	26
Nichols, Catharine, daughter of Cyprian		
Ogden, Clarissa, dau. of Jacob	1794	15
Olcott, John	1794	59
Olcott, Sally	1794	15
Olcott, Roderick	1801	36
Olcott, Jonathan	1753	57
Olcott, Sarah, wife of Jonathan	1776	74
Olcott, Samuel	1781	53
Olcott, Mary	1766	35
Olcott, Mary, wife of Capt.	1792	61
Olcott, Sally	1779	16
Olcott, Clarissa	1704	15
Pitkin, William	1694	58
Phippen, Rachael	1721	2
Pierce, Anna and Samuel, ch. of Pelatiah		
Pratt, Hannah, wife of Daniel	1682	50
Pratt, Zachariah	1805	79
Pratt, Timothy	1783	33
Pratt, George	1805	50
Payson, Nathan (Col.)	1761	41
Porter, John, comptroller of public accounts	1806	48
Perkins, Mary, dau. of James	1806	5
Perkins, Lucinda	1805	3m
Payne, Benjamin	1782	54
Payne, Rebecca, wife of Benj'n	1786	51
Payne, Mary Ann	1797	36
Phelps, Sarah	1758	96
Patten, Lucinda, wife of Nathaniel	1780	35
Patten, Lucinda,)	1807	22
Patten, Fanny, } ch. of Nathaniel	1809	15
Patten, Sally,)	1810	17
Pantry, John	1736	90
Powell, Elizabeth, wife of William	1725	27
Proctor, William	1788	23
Richards, James	1680	47
Richards, Thomas (Dea.)	1740	83
Ridgaway, Naomi, wife of Samuel	1773	68
Robbins, Clarissa	1801	22
Strong, Anna Smith	1784	25
Strong, Anna McCurdy, wives of Rev. Nathan	1780	20
Strong, John McCurdy, son of Rev. Nathan	1806	29
Smith Daniel	1800	29
Smith, Solomon, Jr.,	1787	25
Smith, Solomon (Dea.)	1786	51
Smith, Anna, wife of Dea. Solomon	1784	40

	Died.	Age.
Smith, George	1808	82
Smith, Ann, wife of George	1796	70
Smith, Martha	1756	5
Smith, James	1798	1
Smith, John	1801	9m
Sweetland, Sarah, wife of Benjaman	1805	33
Sweetland, Eleazur	1798	32
Sweetland, Polly, wife of Eleazur	1792	22
Sweetland, Effingham		1
Sargeant, John, son of Jacob	1802	11
Steel, Elizabeth, wife of George	1800	29
Steel, Ashbel	1790	59
Steel, Nabby, dau. of Ashbel	1772	14
Steel, Jonathan	1753	60
Steel, Dorothy, wife of Jonathan	1775	82
Sloan, Samuel	1775	4
Starr, Harriett	1801	11m
Stone, Samuel (Rev.), pastor First Church	1663	61
Sheldon, Joseph	1794	65
Sheldon, George, son of Joseph	1764	2
Sheldon, Deacon Isaac	1749	63
Sheldon, Elizabeth, wife of Isaac	1745	53
Sheldon, Anna, wife of Isaac	1802	73
Sheldon, Daniel	1772	46
Sheldon, Lucretia, wife of Daniel	1772	47
Sheldon, William, son of Daniel	1758	5
Sheldon, Isaac, son of Isaac	1754	2
Sheldon, Sarah, wife of Joseph	1785	50
Sheldon, Isaac	1786	63
Seymour, Israel	1784	49
Seymour, Jonathan	1776	73
Seymour, Thomas	1740	71
Seymour, Thomas	1767	62
Seymour, John	1748	84
Seymour, Mary Ann, wife of Thomas Y.	1782	19
Seymour, Mary, wife of Nathaniel	1758	54
Seymour, Zebulon	1765	65
Seymour, Mary, wife of Thomas	1746	69
Seymour, Jerusha	1753	29
Seymour, Mary Ann	1766	6
Seymour, Elizabeth, wife of Richard	1759	44
Seymour, Prudence, wife of Frederick	1799	30
Seymour, Deliverance, wife of Jared	1799	66
Seymour, Lovisa, wife of Joseph W.	1798	39
Spencer, Obadiah	1741	75
Spencer, Abigail, wife of Disbrow	1725	46
Sanford, Huldah, wife of Robert	1759	28
Sanford, Robert	1728	72
Sanford, Zachariah, son of Zachariah	1683	
Skinner, Stephen	1758	43
Skinner, Joseph	1748	79
Skinner, John	1773	76
Skinner, Mary, wife of John	1771	67
Skinner, Mary, wife of John, Jr.,	1772	42
Skinner, Rebecca, wife of Nathaniel	1780	31
Skinner, Leonard	1746	4
Skinner, Rachael, wife of John	1748	77
Skinner, John	1743	77
Skinner, Sarah	1750	1
Skinner, Abagail	1750	3

THE ANCIENT BURYING GROUND OF HARTFORD. 85

	Died.	Age
Skinner, Abagail, wife of Elisha	1777	19
Skinner, Hepzebah, wife of John	1791	54
Stanley, Bennet, alias Wollterton	1664	
Stanley, Hannah ⎫ Children	1681	7
Stanley, Susannah ⎬ Nathaniel	1683	2
Stanley, Sarah ⎭ { Stanley.	1680	20
Stanley, Sarah, wife of Nathaniel	1716	76
Stanley (one of his Majesty's assistants), Nathaniel	1712	74
Stanley, Joseph	1675	4
Stanley, Anna, wife of Col. Nathaniel	1752	66
Stanley, Nath niel (Hon.), treasurer of Connecticut	1755	73
Stanley, Sarah	1698	44
Stanley, Hannah (wives of Caleb)	1680	45
Stanley, Caleb	1718	75
Stanley, Caleb, son of Caleb	1712	37
Stanley, Mary	1698	6
Stanley, William, gave his property to Second Church	1786	63
Thomas, Rachel	1760	2
Thomas, Lydia, of Marlborough	1758	30
Thomas, Mary	1764	34
Tiley, Walter	1791	9m
Tiley, Susanna, wife of John	1724	43
Thompson, Gideon	1759	56
Tisdale, Emily	1802	7
Talcott, Joseph (Hon.) Governor of Connecticut 1725-1741	1741	
Talcott, John, son of the Governor	1771	73
Talcott, Abigail, wife of John	1784	80
Talcott, Mabel, wife of Samuel	1775	62
Talcott, Joseph, son of the Gov.	1799	62
Toocker, Michael	1801	18
Taylor, James	1772	
Van Norden, Anna, wife of John	1799	40
Woolterton, Gregory	1674	81
Woolterton, Susanna, wife of Gregory	1662	75
Woolterton, Samuel	1668	7m
Wilson, Phineas	1692	64
Wilson, Mary, wife of Phineas	1688	29
Waters, Bevil	1729	97
Wattles, Jonathan S	1779	1
Wattles, Delight S	1780	9
Webster, Sarah, wife of Robert	1725	53
Walker, Marion, wife of John	1762	25
Watson, Ebenezer	1777	33
Watson, Elizabeth, wife of Ebenezer	1770	28
Whitman, Elnathan (Rev.), pastor of Second Church	1777	69
Wilson, Elizabeth, wife of Phineas	1727	87
Welles, Hannah	1683	50
Welles, Blackleach	1788	64

	Died.	Age
Welles, Mary	1795	6
Welles, Julia	1799	15
Welles, Britty, wife of Ashbel	1793	31
Wentworth, Samuel	1711	20
Watson, Sally, wife of John	1796	38
Watson, John	1795	66
Watson, Hannah, wife of John	1799	72
Woodward, John	1793	4
Walker, Marian, wife of John	1795	42
White, Elizabeth, wife of John J.	1804	29
White, Susan S.	1804	7
Williamson, Caleb	1738	87
Williamson, Mary, wife of Caleb	1737	77
Williamson, Anna, wife of Ebenezer	1750	49
Wadsworth, Joanna, wife of Joseph	1762	78
Wadsworth, Daniel	1762	42
Wadsworth, William	1771	49
Wadsworth, Thomas	1716	26
Wadsworth, Daniel (Rev.), pastor First Church	1747	43
Wadsworth, Abigail, wife of Rev. Daniel	1773	67
Wadsworth, Daniel	1750	10
Wadsworth, Ruth	1750	5
Wadsworth, Jeremiah (Col.)	1804	61
Wadsworth, Mehitabel, wife of Col. Jeremiah	1817	82
Wadsworth, Elizabeth	1810	72
Wadsworth, Eunice, daughters of Rev. Daniel	1825	89
Wadsworth, Millicent, wife of Capt. Samuel	1790	67
Willet, Nathaniel	1608	80
Winchester, Elhanan (Rev.)	1797	46
Whiting, Joseph	1715	
Whiting, Anna, wife of Joseph	1735	82
Whiting, Mary	1714	26
Whiting, Abigail	1722	4
Whiting, Calvin (Rev.)	1795	24
Weare, Caty	1791	1
Weare, William T.	1807	10m
Weare, Martha, wife of William	1795	38
Watson, Joseph	1803	29
Watson, Joseph	1806	3
Weeden, Mary, wife of Henry	1803	19
Wood, Lucy	1802	37
Wood, William	1795	4
Wood, Benjamin S.	1793	1
Warner, Azubah, wife of Eli	1774	43
Way, Mary	1701	70
Woodbridge, Timothy (Rev.), pastor First Church	1732	
Woodhridge, Abigail, wife of Rev. Timothy and formerly of Richard Lord	1754	77
Westcoate, Samuel	1775	26

ON THE HOUSATONIC.

AMONG THE LITCHFIELD HILLS.

BY EDGAR DEANE.

At the advice of his physician, who charged only two dollars for telling him, Uncle William was induced to take a short rest from his arduous duties. His consultation with Cousin Jim resulted in their deciding to take a driving trip down the *Housatonic Valley from Canaan. They were to drive as they pleased, with no particular point for destination, and get back when they chose.

Arriving in Canaan rather too late in the afternoon to start the same day down the valley, Uncle William, who had brought his camera, started out to cultivate his artistic eye. His operations were not complete, of course, without " Let's see the picture, mister," from the omnipresent small boy, whom a

---

* As to the meaning of Housatonic, in his book, "Indian Names in Connecticut," Dr. Trumbull says, " Eunice Mahwee (or Mauwehu), the last full-blooded survivor of the Scaticook band, in 1859, pronounced the name *Hous'atenuc,*' and interpreted it 'over the mountain.' The tradition received by the Scaticook Indians of the discovery of the river and valley by those who came over the mountain from the west, establishes this interpretation beyond a doubt." It is also interpreted " River of the Mountains."

companion soon accosted with, "Say, Sammy, yer mother wants yer; you'll ketch it when you git home." This cheerful announcement abated Sammy's ardor in the investigating line, and he hurriedly departed for that place unlike any other. The explanations which would have been necessary to enlarge Sammy's knowledge of photography reminded them of the experience of a dealer in photographic supplies. A purchaser complained of the plates he bought. "Did you follow directions?" asked the dealer. "Oh, yes, very carefully. I loaded the holders, exposed the plates, took them in the dark room

VIEW IN CANAAN.

and looked at them, but not a trace of a picture could I find." "Did you develop them?" "Develop! what's that?" asked he, in utter amazement. This customer must have been related to the young man who bought a printing frame at a store and took it back two days later, mad as the proverbial "wet hen." He gave them to understand that he had bought and paid for a good printing frame and they couldn't push off any second-hand goods on him. They said they were very sorry, they supposed the frame was all right and would do anything they could to rectify a mistake. "Well," said he, pointing to the dial on the back of the frame, used for registering the number of prints, "I had a print in that frame *all day* yesterday, and that pointer never stirred."

As Sammy could not see the picture, neither could Uncle William, and this was the beginning of a series he was taking on faith, the results to be found after his return home, where in the seclusion of his private apartments, "he'd do the rest."

Early the next morning the journey was begun, they starting for Falls Village by the way of Twin Lakes, and from thence to Lime Rock and Sharon, where they stopped for the night.

It has been said that one takes away from a place only what he brings to it. In a certain sense this may be true. One has to have the ability to appreciate what he sees, in order to absorb it. Aside from that he may learn many

TWIN LAKES.

things and gain much knowledge and pleasure from traversing a country new to him, although he will realize what he misses, because it *is* new to him. The wealth of reminiscence which an inhabitant of the region can impart, the historical detail familiar to the student of that section, the abodes or sometime homes, of well-known people,—all these the traveler likes to know about and feels his loss if the knowledge is lacking. The exception to this is when he goes to a cemetery and finds out what a number of saintly people formerly lived in that region. Let the tombstones tell their own story, and have no wily native appear to disillusion the stranger by hinting that so-and-so's epitaph and truth are total strangers.

In few sections of the country of equal area could one find more to interest him when thoroughly familiar with the history of the inhabitants than in Litchfield County. In an address delivered before the Litchfield County Historical and Antiquarian Society, April 9th, 1856, Mr. G. H. Hollister said: "Many of you are doubtless aware that Litchfield County has from the first been distinguished for its intelligence and enterprise, and that its little county townships

CANAAN FALLS.

have contributed more to the forum, the pulpit, the bench, the academic hall, and the professor's chair, not only within our own limits, but in the several states of the union, than in any other portion of the continent occupied by an equal number of inhabitants." He then gives a few brief statistics in support of his statement and goes on to look for the reason, which, after speaking of dissensions in church government and boundary lines inducing the removal of some to Litchfield County in the early times, then known as the "Northwestern Wilderness," he sums up in part as follows: "A variety of other motives led these adventurous men to subject themselves to the hardships incident to a warfare with the rugged obstacles of nature. A desire like that of Rasselas, to see what lay beyond; a love of possessing land, for which the Saxon blood has been famous from the earliest times—that restlessness which belongs to an unsettled state of society; a fearless courage stimulating the emigrant on from difficulty to difficulty, with an appetite which grew by what it fed on; a fervent

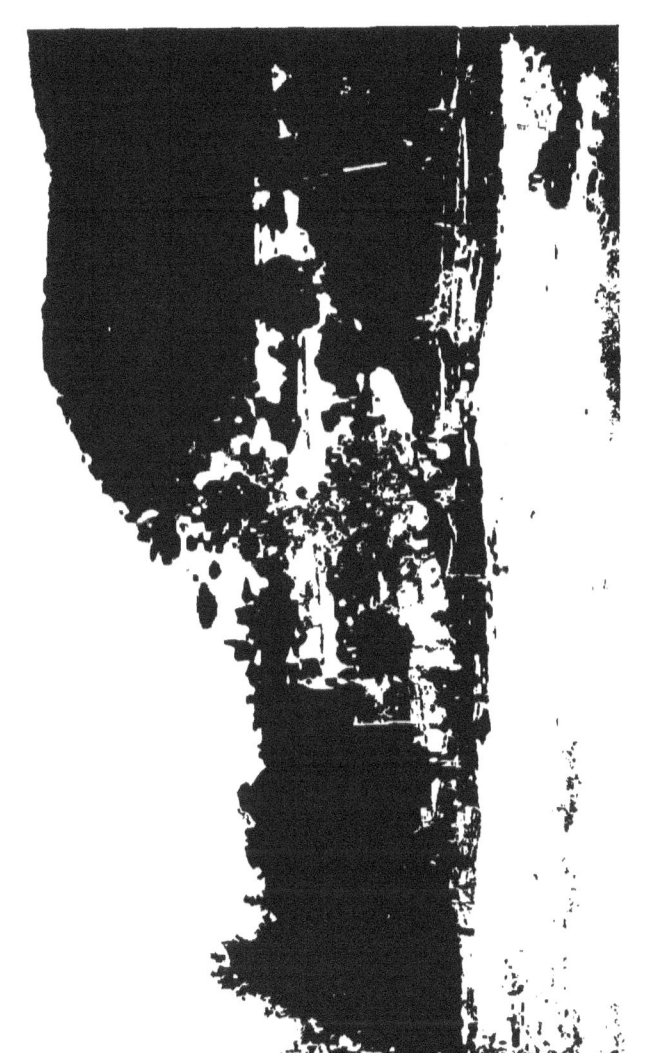

BARRACK MOUNTAIN.—VIEW NEAR LIME ROCK STATION.

imagination which always accompanies religious zeal, and lights up whatever is distant with rays of hope and promises of future glory; a sublime trust in God, who made the winds that howled and the snows that drifted over the wintry waste, to be ministers of His wrath and the servants of His will; these are some of the motives which led to the settlements of the forbidding hill-tops where the oak battled with the elements, and of the more inviting interval where the pine and hemlock sighed amid the tall grass of the hunting-ground. The elasticity of a ball is to be estimated by the length and number of its rebounds. This is true of emigration. The toughness of fiber, the wiry strength of the adventurer's nerves, is best known by the number of removes that he made, and their distance from the secure abodes of his fellow men. Hence you will find that the settlers of Litchfield were from the first, *picked men*. The love of luxury and ease was almost unknown to them. They built their houses on the hills of Goshen, Litchfield, Winchester, Torrington, Watertown and Bethlehem, and made their roads to them from the valleys with a defiance of comfort and civil engineering shocking to the nerves of their descendants."

CHURCH PORTICO, LIME ROCK.

The last statement, anyone who has driven in that region can readily appreciate, for it seems as though the roads were built over the steepest hills that could be found. As another writer, in commenting on the same subject, has said: "Roads were laid out of a liberal width, usually six rods, but in other respects the layout fails to command our respect. To get to the top of the highest hill by the shortest route, and thence to the top of the next, seems to have been the chief object in view, and though many of these old roads have been discarded, yet the traveler, if he has any taste for engineering, still has the opportunity to exercise his propensity."

The pleasant summer morning in a region abounding with enchanting views was thoroughly enjoyed by Uncle William and Cousin Jim, as they journeyed by the Twin Lakes, Washinee and Washining, and thence to that grandest natural phenomenon in the valley, Canaan Falls.

In the afternoon a pleasant time was had at the Barnum, Richardson Co's works at Lime Rock, where the superintendent entertained them by showing them about the shops. A new tire-setting machine interested Uncle William by its wonderful efficiency. To anyone in need of such a machine he would unhesitatingly say, "Look into the merits of this one."

As the stranger drives through the beautiful streets of Sharon, his mind most naturally turns to the biblical phrase, "The rose of Sharon and the lily of the valley," and he thinks that surely those who christened the place must have had that saying in mind. It certainly is one of the most attractive towns in all New England. The extra broad, well-shaded street, or double street, for it is a regular boulevard, with nicely-kept lawns on both sides, extending through the center of the town, and the charming residences, are revelations to the traveler who comes upon it for the first time, having known nothing about it and expecting to find in this far corner of the state, remote from railroads, a primitive country village. It has an air of originality about it, too, that gives it a character all its own. This is evidenced more especially by its soldiers' monument, a huge stone cannon, with the inscriptions on its pedestal, so different from the conventional type of soldiers' memorials elsewhere seen, and by the stone clock-tower in the center of the town, which musically chimes the hours.

From Sharon over the mountain to West Cornwall and on to Kent was but a day's journey, allowing Uncle William ample time to photograph what took his fancy.

The township of Cornwall, though composed of much good farming land, and especially land adapted to the turning out of dairy products, is quite hilly and mountainous.

The Hon. T. S. Gold, in his "History of Cornwall," says: "The rocky surface of Cornwall gave large indications to the early settlers of mineral wealth, and the township was named after the rich mining region in the old country." Furthermore, the same author remarks: "When the question of a county seat was early agitated, and Cornwall put in her claim for the honor, 'Yes,' it was said, 'go to Cornwall and you will have no need of a jail, for whoever gets in can never get out again.'"

CLOCK TOWER, SHARON.

"The old divine who, passing through Cornwall, delivered himself of the following couplet, gave more truth with his poetry than is considered essential:

'The Almighty, from His boundless store,
Piled rocks on rocks, and did no more.'

"Another authority attributes it to Dr. Dwight, president of Yale College, who came up to look at the college lands, and thus expressed himself:

> 'The God of Nature, from His boundless store,
> Threw Cornwall into heaps and did no more.'"

Concerning the names of the several mountains, Mr. Gold gives some interesting information. Besides speaking of a number which were named after men who lived in their vicinity, such as Hough Mountain, Rugg Hill, Waller Hill, Bunker Hill, Dudley Town Hill, and Clark Hill, he says: "About half a mile south from his house (Deacon Waller's, at the foot of Waller Hill), we find another large hill, properly called Tower Dale. This noble name, thus written by the early settlers, has degenerated in common speech, into the insignificant title of Tarrydiddle. Going in the same direction, but a little farther removed from the river, we find Buck Mountain, so called from the great number of deer that used to be found there. The first hill below West Cornwall, and nearer the river, was called Green Mountain before it became denuded of its pines and hemlocks, which in early times covered it densely. Then next south and easterly lies a long and high hill called Mine Mountain, from the minerals it was supposed to contain. Cream Hill, lying in the north middle part of the town, received this appellation from the superiority of its

VIEW IN WEST CORNWALL.

soil and the beauty of its scenery. A pretty lake lies at its foot, and in fair view from its southern aspect, called Cream Hill Lake. A high and steep mountain range lies at the northwest of Sedgwick Hollow, called Titus Mountain, and was so named from a young man of that name who, with others, was amusing himself in rolling rocks down the steep side of the mountain, and who had the misfortune to break his thigh.

"South of Cream Hill rises an isolated hill of no great height, but rough

AMONG THE LITCHFIELD HILLS. 95

and uncomely, to which is given the name of Rattlesnake Hill. I set down here the tradition of fifty rattlesnakes killed at one time on this hill, lest the story grow larger and tax our credulity too much as to the origin of the name. This raid was too much for the snakes, as none have been found there in the period of authentic history.

"Southeasterly from Clark Hill is the most elevated land in the state, lying mostly in Goshen, from the apex of which is a view of Long Island Sound. This is called Mohawk Mountain.

RIVER VIEW AT WEST CORNWALL.

"Three hundred acres of land given by the General Assembly to Yale College, is located in Cornwall, and goes by the name of College Land. Bloody Mountain, so named from a bloody tragedy *not* enacted there, lies north of the old Goshen and Sharon turnpike, northwest from the center of the town.

"From the summits of many of these hills extensive and magnificent views are presented, extending west of the Hudson River and over a large share of Berkshire County in Massachusetts. There are many other minor hills, the beauty and picturesque appearance of which, to be fully appreciated must be seen."

The keynote is struck in the last sentence. It is vain to attempt to describe the endless number of mountain and valley views, each with some special feature of attractiveness, each grand and splendid in itself, that greet the traveler through this region. To attempt the description is mere idle repetition of words that fail utterly to adequately express his feelings.

KENT FALLS.

Such were the sights that met our travelers' eyes throughout their whole drive. From Cornwall their line of travel for the next few days was through Kent, over to Roxbury, and then north through the Shepaug Valley to Washington and Litchfield, then through Goshen back to their starting point at Canaan.

And this short trip was but one of many of equal interest that could be taken in the same region, for the places necessarily omitted in traversing the ground but once, were legion.

The magnificent mountain scenery was diversified by the numerous beautiful water scenes constantly met with on the Housatonic, Shepaug and the smaller streams, with here and there a pretty lake, besides visits to the rugged and picturesque ravines at Kent and Roxbury Falls.

Who of us would not say with Uncle William, when in such a spot as either of the latter places, "Like it? Why I could stay here all day."

Cool, restful and delightful in every way, there the lover of nature is in his element, and few there be of us who do not retain an instinctive passion for such

MAIDEN'S WELL—KENT FALLS.

scenes, though it be, perhaps, what remains to us of the most refined of savage instincts, stifled in vain through a thousand years of civilization.

Perhaps because we associate with the Indian what is most rugged and wild, the mind naturally goes back to the aboriginal inhabitant when contemplating this region, despite all the evidences of the two centuries of the white man's occupancy. And this aside from the Indian names, which we hope will long remain. Barber, in his "Connecticut Historical Collections," tells us that, "Gideon Mauwehu, the sachem of the Scaticook tribe, in one of his hunting excursions came to the summit of the mountain which rises almost precipitously west of Scatacook (Kent), and beholding the beautiful valley and river below, determined to make it the place of his future residence. It was indeed a lovely and desirable place ; there were several hundred acres of excellent land, covered with grass like a prairie, with some few scattering trees interspersed. The river was well supplied with fish, and on the mountain, on both sides, was found an abundance of deer and other wild game. At this place Mauwehu collected the Indians and became their sachem."

Well has Mr. Hollister expressed it when he said, in the address previously alluded to : " All over the country lie scattered these simple mementoes of a race which held dominion over the soil for unknown ages before the English emigrant ever set foot upon it. His implements of war, sharp as the fabled dragon's teeth, but not vital like them, still lie buried in the fields over which he once hunted the wild deer, the bear, the moose and the otter. The plowboy whose mind is filled with stories of the Indian wars, continues to turn them up with the share from year to year, and stops his team with a shuddering chill to handle the serrated arrow and grooved tomahawk. Their household utensils—the stone mortar and pestle, the pots in which they boiled their venison, the pans in which they fried their fish, the stone pipe that sent up its grave offering of peace around the council-fire, their grotesque attempts at sculpture,

FALLS BELOW NEW MILFORD.

representing their grim ideal of a god—are still extant in the country, but fast passing away. Although the war whoop echoes no longer among the cliffs of Cornwall and Scaticook; although the bark palace of the chief of Werauhaumaug has crumbled by the side of the Great Falls at New Milford, and his people no longer frequent the borders of the lake that still bears his name; though the tribe of Pomperaug has melted away like the dew, and the meadows of Weatague are swept yearly by the scythe of the Saxon ; yet here and there in warm sheltered nooks, by river-bank or brook-side, the bones of the warrior rest in the alluvial mould. Whence came this wild fierce people, wandering without being nomadic, cultivating history without the aid of letters, generous without knowing how to forgive, scornful of death when called to look him in the face, yet lurking like the fox to avoid his approach? Whence came they? How long did they remain proprietors of the country, and why did they melt so suddenly away before the rays of civilization?"

AMONG THE LITCHFIELD HILLS. 99

We wish we could answer. Even Uncle William, who was of a reflective turn of mind and had given much thought to such problems, vouchsafed no explanation. Besides the scenery and thoughts of the noble red man, there were many things of more recent historical interest to claim his attention. At Kent and Roxbury the extensive iron works formerly in operation ; the reminder by a monument in the center of the latter town of that hero of the Revolution, Colonel Seth Warner ; at Washington, Litchfield and Goshen, of many things that have made those places well known.

Nor was the trip lacking in amusing and humorous incidents. Such were

ROXBURY FALLS.

the ones, to his regret, that Uncle William failed to get pictures of. But that is the usual way of such things—the biggest fish get away.

In due course of time, in spite of having the laziest horse in the county, Uncle William and Cousin Jim got back to Canaan, returned the horse to the stable, complimented the owner on possessing such a fine animal, and took the train for Hartford.

BOOK NOTICES AND REVIEWS.

I. NOTICES.

Books in preparation or in press. Those interested are invited to communicate with the authors.

Butler—A monograph on some families who descend from Richard Butler of Hartford, Ct. Emily Wilder Leavitt, 10 Joy street, Boston, Mass.

Cleveland and Cleaveland Families—Price $15.00 per set of 3 vols. to subscribers now. Edmund J. Cleveland, 43 Beacon street, Hartford, Ct.

Cone—Descendants of Daniel Cone, 1626-1706. William W. Cone, 1405 Polk street, Topeka, Kan.

Crow or Crowell and Kelley—Early settlers of Yarmouth, Mass. Henry G. Crowell, South Yarmouth, Mass.

Nickerson—Descendants of William of Chatham, Mass. Wm. Emery Nickerson, 12 Pearl street, Boston, Mass.

Rockwell and Keeler Genealogy—James Boughton, 223 Keap street, Brooklyn, N. Y.

Tinker—Descendants of John of New London, Ct. Price, $5.00 per copy. Rev. William Durant, Saratoga Springs, N. Y.

Wakeman—Descendants of John, one of the founders and Treasurer of New Haven Colony. Price, $5.00 per copy. Robert P. Wakeman, Southport, Ct.

Waterbury Genealogy—Early settlers in Stamford, Ct. William F. Waterbury, Stamford, Ct.

Early Mass. Marriages—First book; price, $2.00 postpaid. Frederick W. Bailey, New Haven, Ct. Box 587.

Enfield, Conn., History—Francis Olcott Allen, 340 South 16th st., Philadelphia, Pa.

Staten Island, N. Y., Memorial History—Ira K. Morris, New Brighton, N. Y.

Goshen, Conn., History—Price, $3.25 net, sent by mail. Rev. A. G. Hibbard, Woodstock, Ct. Box 66.

Amenia, N. Y.—Mr. William A. Eardeley-Thomas, 5000 Woodland avenue, Philadelphia, Pa., will publish all the Amenia records as soon as the 100 advance paid-up subscriptions at $5.00 per volume are received. No promises will be noticed. The $5.00 must accompany every subscription. The book can be had only by subscription.

Billings History, in preparation by Mr. C. Billings, Billingsbridge, Ontario, Canada.

"Carpenter Family in America"—550 pp.; not over $7.50 per volume; probably $5.00 if 250 copies are ordered. Mr. Daniel H. Carpenter, Maplewood, N. J.

Case and Hathaway Genealogies—Mr. C. V. Case, Ashtabula, Ohio.

History of Guilford and Madison, Ct.—500 pp., $2.50—Bernard C. Steiner, Baltimore, Md., care of Enoch Pratt Free Library.

Hanford Genealogy—Mr. A. C. Golding, Norwalk, Ct.

Taylor Genealogy—Norwalk, Wilton, Danbury, Bethel, Newtown, New Milford, and Fairfield county generally. Mr. W. O. Taylor, Orange, Mass.

II. REVIEWS.

"Records of the State of Connecticut," Vol. I, 1776-1778; Vol. II, 1778-1780; published by Charles J. Hoadly, LL.D., State Librarian, "in accordance with a Resolution of the General Assembly." They contain the Journal of the Council of Safety from Oct. 11, 1776, to April 23, 1780, and an appendix in each volume. Each volume contains a fine index, and is well printed and bound. These volumes exhibit the results of careful and painstaking labor in reading old documents, for which Dr. Hoadly is justly renowned.

"The Munson Record: a Genealogical and Biographical Account of Captain Thomas Munson (a pioneer of Hartford and New Haven) and his Descendants," by Rev. Myron A. Munson, M. A. Two volumes, royal 8vo., pp. 1267. We are especially attracted by the extent to which research in the original sources is represented, the public records of 74 towns and cities in 9 different States having been studied by the author, besides visiting 39 other places to consult church records and secure personal interviews. The most authentic way of presenting history is by largely quoting public records. Our author has done this, making hundreds of these quotations, many of which touch families of other names. Authencity, already replete, is intensified in eighteen or twenty instances by facsimiles of the original records. We have here a Connecticut subject, by a Connecticut author and printer. Tables of *Contemporary Events* furnish a setting in general history for the family events of the first eight generations—a feature which has been fervently and repeatedly commended. There is an attempt to record the political and religious preferences of all members of the family. A novel diagram is given exhibiting *Munson Migrations* from Connecticut. The great number of geographical elucidations and allusions of an illumine sort surprises one—there are 247 items in the geographical index, such as Ball's Island, Ditch Corner, Landing Tree, Neck Rock, Ox Hill, Stable Point, etc., and likewise a great number of historical matters of a local and general character which are explained or illustrated, e. g, the Connecticut Standing Army, owning baptismal covenant, billeting act, courts of four or five kinds, project for founding a commonwealth at Delaware Bay, "divisions" of land, Quinnipiac ferries, hat-pegs in meeting house, King Phillip's War, first jury, lecture days, "ordinary," horse-book, origin of "towns-men," Long Wharf, whipping post, etc.—rarely has a family history, as a subordinate specialty, attempted to illumine general history. We have three fac-similes of Revolutionary documents, fac-similes of the signatures to the Fundamental Agreement at Quinnipiac and to the Planters' Agreement at Wallingford, and many other matters which are now first given to the public. The work may be had of the author, 202 Exchange street, New Haven, Ct., for $12.00 per set.

"History of Ancient Woodbury, Ct., from the first Indian Deed in 1659 to 1879, including the towns of Washington, Southbury, Bethlehem, Roxbury, and a part of Oxford and Middlebury," is a work in 3 vols. by William Cothren, Esq., of Woodbury, Ct. Volume I is out of print, while the few remaining copies of Volumes II and III may be procured of the author at $4.25 per copy, postpaid. The work is devoted entirely to the genealogical statistics of Ancient Woodbury from 1670 to 1879, and of Ancient Stratford from 1639 to 1728, which then included Bridgeport, Huntington and Monroe. There are nearly 35,000 entries of births, baptisms, marriages and deaths, collated by years. Here is a first-class chance to get these volumes at more than a reasonable price. One is surprised that they can still be obtained at such a low figure.

A. Vital Statistics of Seymour, Ct., Vol. II, pp. 59; $1.00; postpaid, $1.06.
B. History of Oxford, Ct., Part I, mostly a transcript of church and town records of births, marriages and deaths; paper covers, $1.00; postpaid, $1.04. Only one part issued.
C. "The Sharpes," 1893-6; 212 pages; $3.00. Originally published monthly.
These three works were published by W. C. Sharpe, Seymour, Ct., from whom they can be had at the above prices. *A* covers the period from Jan. 1883 to Dec. 31, 1891, is neatly bound and has a good index. *B* also contains burials in Zoar Bridge Cemetery and Old Quaker Farms Cemetery. *C*, we regret to say, has no index. One was prepared, but never published. We are sorry to learn that on account of so little interest being taken in the work, the editor feels compelled to stop publishing "The Sharpes." We heartily commend these works to our readers and friends.

"Samuel Clark, Sr., and his Descendants," by Rev. Edgar W. Clark, A. M., Pana, Ill.; second edition, 8vo., pp. 122; price in muslin, $1.25; paper, 50c. "This has been a gradual gathering of more than twenty years, and a work of love." The family appeared in Bedford, N. Y., before 1681 in the person of William, Sr., son of Samuel, Sr.

"Littleton Historical Society, Proceedings No. 1, 1894-1895," 8vo., pp. 186; $1.50 postpaid The work treats ᵃmong other things of the Garrison House at Nashoba, John Eliot, the apostle to the Indians, the Work of Historical Societies, the Indians of Nashobah, forty-six pages of epitaphs from the Old Burying Ground at Littleton Common, etc., and contains a fine index. A good share of the work has been done by Mr. Herbert J. Harwood, chairman of the committee, to whom much praise is due.

"A Partial Record of the Descendants of John Tefft of Portsmouth, Rhode Island, and the Nearly Complete Record of the Descendants of John Tifft of Nassau, N. Y." compiled by Mrs. Maria E. Tifft, 196 Linwood avenue, Buffalo, N. Y. It is an 8vo. volume, contains pp. 159+14, printed on fine deckel edge paper and rubricated. The work, neatly bound, is a splendid contribution to genealogy and is a credit to the compiler. The work can be had of the author for $3.50.

History of Montville, Ct., formerly the North Parish of New London, from 1640 to 1896, compiled and arranged by Henry A. Baker, Esq.; price $1.00; press of Case, Lockwood & Brainard Company. The book contains 727 pages + viii., is well printed and bound. There are 500 pages devoted to the genealogies of the early settlers and the appendix contains 11 pages more. The work has a good index. There are over 40 illustrations in the work. All that it was possible for the author to obtain has been incorporated.

"The Lineage of Rev. Richard Mather," by Horace E. Mather, Esq., of 747 Asylum avenue, Hartford, Ct., is a work of 540 pages gotten up in an exceedingly attractive style, containing the portraits of the Rev. Richard Mather of Dorchester, Mass.; Rev. Dr Increase Mather, his son, of Boston; Rev. Dr. Cotton Mather, his grandson, of Boston; Rev. Samuel Mather, his grandson, of Witney, Eng.; Rev. Dr. Samuel Mather, his great-grandson, of Boston. Also 17 other portraits of prominent descendants of Richard Mather in the book with other engravings of historic interest. It also gives biographical sketches of these and others connected with the family. Over forty-three hundred of the descendants in the male and female branches are indexed in the work. Mention is also made of a large number of the Mathers of other emigrations from England and Scotland, as well as those who are residents of Europe. The work can be had for $5.00 a copy.

A. "Notes and Additions to the History of Gloucester, second series, by John J. Babson, with an appendix containing indexes to Parts I and II"; pp. 187; price, $1.50.
B. "Inscriptions from the Old Cemetery in Rowley, Mass., copied by Geo. B. Blodgette, M.A."; pp. 78; price, 75c.
C. "Deaths in Truro, Cape Cod, 1786-1826, taken from the diary of Rev. Jude Damon, by John Harvey Treat"; pp. 26; price, 50c.
These three works, of immense value to the genealogist, can still be supplied at the above price by Eben Putnam, Esq., of Salem, Mass. It would be of advantage to those purchasing genealogies and histories to communicate with Mr. Putnam.

"Records of William Spooner of Plymouth, Mass., and his Descendants, Vol. I," is a work of 694 pages, compiled by Thomas Spooner, Esq. The book is bound in green, is printed on good paper, and has a fine index. The foot-notes, scattered through the volume, give the ancestry of the wives or husbands of many of the Spooners, thus making the work of great value to other families. Volume II was prepared, but has never been published. It is already for the printer, and it is hoped that the remaining copies of Vol. I will find a speedy sale, so that Vol. II can be given to the printer. The Vol. I can be had at $3.00 a copy of M. Alice Spooner, Glendale, Ohio.

"Genealogy of the Howes Family in America, Descendants of Thomas Howes, Yarmouth, Mass., 1637-1892, with some account of English Ancestry, by Joshua Crowell Howes, Dennis, Mass., with illustrations," is a work of 209 pages with blank pages for manuscript notes. The arrangement is clear, concise and can be understood by anybody. The work can be purchased from the author; price, $2.00; by mail, $2.12.

"The Descendants of John Porter of Windsor, Ct., 1635-9, compiled by Henry Porter Andrews," is a work of 888 pages in two volumes. The book contains three splendid indexes. The author has wisely traced out the maternal lines to the first comer in the country. This is a splendid work and shows the results of careful research. It can be had for $12 per set of Augusta Porter Wiggins, Saratoga Springs, N. Y.

"The History and Genealogy of the Colegrove Family in America, with Biographical Sketches, Portraits, etc.," by William Colegrove, D.D., LL.D , of Tallula, Menard Co., Illinois, is a 12mo. book of 792 pages, which can be had of the author for $4.00 cloth, $5.00 morocco with gilt edges; postage, 16c. There are over sixty blank numbered pages for manuscript notes, and a good index, in two columns—the males in the left column and the females in the right. The work takes up the line of Francis Colegrove who came from London, Eng., to Warwick, R. I., about 1680. He was probably born at or near Swansea, Wales.

Lane Genealogies—Vol. I, by Rev. Jacob Chapman and Rev. James H. Fitts, contains the descendants of William Lane of Boston, 1648; John Lane of York Co., Maine, 1693, and John Lane of Fishersfield, N. H., 1737. Copies may be obtained of Rev. Mr. Chapman, Exeter, N. H., for $3.50. Vol. II, by Rev. James H. Fitts, contains the descendants of William Lane of Dorchester, Mass., 1635; Robert Lane of Stratford, Ct., 1660; John Lane of Milford, Ct., 1642; John Merrifield Lane of Boston, Mass . 1752; Daniel Lane of New London, Ct., 1651, and George Lane of Rye, N Y., 1664. Copies may be had of Rev. Mr. Fitts. Newfields, N. H., for $3.50. These two volumes, bound in uniform size, present a neat appearance, are well indexed, are illustrated and a credit to the compilers. Vol. III is nearly ready It will contain the descendants of Job Lane, Malden, Mass., 1644, and his brother James of Casco Bay. Maine, 1660. Unconnected families will be added. Additional information should be sent at once to Rev. Mr. Fitts.

"The Genealogy of the Hamilton Family from 1716 to 1894, compiled by Salome Hamilton, Faribault, Minn.;" 8vo , pp. 133+vi, records the descendants of James Hamilton, a Scotch-Irishman who came to Worcester county, Mass., before 1720. The author, of whom this neat volume can be had for $2.00, is still collecting data on all of the name.

"A Peters Lineage — Five Generations of the Descendants of Dr. Charles Peters of Hempstead, compiled by Martha Bockée Flint," of No. 3 Barclay st., Poughkeepsie, N. Y.; price, $2 00; pp. 164 + xi. This is a splendid volume and shows the result of careful compilation.

"A Genealogical History of the Harwood Families Descended from Andrew Harwood, who was born in England and resided in Boston, Mass." (freeman there 1643), by Watson H. Harwood, M. D., of Chasm Falls, N. Y.; price, $2.50; 8vo., pp. 91+x; second edition. Dr. Harwood, we are pleased to say, is collecting additional materialfor a third edition and would especially like to learn where Andrew Harwood was born and the exact year when he came to America.

"Hall Ancestry—A Series of Sketches of the Lineal Ancestors of the Children of Samuel Holden Parsons Hall and his wife, Emily Hulkeley of Binghamton, N. Y., with some account of nearly one hundred of the early Puritan families of New England ; also tables showing royal descents of Mary Lyman and Sarah Chauncy and of their descendants," by Charles S Hall, 86 Court street, Binghamton, N.Y.; price, $5.00 net; pp. 507-x, pica type, laid paper; edition 200 cloth copies ; 8vo., gilt top. It is a splendid volume, and the aim has been to collect all the information accessible as to the Hall-Bulkeley ancestry. There are 16 pedigrees showing descent from Alfred, William the Conqueror and the Edwards; Kings Malcolm and David; Charlemagne and the Louis; Royal Houses of Germany, Spain and Naples.

"Lewis Walker of Chester Valley and His Descendants, with some of the Families with Whom they are Connected by Marriage, 1686-1896, collected, compiled and published by Priscilla Walker Streets," of 109 East 19th St., New York City; price, $5.00; 8vo., pp. 443; illustrated. This is a splendid contribution to Pennsylvania genealogies. The full and very complete index makes it a pleasure to use the book, evidencing as it does careful and laborious research and editing. Lewis Walker came from Wales in 1687 and settled on the Welsh Tract in Radnor and later moved to Chester Valley.

"An account of the Descendants of Thomas Orton of Windsor, Ct., 1641 (principally in the male line)," by Prof. Edward Orton, Ll.D., of 100 Twentieth street. Columbus, Ohio; price, $2.00; 8vo., pp. 220. The attractive make-up of this volume ought to find it a ready sale. It has an index, and the presswork is well done.

"Ancestry of Nathan Dane Dodge and of his wife Abigail (Shepherd) Dodge with Notes," by Mary A. (Dodge) Parsons, is an 8vo. cloth volume, pp. 76. This has a fine index, neatly bound in black, and is illustrated with two portraits. It consists of sketches of the ancestors of the persons named.

COLLECTIONS OF THE CONNECTICUT HISTORICAL SOCIETY. Vol. VI. Hartford, 1897.—Hartford Town Votes, Vol. I, 1635-1716; 410 pages and two plates. The preparatory note signed by Charles J. Hoadley, LL.D., the president of the Historical Society, says: "The records of the town of Hartford were begun with Jan. 1, 1638, or 1639, according to the present mode of accounting. Many of the early leaves (of the original record book) are badly frayed, and possibly some are lost." The town clerk of Hartford certifies over his official seal that the volume "is a true and correct copy of all the records contained in the earliest volume of the town votes of Hartford." The first entries concern the allotment of lands in 1635. It is safe to say that no book has appeared since the publication of the Colonial Records covering this period which will so well repay the student of Connecticut colonial history and the origin and development of its institutions, or the family historian and genealogist. He must be a sorry student indeed who cannot now add to his knowledge of the workings of the little municipality or give leafage and color to the dry boughs of his genealogical tree. The town of Hartford is to be congratulated that such an addition has been made to its available history, while the example set to other of the old towns should not be lost. The town and county history as usually published concerns the living rather than the dead, and the beginnings fade into insignificance beside the accomplishments of "our esteemed fellow townsman." Publish the *records*.

The book is a handsome specimen of typography, but must have been a sore trial to everyone concerned in its production. A manuscript almost illegible; an ortography of puzzling illiteracy, and the attempt to make the printed arrangement conform to the original in the smallest particular—all must have tried the patience of the editor, proof-reader and printer. But the result is a pattern to be followed. To Frank F. Starr, the well-known genealogist, and Albert C. Bates, librarian of the Historical Society, thanks for all this faithful editorial labor is due. An altogether too modest mention is made of Mr. James J. Goodwin, who bore the expense of preparing and publishing the volume.

The desire to quote arises at almost every page. For an instance of that peculiar temperament which has made the Connecticut Yankee famous, see page 236. As showing the danger from fire, under date of 1635: "It is ordered that eury howse shall haue a ladder or tre at Most who shall reach (within) Two ffoote of the Topp of his howse vppon (the) forfetuer of faue shillings A mounth for (each) mounth he shall'want the same." In 1661, "ye Jews who at present liue in Jon Marsh his house haue liberty to soiorne in ye Towne," and some months earlier it is recorded "Ther remaineth in John Allyns hand for the Jews o 10-0" (p. 133,5) for aid (?) A "Husband for ye Towne" was chosen in February, 1660, and "ensine John Tallcott" was the town husband or treasurer.

In 1694 a meeting of the town "Considered ye motion of our Neighbours of the East Side (East Hartford) in referrance to their desire of Setteling of a minister." The good people of Hartford objected, and those pious citizens and church members, after stating that "if the Gen[rll] Court See Cause to Over Rule in this Case (i. e., grant permission for the settling of a minister) we must Submit," then entered the following record: "But those of the East Side that Desire to Continue with us of the west side shall soe Doe, that all the Land on the East side that belongs to any of the people of the West side Shall pay to the ministry of the west side and that all the Land on the west side shall pay to the minister of the west side tho it nelongs to the people of the East side." In 1681 a ferry was established, and it might be presumed that it was to encourage the people of the East side to visit the growing capital. It was to be in the "keepe" of Thomas Cadwell "att the Common Landing place att Hartford." The fare as establisned was "for the Caring ouer horse and man six pence per time in money if they be not of this Towne and two pence for a single man an money; and if they be of this Town thay are to pay a peney in silluer a single person or Two pence in other pay and for a man and horse three pence in silluer or six pence in other pay; and for those of this Towne hee Carrys ouer after the day light is shutt in Thay shall pay six pence a horse and man in money or eight pence in other way; and ffor single persons Two pence in siluer or Three pence in other pay." The spirit of the Golden Rule was even thus early not allowed to interfere with business. Did the people of the east side retaliate in any way?

The omissions shown in the printed text by brackets are very tantalizing. What a pity we are never to know why in 1639-40 "it is ordered that mr Hopkins mr wells mr Taylcot and william Spencer shall Deall with mr Chaplin aboute (   ) are fforfeted into the Towns hands." (p. 13). What had Mr. Chaplin done or left undone and what did he forfeit to the town? Time, the ravager, has blotted it forever from the old record; but we would willingly forgive the learned editors or Dr. Hoadly if they had hazarded a guess at the matter. Here, and in many other places where the meaning is lost or doubtful, a note from the rich stores of knowledge of Dr. Hoadly or the editors would have illumined darkness. Not everyone can read between the lines, and the few notes given whet the desire for more. The honest but unlearned searcher gets little help. For example: In September, 1640, is given to "richard Church the persell of swompe" one end of which "buts vpon the soldyer field." (p. 35.) Neither here or at other references to the soldiers' field is its nature shown. It was not a burial or parade ground, but the choicest meadows in the town, which was divided among those who went against the Pequot Indians in 1637. What was "the diucth hous"* mentioned on p 72?

With so much that deserves the highest commendation, how could the Historical Society of Conn. let the volume go out

*The Dutch fort, or House of Hope, possibly.

with such a badly made index? It fills seventy pages of the volume, but fails to show the subjects a student would turn to first. The index of personal names is very complete and all possible variations in spelling are apparently given. But when will indexers learn that a subject index should show *subjects*, ideas, generalizations, collations, and by references bring together in an alphabetical arrangement related things, not simply make a cumbersome list of prominent words and page numbers. Take the following examples which fail of entry in this subject index: education, taxes, crime or criminals, bounds or boundaries, Indians, town meetings, drainage, civil actions, liens, military, fines, and other matter with which the book is filled. The town had often recurring troubles with neighboring towns over the boundaries. A bright thought may lead the reader to look at the word "line," and there he will find among many references that Windsor was the most harrassing neighbor. Why enter "meeting-house" and not church or religion with a reference? No more interesting subject to the student than the land tenure is found in the record. Here the index, though minute, is not apparently arranged; so you look after "proportions of division" to find "allotment of" lands. The straying cattle, hogs and other beasts occasioned many votes, but under pounds there is no reference to the fines or poundage. Cattle are mentioned but not hogs or horses. "Highways" is also badly digested. Provision was early made against the danger of fire, but one must look under "ladder" to find it. Why both "Ousatunuck" and "Housatunuck" with differing references? It is not a pleasant task to single these out from dozens of others for censure, but the volume deserved a better index. H.

"Historical Sketches of New Haven," is the title of a book written and published by Miss Ellen Strong Bartlett. The articles included are, "The New Haven Green," "A New Haven Church," "The Grove Street Cemetery," "Hillhouse Avenue," and "John Trumbull, the Patriot Painter." The author, in her prefatory note, says: "These papers have appeared by request, from time to time, in THE CONNECTICUT QUARTERLY and the *New England Magazine*, and as some of them are out of print, it has seemed best to bring them together in this volume.

"Although they are an humble contribution to the literature that is accumulating with reference to New Haven, they are the result of loving and careful research in the most trustworthy sources of information, and it is earnestly hoped that everything therein stated as a fact rests on undoubted testimony.

"We cannot too often recount the efforts made in planting the tree, if thereby those who eat the fruit are incited to till the soil about the roots."

This book can be had at book stores, or of Miss Ellen Strong Bartlett, Redford Park, Stamford, Conn. Price, $1.50.

We are glad to see another book from the pen of Rev. Frank Samuel Child, author of "An Old New England Town," "The Colonial Parson of New England," etc. Whatever Mr. Child writes, we may be sure is of highest excellence. His latest book, "A Colonial Witch," is of this order.

This book is a keen and sympathetic study of the social conditions which prevailed in Connecticut between the years 1640 and 1660.

The author is a ripe scholar in colonial history, and has given special attention to the psychology of the witchcraft delusion. His treatment of the theme takes the form of a well sustained and fascinating narrative. Mr. Child has made large use of town and court records, private journals and public documents in the historic setting of the narrative.

The analysis of the witch's character is a deft and subtle piece of literary workmanship, suggestive of the deep problems connected with this popular superstition. Although the theme is a sombre one, the author charms his reader by the play of quaint fancy and genial humor.

The black art was a tragic reality in the opinion of the masses. The colony of Connecticut was one with the whole world in its ready credence. In portraying a remarkable phase of life in this early period of American history, the author has endeavored to incite an interest that shall prove charitable in respect to our ancestors, at the same time that it shall be intelligent in its survey of the subject. 12mo., cloth, gilt top, $1.25. Sent postpaid on receipt of the price by the Baker & Taylor Co., publishers, 5 and 7 East Sixteenth street, New York.

FREE TO SERVE, a tale of colonial New York, by Emma Rayner, with cover design by Maxfield Parish. For the background of this romantic story the author has chosen a little-worked but extremely interesting time and place—New York in the early eighteenth century, when the manners and customs were part Dutch and part English, with Indians and Frenchmen lurking in the shadows. The romance has a new scheme of plot, and hurries on through a series of vivid adventures in the lives of two brothers and the handmaid who is free to serve, but not to plight her troth till the end of the story. A Puritan maid from New England lends a piquant contrast to her Dutch relatives, and thus all types of colonial Americans are on the stage. Large octavo, $1.50. Copeland & Day, publishers, 69 Cornhill, Boston.

PUBLISHER'S NOTES.

With this issue of THE QUARTERLY we begin our fourth year under most favorable circumstances, due to the generous reception accorded it by the public.

This we have tried to deserve, and it is our desire and endeavor to still continue to merit even a greater patronage than we now have.

To this end we have planned for an exceptionally interesting and valuable series of numbers for the coming year. Among other things it is our intention to give more in the line of biographical sketches than we have heretofore. No state in the Union is richer in this field. Of the illustrated sketches of towns, we have several of the most interesting and important in preparation. The article on early text books to be found in this number will be followed up with more extended sketches of those early educators, such as Webster, Olney, Mrs. Willard, Daboll and others. It is fitting in this connection to speak of a man that has been identified with the educational interests of our state and country for a longer period and more prominently than any other, and our next issue will contain an article on Dr. Henry Barnard. Although a great deal has been written about Dr. Barnard of late, we intend to give much information that has never been published.

We also are planning for more short stories of local color, which always interest. With interesting and efficient departments, genealogical, historical notes, etc., we are striving, as we always have been, to make each succeeding year of more value as a historical, literary and picturesque medium of Connecticut. We always keep in mind the ultimate object—to make it so that the file of THE QUARTERLY, as it goes on from year to year, will be of increasing and permanent value

HISTORICAL NOTES.

[Contributed by David Coe, Stratford Conn.]
LETTER OF JOHN COE, SON OF ROBERT COE, TO MARY HAWLEY COE, HIS WIFE.

WESTFIELD, MASS., Aug. 23d, 1708.

My Dear Wife :
Thies come to bring my harty love and efections to you and to tell you of my earnest desiar to imbrace you in the arms of my love hoping they may find you and ouers in health.
I have been very well ever since I left you for which I prays God. The post from Abani last weeke brings news that the enimy disagre and the french indians are turned bak, the scouts from dearfield have not yet discovered the army we look for a post from Albani to morrow after which we are in great hops of being drawn ofe or the greater part of us.
I am just now a going to Northampton to wait on our govener, which makes me in so much hast. So I remain til death your loving husband,
JOHN COE.
Our soldiers here are all well.
Address to Mary Coe
Living | at | Stratford |
| three | d d d

The following, taken from the Utica *Observer*, is of interest in connection with our article in this number on "Early Text Books in Connecticut."

A GREAT BOOK.

There is in Utica an old man of unusual intelligence, who is known to have graduated from no college, and yet whose perfect English, including syntax, orthography and pronuncia-tion, would stamp him as an educated man in any company. One night this old man was seated in the rooms of the Cogburn club, when he consented to be interviewed as follows :
" From whom did you get the foundation of your education?"
" From Webster."
" Daniel Webster ?"
" No, but Noah Webster, through his spelling book. When I was 12, I could spell every word in that book correctly. I had learned all the reading lessons it contains, including that one about the old man who found rude boys in his fruit trees one day, and who, after trying kind words and grass, finally pelted them with stones, until the young scapegraces were glad to come down and beg the old man's pardon."
" Webster's spelling book must have been wonderfully popular."
" Yes." And a genial smile lighted up the ancient face. " There were more copies of it sold than of any other work ever written in America. Twenty-four millions is the number up to 1847, and that had increased to 36,000,000 in 1860, since which time I have seen no account of its sale. Yes, I owe my education to the spelling book."

[Contributed by Edward S. Boyd, Woodbury, Conn.]
The following is a copy of the First Records of the 1st Co. 13th Reg't Light Infantry Connecticut Militia, organized at Woodbury in 1795, and having its first drill July 25, 1795 :
We whose names are underwritten do hereby enlist into the first Light

Infantry Company 13th Reg't and engage and bind ourselfs to conform to all the rules and regulations adopted by sd comp'y

Nathan, Hurd jr	Richard man
Bethuel Tompkins	Judson Morris
Simeon H. Minor	Nathan Galpin
David Roots	James Clark
Samuel Asa Galpin	Truman Foot
Phineas Martin	John Marshall
Samuel Atwood	Ichabod Prentiss
Abram Crouchright	Daniel Mitchel
Daniel Stilson jr	Samuel Spolding
Matthew M. Morris	Christopher Prentiss
Iohn Judson jr	William Lum
Truman Percy	Thady Crammer
Amos Tuttle	David Hinman
Uri Gillet	Dennis Bradley
Oliver Judson	James Moody
Bishop Cramer	Gideon H. Hotchford
Solomon Root	Charles Thompson
Rewben Mallory	Truman Martin
Garrick Bacon	Noah B. Benedict
Peter foot	Samuel Martin
Elijah Calhoon	Amos Smith

The above has recently come into the hands of Edward S. Boyd of Woodbury, as Librarian of the Woodbury Library. The book was presented to the library by Mrs. Carr, daughter of the last captain of the company, and contains the records from 1795 to 1817.

[From the Stafford Press.]
STAFFORD'S EARLY DAYS.

Speaking of the old and new brings to light an interesting reminiscence of Stafford's earlier days. The place halfway between the Springs and the Hollow, on the east road, and now called the Wright place, was originally known as the Old Dr. Stanton place. The house must be an ancient one, for the doctor was a very old man in 1801, but he practiced for some years after that, for just how long we are unable to state. There are at the present time men living in town who positively know that he was practicing in their father's families along about 1800. The late Governor Hyde used to relate many interesting anecdotes of the old doctor which he obtained in his youth. In those days nearly every one rode horseback, and the doctor and his mare was known for miles around,it being stated he always owned the best horse in town. He was a very eccentric old fellow, but withal he must have been a very celebrated physician, as he was often called in council many miles away. The singular fact in connection with the old doctor's life is that he lived to be 115 years of age, and was in active practice at 105. It is further stated as a fact that for the last fifty years of his life that he drank a quart of Santa Cruz rum every day.

The doctor was an inveterate snufftaker, and in connection with this habit quite a remarkable cure of his is related. He was called to Woodstock to attend a lady suffering with a severe attack of quinsy; in fact, so bad was the case that the local physicians had given her up and Dr. Stanton was sent for as the last hope. This lady stood very high in the social circles of that place, and much interest was felt by the townspeople in the result of the doctor's visit. Dr. Stanton arrived and immediately went into the sick room. After a short examination of the patient he took out his snuff-box, and after taking a pinch himself, offered it to the lady, which, of course, she indignantly refused. But the doctor insisted, saying that it was his prescription, and compelled her to fill her nostrils full. Of course she commenced to sneeze, and sneeze she did with a vengeance. During her struggles the swelling broke and all danger to the patient was over. Dr. Stanton, without waiting longer, started for his horse, and as he prepared to mount he remarked to the bystanders, "The absurdity of these fool-doctors sending all the way to Stafford for me to come and save a woman's life, when all she needed was a pinch of snuff."   A. H. S.

PRIVATE HOWE'S FUNDS, AND HOW THEY FURNISHED A PAY DAY FOR A CONNECTICUT REGIMENT.
[From the Youth's Companion.]

When the civil war broke out an immense meeting was held in Bridgeport, Conn., and many men volunteered for the army. To the great surprise, one of the richest men in the state, Elias Howe, the inventor of the sewing machine, arose and made this brief speech:

"Every man is called upon to do what he can for his country. I don't know what I can do unless it is to enlist and serve as a private in the

Union army. I want no position; I am willing to learn and do what I can with a musket."

But it soon proved that the chronic lameness from which Howe suffered incapacitated him from marching with a musket, even to the extent of standing sentry. Determined to be of use, however, he volunteered to serve the regiment as its postmaster, messenger and expressman.

Sending home for a suitable horse and wagon, he drove into Baltimore twice a day and brought to the camp its letters and parcels. It was said that he would run over half the state to deliver a letter to some lonely mother anxious for her soldier boy, or bring back to him a pair of boots which he needed during the rainy winter.

For four months after the Seventeenth Connecticut entered the field the government was so pressed for money that no payment to the troops could be made, and there was consequently great suffering among the families of the soldiers, and painful anxiety endured by the men themselves.

One day a private soldier came quietly into the paymaster's office in Washington and took his seat in the corner, to await his turn for an interview. Presently the officer said:
"Well, my man, what can I do for you?"
"I have called to see about the payment of the Seventeenth Connecticut," answered the soldier.

The paymaster, somewhat irritated by what he supposed a needless and impertinent interruption, told him sharply "that he could do nothing without money, and that until the government furnished some it was useless for soldiers to come bothering him about pay."

"I know that the government is in straits," returned the soldier. "I have called to find out how much money it will take to give my regiment two months pay. I am ready to furnish the amount."

The amazed officer asked the name of his visitor, who modestly replied, "Elias Howe." He then wrote a draft for the required sum—$31,000. Two or three days later the regiment was paid. When Mr. Howe's name was called, he went up to the paymasters' desk and signed the receipt for $28.65 of his own money.

The officers of a neighboring regiment sent over to the Seventeenth Connecticut to see if they could not "borrow their private."

Our attention has been called to the title under one of the pictures in the photographic department of the QUARTERLY, in No. 3, Vol. 3, stating that Dr. Titus Coan was one of the first missionaries to the Sandwich Islands.

Rev. S. W. Whitney of Saybrook, Conn., writes us that the statement is misleading, as "The pioneer group of missionaries to the Hawaiian Islands, which embarked from Boston, Mass., in October, 1819, and arrived there in April, 1820, consisted of Messrs. Hiram Bingham, Asa Thurston, Samuel Whitney, Samuel Ruggles, Thomas Holman, M. D., Elisha Loomis and Daniel Chamberlain. Dr. Coan did not go until more than fifteen years after that, he and his wife being a part of the *sixth reinforcement* of missionaries, which left Boston in Dec. 1834, and reached the islands the following spring."

The following, in reference to a statement on page 436 of the QUARTERLY for 1897 has been sent us:

"Far from sympathizing with the British during the Revolution, the Rev. Benajah Phelps, the first minister of Manchester, then Orford Society, was noted for his loyalty to the American cause.

"He was born in Hebron in this state in 1738, graduated from Yale College in 1761, studied divinity, was ordained in 1765. In response to a request from Cornwallis, Nova Scotia, for a minister, he was sent to that place, and succeeded in gathering a Congregational church there and in the neighboring town of Horton. In November, 1766, he married Phebe, daughter of Colonel Robert and Prudence Denison of Horton, and lived in Cornwallis twelve years after his marriage. In 1778 he returned to New England, having begun to suffer for sympathy with the American Revolution, and having been put to the alternative of leaving the province or taking up arms against his country. The following year he obtained permission to return to Nova Scotia for his family, but was captured by a British man-of-war. After some time he, with others, was put on a boat about fourteen miles from land in very rough weather, and left to the mercy of the seas. He finally reached land, but never returned to Nova Scotia, his family coming to him soon after. In view of his extraordinary sufferings and losses, the General Assembly granted him one hundred and fifty pounds. In 1781 he was installed in Manchester, Conn., the first minister of the church there, and spent the rest of his life in that town, dying in 1817.

"I have quoted very fully from Dexter's 'Yale Biographies and Annals,' also from Trumbull's 'Memorial History of Hartford County,' for it seemed rather a pity, in view of his loyalty and his perilous journey back from Nova Scotia, where he had assuredly done his duty toward his country, that the reverend gentleman should be classed among those who were in sympathy with the British."

E. P. F.

What may have been a typographical error has called out the following interesting letter from one of our subscribers:

"In the very excellent and interesting article on 'Our Neighborhood Churches During the American Revolution' in THE QUARTERLY, Vol. 3, No. 4, are mentioned the Cousins Eells for their adhesion to the cause of the Colonies. In the article the name is spelled 'Eels,' and of that I wish to speak.

"Our ancestor, Major Samuel Eells, of Hingham, Mass., spelled his name Eells. It was he who immortalized his name in denouncing the action of the Trustees of Plymouth Colony in selling the 160 Indians as slaves to the West Indies, an act only eqaal in its infamy and cruelty to that of Judas, who betrayed our Saviour for a price.

"His son, Col. Samuel Eells, of Milford, was for more than forty years in employ of Connecticut provinces in various public offices; at one time secretary of Governor Leete. Nathaniel Eells, of Scituate, a son of Major Samuel, married his wife, Hannah North, an aunt of Lord North, Prime Minister of George III, during the Revolutionary War, but her children were all loyal to the Colonies. Another Nathaniel Eells, of Stonington, an ancestor of Rev. Cushing Eells, the founder of Whitman College; Samuel Eells, of North Branford, a captain in the Revolutionary War, whose father, at the time of the Lexington massacre, preached a strong sermon in favor of the Colonies, dismissed his congregation, came out of his pulpit, opened a recruiting office in the church and raised a company. They chose him as their captain. On account of ill health he declined, and they chose his son for their captain. He went through the Revolutionary War. Rev. Edward Eells, who married Martha Pitkin, 1740, and whose son Ozias was for 29 years pastor at Barkhamsted, all spelled their name Eells. Harvey Eells, born 1801, on account of a foolish quarrel among school children, who made fun of his name and said it was squirmy, foolishly dropped one l, and called himself Eels. Most of his descendants moved to Georgia and sided with the Rebellion, and fought against us in the Civil war. There was one notable exception, Major W. B. Eels, of Milford, of the 19th Connecticut Volunteers and 2d Connecticut Artillery, who was wounded and disabled at the battle of Cold Harbor, made Lieutenant Colonel, but his wounds not allowing him to return to active service, soon after the war he died from the effect of those wounds at Terryville.

"In Stonington there is a Hannah Eells Society, a branch of the Daughters of the American Revolution."

W. E. A.

[We hope to have, sometime in the future, something more complete about this interesting family.—ED.]

FROM THE SOCIETIES.

SONS OF THE AMERICAN REVOLUTION.

The board of managers of the Connecticut Sons of the American Revolution met Monday, Dec. 20, 1897, at New Haven. President Jonathan Trumbull presided. They elected the following members: William Edward Gruman of Hartford, Edwin Comstock Johnson, 2d, of Norwich, Henry Isaac Boughton of Waterbury, George W. Moore of South Windsor, Herman Daggett Clark of New Haven, and William Skilling Mills of Bridgeport; also these last "own sons," their fathers having served in the American Revolution: Justin Hodge of Riverton, and George Dorr Goodwin of Sharon.

Action on the proposed fusion with the "Sons of the Revolution" was made the special order for the next meeting. The next dinner, Feb. 22, will be in New Haven. It will be in a new large hall, capable of seating not less than 400, and a great time is expected. Gen. E. S. Greeley was made chairman of the banquet committee, as Gen. S. E. Merwin will be away at that time. The governors of what were the 13 original states will be invited to the banquet.

A reception will be tendered the invited guests at 11.30 a. m., and dinner will be served at 12.30, in order to give ample time for the addresses. President Trumbull will preside, and Col. Osborn will officiate as toastmaster.

DAUGHTERS OF THE AMERICAN REVOLUTION.

Greenwoods Chapter No. 38, of the Daughters of the American Revolution was organized in this place, Wednesday, Dec. 22, 1897, by Mrs. Sara T. Kinney, the state regent. There are twenty-six charter members, and the chapter is proud and happy to reckon among the number a real daughter. Mrs. Mary Steele Cleveland, who is seventy-nine years old, the daughter of John Steele of Hartford, who entered the Revolutionary army January 3, 1777. Mrs. Cleveland was presented with the souvenir gold spoon of the order, to which every real daughter is entitled. Officers were elected as follows: Regent, Mrs. C. J. Camp; vice-regent, Mrs. George S. Barton; registrar, Mrs. Henry Gay; recording secretary, Mrs. J. H. Alvord; corresponding secretary, Mrs. Alice D. Vail; treasurer, Mrs. David Strong; historian, Mrs. Harvey L. Roberts; assistant historian, Judith B. Phelps; librarian, Mrs. E. P. Wilcox; board of management, Mrs. William G. Coe, Mrs. L. M. Blake, Mrs. George W. Phelps, Mrs. Edward Clarke, Mary B. Dudley; programme committee, Mrs. Emily G. Steele, Mrs. Gertrude S. McClelland, Mrs. John Rippere, Mrs. Edward P. Jones, Mrs. T. M. Clark, Alice Coe.

D. A. R. CENTENARIAN.

Mrs. Abigail Foote Loomis, of East Hampton, who, if she lives, will be 100 years old next June, has been given one of the gold spoons which are presented to all real daughters of the Revolution, by the National Society, D. A. R., of Washington, D. C. Mrs. O. V. Coffin and Mrs. James H. Bunce came over from Middleton to make the presentation on behalf of the society. The spoon is of appropriate design with Mrs. Loomis' initials engraved on the back of the handle, and on the bowl "Presented by the National Society, D. A. R." It was the intention to have a little party of friends and relatives, but this was finally abandoned. Both Mrs. Loomis and her daughter, Mrs. Philo Bevin, with whom the aged lady now makes her home, have been made members of the James Woodworth Chapter, D. A. R., Middleton. Mrs. Loomis is still hale and hearty, and hopes to reach the century mark. On Thursday she sat down with the family to Thanksgiving dinner. She was born in Westchester, her father, Nathaniel Foote, being a descendant from one of the settlers of Wethersfield of that name. Four children are living, Mrs. E. A. Bliss of Hartford, Mrs. Philo Bevin of East Hampton, and Israel and Milton Loomis of Westchester. There are also twelve grandchildren and nine great-grandchildren.

The occasion of the presentation of the charter to the Hannah Woodruff Chapter, D. A. R., of Southington, was an event worthy of record.

The chapter was organized June 25, 1897, was admitted to the national organization October 25th, and the charter was presented to the members Thursday, December 9th, 1897. The order of exercises on the latter occasion was as follows :

Music—The Star Spangled Banner   Chorus
Invocation   Mrs. H. T. Buckley, State Chap.
Music—Trio
   Mrs. W. H. Cummings, Mrs. E. W. Twitchell, Mrs. E. B. Kilbourn
Address of Welcome
   Mrs. F. B. Bradley, Regent
Music—Piano Duet
   Mrs. L. K. Curtis, Mrs. R. G. Andrews
Historical Sketch—Hannah Woodruff
   Mrs. A. M. Lewis
Music—Solo   Mrs. E. B. Kilbourn
Presentation of Charter—
   Mrs. S. T. Kinney, State Regent
Acceptance of Charter,   Mrs. F. B. Bradley
Violin Solo—   Miss Anita Lewis
Recitation—A Daughter of the Revolution
   Mrs. Anna D. Pollard
Music—Trio
Address—   Mrs. S. T. Kinney
Music—America   Chorus

The historical sketch by Mrs. A. M. Lewis, containing much interesting information, Mrs. Kinney's address, full of patriotic sentiments admirably expressed, and the shorter addresses by the regent and others, incident to the meeting, were of more than ordinary merit.

The chapter has four "real daughters," one of whom was present at this meeting.

MAYFLOWER DESCENDANTS.—ANNUAL MEETING OF THE CONNECTICUT CHAPTER, HELD AT NEW LONDON.

The Connecticut Chapter, Society of Mayflower Descendants, was very largely represented at the meeting held in the west parlor of the Crocker House, on Monday evening, Dec. 20, 1897. William Waldo Hyde of Hartford, Governor of the chapter, presided at the business meeting, when reports of the secretary, treasurer and historian were read and approved.

The old board of officers was re-elected as follows ; Governor, William Waldo Hyde of Hartford ; secretary, Percy C. Eggleston of New London ; historian, Edward A. Hill of New Haven ; treasurer, Laurance W. Miner of New London.

At the close of the business meeting George W. Stone of Boston, a member of the Massachusetts Chapter, read an original paper on "Pilgrim Days." Mr. Stone has presented this paper before the chapters of New York and Philadelphia, and his reading gave pleasure to all. It was full of interest to the chapter members.

An informal banquet followed. There was a gratifying attendance of the society members.

GENEALOGICAL DEPARTMENT.

Of the "Genealogical History of Families" Sir Robert Atkyns writes: "This has its peculiar use; it stimulates and excites the brave to imitate the generous actions of their ancestors; and it shames the debauched and reprobate, both in the eyes of others and in their own breasts, when they consider how they have degenerated." Page 11, 2nd ed., folio, London 1768, Preface to the Ancient and Preserved State of Gloucestershire.

Querists should write all names of persons and places in such a way that they cannot be misunderstood. Always enclose with queries a self-addressed stamped envelope and at least *ten cents for each query.* Querists should write only on one side of the paper. Subscribers sending in queries should state that they are subscribers, and preference in insertion will always be given them. Queries are inserted in the order in which they are received. On account of our limited space, it is impossible that all queries be inserted as soon as querists desire. Always give full name and post-office address. Queries and notes *must* be sent to Wm. A. Eardeley-Thomas, 50th street and Woodland avenue, Philadelphia, Penn. The editor earnestly requests our readers to assist him in answering queries. His duties are onerous enough in other directions, so that only a limited amount of time can be devoted to query researches.

Notes.

36 *Abington, Ct., Cong'l Ch. Deaths.*
[Continued from page 482.]

1793.—Nov. 3, widow Stowel, in the 86th year of her age.

1794.—Nov. 18, Hezekiah Griggs.
Dec. 6, Elliot, child of Dr. Jared Warner, aged 2 years.

1795.—March 27, Hannah Griggs, 17, and March 28, Elizabeth Griggs, 12, daus. of Mr. Sam'l Griggs.
Oct. 6, Marcia, child of Mr. Amasa Goodell.
Oct. 17, Mr, Pelatiah Lyon.

1796.—Jan. 17, Esther, wife of Lieut. Joshua Grosvenor, æt. 65.
Jan. 31, Miss Nancy Sumner, æt. 32.
Feb. 6, infant child of John Morse.
March 29, Sally Griggs, 15, and March 31, Polly, wife Samuel Bowing, daughters of Mr Sam'l Griggs and Elizabeth, his wife.
April 2, the youngest child of Samue, Bowing.
April 10, Betsy, daughter of widow Hannah Lyon.
May 25, Mr. Amsdell, an old man who moved from Southboro, Mass.

Aug. 20, Mr. John Morse.
Aug. 22, the wife of Mr. Uriah Kingsley.
Sept. 12, Jerusha, the wife of Oliver Goodell.
Oct. 10, Walter, child of Deacon Joshua Grosvenor.
Oct. 13, Joseph Crafts, aged 22.

1797.—Jan. 9, the wife Mr. Thomas Dennison.
May 17, the wife of Mr. Levi Day.
Oct. 27, infant child of Amasa Goodell.
Dec. 28, Mr. John Wheeler.

1798.—Within the local Bounds of the Parish of Abington:
Jan. 6, M. infant child of Capt. Peter Cunningham, aged 1 hour.
Feb. 22, M. child of Appleton Osgood, aged 7 weeks; hooping cough.
April 29, F. infant child of Stephen Utley, jun'r, aged 4 days.
June 8, Mr. Benj'n Hicks, aged 88; disease, dropsy.
Aug. 9, F. child of Daniel Ingals, aged 3; supposed worms.
Aug. 11, Mr. John Bennet, supposed to be nigh 100: old age.

1799—Jan. 3, Mr. Amos Grosvenor, aged 75; consumption.
Jan. 6, M. Nelson, child of Wil'm Trowbridge, æ. 5 weeks; convultion Fits.
Jan. 17, Mr. Sam'l Carpenter, æ. 82; mortification.
Feb. 6, F. A., child of Isaac Farnham, æ. 4 months; plague in the Bowles.
Mar. 30, Miss Lucinda Goodell, æ. 35; consumption.
June 5, Widow Griggs, æ. 82; old age.
June 13, Leiut. Zachariah Goodell, æ. 62; palsy.
June 14, the wife of Capt. Nathan Paine, æ. 39; consumption.
Oct. 21, Leiut. Joshua Grosvenor, æ. 74; fever.
1800—Jan. 14, F. child of W'm Trowbridge, æ. 6 weeks; consumption.
Feb. 2, F. child of D'n Joshua Grosvenor, æ. 5 weeks; rattles.
July 7, wife of Mr. Amasa Goodell in the 46th year of her age; died in Travail.
Aug. 29, wife of Mr. Sam'l Sumner in the 67th year of her age; Bilious Fever.
Oct. 11, Mr. Benj'n Ingals, æ. 85.
Oct. 12 wife of Mr. David Ingals, æ. 55.
Oct. 14, child of Silas Rickard.
In this year died Widow Chandler, mother of Silas Chandler, not recorded in the season of it.

[To be continued.]

37. Inscriptions from gravestones in Lieutenant Henry Bennett's Burying Ground in Sherman, Ct., copied and contributed by Wilford C. Platt, Esq., New Fairfield, Ct.

[In this burying ground some of the stones are standing, some pulled up and set by the wall, and when it was ploughed a great many years ago it is thought some of the stones were broken up and put in the stone wall and some used for steps to houses, so that very few are left. One very large stone was so heavy that it could not be moved to read the inscription, and as Samuel Ackley's stone was back of it the date of his death could not be obtained. The stones of Nathan Hubbell, Mabel Stewart and Alexander Stewart were probably the foot-stones, and as the head-stones were not found it is thought they were destroyed.]
Aaron Osborn, died Nov. 18, 1814, in his 75th year.
Phebe Osborn, wife of Aaron, d. April 22, 1809, in her 57th year.
Massa Osborn, daughter of Aaron and Phebe, d. Jan. 23, 1803, in her 25th year.
Lieut. Henry Bennet d. Sept. 19, 1784, in his 73d year.
Mr. Benjamin Bennett, deacon of Christ Church, died Feb., 1792, in his 79th year.
Mrs. Mary Bennet, wife of Deacon Benjamin, d. Jan. 25, 1795, aged 70 years.
Mrs. Rebekah Northrop, wife of Mr. David, d. March 30, 1791, aged 29 years 2 months.
Capt. Daniel Noble, deacon of Christ Church in New Fairfield, d. Oct., 1757, aged 37 years.
Sally B. Clark, wife of Adam S., died May 15, 1803, in her 32d year.
Katherine Cowdrey, wife of John, d. Sept. 9, 1806, in her 57th year.
Mrs. Mary Sill, wife of Rev. Mr. Elijah, d. Aug. 30, 1761, aged 27 years.
Thomas Major Hickling, son of Mr. John and Caty Hickling, d. July 25, 1773, aged 1 year 7 mos. 15 das.
Johannah Hubbell, wife of Esq. Ephraim, d May 17, 1781, in her 64th year.
Dennis Hubbell, d. July 19, 1786, aged 43 years.
Mr. Levi Hubbell d. Dec. 12, 1773, aged 25 years.

[To be continued.]

38. Quaker Hill, N. Y. Friends Records (copied by Wm. A. Eardeley-Thomas) with original pagination: P. 228, List of Heads of Families on the Verge of our Monthly Meeting held on the Oblong and in the Nine Partners Circularly taken in the 3rd mo., 1760:

PAGE 228.

1ST—AT NEW MILFORD.

Dobson Wheeler & wife
Aaron Benedict
Joseph Ferriss
Gains Talcott

James McKenney
Lydia Norton
Anne Phillips

2d—AT OBLONG.

John Hull and his wife
Wing Kelley   "
Oliver Tryon   "
John Wing   "
John Hoag ye 2nd & wife
Benj'm Hoag & his wife
Abner Hoag & wife
Benj'm Hoag Senr & wife
Philip Allen   "
Moses Hoag   "
George Soule   "
Wm. Russell   "
David Hoag   "
Ebenezer Peaslee   "

Nehemiah Merritt & wife
                     " Jr. "
Elijah Doty   "
Henry Chase   "
Abraham Chase   "
Benj'm Ferriss   "
Timothy Dakin   "
Elisha Akins children
Reed Ferriss & wife
Zebulon Ferriss & wife
John Hoag, Sen'r   "
John Hoag, Jr.   "
Jedidiah Wing   "
Josiah Akin   "

PAGE 229.

Stephen Hoag & wife
James Hunt   "
Prince Howland   "
Isaac Haviland   "
Nath'n Birdsall   "
Nath't Birdsall Jr.   "
Daniel Chase   "
Edward Wing   "

Abraham Thomas
Isaac Bull
Patience Akin
Desire Chase
Mary Allen, Widdow
Mersey Fish
Margaret Akin
Margery Woolman

[To be continued.]

39. Danbury, Conn., Town Records of births, marriages and deaths (copied by William A. Eardely-Thomas.) The records of Danbury were burned by the British in the Revolution when the town was burnt. Only the recorded copies of the wills were saved. The following are from vol. 1 and were re-recorded as soon as possible after the burning. The original pagination is preserved here.

p. 356, Hodges, James, son of Ezra, m. Sept. 14, 1803, Annis, 6th dau. of Eleazer Benedict.

Benedict, Amos son of Theophilus, b. Nov. 11, 1778, m. Mar. 12, 1800, Sarah dau. of Jonas Benedict, b. Nov. 23, 1780 and had 1, Nancy, June 3, 1801. 2, Thomas Brigham, Sept, 25, 1803.

Bailey, Lemuel B., son of Samuel, m. Sept. 20, 1801, Abby, dau. of Abraham Gregory of Norwalk, dec'd, and had 1, Caroline, July 12, 1802. 2, Hannah Lurana, June 14, 1804.

p 357, Ezra Hamilton, 5th son of Joseph, b. Dec. 3, 1768, m. Sept. 15, 1793, Polly 4th dau. of Matthew Barnum and had 1, Daniel Ezra, Aug. 31, 1794.

Levi Weed, son of Asa, m. Apr. 12, 1803, Rachel, dau. of Benjamin Crofut all of Danbury.

Abijah Peck, jr., 2d son of Abijah of Danbury, b. Sept 30, 1768, m. Oct. 4, 1790, Clarissa, dau. of Thomas Stedman of Hampton, and had :
1. Henry, b. Nov. 21, 1791.
2. Frederick, b. Sept. 18, 1793.
3. Sophia, b. Jan 16, 1796.
4. Edwin, b. Mar. 18, 1798.
5. Abijah, b. Mar. 9, 1800.
6. James Stedman, b. Apr. 19, 1802.

Abijah Peck, the elder, d. Feb. 5, 1804.
[To be continued.]

40. Marriages on records of St. John's Protestant Episcopal Church, Stamford and Greenwich, (copied by Wm. A. Eardely-Thomas.)

Oct. 26, 1748 the missionary arrived at the mission. The records are missing for almost ten years.

1758—Mar. 28, Stephen Fowler and Hannah Fowler, both of North Castle.

Apr. 18, Samuel Seward and Phebe Ghorum both of Stamford.

May 25, Abijah Seely and Lucy Hait both of Stamford.

June 27, John Ketchum and Elizabeth Brown both of Norwalk.

Dec. 25, John Hoy, a soldier and Hannah Welch of Stamford.

1759—Jan. 4, Thomas Bekell, a soldier and Mary Dibble of Stamford.

Feb. 11, Bezaleel Brown and Rachel Mead both of Stamford.

Aug. 23, James King of New Castle in one of ye Southern Provinces and Keziah Cory of Greenwich.

Dec. 13, Lemuel Raymond of Salem and Lydia Seely of Stamford.

1760—Jan. —— Ezekiel Seely and Catherine Welch both of Stamford.

(torn), John Holly and Elizabeth King both of Stamford.

Apr. 6, Platt Townsend of Oyster Bay, L. I., and Elizabeth Hubbard of Stamford.

Aug. 10, Nathaniel Sacket and wid. Sarah Lockwood both of Greenwich.

Oct. —— John Loder and Hannah Sherwood both of Stamford.

(torn) Nathan Smith of Stamford and Elizabeth Betts of Greenwich.
1761—July 23, Wm. Hunt of Westchester and Susanna Fowler of North Castle.
Aug. 1, Stephen Platt and Jane Rogers both of Stamford.
Aug. 22, Selleck Holly and Abigail Waterbury both of Stamford.
Oct. 18, Henry Johnson and Amer Peck of Greenwich.
Nov. 10, Nathaniel Seely and Elizabeth Scofield both of Stamford.
1762—Jan. 7, Israel Knap and Elizabeth, wid. of Dr. Hngford both of Greenwich.
Feb. 2, Sands Sutton and Mary Fowler both of North Castle.
Apr. —— Nath'l Jessup and Sarah James both of Greenwich.
1763—June 18, Fyler Dibblee and Polly Jarvis both of Stamford.
June 27, Epinetus How and Elizabeth Cramner both of Stamford.
July 25, Wm. Dodge of New York and Jamima Mead of Greenwich.
Jan. 1, William Thompson and Hannah Pangbon.
Oct. —— Silas Lockwood and Deborah Lockwood both of Greenwich.
[To be continued.]

Queries.

113. *Bishop,* Silvanus M., Nov. 16, 1761, Sarah Beecher in New Haven. This is the first record we have of him. They are both buried in Danbury, Ct. He d. Sept. 2, 1824, aged 86. Who were his parents? A tradition not yet authenticated, says he came from about Middletown.
B. B. H.

114 (*a*) *Alling,* Asa, b. Jan. 18, 1723. N. Haven, son of Caleb first, settled at Nine Partners, Dutchess, Co., N. Y., where he was living in 1755, since which his record and that of his family is lost. There are or were Allings in Dutchess Co., claiming descent from Roger Alling, one of the original settlers of N. Haven. Have they not sprung from this Asa?

(*b*) *Alling,* Ruth (second wife of the 3d Roger m. abt. 1713) and Keziah (wife of Samuel, son of the 3d Roger, lived in Woodbridge, Conn., m. abt. 1736); who were parents of Ruth and Keziah?
G. P. A.

115. *Payne,* Joseph of Columbia, Conn., now called Prospect, d. there in 1805. His ancestry is desired. Was he a descendant of William Payne a freeman of the New Haven Colony 1669?
A. L.

116. *Wyman,* Dr. Solomon, b. Mar. 12, 1766, d. June 20, 1857, m. 1st, Clarissa, dau. of Enoch and Phoebe (Owen) Ashley. He graduated at Lebanon, N. H. medical school, married at Milton, Vt., and had son Ashley b. there Dec. 19, 1801. His wife d. soon after. He settled in Constable, Franklin Co., N. Y., 1805. He was a practicing physician, a leading and highly respected citizen, and d. there at the age of 91. Who were his parents and where was he born? His mother's name is said to have been Elizabeth Hazen. Who were parents of Enoch Ashley and Phoebe Owen, where and when were they born?
F. W. A.

117 (*a*) *Adams,* John of Plymouth, came in the Fortune, m. Ella Newton and had James, who m. a Vassall and had 1, Richard, the Indian fighter, and 2, William——William was at one time in Norwich and had a son James. James of Westerly cannot be accounted for nor James, son of William, disposed of. It is desired to prove them one and the same person.

(*b*) *Hancox,* Abigail, m. 1759 in Stonington, Wm. Middleton. Was she dau. of William and Hepzibah (Winslow) Hancox?

(*c*) *Cole,* Lucy, b. Sept. 16, 1773, m. Mar. 11, 1792, Joseph Bennett. Who were parents of Lucy Cole? Her father was a Revolutionary soldier. The Bennett's were from Lebanon, Ct.

(*d*) *Allen,* Hannah, m. Apr. 17, 1738, James Comstock; she was 63 years old in 1781; perhaps dau. of Samuel Allen. What was her ancestry?

(e) *Brown*, Hannah, b. 1691, d. June 6, 1771, m. 1708, Edward Cogswell, b. in Gloucester, lived for a time in Preston, Ct., and d. 1773 in New Milford, Conn. What was her ancestry?

(f) *Wheeler*, Hannah, b. May 12, 1707, m. Jan 23, 1731, Nathaniel Adams. Was she dau. of David Wheeler of Groton. F. P. B.

118. (a) *Williams*, William, b. Oct. 12, 1710, m. Tabitha Parsons, b. Mar. 11, 1713. Where were they born and who were their parents? Their son William Williams, b. June 11, 1738, commanded a regiment at Bennington in the Revolution; he m. Zilpah or Zipporah ———; both d. in 1822, in Stewartstown, P. Q. What was the family name of Zilpah? Zipporah Williams dau. of William and Zipporah m. Gilbert Parmelee of Wilmington, Vt., who was b. at Killingworth, Ct., Jan. 23, 1764. Wanted date of m. and place of b. of Zipporah (Williams) Parmelee.

(b) *Parmelee*, Nathaniel, (great grand-father of above Gilbert) m. Esther supposed to be dau. of John Ward and grand-dau. of Andrew and Esther Ward. According to Middletown, Conn., Town Records, this Esther Ward m. William Cornwall. Can any descendant of Nathaniel and Esther Parmelee tell me the maiden name and parentage of Esther?

(c) *Button* or Bouton, Mary (or Deborah) m. Thomas French of Charlestown, Mass., (1638) who d. abt. 1665 at Guilford, and had Sarah French mother of Nathaniel Parmelee. Who were the parents of Mary (or Deborah) Button (or Bouton)?

(d) *Field*, Zachariah of Hartford, moved to Hadley in 1659, m. Mary Stanley. Who was she?

(e) *Parmelee*, Lemuel, son of Nathaniel and Esther, b. 1704, m. Sarah Kelsey. Her mother was Jane ——— ———. What was the maiden name of Jane? E. M.

119. *Austin*, Anthony[1] came from Eng. in 1638 with parents and settled in Charlestown, Mass.; Nathaniel[2] 1678, Suffield, Conn.; Capt. Daniel[3] 1720, Suffield; Linus[4] 1773, Wilmington, Vt.; Alvin[5] 1806, Xenia, Akron and Cincinnatti, Ohio, and Chicago; Andrew C.,[6] Detroit, St. Louis and Kansas City. How did Daniel get the title of Captain?
F. D. A.

120. (a) *Shepard*, Jonathan of Coventry, Ct , his genealogy is being compiled and information is desired. He married 1st, Love Palmer of Stonington, Ct., and had : 1. Jonathan. 2. Oliver. 3. Nathaniel. 4. Amos. 5. Simeon. 6. Joshua. 7. Rosswell. 8. Prudence. (m. in Coventry, John Ladd.) 9. Anne (m. Silas King of Coventry). 10. Love (m. in Alstead, N. H., Daniel Marley of that place). Jonathan m; 2nd Polly Underwood and had one daughter. Jonathan, jr., m. Hannah Benjamin of Hartford and had 6 sons and 1 dau. Information desired about Polly Underwood and her dau. Prudence (Shepard) Ladd, Anne (Shepard) King, Jonathan Shepard, jr.

(b) *Hamblin*, Joel, m. Polly Channing and had Oliver, b. Sept. 3, 1731 in Enfield, Ct., m. 1777 at Tolland, Ct., Rachel Cleveland—moved to Brookfield, Vt. The descent from Oliver and Rachel is traced to the present day. I wish to learn more about the Hamblin family.
V. E. C.

121. *Skinner*, Richard, b. abt. 1688, d. 1758, came to Haddam, Ct., and established there the family of that name. From whence did he come and who were his parents?
E. A. S.

122. *Curtis*, Daniel, of West Hartford, Ct., m. Oct. 14, 1736, Rebekah ———. His ancestry is desired. It is believed he was a son of Thomas Curtis of Wethersfield. Would like to know how he is connected with the Stratford Curtis family.
G. H. T.

123. (a) *Maltby*, Timothy of Conn., m. Mabel Dimmock. What was his ancestry and who were his children?

(b) *Parmelee*, Rhoda, dau. of Jeremiah of Wilmington, Vt.; Rhoda, b. 1744, d. 1784, dau. of Asahel; Rhoda bapt. Apr. 17, 1767. Newtown, Conn., dau. of Stephen. Who did these three Rhodas marry and what children did they have?
(c) *Terry*, George, m. Abigail, dau. Robert and Hepzebiah Gibbs. Who were parents of George and Robert?
(d) *Slade*, Henry, m. 1776 Naomi Chase. Who were their parents and what children had they? J. W. E.

CORRECTIONS AND ADDITIONS.

Query 103, p. 485, OCTOBER QUARTERLY, should be John T. Peters, not John S. Sarah Farnham m. *Zelotis* Lord. There was a Sarah Farnham m. Wyllis Lord but we want information about Sarah and Zelotis.
W. L. M.

CHASE GENEALOGY.

[From " A Chase," Providence, R. I.]

12. Thomas Makepeace, m. 2nd, Jan 10, 1697-8, Mary Burt by Thomas Leonard of Taunton. Mary Chace probably d. 1697.

13. Austin (p. 309 Gen. Dict.) an Freetown records say that Benjamin Grinnell was b. Jan. 12, 1696, instead of Daniel.

14. "Ensign" Jacob⁴ (John³, John¹, Nicholas¹,) and Philip (Chase) Hathaway had:
  1. Jacob, m. wid. Deborah (Kent) Hathaway.
  2. Philip, m. Martha Simmons.
  3. Joseph, m. Alice Strange.
  4. Isaac, m. Rebecca Warren.
  5. Melatiah, m. 1st, Anna Hoskins.
           2d, wid. Sarah King.
  6. John, m. Merriba Simmons.
  7. Benjamin, m. Mary Davis.
  8. Guilford, m. Lydia Simmons.
  9. Ja (el?) m. 1st, Rebecca Simmons.
           2d, Elizabeth
  10. Hannah, m. Lot Strange.
  11. Betty, m. John Winslow.

17. Bethiah³ Chase m. Joseph Dunham of Edgartown, Mass. He was a carpenter. They lived in Freetown, Norton and Middleboro, Mass., the last place was where she d. May 20, 1753, a widow. She was one of the original members of the Congregational Church of Christ in Freetown. Joseph the husband was one of the original members of the Church in Norton, Mass. They had:
  1st, Hannah⁴, June 1, 1707. Whom did she marry?
  2d, Stephen⁴, May 5, 1709. What became of him?

OTHER CHASE ADDITIONS AND CORRECTIONS.

5. There is no possibility of Mary Hall having m. a *Wm.* Chase; she m. either Jacob³ or was 2d wife of John³.

9. Sarah, wid. of Joseph Chase, m. 8 m, 3, 1737, Sw. Fr., John, son of John Reade of Freetown; he was dead before 1-25-1742.

10. Amey, died before Feb. 24, 1715-6 as stated by John Borden, her father, in his will made at this date.

11. Samuel Sherman was son of Philip not of John. Philip⁴ Sherman (Samuel³, Henry², Henry¹) m. Sarah Odding, and had among others:
  vi. Samson⁶ m. Isabel Tripp and had 2, Sarah⁶ m. 1st, Joseph⁵ Chase (William², William¹); m. 2d, John, son of John Reade.
  viii. John⁵ m. Sarah Spooner and had 3, Abigail⁶ m. Nathaniel⁴ Chase (William³, William², William¹.)
  x. Hannah⁶ m. William³ Chase (William², William¹.)
  xi. Samuel⁵ m. Martha Tripp and had 1, Sarah⁶ m. Samuel³ Chase (William², William¹.)
  xiii. Philip⁵ (pe) m. Benjamin⁴ Chase (William¹.)

27. Thomas and Mary⁴ (Chase) Woodmansee, had also a dau. vi. Hannah *Woodmansee*, b. Nov. 15, 1730, m Jan. 15, 1756, Nicholas Cornell.

24. T. R. Chase of Detroit, Mich., says he never heard of an Ezekiel in this family. I am certain I had this on reliable authority. Mr. Chase also says that No's 114 and 115 both married men named Peleg Sherman. He says there were 3 cousins of that name living at this time. It seems to me that Dartmouth T. R. would have said Elizabeth Sherman d. 1747, if she, No. 125 had mar. a Sherman. I concluded that because Dartmouth T. R. said Elizabeth Chase d. 1747, that therefore she was not married.

DESCENDANTS OF WILLIAM CHASE OF YARMOUTH.

BY WILLIAM A. BARDFLEY-THOMAS.

PART IV.

185—iii. Mary,[5] May 6, 1735; m. int. June 25, 1770 (Rehoboth T. R.), Thomas Horton, and had there 1. Thomas,[6] Aug. 9, 1773. What became of him? 2. Hozia,[6] Feb. 1, 1775. What became of this person?
186—iv. Sarah,[5] ——————— —— ———. What became of her?
187—v. Ann,[5] ——————— — ————. An Anne Chase, b. ——, 1737, d. Sept. 13, 1807, m. Nov. 23, 1760, in Scituate, R. I., Robert[4] (b. 1715, d. Aug. 1792), son of Peleg[3] (Daniel,[2] Roger[1]) and Elizabeth (Carpenter) Williams, and had, 1. Ephraim; 2. Wilbour; 3. Robert; 4. Sarah.
188—vi. Samuel,[5] June 15, 1741. What became of him?

32. **Hannah[4]** (Jacob[3] Chase, William,[2] William[1]) *Read* m. Dec. 1, 1720 (Sw. T. R.), Benjamin (b. 1700, d. Mar. 19, 1733), son of Joseph Read. Ch. b. Swansea:

    i. Benjamin[5] *Read*, May 31, 1721.
    ii. David[5] *Read*, Jan. 20, 1722-3.
    iii. Barnard[5] *Read*, Feb. 12, 1724-5.   What became of these
    iv. Hannah[5] *Read*, Jan 29, 1729-30.   children?
    v. Samuel[5] *Read*, April 7, 1727.
    vi. Stephen[5] *Read*, Nov. 7, 1732.

33. **John[4]** Chase (John,[3] William,[2] William[1]) d. Nov. 26, 1755; m. July 17, 1700, Swansea, Sarah Hills; she d. May —, 1757. Who were her parents? On p. 455 of Otis Barnstable it is stated that *John* Chase m. Mercy, dau. of Gershom and Bethia (Bangs) Hall. I can find no authority for the name of *John* Chase. Bethia Bangs was b. 1642 (d. 1696, æt. 54), m. abt. 1665 (as her second child Samuel was b. 1669) Gersham Hall, b. 1647 (d. 1732, æt. 85). Their dau. Mercy was b. 1671. I incline to the belief that she m. Jacob[3] Chase (5), as both were of age by 1689 and his wife was named Mercy. Still she may have m. John[3] Chase (6) as his second wife; but she certainly did not m. (before 1727, date of father's will) John[4] Chase (33), since his wife Sarah did not die before 1757. Ch. were:

189—i. Charity,[5] 1701. What became of her?
190—ii. Ebenezer,[5] 1704. What became of him?
191—iii. John,[5] 1706; m. pub. Jan. 19, 1732-3, Thinkful Berry.
192—iv. Benjamin,[5] 1708. What became of him?
193—v. Earle,[5] 1711. What became of him?
194—vi. Elisha,[5] Dec. 15, 1712; m. Jan. 30, 1733, Sarah Deen.
195—vii. Judah, ——————; d. Nov. 7, 1791; m. 1st, April 11, 1734 (Taunton T. R.) Sarah Macomber of Taunton (who were her parents?); m., 2d, April 24, 1737, Judith Leonard of Raynham; then he joined the Friends in Swansea; (who were her parents?); m., 3d, 2 m, 11, 1749, Sw. Fr., Lydia[5] Chase (116). Did he have any issue?
196—viii. Rebecca,[5] ——————; m. April 19, 1736 (Sw. T. R.), Ezekiel Chase. Was he Ezekiel[5] (No. 115)? It is said he had a family in Dartmouth, but they do not appear on the T. R. What children did he have?
197—ix. Elizabeth,[5] ——————. ——————. What became of her?

34. **Thomas[4]** Chase (John,[3] William,[2] William[1]) m. abt. 1704-5, Sarah ——————. ——.. It is said her name was "Guell," but I have no authority for this outside of the fact that the first child is named "Guell" Chase on Yarmouth Town Records, while several printed works call the name "Gowell." I have been able to learn nothing of her ancestry. Yar. Town Records—Jonathan Whilden, Thomas "Chaise" and Joseph "howes" grand jury men Mar. 23, 1724-5; Thomas "hallet," Jofhua Tay-

(17)

lor, Thomas "Chaife" and John Crowell grand jury men Jan. 20, 1728-9; Thomas Bray jun., James; Taylor, Thomas Tobey jun. and Thomas "Chace" "pettitt" jury men Mar. 1, 1736. A Thomas Chase received 7½ shares of common lands in 1712 (pp. 129 and 130 Yar. T. R.); also a Thomas Chase owned land in Yarmouth Jan. 21, 1739 (p. 142 Y. T. R.). His will dated Sept. 1, 1767, in Y., names wife Sarah; 3 daus. and 3 sons; gr. son Thomas of son Guell deceased; 2 gr. children "Basheba" and Guell, heirs of gr. son Guell deceased (p. 321, Vol. 13, Barnstable Probate Rec.). His inventory Dec. 5, 1768—£37 s18, p. 388, B. P. R.

Children's births, p. 27, book 3, Yar. T. Rec.:

198—i. "Guell,"[5] Jan. 22, 1707-8; m. Nov. 28, 1727, Jane Philips. Who were her parents?
199—ii. "Hanah,"[5] May 24, 1712; not named in her father's will. Did she die unmarried?
200—iii. Phebe,[6] July 4, 1713; m. Aug. 2, 1733, Thomas Baker.
201—iv. Richard,[5] Mar. 3, 1714-5; m. Jan. 21, 1734-5, Mrs. Thankful Chase, wid. of John 191.
202—v. Joseph,[5] Mar. 17, 1718-9; m. Jan. 19, 1733-4, Sarah O'Kelley.
203—vi. "Precilah,"[5] April 10, 1720; m. Oct. 12, 1739, in Yarmouth, Mass., Christopher Ellis· Did he have any children? Who were his parents?
204—vii. Sarah,[5] May 20, 1722; m. Aug. 23, 1739, in Y., Nathaniel Basset of Chatham, Mass. Did he have any children? Who were his parents?
205—viii. Abner,[5] June 22, 1729; m. Oct. 27, 1748. Deborah Baker.

35. Jonathan[4] Chase (John,[3] William,[2] Wiliiam[1]) mar. July 6, 1709, at Basnstable, Mass., Sarah Green. Who were her patents? He lived in Newport, R. I.; he was admitted as freeman in R. I., May 2, 1727—then "viewer" of Fishoil and Whalebone. Did he marry a second wife Mary _____ and live in North Kingston R. I?

Children's births, book 3, p. 81, Y. T. R. ("Chaise"):

206—i. Joshua,[5] Nov. 16, 1709. What became of him?
207—ii. "Unis,"[5] July 15, 1711. "A Unis Chase of Yar. m. Mar. 7, 1741-2, in Dighton, Mass., Benjamin Hilander of Sheffield, Eng." Did he have children? Who were his parents?
208—iii. Caleb,[5] Sept. 25, 1713; m. pub. Nov. 17, 1734, in Y., Priscilla Godfrey. Who were her parents? m. 2d, Sept. 8, 1736, in Y., Mary Wixon. Who were her parents? Did he have children?
209—iv. Jonathan,[5] Aug. 10, 1716; m. pub. Feb. 1752, in Y., Experience Arey of Harwich; m. pub. Feb. 22, 1752, in Harwich, Experience Ary, late of Truro (who were her parents?); m. pub. Mar. 2. 1754, in Y., but mar. Mar. 18, 1754, in H., Elizabeth Smith. Who were her parents?
210—v. "Sarah Chase of Jonathan" (North Kingston, R. I., T. R.) m, Nov. —, 1748, Benjamin Congdon.
211—vi. John,[5] ——— . ———-(according to T. R. Chase), m. Nov. 11, 1759, in Providence, R. I., Edith Jones. · Did he have children? Who were her parents?
211 a—vii. Mary,[5] (perhaps) m. Nov. 23, 1766, in Providence, R. I., Jabez Pursye. Did he have children? Who were her parents?
Jonathan and Mary ( ) Chace had 2 children in North Kingston, R. I.
212—viii. A child, May 20, 1733; perhaps "Phebe Chase of North Kingston, R. I. (T. R.) dau. of Jonathan who mar. Feb. —, 1753 (No. Kingston T. R.), Jeremiah Harrington," was this child. Did he have children? Who were his parents?
213—ix. A child[5] May 23, 1735; perhaps it was the Esther Chase who m. ——— ———

Ephraim (b. Nov. 18, 1733; d. March 17, 1800), son of John and Comfort (Hart, Gifford, and had (vide Gifford Gen.):

1. Jonathan *Gifford*, Aug. 5, 1757; m. April 29, 1779, Locs Eddy.
2. William *Gifford*, Feb. 24, 1762; m. Hannah ___ ___
   Who were her parents?
3. Lydia *Gifford*, May 27, 1764; m. Philip[3] Chase (James,[4] James,[3] Isaac,[4] William,[3] William,[2] William[1]). Did he have children?
4. Esther *Gifford*, Nov. 12, 1769. What became of her?

HALL'S VEGETABLE SICILIAN HAIR RENEWER

Hair Like This...

Long, luxuriant, silken, soft, is the result of the use of Hall's Vegetable Sicilian Hair Renewer. This preparation renews the hair by renewing the conditions under which growth alone is possible.

HALL'S HAIR RENEWER feeds the hair, enriches the soil of the scalp, and so restores the color to gray and faded hair, stops hair from falling, removes dandruff, and promotes a healthy growth.

♦♦♦♦

From the Highest Medical Authority in Sweden.

I have had occasion to see several persons who, for some time have used HALL'S VEGETABLE SICILIAN HAIR RENEWER and know that it has restored the original color to the hair, as well as being efficient in removing the itching and dandruff that accompanies the falling of the hair. I consider it my duty to acknowledge the same.

VINCENT LUNDBERG,
Physician in Chief to the
King of Sweden.

R.P. HALL
AND
COMPANY
PROPRIETORS
NASHUA
N.H.

A FINE HAIR DRESSING

HERALDRY...

Family Crests, Coats of Arms
Properly Emblazoned.

✤ ✤ ✤ ✤ ✤ ✤

E. A. SHERMAN,

Room 32, Trust Co. Building.   HARTFORD, CONN.

SMOKE A CIGAR

Made of Tobacco---Not Drugs.

LA ROSA BACCO IS MADE OF

NATURAL CURED TOBACCO.   NO ARTIFICIAL FLAVOR.

LET US SEND YOU A BOX (By Mail).

LA ROSA BACCO :
50 Perfectos.   (Large) $3.75
50 Operas or Coquettas (Small) 2.00
25 Operas or Coquettas "   1.00

BEE CIGAR CO., 220 State St.   A. MARWICK, Jr., Druggist, 377 Asylum St.
HARTFORD, CONN.

...Carriages Harness and Horse Goods.

ESTABLISHED 1868---Just thirty years ago.
OLDEST HOUSE IN OUR LINE IN THE CITY.

Our goods must be seen to be appreciated. Those who have dealt with us NEED no invitation; to others we simply say

COME TO 393 ALLYN STREET,

100 feet from east entrance to
Union Passenger Station.

Hartford, Conn.   **F. M. WARREN.**

Mention THE QUARTERLY

ORGANIZED 1866.

J. M. ALLEN,
President.

F. B. ALLEN,
2d Vice-President.

WM. B. FRANKLIN,
Vice-President.

J. B. PIERCE,
Sec'y and Treas.

Thorough Inspections

And Insurance against Loss or Damage to Property and Loss of Life and Injury to Persons Caused by....

Steam Boiler Explosions.

MORE THAN 62,000 STEAM BOILERS NOW UNDER THE INSPECTION CARE OF THE COMPANY.

87th Semi-Annual Financial Statement of the

Phœnix Insurance Company,
OF HARTFORD, CONN.
....JANUARY 1st, 1898....

Cash Capital, - - - - $2,000,000.00

Assets Available for Fire Losses, **$5,538,379.50** As Follows:

Cash on Hand, in Bank and with Agents,	$747,147 73
State Stocks and Bonds,	29,250 00
Hartford Bank Stocks,	569,280 00
Miscellaneous Bank Stocks,	359,907 00
Corporation and Railroad Stocks and Bonds,	2,774,416 00
County, City and Water Bonds,	341,270 00
Real Estate,	527,696 67
Loans on Collateral,	20,200 00
Real Estate Loans,	132,340 70
Accumulated Interest and Rents,	33,871 40
TOTAL CASH ASSETS,	$5,538,379 50

LIABILITIES.

Cash Capital,	$2,000,000 00
Reserve for Outstanding Losses,	375,170 73
Reserve for Re-Insurance,	2,139,093 40
NET SURPLUS,	1,022,915 38
TOTAL ASSETS,	$5,538,379 50

Surplus to Policy-holders, . . . $3,022,915.37

Total Losses Paid Since Organization of Company,

$41,385,760.27

D. W. C. SKILTON, PRESIDENT.
EDW. MILLIGAN, SECRETARY.

J. H. MITCHELL, VICE-PRESIDENT.
JOHN B. KNOX, ASS'T SECRETARY.

1898.   THIRTY-FOURTH ANNUAL STATEMENT   1898.
...OF THE...

Travelers Insurance Company.

Chartered 1863. (Stock.) Life and Accident Insurance.

JAMES G. BATTERSON, President.

Hartford, Conn., January 1, 1898.

Paid-Up Capital, - $1,000,000

ASSETS.		LIABILITIES.	
Real Estate,	$1,994,465.31	Reserve, 4 per cent. Life Department,	$16,650,062.00
Cash on hand and in Bank,	1,345,412.83	Reserve for Re-insurance, Accident Dep't,	1,385,817.22
Loans on bond and mortgage, real estate,	5,906,610.72	Present value Installment Life Policies,	420,288.00
Interest accrued but not due,	227,770.38	Reserve for Claims resisted for Employers,	299,066.30
Loans on collateral securities,	915,400.94	Losses unadjusted,	269,794.94
Loans on this Company's Policies,	1,106,686.51	Life Premiums paid in advance,	25,330.58
Deferred Life Premiums,	209,966.10	Special Reserve for unpaid taxes, rents, etc.,	110,000.00
Prems. due and unreported on Life Policies,	228,448.75		
United States Bonds,	14,000.00	Total Liabilities,	$19,140,359.04
State, county, and municipal bonds,	3,612,546.78		
Railroad stocks and bonds,	4,664,205.75	Excess Security to Policy-holders,	$3,722,635.12
Bank stocks,	1,064,047.00		
Other stocks and bonds,	1,449,455.00	Surplus to Stockholders,	$2,722,635.12
Total Assets,	$22,868,994.16		

STATISTICS TO DATE.

LIFE DEPARTMENT.		ACCIDENT DEPARTMENT.	
Life Insurance in force,	$91,882,310.00	Number Accident Claims paid in 1897,	18,611
New Life Insurance written in 1897,	14,507,249.00	Whole number Accident Claims paid,	307,000
Insurance issued under the Annuity Plan is entered at the commuted value thereof as required by law.		Returned to Policy-holders in 1897,	$1,381,906.81
		Returned to Policy-holders since 1864,	21,210,005.96
Returned to Policy-holders in 1897,	1,235,585.30	Returned to Policy-holders in 1897,	$2,617,492.20
Returned to Policy-holders since 1864,	13,150,350.57	Returned to Policy-holders since 1864,	34,360,626.53

GEORGE ELLIS, Secretary.
JOHN E. MORRIS, Assistant Secretary   J. B. LEWIS, M D, Surgeon and Adjuster.
EDWARD V. PRESTON, Supt. of Agencies.   SYLVESTER C. DUNHAM, Counsel.

THE LEADING
FIRE INSURANCE
COMPANY
OF AMERICA.

INCORPORATED
1819.
CHARTER
PERPETUAL.

CASH CAPITAL,	$4,000,000.00
CASH ASSETS,	12,089,089.98
TOTAL LIABILITIES,	3,655,370.62
NET SURPLUS,	4,433,719.36
LOSSES PAID IN 79 YEARS,	81,125,621.50

WILLIAM B. CLARK, President.

W. H. KING, Secretary.   E. O. WEEKS, Vice-President.
A. C. ADAMS,   } Assistant Secretaries.
HENRY E. REES,

WESTERN BRANCH, 413 Vine St. Cincinnati, Ohio,   -   KEELER & GALLAGHER, Gen'l Agents.
NORTHWESTERN BRANCH, Omaha, Neb.,   -   -   { WM. H. WYMAN, Gen'l Agent.
                                             { W. P. HARFORD, Ass't Gen'l Agent.
PACIFIC BRANCH, San Francisco, Cal.   -   -   BOARDMAN & SPENCER, Gen'l Agents.

INLAND MARINE DEPARTMENT:

| CHICAGO, ILL., - | 145 La Salle Street | BOSTON, - - - | 12 Central Street, |
| NEW YORK, - | 52 William Street | PHILADELPHIA, - | 229 Walnut Street |

1851   1897

The Phoenix Mutual Life Insurance Company,

OF HARTFORD, CONN.

HOME OFFICE
PHŒNIX MUTUAL LIFE INSURANCE CO.
HARTFORD, CONN.

Issues all the modern forms of Life and Investment Policies.

Examine our new EXCHANGEABLE LIFE and RETURN PREMIUM contracts, also our 5 per cent. 20 YEAR INCOME BOND Policy.

Send your age to the Home Office, and we will send you a sample policy, showing just what we have to offer.

JONATHAN B. BUNCE, Pres.   JOHN M. HOLCOMBE, Vice-Pres.
CHARLES H. LAWRENCE, Secretary.

JAMES E. SMITH,

General Special Agent,

No. 49 Pearl St., Hartford, Conn.

We Have Enlarged Our Plant,
Put in New Machinery,

to meet the demands of our growing business, and now, with one of the best equipped establishments, we are prepared to do all kinds of Photo-Engraving in a First-class manner.   Give us a call.

✦✦✦✦✦

The Hartford Engraving Co.,

66 State Street, Courant Building,

HARTFORD, CONN.

Engravers for the
CONNECTICUT QUARTERLY

"*The Grate That Heats.*"

Jackson Ventilating Grate.

Heats on two floors.

Highest Award, World's Fair, '93.
Thousands now in use.
Our customers are our references.
Do not regard this grate as simply a luxury for Spring and Fall. It will heat two large rooms when the mercury outside is at zero or below, and will thoroughly and constantly ventilate the rooms without an open window or any draught.

Favor yourself and us by proving the luxury, the cheerfulness, the healthfulness and the economy of these grates.

Call and investigate or send for an illustrated catalogue.

Stoughton & Taylor,
38 Ann St.,
Hartford, Conn.

Mantels, fireplace fixtures, tiles, delft, Kenton Vitrea, etc.

Huntsinger's Business College

Is the leading school of Connecticut for business or short-hand training. Day attendance over 290 pupils. Seven skillful, polite and obliging teachers. This school has placed 122 graduates in good-paying positions the past thirty-seven weeks.

No term divisions and new pupils enter every week. We do all that can be done to place graduates in situations. Full information for the asking. Visitors welcome.

M. Huntsinger

✢ Where to go for Good Printing and Bookbinding. ✢

The Horton Printing Co.

Have one of the best equipped plants in the state for turning out the highest class of work at lowest prices.

. . SPECIAL ATTENTION . .

Given to Original Designs in Printing and Bookbinding.

We carry a Special Line of . . .

✢ FINE STATIONERY ✢

Which for variety and low prices cannot be equalled.

Steel Plate Engraving and Printing,

IN UP TO DATE STYLES.

OPERA HOUSE BLOCK, MERIDEN, CONN.

THE CONNECTICUT QUARTERLY

Illustrated Articles in this Number:

The Last Shot in the Arctic,
Ellington,
Henry Barnard,
Slater Memorial, Norwich,
Bristol Historical Society,
Augustus H. Fenn,

Etc., Etc.

See Contents on First Page.

$1.00 a Year.   HARTFORD, CONN.   25 cts. a Copy.

The Philadelphia, Reading and New England R.R.

⁕Summer Home Book for 1898

IS NOW READY FOR DISTRIBUTION.

It contains over one hundred attractive half-tone illustrations and is without doubt the handsomest book of the kind ever issued by any railroad. It contains an increased list of Hotels and Boarding Houses, gives rates for board and all information sought after by those intending to summer in the country. Don't neglect getting a copy—sent free for postage, 6c., to

W. J. MARTIN, Hartford, Conn.

The Connecticut Quarterly

AN ILLUSTRATED MAGAZINE

Devoted to the Literature, History, and Picturesque Features
of Connecticut

PUBLISHED QUARTERLY
BY THE CONNECTICUT QUARTERLY COMPANY
66 STATE STREET, COURANT BUILDING.

GEORGE C. ATWELL, EDITOR   HARTFORD, CONN.

CONTENTS.

Vol. IV   April, May, June, 1898.   No. 2

Henry Barnard, LL.D.	From a painting by A. C. Fenety.	*Frontispiece*	
Henry Barnard, Educator.	Illustrated.	*Frederick Calvin Norton.*	123
The Lesson of the Rain.	Poem. Illustrated.	*Louise P. Merritt.*	138
The Tories of Connecticut.		*James Shepard.*	139
The House of the Kindly Smile.	Poem. Ill.	*Mary A. Hoadley.*	151
A Reminiscence of the Snowstorm of February 1, 1898.			
	An illustration drawn by	*H. Phelps Arms.*	152
The Black Dog. Story.	Illustrated.	*W. H. C. Pynchon.*	153
Arbutus. Poem.		*Sarah E. Bel.*	161
Mistress Mary's Wedding Apron.	Poem.	*Ellen Brainerd Peck.*	162
The Last Shot in the Arctic.	Illustrated.	*Charlotte M. Holloway.*	163
The Sea was in Frolicsome Mood To-day.	Poem. Ill.	*Arthur Cleveland Hall.*	171
Nerva. Story. Part II.	(Concluded.)	*Milo Leon Norton.*	175
A Midnight Song. Poem.		*Minnie Louise Hendrick.*	179
List of Burials, Center Church Burying Ground, Hartford.			
	Copied and annotated by	*Mary K. Talcott.*	180
Ellington,	Illustrated.	*Alice E. Pinney.*	189
Tempest. Poem.		*Delia B. Ward.*	196
Augustus H. Fenn.	Illustrated.	*Joseph H. Vaill.*	197
Art Education in the "Rose of New England."	Ill.	*Alice W. Cogswell.*	201
The Bristol Historical and Scientific Society.	Ill.	*Piera Root Newell.*	208
	Pen and ink sketches by Antoinette Newell.		
Departments.—GENEALOGICAL DEPARTMENT.			218
HISTORICAL NOTES.			226
DESCENDANTS OF WILLIAM CHASE OF YARMOUTH.			227
EDITORIAL NOTES.			229
PUBLISHER'S NOTES.			231
FROM THE SOCIETIES.			231
BOOK NOTICES AND REVIEWS.			233

Copyright, 1898, by GEO. C. ATWELL. (*All rights reserved*).
Entered at the Post Office at Hartford, Conn., as mail matter of the second class.

Blickensderfer Typewriting Machines

Equal any of the high-priced machines in capacity and quality of work and excel them in convenience. Practical, low-priced, portable, keyboard machines. Have 84 letters and characters all on a type-wheel weighing less than one-quarter of an ounce.

Scientific Keyboard,
No. 5. $35.00

H. C. HAYWOOD & CO.,
GENERAL AGENTS.

Meriden, Conn.

No Ribbon. Writing always in sight. Type interchangeable. Direct inking and printing. Unequalled in manifolding power. Acknowledged simplicity of construction. Most durable machines made. Weight only six pounds.

Either Scientific or Universal Keyboard
No. 7. $50.00

Comprehensive in Plan,

Moderate in Price, Thorough in Practice, Famous for Results, with a corps of Teachers who are Masters in their Special Departments.

New England
CONSERVATORY
OF MUSIC
(Founded 1853 by Dr. E. Tourjée)

offers unequalled advantages to students seeking Thorough Instruction in **Music, Musical Composition and Elocution.**

G. W. CHADWICK, Musical Director
SCHOOL YEAR BEGINS SEPT. 9.
PROSPECTUS FREE. Address
FRANK W. HALE, General Mgr., Franklin Sq., Boston

Provide for the Future

The **FIRST** payment upon shares in Class A or B in the Connecticut Building and Loan Association secures to a shareholder's family protection to as large an amount as would take twenty years to accumulate by saving.

Ten dollars a month for 120 months in Class A, or for 108 months in Class B, will produce $2,000, or pay that amount to one's estate in the event of prior death.

Assets, over $800,000.00

Guarantee, Reserve
Fund and Surplus, **$102,700.85**

**The Connecticut
Building and Loan
Association...**

252 Asylum Street, Hartford, Conn.

The Religious Herald

336 Asylum Street,
Hartford, Conn.

Congregational Weekly
of Connecticut.

Single Subscriptions and Renewals, $1.00
New Subscribers (in clubs of five), 50c

REUBEN H. SMITH,
Editor and Proprietor.

*C*HURCH SOCIETIES, Fraternal Organizations, Clubs, etc., desiring entertainment of any kind, or PERFORMERS DESIRING ENGAGEMENTS, should correspond with the...

⁕Connecticut Entertainment Bureau⁕

252 ASYLUM STREET
HARTFORD, CONN.   P. O. Box 588

We furnish at short notice solo artists for concert, oratorio and opera; readers, humorists and lecturers for entertainments; choir singers, and organists for church poitions; directors for opera or choral societies, and experienced coaches for dramatic work.

WRITE US for prices and particulars; all correspondence will receive prompt attention

---

⁕ The Connecticut Quarterly. ⁕

$1.00 a Year.   25 Cents a Copy.
Payable in Advance.

All subscriptions taken with the understanding that they expire after four numbers have been sent. Unless renewed we discontinue sending.

When change of address is desired give both old and new address and we should receive notice at least two weeks before the first of the first month of the quarter.

Vol. I and Nos. 3 and 4 of Vol. II out of Print. We have a few of Nos. I and 2 of Vol. II. Price, 25 cents a copy.

Remittances should be by Check, Express Money Order, P. O. Money Order or Registered Letter. Money by mail at sender's risk. We promptly acknowledge by postal card all subscriptions received by mail.

HENRY S. HOUSE, Mgr. Subscription Department.

We can have Your Numbers Bound for you.

Price $1.00 and 1.25, according to style of binding.

NOTICE—Do not subscribe of **a person unknown to you.** Our authorized agents have full credentials.

The ÆTNA LIFE Insurance Company, Hartford, Conn.,

with Assets of over $47,000,000 and Surplus over liabilities (upon a conservative basis) of $7,000,000, has unparalleled Strength, Lowest Rates, Largest Dividends, and is the only Company in existence which has increased its Dividends to its Insured each year for the past twenty-five years. Its policy contracts are Incontestable, Non-forfeitable, and have Cash and Loan Values.

AN UNRIVALLED RECORD.

JOHN GEMMILL, a Merchant of Hartford, Conn., insured in the ÆTNA LIFE, under Policy No. 70,088, for $5,000 on the Thirty Year Endowment Plan. The policy was taken out in 1870 (he was then thirty years of age) and will mature and become payable to the insured in the year 1900. His twenty-eight annual payments aggregate $4,330.20. His twenty-seven annual cash dividends amount to $1,481.23. The cost to date is $2,848.97. He has two more premiums to pay, amounting to $309.30. If the Company's present rate of dividends is maintained he will receive $333.82, or $24.52 more than his two required annual payments, reducing the net cost of the policy at its maturity to $2,824.45. He will receive in the year 1900, $5,000, being $2,175.55 in excess of the net cost of the policy, $177.02 for each $100 paid to the company. Other as favorable examples will be given if requested.

The ÆTNA LIFE writes every approved form of Life, Term, Endowment and Accident Insurance.

MORGAN G. BULKELEY, President.
W. S. ROBERTS, Manager for Eastern New York Agency,
35 and 37 State Street, ALBANY, N. Y.

C. E. SHEPARD, General Agent, Life Department.
J. L. HUTCHINSON, General Agent, Accident Department.

HOME OFFICE, HARTFORD, CONN.

The Connecticut Quarterly.

"Leave not your native land behind."—*Thoreau.*

SECOND QUARTER.

VOL. IV.   APRIL, MAY, JUNE, 1898.   NO. 2.

HENRY BARNARD, EDUCATOR.

BY FREDERICK CALVIN NORTON.

"I consider a human soul without education like marble in the quarry, which shows none of its inherent beauties until the skill of the polisher fetches out the colors, makes the surface shine, and discovers every ornamental cloud, spot, and vein that runs through the body of it. Education after the same manner, when it works upon a mind, draws out to view every latent virtue and perfection, which, without such helps are never able to make their appearance. What sculpture is to a block of marble, education is to the human soul."
—*Joseph Addison.*

On the 24th of January, 1897, there was gathered in the hall of representatives at the State Capitol at Hartford one of the largest assemblages of public educators and friends of education ever convened in this country, and all to do homage to one man. It was primarily a State demonstration, yet by looking over the audience one might notice the representative of the United States Government, William T. Harris of Washington, commissioner of education ; the Hon. James L. Hughes, inspector of schools in Toronto, Canada ; Professor William G. Sumner, one of the most distinguished scholars and writers on political economy that Connecticut has ever produced ; the Hon. Charles R. Skinner, superintendent of public schools of New York ; President Adams of Wisconsin University;

FROM THE FIRST PORTRAIT OF DR. BARNARD—MADE IN 1836.

Thomas C. Stockwell commissioner of schools in Rhode Island; the Rev. Thomas Shahan, D.D., of the Catholic University of America; and George H. Martin, superintendent of the schools in Boston. Thus the celebration assumed a national rather than a local character.

At 10.30 a. m. the governor of the commonwealth, Hon. Lorrin A. Cooke, called the assemblage to order, and a chorus from the Hartford High School sang the following ode composed by Richard Burton for the occasion:

> "In the early days in the morning haze
> The builder builded his wall;
> He heard the cry of the By and By,
> He harked to the future's call,
> He saw the hall
> Of learning uplift fair and high.
>
> And now our sage in his beautiful age
> Is pillowed in memories great;
> His work is blest, for his high behest
> Was the nurture of the State.
> Then let the children for whom he wrought
> Hail him as Hero now;
> The sure-eyed seer, the pioneer,
> With the silver sign on his brow."

THE HOME OF DR. BARNARD, HARTFORD — FROM A DRAWING MADE IN 1860.

Governor Cooke then congratulated those present and also the State of Connecticut upon the remarkable and unique celebration. "This assemblage is to celebrate an individual birthday," said he. "The man we honor to-day was a pioneer and a hero. It was his hand that blazed the way for state supervision of public schools in our own and other states. The leaven introduced by him more than fifty years ago has continued to work until we have the present free school system, and still our educators, in the spirit and example of their great predecessor, are marching forward to other and improved conditions." After this the mayor of Hartford welcomed the visitors, and added: "Seldom is the opportunity given a community to honor itself by doing honor to one of its most distinguished sons in his day. But we have such an opportunity, and on this day we do by fitting ceremonies demonstrate the apprecia-

> *State of Rhode Island and
> Providence Plantations.
> In General Assembly
> January Session of 1849*
>
> *Resolved unanimously, That the
> Thanks of this General Assembly be given to the
> Hon. Henry Barnard for the able, faithful and
> judicious manner in which he has for the
> last five years fulfilled the duties of
> Commissioner of Public Schools in the State
> of Rhode Island.*
>
> *Resolved, That the Governor be requested to
> transmit to the Hon. Henry Barnard a copy
> of the foregoing Resolution under the Seal
> of the State.*
>
> *True copy of Record - witness
> Henry Bowen Secy*

TESTIMONIAL FROM THE GENERAL ASSEMBLY OF RHODE ISLAND TO DR. BARNARD.

tion and esteem we have for our fellow honored townsman, the anniversary of whose birthday we celebrate and whose deeds fruitful for our good and that of all people call for our most profound veneration and gratitude." Following the mayor distinguished men testified in eloquent words to their appreciation of the life work of this one man, and in the evening his praises were still further sung by those high in the educational circles of state and country. The man whose birthday this large and intelligent body of American citizens had gathered to celebrate was Doctor Henry Barnard of Hartford, whose wonderful career began sixty years before. As he sat on the platform before that audience the school children throughout the length and breadth of the State were listening to the story of noble efforts made in their behalf two generations before by the "Nestor of American Education."

Henry Barnard, known in this country and Europe as the greatest living educator, was born in the house where he now lives, at Hartford, on the 24th of January, 1811. His family, which was an old one, had lived in Hartford from the first settlement of the colony. As a boy he attended the "district school," and he has often said that it took half of his long life to rid himself of the bad mental habits acquired there, notwithstanding which he has always

FROM A DAGUERREOTYPE OF DR. BARNARD,
Taken about

PORTRAIT OF DR. BARNARD MADE IN 1854.
Engraved for the Conn. State Teachers
Association

remained deeply attached to this early seat of learning, not because of the quality of education it dispensed, but because the institution represented the best ideal of American citizenship, where the children of the wealthy and poor were brought together on terms of absolute equality.

PROF. H. GLICK.

In late years when he had become a great reformer, he valued the personal knowledge which qualified him to speak of the defects of the district school. His especial college training was had at the Monson Academy (Mass.) and the Hopkins Grammar School in Hartford, and in these he formed the opinion held throughout his life that all subjects taught in institutions of their class could be easily introduced into a common or public high school. He has lived long enough to see the hope of his boyhood days fully realized.

Dr. Barnard was graduated with high honors at Yale College in 1830 in the class with Edward Hammond, Prof. Elias Loomis, Prof. A. D. Stanley, Judge Woodruff, and John C. Smith. During his course at Yale he paid particular attention to English Literature and to the practice of English Composition, for which the class room exercise and the literary societies of the colleges then furnished such an inviting arena. The old Linonian Society received a large share of his interest and he was at one time president of the association.

Having determined to prepare himself for the practice of law, he began, after leaving college, reading for that purpose. In the office of Hon. Willis Hall, afterward attorney-general of New York, and W. H. Hungerford, Esq. of Hartford, he continued his studies of Kent, Blackstone, and other legal writers.

Besides the law he pursued a course of general reading, and thus at the age of twenty-seven, he had gained a knowledge of ancient and modern literature rarely attained by professed scholars.

Upon the suggestion of President Day of Yale, as a means of reviving and making permanent his knowledge

The Faculty of the University of Wisconsin
to
Henry Barnard, LL.D., L.H.D.,
Sometime Chancellor of the University of Wisconsin

Greeting:—

The Faculty of the University you once served gladly take advantage of your eighty-sixth anniversary to extend to you their cordial congratulations. We join with the whole nation in recalling the invaluable work which you have accomplished for the cause of education in this country.

But in particular, we, who have entered into the fruits of your early work, recall your enthusiastic labors in preparing the way for higher education in this state. Your sagacity early recognized that the foundations of a state university must be laid among the people, and you devoted yourself with contagious zeal to the upbuilding of the schools of this Commonwealth.

We beg you, therefore, to accept this expression of our kindly remembrance and our gratitude for these conspicuous services.

C. K. Adams,
President.

W. L. Howard,
Secretary

TESTIMONIAL FROM THE UNIVERSITY OF WISCONSIN.

of the ancient classics, Mr. Barnard now took charge of the preparatory school at Wellesboro, Pa., which he found on about the same plane as the "district school" of his native state.

Here he read and thought much upon the subject of perfecting the course of study, and also gained that wonderful practical knowledge of schools which afterward proved to be of such incalculable service to him. Returning to Connecticut in the winter of 1835, he was admitted as attorney and counsellor at law, but before entering upon his practice he decided upon a visit to Europe for the twofold purpose of study and travel. He carried letters of introduction to Wordsworth, Lockhart, DeQuincey, Carlyle, and other prominent literary characters.

Mr. Barnard returned from Europe more than ever attached to American

BRONZE MEDAL - AWARDED—VIENNA, 1873.
Two-thirds actual size.

institutions, and in an address soon after uttered those memorable words: "Here at least no man can live for himself alone. Individual happiness is here bound up with the greatest good for the greatest number. Every man must at once make himself as good and as useful as he can, and help at the same time to make everybody about him and all that he can reach better and happier."

This was the ruling sentiment of his life. This it was that induced him to abandon the prospects of professional eminence and a lucrative practice, and after a brief but noteworthy career in the legislature to devote himself to the work of educational reform.

While a member of the General Assembly in 1837 he originated and secured the passage of a resolution requiring the comptroller to obtain from school visitors official returns respecting public schools in the several school societies; and in 1838, of an "Act to provide for the better supervision of the common schools."

At the time of which we write (1838), doctors', lawyers' or clergymen's sons were not sent to district schools to prepare for college, because only the ordinary branches were there taught; they were obliged to attend private institutions of a rather exclusive character. This state of affairs had been carefully noted by Dr. Barnard, who now began a systematic campaign to revive educational matters in the state. "A Board of Commissioners for Common Schools " was organized by this act, and Mr. Barnard was chosen the first secretary after the Rev. Dr. Gallaudet had declined. He devoted all the resources of his intellect to the severe duties of this office until 1842, when, by adverse political action, the board was abolished. But during four years of arduous labor he had fought an uncompromising battle for school reformation. That he was the man destined for the work is evidenced by the words of a writer of the time who spoke of Henry Barnard as "possessing fine powers of oratory, wielding a ready and able pen, animated by a generous and indomitable spirit, willing to spend and be spent in the cause of benevolence and humanity."

Horace Mann, his great coadjutor and friend, said in the *Massachusetts Common School Journal:* "It is not extravagant to say that if a better man be

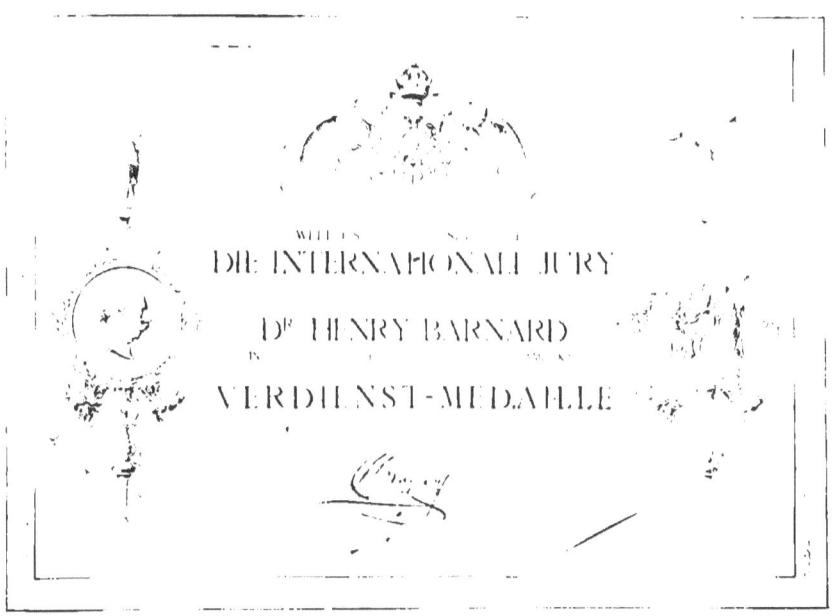

DIPLOMA AWARDED BY VIENNA EXPOSITION, 1873.

required we must wait at least until the next generation, for a better is not to be found in this present." These remarks of a fellow worker's were justified by the four very able "reports" presented by him to the legislature, and the four volumes of the *Common School Journal.* The reports have been very highly prized by the leading educators in this and other lands. Chancellor Kent, the great jurist, in his "Commentaries on American Law" (1844), said of the first report: "It is a bold and startling document founded on the most painstaking and critical inquiry." Commentating on subsequent reports, the same distinguished writer refers to Mr. Barnard as "the most able, efficient and best informed officer that could perhaps be engaged in the service." His publications, he said, contained "a digest of the fullest and most valuable information that is to be obtained on the subject of common schools both in Europe and the United States."

During the four years of his incumbency the state allowed Dr. Barnard $3,747 out of its treasury, but the entire amount of this salary he expended in promoting the prosperity of the schools. After his retirement from the board he visited every portion of the country, collecting data for a book he intended to write, entitled "A History of Public Schools and the Means of Popular Education in the United States." Boston, New York, Cincinnati, and New Orleans invited him to superintend their schools, and positions of a similar nature came to him from all parts of the land. His literary project was postponed by an invitation from Governor Fenner of Rhode Island to accept the position of superintendent of education in that state. In five years he revolutionized the educational views of the people, vivified their existing edu-

GOLD MEDAL—PARIS EXPOSITION, 1878.
Four-fifths actual size.

cational system, framed and secured the enactment of the first efficient school code adapted to the wants of the state, organized upon it an excellent system of popular education, and on retiring from office in 1849 received the unanimous thanks of the state legislature and a grateful testimonial from the teachers. Through him, for the first time in the history of Rhode Island, taxation for the support of the schools was obtained.

During this very busy period Mr. Barnard published many pamphlets and several volumes to arouse sentiment and advance the schools of Rhode Island. He also edited (1845-9) the *Journal of the Rhode Island Institute of Instruction.*

Before accomplishing all his plans Dr. Barnard was forced to retire from office, owing to the precarious state of his health, yet even during this retirement he received invitations to professorships in two colleges and to the superintendence of schools in three states.

But a work far more congenial in every way, and in his native state, awaited his restoration to health. By the year 1849 every individual measure destroyed by the political schemes of 1842 had been restored, not only on the statute books, but in the minds of the people as well. The work commenced by the courageous, self-sacrificing educator twelve years before, had brought forth an abundant harvest. Dr. Barnard was then considered one of the ablest living educators, and Thomas Rainey, editor of the *Ohio Journal*, wrote in 1852: "He has done more than any other ten men in New England for education."

HENRY BARNARD, EDUCATOR.   131

In 1849 an act was passed to establish a State Normal School, the principal of which should be the superintendent of common schools. Dr. Barnard was the only man for the place, and he accepted on condition that an assistant be appointed to take charge of the Normal School.

And now, after struggles and disappointments innumerable, Dr. Barnard saw Connecticut foremost among the States in the cause of education.

From 1850 to 1854 he served in the dual capacity of principal of the Normal School and state superintendent of the common schools, again editing the *Connecticut School Journal* during that period. As an instance of the repute in which he was held at this time as a great educational reformer may be noted

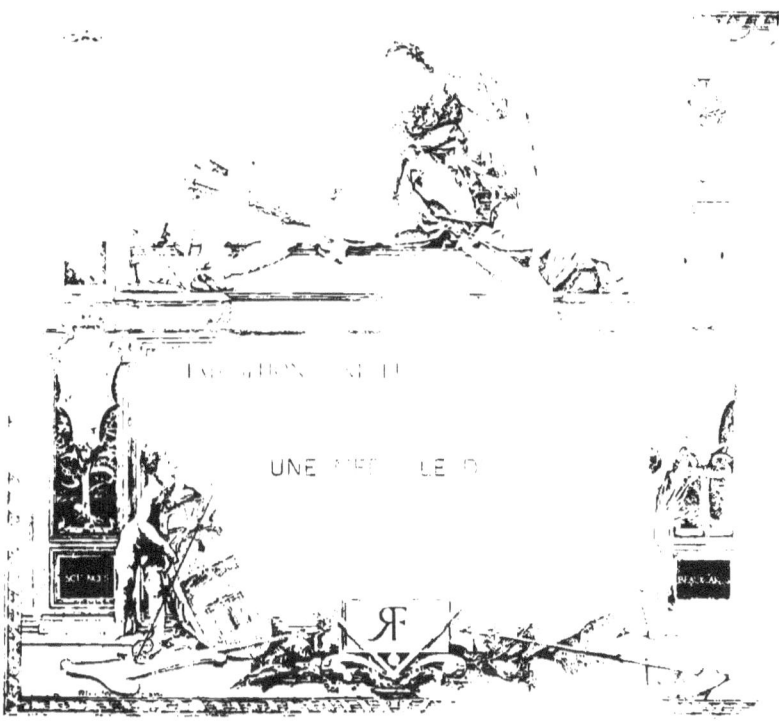

DIPLOMA—PARIS EXPOSITION, 1878.

the fact that each of the corporations of Union, Harvard and Yale colleges in 1851 bestowed upon Mr. Barnard—then only forty years of age—the honorary degree of Doctor of Laws. Dr. Winmer, a famous German scholar and writer, called him "the veritable reformer of popular education."

In 1855 he was unanimously chosen president of the American Association for the Advancement of Education, which had originated in 1849 through his own efforts, and which he endeavored to imbue with a large national policy as the central agency for school statistics and for the promulgation of reformatory measures in our state and city systems and institutions of learning. About this time he commenced the publication at Hartford of a quarterly review, *The American Journal of Education*. This encyclopædic work was conducted by Dr. Barnard until a short time ago. For a year or more he occupied himself with literary work connected with the *Journal*. In 1858 he became chancellor of the University of Wisconsin. It has been said that his principal reason for undertaking the office of chancellor was to unify educational interests throughout the state from the kindergarten to college halls, making them all free. While laboring here with his old-time zeal to establish an institution where young men or women might be prepared for college or a business life, he at the same time endeavored to raise the standard of the schools in order that these young men and women might be better prepared for admission to the colleges.

Early in the year 1860 he was attacked with nervous prostration, and after sending his resignation—which was reluctantly accepted eight months later—he remained idle for two years, being utterly incapable for work. But a Cen-

DIPLOMA--MELBOURNE EXPOSITION, 1880.

tral Normal School and the Teachers' Institute were the direct products of his energetic campaign in Wisconsin for a change in the school system of that state. He also published four volumes, being the first of the series, "Papers for Teachers," and intended as a guide for teachers in the instruction of their pupils. His work in Wisconsin alone was enough to win for any man fame of the most endurable character—nor is it forgotten, although a generation has passed since the performance of those labors. In 1866 Dr. Barnard became president of St. John's College, Annapolis, Md., where he remained a short time only, for the year following (1867), when the United States Bureau of Education was formed, he was chosen as first commissioner.

He himself had for almost thirty years pointed out the need for such a bureau, and as James L. Hughes of Toronto wrote : "It was but fitting that the

DIPLOMA NEW ORLEANS EXPOSITION, 1884

man who had done most to organize the state and city school systems of the United States, who had conducted the first County Teachers' Institute on lines similar to the present summer schools, who had championed the cause of woman by demanding for her equal educational privileges with man as a student and as a teacher, who had established the first state system of libraries, who was the first to propose a national organization of teachers, and who had published more educational literature than *any other man in the history of the world*, should be the first Commissioner of Education appointed by the government of the United States."

He remained in Washington four years, and performed the duties of that high and honorable office with distinction.

It has been said by the same writer (Mr. Hughes) that nearly every reform advocated by Dr. Barnard in his first report as Commissioner of Education has since been adopted by the United States.

A separate article of great length would be needed to treat of the enormous amount of literary work Dr. Barnard executed during the sixty years of his active life. We can give only a very brief sketch of his publications, all of which were originally written to assist him in his work of educational reform.

In 1839 he published "School Architecture," of which over 130,000 copies were printed by legislative authority; in 1851, "Normal Schools;" in 1854, "National Education in Europe," a volume containing over 900 pages, which has been described as an encyclopædia of educational systems and methods. The *Westminster Review* said it "contained more valuable information and statistics than could be found in any one volume in the English language, and it grouped under one view the varied experiences of all civilized countries." His "Educational Biography," a monumental work and a veritable thesaurus of pedagogical literature, data, reminiscence and statistics appeared in 1857. "Reformatory Education" was published in the same year; "Object Teaching" in 1860, and "Military Schools" in 1862. Later volumes of his works are "Technical Schools and Education," "Universities and Colleges," "German Teachers and Education," and "Pestalozzi."

FROM PHOTO TAKEN 1870.

The crowning work of his long and busy life, however, is the *American Journal of Education*, beginning, as before stated, in 1856, and edited by him until 1893. This remarkable publication, which has now reached over thirty-one large octavo volumes of about eight hundred pages each, won for him a distinguished place in Europe and fame in all civilized countries. It is the only general authority in respect to the progress of American education during the past century. It includes statistical data, personal reminiscences, historical sketches, educational biographies, descriptions of institutions, plans of buildings, reports, speeches and legislative documents. These books contain facts, arguments and practical methods which no teacher or organizer can afford to be without. The *Westminster Review* said England had nothing in the same field worthy of comparison with it, and the *Britannica* says of it : "The *Journal* is by far the most valuable work in our language on the history of education." Besides devoting his time to the preparation of these works, Dr. Barnard spent more than forty thousand dollars from his private fortune to keep up the publication of them when other means failed. There have been several attempts to purchase the plates of the *Journal* (which are piled up in the cellar of his house in Hartford) and thus partially compensate this noble altruist for the large sacrifices he has made. Everybody admits the worth of this *Journal*, and Prof. Quick, the famous English educator, when he heard of the probable destruction of the plates, wrote to Dr. Harris: "I would as soon hear that there was talk of pulling down one of our English cathedrals and selling the stone for building materials." But in making this large financial sacrifice Dr. Barnard was only following out the spirit of his own memorable words uttered near the beginning of his career: "So far back as I have any recollection, the cause of true education, of the complete education of every human being without regard to the incidents of birth or fortune, seemed most worthy of the consecration of all my powers and, if need be, of any sacrifice of time, money and labor which I might be called upon to make in its behalf."

What else save for his love of humanity could have prompted a man to leave a profession in preparation for which he had devoted a large amount of time and money, in which he was sure to win fame and fortune, to leave all this and devote his time and all of a large fortune "simply to make accessible in book form what is recorded of the wisdom of the race as it relates to the instruction of children."

Pestalozzi—Froebel—Mann—Barnard! To these men, especially to Barnard, the United States owes its "new education." Have we as a people, as a state, as a nation, forgotten the debt we owe this man, whose self-sacrificing devotion founded our present magnificent school system?

No, Connecticut has not forgotten, nor has the nation; but both recognize the brilliant work Dr. Barnard has done for them. Probably no American, certainly no Connecticut man, ever received during his lifetime such universal and continued recognition. In forming an estimate of him, let us look at the opinions of his ablest coadjutors. More than a generation ago the Hon. John D. Philbrick said of him: "The career of Henry Barnard as a promoter of the cause of education has no precedent and is without a parallel. Mr. Barnard stands before the world as the national educator."

"His Rhode Island work," wrote Horace Mann, "is the greatest legacy yet left to American educators." Dr. Noah Porter wrote his opinion of Mr. Barnard's work in the *Connecticut School Journal* forty-three years ago. These are his words published in January, 1855: "But we will not forget in our hour of success the earnest and able advocate of that cause when neglected and unpopular. We will not forget the generous and indomitable spirit which prompted him in the outset of his public life to plead that cause without fee or reward, which induced him to abandon a

FROM PHOTO TAKEN 1886.

professional career and in which steadily pursued he was sure to bring distinction and wealth, which has enabled him to turn a deaf ear to the voice of political ambition and to close his heart to the seduction of popular applause so easily gained by one possessed of his power of oratory in the discussion of questions of temporary interest; which has led him to decline positions of the highest literary dignity in college and university that he might give himself up unreservedly to the improvement of common schools—the long forgotten heritage of the many. His labors were arduous enough in themselves, being none other than to awake a slumbering people, to encounter prejudice, apathy and sluggishness, to tempt avarice to loosen its grasp, to cheer the faint-hearted and to sustain hope in the bosom of the desponding. The teachers of Connecticut and of the country can never forget his valuable services to them—to many of them individually—and to the measures and agencies which he has advocated and to some extent projected for the advancement of their profession."

Professor Quick wrote twenty-two years ago: "Those who know the wealth of German pædeutical literature often lament the poverty of our own. Indeed the history of education and treatises upon everything connnected with education may now be read without having recourse to any foreign literature whatever. A great deal of this literature owes its origin to the energy and educational zeal of one man—the Hon. Henry Barnard."

Another English writer said of him: "He gave himself to the work with the enthusiasm of an apostle. Probably no man in the United States has done

BRONZE MEDAL. WORLD'S FAIR, CHICAGO, 1893.
Two-thirds actual size.

so much to advance, direct and consolidate the movement for popular education. In looking back to the commencement of his lifelong labor, it would seem that he must contemplate with eminent satisfaction the progress of public sentiment and the good results already attained, as well as the brightening prospects for the future. He has done a work for which his country and coming generations ought to thank him and do honor to his name."

The following is the deliberate opinion on Dr. Barnard's work by the Honorable William Torrey Harris, LL.D., United States Commissioner of Education: "It is deemed a piece of good fortune that we are able to recognize and acknowledge the services of a public benefactor while he is yet living in our midst. Most recognition comes too tardy for the purposes of comfort and consolation of the hero himself. We build high the monument and place the portrait statue in our public square, not only to commemorate the patriotic citizen who benefitted us by his life, but also to confess our churlish neglect of his service while he lived.

"The nation rejoices with Connecticut in paying the tribute of respect to the great educational counsellor of the past fifty years—for Dr. Barnard has always been retained as a counsellor on all difficult educational questions by state legislatures, municipal governments and the founders of new institutions of learning. The nation assists you to-day in this celebration of the man who has expended his time and fortune to print and circulate an educational course of reading of 24,000 pages and twelve million of words. It assists you (Connecticut) in bearing testimony to Henry Barnard as the missionary of improved educational methods for the schools of the people, the schools which stand before all other philanthropic devices, because they alone never demoralize by giving help—they always help the individual to help himself."

Although Dr. Barnard has reached the eighty-eighth year of his life, he retains his old-time custom of rising at 5 o'clock every morning, and accomplishing his study and literary work before breakfast. It was the writer's good fortune, recently, to spend an early morning hour in his company. To see him in his ripe old age, with elastic step, upright form, manly and scholarly countenance; to hear the words of warm and courteous welcome with which he receives all who enter his home; to listen to the discourse with which he charms them, is truly a great pleasure and a great boon.

Every teacher and pupil in the State should remember him and his sacrifices in their behalf.

In the words of Dr. Oliver Wendell Holmes, one of the last of Dr. Barnard's early friends to leave him, we exclaim:

> "Before the true and trusted sage,
> With willing hearts we bend,
> When years have touched with hallowing age
> Our Master, Guide and Friend.
>
> "But when untamed by toil and strife,
> Full in our front he stands,
> The torch of light, the shield of life,
> Still lifted in his hand.
>
> "No temple, though its walls resound
> With bursts of ringing cheers,
> Can hold the honor that surround
> His manhood's twice told years!"

THE LESSON OF THE RAIN.

BY LOUISE P. MERRITT.

Through long days of darkness
Fell the sad-voiced rain,
Till the world seemed weeping
Like a soul in pain.

Yet we knew that slowly,
Surely, hour by hour,
Grew to full perfection
Many a leaf and flower.

Thus our days of darkness,
Sorrow, pain, and woe,
Are God's ways of making
Wayward spirits grow.

Then there came a Sunday,
Clear with heaven's own blue,
Fresh with bursting leaflets,
Bright with crystal dew.

Trees with feathery branches
Caught the sun's bright rays,
Softly sang the wild birds
To their Maker's praise.

Shy and sweet the violets
Grew beside our way,
And we knew that surely
Spring had come to stay.

Thus God grant our natures
May attain full powers,
By the loving chastening
Of affliction's showers.

THE TORIES OF CONNECTICUT.

BY JAMES SHEPARD.

During the first few years of the revolutionary war, this state was literally full of Tories. They filled our jails to overflowing; many of them were confined within the court-house at Hartford, and others were confined under guard or within certain limits on parole in various parts of the state where they would be out of contrast with the British, while many others of fighting age and burning zeal for their King left their families, property and homes and took up arms against the American cause.

In addition to our own Tories those of other states were sent here for confinement. The Tories were so numerous that it would be impossible to notice them all in one paper and besides it would be an almost endless task to find in the voluminous manuscript records of the state, the various superior courts and towns, the names of those who were brought to answer. And even if one should do all this, there were many more bearing coldness or hatred to the American cause who by a judicious self-control kept their hands and tongues from committing any overt act and thus left no history.

A Tory was an American who adhered to the King, and by sympathy or otherwise favored the part of Great Britain in the revolutionary war. They were sometimes called Loyalists, but the terms Loyalist and Tory mean precisely the same thing, excepting as the word Tory may carry with it an element of contempt. Those who strenuously insist on saying Loyalist instead of Tory would be very likely to apply the name Rebel to our revolutionary Patriots. The Tories were certainly loyal to their King, they upheld the existing state of affairs—in fact one of the principles of Tories in any country has always been " the maintenance of things as they were."

In May, 1775, the Colony of Connecticut passed an "act regulating and ordering the Troops that are or may be raised for the Defence of this colony,' which act was called the articles of war. In December, 1775, an "act for restraining and punishing persons who are inimical to the Liberties of this and the rest of the United Colonies " was passed, which provided among other things "that if any person by writing, or speaking, or by any overt act, shall libel or defame any of the resolves of the Honorable Congress of the United Colonies, or the acts of the General Assembly of this Colony, and be thereof duly convicted before the Superior Court, shall be disarmed and not allowed to have or keep any arms, and rendered incapable to hold or serve in any office civil or military, and shall be further punished by fine, imprisonment or disfranchisement." The same act provided also for the confiscation of real estate. At a special session in June, 1776, this act was amended to cover the confiscation of both real and personal estate of all convicted Tories. The year of the King's reign headed the record of this act of '75 opposing the King, but that was the last time that such dating appears in the journal.

The Governor and Council of Safety on July 18, 1776, voted that, "Whereas many persons inimical to the United States do wander from place to place with intent to spy out the state of the colonies," etc., and "no person be allowed to pass unless known to be friendly, or unless by proper certificate or otherwise they can prove themselves to be friendly to America." A more stringent act of the same nature was passed in May, 1777.

In October, 1776, an act for the punishment of high treason and other atrocious crimes against the state was passed which provided "That if any person or persons belonging to or residing within this state and under the protection of its laws, shall levy war against the state or government thereof, or knowingly and willingly shall aid or assist any enemies at open war against this state or the United States of America by joining their armies or by enlisting or procuring or persuading others to enlist for that purpose * * * or shall form or be in any way concerned in forming any combination, plot, or conspiracy for betraying this state or the United States into the hands or power of any foreign enemy, or shall give or attempt to give or send any intelligence to the enemies of this state for that purpose, upon being convicted shall suffer death." At least six persons were convicted of high treason under this act, but Moses Dunbar of Waterbury is the only person who was ever executed in Connecticut under the civil law.

It was further provided in May, 1777, "that all Tories confined within this state may at all times be taken for debt, provided they are returned after having worked out their indebtedness." In October, 1777, it was enacted "that no person can be administrator on any estate till he has taken the oath of fidelity, and that anyone who refuses to take the oath of fidelity shall not be capable to purchase or hold or transfer any real estate without license from the General Assembly."

It was not necessary that a man should be convicted of toryism by a justice of the peace or a judge before he could be confined or removed and compelled to pay the cost of removal. In October, 1776, the General Assembly voted "That the civil authority, selectmen and committee of inspection within the several towns of this state shall have power to confine within certain limits or remove all such persons as they shall upon due examination judge to be inimical and dangerous to the United States, at the cost of such persons, and that His Honor the Governor and Council of Safety shall determine the place or places of confinement."

In August, 1777, it was enacted "that any person convicted under the act relating to treason shall not be allowed liberty on bail, but shall be imprisoned until delivered by due course of law."

The first record I find of any Tory in the doings of the General Assembly is that of Abraham Blakesly of New Haven, captain of a military company in the second regiment of this colony, who was complained of before the General Assembly in March, 1775, "for being disaffected to this government by speaking contemptuously of the measures taken by the General Assembly for maintaining the same." His case was referred to the next session, and in the following May he was cashiered. In October, 1775, it was represented that Benjamin Stiles of Woodbury "hath publickly and contemptuously uttered and spoken many things against the qualification of the three delegates of the colony now belonging to the Continental Congress, &c., &c., whereof he hath openly showed his inimical temper of mind and unfriendly disposition." He was cited to appear before the General Assembly at their next sessions.

It was also reported that a major part of one company in Northbury (now Plymouth) was inclined to toryism, and a committee was appointed to inquire and report.

In November, 1775, "The Brigatine Minerva, an armed vessel in the service of the colony, was ordered on a cruise to the northward on an important enterprise for the defense and safety of the colony, when all hands on board except ten or twelve utterly declined and refused to go, so that the expedition wholly failed." All these disobedient hands were discharged and their title to receive their wages was suspended.

In December, 1775, Lieut. Benjamin Kilborn of Litchfield was complained of as declaring "that he wished there were ten thousand regular troops now landed in the colony and that he would immediately join with them in order to subdue the Americans who were in a state of rebellion, that he was determined to join the Regulars and would kill some of the inhabitants of said colony! that the late oppressive measures of the British respecting America were constitutional and right and that the conduct of the United Colonies were unconstitutional and rebellious," etc. He was cashiered and directed to be prosecuted in law for what he would call his firm adherence to the King, and yet the complaint against him was brought by the "Attorney of our Lord the King." The forms of various processes, oaths, etc., were soon afterwards changed to avoid all reference to the King.

In June, 1776, Capt. Daniel Hill, Lieut. Peter Lyon and Ensign Samuel Hawley, all of the 11th Company, in the Fourth Regiment, and Hezekiah Brown of the 12th Company, in the Tenth Regiment, were ordered to appear before the General Assembly for disobedience, etc. John R. Marshall of Woodbury, missionary, was cited to appear before the General Assembly for toryism. Capt. Isaac Quintard and Filer Dibble, both of Stamford, were suspected of assisting a British officer to the possession of certain barrels of powder stored at said Quintard's house, but Quintard claimed to be innocent and Dibble published a confession and recantation of toryism. He afterwards joined the British army. Capt. Nathaniel Shayler of Middletown refused to muster his company and march to assist George Washington at New York. He was cashiered and declared unfit to hold office. Thomas Brooks of Farmington, a lieutenant, openly professed that he could not join the army against Great Britain or against the King, and was therefore suspended. Jacob Perkins, captain of the First Company, in the Twentieth Regiment, and Samuel Wheat, captain of the Second Company, in said regiment, refused to muster and march for the defence of this state and were ordered to be brought before the General Assembly, but in December, 1776, upon satisfactory information that they had acknowledged their fault, "have since complied and declared themselves sorry and are now ready to defend their country with their lives and fortune, *this assembly ready to forgive* have and do revoke the aforesaid order." In January, 1778, Capt. James Landon of Salisbury, for neglect of duty and great unfriendliness to the American cause, cited to appear before the Assembly and later was cashiered. Capt. Solomon Marsh was also cashiered for the same cause, while John Marsh the 3rd declared his willingness to risk his life for America and the complaint against him was dismissed. "Epaphras Sheldon, Esqr., Colonel of the Seventeeth Regiment of militia, was dismissed for disobedience and Lieut. Ira Beebe of Waterbury was dismissed for leading off a number of his company from Fishkill last October."

In February, 1778, it was represented to the General Assembly "that Robert Martin hath been chosen Captain of the 15th Co. 10th regiment, and Reuben Rice, junr. Lieut. and that they are unfriendly to the liberties of America and its independence." A committee was appointed to examine them, but they subsequently received their commissions.

In May, 1778, "three alarm list Companies of Newtown made choice of persons for their officers that were inimical to this and other of the United States, and for that reason their commissions were refused and a new election ordered."

Fairfield county was a Tory center. The first Episcopal church in Connecticut was founded at Stratford in November, 1722. The Rev. John Beach, rector of the churches at Reading and Newtown, said in 1767: "It is some satisfaction to me to observe that in this town (Newtown) of late in our elections the church people make the major vote, which is the first instance of this kind in this colony, if not in all New England." This was the only town in the state in which Episcopalians were in the majority during the war. In 1775, it was represented to the General Assembly "that the towns of Ridgefield and Newtown had come into and published certain resolutions injurious to the rights of this colony and of a dangerous tendency." A committee was appointed to examine said matter and report. In October, 1777, it was represented to the General Assembly "that a number of inimical persons in the western towns in the state are forming dangerous insurrections and taking every method in their power to communicate intelligence to comfort, aid, and assist the enemies of these United States and to distress the inhabitants of said towns," etc. Whereupon a committee was sent to these towns to "examine all such persons *with full power to confine them* as deemed best." The town officers may have been Tories, or the towns may have instructed them not to take any action. Such votes were passed in several towns. Even in Middletown several resolutions to have the town authorities take action against the Tories were voted down. That place was probably a Tory center, for in July, 1776, the Council of Safety voted "that none of the prisoners residing at Hartford or Wethersfield be any longer permitted to go into the town of Middletown without a special license."

In October, 1776, Ralph Isaacs and Abiatha Camp, both of New Haven, were before the Assembly and adjudged to be "so dangerous to the state that they ought to be removed." They were sent to Eastbury, in the town of Glastonbury, to be retained there in care of the civil authority of the town, and it was further resolved, "That if said Isaacs and Camp shall receive any letter or letters from any person or persons, or send any, they shall offer such letters to some one of said civil authority or selectmen to be by them read and inspected." It was also provided that in case they should leave Eastbury, any officer can take them and put them in jail. In December following, Isaacs asked permission to reside in Durham under the same conditions. His petition was granted, but still discontented, in February, '77, he complains of his quarters, and at his own request he is ordered to Wallingford. In response to another petition the following June, the still discontented Isaacs is removed to his farm in Branford. In October of the same year he is "granted liberty to attend any of the Superior Courts in this state in which he has any action depending for tryal upon first taking the oath of fidelity. In January, 1778, he states that he is the executor of his father's and brother's wills, that these estates and his own affairs suffer greatly by reason of his confinement, that he has taken the oath of fidelity and done much to promote the good of the United States, whereupon he was "discharged and set at liberty."

His fellow prisoner remained for a while at Eastbury, and while there, Davis's History of Wallingford says that he applied to the General Assembly for "permission to be indulged the free exercise of his religion on Sundays at Middletown in attending religious worship by the Church of England, of which he was a professor and member," but the petition was denied. In December, 1777, he asked to be removed either to his farm in North Branford or to his house in Wallingford. He was sent to Wallingford to stay within the limits of the Parish. He does not, however, appear to have been well received for the town "Voted, that Abiatha Camp, formerly of New Haven, now being in the town of Wallingford, shall not dwell in said town nor be an inhabitant of said town. Voted that the Selectmen of said town Go and Warn Said Camp immediately to Depart said town." He was certainly in a straight betwixt two. He could stay only in defiance of the town, he could leave only in defiance of the state. The state came to the rescue and discharged him in January, 1778. He finally went to St. John, New Brunswick, and died there in 1841. The selectmen of Stamford, when they warned Tories out of town, added the injunction that they were "never to return."

On January 22, 1777, Ebenezer Hall of Fairfield was by the authorities of that town brought before the Governor and Council as a person dangerous and inimical to this and the United States that his place of confinement might be determined. His Honor the Governor fully instructed him in the nature of the dispute between Great Britain and these states and of the measures taken to prevent any rupture or disaffection between this and the mother country long before the commencement of any hostilities. The said Hall then declared himself fully convinced of the justice of the American cause and of her rights to take up arms in defence, whereupon he was released and allowed to return to his family on giving bail, etc. A similar petition and action was had as to Capt. Isaac Tomlinson of Woodbury.

January 22, 1777, Lazarus Beach, Andrew Fairfield, Nathan Lee, Abel Burr of Reading and Thomas Allen of Newtown, being Tory convicts confined in the town of Mansfield to prevent any mischievous practice, having made their escape, and being taken up, were remanded back to the Governor and Council. They were all sent to jail in Windham "to be safely kept until they come out thence by due order of the General Assembly or Governor and Council." A Thomas Allen of New London was sent to Windham as a Tory in March, 1777.

On January 28, 1777, Rev. John Sayer of Fairfield was before the Governor and Council as a Tory that he might be ordered to some safe place for confinement. He was sent to the parish of New Britain to be under the care of Col. Isaac Lee, and not to depart the limits of said society until further orders. In July of the same year the wardens of the Episcopal church and others at Fairfield, with consent of the selectmen and committee of inspection, petitioned for his release and return to his people to remain within the limits of Fairfield and give bond with surety for good behavior, which petition was granted. He was probably the first Episcopal clergyman that ever resided in New Britain. In a letter he subsequently said: "I was banished to a place called New Britain, where I was entirely unknown except to one poor man, the inhabitants differing from me both in religion and political principles; however, the family in which I lived showed me such marks of kindness as they could, and I was treated with civility by the neighbors."

In January, 1777, Ebenezer Holby, Elliot Green, Jonathan Husted, Josiah Seely, Benjamin James, Isaac Hubbard, Jacob Scofield of Stamford, Nathan Fitch, Frank Smith, Gold Hoit, Stephen Keller and John Betts of Norwalk, convict Tories, were permitted to return home upon giving bond of £1,000 each for their good behavior, and not to give any intelligence nor do or say anything against the interests of the U. S. A.

John Sanford, a person confined in Mansfield as an enemy to his country, was permitted to go to Reading to settle his mother's estate on giving bond for £1,000 to be forfeited if he did anything against the interest of this state or the other of the U. S. A.

In February, 1777, Capt. Hall of Wallingford took considerable time of the General Assembly on business about Tories, and the 24th of that month was a day appointed for Tories to bring their cases before the General Assembly. Job Barnlock, Enoch Warren, Jos. Olmstead and Richard Patrick of Norwalk, residing in Coventry, Frederick Dibble and Stephen Wilson of Stamford, residing at Lebanon, were permitted to return home, having signed a full and ample declaration of the justice of the American cause with profession of their friendship to it. The next day three more Tories, viz., Gardner Olmstead of Norwalk, Nathaniel Munday and Samuel Crissey of Stamford came and signed the same declaration and were discharged. William Fitch of Stamford was also allowed to go home. John Wilcocks, Ira Ward and James Ward, all of Killingsworth, and confined in Willington, repented and were released. George Folliot of Ridgefield, having been confined first in Fairfield jail and then in Hartford jail, was released on paying cost, etc. One Hubbard and Jno. Wilson, of Stamford, visited houses and persons infected with small pox and then went about among people not so infected. They were consequently put in charge of the selectmen of Lebanon.

Hanford Fairweather of Norwalk, sentenced to Windham jail for two years, had the privilege to work out days, but had to return to jail at night, asked permission to stay outside of the jail and also to go to Norwalk and remove his family to Windham to reside there with him. His request was granted.

Of Tory property that was confiscated, we find but little in the published state reports. In December, 1776, the property of John McKey of Norwalk was confiscated, and he was sentenced to two years' imprisonment for harboring and secreting persons who were about to go over to the enemy. In May, 1777, he was released and his estate restored to him.

Sundry farms in Hebron, belonging to Barlow Trecothick and John Tomlinson of Great Britain and to the Rev. Samuel Peters, then in Great Britain, were confiscated in May, 1778, and the State Attorney for Hartford County was empowered to lease the said farms for the benefit of the state.

In May, 1777, Mary Hoyt, wife of Isaac Hoyt, late of Danbury, represented to the General Assembly that she had ever been a true friend to the rights of her country, but that her husband, being an enemy to his country, joined the British during their raid on Danbury and thereby justly forfeited all his estate, both real and personal, which had been seized and left her without the necessities of life. She requested that she might be allowed one-third part of said estate, which request was granted. Nicholas Brown of Hartford went over to the enemy in New York and left his wife Hannah and four children. She was given liberty to follow him with her children to New York at her own pleasure and expense. Hannah Church, the wife of Asa Church of Danbury, was also given permission to follow her absconding husband to New York.

In February, 1778, it was represented to the General Assembly that the property of Samuel Doolittle of Waterbury had been confiscated, leaving a wife Eunice and three children to be supported by her father, Thomas Cole, and that a certain round table and other articles of the confiscated property were her wedding portion. It was therefore resolved "that the said round table and other articles, being 1 quart cup, 3 pewter platters, 6 plates, 1 pint cup, 3 pewter basins, 3 porringers, 1 teapot, 1 pepper box, 5 spoons, 3 knives and forks, 6 plain chairs, 1 great wheel, 1 Dutch wheel, 1 feather bed, 1 bed quilt, 2 blankets, 2 pair of sheets, 1 iron pot, 1 looking-glass, 1 beer barrel, 1 churn, 1 pair of flat-irons, 1 clock-reel, 1 bed tick, 1 meal sive, 1 frying pan, 1 chest with drawers, 6 black chairs, 1 warming pan, 1 brass kettle, a cow and a calf and ten sheep, which are now held in custody of Samuel Hickox, constable, be delivered to said Thomas Cole for the use and support of said Eunice and her children.

In August, 1779, the town authorities of Derby applied to the General Assembly in behalf of the family of Azariah Prichard, who had gone to Canada and joined the enemy, and permission was granted his wife and children with wearing apparel and a bed and furniture to be removed to Canada.

In May, 1778, the confiscation act was so amended that the constable was not compelled to take household goods away from the families, and all confiscated estates were thereafter brought before the probate courts, who were instructed to grant administration as in other estates, whereby a proper allowance for the wife and children could be made and also provision for the payments of debts.

In January, 1780, the administrators of the confiscated estate of Joseph Hanford of Fairfield, and of William Nichols of Waterbury, asked the General Assembly for certain instructions. In 1777 the town of Wallingford voted "That the families of all those who are convicted of Toryism and the heads of all the families that have absconded to Lord How, they and their families shall be removed to Lord How. Also voted that the selectmen of said town secure the estates of all those persons that are inimical to the States of America."

In 1780, Pomp, a negro slave belonging to the confiscated estate of Rev. Jeremiah Leaming, formerly of Norwalk, represented to the General Assembly that he was "liable to be sold for the benefit of the state and to be continued in slavery by act of the government, praying to be emancipated and set at liberty." The petition was granted. In the case of a certain negro calling himself James Cromwell, who fled from his master, Major Hudson, a Tory enemy at Long Island, the Governor and Council voted that "he may be and ought to be protected until the pleasure of the General Assembly may be known."

In February, 1778, "upon the memorial of Moses Northrup, Patience his wife, and Eunice Northrup his daughter, all of New Milford, showing to this Assembly that the said Patience and Eunice are confined in Litchfield goal upon suspicion of *treason against this state*, that no court proper to try them will sit in said county till August next and that their services are greatly needed at home," praying to be admitted to bail as they could not be under the law. This petition was granted.

Various records show that those who were once Tories were not always Tories. The Loyalists of '75 and '76 were often the Patriots of '77 and '78, and in fact on or about 1780 the Tories were mainly banished or repressed. It is, however, seldom that a Patriot has been converted to Toryism, but a few such cases are found, although they generally returned again to the American cause. Nearly all the petitions for favor that we find appear to be from good Tories or those who are weak in the faith. Our state reports are published only to May, 1780, and they contain only such resolutions as received an affirmative vote. Tory petitions that were denied are not placed on the records of the General Assembly and can be found only in various manuscripts, and the trials of the incorrigibles who would suffer anything rather than ask a favor of their opponents can be found only in various court records.

In May, 1777, Joseph Seely junr. had been sentenced to two years in jail and a fine of £20. He says "that he had served the U. S. in the present war with faithfulness, and professing repentance for his evil conduct, promising reformation in the future" prays for release upon his enlisting into the continental army. Granted, upon his so enlisting and paying or securing the cost of prosecution arising against him.

Nathan Daton of New Milford took an active part on the side of his country at the beginning of the war, yet in November '76, having his mind from some disastrous incidents of the war filled with gloomy apprehensions, sundry of his acquaintances, by the stratagem of magnifying the dangers of this country and by the strongest assurances of the safety and peace he might enjoy under the protection of the regulars on Long Island, deluded and seduced him to so far join them as to put himself under their protection, but Col. Delancy, then commander, tyrannically forced him to bear arms under pain of military execution. He finally escaped, returned to New Milford and was then sent to Litchfield jail. He was released and pardoned.

Joshua Stone, confined in Hartford jail, was a hearty friend to his bleeding country at the beginning of the war, but by the crafty insinuations and persuasive arguments of his near relatives to the contrary and the persuasion of his unfortunate father, he was influenced to go to the British at New York, where he was confined as a spy, but soon after made his escape to Stamford, where he was taken, bound over to the superior court of Fairfield county, then sentenced to three months' imprisonment and a fine of £20, which he peacefully endured, but in working out the fine he was permitted to labor for one Elisha Wadsworth, who, being an enemy to the United States, persuaded him to run away. He was apprehended and confined in Hartford jail. "But by the powerful arguments of a worthy member of the General Assembly on the justice of the American cause, he is fully sensible of his error." He was discharged

THE TORIES OF CONNECTICUT.   147

on paying cost, etc., and further that he "may enlist in the continental army for three years."

Marchant Wooster, of Derby, represented that he was "always a friend to the United States and faithfully served as a soldier in '76, but was afterwards unhappily seduced by one Major French, a British officer, to join the enemy, where he was taken a prisoner of war." Professing a hearty and sincere repentance, he was discharged on taking the oath of fidelity.

"John Elliott junr. of Middletown hath ever been friendly to the U. S., but by means of a most trying scene of disgrace and disappointment he had met with, he rashly and unadvisedly went to New York, and, expressing deep remorse and penitence, his request for a stay of prosecution was granted." From these and similar petitions, it appears that all able-bodied Tories who went into the territory in possession of the British were forcibly impressed into the service.

Persons were sometimes unjustly detained as suspected Tories. Col. Wadsworth reported three prisoners of whom it was "highly probable that they had never shewn themselves inimical to or being active against the United Colonies," and consequently they were released.

Benjamin Betts of Stamford was taken from his bed, carried to Long Island and forced into the British service. He subsequently escaped, and was then arrested, fined and imprisoned for Toryism.

Twenty-six other prisoners whose cases require no special mention were before the General Assembly in various ways as follows: Seth Hall, Ebenezer Sturgess, Timothy Beach, Gurdon Wetmore (probably of Middletown), David Adams junr., Squire Adams, Gideon Lockwood and Albert Lockwood, all of Fairfield; Daniel Lockwood, Isaac Peck, Gilbert Lockwood, Solomon Wright, Isaac Anderson, James Merrill, Benjamin Wilson and Nathan Merrill, all released on request of the selectmen of Greenwich; David and Benjamin Peet, of Stratford; Jabez Sherwood, junr., Hezk. Holby, Solomon Merrit, junr., Silas Knap, Wm. Marshall, Joseph Galpin and Jonathan Mead, of Greenwich, and Roger Veits of Simsbury.

In October, 1777, "Eight Disciples of Robert Sandeman, viz., Daniel Humphreys, Titus Smith, Richard Woodhull, Thomas Goold, Joseph Pyncheon, Theophilus Chamberlain, Benjamin Smith and Wm. Richmond, all of New Haven, who, on account of their religion, were bound in conscience to yield obedience to the King, signified their desire, if they may not continue at New Haven, to remove to some place under the dominion of the King." The request was granted under certain conditions, excepting as to the daughter of Richard Woodhull, "who shall not be removed," as she was heiress to considerable real estate in New Haven.

Seventeen prisoners from Farmington—Nathl. Jones, Siemon Tuttle, Joel Tuttle, Nathaniel Mathews, John Mathews, Riverius Carrington, Lemuel Carrington, Zerubbabel Jerom, jr., Chauncey Jerom, Ezar Dormer, Neheniiah Royce, Abel Royce, George Beckwith, Abel Frisbie, Levi Frisbie, Jared Peck and Abraham Waters—were released on taking the oath of fidelity and paying costs. The committee who examined these prisoners found that they had been much "under the influence of one Nichols, a designing church clergyman (the Rev. James Nichols of Bristol), that they had refused to go in the expedition to Danbury, that Nathaniel Jones and Simeon Tuttle each of them have as they believe a son gone over to the enemy, that they were grossly ignorant of the true grounds of the present war, and that they were convinced since the Danbury alarm that there was no such thing as remaining neuters." Poor Mr. Jones thought that his son John was in the British service as captain of the marines, but he had been killed in his first engagement about six months before this time.

Dr. William Samuel Johnson of Stratford was one of the most noted men of Connecticut ever arrested for Toryism. In military affairs he was first appointed a lieutenant in 1754, afterwards a captain, and in 1774 was made a lieutenant-colonel. He was a member of the General Assembly at various times from 1761 to 1775, serving in both houses. He was a representative from Connecticut to the Stamp Act Congress at New York in 1765. He drew up the petitions and remonstrances to the King, and about one year thereafter, when the Stamp Act was repealed, he drafted the "Address to the King" for the colony, "returning their most grateful tribute of humble and hearty thanks." He was made a Doctor of Laws by the University of Oxford, January 20, 1766. In February of the same year he was appointed special agent of Connecticut before the King and Lords in Council at London, where he remained until 1771. He was a judge of the superior court of the colony from 1772 to 1774. He was chosen to represent Connecticut in Congress at Philadelphia, in 1774, but other duties prevented him from accepting. After the Battle of Lexington, in 1775, he was appointed by the unanimous voice of the Assembly one of the committee to enter Boston under a flag of truce with a letter from the Governor to General Gage, then in command of the British forces, pleading for a stay of hostilities. After the Declaration of Independence he persuaded himself that he could not join in a war against England, and resolved to remain neutral. In the midsummer of 1779, after General Tryon raided Fairfield and Norwalk, it was rumored that Stratford was also to be destroyed. Knowing Dr. Johnson to be well acquainted with the British general, the frightened people insisted that Johnson should seek an interview with Tryon to dissuade him from burning the town. He reluctantly consented. Major General Wolcott, in command of the Continental forces along the coast, sent an officer with a detachment of troops to arrest Dr. Johnson and send him under guard to the town of Farmington. The arrest was made, but Johnson persuaded the officer to accept his word of honor to proceed at once to Farmington and place himself in the custody of the selectmen. On arriving there, one of the selectmen proved to be an acquaintance of Mr. Johnson, and they declared that they "had no business with him," but at Johnson's request they accepted his parole and permitted him to go alone to Lebanon and present himself to the Governor and Council. Johnson solemnly declared "that he never hath communicated with the enemies of this state in any way, nor done or said anything in prejudice of the rights and liberties of this state." He had even "hired a soldier to serve during the war," that in the Stratford matter he only yielded at the "pressing importunity of the people." The board disproved of the course taken by the people of Stratford, commended the measures taken by General Wolcott as prudent and necessary," etc., but nevertheless, being satisfied with Dr. Johnson's word and oath, he was released.

But this arrest did not prevent him from receiving further positions of honor from our state. He was one of the three counsellors of Connecticut in the Susquehanna case, was a member of the Continental Congress from 1784 to 1787, he aided in drafting the Federal Constitution, and Dr. Beardsley says that "the first action of the Legislature of Connecticut under the new Federal Constitution was the election of Dr. Johnson as a Senator in Congress." He held this office from 1789 to 1791, and was then president of Columbia College till 1800:

The motives that may have induced many to join the enemy are set forth in an act of the General Assembly passed at its May session in 1779, which, after referring to the crime of treason when committed with deliberation as justly deserving the most severe and exemplary punishment, they say: "But whereas it is apprehended that very different motives and principles have influenced the conduct of the deluded few who have taken part against their country—some through ignorance of the nature and grounds of the dispute between Great Britain and America, some through particular prejudice, prospects of reward and gain, others deceived by the treacherous acts of subtle and secret enemies, have without deliberation given way to the force of various temptations, which persons are now convinced of their error and lament their folly. This Assembly, taking the matters aforesaid into consideration and ever willing to exercise leniency and mercy according to the genius of this free and happy constitution as far as may be consistent with justice and public safety, do therefore in tenderness and compassion to such deluded persons resolve and declare, that any and all such persons who shall return into this state on or before the first day of October next and deliver themselves up to the civil authority of the town to which they belong, may and shall be suffered to remain and dwell in safety in such town, provided," etc. And His Honor the Governor was advised to issue a proclamation accordingly.

But it appears that in the following August, the Governor, through a press of more important matters, had not issued said proclamation, and whereas it appeared that "the inimical persons described in said act both in this and the other states have been very active of late in favor of the detestable cause which they have chosen, and many of them on board and assisting the fleet and army who have lately committed the inhuman destruction of several important towns in this state, and otherwise discover great malignity against their country," etc., they advise "his Excellency the Governor not to issue said proclamation until otherwise advised "

Resolutions desiring the Governor to issue a proclamation of pardon had been passed at the May session in 1777. General Putnam had also issued such a proclamation.

Seventeen persons, in addition to those hereinbefore named, escaped from the British and received pardon, as follows: Pardon Tillinghast Taber, of New London; Elijah Elmore, of Stratford; Israel Rowland and Samuel Hawley, of Redding; David Manvill, Jesse Tuttle, Seth Warner, Ephraim Warner, Richard Miles and Daniel Finch, of Waterbury; John Moorehouse and Comfort Benedict, of Danbury; James Benham, of Wallingford; Michael Ames, of New Haven; John Davis junr., of Derby; Elisha Fox (residence not stated) and Nathan Fitch, of Greenwich.

In January, 1778, David Washburn of New Milford represented to the Assembly that he was under the sentence of death, having been convicted in November, 1777, of high treason, and that the particular species of treason for which he was condemned was going on board an armed brig belonging to the enemy. His sentence, with that of David Whelpley, Solomon Ferris and Wm. Peck, all of whom were to be executed on the 10th of November, 1779, for high treason, was suspended until the first Wednesday of March, 1780; but before that time it was arranged to have these persons exchanged as prisoners of war. Probably they were not executed through fear that the British would retaliate.

In January, 1779, Nehemiah Scribner of Norwalk, being under sentence of death for high treason, had his sentence changed to confinement and labor at Newgate prison "during the pleasure of the General Assembly." Other persons whose names are not published in the state reports were held for high treason, as a resolution was passed in January, 1779, that all persons so held in the New Haven, Fairfield and Litchfield jails be transferred to the jail at Hartford.

Moses Dunbar was hung for high treason at Execution Hill, Hartford, near the present site of Trinity College, on March 19, 1777. His treason consisted mainly of enlisting men for the British army and having a captain's commission for that purpose. A full account of the affair, including his farewell letter to his children and his dying speech, may be found in the new History of Waterbury. His widow retired to the British army for a time, but afterwards returned to Bristol.

Referring now to non-resident prisoners, Dr. Benjamin Church of Boston, a member of the 1774 Congress, was confined at Norwich from November, 1775, to May, 1776, with the privilege of going into the jail-yard once a week. He was a supposed Patriot, but was sentenced for treasonable correspondence with the enemy, a letter written in cipher having been found on his person. Many Tories were sent here by order of the New York convention. In May, 1776, a newspaper says that "forty-nine dirty Tory prisoners, taken at Johnston, N. Y., were brought under guard from Albany to Hartford, and others were on the way."

Gov. William Franklin, a natural son of Benjamin Franklin, arrived here in July, 1776, and was confined for a time at Wallingford and afterwards at Middletown. He was the last royal governor of New Jersey, and was sent here by the New Jersey convention as a person "that may prove dangerous." In August, 1776, nineteen Tories from Albany arrived here and were sent to New London, and a little later were removed to the town of Preston. Mr. Mather, the mayor of New York, was confined at Litchfield. John Munroe and Henry Van Schaack, Tory prisoners from Albany, were sent to East Haddam; Munroe had served in the British army and Van Schaak had talked too much. He was released in January, 1777. Judge Jones, who afterwards wrote the History of New York in the Revolutionary War, was at one time a prisoner in Connecticut. In the latter part of 1776 it was found that these non-resident Tories were a great burden, owing to the scarcity of food. In fact, our own people were really suffering, and by the force of circumstances were compelled to send these non-resident prisoners home with the request that they deliver themselves up to the authorities who sent them here. This was done without the knowledge or consent of those who had placed these prisoners here for safe keeping.

Nearly all the names thus referred to in this paper are found in the published colonial and state records, but they include only a small per cent of the

Connecticut Tories. The new history of Waterbury republishes from Bronson's history the names of sixty-eight persons who left Waterbury to join the enemy. I find only seven of these names in the colonial and state reports. The History of Stamford names sixty Tories of that town, only five of whom I find in the state reports. No mention has been made of court martials nor of deserters who did not go over to the enemy."

[To be concluded.]

THE HOUSE OF THE KINDLY SMILE.

BY MARY A. HOADLEY

It stands by the road of every day
This House of the Kindly Smile,
About its porch the roses sway
And butterflies flit the while.

The heart bowed down by weight of woe
Looks up when passing by,
And its burden melts like April's snow
When it meets the friendly eye.

For she who dwells in this wayside house
Well knows the way is rough.
She gives the traveler heart again;
She smiles—and it is enough.

From a drawing by H. Phelps Arms.   A REMINISCENCE OF THE SNOW STORM OF FEBRUARY 1, 1898.

THE BLACK DOG.

BY W. H. C. PYNCHON.

" And if a man shall meet the Black Dog once it shall be for joy; and if twice, it shall be for sorrow; and the third time he shall die."

IN a corner of our country not far removed from two of its great cities, there is a low range of mountains, the hoary evidences of ancient volcanic action. Countless years have elapsed since the great tide of molten lava rolled over the region. Years fewer, but still countless, have passed during which the shattered and tilted remnants of the lava sheets have watched over the land. Deep gorges divide the masses into separate mountains, lonely and desolate, and the most desolate and the most conspicuous of all is the West Peak.

The West Peak stands at an angle of the range. Though it is not very high by measurement, yet, by its wild and savage aspect, it makes a stronger impression on the traveler than many mountains of much greater altitude. On the northeast it presents a long, heavily wooded slope agreeing with the incline of the ancient lava sheet, but its southern and western faces and its eastern flank are topped with perpendicular cliffs, their feet buried in a vast mass of broken rock, the wreck of ages, which the frost has rent from the face of the mountain. When summer is on the land, the gray cliffs rising from the forest which covers the base of the mountain give an impression of hoary antiquity that is almost oppressive. But when the winter winds roar through the stunted cedars and whirl the snows from the summit, when the rocks stand out black through the drifts that pile up under the lee of the cliffs, then the West Peak has a look of menace hard to describe. So it is not strange that weird tales have sprung up concerning this mountain, tales that are told about the firesides in the few houses that stand on the lonely roads that traverse the region. There is one tale that is especially to be mentioned—the story of a black dog that is seen at times upon the Peak. Many have seen him once, a few twice—none have ever told of the third meeting. It is a short haired black dog of moderate size, with nothing particularly noticeable in its actual appearance. Yet there are two signs by which it is ever known:—men have seen it bark, but have heard no sound; and it leaves no footprint behind it on the dust of summer or the snow of winter. Yes, there is a third sign. It is told in different words by different people, but the meaning is always the same, and the words with which I have begun this narration are my own ren-

"THE MOST DESOLATE OF ALL IS THE WEST PEAK."

dering of the common tradition. It may seem strange that a man of science should believe a thing of this kind—an idle tale for the ignorant and superstitious, you will say,—but I do believe it. And if you would know why, listen :

It was late in the spring of 18— that I visited West Peak for the first time. I was then a student at Harvard, and the work in geology that I had taken up made it desirable for me to visit the locality. At that time I had heard nothing of the legend. In the town of Meriden, which lies a few miles distant from the mountain, I hired a horse and wagon suitable for the trip and started out for the Peak in the best of spirits. From Meriden the road runs for about two miles in a generally northwest direction and then turns north into a deep valley lying between West Peak on the west and Notch Mountain, as it is called, on the east. At the farther end of this valley there is a seldom used road which turns toward the southwest again and winds up the easy slope at the back of the Peak. Guiding myself by the maps which I had brought with me,

I reached this road and there got out of the wagon to examine the vesicular lava of which there was a good outcrop at that point. I had been on my knees pounding away for dear life in my endeavor to get off a good cabinet specimen and had just gotten up to straighten my back, when I noticed trotting up the road a dog. I suppose he might have been called black, but it was the same degree of blackness that you see in an old black hat that has been soaked in the rain a good many times. His lineage was evidently uncertain. I think that, like the young man mentioned by Tennyson, he was "too proud to care from whence he came." But he seemed friendly, and when I drove on he insisted on following the wagon. So I let him go with me for the sake of his good company. Certainly that dog was a philosopher. In all that long day's journey—for after we left the Peak we went many miles beyond to visit other fragments of the lava-sheet—he followed the wagon. But this did not inter-

"ITS WESTERN FACE TOPPED WITH PERPENDICULAR CLIFFS."

fere with his pursuing "original investigation." There was not a brook on the route which that dog did not wade. He scoured every patch of woods, he poked his inquisitive nose into every hole and behind every stump. We made a jolly trio—the rough, strong old horse, the faded dog, and the man whose appearance was not one whit better than that of his companions. At the little village of Southington we stopped for dinner and then pushed on until, under the shadow of yet more western hills, I found the last point to be reached in the day's march. Then we turned back and started for home, the dog running on ahead. I took a great liking to that dog. In the first place he was so quiet,

Not once in all that day did I hear him bark, even when a calf beside the road tried to coax him into a fight. And he was so light of foot! Though the roads were very dry, yet I did not see a puff of dust rise from his feet as he trotted along ahead of the horse. On the return journey we traversed the same route that we had come in the morning instead of taking the direct road to Meriden, which passes south of West Peak. As we came toward the Peak, the last light of the setting sun was just touching the highest rocks, and by the time we had entered the valley of which I have spoken night had almost closed in. The dog still trotted on ahead until we came to the place where I had met him in the morning. Then he stopped, looked back at me a moment, and quietly vanished into the woods. I stopped and whistled and whistled again, but no dog appeared. So I drove on without much regret, as it is rather hard to tell what to do with a tramp dog even when he is a philosopher—particularly when he is a very homely dog. There is a chance that your friends will not appreciate his philosophical attainments as highly as you do.

The old horse knew that he was bound for home and he took the road at a very good gait. Soon the sharp summits of West Peak and Notch Mountain showed against the sky well behind us, and half an hour more brought us to

"WHEN THE ROCKS STAND OUT BLACK THROUGH THE TREES."

Meriden again. After supper I sat before the open fire at the Winthrop—for the evenings were still cool enough to make a fire almost a necessity—and thought over the whole day's trip. I am supposed to be a civilized individual, but there is a great deal of the tramp in me for all that, and for that reason I had enjoyed the day all the more. The change from close laboratories to the fresh air of the hills was alone enough to pay for all the trouble I had taken. That, no one could fail to enjoy. But the long drive through the beautiful mountain region, fresh with the beauty of spring, appealed particularly to the tramp in me. Many a time since then, when I have been weary and discouraged, I have gone back in memory to that long day's drive through the sunny valleys and over the breezy hills, and have felt the old gray horse rub his nose against my arm, and have seen the tramp dog look up into my face with his knowing brown eyes. It is curious how often it is that the little things leave the greatest memories behind them.

And this is how I met the Black Dog the first time—for joy.

*   *   *

I don't know just how we came to do it. I think it must have been that that spring visit to the West Peak gave me a desire to see how it

"THE WEST PEAK HAS A LOOK OF MENACE HARD TO DESCRIBE."

"WHEN THE WINTER WINDS WERE HOWLING OVER THE HILLS."

would look when its flanks were wreathed in snow and when the winter winds were howling over the hills. At any rate, the evening of February 5th, in the third year after my first visit, found me and my friend, Herbert Marshall, sitting again before the fire at the hotel where I had stopped before. It was then that I heard for the first time the story of the Black Dog. Marshall had been all over the region thoroughly in his work for the United States Geological Survey and he had climbed West Peak many times and at all seasons of the year.

We talked till late that night, and, as the fire died down to a mass of glowing embers, he told me how he himself had twice seen a black dog upon the mountain, but he laughed at the legend, saying that he did not believe in omens unless they were lucky ones. So we turned in and forgot all about omens, good or bad, until long after sunrise the next morning.

The morning was clear and bright but very cold, and the light on the snow was dazzling. We started for West Peak at about nine o'clock. We both wore hip boots and had on leather jackets under our overcoats. We carried with us, beside our lunch and a coil of rope, a hand camera—for I had determined to get some views from the top if possible. We found it heavy walking, for the snow was light and fine and fully a foot deep.

"A DEEP VALLEY LYING BETWEEN WEST PEAK AND NOTCH MOUNTAIN."

We did not reach the Peak until about eleven o'clock, and then we found the woods on the back so choked with snow that it was impossible to make any considerable progress through them, so we determined to try to make the ascent on the southern face. This portion of the mountain is much steeper, but it is free from forest, and the mass of broken fragments of rock which runs up to the foot of the cliffs affords a fairly good foothold. The cliffs themselves are pierced by many clefts broad enough in many cases to admit a man, while in some instances the clefts have been broadened by erosion into actual gorges.

The sharp, bracing air put life into us and we went at the ascent with enthusiasm. It was hard work, for many of the fragments were insecure, and snow is always uncertain stuff under the best conditions, but in the course of

an hour we were at the top of the "talus" and under the foot of the cliffs.
Here we found one of the narrow ravines of which I have spoken, which gave
a chance for further ascent, and then the fun began. But at last, by scram-
bling, crawling and wriggling, we got to the top and pulled the camera up
after us with a rope, much to the detriment of the former. Our lunch we left
at the foot of the ravine until we should come down. Arriving on the top of
the cliff, we found that the wind had risen and was blowing fiercely from the
northwest, whirling the snow in great clouds over the plain below us. Nevertheless, we determined to try for a few photographs, and here was where we
made our fatal error. We had become very warm in climbing the Peak, but
during that few minutes' halt on the summit the bitter wind chilled us to the
bone. Our gloves, which we had laid aside while taking pictures because they
were soaked with melted snow, froze, and it was with aching hands and feet
and with stiffened
limbs that we began
our descent into that
little gorge through
which we had come
up, the gorge of
which I never think,
since that fearful day,
save as the Valley of
the Shadow of Death.

So long as we
were in the sunlight
we went on with some
courage, but when we
passed into the shad-
ow of those black
cliffs, courage seemed
to die in our hearts
and we struggled on
blindly through the
drifted snow, hoping,
it seemed sometimes,
almost against hope.
Marshall was in the
lead, and I was fol-
lowing as best I
could, when he sud-
denly stopped and
without a word point-
ed to the top of the
cliff. There, high on
the rocks above us,
stood a black dog

"THE CLIFFS THEMSELVES ARE PIERCED BY DEEP CLEFTS."

like the one I had seen three years before, except that he looked jet black
against the snow wreath above him. As we looked he raised his head
and we saw his breath rise steaming from his jaws, but no sound came through

the biting air. Once, and only once, he gazed down on us with gleaming eyes and then he bounded back out of sight. I looked at Marshall. His face was white and he steadied himself against a rock, but there was not a tremor in his voice as he said:

"I did not believe it before. I believe it now; and it is the third time."

And then, even as he spoke, the fragment of rock on which he stood slipped. There was a cry, a rattle of other fragments falling—and I stood alone.

Later—I cannot tell how much later—there is no measure of hours and minutes at such a time—bruised, bleeding, almost frozen, I stood by all that was left of my friend. He was dead; his body was already stiff, and I knew that unless I would share this, his last sleep, I must hasten. So I bent over him in a hasty farewell and then staggered on.

HERBERT MARSHALL.

What followed I cannot say. I only know that I came to a house and was taken in and cared for. Before long I was so far revived as to tell what had happened, and a party of men from the neighboring farms sought and brought back the body of poor Marshall. They found him where I left him, and by the body watched a black dog that as they approached fled swiftly back into the shadows and of the lonely ravine where the brave life had ended.

I believe the story of the Black Dog. Can you wonder that I do? Moreover, I know that some time I shall see it again—

"THE VALLEY OF THE SHADOW OF DEATH."

for the third and last time—and shall go even as my friend went. It may be years before my doom comes. The Survey cannot spare my services on the West Peak area. I must die some time. Why should I shirk my duty? Yet, when I am gone, this paper may be of interest to those who remain, for, in throwing light on the manner of my death, it will also throw light on the end of the many victims that the old volcanic hills have claimed.

* * * *

(From the New York Herald, November 13th, 1—.)

"The body of F—— S———— of the U. S. Geological Survey was found on West Peak, near Meriden, Conn., yesterday. Mr. S————, who was at the head of the work on the West Peak area, disappeared on November 2nd, and all search for him has proved unavailing until yesterday, when his body was found at the foot of the southern cliff of the Peak. Apparently he had fallen from the top, a distance of some forty feet. It is a singular fact that the body was found on almost the identical spot where his friend, Herbert Marshall, met his death six years before. This makes the fifth man who has lost his life on the range within thirty years."

———

ARBUTUS.

BY SARAH J. BEL..

Treasure of wooded banks,
    Sweet is thy breath to me;
Fragrance of sunny nooks,
Neighbor of laughing brooks,
    Joy of the fields so free.

Springing on red-brown stems,
    Fresh are thy leaves so green;
Bright are thy pink-white flowers,
Kissed into life by showers,
    Sweetened by breath unseen.

Beauty is all around!
    Life is the same sweet thing,
In birds of the air,
In children so fair,
    Or the sweet flowers blossoming.

MISTRESS MARY'S WEDDING APRON.

BY ELLEN BRAINERD PECK.

On Mistress Mary's wedding day,
   In the old colonial time,
Sweet, the gardens were, and gay,
   Blooming, in their fragrant prime.

They tell me roses were ablow,
   Making pink the country-side,
In those hedges, long ago,
   Fitting for so fair a bride.

I wis, the birds began to sing,
   When Mary to her marriage stepped,
A vision, radiant of the spring,
   As down the quaint old hall she swept.

And o'er her grand frock, daintily,
   In housewife fashion, fair of old,
She wore an apron, brave to see,
   Embroidered, all, in pink and gold.

The years, with tender touch and light,
   Have brushed its satins golden hue,
The broidered roses still keep quite,
   Their first deep blush tint, too.

Oh, relic rich in family lore,
   What pride of ancestry you bring
Through generations passed before ;
   You almost seem a living thing.

A gathered wealth of old romance
   Enfolds you with ancestral thought,
The old-time beauty to enhance,
   As moonlight in a soft mist caught.

And storied memories ever seem,
   That cluster round a dear heir-loom,
As fragrance, faint, as in a dream,
   Of flowers that fade, no more to bloom.

[NOTE: This beautiful apron is in the possession of Mrs. Carrie K. Bill, whose husband is a lineal descendant of the maker of the apron, Mary Wright of Norwich, Conn., who was wedded to Amos Geer on June 14th, 1757.]

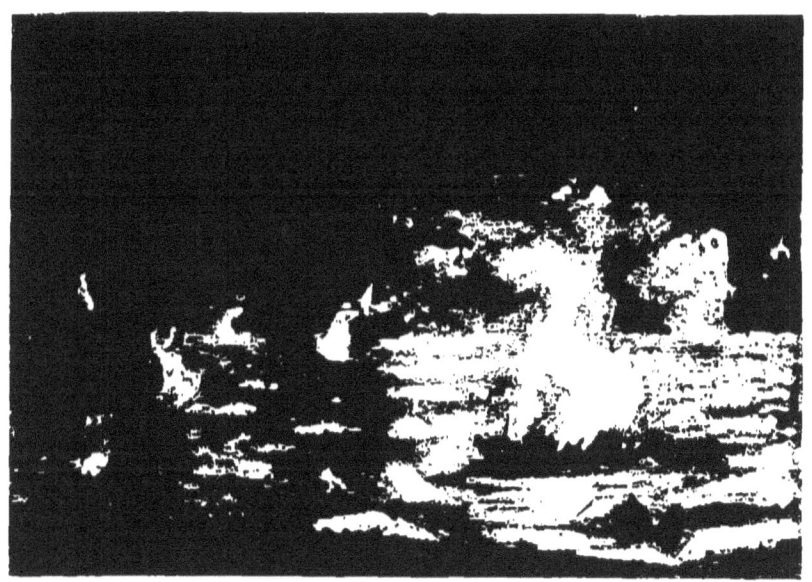

THE LAST SHOT IN THE ARCTIC.

BY CHARLOTTE MOLYNEUX HOLLOWAY.

AS one walks along the winding streets of New London, one cannot help being impressed with the solid comfort and beauty of many of the homes and the impression deepens into admiration when it is learned that the major portion are the result of the courage ("grit," he would call it), skill and endurance of the whaler of the days gone by. He began life on some sterile farm in Waterford,—take New London as centre and nearly the whole of the circle is Waterford,—and at fourteen, or before, tightened up his "galluses," put on his "Sunday go to meetings" and went into town to ship before the mast on some whaler bound for a cruise of two or three years. Then, if there was good stuff in him, he rose from boat-steerer to mate and "Cap'n," and had the felicity and profit of standing on the deck and roaring at the men in the choice vernacular of the seaman.

But the captain had often the most perilous part of the work of capturing the whale. He generally went in the first boat and quite often the whale "milling" gave the men a race for life rather than lucre.

But they count their hardships small now that years have softened their

NEW LONDON HARBOR.

horrors, and they enjoy all the comforts of home with the consciousness, which is keenest pleasure to every true man, that it has all been earned by themselves.

It is a long time since New London saw a whale ship depart from her wharves, and to the present generation stories of whaling days have the flavor of antiquity. The Charles Colgate, belonging to one of the biggest and most successful firms in the business, Lawrence & Co., lies stripped and rotting, a veritable curiosity; but for tangible evidence of what whaling has done for the town, look at its Soldiers' and Sailors' Monument, its Public Library, its handsome female academy, the two parks and the rows of substantial looking private houses which are sure to be well supplied within with mementoes of their owners' voyages in the shape of pictures etched on whales' teeth, eggs of penguins, and ostriches, feathers, stuffed birds, shells — all the thousand tokens of loving thought that the absent one gathers for those at home.

On the street you will meet a hale old man carrying his three score and ten with ease, bluff and simple of speech, with the roll of the sea in his gait, and contempt for creased trousers in his attire. Or step into a bank and ask for the president. In the prosperous money class are many of the salts of the past, though a few have always failed to win fortune's favor. Stop one of these old sea dogs and start him away from his favorite occupation of worrying over the safety of his securities and bring him back to the days of "auld lang syne." The eye will brighten and the cheek gain color while the ring of the sea sounds clearer in his voice as he tells of the struggles and successes of his life. It is a yarn well worth hearing and having little of exaggeration, for these old heroes are modest and truthful men who religiously believe it was easier for the whale to swallow Jonah than a church member a landsman's fish story.

About the best preserved and oldest of the whaling captains in the country is Capt. Samuel Greene, who for more than forty years never staid on land longer than was required to fit out a vessel. Captain Greene celebrated his golden wedding seven years ago, and his friends aver he is younger and heartier looking to-day than then. He was born

HULK OF THE CHARLES COLGATE.

in Waterford, November 11, 1815 and went before the mast in the Neptune under Capt Nat. Richards in 1829, and after seven voyages in various ships he came at the age of 23 to his first vessel, the Neptune, as master. He married at 25 a very estimable lady, who, with two of his three children, bears him companionship. The captain's home may be said to have all the heart desires but as he rides his grandson on his knee, he turns back to the days of hardship and peril with a sigh of regret that he stands alone of all the men who shared their struggles together in the beginning.

RESIDENCE OF CAPT. JAMES SMITH.

In the log book of the captain's memory is many a stirring tale, but none more exciting, more certain to arouse deepest feeling, than that of his capture by the Shenandoah in 1865.

"Maybe it is a good thing, but I guess if you ask any old fellow to go back to the days of the war, it will seem to him as if it was so far off that it is dimlike and unsubstantial; but just give him a sight of Old Glory, and let him hear 'Marching Through Georgia' and he'll sniff the air like a battle horse. Anything like Grant Day is sure to make the blood tingle and quicken the memory till it all sweeps past like a grand panorama. It is a grand thing to be able to say that you have done something for the defence of the Union, but the whalers had not the least idea that the war was coming. They had little accurate knowledge of the progress of events which swept away all the weak subterfuges of compromises. Their business left them little chance to talk politics. And when the sudden storm burst the men who were out on voyages, voyaging four years at a time and only once or twice a year touching ports where they received stale news, were the very last to believe there was any chance of any section trying to break up the Union.

"Not that we need complain, though. I'd like to see some of these big bonus winners do a neater job than some of the old whalers that were almost condemned when Uncle Sam pressed them into service. Even their old hulks did their share in Charleston harbor.

"Ever heard of the stone fleets Nos. 1 and 2? No? Well, the rebels did.

"Just as soon as the Confederates began to fit out privateers to cruise against Union commerce and destroy the whalemen in the Pacific, the owners of the latter were alarmed and withdrew all their ships which they could reach from service. If there was one thing which Uncle Sam did not have at the

RESIDENCE OF CAPT. SAMUEL GREENE

beginning of the struggle it was ships, and he eagerly accepted the offer of some of these well built vessels, which were used for blockade runners. A good use was found for the veterans which had been so long in service that they were thought deserving of retirement. The United States bought forty, and filling them with stone to the deck, divided them into two fleets and sunk them off Charleston harbor in 1861 and '62 to prevent the escape of privateers and the entrance of blockade runners.

"It is worth while stopping a bit to think of the famous history that belonged to some of these old ships which had so glorious an end. Many of them had been famed in the China and European trade. The Herald was nearly one hundred years old. The Corea was an armed store ship belonging to the English navy, and in the Revolution was driven into Long Island and an expedition of one hundred men and boys was planned from New Bedford to capture her. When their schooner neared the Corea, all on board hid below excepting four men and a boy who seemed to be engaged in fishing. The Corea fired a gun, and bearing down upon them ordered them alongside. They grumblingly obeyed and were despoiled of their fish and the Corea's crew swarmed on their deck. The captured fishermen threw the fish into the sea, and at the signal the secreted men rushed forth, overpowered the Englishmen, captured their vessel and brought it in triumph into New Bedford. The Corea, Fortune, Tenedos, Lewis and Phœnix, of New London; Meteor and Robin Hood, of Mystic; Timer, of Sag Harbor; Amazon, Harvest and Rebecca Sims, of Fairhaven; Potomac, of Nantucket; American, of Edgartown; and Archer, Courier, Cossack, Frances, Henrietta, Garland, Herald, Kensington, Leonidas, L. C. Richmond, Maria Theresa, and South America, of New Bedford, were the first stone fleet. To the second fleet New Bedford sent the America, India, Valparaiso and Majestic; New London, the Montezuma, New England, and Dove; Newport, the William Lee and Mechanic; Sag Harbor, the Emerald and Noble; Salem, the Messenger; and Gloucester, the Newburyport.

CAPT. JOHN HAYNES.
Organizer of the Jib Boom Club.

"The Calhoun was the first in the Pacific whaling grounds to destroy the

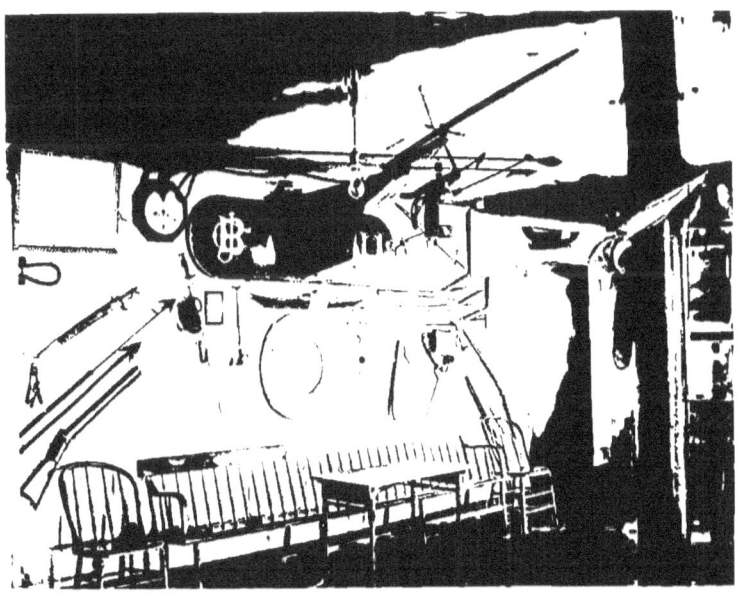

WHALING AND WAR RELICS.—JIB BOOM CLUB.

whalers, and three from Provincetown —the John Adams, Mermaid, and Parana—were captured and the vessels with their cargoes of oil set on fire and the sixty-three men composing their crew brought to New Orleans and set adrift.

"The most formidable and destructive were the famous Alabama and the Shenandoah. These scourges of the sea ranged along the Atlantic Ocean and intercepted returning whalers. The Alabama was particularly clever in devices for alluring the unsuspecting into her power. After capturing a vessel she would wait until night and then set it on fire. All the whaleships seeing the blaze would start to rescue the men whom they thought were in peril, and thus fell into the trap. The Alabama decoyed and burned the ships Benjamin Tucker, Osceola, Virginia, and Elisha Dunbar, of New Bedford; Ocean, of

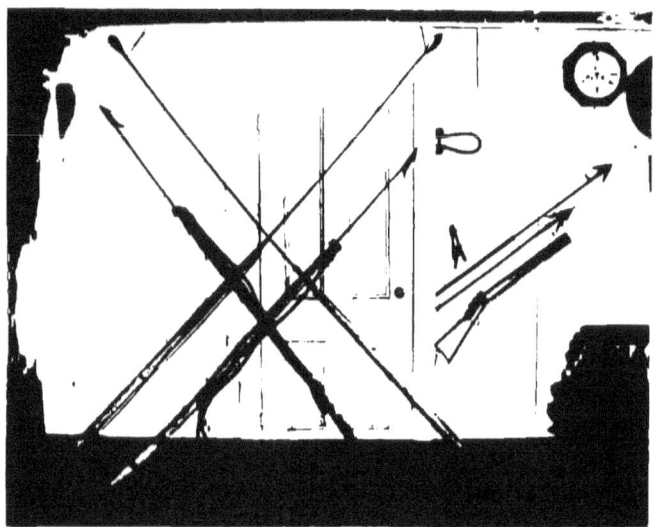

HARPOONS, LANCES AND BOMB-LANCE GUN.

Sandwich; Alert, of New London; and the schooners Altamaha, of Sippican, and Weather Gage, of Provincetown, who had hastened to rescue the men of the Ocean Rover, of Mattapoisett, which they thought had caught fire through accident. Many of the whalers would go into friendly ports and wait until the privateers went on their way; others were blockaded, and a good many excellent ships manned by resolute men gave the Confederates good doses of lead. The United States navy was largely recruited from the merchant and whaling services.

"The men who went out in '60 and '61 had no way of getting to their home ports, and mighty few of them did; they used to go to Honolulu and San Francisco. Then some daring spirits did get out from New Bedford and New London and managed to make very good voyages.

"There wasn't any more profitable season since the fifties than that ending in the spring of '65, and there was a big fleet of whalers in the Northern

THE LAST SHOT IN THE ARCTIC.

Pacific and Behring Straits waiting for the advancing spring to let them start for home. Some had been out six months, some eighteen, some two years. Many had every bit of space filled, and others had just enough of success to make the men comfortably happy. None of them had any late home news. The latest comer, the Nassau of New Bedford, Captain Greene of New London, had brought the satisfactory tidings when she left the States in December, 1864, that there wasn't much comfort ahead for Johnny Reb. No one thought that there was a confederate privateer within a thousand miles. But the Shenandoah, under Waddell, was in the sea of Ochotsk, ruthlessly destroying every ship she met. There the Abigail of New Bedford, Capt. Ebenezer Nye, was her first victim in the middle of June. The Abigail was becalmed and all hands were at work clean-
ing up when the lookout announced a ship in sight. The first mate after some scrutiny announced that it was a United States gun-
boat. 'Give me the glass,' said Capt. Eb.. 'It's darned suspicious that there ain't any flag. No United States skipper'd forget that in these times.' 'She's making for us,' he added after a few moments.

THE HIBERNIA.
The largest of the New London Whalers.

'We'll find out pretty quick. I wish we carried a gun to pepper 'em if they are enemies and salute 'em if they are friends.' 'We could pelt 'em with biscuit,' said the mate, who was sure they were friends.

"As the stranger neared them, she ran up the stars and bars and they could see her ugly guns and her deck swarming with men.

"'Good God!' cried Capt. Eb., 'it's one of them devils, and we're done for.' A boat was lowered from her and pulled directly toward the whaler. It halted a few boat's lengths away at the hail of the captain.

"'The Shenandoah, and if you don't surrender at once we'll blow you to kingdom come !'

"'God help us !' groaned Nye. 'There's nothing else to be done. It is hard to be in a hole like this, but we shall be the only victims if I can help it. Get out two boats, men, while I parley with this fellow. We'll start off and risk it. There's about thirty ships in the straits, and maybe we can warn them.'

"'What do you want to interfere with us for?' he shouted. 'Nice, manly work it is for you. There ain't any fighting going on here, and you'd better have stayed where there was. You can burn this ship, but it ain't going to do you a sixpence of good.'

"To his surprise the men in the boat looked listless and dispirited, and after he had said all that he could think of to take up the time, the officer only answered: 'Listen to the Yank scold ! He can do better at that than at fighting.' 'Oh, that's in line with your work,' cried Nye. 'You'd see what I'd do if I had a chance." 'You are going to surrender, sensibly? We don't want to spill any blood.' 'Yes.' The boat turned back, and Nye, asking his men to keep the Shenandoah occupied as long as they could, hastened to the boats with those who had signified their willingness to go. They had pulled a good distance from the Abigail ere the Shenandoah noticed their departure and trained one of her guns upon them, but the shot went wide. The men had tried to bring with them their precious possessions, and Capt. Nye had judged it best not to seem to notice how heavily laden were the boats. They kept together for a time, not a word in either boat, but every man was stealing furtive glances back for the light he dreaded to see. It came at last, and a long drawn sob of agony burst from every throat. A moment they paused, then thought of others to save. Hope to foil the privateer stimulated them, and under the impetus they made rapid headway. Darkness prevented their keeping together and when morning dawned the boat in which was Capt. Nye could descry no sign of her mate. It was hard to keep up the spirits of the men, and a calm and thick fog added to their gloom. On the fourth day they had reached a point off the eastern coast of Siberia, about fifteen miles south of Cape East, and Capt. Nye, now that the fog through which they had been helplessly drifting had lifted, kept a sharp look out for sight of the fleet of whalers which he knew must be in this region. It was late in the afternoon of the 26th of June when they were overjoyed at seeing a ship which hoisted the stars and stripes in

WHALES' AND WALRUS' TEETH.
The three Barnacles here shown were taken from the Heads of Whales

response to their signal. They were soon on board and received her sad news. She was a New Bedford whaler lately constructed, and her superior steam equipment had enabled her to escape the ravages of the Shenandoah, which that very morning had captured and burned the Isabella, Gypsy, Catherine, General Williams, and William C. Nye.

"This news completely prostrated the captain, whose grief that he had vainly abandoned his ship was most poignant. But they cheered him up, saying he ought to be glad that he had escaped the mortification of being made a prisoner. As for the Shenandoah, it wasn't likely she would think there were more than the little fleet upon which she had pounced. But the Shenandoah was leaving nothing to presumption. Laden with everything of value from her five victims, she was steaming leisurely about, confident that she would find further prey, and, smarting under the knowledge of continued and irretrievable reverse to the Confederacy, vengefully determined to make the Yankee victory as dear as lay in her power. Fate seemed to delight in affording her opportunity. The 27th of June she spied a large fleet of whalers near Cape East apparently waiting for a wind. The sea was jammed with ice, and they had gathered there to assist the Brunswick, a New Bedford ship that had been badly jammed. To the powerful craft the ice was a mere shell, and she steamed her way toward them. Not one endeavored to escape, for the idea unaccountably possessed them that she was a government survey vessel. So sure were they, that impatience to hear the news from the States forced them to send Capt. Ludlow of Long Island to meet her. The Shenandoah disdained to resort to any of her usual tactics of concealment, and, exulting in the consciousness of the utter helplessness of her quarry, lay to and waited for the embassy. Ludlow had not put his foot on deck when he saw his mistake, but he boldly stated his errand. Waddell speedily convinced him of his error, and angrily ordered him to return with the intelligence from the Shenandoah that their Union sympathies would not save their ships. 'Well,' said Ludlow undauntedly, reckoning he might as well be hung for a sheep as a lamb, 'We won't begrudge them to Uncle Sam.'

THE GEN. WILLIAMS.

"A hurried council was held on his return. There were the Hillman, Isaac Howland, Nassau, Brunswick, Waverly, Martha 2nd, Congress, Covington, Milo, General Pike, Nile, James Maury, Nimrod, and Favorite. Their crews numbered 400 men, but, according to the careless custom of the times before the Civil War, none of them had arms, guns, or facilities for running away from the formidable gunboat which could so easily annihilate them. So it was resolved to swallow their bitter pill with what grace they could muster, with the hope that Waddell would be merciful enough to bond some of the ships and let them go.

"They had good fighting blood in them, these old sea dogs, and it was like pulling a double molar to get some of them to consent. But the prudent won the day, save with old Tom Young of Fairhaven, who swore in a way that would have made a Parkhurst jump, if the Fates had not mercifully foreborne to deal out Parkhursts in those days of affliction.

"Capt. Thomas G. Young was captain only in name, for he was close upon the patriarch's three score and ten, but his spirit was high, his heart full of courage and patriotism, and he swore with a deep and satisfying oath that no Johnny Reb could ever receive his surrender. If Waddell should destroy his vessel without his protest, he would never forgive himself.

"'Damn it all, men,' he said, 'don't let us be chickens. We can fight for the Union just as good here as anywhere. I've sailed with you all many a year, and the Favorite always knew she had a good crew and respected 'em. No true Yankee skipper'll give up his ship.'

"But officers and men took a different view. They knew that Capt. Young was part owner of the Favorite, and that, personally, they would gain nothing by a resistance which might imperil their lives. To sacrifice their kits and all their treasures appeared enough to the men who had incentives to life in distant wives and children. Vainly they urged the captain to reconsider his decision. But he appealed again to them to make a determined resistance, and finding them obdurate, loaded his bomb guns and fire arms and took his stand upon the cabin roof. In the meantime the other ships were submitting quietly to the Shenandoah, and, as they saw the stand of the Favorite, the men were apprehensive lest a human sacrifice result. When the Shenandoah's boat brought the demand to surrender to Capt. Young, he yelled out : 'Stand off! I'm going to shoot Waddell to-day!'

THE CHELSEA.
A typical Whaler of about 1890.

"The sight of the guns, the look of his eye, were sufficient to emphasize his admonition, and the envoy precipitately returned. Waddell had already divined the Favorite's intention and had given orders to fire upon her, but the returning boat was in range. The captain of the Favorite was now surrounded by his crew imploring him to desist, but being sharply repulsed, they removed the caps from the loaded arms, carried off the ammunition and rushed for the boats. The Shenandoah's boat had reported progress to Waddell, also Capt. Young's declaration that he would shoot him. Waddell laughed. 'It isn't worth while wasting shot on the tub,' he said, contemptuously; 'let two boats go after him, and if the old devil is obstinate, pick him off.'

"They pulled off with alacrity and were soon alongside. Alone, grim and gaunt, the old man stood on the cabin roof, one hand holding a pistol, a pile of small arms at his feet. He was ready to fire his bomb guns after the parley he expected. Not a thought of personal danger came to him, he was only sor-

THE LAST SHOT IN THE ARCTIC.

ry that Waddell was not there. As the boats neared, the commanding officer called, 'Pull down your colors, resistance is useless.' 'I'll see you damned first,' retorted Young. 'If you don't,' said the officer of the boat, I'll shoot you.' 'Shoot and be damned!' invited the old hero, as he drew forth from behind him a small flag, and, waving the stars and stripes around his head, gave three cheers for the Union. Wrapping the flag about him he rushed to fire his guns. From one to the other he went. He had been betrayed! He snapped his pistol. That too had been tampered with. The privateer's crew were swarming over his deck. With a scream of agony, the brave old skipper grasped a gun by the barrel and rushed forward to die fighting. A dozen strong young hands seized and disarmed him. He was put in irons in the top gallant forecastle, and, though some were inhuman enough to suggest burning the ship, his captors contented themselves with tearing the flag to shreds before his eyes, taking from him his money, watch and shirt studs, and leaving him bound.

"Some hours after the Shenandoah had gone sated with plunder, a crew which had left one of the ships, preferring the mercies of the seas to that of the privateer, rescued Capt. Young.

"The Shenandoah burned thirty-four ships in all and bonded four—the Milo, General Pike and James Maury and the Nile of New London. These, loaded to suffocation with her despoiled victims, including Capt. Samuel Greene of the Nassau, proceeded to San Francisco. Thence Capt. Greene came home by the Panama route, to engage, after rest, in but one more thrilling experience ere he devoted himself to the enjoyment of the home he had gained by his unremitting patience and skill.

"In the interim the Shenandoah went her way looking for other spoil. The afternoon of her wanton destruction of the whaling fleet she saw a pert steam whaler rapidly steaming through the straits and promptly gave chase. To her astonishment, as soon as she was seen by the whaler, the latter veered about and came toward her, running up the United States flag, and a boat was lowered and set out for her. Waddell waited, constructing an insolent reply to the entreaty for mercy he expected. The captain and one of the officers of the whaler came on board. There was a bright light in his eye and perfect

THE TUSCARORA.

assurance in his voice as he asked for Waddell. 'You come to surrender?' queried the latter, after they had exchanged greetings with exaggerated politeness. 'Surrender be blowed,' answered the bluff old tar, 'I ain't even going to ask you to do that. I bring you news. The jig's up. Do you see that?' pulling out a paper and waving it before Waddell's eyes. 'Lee has surrendered to Grant at Appomattox. The Confederate States are in Davy Jones's locker'. 'I don't believe it,' blustered Waddell. 'Take them prisoners.'

"But his officers protested as one man: 'We are willing to fight for a cause, but we are not butchers or buccaneers.' 'That's right,' said the whaler, as he took his leave. 'There's no cause since the ninth of April. It's buried under the apple tree at Appomattox.'"

THE SEA WAS IN FROLICSOME MOOD TO-DAY.

BY ARTHUR CLEVELAND HALL.

The sea was in frolicsome mood to-day,
And tumbled the pebbles within her reach,
Across the sands of the curving beach,
Like puss with a bundle of yarn at play.
Far out on the blue I could see the spray
Of the white caps, nodding each to each,
I could hear the sea gulls' plaintive screech,
As it circled, seeking its finny prey.
And the sun shone bright for the sea's delight
He has loved and wooed for ten thousand years,
But the gay coquette is but laughing yet,
Though her cloudy lashes seem wet with tears;
Oh! the sun may smile and the moon beguile
But she clings to the old Earth all the while.

NERVA.

A Story of Pastoral Connecticut.

BY MILO LEON NORTON.

PART II.—RESTORATION.

Not for many years had there been so much activity displayed in the vicinity of Indian Hollow as took place during the summer and autumn following the purchase of the Weston farm. The dwelling had been put in good repair inside and out. The barns had been newly covered and painted and stored with hay and grain. The capacious wood-shed was filled with wood ready for the fire. The cellar was stored with vegetables. The fences were repaired, the brush in the pastures and by the roadside had been cut and burned, the fruit trees pruned, and the unkempt grounds about the house had been graded and seeded down.

The few thousand dollars that Nerva had at her command when she undertook the restoration of the old farm seemed to her a meagre sum indeed. But the neighboring farmers looked upon the newcomers as wealthy city people, with unlimited resources, driven to take up a residence in the country on account of the poor health of the father. Attempts at familiarity, or shrewd efforts to obtain information as to their antecedents, met with no encouragement by the discreet young lady. She was gracious and cordial in her intercourse with her neighbors, but reserved and non-committal.

There was one exception, however.

In a previous chapter I mentioned that one of the residents of Indian Hollow was a young man of progressive ideas, who had worked his way through an agricultural college and had adopted methods of farming unfamiliar to his neighbors. This young man, left to his own resources at majority, was the nearest neighbor of the Smiths, and to him Nerva looked for advice and assistance.

Although five and twenty, and of pleasing manners and appearance, he had never married. His widowed mother kept house for him, and whether it was because he found her society all-sufficient, or because of his native bashfulness, or because he was wedded to his books and studies, that he had not taken a wife, I will not undertake to say. At any rate, he was considered a great "catch" by the rural belles of the vicinity, but they had never been able to make much impression upon him.

People misjudged Leslie Burton. He was pronounced "stuck up" by the young people. Yet there was nothing of egotism in his disposition. He was retiring, thoughtful and studious, rather than social and demonstrative. He was misunderstood.

Being Nerva's confidential adviser and largely the originator of the Weston farm improvements, he was necessarily thrown into her society almost daily. These frequent visits, of course, set all the feminine tongues wagging, but this was entirely unknown to Nerva, as she mingled with her neighbors but little. Leslie was to her an adviser, and she had found his advice invaluable, but she had not thought of him in any other light.

On the other hand, Leslie had looked upon Nerva as a superior being. Her refinement of manner, her reserve, her station as the daughter of a retired millionaire (as he supposed her to be) placed her so far above him that he never once permitted himself to think of her in any other light than as a wealthy city girl with quiet and eccentric tastes. Why she should prefer a residence in the wilderness rather than at some fashionable watering place he could understand only as an eccentricity.

One year had passed quickly away since Nerva had become the owner of the farm. The year had brought great changes to the old place. The house with its fresh paint and broad verandas; the neat barns; the rustic mill, where the fuel for the fires was prepared, and the corn and rye and oats were ground for the farm stock and poultry; the cultivated fields, and the smooth lawn, presented a marked contrast to the desolation of former years.

Nerva sat one May morning on the broad veranda. A cow-bell was tinkling in the pasture. Bees were humming in the cherry trees that were in full bloom. Humming-birds were flitting from flower to flower. Robins were piping in their cheery way, and the woods were ringing with the music of the song birds. It was a beautiful scene that greeted her eyes. She had been very busy the past year, and had hardly taken time to think. But now, when everything had been reduced to a routine and she began to have more leisure, a feeling of loneliness took possession of her. She was thinking of other days.

As she sat thinking, the "hired man," as the New England farmhand is called, drove up on his return from the distant village creamery, where the cream from the farm herd was taken. He tossed a letter upon the veranda as he passed, which Nerva quickly secured and read.

It was from an old schoolmate, one of the few of her old associates who had not forgotten her since her change of fortune. It brought the welcome intelligence that she was coming to pay her old friend a visit.

The next week Alice, the friend, arrived, making the whole place ring with her laughter, and declaring it "just the sweetest old place in the world!"

Alice Van Brunt possessed one of those natures made of frolic and sunshine that a kind Providence has wisely bestowed upon a few choice favorites as a blessing to mankind. They make everyone happy and joyful wherever they go. They see only the sunny side of everything, and when they go into shadowy places they light them up, disperse the gloom, and drive away haunting melancholy.

Alice was so delighted with this quiet nook in the country that she soon sent for her mother and two young lady cousins. As a natural consequence, masculine relatives found time to pay them a flying visit; and two young men, enamored of the two young lady cousins, also concluded to spend a two weeks' vacation there, finding lodgings at neighboring farm-houses.

Nerva thus found herself obliged to play the hostess, which she did gracefully, besides adding to her little store of cash something substantial in the way of remuneration.

Adjacent lands were purchased by some of the visitors attracted to the locality by the glowing accounts of the summer sojourners; and Nerva parted with some of the waste lands bordering the mill pond at a good profit. This land was improved by the purchasers, who also contracted for the erection of two summer cottages in time for use during the following summer.

Following the advice of Leslie, Nerva cleared up adjoining lands, built a drive around the pond and through the neighboring wood, built a neat summer house upon the summit of the cliff overlooking a wide extent of country, and erected three neat cottages to be rented or sold the following season. An ice house was also erected in an out-of-the way nook convenient to the lake, which was filled during the winter.

Nerva was not disappointed in her expectations. All the preparations she had made were needed the following summer, for people came and went, taxing the accommodations of the place to the utmost. More cottages were built, more lots sold, and greater improvements made. A large, marshy meadow adjoining the lake was excavated, the muck being utilized as an absorbent for fertilizing purposes, and the capacity of the lake was doubled. Light row-boats were added to the attractions of the place, and a small wharf was constructed.

The fourth summer brought a still greater influx of city people, and the place experienced quite a real estate boom. Building lots brought nearly as much as the whole original farm. All the milk, butter and eggs that could be produced were needed for the consumption of the summer residents. Vegetables and fruit were in great demand. Butchers, bakers and grocerymen made daily trips for orders, and Indian Hollow became a flourishing summer resort.

It was on a bright October day after the season was ended, and Nerva had settled down, rather enjoying the solitude after the excitement and rush of the summer, that she received a letter from her former lover. He had heard from friends of the success she had achieved as a manager, and it occurred to him that such a woman would make a valuable wife, particularly as he had experienced reverses in business and found himself financially embarrassed. The letter was full of well-worded contrition for his hasty acceptance of his release from their engagement, and stated that he should follow up the letter with a personal appeal if she would consent. Very cautiously he also inquired if among her father's papers there were any bonds of a certain railroad, worthless, as he explained, but which might be made available at a very low figure toward reorganizing the road. If she would take the trouble to look them up, he would be able to offer a small sum—five hundred or so, for what had cost ten thousand dollars!

Nerva had not developed so much business talent during the past four years for nothing, a talent no doubt inherited from her father and which would undoubtedly have remained dormant but for the necessity that brought it out. Before replying she reflected. She believed her former lover to be mercenary and heartless. Of this she had had ample proof. Why this solicitude on his part concerning the bonds? Questioning her father, she obtained such information as he could recall with much effort, for a haze still hovered over his intellect. Correspondence with a former legal friend of the family ensued, and the result was that the hitherto supposedly worthless bonds were exchanged for their face value in cash.

Nerva had now ample capital for the development of her enterprise, and she invested it wisely.

Again and again in quick succession she had been importuned by her former lover for the privilege of a personal interview, but she had answered evasively. Perhaps there was a spirit of retaliation brewing in the quiet little lady's heart. Perhaps it was something else. At any rate, confidential consultation with Leslie Burton was of frequent occurrence, and if that individual only had eyes to see, he might have seen that Nerva had a deeper interest in him than she would have had in a mere adviser.

But Leslie was so deeply impressed with her superiority that he dared not even permit himself to think of her as ever holding any other relation to him than as a friend. Besides, he did not understand women. Books he could read, but women were sealed books to him.

Nerva saw that if her plan was to be carried out—for she had thought out a plan—she would have to, Priscilla like, offer some encouragement that could not be misunderstood.

Putting on her hat and a light wrap one sunny afternoon late in October, she set out, basket in hand, in search of chestnuts. Perhaps she did not know that Leslie was finishing up some fall seeding in a field adjoining the chestnut grove. It might have been a coincidence, of course. Perhaps it was her eagerness to obtain chestnuts that caused her to throw stones and sticks with all a woman's proverbial dexterity up into a tree in full view of the young farmer. Perhaps it was mere gallantry that made the young farmer aforesaid hasten across the field, climb up the tree like a squirrel and shake the brown nuts from their prickly burs with his strong arms. Perhaps it was fear that she would injure her delicate hands with the sharp burs that made him stop, in spite of her protestation, to help fill her basket. Perhaps when this had been done and they stood at the barway together, it was her respect for him as a counselor that made her, somewhat shyly, request his advice on a very delicate subject.

"I have had an offer of marriage," she said, "and you have been so good an adviser and so kind a friend that I wish to obtain your opinion about it."

Poor Leslie turned pale an instant and then flushed a bright crimson. He could have sunk in his tracks. It was easy to persuade himself that he did not care for his pretty, confiding neighbor, but standing here as a disinterested judge on the merits of another man—that was another matter. Of course, she did not appear to notice his confusion.

"If I only dared!" he thought.

But he stammered out something about his inability to advise in such a case. She must consult her own heart.

"That is just the trouble," she said. "I do not love the man. He has proved false to me once, but now professes to be very penitent. Indeed, my regard has gone out for another and a worthier man, but he does not—at least he has never spoken."

She was almost frightened at her boldness. But it was a desperate case Leslie was not a coward. Who this other man was he could not guess. But something was choking him. A great lump was crowded into his throat, and he must speak or die!

"Miss Smith," he finally stammered. "I—I know I ought not to say it. I—I know you will despise me after it, you who are so far above me; you who seem to me as much above me as the stars (once his tongue was loosened he waxed eloquent; but I must speak even if you spurn me and never speak to me again in all your life. Miss Smith—"

"You may call me Nerva, Leslie," said she gently, raising her hand which somehow came in contact with his and was seized with the grip of a vice.

" Then you don't hate me ?" he asked eagerly.
" No indeed !"
" And you won't think me a fortune hunter who cares nothing for you but ; money ?"
" No, Leslie, particularly as I have no fortune. It is because we have lost ·ly everything that we are here. I am worth no more than you are, but are worth more to me than—"
When she recovered her breath she exclaimed, " You are a great bear, ie !" But she didn't seem to be displeased.
Leslie's horses, tired of waiting for their driver, had dragged the harrow hich they were attached across the field and were industriously grazing 1 the headland at the margin of the field. It was a long time before they ? disturbed.

Mr. and Mrs. Burton now make their winter home in the city, but spend greater part of the year on their united farms at Indian Hollow. The er's intellect and health being fully restored, he devotes his declining years ie care of his two lovely grandchildren—two as rugged, healthy, romping ; urchins as one could find in the country.
On every Thanksgiving day the entire family gather around the well-filled d at Weston farm. I say the entire family, for the elder daughter, whose er as a countess came to a disastrous end by the squandering of her own her mother's fortune by her titled but dissolute husband, was only too , with her humbled and repentant mother, to accept the hospitality of a e they would once have spurned.
So, on every Thanksgiving day, the entire family gather round the festive d and devoutly thank God for the restoration of family ties brought about ugh the restoration of an abandoned Connecticut farm.

A MIDNIGHT SONG.

BY MINNIE LOUISE HENDRICK.

I awaked at midnight, through the city streets
Came the sound of music rare and sweet.
The song was of love, and rest, and peace,
Like an angel's song to a restless throng,
It fell on the city's star-lit streets,
Like a benediction, so complete;
It filled my heart with song.

LIST OF BURIALS, OR "SEXTON'S LIST," OF THE CENTER CHURCH BURYING GROUND, HARTFORD.

PREPARED FOR PUBLICATION AND ANNOTATED BY MARY K. TALCOTT.

I.

[It was announced in our October '97 and January '98 numbers, that the Sexton's List of Burials in the Center Church Burying Ground, Hartford, would be published in the QUARTERLY. This valuable list, as has been previously stated, is from a copy made by Dr. C. J. Hoadly, by whose kind permission we are enabled to use it. The remainder of the names will appear in subsequent numbers of this magazine.]

1749-50.
Feb. 22 Infant child of Joseph Shepard.
Mar. 24 The wife of Joseph Shepard.
1750.
April 4 John West.
  21 Abigail, daughter of Daniel Skinner, born Sept. 22, 1729.
Mar. 7 Jonathan Ashley [son of Jonathan and Sarah (Wadsworth) Ashley, b. Aug. 23, 1674].
June   Jonathan Shepard.
July 8 John Spencer.
  21 Sarah, dau. of Daniel Skinner [bapt. June 3, 1749].
  24 Justus Dickinson.
Aug. 5 Abigail, dau. of William Nichols [bapt. April 7, 1745].
  8 Anna, the wife of Ebenr Williamson [Anna Cadwell].
  8 Elizabeth Wyllys [b. July 15, 1705, dau. of Hezekiah and Elizabeth (Hobart) Wyllys].
  14 Maryan, infant dau. of Richard Edwards.
  19 Rebecca, dau. of William Cadwell.
  21 Andrew, son of Andrew Mumford.
  25 Thomas Wells [b. Oct. 16, 1690, son of Thomas and Mary (Blackleach) Welles].
Sept. 5 Widow Abigail Butler.
  5 Sarah, the wife of Thomas Burr [dau. of Thomas Wadsworth].
  11 John Barnard.
  15 Elisabeth, wife of Daniel Miles.
  15 Elisabeth, wife of Jonathan Taylor.
  25 Widow Lydia Dodd [dau. of Lam-

orock and Lydia (Smith) Flower, b. Mar. 22, 1686-7; mar. in 1705 Edward Dodd].
  25 William, son of Richard Goodman [bapt. Sept. 21].
Oct. 12 Mary, dau. of Samuel Flagg.
  16 Sarah Burr [dau. of Thomas and Sarah Burr, b. 1681].
Nov. 2 Daniel, son of the late Rev. Daniel Wadsworth [b. June 21, 1741].
  4 Infant dau. of Daniel Wadsworth.
  6 Anna, wife of Thomas Andross.
  8 Catherine, dau. of Widow Rachel Cadwell.
Dec. 18 Abigail, wife of Capt. Jabez Talcott (?).
  20 Widow Hannah Collyer.
  27 Ruth, dau. of the late Rev. Daniel Wadsworth [b. July 1, 1746].

1750-51.
Jan. 9 Normand, son of Roderick Morrison.
  20 Susanna, dau. of Roderick Morrison.
Mar. 28 Infant dau. of Capt. John Knowles.
1751.
May 26 Moses Ensign.
June 14 Elijah Cadwell.
  23 Nehemiah Cadwell [son of Edward and Deborah (Bunes) Cadwell, b. April 8, 1711].
July 7 James, son of Caleb Bull [b. Sept. 29, 1750].
  29 Abigail, wife of Dan'l Wadsworth.
Aug. 10 Hezekiah, son of Capt. Daniel Goodwin [bapt. Aug. 20, 1750].

CENTER CHURCH BURYING GROUND, HARTFORD. 181

Sept. 2 William, son of Col. Samuel Talcott [bapt. Dec. 18, 1743].
3 Edward Cadwell [son of Edward and Elizabeth Cadwell, b. Sept. 24, 1681].
4 Mary, dau. of Elijah Cadwell.
5 Hannah, wife of Charles Kelsey.
9 James, son of Col. Samuel Talcott [bapt. Sept. 1, 1745].
9 Daniel, son of Roderick Morrison.
Oct. 2 James McLeroy [formerly of Northampton; married Dec. 12, 1736, Helena, dau. of Cyprian Nichols].
31 Christian Farnsworth.
Nov. 26 John, son of John McNight.
Dec. 9 Jonathan Taylor.
1751-52.
Feb. 26 Elizabeth, daughter of William Skinner.
29 Christian Mix [dau. of Rev. Stephen and Mary (Stoddard) Mix of Wethersfield].
1752.
April 14 Abigail, dau. of Capt. William Nichols [bapt. April 7, 1751].
24 James, son of Ezekiel Ashley.
July 14 Infant child of Jonathan Watson, Jr.
Aug. 27 Thomas Ensign.
Sept. 25 Widow Mary Carter.

RECORD OF BURIALS IN THE OLD YARD FROM 1752 TO FEB. 24, 1801, COLLATED WITH THE RECORD OF THE FIRST CHURCH DOWN TO 1771.

1752.
Oct. 22 A child of Mr. Burlison (named Charles).
Nov. 12 Abigail, dau. of Sam'l Farnsworth.
17 Widow Warren.
26 John, child of John Knowles.
28 Husband of Mary Olive.
Dec. — Child of Daniel Marsh.
23 Mrs. Mary Shepard, aged 90.
— Mr. Steele.
1753.
Jan. 19 William Pratt [son of John and Hannah (Sanford) Pratt].
— Child of Thomas Seymour.
Feb. 8 Child of William Nichols (infant).
14 Child of John McKnight (Robert).
April 28 Sarah Marshall.
29 One of the family of Sarah Marshall.
May 11 Jno. Simons, son to the wife of Sam'l Weed.
— A child of the wife of John Weed.
June 10 Child of Caleb Binton.
30 The mother of Ozias Pratt [Hannah Norton of Farmington, widow of John Pratt, Jr.].

July 23 Child of Samuel Drake.
24 Mr. Jonathan Olcott [son of Thomas and Hannah (Barnard) Olcott; bapt. Dec. 29, 1695].
Aug. 6 Anna Hosmer [Ann Prentiss, wife of Capt. Thomas Hosmer; mar. Dec. 24, 1700].
14 Child of John Lawrence (Margaret, infant).
25 Mary Austin, wife of John Austin, aged 76. [Mary, dau. of Nathaniel Stanley, b. Oct. 8, 1677; mar. 1st, Nathaniel Hooker; 2d, in 1713, John Austin].
Sept. 4 Child of Jonathan Seymour.
4 Two children of John Condry (Charles and George).
19 Child of David Bull (Lovina).
21 A child of Elisha Pratt (Levi).
22 Child of Widow Mary Watrous.
27 Child of John Skinner, Jr. (infant).
Oct. 3 Child of Aaron Bull.
22 Child of John Watson, Jr.
28 Child of Doct Neal McLean (Catherine).
28 Child of Sam'l Wadsworth (George).
28 Wife of Joseph Holtom [Abigail Hastings, prob. dau. of Benjamin Hastings of Hatfield].
Dec. 1 Joseph Hartee (Hartoppey), stranger at house of Dav. Bull.
13 Child of Elisha Butler (infant).
14 The husband of Hannah Knowles [Capt. John Knowles, b. in Eastham, Mass., April, 1692].
1754.
Jan. 2 Mrs. Abigail Woodbridge [Abigail Warren, born in Boston, May 10, 1676, dau. of John Warren].
7 The husband of Amy Gross [Samuel, son of Josiah and Susannah (Howard) Gross, born Jan. 24, 1719-20].
7 Child of Roderick Morrison (Susannah).
8 Rebecca Bigelow [dau. of Jonathan and Mabel (Edwards) Bigelow, bapt. Dec. 5, 1708], aged 44.
— Mary, dau. of Lemuel Marsh, dec'd, and Bathsheba, his wife.
15 Child of Isaac Sheldon.
17 Child of John Condrey (Charles).
Mar. 29 Joseph Ashley [son of Jonathan and Sarah (Wadsworth) Ashley, born about 1677].
May 7 Anna Collier [dau. of Capt. Hez.].
15 Mrs. Seymour [Elizabeth, wife of John Seymour and dau. of Lieut.

LIST OF BURIALS,

Robert Webster, m. Dec. 19, 1693].
16 Josiah Bigelow [son of Joseph and Mary (Spencer) Bigelow, b. Jan. 3, 1726].
June 14 James Ensign [son of David and Mehitabel (Gunn) Ensign, aged 88.
21 Child of Clark Bets Jeriden.
July 8 Wife of John Barnard.
30 Sarah Hosmer [dau. Capt. Thomas and Ann (Prentiss) Hosmer, b. Sept. 7, 1707].
Sept. 13 Child of Edward Cadwell (Ruth). Died Sept. 12, Thomas Andross.
22 Susannah Andross, aged 83.
Dec. 15 Benjamin Richards.
28 Child Widow Jerusha Brace.
1755.
Jan. 1 Child of Joseph Shepard, Jr. (Elizabeth).
3 Nathaniel Skinner.
14 Dr. Roderick Morrison [brother of Dr. Normand Morrison, married Jan. 16, 1744-5, Susannah Gross].
16 Jonathan Butler, aged 77 [son of Samuel and Elizabeth].
16 Isaac Seymour [born Oct. 10, 1723, son of John and Lydia (Mason) Seymour].
— Child of Ebenezer Burlison (Charity, dau.).
Feb. 14 Child of John Thomas (infant).
21 Child of Stephen Turner (John, infant).
27 Son of Capt. Aaron Bull.
Mar. 29 Stephen Brace (the aged) [son of Stephen Brace, Sr.].
April 7 Child of Abijah Clark (Lucy, infant).
23 Wife of Dr. Neal McLean (Hannah Stillman) aged 52, formerly wife of the first John Caldwell, mar. Dr. McLean, January 5, 1737].
May 12 Moses Benton [son of Samuel Benton, b. April 26, 1702].
13 Caleb Bull [son of Joseph and Sarah (Manning) Bull, b. Feb. 1, 1679].
14 Father of Gideon Merrills [Wilterton Merrills, b. June 28, 1675, son of John and Sarah (Watson) Merrills].
15 Child of Elisha Butler (infant dau.)
23 Child of Nathaniel Pease [infant dau.).
— Dill Rament:

July 16 Widow Hannah Olcott, aged 93 [dau. of Bartholomew Barnard and widow of Thomas Olcott, mar. Nov. 11, 1695].
Aug. 1 Child of Jonathan Seymour, Jr.
19 Col. Nathaniel Stanley [son of Nathaniel and Sarah (Boosey) Stanley, b. July 9, 1683; treasurer of the Colony of Connecticut, 1749-1755; Lieut.-Col. of First Regiment, 1739, and later; Assistant, 1725-1749].
Sept. 17 Child of Rachel Collyer.
19 Child of Jonathan Bigelow.
21 Child of Zachariah Seymour. Died Nov. 9; Child of Col. Samuel Talcott [Elizabeth, bapt. Oct. 5, 1746].
Nov. 21 Child of Samuel Farnsworth.
Dec. 2 Mother of Samuel Howard [Susannah, dau. of Thomas and Susannah (Bull) Bunce].
12 Wife of Joseph Day (Deborah Andrus).
— Father of Caleb Turner.
14 Jerusha Seymour [dau. of Thomas and Mary (Watson) Seymour, bapt. 2d ch., Dec. 29, 1723].
28 Daughter of the widow of Amy Pratt (Esther).
1756.
Jan. 3 Capt. Cyprian Nichols [Aged 84; son of Cyprian Nichols, who came to Hartford in 1664 from Witham, Co. Essex, England].
6 Child of Geo. Smith (Martha).
19 Hannah Shepard.
23 Child of John Sheldon (Samuel).
Feb. 15 Child of James Shepard (infant).
17 The widow Mary N., mother of Lieut. James Nichols [Mary, dau. of Samuel and Mary (Richards) Spencer; mar. May 24, 1705] (Cyprian Nichols' wife), 75.
20 Child of Hezekiah Wadsworth (Hezekiah).
21 Thomas Warren.
29 Two children of John Cole 2d.
April 5 Wife of Ebenezer Balch.
May 11 George Masters.
14 Child of Daniel Brace, Jr. (James, infant).
21 Child of Samuel Weed (Jerusha).
July 2 Child of Aaron Hopkins (infant).
6 Child of John Jones (Joseph, infant).
9 Child of Thomas Warren.
31 Two children Benjamin Bigelow

CENTER CHURCH BURYING GROUND, HARTFORD. 183

	(Jonas, d. July 30; Lovina, d. Aug. 3). The aged Widow Elizabeth G.		drowned with Dr. Langrell].
		June 16	Jonathan Ensign.
		16	Dr. Thomas Langrell 2d [b. Mar. 6, 1727-8; Harvard College, 1751; an apothecary in Hartford].
	16 Remember Grandmother Gilbert was buried.		
Sept.	3 Wife of John Benton.	24	A French Woman Interred at the expense of the Town of Hartford.
	7 Son of Daniel Brace (Timothy).		
	16 Aaron Hopkins (son of Thomas and Mary (Beckley) Hopkins, b. July 14, 1720].	Aug. 2	John Brooker of Saybrook, suddenly in a fit.
Oct.	3 Child of Capt. John Lawrence (Marian).	25	Black Betsey, Indian woman, buried at her own expense.
	3 Timothy Andrus.	Sept. 7	Mr. William Smith of Haddam, interred at expense of Eliza Wadsworth.
	11 Child of Jared Bunce (Huldah, infant).		
	13 Dr. Thomas Hooker [aged 64; son of Rev. Samuel and Mary (Willett) Hooker of Farmington].	9	Gideon Merrills [son of Wilterton Merrills].
		Oct. 20	Child of Ebenezer Catlin (Lewis).
	22 Child of John Watson, Jr. (Elizabeth, infant).	Nov. 10	Wife of David Seymour (Mary). [She was the dau. of Peter Harris of New London, and mar. D. S., Oct. 20, 1757; she d. of small pox, which she took at New London.]
	Child of Daniel Hinsdale.		
Dec.	26 Phebe Booth, aged 73.		
	29 The husband of Hannah Watson (John).		
1757.		14	Wife of Daniel Bigelow (Abigail).
Jan.	Child of John Lord (Daniel, infant).	20	Child of John Filley (Lucretia).
	26 Child of Ebenezer Burleson (Hezekiah, infant).	Dec. 3	Child of John Barnot, Jr.
		1758.	
Feb.	5 Child of Daniel Bigelow (Rachael).	Jan. 15	Joseph Morris of Coventry. Interred at the expense of Peletiah Pierce.
	5 Reuben Coe.		
	12 Fuller, who died in prison. "The aged." He belonged to Colchester.	18	Child of Daniel Sheldon.
		25	Grace Whaples.
Mar.	11 Old Robin.	Feb. 19	Mrs. Phelps (the Widow Sarah). Interred at expense of Timothy Phelps, Jr. Aged 96. [Dau. of John Pratt, born 1668; mar. Timothy Phelps, Nov. 13, 1690.]
April	6 Ebenezer Williamson [b. in Barnstable, Mass., April 4, 1697, son of Lieut. Caleb and Mary (Cobb) Williamson).		
	7 Child of Ozias Goodwin, Jr. (Job, infant).	Mar. 1	Wife of Nathaniel Seymour [Mary, dau. of Capt. Thomas and Ruth (Norton) Seymour, b. Nov. 3, 1703].
May	2 Samuel Flagg. [He kept Flagg's Tavern, where the Universalist Church now stands.]		
		14	Child of Moses Dickinson (infant).
	23 Child of Betzy, Indian.	26	Wife of Joseph Bunce.
	25 Wife of John Coleman (Deborah) aged 24. [Deborah, dau. of John and Deborah (Youngs) Ledyard, bapt. July 9, 1732].	Feb. 7	Joseph Wadsworth, Jr. [son of Joseph and Joanna (Hovey) Wadsworth], born 1717.
		May 6	The Mother of John Sheldon (the aged widow Elizabeth S). 89.
	29 Child of Samuel Wadsworth (Samuel, infant).	30	Child of Anna Barret.
	30 Child of John Skinner (infant son d. soon after birth).	June 2	Child of Jonathan Wells.
		9	Dorcas Brownson.
June	11 Child of Samuel Drake (Martha, infant).	18	The wife of Aaron Bull
		July 11	Child of John Skinner, Jr. (d. soon after birth).
	16 A Drowned Man—grave dug at expense of Benjamin Bigelow. [Wm. Harpy of Harvard, Mass.,	11	Stephen Skinner [son of Joseph and Elizabeth (Olmsted) Skinner; bapt. Mar. 11, 1715].

LIST OF BURIALS,

Sept. 20 Child of Thomas Ensign (Thomas).
Sept. 10 A Sister of Benjamin Bigelow (Lydia Thomas). [Probably sister of his wife, Levinah Thomas, who was b. in Marlboro, Mass.]
Oct. 3 John Butler, Jr.
William Day, Jr., died in the army. [Son of William and Elizabeth (Andrus) Day.]
6 Daughter of Joseph Bigelow.
9 Child of Jared Bunce (Jared).
9 Child of James Mookler (infant, still born).
11 Child of Zachariah Seymour.
11 Child of Uriah Shepard (Nathaniel).
17 Child of Elisha Bigelow (Normand).
24 Child of Elisha Bigelow (Samuel).
24 Child of Richard Goodman (Sarah).
25 Child of Joseph Hosmer.
31 Child of Alexander, the Frenchman.
Nov. 4 Widow Mary Richards, aged 90.
6 John Caldwell (Capt.). [Son of John Caldwell, who came to Hartford about 1725, from Beith, in North Britain; bapt. Jan. 30, 1757.]
9 Child of Lieut. Richard Goodman (Hezekiah).
13 Child of Alexander, the Frenchman.
Dec. 20 Child of Matthew Webster.
1759.
Jan. 16 Child of Thomas Noble.
26 Child of Samuel Shepard.
27 Child of Lieut. Richard Goodman (Huldah). [Bapt. July 22, 1753.]
Feb. 23 Child of Samuel Shepard (Hannah).
24 Child of Capt. John Lawrence (Edward).
28 Child of Robert Sanford (infant dau. still born).
March 6 Stephen Watson.
7 The Wife of Thomas Hopkins [Mary, dau. of Nathaniel Beckley of Wethersfield; born 1696].
13 The Wife of Robert Sanford (Huldah).
14 Two Children of Caleb Bull in one grave.
17 Child of Thos. Hopkins (still born).
17 Child of Lieut. Hezekiah Marsh (infant).
26 The Wife of Zachariah Seymour [Sarah, dau. of Jonathan and Dorothy (Mygatt) Steele].
28 Child of James Shepard (Epaphras, infant).
30 The Wife of Thomas Hopkins, Jr. (Anne).
April 2 Widow Rachel Cook ("the aged"). [mar. Oct. 8, 1705, Joseph Cook, dau. of Samuel and Sarah (Richards) Spencer, Jr.]
2 James Barnot, a son of John Barnot.
April 19 Child of Widow Elizabeth Wadsworth (Elizabeth, infant).
27 Ziba Warren, son of Thomas Warren.
May 12 Maynard Day [son of John and Sarah (Maynard) Day].
22 Gideon Thompson, Esq.
July 3 Child of Col. George Wyllys (George). [Bapt. Dec. 19, 1756.]
14 Child of Jonathan Olcott (Anna). [Born 1754.]
23 Uriah Shepard.
Aug. 2 Child of Thomas Burr, Jr. (Thomas).
10 Child of Richard Seymour.
14 Child of Elijah Clapp.
24 Child of John Skinner (infant).
27 Child of Charles Kelsey, Jr. (Huldah).
29 Daughter of Daniel Butler (Thankfull).
— John, son of Richard Edwards and Mary Butler, his wife [b. July 31, 1757].
31 Isaac, son of Isaac Bunce [bapt. Oct. 1, 1758].
Sept. 9 Anna, daughter of Daniel Butler.
10 Child of Joseph Barrett.
13 Child of Moses Taylor.
13 Child of Benjamin Watrous.
14 Child of John Sheldon (Samuel).
15 Child of Edward Dodd (Lydia).
23 Child of Edward White (Edward).
30 Child of Persis Bunce.
Oct. 8 Son of Richard Seymour.
12 Wife of Richard Seymour [Elizabeth, dau. of Joseph and Joanna (Hovey) Wadsworth.
Nov. 17 Child of Levi Jones (Mille).
26 Child of Eunice Cross.
Dec. 6 John Sperry, belonging to New Haven.
6 A Soldier who died at the Widow Pratt's.
6 Prudence Ayres, a child interred at the expense of John Barnot, Jr.
1760.
Jan. 8 Elijah Cadwell.
19 Child of Widow Catherine Bruce.
24 Child of John Pantry Goodwin (Hezekiah). [Bapt. Feb. 13, 1757.]
Feb. 4 Child of Lieut. Richard Goodman

CENTER CHURCH BURYING GROUND, HARTFORD. 185

		(Sarah). [Bapt. Dec. 30, 1759.]
	28	Child of John Lord (infant).
April	3	Child of John Thomas (Rachael, died before baptism).
	14	Hezekiah Merrills [son of Deacon Daniel and Susanna (Pratt) Merrill].
	21	Child of Isaac Bunce (infant son, still born).
May	21	Abigail Gilbert.
	31	Caleb Church [son of John and Abigail (Cadwell) Church, b. 1703].
July	4	Child of John Sheldon (still born).
	7	Widow Olcott (the aged widow Sarah). [Dau. of Sergt. John and Mary (Barnard) Bunce, bapt. Jan. 1, 1681-2.]
	13	Mary Burkett (dau. of Uriah).
	28	The mother of Gideon Bunce [Amy, widow of Joseph Bunce].
Aug.	10	Mary Ann, dau. of Capt. John Lawrence.
Sept.	8	John Cole.
	5	Child of Caleb Bull (Martha). [Born Feb. 27, 1760].
	4	Abigail, wife of Capt. Timo Phelps.
Oct.	7	Child of James Ensign.
	25	Abigail Thornton.
Nov.	10	Child of Jacob Seymour (Abigail, d. before baptism).
	10	The Mother of Samuel Bunce [Brace?] (the aged widow Sarah Brace).
	11	Child of Thomas Ensign (Elizabeth).
	17	Richard Shaw.
Dec.	1	Joseph Buckingham, Esq. [b. Aug. 7, 1703, son of Rev. Thomas and Ann (Foster) Buckingham; Yale College 1723].
	2	Lieut. Samuel Catlin (the aged). [Son of John and Mary (Marshall) Catlin, born Nov. 4, 1672.]
	4	Thomas Mygatt. Died with small pox. [Son of Zebulon and Dorothy (Waters) Mygatt, born 1730.]
	7	George Steele. Died with small pox.
	13	William Powell [mar. Elizabeth, dau. of Cyprian and Helena (Talcott) Nichols].
	19	Persis Bunce. Died with small pox.
	22	Child of Joseph Rogers (infant).
	27	Widow Hannah Butler (the aged.)
1761.		
Jan.	4	John Nichols ("the aged").
	4	Child of Samuel Day (infant).

	7	A son of Dr. Norman Morrison died by small pox (Allan.). [Buried in St. Paul's churchyard, then a part of Dr. Morrison's homestead]
	9	Phineas Foster. Died with small pox.
	27	Mrs Sarah Bunce ("the aged widow"). [Sarah, dau. of Zechariah Sandford, widow of Jonathan Bunce.]
	31	The Wife of Mr. David Bull (Mary).
	31	The Widow Sarah Grover. Died with small pox.
Feb.	7	Johanna Merrill. Died with small pox.
	12	Widow Jerusha Brace.
	14	Ensign Nathaniel Seymour [born Nov. 17, 1704; son of John and Elizabeth (Webster) Seymour].
March	1	Richard Wallis.
	8	Dositheus Humphrey. Died with small pox. [Son of Dositheus and Anne (Griswold) Humphrey; born Nov. 27, 1727.]
April	4	The Wife of Jonathan Burket Sarah Burket).
	6	Daughter of Stephen Turner (Susanna).
	10	Dr. Norman Morrison (d. small pox). [Buried in St. Paul's churchyard, near his son Allan.]
	17	Child of Samuel Farnsworth.
	18	Child of James Shepard.
	20	Col. Nathan Payson.
May	4	Child of Mary Burke (Thomas).
June	9	Child of John Skinner (Susanna, infant).
	11	Child of Pelatiah Pierce (Samuel, infant).
	27	Child of Samuel Tilley (Walter).
July	16	Sister of Daniel Butler (Deborah).
	16	Child of Pelatiah Pierce (Anna, infant).
	—	Son of Stephen Turner (Stephen).
Aug.	28	Child of Jared Bunce (son, still born).
Sept.	4	Dr. Samuel Hooker.
	7	John Butler ("The aged Mr")
	15	John Hosmer [son of Capt. Thomas and Ann (Prentiss) Hosmer].
	16	Abigail Whaples.
	16	Child of Jonathan Taylor (Ann, infant).
	30	Child of Josiah Shepard.
Oct.	1	Child of Timothy Phelps, Jr. (Richard).

LIST OF BURIALS,

Nov. 2 Child of James Cadwell (Gurdon).
8 Thomas Burr ("The aged Mr.")
19 Child of Ezra Andross.
Dec. 14 Two infant children of Samuel Olcott (Samuel, James).

1762.
Jan. 1 Child of Capt. John Lawrence (Peggy).
14 Wife of James Shepard (Sarah).
18 Elisha Johnson of Colchester, died in Goal. Burial charged to Jared Bunce.
18 Child of David Shepard (David, infant).
22 Joseph Shepard.
Feb. 1 Evander Morrison (Revd. died Jan. 30th. [Brother of Dr. Norman Morrison; for a time minister at West Simsbury, now Canton.]
8 Wife of Joseph Wadsworth (Joanna). [Born about 1684; dau. of Lieut. Thomas and Sarah (Cook) Hovey of Hadley.]
12 Wife of Thomas Long (Helena) [Dau. of Cyprian and Helena (Talcott) Nichols, born 1701.]
26 Daniel Wadsworth (born 1720. [Son of Joseph and Joanna (Hovey) Wadsworth.
Mar. 15 Child of David Bull (infant).
April 13 William Baker, aged 84. [Son of John and Lydia (Baysy) Baker.]
17 Jonathan [Qu. John?] Carter (brother of Joshua.) (felo di se.)
June 3 Child of Joseph Hosmer.
28 Wife of George Olcott (Dorothy). [Dau. of Joseph and Elizabeth (Olmsted) Skinner; bapt. March 30, 1718.]
July 11 Widow Brameson. Intered at expense of Gideon Bunce. [Ahigail, dau. of Joseph and Amy Bunce; bapt. Mar. 28, 1731; mar. Patrick Bainingham.]
31 Child of Thomas Burr (Eunice).
Aug. 5 Child of Mary Burk.
9 Child of Daniel O'Lent ?
11 A brother of Jonathan Butler.
Sept. 13 Child of Phineas Cole (James).
15 Child of George Lord.
18 Child of Josiah Clark.
Oct. 2 Child of Samuel Watrous.
5 Wife of John Walker (Marion). [Dau. of Dr. Normand and Ann (Smith) Morrison; bapt. Mar. 26, 1738].
11 Wife of Thomas Sanford (Amy).

2 A Child of Peggy. Interred at expence of the Town. Infant child of Margaret Kelley.
13 The Mother of Col. George Wyllys (The aged Mrs. Elizabeth.) [Dau. of Rev. Jeremiah and Elizabeth (Whiting) Hobart of Haddam, Ct.]
Nov. 1 Child of John Skinner, Jr. (Charles) [Bapt. Oct. 17, 1762.]
15 Son of James Bunce.
24 Mrs. Grose Intered at expence of Daniel Sheldon. (The widow Susanna). [Dau. of Samuel and Susanna (Bunce) Howard; mar. Jonah Gross, Mar. 13, 1717-18.]
Dec. 4 Child of Abijah Clark (Mary, infant).
31 The following persons belonging to this Society died in the Army in the Summer past:
Ebenezer Burlison
Ebenezer Holmes
Edward Cadwell
Daniel Brace Jr.
—— Brace
Timothy Bigelow [son of Lieut. Timothy and Abigail (Olcott) Bigelow, born May 22, 1730, died at Charlestown, N. H. A private record states that he died in the army at Fort Stanwix in the summer of 1762.—Bigelow Gen., '87].

1763.
Jan. 25 Capt. Nathaniel Hooker [b. Oct. 5, 1710; Yale College, 1729; son of Nathaniel and Mary (Stanley) Hooker].
31 Widow Anna Morrison [Anna Allwood, born in England, widow of Dr. Norman Morrison, and formerly wife of Capt. John Smith, a sea captain who died on the voyage to Ireland about 1731].
Feb. 14 Mrs. Anna Hyde, widow. [Anne Basset, born about 1701; married April 24, 1722, Capt. William Hyde of Norwich.]
March 3 Child of Samuel Olcott (still born).
11 Child of Samuel Marsh (still born).
15 The Father of William Hooker.
April 7 Stephen Turner is Charg'd the Burial expences of Daughter Rachael's Child (still born).
May 16 Widow Mary Cole.
18 The Wife of Jared Bunce (Mary). [Dau. of Timothy and Mary (Mygatt) Stanley; bapt. June 2, 1735.]
23 Dositheus Humphrey [son of Na-

CENTER CHURCH BURYING GROUND, HARTFORD.

       thaniel and Agnes (Spencer) Humphrey, b. Dec. 4, 1709].
31 Mary Ellery. [Probably Mary, dau. of John and Mary (Austin) Ellery, b. April 28, 1742.]
June 14 The Wife of Benjamin Hopkins (Rachael). [Bapt. Sept. 4, 1737; dau. of Eliphalet and Katherine (Marshfield) Steele.]
    23 Child of George Lord (infant).
    26 James Curry.
    27 Child of Thomas Hopkins, Jr. (Mary, infant).
Aug. 6 Thomas Collyer [b. in 1730, son of Abel and Rachel Collyer].
    18 Josiah Shepard.
    28 Mary Hooker Daught Eunice [dau. of Capt. Nathaniel and Eunice (Talcott) Hooker].
Sept. 22 Child of Mehitabel Shepard.
    25 Child of John Skinner, Jr. (infant).
Oct. 2 Child of James Taylor.
    8 Child of Ebenezer Barnard (Daniel).
    19 Child of Moses Kellogg (Jerusha).
    12 Joseph Warrin.
    23 Child of Charles Kelsey Jr. (Sarah).
Nov. 8 Samuel Burr ("The aged"). [Son of Samuel and Mercy Burr; born May 4, 1697.]
    17 The Mother of Joseph Wheeler.
    22 Lieut. Richard Goodman [b. Nov. 4, 1704, son of Richard and Abigail (Pantry) Goodman].
Dec. 10 Child of Jonathan Easton (Mary).
    16 Hezekiah Collyer (Capt.) [Born Mar. 22, 1707, son of Joseph and Sarah (Forbes) Collier.]
    26 Hannah Burr ("The aged").

1764.
Jan. 10 The Wife of James Sutor (Mary).
    29 Child of Moses Shepard (Moses).
Feb. 10 Ebenezer Benton, Jr.
    18 Child of Silas Andrus (infant).
March 1 Child of Timothy Dodd (Mary, infant).
    5 Wife of Timothy Dodd (Abigail).
    6 Benjamin Hopkins [bapt. May 11, 1734; son of Thomas and Mary (Beckley) Hopkins].
    11 Child of John Ellery.
    11 Wife of John Joy (Sarah).
    23 Catherine, infant dau. of Benjamin Hopkins, died.
    24 Benjamin('s) Child Intered at Expence of Moses Hopkins.
April 8 Child of Joseph Sheldon.
    16 John Ellery [b. April 17, 1738; son of John and Mary (Austin) Ellery].
    18 Child of Elisha Bigelow (Edward).
    23 Child of Mahitabel Shepard.
May 3 Thomas Hudson.
    9 Wife of James Taylor.
    11 Hannah Ensign (Widow) [of Thomas Ensign].
    16 Child of John Cook, Jr. (John, infant).
June 6 Robert Nevins.
    10 Child of John Walker (infant, unbapt.).
    16 Wife of Elisha Andrus (Deborah).
    18 Thomas Hopkins [son of Stephen and Sarah (Judd) Hopkins, born 1692].
July 8 Collin Mc.
    14 Wife of John Thomas.
Aug. 2 Child of Thomas Sloan (Susannah).
    11 Child of Ezra Corning (Mary, infant).
    20 Widow Hannah Bigelow [born May 19, 1738, at Norwich; dau. of William and Anne (Basset) Hyde].
    24 Wife of Cyprian Powell.
Sept. 17 Child of John Skinner, Jr. (infant).
    28 The Mother of Zebulon Spencer, Jr. (aged widow Sarah).
Oct. 5 Mrs. Anna Burnham or Buckingham. [Ann Foster, dau. of Rev. Isaac and Mabel (Wyllys) Foster, wife, first of Rev. Thomas Buckingham, second of Rev. William Burnham of Kensington; born in 1739, dau. of Hon. Daniel and Sarah (Hooker) Edwards.]
    12 The wife of George Lord (Sarah).

1765.
Jan. 14 Mary Hooker.
    21 Still born dau. of Elisha Wadsworth.
Feb. 5 Zebulon Seymour [b. May 14, 1708, son of John and Elizabeth (Webster) Seymour].
    10 Mary Burr Intered at Expence of Town.
    20 Lorenzo Gross [son of Jonah and Susanna (Howard) Gross, bapt. Dec. 14, 1729].
    21 Child of Lieut. John Cole.
    32 Child of Ebenezer Barnard (Chas.)
March 6 Child of Jonathan Seymour, Jr.
April 5 [Dr.] Jonathan Bull [son of Major Jonathan and Sarah (Whiting) Bull, b. July 14, 1696].

[To be continued.]

MAIN STREET, ELLINGTON

ELLINGTON

BY ALICE E. PINNEY.

Ellington was originally a part of the ancient town of Windsor, and the little collection of farms around the Great Marsh, or, as the Indians called it, Weaxskashuck, was known as Windsor Goshen. In early times an idea was prevalent that the land around the Great Marsh in the valley was unhealthy, and, in consequence, the first settlers from Windsor passed by it to the hills beyond. At that time the marsh consisted of a large sheet of water surrounded by woods and underbrush. It has since been ditched and drained, the underbrush cleared away, and the greater part of it improved into good tillable land and pastures.

There is a belief among geologists that Ellington valley is an ancient lake bed, and that the marsh is all that is left of a prehistoric lake. This may account for the fertility of the soil, the smooth level sweep of land all over the valley, and the absence of rocks and stones. That it was a favorite resort of the Indians is proven by finding numberless Indian relics, such as arrow and spear heads, pestles, gouges, and other stone implements in the fields near by.

The earliest purchase of land within the limits of Ellington was made in 1671 by Thomas and Nathaniel Bissell of an Indian named Nearawonuck. The first resident was Samuel Pinney (son of Humphrey Pinney, the emigrant), who had for several years been engaged in surveying lands east of the Connecticut river. He purchased of the Indians in 1717 a tract of land one and a half miles from east to west by one mile from north to south in the southwestern part of the town, including the greater part of what has since been known as Pinney street and the village of Windermere. A part of this tract is still in the hands of his descendants, including the spot where Samuel Pinney built the first log house, and it is the only tract of land in the town which has never been conveyed by deed away from the descendants of the original holder. No title can be found but the Indian title to Samuel Pinney.

In 1768 all the territory lying east of the Connecticut river was made a town distinct from Windsor and became known as East Windsor, while in 1786 Ellington had so increased in population that it was set apart as a town by itself and was known as Elenton, the name receiving its present spelling at a later date.

Some claim that the name was originally Ellington, since the town was an "ell" or addition to the towns of Windsor and East Windsor. Others suppose the town to have taken its name from a long, narrow strip of land extending to the eastward. This narrow strip of land was formed before Ellington was set apart as a town. At the time when the boundary line between the colonies of Connecticut and Massachusetts was fixed, 7,259 acres of land were taken from the old town of Monson and given to the towns of Enfield and Suffield.

The General Assembly of Connecticut agreed to give to the town of Monson, as an equivalent for what had been taken from it, certain lands in the northeast corner of East Windsor, and James Wadsworth and John Hall in 1713 laid out 8,000 acres for this purpose, leaving only the long narrow ell extending to the Willimantic river, from which the town doubtless derived its name.

Governor Wadsworth's descendants afterwards settled in the northeastern part of the town. The old Wadsworth homestead, one of the oldest houses in Ellington, is still standing and is owned by the descendants of the builder. Though it may not be the oldest house in Ellington, it is the only one that can prove its age, for it has a white stone tablet set in the front of the old chimney bearing the date of its erection, 1783, and the Wadsworth initials. The attic is rich in relics. Specially worthy of mention are a mirror made in 1749, an old musket carried by the present owner's grandfather at the storming of Quebec in the French and Indian War, and a bronze powder flask. A beautiful white stone platter, brought from Germany, was a portion of the wedding dowry of a Mrs. Wadsworth of a hundred years ago.

A stone in the old Ellington cemetery marks the resting place of a certain "Dr. Joseph B. Wadsworth who departed this Life March ye 12, A. D. 1784 in ye 37th Year of his age." He graduated from Yale College in 1766, and was a surgeon in the Revolutionary Army. He was a native of Hartford, and subsequently settled about a mile northeast of Ellington Meeting House. He was described, as the handsomest and most polished gentleman of that day, a peculiar elegance and neatness of taste and style being a marked characteristic. He wore a three-cornered hat, scarlet coat, white or yellow vest and breeches and topped boots, a costume peculiar to those who occupied a high rank in society.

CONGREGATIONAL CHURCH, ELLINGTON.

Ellington cemetery was set apart early in 1700. The first deaths recorded in Ellington were those of Lieut. John Ellsworth in 1720, who was buried in Windsor, and of "Isibel Pinye," believed to have been an infant daughter of Samuel Pinney, the first settler.

Ellington cemetery is described as being at that time a forest, and a tree was cut down to make room for the first grave. This fixed the place for a burying ground. Here lie two of Ellington's early pastors, namely, the Rev. Seth Norton, who died in 1762, and the Rev. John Bliss, who died in 1790. Ellington's first pastor, the Rev. John McKinstrey, who died in 1754 was buried in a separate lot laid out for the purpose back of the first church. This lot, protected by a stout iron fence, has served for a burial place for his descendants from that time.

THE MCKINSTREY CEMETERY.

In the year 1725 the church at Windsor voted that the people of Ellington should be exempt from paying a minister's tax, if they would provide preaching for themselves. So, in 1726, the town granted thirty acres for a minister's home lot and forty acres in the "equivalent." There were only a few families in the parish and they were so poor that two or three years elapsed before any one came to preach for them. In 1730 there were only eleven families, but a year later they hired the Rev. John McKinstrey, a graduate of Edinburgh University. In 1733 they settled him

THE BROCKWAY HOUSE.

for £40 a year and his fire wood. He was the ancestor of the family in Ellington bearing the name. For some reason the people were still taxed by the church at Windsor, and in 1734 they petitioned the Assembly for exemption from these taxes. This was granted, and in 1735 Ellington was set apart as a separate parish. It was still difficult to raise the salary, though Mr. McKinstrey gave the people credit for being more benevolent than able.

In 1736 they voted to build a meeting-house 45 feet long by 35 feet broad, with posts 20 feet high. The location was at the fork of the roads, west of the park of the present day and near the elms. The house, which faced the east, was not plastered, but was ceiled up to the rafters. It was unfinished overhead and had neither bell nor stove. A few of the wealthiest parishioners were the happy possessors of foot-stoves, but the rest of the congregation had to endure the cold as best they could. This house stood until the new one was built in 1804.

JUDGE SAMUEL PINNEY.

The Rev. John McKinstrey resigned some time before his death, in 1754. For several years following the Revolutionary War the people were very poor and were unable to pay a settled minister. So, for a time they "candidated," paying the candidates in produce. In 1791 they again settled a minister, who remained eight years, until the coming of Rev. Diodate Brockway, Ellington's most celebrated and best beloved pastor.

The Rev. Diodate Brockway was ordained in 1799, his father preaching the ordination sermon; and, as the church was small, the services took place on the green before the church, the steps serving as a pulpit. He remained an active pastor thirty years, but was connected with the church fifty years, during which time it was very prosperous.

In 1804 a new church was built costing about $7,000, Col. Samuel Belcher, a noted builder of Hartford, being the contractor. It stood on the park, opposite the church of the present day. During the building of the church, Mr. Brockway, in ascending the cupola, fell a distance of sixty-five feet and was quite seriously injured. In consequence he was always lame, and he was forced to preach the dedication sermon, in 1806, sitting in a chair. In 1813 he felt obliged to resign because his salary would not support him. As he was greatly beloved, his salary was raised; but when, four years later, the hard times came, he relinquished a part of it. This was an example of the manner in which he and his people shared together their prosperity and adversity. He was heard

THE PINNEY HOMESTEAD.

to say that his marriage fees were invariably according to the circumstances of the parties. The largest fee he ever received was twenty dollars, and the smallest an old-time twenty-cent piece, while at times he performed the ceremony for nothing. He died in 1849, having had charge of the church, with the aid of colleagues, until five years before his death.

FRANKLIN HOUSE.

The present Congregational church which stands opposite the park was dedicated August 26, 1868, after which the old church of 1804 was taken down and removed to Rockville. There it serves as an opera house, the lower story being occupied by the Rockville *Journal*. The first deacon of the Ellington church, Isaac Davis, was chosen before the church was fairly organized.

Although Ellington was not incorporated as a town at the time of the Revolution, yet she did her part nobly in sending men to the war. Among the most noted of these was Lieut. Eleazer Pinney, son of Capt. Benjamin

Pinney and grandson of Samuel Pinney. He was twenty-three years old at the beginning of the war. In the campaign against Burgoyne he was sergeant in a corps of Connecticut militia that distinguished itself. He took part in the battles of Stillwater and Saratoga. He was one of the division that stormed Burgoyne's camp and he witnessed the surrender. Other soldiers from Ellington were Lemuel Pinney, Jonathan Buckland, Sr., Jonathan Button, Wareham Foster, Daniel Sanger, Paul Hamilton, and Daniel Pierson who not only served as a volunteer but also furnished a man for the regular army at his own expense. Daniel Pierson and Samuel, his brother, took part in the Battle of

ELLINGTON'S FIRST TAVERN.

Long Island, and were with Washington in the retreat that followed. Dr. Joseph Kingsbury served as surgeon from Ellington, while Ebenezer Nash, one of the early settlers, was a member of the Constitutional Convention of 1787.

The first merchant within the limits of what afterwards became the town of Ellington is said to have been a Mr. McLean, who kept a store on the old road formerly leading to Job's Hill, west of the old Daniel Warner place, in the northern part of the town. This appears at that time to have been a central location, for it is also recorded that the first blacksmith shop was located about eighty rods northeast of the same house. John Hall, Sr., was probably Mr. McLean's successor as merchant, and is reported to have become very wealthy. He used to travel to and from Boston on horseback, and much of his stock was brought from that city in the ponderous saddle bags which he carried.

He died at the beginning of the present century, and his son, John Hall, Jr., the founder of the old High School, inherited much of his wealth.

The first tavern in Ellington, built about 1790, is still standing, and is now occupied as a farmhouse by Mr. Fenlon Dow. A few years later, a hotel was kept at the house long known as the Horace Chapman place on the east street. It was in a good location, on the old stage road from Vernon to Somers, at its junction with one of the first surveyed roads leading from Ellington to Tolland. The first proprietor of this hotel was Wareham Foster, an old Revolutionary hero, and his successor was Gordon Smith of Enfield. Gordon Smith sold the property to John Chapman, who continued to keep the hotel for some time, but eventually turned it into a farmhouse.

In 1823 the present hotel was built and was named the Franklin House, its first proprietor being William Ransom of Vernon. It is situated in the center

THE GREEN, SHOWING SITE OF SECOND CHURCH EDIFICE.

of the main street instead of on the stage turnpike, and doubtless did a rival business to the hotel on the corner. This house is still used as a hotel, and the old sign bearing the portrait of Benjamin Franklin still swings from the large elm before the door.

About the beginning of the present century the business of the town changed its location again to a point on the old turnpike a mile east of the present center, near the junction with the road leading to Stafford, where a thriving store was kept in an old red gambrel-roofed house by Dr. James

Steele of Tolland. Although he bore the professional title of doctor, he is recorded as being a merchant and a farmer. He died in 1819. Lucius Chapman is said to have kept the store from 1825 until 1856, when he sold out and went West and the place was abandoned for store purposes.

Early in 1829 the famous Ellington High School was built by the Hon. John Hall. He was not only the founder of the school, but he was also its first principal, and he may justly be termed the pioneer educator of Tolland County. The school was first started in a small one-story building, which was afterward sold and moved to Pinney street at the time of the erection of what afterwards became the famous High School. This second building soon became famous as a high grade boarding and day school. After the death of Dr. Hall it changed hands several times, and finally, after standing vacant for several years, was destroyed by fire in 1875.

Ellington in its primitive days was noted for its extensive rye fields, which supplied the neighboring distilleries with grain, a single lot containing sometimes as much as a hundred acres, and the pastures were covered with flocks of sheep and herds of cattle. But times have changed and the former rye fields now yield crops of tobacco, corn, potatoes and fruit, until, as a recent historian says, "the whole valley is a well cultivated garden." And with the rye fields have vanished the distilleries for which they formerly supplied the grain.

TEMPEST.

BY DELIA B. WARD.

They sing, weird voices, of the past,
Ah, wailing rhapsody, thou hast
A soft refrain for every woe,
A sympathetic cadence low;
While rushing winds, in phantom glee,
Retune the chords to revelry.
Oh, mad carousal! Where is he
Who can create such symphony
Of clashing sounds, and direful moans,
And underlying monotones?

SKETCH OF AUGUSTUS H. FENN.

BY JOSEPH H. VAILL.

Augustus Hall Fenn, member of the Supreme Court of Errors, whose death occurred in Winsted, September 12, 1897, was born at Plymouth, Conn., January 18, 1844. His parents were Augustus L. and Maria Hall Fenn. His ancestors settled in New Haven in 1639, and the sterling characteristics he exhibited indicate inheritance from sturdy ancestry of colonial days.

The foundation of his education was laid in the common school of his native town, upon which he built, later on, at the Waterbury high school. He early showed unusual literary talent, and at fifteen published a volume of poems, which he studiously hid from the public eye, however, in later years.

He began the study of law at the age of eighteen with Hon. Ammi Giddings in his native town, but relinquished it after a few months to enlist in the army. He entered the military service as lieutenant in the 19th Conn. Volunteers, in July, 1862. The following year, when his regiment became the 2nd Conn. Heavy Artillery, he was advanced to a captaincy. The adjutant and historian of his regiment says of him: "He proved himself one of the best drill masters and disciplinarians in the regiment, and one of the most competent officers in every position." He served for a time on the staff of General Emory Upton, and was five times detailed as judge advocate. At the battle of Cedar Creek he lost his right arm. Hospital surgeons who attended him proposed to muster him out for disability, but he protested, and through the influence of Gen. Ranald S. Mackenzie he was retained. "In less than seven weeks from the time his arm was taken off at the shoulder he reported for full duty," writes his regimental historian, and he subsequently participated in several engagements. He was promoted to major in January, 1865, and was brevetted lieutenant-colonel and colonel for conspicuous instances of bravery.

JUDGE AUGUSTUS H. FENN.

Colonel Fenn was mustered out of the military service with his regiment August 18, 1865, and the following month resumed the study of law with Gen. S. W. Kellogg in Waterbury. He was admitted to the bar of Litchfield county, February 15, 1867, after which he pursued a course of study for a year at the Harvard Law School, from which he received the degree of bachelor of laws. After practicing a year in Waterbury, he opened an office in his native town, where he continued in the practice of his profession until 1875. He was judge of probate several years in Plymouth, holding also several other minor public offices. In 1875 he was Republican nominee for secretary of state, but his party ticket was unsuccessful in that election.

In 1876 he removed to Winsted, which since that time has been his home. He had become an ardent admirer of Samuel J. Tilden in his fight against the "Tammany ring" of New York, his admiration being so strong as to lead him to remark that if Tilden should be a Presidential candidate, he should support him. He was true to his word, and thus became allied with the Democratic party. He was judge of probate in the district of Winchester several terms, and by the careful study of that branch of his profession, became known as one of the best authorities of the state on probate law.

BOYHOOD HOME OF JUDGE FENN, PLYMOUTH, CONN.

In 1884 he represented Winchester in the General Assembly, serving on the judiciary committee and as chairman of the committee on forfeited rights. In 1885 he was appointed by the Governor member of a committee to revise the statutes, a task of which he performed his full share.

Notwithstanding his changed political affiliations he continued to hold the highest esteem of his former political associates, for he was never regarded as strenuously partisan. He was nominated judge of the Superior Court in 1887 by a Republican governor, and as associate justice of the Supreme Court of Errors in 1892 by another governor of the same party. His appreciation of these advancements at the hands of his political opponents was such as to lead him to say—when his name was mentioned in various newspapers in connection with gubernatorial honors—that he should never allow himself to accept nomination for any position which would bring him into competition with any Republican. He had been advanced in his profession by his political opponents and felt that it would indicate lack of appreciation, or ingratitude, were he to take advantage of his promotion to the bench as a stepping-stone to further political preferment.

It may be well doubted if there can be recalled, within the remembrance of the present generation at least, another equally conspicuous instance showing firmer or more intimate friendships than existed between Judge Fenn and those who differed with him politically. His relations with his townspeople, with his professional associates and with his comrades of the war were such as to indicate that political differences were not thought of, or if thought of were no bar to the most intimate confidences. His loyalty to his personal friends and neighbors was not unlike that he exhibited to his country—firm and unwavering. In the Presidential campaign of 1896 he affiliated with the Republican party.

As an advocate, Judge Fenn is remembered as possessing gifts which, if they did not draw spectators to the court room, at least prolonged their stay. His addresses were listened to with an attention rarely warranted by the merits of the cause at issue. His language was concise, and he had such excellent choice of expression as to make his arguments models of diction. It was clear to the listener that he had the main points of his argument well arranged in his mind. His citations from authorities indicated not only a well read lawyer, but the happy faculty of weaving them into the warp and woof of his argument with harmonious effect. His success as an attorney was so fully recognized during his period of practice that he was never without a long list of clients.

Judge Fenn first sat on the supreme bench as a regular member at the May term in Norwich, in 1891, although his appointment by the Legislature was not completed until the 2d of February, 1893. His last duty was at the May term in Norwich, 1897. He was regarded by his associates of that tribunal as an agreeable companion, cheerful, kindly, sympathetic and generous. He had unusual power to acquire knowledge, a singularly clear and retentive memory, great industry and wonderful endurance. He had read not only the common books of the law but some which are not commonly looked at. He had read most of the text of Littleton in the Norman French, Fearne's Contingent Remainders, and had gone over Coke's second, third and fourth Institutes. His mind worked rapidly and he came to conclusions quickly. It is said of Lord Eldon that he was never quite ready to decide a case, because he always doubted. Judge Fenn, while he was always conscious that all human judgments are liable to error, gave to every case his best judgment, came to that conclusion which he deemed to be the correct one, and then laid it aside. He

JUDGE FENN'S HOME IN WINSTED.

never seemed to be distressed by doubts. He had very little pride of opinion, and not any pride of position.

In consultation, Judge Fenn was always considerate and forbearing. He listened to others with the greatest patience, and was always ready to yield, so far as possible, in order to secure a unanimous judgment. It is difficult to recall a dissenting opinion written by him; he has joined another judge sometimes in a dissent. He was a favorite with lawyers who argued before the court, because he was always attentive. His written opinions are regarded as a pretty accurate reflex of his mind. He worked rapidly; his opinions indicate that quality, and some of them show a want of careful revision. His relations with his associates on the bench were always intimate and confidential rather than professional, and he appeared to be regarded as a younger brother rather than as a rival in the profession or in the struggle for preferment, and his death came to them like a personal affliction.

Judge Fenn was president of the Connecticut Army and Navy Club at

LIBRARY IN WINSTED RESIDENCE.

time of his death, a member of the Grand Army of the Republic, and of the Loyal Legion. His patriotic impulses found their best medium of expression in public addresses on Memorial Day and on similar occasions. He was president of the Winchester Memorial Park Association, trustee of the Gilbert School and Home, and identified with various other local organizations. He possessed a reverent nature, and, though not a communicant, was a regular attendant of the Congregational church. His domestic relations were of an agreeable character, and to him there was "No place like home." He was twice married—in 1868 to Frances M. Smith of Waterbury, and in 1879 to Mary E. Lincoln of Winsted. His widow and four children survive him—Emory, Augusta, Lucia and Lincoln—two by each marriage.

ART EDUCATION IN THE "ROSE OF NEW ENGLAND"

BY ALICE W. COGSWELL

THROUGH articles which have recently appeared in the pages of this magazine, as well as in other ways, many readers of the QUARTERLY have been made familiar with the interesting landmarks of "ye ancient town of Norwich" and with the quaint or stately figures who have played well their parts in its history in days gone by. To many others, doubtless, it is also well known as an educational center through its admirably equipped preparatory school, the Norwich Free Academy. Perhaps, however, fewer people throughout the state have thought of the little city on the Thames as an art center. Never-

SLATER MEMORIAL AND NORWICH FREE ACADEMY.

theless, it is slowly but surely winning public recognition as such through its Art Museum and its Art School, which are both closely allied to the Free Academy.

Both of these have their home in the Slater Memorial Building, a gift to the institution from a former student of the Academy and a public spirited citizen of the town, "in grateful recognition of the advantages there enjoyed" and in memory of his father, for many years a member of the board of trustees. The same generous friend also equipped the Museum with a collection

ENTRANCE HALL — SLATER MEMORIAL

NIKE (VICTORY) OF THE THIRD
CENTURY, B. C.
Found in the Island of Samoth-
race, 1863.

of casts, now numbering nearly four hundred, representing the best sculpture of the Classic and Renaissance periods, and also a collection of very fine photographs of the world's best art in painting and architecture. These were very carefully selected under the supervision of Mr. Edward Robinson, curator of the Boston Art Museum, and are most admirably arranged to display them to the best possible advantage both for the general public and for the student. The Museum was formally dedicated in 1888.

The donor of this noble gift, as well as the board of trustees of the Academy, realized that much yet remained to be done to make the Museum fully exert its due influence on the community, and to meet this recognized want the foundation of the Art School followed two years later.

The aim of the trustees was to offer a thorough training in art to those residents of the town and of this section of the state who desire to develop "the power to understand, to enjoy or to create the beautiful." Five rooms in the Memorial Building were set apart for the use of the School. Both day and evening classes were established, the day classes intended for those students who could give much time to study, the evening classes mainly—but by no means solely—for wage earners who were occupied during the day, but who desired a training in art either simply for personal education or as a means to increase their ability in their chosen fields of labor. The school pursues its work along three main lines—drawing and painting, modelling, and design.

All new movements in any community at first awaken great popular enthusiasm, and Norwich was no exception to the rule. Art became a fad for a time, applications for membership were very numerous the first year—especially for the evening classes—and the student with the customary roll of charcoal paper was as familiar a figure as the granite soldier on Chelsea Pa-

PECK LIBRARY

rade. But alas, many of these would-be artists soon discovered that "Art is long," lost patience and fell by the wayside, finding it a far cry from drawing "block" hands and feet to representing the Venus of Milo or the Praxiteles Hermes. Next year the inevitable sifting process followed. This scattered the chaff and left a residue of earnest workers who had counted the cost and believed that the pleasure the pursuit of art brings with it is worth the sacrifice and self-denials it demands. Since that time the school has been on a sound working basis. Year by year since its foundation it has grown steadily in earnestness of purpose, in directness of aim and in *esprit de corps*, and its small but steady increase in numbers since the second year shows a slow but healthy growth.

I wish I might take my readers on a tour of inspection of the large, well-lighted rooms in the Slater Memorial Building which are devoted to the use of the Art School. On the right, after the great entrance door swings open and admits us into the lofty entrance hall, we should first enter the evening class room, a large apartment divided into alcoves by screens hung with casts, and well arranged for artificial light. A stroll about would show us that the room, which is deserted by day, must, in the

PREPARATORY ROOM.

three evenings of the week when it is occupied, be a hive of industry, for many of the unfinished drawings on the boards show how much may be accomplished in even a limited amount of time when energy is directed to one aim alone.

Let us ascend one flight of stairs—and we reach the Design Room, where, if our visit is made in the morning, we shall find busy students working at large tables either drawing in first drafts of problems in charcoal or filling in the prepared pencil outlines with water colors. A glance over the shoulders of the pupils or at the walls of the room will show us what these "problems" are. Persian rugs, tiles, placques, fans, grille work, etc., hanging on the walls are an evidence of the kind of work done here. No (so-called) original work of any kind in this department can be done, however, without a firm grasp of the principles used in decorative work by the nations which have preceded ours on the stage of history. A course covering many months in the History of Ornament, from the first efforts of savage tribes down to the best achievements of the Renaissance, is required of every pupil who enters this department and wishes to reach success in it.

A satisfactory course in Historic Ornament would be impossible were not a large and well equipped collection of casts, books, prints and photographs available. Such a collection, however, is always at hand in the Peck Library, located in a beautiful room, spacious and well-lighted, on the same floor. This library is very rich in literature and photographs relating to art; and large tables, with racks for holding the pictures, afford the best opportunities for sketching. These collections are always accessible to students of the Art School and are in constant use.

To make the art treasures of the building still more useful to the students and to the public, courses of lectures on sculpture, painting, architecture or decoration are held each winter and are illustrated by the casts and photographs.

Leaving the library, another flight up brings us to the Preparatory Room, where, if it is the first of the school year, we shall find students at all stages of progress, from those who are drawing from casts of block hands and feet to those who are working from the most delicately modelled heads. When a scholar in the judgment of the teacher has gained proficiency enough in drawing from the head, he is promoted to the Museum to draw from the full-length figure.

Still one more flight up, and under the roof we find another knot of pupils working in oil or charcoal from the living model.

On Thursday afternoon of each week the sketch class also works for two hours from a model in pencil, pen and ink, or water color. This class was

CLASS IN DESIGN

started and is maintained by the students themselves, each member in turn providing a model for the afternoon.

No mention of the Art School would be complete without a word about

the Children's Class which has proved such a success in the School. The idea
of the possibility of training young children in the elements of art and thus
fitting them to know and appreciate the beautiful is not a very new one, as it
is recognized more or less in the public schools of most progressive cities of
any size throughout the country. But of course any thorough instruction in
this line cannot be carried on in the common schools, owing to the lack of time
and the requisite facilities. Several art schools in the country, however, have
opened classes on Saturday for children between the ages of eight and thirteen years, in order to give them a more comprehensive art education than is
possible in the public schools. Such a class was opened here in 1895. The

ART MUSEUM.

lessons, which the little pupils enjoy thoroughly, include drawings from objects and from casts, composition from subjects given by the teacher, rapid
sketching, and painting in water color and pastel. In the spring term they
also model in clay.

Not the least valuable are the walks in the Museum with the teacher,
where a cast is pointed out, its story both historical and mythical told, and
then it is sketched by the young art students. Knowledge gained in that way
is absorbed without conscious effort and as a pleasure rather than a task. That
this training of eye and hand is appreciated by the parents is shown by the
applications for admission which became so numerous this year that a second
class was formed.

For six weeks in the Spring a teacher from New York gives instruction in modelling, and for that time the preparatory and antique classes devote
their time to that.

Each year exhibitions of art work of various kinds are held by the school for the benefit of the students themselves and for the broadening influence they may exert on the community. Such exhibitions have included both pictorial and industrial art. Furniture, rugs, porcelains, book bindings, stained glass designs, magazine illustrations, pictures, etc., have been some of the phases of art work represented. That these displays and the atmosphere of the Art School as a whole are slowly but surely exerting an influence upon the people of the town is shown by the increased interest in, and the more intelligent comprehension of the work of the school shown at the annual exhibitions each year.

There is also a very pleasant social side to the life of the School, which is not yet so large but that a spirit of *camaraderie* exists among the students. With the purpose of furnishing a bond of union between those pupils who are working in other places and those still in the school or in the town, a flourish-

LIFE CLASS.

ing "Art Students' Association" was formed three years ago which holds monthly meetings where papers on art topics are read and discussed. It is also pledged to forward in any way possible the interests of the Art School.

With one exception, this is the only art school in the country in which a scholarship given free for one year has been offered by the Art Students' League of New York. This example was followed by a like offer from the Boston School of Design. To obtain these scholarships drawings are submitted to the authorities of these schools, the best set, of course, receiving the award.

The good work done in the Norwich Art School is recognized by the large metropolitan schools; and the students who go from it, either to such institutions or to labor independently, show the effect of the thorough training they have received here.

THE LIGHT OF OTHER DAYS.

THE BRISTOL HISTORICAL AND SCIENTIFIC SOCIETY.

BY PILRA ROOT NEWELL.

Pen and ink sketches by Antoinette Newell.

The Bristol Historical and Scientific Society had its beginning at the Bristol Centennial in 1885, and received its initial impetus from the addresses delivered on that occasion by Prof. Tracy Peck of Yale and by Senator Joseph R. Hawley, who suggested that the collection of articles loaned for exhibition at that time should be made the basis of a permanent historical museum.

But while due honor should be given to those who proposed laying the foundations of a museum, to three so-called antiquarians of Bristol, Dr. Fred-

MR. AND MRS. THOMAS BARNES, Descendants of Bristol's first settlers.

erick H. Williams, William C. Richards and Edward E. Newell, the credit belongs of following these suggestions and forming the Bristol Historical and Scientific Society.

On June 18, 1890, about one hundred citizens of Bristol met in the Court Room of the Town Hall to consider the advisability of organizing such a society and to appoint a committee to draft a constitution and by-laws and present them for action on the second of July following. The adjourned meeting was held and the constitution was adopted and a president and a board of directors were elected. On August 28 a meeting of this board was held and a committee appointed to hire the upper

REEL AND SWIFT.   FLAX WHEEL.

room in a block which had just been completed and to have charge of all articles donated to the Society.

In 1891 the cause of history and science seemed to languish, for at the annual meeting there was not a quorum present.

September 27, 1892, is the date of the last minutes recorded with this dying wail, "Annual meeting adjourned for want of quorum."

In spite of all obstacles, want of encouragement from the public and need of money to carry on the enterprise, two faithful souls toiled on, collecting, labeling and arranging. Just as they were on the verge of despair, seriously contemplating the wisdom of letting the Society die a natural death, Mrs. Randolph DeB. Keim, the organizing regent of the Connecticut Daughters of the American Revolution, visited the rooms. By her appreciation and interest in the collection she so inspired the Bristol Daughters that they voluntarily assumed the care of the relics of "ye olden time."

After this preamble, come with me and see how our great-grandmothers lived and toiled and moiled, and perhaps we shall come away thankful for our mercies that we did not live in those "good old days."

Up one flight of stairs; up two flights of stairs; at the third we pause for contemplation and possibly—breath, wondering if these stairs have not something to do with the indifference of the public to this Society.

A glimpse of a scarlet cloak in the room above, a bit of "grandfather's clock" and a big wheel attract our attention at once, and we mount the last flight. A bewildering array of wheels, looms and all kinds of kitchen utensils meets our eyes; but we must first visit the portrait gallery, for, "in treasuring the memory of the fathers, we best manifest our regard for posterity." Here are the pictures of representative men of the town whose labors are ended, with some particularly interesting portraits of a few of the early settlers of Bristol.

Passing out of the gallery we notice at the left a rotary stove, which was a sort of labor-saving machine, for the pots and kettles were not lifted off the stove, but gracefully swung around the circle. Standing near are several foot stoves, many of which, no doubt, have often been carried to

FLAX-BREAK   ROTARY STOVE.

"the meetin' house on the hill," in those days when it was considered a means of grace to shiver and shake with cold while receiving spiritual food.

On the beam at our right hangs a row of lanterns appropriately labeled "The Light of Other Days." Some of these are really valuable, even though they have a battered and woe-begone appearance and look as if they had been out very late o' nights. Here is a flax-break; in the corner stands a carpet-loom, one of the many treasures acquired by the unremitting labors of the collectors for the Society.

Near the loom stands a target, an Indian in war paint and feathers, used by a rifle company, the "Old Bristol Blues."

This queer-looking barrel was made from the trunk of a pepperidge tree and was used for holding salt. A tall old-fashioned clock looms up before us. It was made by Gideon Roberts, the founder of the clock industry in Bristol. It is said he owned the first chaise in Bristol, and it is pleasant to think of him driving over the hills with his bride, Falla Hopkins, from Hartford. We trust he was not so much absorbed in thoughts of "those parts of eighty clocks which he meant to put together by May 1st," and in "collecting timber for one thousand more," that he could not notice the lights and shadows on the hills as they drove back to their substantial house on Fall Mountain.

On the table near the north wall can be found kitchen utensils of all kinds, farming implements, water bottles, canteens, cow-bells, saddle-bags, churns, mortars and pestles and many articles for domestic use. A long-handled wooden peel brings up visions of the old brick oven; a hanging griddle, toasters and tin bake-ovens call back the days when our great-grandmothers cooked by an open fire.

Here are candlesticks galore. It does not take much imagination for us to see great grandfather reading *The Hartford Courant* by the flickering light of a tallow candle. On this table is a carved oak chest which looks as if it might have come over in the Mayflower. At the head of the table is a lap organ; the bellows were worked by one arm, and at the same time the player was supposed to use both hands in playing!

It requires little imagination to transfer ourselves to the other side of the

TOW BASKET, STRAW BEE-HIVE AND CHEESE BASKET.

world as we gaze upon the Austrian piano, with its harp-shaped back, scarlet silk, and altogether regal air. Its history is shrouded in mystery and romance.

Here are cases containing china and glass, minerals, shells, birds' eggs, old deeds, paper money, Indian relics from New England, Florida and New Mexico; Indian and Mexican pottery, and many interesting things from California.

One case has an unusually fine exhibition of Indian relics. Here can be seen a spear-head fourteen inches long, one of the largest known in this country, found in Southington; also two pipes from Mt. Lamentation, near Meriden. One is of the Haidah Indian type, of Victoria, Vancouver. There are none like it found in this vicinity, and its presence is a mystery—unless the Haidah Indians came down to spend Thanksgiving with the Tunxis tribe and left this pipe behind them! The other pipe, which resembles a crow, is exceedingly rare and valuable. At the back of the case hangs a stone pestle in the form of an eel so cunningly fashioned that when it was found it was believed to be a petrified eel.

In the next case can be found, among many other interesting articles, a white stiffly-starched linen cap with this printed label sewed upon it: "Deacon

Manross, with a neat white Holland cap upon his head, starched and ironed with care and neatness. Oh! how proud was the wife, of her husband's cap!" This cap was worn by Elisha Manross, in 1765, in his honored position as deacon of the Bristol Congregational Church.

Dr. F. H. Williams, one of the originators of this Society, has the finest exhibit in the room. In his ethnological collection are casts of reindeer bones which were engraved by prehistoric men, curios from the Cliff Dwellers in Arizona, and a basket containing mummied bones, spindles with yarn and other articles from a prehistoric cemetery in Peru. He also exhibits grotesque images from Mexico and Egypt, Aztec household goods, an ancient lamp from Asia Minor, casts of idols, and cowry shells or African money, one hundred of which will buy a wife.

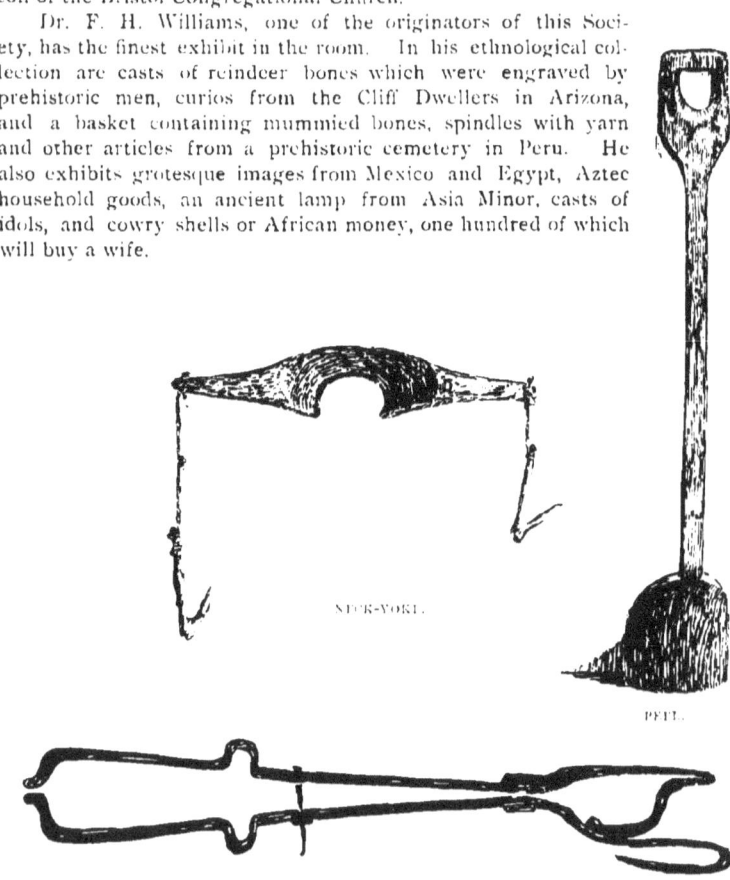

NECK-YOKE.

PEEL.

PIPE-TONGS.

On a round three-legged table standing before one of the windows is a case of Silurian fossils. On a card with two shells is this label: "These two shells were once in the private collection of Washington at William and Mary College."

We must not overlook the old hats and bonnets, the green calash and gum shoes, the pointed slippers, shell combs and other frivolities of our foremothers.

Here is a chaise and harness once the property of Governor Trumbull, the "Brother Jonathan" of the Revolution, and now owned by W. G. Bunnell of

Burlington; and here is a dugout canoe, said to be prehistoric. Over the spinning-jenny hang two scarlet cloaks, one of which was exhibited at the Atlanta Exposition.

On the south wall is a shelf filled with churns, chairs and clocks, bake-ovens, bee-hives and hair trunks. On the wall are maps, charts, mirrors, photographs, sconces, candle-holders, bellows, snow-shoes, cheese-baskets, ladders, presses, antlers, tusks, horns, and — a boot-jack! This boot-jack does not seem to be proud or haughty in any respect, although the "immortal Washington" used it during the Revolution.

We must not omit mentioning the old Bristol newspapers, although they are hardly worthy of notice, as they are mostly of a scurrilous nature, not papers "for the home and fireside." These were only occasionally printed and quietly scattered in the community. Such were *The Bristol Times*, printed in 1831; *The Bristol Lash;* *The Bristol Bull-Let-In*, 1844; *Monthly Review*, 1845; and *The Old Guard*, 1855.

MORTARS AND PESTLES.

In the case in the middle of the room are some most interesting articles, such as one of the first electrical machines, an early form of the sewing machine, colonial lamps and ancient fire-arms.

Perhaps the most interesting article in this room is a cane once owned by Napoleon Bonaparte and used by him on board the Bellerophon while on his way to St. Helena.

Near the wall is a set of surgical instruments once used by Dr. Jared Pardee, a famous Bristol physician; and in the corner is a case full of ancient books, papers and documents valuable and interesting. Here can be found old bibles, almanacs, newspapers, magazines, school books, music books, the first *Connecticut Courant*, printed in 1764; a fac-simile of Washington's account with the United States from 1775 to 1783; an English Diction

FOOT STOVES.

ary, "Being also an Interpreter of Hard Words;" sermons, licenses and sales of slaves; the Greek Testament and lexicon owned by the Rev. Samuel Newell, Bristol's first minister; and "Letters to a Young Lady on a Variety of Subjects, Calculated to Improve the Heart, to Form the Manners and Enlighten the Understanding," printed in 1792. To these may be added "The Experienced Fowler, or the Gentleman's Recreation," containing "The True Art of Taking Water and Land Fowl with Divers Kinds of Nets, &c. &c.," printed in 1704; a book of sermons "On the Education of Children," printed in 1812, and, it is needless to say, the historic "New England Primer."

AUSTRIAN PIANO

Among the old papers we find a blank warrant for the arrest of "Treasonable parties against this and the United States," signed by Governor Trumbull and dated 1779. These warrants were issued by Capt. Simeon Newell, who was the only person authorized to fill in the blanks, and were aimed particularly against the Tories. Capt. Newell was at this time very energetic in the prosecution of the Tories, and on this account the blank warrants were issued to him, giving him unlimited power to arrest persons suspected of treasonable practices. Through the information which he obtained in these prosecutions, he learned enough of the intended treachery of Arnold to induce "Our Great Washington"
— as the record in the Wadsworth Athenæum in Hartford says — "to fly as with the wings of an eagle to West Point."

The following extract from a letter of Prof. Mason, curator of the National Museum at Washington, is a handsome tribute to the real excellence of the collection of the Bristol Historical Society: "What interested me most in your collection was the saving of rare specimens of old machines worked by hand that pre-

CRADLE

ceded in colonial life the present great factories. I was delightfully surprised to see two specimens of a curious kind of belt loom of which at that time I only knew of the existence among the Indians of New Mexico, but stimulated by finding your specimens I have corresponded on the subject until we have pictures and

CHURN

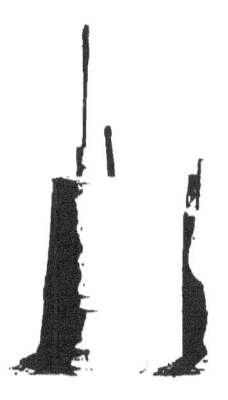
CHURNS

BREAD TOASTERS.

FLAT IRON   CANDLE MOULD.   CANDLE SCONCE.   BELT LOOM.

specimens from Maine, Connecticut, New York, Pennsylvania, Northern Germany, Italy and Lapland. I shall soon publish a paper on the spread of this interesting little apparatus."

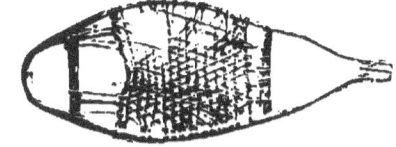
SNOW-SHOE.

One of these looms, together with several other objects from the Bristol Historical Rooms, is now on exhibition in the National Museum at Washington.

But we have already lingered too long, so we can only glance at a dingy card — an invitation to a Columbian Ball given in Bristol, May 4th 1813 at Mr. Abel Lewis' ball room at 10 o'clock p. m.

DEACON'S CAP.

BOOTJACK,
Loaned to Washington

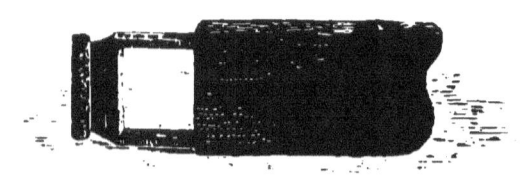

PITCH-PIPE.

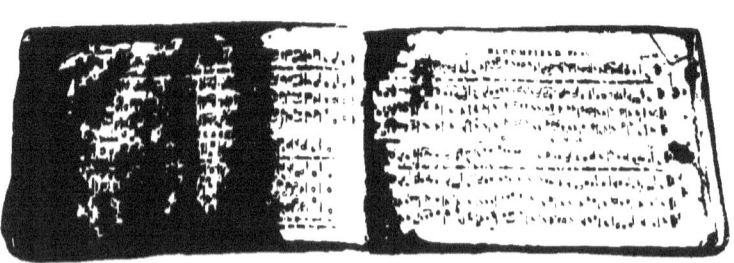

OLD MUSIC BOOK.

BRISTOL HISTORICAL AND SCIENTIFIC SOCIETY. 217

WATER BOTTLES.   BONNET

We must leave the beaus and belles dancing in the old tavern, and although the half has not been told, register our names in the visitors' book, which is ever guarded by the sad-faced idol from Panama.

NOTE.—Since the foregoing article was written the society has removed the collection from the room in the business block mentioned, to the Bristol High School building.

GOVERNOR JONATHAN TRUMBULL'S CHAISE

GENEALOGICAL DEPARTMENT.

Querists should write all names of persons and places in such a way that they cannot be misunderstood. Always enclose with queries a self-addressed stamped envelope and at least ten cents for each query. Querists should write only on one side of the paper. Subscribers sending in queries should state that they are subscribers, and preference in insertion will always be given them. Queries are inserted in the order in which they are received. On account of our limited space, it is impossible that all queries be inserted as soon as querists desire. Always give full name and post-office address. Queries and notes must be sent to Wm. A. Eardeley-Thomas, 50th street and Woodland avenue, Philadelphia, Penn. The editor earnestly requests our readers to assist him in answering queries. His duties are onerous enough in other directions, so that only a limited amount of time can be devoted to query researches.

Notes.

41. CONNECTICUT FOUNTAIN FAMILY.
(*Continued from page 480, Vol. III.*)
Compiled by Wm. A. Eardeley-Thomas.

5. *Moses*² Fountain (Aaron¹) m. Aug. 13, 1719, in Norwalk, Ct. (Hall's History) the widow Elizabeth Gregory. Rev. Chas. M. Selleck of Norwalk, Ct., says she was dau. of Joseph Ketchum. Who was wife of Joseph Ketchum? What was the first name of Mr. Gregory? Jan. 1732-3, Moses Fountain sold to Abraham Smith of Norwalk for £9 all claims to the meadow called "Gregory's Boggs," about two acres (Norwalk Land Records). March 14, 1738-9, Moses Fountain and Elizabeth, his wife, sold land for £647 to William Johnson (N. L. Rec.). Sept. 21, 1741, Moses Fountain was a freeholder in Bedford, N. Y. (p. 37, Vol. I, Bolton's Westchester Co. History, 1881). July 1, 1741, John Copp of Norwalk for £650 New England money sold land in Bedford to Moses Fountain, wit. Zebadiah Mills and John Sherwood (p. 61, Vol. III, Bedford, N. Y., Town Records). "To all people to whom these presents shall come, etc.": ".....Moses Fountain, Sr., of the town of Bedford" to Matthew Fountain a certain tract of land in the New "purchase," 1756, Dec. 28, wit. Nathaniel Knap and Lewis McDonald (p. 55, Bed. T. Rec., Vol. III). I think the above deeds prove conclusively that the Westchester Co. Fountains came from Conn., and the early generations as Bolton has them are entirely wrong. James H. Fountain, Esq., of Riverside, Cal., says that Moses mar. a Miss **Whelpley**, but I can find no authority for such a statement. March 1770-1, "Moses Fountain, a Baptist, who lately came to this place" (p. 324 Stamford History, Rev. E. B. Huntington); Dec. 27, 1773, by a vote of the Cong'l Society, it abates the society rates for the year 1771 for Moses Fountain, a Baptist (p. 325, Huntington). Sept. 16, 1777, he took the oath of fidelity to the State of Connecticut in Stamford. He was a tything man in Stamford, Dec. 13, 1779. Oct. 22, 1788, Moses Fountain received about half an acre of land from Joshua June (p. 54, vol. M. Stam. Land Rec.). March 2, 1792, Moses Fountain of Smith's Clove, N.Y., for £20 sold land in Stamford to Daniel Nichols, Jr. (p. 626, Vol. L, Stamford Land Records). Ch. Norwalk, Ct. Records, (Hall's History.)

18—i. Moses,³ b. Sept. 7, 1720; mar. Mary, dau. of James

and Ruth ( ) June. James was prob. son of Peter June, and (if so) born June 29, 1687, in Stamford. Page 52, Vol. III, Stamford Probate Records, contains the distribution of the estate of James June on Jan. 26, 1762: he left, 1. James. 2. Joshua. 3. Thomas (prob. father of Nathaniel and Sarah, grandchildren). 4. Ruth, wife of Stephen Clason. 5. Deborah, wife of Samuel Banks. 6. Mary, wife of Moses Fountain. 7. Hannah, wife of John Palmer.

Bedford Town Records, p. 29, Vol. III, the ear-mark of Moses Fountain Jr., is entered Jan. 24, 1748-9, Reuben Holmes, clerk. Oct. 31, 1767, Moses Fountain and Mercy, his wife, of New River, Onslow Co., North Carolina, for £28 sold land in Stamford to Joshua June (p. 202, Vol. H, Stamford Land Records). I have not yet been able to learn anything from North Carolina. This family has undoubtedly got mixed up with the Va. family in which the name Moses was quite common.

19—ii. Joseph,[3] b. Dec. 4, 1723. Nothing further is known of him.

20—iii. Samuel,[3] b. Mar. 7, 1725-6; m Jan. 20, 1746-7, in Wilton Cong'l Ch., Abigail, dau. of John Stuart (vide Norwalk, Ct., Land Records, Dec, 1748). He is mentioned in 1756 in Wilton store accounts—William Sterling was the storekeeper. Sept. 16, 1777, he took the oath of fidelity to the State of Connecticut in Stamford. He was surveyor of highways Dec., 1777, in Stamford; and again Dec. 13, 1779. Feb. 21, 1784, Martha and Samuel Fountain for £54 sold land to Jonas Scofield (p 538, Vol. K, Stamford Land Records). I have not been able to learn anything further about him.

21—iv. Matthew,[3] b. Mar. 4, 1730-1; m. Elizabeth Hoyt.

[To be continued.]

42. Descendants of Ezra[1] Perry, compiled by Wm. A. Eardeley-Thomas (continued from page 480). The editor thinks it best here to publish such Perry items as he has not been able to place. Some one may be able to place these items.

MARRIAGES IN SANDWICH, MASS.
(PER TOWN RECORDS.)

Perry, Ann to William Raymond, Mar. 2, 1765-6.
Anna to Ebenezer Raymond, Mar. 2, 1766.
Celia to Samuel Blackwell, Jr., Feb. 19, 1797.
Charles to Mary Nye, Sept. 27, 1823.
Deborah to Hicks Jenney of Dartmouth, Nov. 5, 1767.
Deliverance to John Bourne, Nov. 26, 1801.
Elizabeth to Peleg Barlow, July 25, 1717.
Elizabeth to Job Foster, Oct. 27, 1753.
Elizabeth to Joseph Foster, Nov, 15, 1753.
Eleazer to Elizabeth Freeman, Feb. 12, 1754.
Eliphal to Stephen Harper, Nov. 5, 1728 (Fr. Rec.).
Hannah to Samuel Gibbs, Jr., Sept. 10, 1744.
Hannah to Samuel Gibbs, Mar. 20, 1746.
Hannah to Jabez Swift of Falmouth, Jan. 30, 1755-6. Published May 25, 1754, in Falmouth.
Hannah to Samuel Money, January, 1805.
Joanna to Joseph Bennett of Middleboro, Dec. 18, 1807.
John to Hannah Sanders of Dartmouth, Oct. 19, 1728.
John, Jr. to Abigail Tupper, Oct. 26, 1769.
John to Mary Swift of Falmouth, Jan. 20, 1793.
Lydia to Ellis Tobey, Jan. 11, 1759.
Meribah to John Barber, June 3, 1731.
Martha to William Bourne, July 25, 1793.
Patience to Capt. Moses Hatch of Falmouth, Mar. 12, 1739-40. Published Jan. 19, 1739-40, in Falmouth.
Rebecca to Jonathan Fuller of Barnstable, Mar. 3, 1718
Rebecca to Gideon Ellis, Jr., Feb. 9, 1748-9.
Rebecca to Philip Ellis, Nov. 20, 1771.
Reuben to Elizabeth Tupper of Barnstable, Mar. 3, 1790 91.
Ruth to Jesse Gifford, June 2, 1774.

Sarah to Seth Sturtevant of Wareham, Feb. 25, 1802.
Seth to Mercy Freeman, May 3, 1757.
[To be continued.]

43. *New Fairfield Families—III.*

PEARCE (concluded).
Contributed by Edward H. Pearce of New Fairfield.

David[1] Pearce, b. 1739, d. 1801; m. Phebe, b. 1743, d. 1819, dau. of Nathan and Elizabeth Stevens, and had: Nathaniel Stevens[2] Pearce, b. Feb. 23, 1781, d. May 13, 1822; mar. Rebecca, b. Sept. 10, 1782, d. Feb. 22, 1825, in N. F., dau. of Abel and Keziah (Hodge) Sherwood. Nathaniel S.[2] and Rebecca (Sherwood) Pearce had:
i. Alvah Sherwood,[3] May 9, 1803, d. May 6, 1875; m. Amy, b. 1801, d. 1838, dau. of Ebenezer (David) and Betsey (Nash) Barnum, and had Amzi H.,[4] b. 1829; m. F. Jane, dau. of Ira (Thaddeus, David) and Betsey (Bradley) Barnum.
ii. Ambrose Bryant,[3] Oct. 20, 1805, d. June 22, 1879; m. Evaline, dau. of Thaddeus and Abigail (Stevens) Barnum.
iii. Harrison,[3] Feb. 23, 1813, d. Sept 16, 1816.
iv. Mary,[3] Dec. 1, 1820, d. Aug. 12, 1821.
Ambrose B.[3] and Evaline (Barnum) Pearce had:
i. Ira Barnum,[4] Jan. 24, 1827, d. Nov. 13, 1827.
ii. Harriet Ann,[4] April 26, 1828; mar. May 9, 1853, Eli, son of Lyman and Sally Betsey (Elwell) Jennings. No issue.
iii. Mary Jane,[4] Mar. 18, 1830, d. April 10, 1833.
iv. David Barnum,[4] May 21, 1832, d. Oct. 8, 1867; m. Oct. 13, 1853, Hannah, dau. of John and Clara Elwell. 1. Alphonso[5] went to Minn. and mar., but left no issue surviving. 2. Theodore[5] died young.
v. Ira B.,[4] Dec. 13, 1835; m , 1st, Dec. 1, 1858, Orpha, dau. of Lyman and and Sally B. Jennings, and had : 1. Harriet Ann,[5] Sept. 22, 1863, m. Asa Briggs, and d. Mar. 25, 1885, without heirs. 2. Evaline,[5] June 29, 1872; m. Charles Woodin, who died July 8, 1893, and had Harriet,[6] April 16, 1893. Ira B.[5] m., 2d, March 21, 1894, Cornelia Benham, wid. of Oliver Barnum.
vi. George Nathaniel,[4] Dec. 17, 1838; m. Dec. 21, 1859, Lydia Ann, dau. of Dimon and Jane (Hoag) Disbrow and d. Mar. 7, 1893, s. p.
vii. Philo Stevens,[4] Oct. 12, 1843; m. Oct. 27, 1869, Orva Lavenda, dau. of John (b. 1821) and Jane (Ramsdell) Barnum, and have : 1. Thaddeus Bernard,[5] Sept. 6, 1870; m. Jan. 1, 1894, Louis Hortense Newton, and have Ethel Margerite,[6] Mar. 8, 1895. 2. David Arthur,[5] Oct. 2, 1873. 3. Lena Jane,[5] Dec. 3, 1882. 4. Ambrose,[5] Jan. 19, 1886.

44. *Fountain Family of Staten Island.*
By William A. Eardeley-Thomas.
[Continued from page 482.]

25. Anthony[4] Fountain (Vincent,[3] Vincent,[2] Antone[1]) d. about 1813, aged 90; m., 2d, between 1752 and 1756 by Rev. Charlton Chorch of Richmond, S. I., to Hannah (Anaatje) Garrison, or Gerretson (p. 95, 1894 N. Y. Gen. Biog. Rec. I have not not been able to learn who were the antecedents of Hannah Gerretson. It would seem that Anthony must have had a wife before Hannah, as a Vincent F. born 1748 was son of Anthony, and this is the only place where he will fit. Anthony m., 3d, in old age Elizabeth ____ who was much younger than himself. She died Nov. 15, 1821. He was known as a man of very large stature, probably 6 ft. 6 in. and huge in proportion. He is probably the man of this name who was supervisor of Southfield, Richmond Co., N. Y., in 1767, 1769 and 1784; a member (p. 169, Clute's Annals says associate judge) of the first court held after the Revolution, in Sept., 1794 (p. 148, Clute). Anthony, Sr., bapt. August 27, 1785, in Baptist Church on Staten Island; also Belichy and Hannah (p. 282, Clute). These three were incorporators on Dec. 3, 1785, of the old Baptist church, "Old Clove Church" (page 405, Baylie's Hist. Richmond Co.). His will Feb. 7, 1813, Liber A, p. 457, Richmond Prob. Rec., names wife Elizabeth and daus. Ann Magee Fountain and Phebe Baldwin Foun-

tain; makes a bequest unto John, son of Jacob Fountain; executors, John Garretson and Christopher Parkinson; witnesses. Joseph Perine, James Fountain, M. D., and Charety Baker.

By 1st wife:

40—i. Vincent,[5] b. 1748; m., 1st, Amy Fettie; m., 2d, Alice Jennings. Who were their parents?

By 2d wife, bap. Dutch Ref. Church:

41—ii. Antone,[5] bapt. Nov. 3, 1754; m. 1st, Catherine Journeay; m., 2d, Clara ———. Who were their parents?

iii. Maragrietye,[5] bap. Mar., 1756; m. Cornelius Kruzer (so writes Mr. Wm. A. Harding of Brooklyn, N. Y.)

42—iv. John,[5] bapt. Nov. 20, 1757. What became of him?

43—v. Charles,[5] born Sept. 25, 1756, son of Anthony and Susannah (St. Andrew's Prot. Epis. Ch. Records). What became of him?

44—vi. Cornelius,[5] bapt. Dec. 23, 1759; m. Elizabeth Vandeventer.

45—vii. Garrett,[5] born Dec. 5, 1765 (date from tombstone); m. Anne Betts of Ridgefield, Ct. Who were her parents?

viii. Gideon.[5] Left home and never heard from.

46—ix. Jacob,[5] born March 13, 1772. Whom did he marry? I place him here because he is named in will of Anthony, whom I think was his father.

x. Margaret,[5] b. ——, m., 1st, (Joseph?) Perine, and had: 1. Margaret Ann. What became of her? 2. Joseph. What became of him?

By 3d wife:

xi. Ann Magee,[6] b. about 1801, d. unm. before July 10, 1832 (account book of Isaac Nichols).

xii. Phebe Baldwin,[6] b. March 3, 1804, d. May 3, 1857, æt. 53 yrs. 2 mos., and is buried in Mt. Pleasant Cemetery, Newark, N. J.; mar. ———, Aaron J—— (b. ———, 1803; d. Feb. 4, 1861, æt. 58), son of Isaac Nichols, and had: 1. Dr. Isaac A——,[6] b. —— 1827, d. Nov. 26, 1880, æt. 53. Did he have any issue?

[To be continued.]

Queries.

124. *Griswold,* Elias of Wethersfield, Ct., b. Oct. 6, 1750, m. Dec. 8, 1773, Rhoda, dau. of Joseph Flowers, and had Elias b. June 14, 1775, m. his cousin Wealthy Flowers, b. Apr. 5, 1775, at Ashfield, Mass. The given names of her father and mother are desired. Also her mother's maiden name. A. E. V.

125. *Hilliard,* Joseph, b. Jan. 15, 1738, Norwich, Conn., m. about 1756 Sarah ———— It is supposed they were married in Tolland, Ct., and it has always been thought she was Sarah Burr. Proof is desired. S. H. H.

126. (*a*) *Babbitt,* Zephaniah. mar. Abigail Hamlin. Who were the parents of Zephaniah and Abigail?

(*b*) *Olmstead,* Sarah M., b. 1794, in Sharon, Ct., dau. of Hezekiah. Who were his parents? C. O. B.

127. *Perry,* John, and Elizabeth his wife (neé Corbin) of Ridgefield, for £11 bought land May 9, 1794, for Nathan Whitney. Who were their parents? What children did they have? W. A. E. T.

128. *Smielau,* John had a son Henry John Smielau mar. Mary Meyer; they had a son, Franklin Smielau, b. Aug. 27, 1876, Cincinnati, Ohio. Whom did John marry and who were his parents? S. F.

129 (*a*) *Burton,* Dr. Patrick, b. Lynchburg, Va.; mar. as 1st wife Emily Scott of Va. Who were parents of Dr. Patrick and Emily? It is said that the mother of Dr. Burton belonged to a Conn. Mercer family. Dr. Patrick and Emily had, 1. Dr. Selden Mercer Burton, b. 1822, d. about 1854; m. about 1850 Phebe Stillè, b. 1820, dau. of John Stillè of Phila. 2. Mary Scott Burton, m. Abraham Weaver. 3. Emily Burton. Dr. Patrick had two or three wives.

(*b*) *Stillè,* John, b. Phila., m. Maria, dau. of Tobias Wagner, and had Phebe Stillè, b. Phila; m. Dr. Selden M. Burton and had Maria, b. 1852; m. 1875 Prof. William Morton Easton. Who were parents of John Stillè and Tobias Wagner? Are these Burtons, Scotts, Stillès or Wagners eligible to the Revolutionary societies? M. B. E.

130. *Way*, William of Conn., m. Sarah Cole of Conn.; moved to Madison Co., N. Y., and had William b. there 1816. Who were the ancestors of this Cole and Way family?
W. F. L.

131. *Hills*, Amos, b. abt. 1744, m. Rachel Lewis of Middletown, 1773. Who were his ancestors? Where was he born and where did he die? Family records say of East Hartford or Farmington. J. L. C.

132. *Hoskins*, Samuel, m. Mary Blake, and had Ebenezer, b. 1752, moved about 1790 to N. Y. State. Ebenezer and Samuel both lived in Groton, Conn. Who were parents of Samuel? C. L. H.

133 (*a*) *Scofield*, Elnathan, about 1800, went to Ohio; he was b. about 1775, and went to Ohio from Litchfield Co., Conn. I wish to learn from what town he went? He was possibly son of Elnathan Scofield, b. 1746 in Stamford, Conn.

(*b*) *Hopkins*, Elizabeth, b. about 1600 in Eng.; m. there Jan., 1629, John Wakeman, and came to New Haven Colony 1640-41, buying the place of wid. Baldwin, who moved to Milford. Who were the parents of Elizabeth? When and where did she die?

(*c*) *Wakeman*, Sarah, b. 1593 (sister of John); m. 1621, Richard Hubbell, and had a son Richard, Jr., b. 1623. Is he not the one who is called the emigrant of Fairfield, Ct.?

(*d*) *Williams*, Thomas, left Plymouth, Mass., in 1638; m. Elizabeth Tart (or Tait) of Scituate, and settled in Eastham, Mass. Was he the son of Thomas Williams, signer of the Mayflower Compact or even the signer himself? Is there positive proof that Thomas, "the signer," died the first winter and left no children? If so, then who was this Thomas who left Plymouth 17 years after the Pilgrims landed?

(*e*) *Briggs*, Capt. Daniel of Stamford, Conn., who was there in 1711-12 From whence did he come and who were his parents? He m. 1704, at Rye, N. Y., Elizabeth Newman. Is he descended from the Briggs family who descended from Francis Cooke?

(*f*) *Jennings*, John, was in Hartford, Conn., as early as 1640, and is said to have died there in 1641. Where did he come from and when did he die? Was he father of Joshua Jennings who in 1656 settled at Fairfield, Conn. and who went there from Hartford? Joshua m, 1647, Mary Williams of Hartford. Who were her parents? When and where was she born? When was Joshua and Matthew Jennings born? Which of Matthew's two wives was the mother of Jeremiah, b. 1703? When did Jeremiah die?

(*g*) *Hyde*, Humphrey, m. Ann———. Who were parents of each?

(*h*) *Meigs*, John of Guilford, m. 1632, in Weymouth, Eng., Tamasin Fry; their dau. Mary b. at Weymouth, 1633, and their son John in America in 1640. They had besides 3 daus. Elizabeth, Concurrence and Tryal, who were probably born in America between 1640 and 1650. The family came to America in 1639, but where they first settled is not known; it was probably in Mass. John came to Hartford, and from there to New Haven 1645 or 6, where he bought a lot on corner of Church and Chapel Sts. of Wm. Jeans, 1648. Were not the 3 daus. born in New Haven? The birth of Elizabeth and the date of her marriage to Richard Hubbell of Fairfield, Conn., particularly desired. C. L. S.

134. *Anderson*, George of Willington, Conn., m. March 23, 1749, Abigail, dau. of Capt. Stephen and Abigail (Rugg) Brown and g-g dau. of Capt. John Mason of Pequot fame. He is supposed to be connected with the Scotch who settled for a time in Londonderry, Ireland, and then came in 1725 to America and settled in Worcester, Pelham and Palmer, Mass. He with his two sons, Stephen and Thomas, were in the company of Capt. Thomas Knowlton, from Ashford, at the battle of Bunker Hill. He died in 1816 at Willington. His sons, Lemuel and Wil-

liam joined the Revolutionary army later. It is a family tradition that he had a brother Adnah in Nova Scotia. Wanted: any definite clews to his ancestry, place or date of birth.   F. W. A.

135. (a) *Adams*, Richard, m. ——— and had Richard, b. April 26, 1763, in Pomfret, Conn. Who was his mother?

(b) *Warner*, William, died Feb. 28, 1714, in Wethersfield, Conn., and left two sons, 1. William, b. Jan. 25, 1672, and 2. Daniel, b. Jan. 1, 1680. William Jr. had a son William b. Dec. 4, 1717. Daniel had a son William b. Oct. 1, 1715. About 1739 William Warner m. Rebecca Lupton. About the same time William Warner m. a wife—name not known to me—and for his 2d wife, Mar. 25, 1752, Prudence May. Who was father of the William who mar. Prudence May?   A. L. F.

136. *Moss*, John of East Haven, Conn., one of the original founders of the New Haven Colony. From whence and when did he emigrate? And any other facts of his ancestry?
   C. C. W.

137. (a) *Bigelow*, Patience, mar. 1734 Lieut. Samuel Lawrence. What was her paternal ancestry? What was her maternal ancestry?

(b *Lawrence*, Zeruah, b. May 20, 1754, d. Feb. 24, 1832, dau. of Lieut. Samuel and Patience (Bigelow) Lawrence. Wish the paternal and maternal lines of this Samuel Lawrence.

(c) *Hathaway*. Capt. Clothier, mar. Mary Borden and had Sarah, b. Sept. 12, 1790; d. June 22, 1859; m. Capt. Holder Chace. Would like ancestry of Capt. Clothier.

(d) *Smith*, Jeremiah, b. 1704, d. Sept. 20, 1793; m. Martha Williams and had Jonathan, b. Jan. 24, 1746; of Preston, Conn. Would like ancestors of Jeremiah. His father might have been Asa.

(e) *Williams*, Martha, b. 1711, d. Feb. 9, 1786, m. Jeremiah Smith. Would like names and dates of her ancestors.

(f) *Witter*, William, m. ——— and had Hannah, b. May —, 1750, d. May 29, 1823, m. Nov. 23, 1769, Jonathan Smith. I have a book printed in 1618 which belonged in 1735 to Wm. Witter. Wish dates of his birth, marriage, death and ancestors back. Also same of his wife.   C. V. C.

138. *Hubbard*, Thomas, mar. Phebe Oakley of Westchester Co, N. Y., whither he had removed. He is said to have been a Conn. man and in the battle of White Plains. Wanted, his parentage. Who was the Thomas Hubbard in White Plains if not this one? Anna Hubbard m. about the time of the Revolution, Hozea Hamilton, and moved from Conn. to N. Y. Who was she?   E. P.

139. (a) *Badger*, Enoch[4] (Nathaniel,[3] John,[2] Giles[1]) b. 1714, settled in Coventry, Conn. Family may have lived in Windham and Norwich previous to 1748; mar. Mary ———. Who were her parents? Enoch[4] d. 1793. His son Enoch, b. 1750, mar. Feb. 11, 1773, Mary Lamphear. Who were her parents and grandparents?

(b) *Warriner*, Abner[5] (Moses[4], William,[3] James,[2] William[1]), b. Dec. 12, 1752, m. 1778 Elizabeth Wright or Knapp. They resided in Wilbraham, Mass., but she d. at Enfield, Conn., aged 93. Who were her parents and grandparents?
   F. H. H

140. *Gorham*, Jabez,[4] son of John and Desire (Howland) Gorham, b. Aug. 3, 1656; m. Hannah ———, and he d. May 18, 1725. Jabez and Hannah (———) Gorham had Isaac, b. Feb. 1, 1689, who m. 1st, Mary ——— and she died Sept. 2, 1716; m. 2d, Hannah Miles, May 23, 1717, and she d. before 1756. Can anyone give the names of the parents of Hannah who mar. Jabez Gorham,[4] and the names of the parents of Mary, the first wife of Isaac Gorham? Was the said Hannah, or Mary, a lineal descendant of Elder William Brewster? Would like the lineage of the said Hannah and Mary? E. C. J.

141. *Durkee*, Lydia, b. ———, d. Oct. 3, 1820, in Ind.; mar. at Norwich, Conn., May 1, 1785, William Lord, b. June 20, 1763, at Norwich, d. Oct.

3, 1820, in Ind. Wanted, Lydia Durkee's birth and parents.   E. J. E.

142. *Chase*, Constant, my grandfather, joined the privateer brig Argus in Savannah, Ga., as Prize Master. She was a *Lettre de Marque*. John Howe (or George) was commander, James Fairfield of Salem, Mass., was 1st officer. The brig was taken shortly after she sailed from Savannah by a British 74—"St. Domingo." The ship's company was taken to Plymouth, England, thence marched to *Dartmoor Prison*. Chase was in Prison No. 5; was among those fired upon by order of Capt. Shortland and was sent home in a cartel and landed in N. Y. 1815, after the peace. Can anyone cite me to any document which will legally prove the above statement?   C. C.

143 (*a*) *Abernathy*, Elizabeth, b. June 24, 1777, d. July 23, 1828; m. Nov. 10, 1793, Amos, son of Elisha Tuller, of Simsbury, Conn. Desire her ancestry. Was this Elisha in the Revolution?

(*b*) *Bunce*, Martha, m. Joseph Tuller of Simsbury, Conn. Was she the Martha Bunce who with twin Mary was bapt. 1720 and daus. of Joseph and Amy (———) Bunce?

(*c*) *Tuller*, John of Simsbury, m. 1684 Elizabeth, wid. of Joseph Lewis and dau. of John Case of Simsbury. Wanted, ancestry of John Tuller with dates.   M. C. T.

144. (*a*) *Bullard*, Abigail, m. abt. 1723, Ephraim Spalding, both of Plainfield, Conn. Who were her parents?

(*b*) *Thompson*, Eunice, m. June 19, 1739, Ebenezer Carpenter, both of Coventry, Conn. Who was her father?

(*c*) *Madison*, Mary, said to be a cousin of President Madison, m. Mar. 6, 1766, Foster Whitford of West Greenwich, R. I. Does any one know of her and her family? Tradition says they were of Conn. Whitford and wife moved to Saratoga Co., N. Y., before the Revolutionary War.   G. B. S.

145. (*a*) *Bishop*, Rebecca, dau. of Lt. Gov. James Bishop, m. Nov. 14, 1695, Samuel Thompson (gr. son of Anthony, the emigrant to New Haven, 1638) and lived in Westville, Conn. What is date of her birth and death?

(*b*) *Wilmot*, Hannah, mar. May 30, 1723, James Thompson, b. June 15, 1699 (son of above Samuel) and lived in Westville, Conn. Who were her parents?

(*c*) *Booth*, Elisha, b. prob. about 1700, in Southampton, L. I.; m. Hannah, dau. of Alexander Wilmot of Southampton, L. I., and formerly of New Haven, Conn. These two Hannah Wilmots may have been cousins. This Elisha Booth was probably a grandson of John Booth who came from Eng. to Southold, L. I., 1651. If so, which of John Booth's four sons, Thomas, John, Charles and William, was his father? Or whose son was he?

(*d*) *Sackett*, Jonathan, mar. Ruth Hotchkiss and had Sarah, b. Aug. 9, 1721, in New Haven, who m. Elisha Booth (son of above Elisha) and had 1. Jonathan, and 2. Hannah. They lived in the vicinity of Westville, Conn., or in Hamden, Conn. Who were parents of this Jonathan Sackett? Who were parents of Ruth Hotchkiss? Who were gr. parents of Jonathan Sackett? In Vol. 9, p. 10, N. Y. Genealogical and Biographical Record, it says : " John Booth, before coming to Southold in 1651, was at Barbadoes. He left England with merchandise which was wrecked in the Swallow; probably the vessel commanded by Capt. Jeremy Horton." Where is the authority for this statement found by Mr. Moore?

(*e*) *Cooper*. i. Triphena, d. Apr. 10, 1818, æt. 81, unmarried. ii. Sarah, m. James Gilbert. iii. Rebecca, b. 1744; m. Jonathan Booth, b. 1747, son of Elisha, Jr. iv. Samuel, m. Rachel Ford. These 3 sisters and brother lived in S. W. part of Hamden Conn., or in that vicinity. Who were their parents?

(*f*) *Booth*, Sir Henry of Harlaston, Derbyshire, Eng., d. 1424, had a dau. Alice who mar. Sir Nicholas Fitzhubert of Norbury, Derbyshire, knight of the shire of Derby, 1434, 1446 and 1452, and sheriff of the county in 1448 and 1466 Who were parents of Sir Henry? On the spindle side I trace my ancestry to this Alice and Sir Nicholas, and hence my interest in Sir Henry. Sir Thomas Booth of Barton (in Lancashire?) Knight, was living in the time of Edward III. He gave to his second son Henry all his lands in Jowell. Whether this second son Henry and Sir Henry of Harlaston *are one person*, I cannot determine, though they may be, as Sir Henry of Harlaston has about the same coat-of-arms as Sir Thomas? W. S. B.

146. (*a*) *Briggs*, William of Boston and Lyme, Conn. His early family history desired. His wife's full name. Did he render any colonial services, civil or military? His dau. Hannah m. Wolston Brockway. She d. Feb. 6, 1687. When was she born?

(*b*) *Birchard*, Thomas. Early family history; wife's full name; dates of their b., m. and d.; his dau Hannah, m. Apr. 12, 1653, at Guilford, Ct., John Baldwin and moved to Norwich, Ct., in 1660. When and where was Hannah born? Did Thomas render any colonial services, civil and military?

(*c*) *Hawkins*, Claraina, m. Feb. 26, 1776, Benjamin Twichell (of Oxford, Conn, it is thought). Desired, her early family history, dates of birth and death, and where each occurred. Also names of her father and mother with dates of their b., m. and d. A. I. H.

147. *Kilburn*, Samuel, b. Feb 21, 1783, Sterling, Mass.; m. Mary Beaman and had: i. Mary. ii. Uri. iii. Elmira. iv. Manda. v. Fernanda. vi. Dexter. vii. Susan. viii. Emily. ix. Anda (my father), and x. George. This record is given in Kilburn Gen., 1856, by Durrie & Peck. Who was father of Samuel? Was Mary Beaman a descendant of Gamaliel Beaman who settled Lancaster (now Sterling) as early as 1659, and d. in 1707. A. K. K.

148. (*a*) *Johnson*, Sylvester, b. 1728; m. Mary ———; Lisbon, Ct. Who was his wife and what was his ancestry? He had: i. Stephen, b. 1757, m. Experience Wheeler; ii. Nathan. Stephen and Experience had Sylvester b. 1800, Ephraim, Mary, Benjamin and Eliza.

(*b*) *Wood*, Joseph, m. Elinor Tusten; lived at Goshen, N. Y., and had Julia 1775, John 1778, James 1779 m. Charlotte, dau. of Ebenezer and Martha Davis) Duning (or Dunnig). Was Joseph descended from the Long Island Woods? F. B. K.

149. *Blague*, Henry appeared in Boston as early as 1642 and d. in 1662; was buried in Old South Church. His wife was Elizabeth ———. He had sons Henry, Philip, Nathaniel and Joseph; daus. Elizabeth, Rebecca and Martha. My known ancestor, Joseph Blague, was in Saybrook, Ct., as early as 1680. Was he a son of Henry of Boston? Did any of Henry's sons settle in Braintree, Mass.? From whence did Henry come? We have always supposed he was from England, as we have found the name in English history only, time of Henry VIII.
C. C. B.

150. *Woodruff*, Matthew Sr. of Farmington, Conn., 1640. What relation was he to Benjamin Woodruff of Essex and Old Norfolk counties, Mass.? In the old cemetery at Farmington, Conn., are tombstones: "Mr. Joseph Woodruff d. Oct. 7, A. D. 1799, in the 84th year of his age." Also "In Memory of Mrs. Hannah Woodruff, consort of Mr. Joseph Woodruff, who died Oct. 11, 1799, in the 77th year of her age." (Savage says she was "Hannah, dau. of John Clark," but beyond that he was ignorant.) Who were parents of this Joseph, or what was his relation to Benjamin or Matthew, Sr.? E. E. S.

151. *White*. Can anyone give information concerning the White family of Lebanon (Crank), Conn., or tell where such information can be found? Especially as to the name of the pioneer. Nathaniel seemed to be a favorite name. E. L. H.

152. *Brewster*, Anne, b. Dec. 16, 1755, in Duxbury, dau. of Nathan Brewster, b. Dec. 21, 1724, in Duxbury, and Hannah Partridge) Brewster. Anne Brewster mar. Solomon Lee of Lebanon, Ct. Can anyone give the lineage of said Nathan Brewster? F. E. W.

HISTORICAL NOTES.

The following extract bearing upon negro slavery in Connecticut was copied from some old papers found in a desk purchased in Middletown, Conn., by James F. Savage of Lowell, Mass., and is contributed to this department by him:

BILL OF SALE FOR ROSE THE NEGRO GIARL
Sep^t 8th 1747.

Know all Men That I James Ward Junr of Middletown in the County of Hartford, for the Confideration of the Sum of One Hundred pounds old tenor bills to me well & truly paid by John Eafton of Middletown aforefaid Do by thefe prefents fully freely and abfolutely, Give, Grant, Bargain, Sell and Deliver unto the said John Eafton his Heirs and Assigns, One Certain Negro Girl named Rofe, aged five years Last January. To Have and To Hold the said Negro Girl for and Dureing the term of her Natural Life unto him the f^d John Eafton his Heirs and Assigns, to be to his & their only ufe benefit & behoof; And I the S^d James Ward for myfelf and my heirs, Do hereby Covenant, Declare and warrant that the S^d Rose is in health & well and that fhe hath the free ufe of her Limbs and fenses, and that I and my heirs will and fhall Warrant the title of the faid Negro Girl unto the faid Eafton and to his heirs & Affigns. In witness whereof I have hereunto fet my hand & Seal this eighth Day of Septem^r A D, 1747. JAMES WARD.

Signed, Sealed & Del^d
In prefence of
THOMAS EMMES.
WM. ROCKWELL.

Mr. Conant and Mr. Fenn, the clerk and asssistant clerk of the Superior Court of Hartford County, have discovered, packed away in old trunks in the attic of the county building, the ancient law records of the county dating back to 1718. Among them are the records of the judgments given from 1774 to 1798, generally believed to have been lost and so reported to the Legislature in 1889. These papers are now being sorted and carefully stored in the vaults, safe from danger of fire and from further ravages of mice and vermin. It is a strange thing that these valuable records should have been forgotten after their removal from the old State House, and much credit is due to Mr. Conant and Mr. Fenn, who are spending their spare time in preserving this rich mine of historical information.

EXPEDITION TO CUBA.
What the Campaign of 1762 Cost in Lives.

"E. C. C.," arguing for peace, writes to the Hartford Courant as follows:

In an address, delivered before the Tolland County Historical society at Tolland, August 27, 1861, the Hon. Loren P. Waldo, president of the society, said:

In the year 1762, the King of England (George III) made a requisition upon the colony for troops to join the expedition against the island of Cuba, and a company was raised in the eastern part of the state, of which Colonel Israel Putman was, by one of formalities of the service, nominally captain, but really under the command of Solomon Wells of Tolland. This company went to the island of Cuba, and was present at the seige and capture of Havana, but was not in any serious engagement. When I was a boy, I was informed, by a man whose name was on the roll that, after the principal fort had been undermined and blown up, so that a column of British regulars carried it by assault, this company had the sad duty to perform of clearing the fort, and burying the dead. The destruction of life was very great; the dead were represented as lying in windrows. Although the company was not under fire during the whole of this campaign, the mortality of its members was unprecedented. Of ninety-eight persons of which the company was composed, and who actually reached the island, only twenty-two returned to their native land. Among the list of dead we read such familiar names as Daniel Brown, William Case and John Curtis."

The same story comes from the town of New Hartford, Ct. :—

"A detachment of sixteen young men, from New Hartford, went on an expedition against Havana, under General Lyman, in 1762, only one of whom, Benjamin Merrill, lived to return. This expedition, which reached Havana in the month of August, was fatal to more than two thirds of the men who composed it, chiefly by reason of sickness incident to the climate of that season. Of a regiment numbering, August 10, 802 men, but 30 were reported fit for duty October 2, and part of those who lived to embark for home died on the voyage, or suffered shipwreck."

DESCENDANTS OF WILLIAM CHASE OF YARMOUTH.

[Continued from last number.]

36. William[4] Chase (John,[3] William[2], William[1]) d , 1771, æt. 98 or 99; m., 1st, Sept. 20, 1715, in Y., Dorcas Baker;* m., 2d, Oct. 15, 1747, in Harwich, Patience,[4] dau. of Jabez[3] (William[2]) and Sarah (Snow) Walker; p. 148, Vol. 47, New Eng. Gen. Reg. has Elizabeth Snow as wife of Jabez Walker. William[4] Chase lived in Harwick and was a Friend in 1743. A William Chase in 1712 received 7½ shares of common lands (pp. 129 and 130, Y. T. R.). Also owned land in Yarmouth Jan. 21, 1739 (p. 142, Y. T. R). His will dated Sept. 17, 1771, at Harwich, names wife Patience; 8 daus. and 4 sons.

First 3 children on p. 77, book 3, Y. T. R.

214—i. "Lydiah,"[5] March 27, 1716; m. , Philip Leonard. Did he have children ? Who were his parents ?
215—ii. Elizabeth,[5] Oct. 6, 1718; m. pub. Dec. 4, 1731, in Y., Joshua[2] Wixin. Did he have children ? Mr. "Rt."[1] Wixin had Barnabas,[2] m. Sarah._____ _____ and had Joshua,[3] b. March 14, 1695.
216—iii. Thankful,[5] March 6, 1720-21; m. March 25, 1743, Stephen[4] O'Kelley (Joseph,[3] Jeremiah,[2] David[1]).
217—iv. Deborah,[5] ; m. May 2, 1751, in Harwich, Henry Hewet of Taunton. Did he have children ? Who were his parents ?
218—v. Dorcas,[5] ; m. pub. Sept. 14, 1744-5, in Y., but m. Jan. 1745-6, in H., Reuben Wixon. Did he have children ? Who were his parents ?
219—vi. Mary,[5] ; m. , Chace. Did he have any children ? Who were his parents ?
220—vii. William,[5] Oct. 16, 1732; m. Feb. 19, 1757, Mercy Chase. Who were her parents ?
221—viii. Sylvanus,[5] _____ ____ ___ -; m. 1757, Charity[5] Chase 242.
222—ix. Job,[5] _____ , 1736 (d. 1833, æt. 97); m., 13t, 1760, Edith Bassett (who were her parents?); m. 2d, 1775, Mrs. Hope (Sears) Howes; m. 3d, Hannah Dimmick. Who were her parents ? What children had this Job ?
223—x. Edmond,[5] ; mar., 1762, Abigail Farris. Who were her parents ?
224—xi. Patience,[5] __ ___ .. She was under 18 in 1771. What became of her ?
225—xii. Meribah,[5] ... ... _____ ___. She was under 18 in 1771, a Meribah m. Jan. 4, 1781, in H., James Ellis. Who were his parents ? Did he have children ?

37. Jeremiah[4] Chase (John,[3] William,[2] William[1]) m. Sept. 11, 1719, in Y., Hannah[4] b. Jan. 11, 1699, in Y.), dau. of John[3] (John[2], Francis[1]) and Hannah (Jones) Baker.

*William[2] Baker (Francis,[1] vide p. 8) d. , 1727, Y.; m.
Mercy ; she d. Nov. 26, 1753, Y. Who were her parents?
Children born in Y.:
i. Mercy,[3] Jan. 3, 1692; m. Feb. 17, 1713, Samuel Smith. Did he have children ?
ii. William,[3] Jan. 8, 1694. What became of him?
iii. Dorcas,[3] Nov. 15, 1696; m. William[4] Chase.
iv. Experience,[3] Jan. 8, 1698.
v. Judah,[3] March 23, 1700-1; m. , Jane __ __.
vi. Elizabeth,[3] Feb. 11, 1702-3; m. Feb. 5, 1718-19, Robert Wixon.
vii. Josiah,[3] Dec. 14, 1704; m. Sept. 25, 1729, Charity Eddy.
viii. Joanna,[3] Feb. 18, 1706-7; m. Aug. 25, 1726, Michael Phillips.
ix. Patience,[3] Feb. 1708-9; m. June 29, 1726, Benjamin Smalley.
x. Elisha,[3] Dec. 11, 1712; m. , 1714-5, Mercy Cahoon.
xi. James,[3] May 20, 1715; m. . , 1737, Keziah Eldridge.
xii. Thankful,[3] Dec. 6, 1710; m. March 8, 1743-4, Daniel Baker.

Jeremiah received, in 1712, 7½ shares in common lands (pp. 129 and 130 Y. T. R.) Capt. "Shuball baxter," James Lewes, Ebenezer "berry" and Jeremiah "Chaice" jury of trials at next inferior court at "barnstable"—Y. T. R. He was a Quaker at Harwich, 1743.

Children's births, book 3, p. 103, Y. T. R. ("Chaise"):

226—i. Jeremiah[5] Aug. 28, 1720; m. Jan, 28, 1741-2, Lydia Paul. Who were her parents?
227—ii. Ebenezer,[5] Sept. 25, 1722; m., 1744, Susanna Berry. Who were her parents?
228—iii Jabez,[5] March 15, 1726-7. What became of him?
229—iv. David,[5] March 15, 1728-9, m. pub. Sept. 5, Y., and Sept. 15, H., 1752, Susanna[4] (b. June 4, 1734, in Y.), dau. of Silas[3] (Nathaniel,[2] Francis[1]) and Deliverance (O'Kelley) Baker of Harwich. What became of this David?
230—v. Elizabeth,[5] July 1, 1731; m., 1750, Joseph O'Kelley, Jr.

38. Isaac[4] Chase (John,[3] William,[2] William[1]) d. May 22, 1759, in Y.; m., 1st, May 23, 1706, in Y., Mary* Baker; she died April 5, 1727; m., 2d, Aug. 3, 1727, in Y., Mrs. Charity, wid. of Jeremiah O'Kelley and dau. of Matthew and Hannah (Marchant) Pease, and she was born Dec. 9, 1696, in Y. An Isaac Chase received 18½ shares in common lands, and "Ye tenement for Isaac Chase to his father, 9 shares" (pp. 129 and 130, Y. T. R.) Inventory of his estate, £39.11, was presented by Barnabas Chase, June 21, 1759 (Vol. IX, p. 425, Barnstable P. R.) Joseph "howes" jun., Isaac "Chaife" and Nathan Taylor—jury men for "April" Court at Barnstable "april" 1720; William "hedge," Silas Sears, Isaac "Chaife" and Isaac "chapman"—jury men for July "court" next at Barnstable, May 24, 1724; Isaac "Chaife" and Thomas Crowell jun. "hog Reefes," Mar. 23, 1724-5; Isaac "Chaise" and Jacob "parker," grand jury men, Mar. 11, 1727-8; Isaac Chafe and John "matthews"—Hog "reefer" Mar. 6, 1737; Isaac Chase and Matthias Gorham—"Hog Rever" Mar. 13, 1740-41.

Children's births, book 3, p. 68, Y. T. R.:

231—i. "Hesaciah,"[5] Dec. 9, 1706; probably lived in Chatham, Cape Cod. Did he have children?
232—ii. "Obediah,"[5] Sept. 16, 1708; m., 1732, Mary Smith of Chatham. Who were her parents?
233—iii. Thankful,[5] Feb. 14, 1711-12; m. Oct. 19, 1732, Jacob Baker.
234—iv. Isaac,[5] Mar. 28, 1714; m. Nov. 17, 1737, Thankful Maker.

*Richard[1] Berry, buried Sept. 10, 1676 (Y. R.), m. ———, Alice ———
 Richard and Alice (   ) had children born:
1. ———, Mar. 20, 1652 (John d. 1745, æt. 93).
2. ———, July 11, 1654.
3. ———, Mar. 5, 1656.
4. ———, April 11, 1657 (perhaps Eliza)
5. ———, May 12, 1659.
6. ———, Aug. 22, 1661.
7. ———, Oct. 18, 1663.
8. ———, Oct. 5, 1668 (father called Sr. in Court Records March, 1678-9).
9. ———, June 1, 1673.
10. ———, Oct. 31, 1675.
11. ———, Dec. 12, 1677.

The record is so defaced that the names can't be made out. Among these children were: Nathaniel (d. Feb. 7, 1694), Richard Jr., Samuel, Joseph, John, and Eliza who m. Nov. 28, 1677, Josiah Jones.
 John[2] Berry (Richard[1]) d. ———, 1745, æt. 93. John had:
 i. Judah,[3] b. about 1676; moved to Harwich. Did he have children?
 ii. Ebenezer,[3] b. about 1678; m., 1st, Rebecca ———; m., 2d, Joanna Phillips; m., 3d, Hannah Lovel.
 iii. Elizabeth,[3] b. about 1680; m. July 15, 1702, Samuel[3] Baker (Nathaniel,[2] Francis[1]).
 iv. Experience,[3] b. about 1682; m. ———, Jonathan Bangs.
 v. Mary,[3] b. about 1684; m. May 23, 1706, Isaac[4] Chase 38

EDITORIAL NOTES.

"The first meeting of the Audubon Society of the State of Connecticut, the pioneer organization of the state, was held on Friday afternoon, January 28, at the house of Mrs. William B. Glover, in Fairfield.

"The motive of the society is the protection of wild birds, discouraging the use for millinery purposes of all bird feathers other than ostrich plumes and the feathers of domestic fowls and game birds used for food, already protected by law.

"The society expects to have public talks upon birds during the coming season, to distribute leaflets and to furnish lists of books to others desiring to study native birds, animals or plants, as but little is at present understood about the value of birds in their relation to agriculture."

It would seem as if this society, if it will avoid too radical steps, might do a very great deal of good in the state. Any movement for the protection of the birds and for promulgating information concerning their value to the agriculturist should be most heartily encouraged. It would seem as if the legislators of the state, also, were waking up to this fact, for the revised statutes for the year 1897 show a distinct advance, with perhaps one exception, in the matter of the bird and game laws. The law, as it exists now, is much more strict than formerly, and distinctly prohibits the destruction of a large number of varieties of birds for any purpose whatsoever. It also protects the nests and eggs as well as the birds themselves. It might be said, however, that the law-abiding gunner will have to carry an ornithology in one pocket and a copy of the Statutes of Connecticut in the other, to be able to decide what he may and what he may not shoot. The cautious hunter will confine himself to English sparrows. It seems as if it would be well if the law could embrace in its protection many other groups of birds popularly supposed to be injurious to agriculture, but really advantageous, if we may trust the word of those who have made a study of the subject. Among this number come the hawks and owls, who more than pay for the occasional theft of a chicken by their unremitting warfare on crop-devouring vermin. This addition would also simplify the wording of the statute. But while the law is to be praised, it is a pity that there is not some exception made for the killing of birds for scientific purposes. A system of limited permits granted to persons properly accredited would fill this need fully.

It is perhaps an interesting question why killing birds for their feathers should be regarded as a worse offence than killing birds for so-called sport. No one is dependent upon partridge, quail, or reed birds for sustenance. Why should it be regarded as worse to take one life to obtain an ornament which will last a whole season than to take several lives to obtain a luxury for one meal? If one is anxious to become a good shot, he will find that a "blue rock target" in a high wind will give him all the practice he wants. And there is this additional advantage, that his reputation for veracity will be in much better condition after a day at "the traps" than after a day in the field.

May the Audubon Society prosper, and may it be instrumental in obtaining wise, firm, and well informed legislation in behalf of the birds.

Those who are fond of arguing the "Good Roads Movement" pro. and con. will find new material for discussion in the report of the Highway Commissioners for 1898. The report is an interesting *resumé* of the work done by the Commission during the previous six months and of the various methods of road construction employed in the different parts of the state. The commissioners seem to have used wonderfully good judgment in the matter of adapting the method of construction to the facilities furnished by the given locality. While they recommend a Telford or Macadam road, with trap as road metal, they allow, as far as possible, the use of other stone in localities far removed from the trap area; and, in regions where stone cannot be readily obtained, they encourage the building of excellent gravel roads. The system of allowing the towns to bid for the contracts within their limits has aroused local interest in the work and has served to reduce costs considerably.

That good roads are a great advantage where there is much teaming to be done no one can deny who has watched the great stream of market wagons that moves towards New York every day over the great Jericho Turnpike of Long Island. But the question arises, how much teaming is done over the ordinary Connecticut road? Investigation will probably show that, while there is a great deal of traffic in the vicinity of the cities, on the roads of the outlying districts there is comparatively little activity even at the time of year when they are in good order. When the highway is so little used, does the advantage of the Macadam road equal the expense of its construction? Will not a good gravel road answer all the needs of the community, especially *if every teamster complies with the "wide tire" law?* There are unquestionably places in all highways which are bad at any time of year. These places would seem to demand a Macadam bed of the best type, but such stretches of road are usually very limited. With the exception of these limited localities, will not the excellent gravel roads, such as the Commission is constructing in many places, serve all needs as well as the expensive stone roads?

It may, perhaps, be fairly asked, if the government is willing to expend so much for water-way travelers in the improvements of rivers and harbors, why should it not spend as freely for highway travelers in the improvement of the roads? In answer it may, however, be suggested that many waterways are as little worth expensive improvement as are some of our highways.

Perhaps the simplest solution of the problem is to be found in Mr. MacDonald's suggestion to build two trunk lines across the state, one from north to south and the other from east to west, following the lines of present important turnpikes. The traveler will then make his was as speedily as possible by roads more or less improved, as the case may be, to these great thoroughfares where he can journey as far as he desires on the best Macadam road that can be built.

The preparations, which the Government is making along the coast to meet the present crisis, bring us seriously to the consideration of the question, what does war mean for Connecticut?

That the Government is making every effort to protect the entrance of the Sound, there is no doubt; but the history of our late war leaves in our minds serious doubts of the ability of forts and mines to stop a fleet or of a blockade to intercept all privateers. The thought that ships of the Spanish navy, as well as privately equipped vessels, may devote themselves to the work of harrassing the coast adds gravity to the situation. The ordnance and cartridge works at Bridgeport and the arms factories at New Haven and Hartford are prizes well worth effort and danger, and the large supplies of coal stored along the water front of these cities may prove a prize almost equally valuable. The Rodman guns, which are to guard harbor entrances, are justly valued by the old gunners who know their good points well, but these guns are few in number, slow of action and of comparatively short range.

In view of these facts it is possible, though by no means probable, that hostile forces might attempt operations by land as well as by sea. Such a movement the state troops will be prepared to meet. Yet, in a long and irregular coast like ours, it sometimes happens that an attack masterfully led may prove a most disastrous surprise. Under these conditions it is an interesting question what part the ordinary citizen is to play; and the mind instinctively goes back to the way in which the farmers met the British regulars in the early days of the Revolution. It is to be remembered that while warships have put on armor, troops have not, and that at short range a Springfield musket is as effective as the latest Winchester. While we anticipate no trouble of the kind, when one considers the steep hills and narrow defiles and the wooded and tortuous roads of Connecticut, is not the story of the Retreat from Concord full of suggestion? Cannot the single citizens of to-day, with hearts full of patriotism, render as effective service in emergency as did their forefathers a hundred and twenty-three years ago?

The dedication of the Hunt Memorial on Prospect street, Hartford, which took place on the evening of February 1, commemorated in a most fitting manner the completion of the Hartford Medical Society's first half-century of usefulness. Through the generosity of the late Mrs. Mary C. Hunt, widow of the late Dr. Ebenezer Hunt—in memory of whom the gift is made—the Society has now a building fitted in the best way to be its laboratory, its library, and its home.

At the opening exercies, after the prayer of dedicaton by the Rev. Dr. Samuel Hart of Trinity College, Dr. Melancthon Storrs delivered an historical address and formally presented the Hunt Memorial to the board of trustees, Dr. Gurdon W. Russell accepting it in behalf of that body. This was followed by an original poem by Dr. Nathan Mayer. After the poem the oration of the evening was delivered by President Daniel C. Gilman

of Johns Hopkins University. President Hartranft of the Hartford Theological Seminary closed the exercises with the benediction.

After the exercises the many visitors enjoyed themselves in examining the building and the portraits which decorate its walls, especially the ones by Mr. Charles Noel Flagg of Dr. Hunt and of Dr. Horace Wells, the discoverer of Anæsthesia.

The importance which the opening of the Hunt Memorial has in the medical history, not only of Hartford but also of the State, may perhaps be best understood from the following words of President Gilman: "As a center of life and light it will be an example to other parts of the State, and even at a distance. Dublin, Edinburgh and London have their halls of medicine where portraits, statues and other memorials of illustrious physicians and surgeons are the ornaments of libraries, museums and laboratories The beginnings of like institutions may be found in Boston, New York, Philadelphia and Baltimore, but Hartford (so far as I know) is the first to establish at a distance from a school of medicine a place of assembly for the members of the profession, where they can know and advise with one another, gather up the experiences of the past, become acquainted with current journals and memoirs, and make such accurate scientific observations as in these days are essential to those who practice the healing arts."

PUBLISHER'S NOTES.

On page 180, in the introduction, we speak of the "Sexton's List" as being copied by Dr. Hoadly. It seems that we were in error and the statement should read, from a list "owned by Dr. Hoadly."

In our last issue, mention was made in our Book Notes, of History of Montville and price quoted as $1.00 a copy. This should have been $4.00 a copy.

FROM THE SOCIETIES.

SONS OF THE AMERICAN REVOLUTION.

At a meeting of the National Society of the Sons of the American Revolution held at Cincinnati in October, 1897, it was voted that steps be taken to form a union between this society and the Sons of the Revolution. This necessitates some changes in the constitutions of the two bodies, and, while the plan has been generally approved by the members of the S. A. R., it has not found so great favor with the other order. At a meeting of the board of managers of the Connecticut Society, S. A. R., held at the Colonial Club, Hartford, recently, it was unanimously voted that the question be referred to the annual meeting to be held on May 10, with the recommendation that the plan as formulated at Cincinnati be not adopted. President Jonathan Trumbull of Norwich presided over the meeting of the board, and in the absence of Col. Louis R. Cheney, secretary, Mr. Frank B. Gay was chosen to fill his place.

DAUGHTERS OF THE AMERICAN REVOLUTION.

The thirtieth general meeting of the Ruth Wyllys Chapter, D. A. R., was held on February 12 in the rooms of the Historical Society at Hartford. An important feature of the meeting was the presentation of a paper by the Hon. Henry C. Robinson on "Jonathan Trumbull." Another notable incident of the meeting was the admission to membership of a real daughter of the Revolution, Mrs. Statira Beardsley. Her father, Philo Hodge, a native of Roxbury, Conn., enlisted in 1776 and served in several of the Connecticut regiments.

The delegates chosen to attend the National Convention of Daughters of the American Revolution at Washington were the regent, Mrs. John M. Holcombe, Mrs. William H. Palmer, Mrs. Francis Goodwin, Mrs. William C. Skinner, and Mrs. Charles E. Gross.

At a recent meeting of the Katherine Gaylord Chapter, at Bristol, the regent, Mrs. John M. Holcombe, made a report in behalf of the committee appointed to consider the advisability of erecting a memorial to the Connecticut women of the Revolution.

Mrs. Holcombe reported that the committee have been in some doubt as to the nature of the memorial to be erected, whether it should be a statue of some special heroine from the history of the State, or whether it should be an ideal figure of the woman of '76. The latter plan has found the most favor, and a site has been suggested just north of the State Capitol in Hartford. The statue is to cost not less than $10,000 and is to be executed in the very best manner possible. To this end communication has been opened with Mr. Macmonnies and Mr. St. Gaudens.

The Seventh Continental Congress of the Daughters of the American Revolution was held at Washington and extended from Monday, February 21, to Saturday, February 26. Over seven hundred regents and delegates were present.

The president-general, Mrs. Stevenson, reported an increase in membership for the past year of 5,059 and a total membership of 23,292. The registrar-general reported that during the last year sixty-nine patriots' daughters had been added to the order, making a total of two hundred and sixty-eight. A financial report showed the assets of the order to be $38,090.44, an increase of $12,634.33 for the year. A report was made by the committee appointed for the erection of Continental Hall—the proposed memorial to the victims of the prison ships. Nearly the whole sum needed for its construction has been raised and Congress has promised a site for the building.

On Thursday, February 24, Mrs. Daniel Manning, former regent of the chapter at Albany and a vice-president of the National Board, was elected president-general. Mrs. Stevenson, who retires from that office, was elected honorary president-general.

One of the pleasantest incidents of the meeting occurred at the reception on Thursday evening, when the gold medals voted by the congress of 1896 were conferred upon the four originators of the order, Mrs. Walworth, Miss

Desha, Miss Washington and Mrs. Lockwood. Another pleasing incident of the session was the presentation of a loving cup to Mrs. Stevenson, the retiring president-general.

The meetings of the congress took place in the Grand Opera House, and the building was filled to overflowing with interested spectators.

BOOK NOTICES AND REVIEWS.

I. NOTICES.

Books in preparation or in press. Those interested are invited to communicate with the authors.

Aldrich Genealogy. M. M. Aldrich, Mendon, Mass.

Miss Emma C. Jones, of Walnut Hills, Cincinnati, Ohio, is compiling a genealogy of the descendants of Elder Brewster. Upon application she will furnish circulars to those who are interested.

William Carpenter of Providence, R. I., and His Descendants, from 1637 to present time; 550 pp.; $7.50 per vol. Mr. Daniel H. Carpenter, Maplewood, N. J.

Curtiss Families of New England. Mr. F. H. Curtiss, B'way National Bank, Boston, Mass.

Thomas Fairchild, Stratford, Conn., 1639, and His Descendants—200 to 250 pp.; $3.00 per copy. Mrs. Annie Fairchild Plant, Milton, Vermont.

Genealogy and Biography of the Huntings of Dutchess County, N. Y., by Isaac Huntting, Pine Plains, N. Y.

Lewisiana or the Lewis Letter, a monthly inter-family paper; 10 cents per copy, $1.00 per year. Carll A. Lewis, Box 24, Elliott, Conn.

Mason Genealogy. Alverdo H. Mason, East Braintree, Mass.

South Britain (Conn.) History, containing genealogies of Guthrie, Platt, Van Hahm and Wagner families; probably others, but not intended to touch families treated in Cothren's Woodbury. William C. Sharpe, Seymour, Conn.

Trowbridge Genealogy; revised, enlarged and up to date, by Mr. Francis Bacon Trowbridge, New Haven, Conn.

Perry Family History. H. Pearl Perry, Westfield, Mass.; also Hext M. Perry, Greenville, South Carolina.

Sherwood Genealogy. Wm. L. Sherwood, 295 Ferry St., Newark, N. J.

Wiggin Genealogy. Levi Jewell Wiggin, 96 Salem St., Malden, Mass.

Probate Records of Essex Co., Mass.; monthly parts of 32 pp., 10 or 12 parts to a volume, at $5.00 per volume. Eben Putnam, Salem, Mass.

Harvey and Nesbit Families. Oscar J. Harvey, 47 Union Street, Wilkesbarre, Pa.

History of Family of Mathias St. John (Sension, Sention, Sinjen) of Norwalk, Conn., whose children were born 1634-1659. It is desired to publish the work during the year 1898. Rev. Horace Edwin Hayden, Wilkesbarre, Pa., and Mrs. Lawrence D. Alexander, New Canaan, Ct.

History of Martha's Vineyard, Mass., by Charles Edw. Banks, M: D., Vineyard Haven, Mass.

Genealogies of the Families in Dutchess County, N. Y,, before 1800, including what is now in Putnam County. Contributions desired. Wm. A. Eardeley-Thomas, 5000 Woodland Ave., Philadelphia, Pa.

II. REVIEWS.

HISTORY AND GENEALOGY OF THE KNOWLTONS OF ENGLAND AND AMERICA. By Rev. C. H. W. Stocking of Freehold, N. J. New York, 1897. A royal octavo volume of six hundred printed pages and many full-page illustrations. Price, $10.00. The volume is a collection of about 7500 Knowlton names and several thousand names other than Knowltons, with whom the latter intermarried, showing the descent of the persons named and in most cases the dates of their births. Some interesting notes relating to the family in England are given; also one of the more or less mythical lines of descent from the god Odin; also (which is not noted in the table of contents) "a partial list of the Knowltons who performed military services for their country;" also a section devoted to the "Royal Descents." Although there is no index, the author explains in an announcement that this will be prepared at an early date, as the "large size of the present history made it impossible to carry, in cloth binding, the additional matter of an index of many thousand names."

COE-WARD MEMORIAL AND IMMIGRANT ANCESTORS. This volume, of which only 150 copies are published, is the work of the Hon. Levi E. Coe of Meriden. The work, as must be the case with any similar work which traces back all the ancestral line of a certain family, is published primarily for the gratification of the worthy pride which the compiler feels in the ancestors of himself and wife. The book, however, has a wide historical and genealogical value, and will be of interest to many. The sketches are carefully written and bear evidence of much research. The lines run back to such well-known Connecticut families as Cornwall and Peck of Hartford, Coe of Wethersfield, Eggleston of Windsor, Camp of Milford, Robinson of Guilford, Atwater of New Haven, and Barns, Kirby, Miller and Ward of Middletown. The appendix contains considerable Coe and Miller genealogy, and the whole 130 pages is well indexed.

HISTORY OF GOSHEN, CONN., by Rev. A. G. Hibbard, Woodstock, Conn. A medium octavo volume of 600 pages and many full-page illustrations. Price, $3.25 by mail, net. In this volume, a history of one of the hill towns of Litchfield county, Conn., there is much that is important and interesting in the field of history—a field made prolific by the palmy days of those towns before the population had flocked to the cities and the railroads had revolutionized the manner of living. The book is enlivened by numerous anecdotes and biographical sketches beside the historical narrative. There are also two hundred pages devoted to genealogies of the early Goshen families. Altogether, Mr. Hibbard has made an interesting and readable as well as a valuable book.

THE CHORDS OF LIFE—A book of poems by Charles H. Crandall, Springdale, Conn., show a true poet and lover of nature. They are much above the average usually found in such books, will take rank with the best and are entertaining reading, while the expression, thoughts and versification are up to an ideal standard. The book contains over 150 pages, and has several neat half-tone illustrations. This first edition is limited to 500 copies, and may be had of the author, Charles H. Crandall, Springdale, Conn.

"SUMMER HOMES AMONG THE MOUNTAINS" is the title under which the annual guide book of the Philadelphia, Reading & New England Railroad comes to us. It is as valuable as ever to the person who has a vacation to plan for, and those who have souls which appreciate the artistic will find it twice as handsome as any of its predecessors. This beautiful book of nearly two hundred pages bears the creditable stamp of the Plimpton Manufacturing Company, and its typographical and press work is of the highest quality. It bears an embossed cover, the figure of which we judge to be Diana. The illustrations are typical of the unexcelled scenery to be found along the line of this road. The vacation problem becomes an analyzed fact, and all the troublesome features as to proper accommodations are done away with. Superintendent Martin's progressive ideas and management show in the improvements he is making each year, and are to be commended.

HALL'S VEGETABLE SICILIAN HAIR RENEWER

Hair Like This...

Long, Luxuriant, silken, soft, is the result of the use of HALL'S VEGETABLE SICILIAN HAIR RENEWER. This preparation renews the hair by renewing the conditions under which growth alone is possible.

HALL'S HAIR RENEWER feeds the hair, enriches the soil of the scalp, and so restores the color to gray and faded hair, stops hair from falling, removes dandruff, and promotes a healthy growth.

♦♦♦♦

From the Highest Medical Authority in Sweden.

I have had occasion to see several persons who, for some time have used HALL'S VEGETABLE SICILIAN HAIR RENEWER and know that it has restored the original color to the hair, as well as being efficient in removing the itching and dandruff that accompanies the falling of the hair. I consider it my duty to acknowledge the same.

VINCENT LUNDBERG,
Physician in Chief to the
King of Sweden.

R.P. HALL
AND
COMPANY
PROPRIETORS
NASHUA
N.H.

A FINE HAIR DRESSING

HERALDRY...

Family Crests, Coats of Arms
Properly Emblazoned.

E. A. SHERMAN,

Room 32, Trust Co. Building.   HARTFORD, CONN.

Maps and Street Guides of the City of HARTFORD.

FOR SALE BY

SMITH & McDONOUGH, 301 Main Street.
L. A. CHAPIN, 347 Main Street.
E. M. SILL, 89 Trumbull Street.
N. Y. & N. E. NEWS CO., R. R. Station.

ELIHU GEER'S SONS,

Printers and Publishers,

16 STATE ST., HARTFORD, CONN.

"The Grate That Heats."
Jackson Ventilating Grate.
Heats on two floors.

Highest Award, World's Fair, '93. Thousands now in use. Our customers are our references. Do not regard this grate as simply a luxury for Spring and Fall. It will heat two large rooms when the mercury outside is at zero or below, and will thoroughly and constantly ventilate the rooms without an open window or any draught.

Favor yourself and us by proving the luxury, the cheerfulness, the healthfulness and the economy of these grates.

Call and investigate or send for an illustrated catalogue.

Stoughton & Taylor,
38 Ann St.,
Hartford, Conn.

Mantels, fireplace fixtures, tiles, delft, Kenton Vitrea, etc.

Huntsinger's Business College

Is the leading school of Connecticut for business or short-hand training. Day attendance over 200 pupils. Seven skillful, polite and obliging teachers. This school has placed 198 graduates in good-paying positions the past fifty-one weeks.

No term divisions and new pupils enter every week. We do all that can be done to place graduates in situations. Full information for the asking. Visitors welcome.

Where to go for Good Printing and Bookbinding.

The Horton Printing Co.

Have one of the best equipped plants in the state for turning out the highest class of work at lowest prices.

. . SPECIAL ATTENTION . .
Given to Original Designs in Printing and Bookbinding.

We carry a Special Line of . . .

FINE STATIONERY

Which for variety and low prices cannot be equalled.

Steel Plate Engraving and Printing,
IN UP TO DATE STYLES.

OPERA HOUSE BLOCK, *MERIDEN, CONN.*

PRINTERS OF
THE CONNECTICUT QUARTERLY

Vol. IV.   July, August, September, 1898.   No. 3.

THE CONNECTICUT QUARTERLY

Illustrated Articles in this Number:

Washington.
New Haven Coast Defenses.
Peter Parley.
Glacial Action in Connecticut.
Old Time Music and Musicians.

See Contents on First Page.

1.00 a Year.   HARTFORD, CONN.   25 cts. a Copy.

The Philadelphia, Reading
....and New England R. R.
⁂Summer Home Book for 1898

IS NOW READY FOR DISTRIBUTION.

It contains over one hundred attractive half-tone illustrations and is without doubt the handsomest book of the kind ever issued by any railroad. It contains an increased list of Hotels and Boarding Houses, gives rates for board and all information sought after by those intending to summer in the country. Don't neglect getting a copy sent free for postage, 6c., to

W. J. MARTIN, Hartford, Conn.

The Connecticut Quarterly

AN ILLUSTRATED MAGAZINE

Devoted to the Literature, History, and Picturesque Features
of Connecticut

PUBLISHED QUARTERLY
BY THE CONNECTICUT QUARTERLY COMPANY
66 STATE STREET, COURANT BUILDING

GEORGE C. ATWELL, EDITOR.   HARTFORD, CONN.

CONTENTS.

Vol. IV   July, Aug., Sept., 1898.   No. 3

Washington Green.		*Frontispiece*
Washington. Illustrated.	*Dwight C. Kilbourn*.	237
The Tories of Connecticut.	*James Shephard*,	257
When Youth is Done. Poem	*Elizabeth Alden Curtis*.	263
List of Burials, Center Church Burying Ground, Hartford.		264
Copied and annotated by	*Mary K. Talcott*.	
New Haven Defenses in the War of the Revolution and in the War of 1812. Illustrated.	*M. Louise Greene*.	272
Blind-Fold. Poem	*Anna J. Granniss*.	290
Succory. Poem. Illustrated	*Louise P. Merritt*	291
A Pastoral. Poem. Illustrated	*Herbert Randall*	292
Some Common Evidences of Glacial Action in Connecticut. Illustrated.	*W. H. C. Pynchon*	294
Twilight. Poem. Illustrated.	*Sally Porter Law*.	303
Peter Parley– As Known to His Daughter. Illus.	*Emily Goodrich Smith*.	304
An Old Daguerreotype. Poem.	*Anna M. Tuttle*.	315
A Social Struggler. Story.	*Jane Morton*.	316
Old Time Music and Musicians. Illustrated	*N. H. Allen*.	319
Departments.—GENEALOGICAL DEPARTMENT.		329
DESCENDANTS OF WILLIAM CHASE OF YARMOUTH.		335
PUBLISHER'S NOTES.		337
HISTORICAL NOTES.		337
FROM THE SOCIETIES.		338
CONNECTICUT FORESTRY ASSOCIATION.		341

Copyright, 1898, by GEO. C. ATWELL (*All rights reserved*).
Entered at the Post Office at Hartford, Conn., as mail matter of the second class.

Profitable Investments

$10 a month for 120 months, paid on the shares of The Connecticut Building and Loan Association, of Hartford, Conn., will produce $2,000. If death occurs in the meantime the shareholder's heirs, or his estate, will receive the $2,000, and, besides, the book value of his shares.

Income-producing city and village real estate, and a paid-in-cash guarantee (Reserve) Fund of $100,000.00 form together the security offered to shareholders. Assets over $800,000.00. Accredited agents throughout Connecticut and in other States. Correspondence solicited.

E. C. LINN, Secretary,
252 Asylum St.,
Hartford, Conn.

The Religious Herald.

336 Asylum Street,
Hartford, Conn.

Congregational Weekly of Connecticut.

Single Subscriptions and Renewals, $1.00
New Subscribers (in clubs of five),   50c

REUBEN H. SMITH,

Editor and Proprietor.

Blickensderfer Typewriting Machines

Equal any of the high-priced machines in capacity and quality of work and excel them in convenience. Practical, low-priced, portable, keyboard machines. Have 84 letters and characters all on a type-wheel weighing less than one-quarter of an ounce

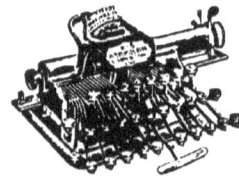

Scientific Keyboard,
No. 5. $35.00

H. C. HAYWOOD & CO.,
GENERAL AGENTS.
Meriden, Conn.

No Ribbon. Writing always in sight. Type interchangeable. Direct inking and printing. Unequalled in manifolding power. Acknowledged simplicity of construction. Most durable machines made. Weight only six pounds.

Either Scientific or Universal Keyboard
No. 7. $50.00

❦ The Connecticut Quarterly. ❦

$1.00 a Year. ❧ 25 Cents a Copy.
Payable in Advance.

All subscriptions taken with the understanding that they expire after four numbers have been sent. Unless renewed we discontinue sending.

When change of address is desired give both old and new address and we should receive notice at least two weeks before the first of the first month of the quarter.

Vol. I and Nos. 3 and 4 of Vol. II out of Print. We have a few of Nos. 1 and 2 of Vol. II. Price, 25 cents a copy.

HENRY S. HOUSE, Mgr. Subscription Department.

BOOK NOTICES.

Historical Collections relating to Gwynedd, a township of Montgomery County, Penn., settled 1698 by immigrants from Wales, with some data referring to the adjoining township of Montgomery, also settled by Welsh ; by Howard M. Jenkins, 921 Arch street, Philadelphia, Penn.; second edition, 464 p.p., 8 vo., 8 illustrations ; $4.00 net, postage 20 cents additional ; price will be advanced to $4.50. Accounts of the Boone, Evans, Foulke, Roberts, Williams and many other families are given. This second edition fills a long felt want, and we are sure the book will find ready and continuous sale.

A Genealogical and Biographical Record of the Savery Families (Savory and Savary) and of the Severy families (Severit, Savery, Savory and Savary) decended from early immigrants to New England and Philadelphia, with introductory articles on the origin and history of the names, by Judge A. W. Savary, M.A., Annapolis Royal, Nova Scotia ; p.p. xx + 266 ; good index ; price $5.00, and 15c for postage ; for sale by the author ; 21 illustrations ; well printed, neatly bound, clear style, and carefully compiled.

History of the County of Annapolis, including old Port Royal and Acadia, with memoirs of its representatives in the Provincial Parliament and Biographical and Genealogical Sketches of its early English settlers and their families, by the late W. A. Calnek, edited and completed by Judge A. W. Savary, M. A., with portraits and illustrations. 8 vo. p.p. xiv. + 660 ; price $3.25 post paid, for sale by the author. It is with great pleasure that we note the large amount of genealogy in this volume. It will be particularly valuable to Americans compiling family histories, since many loyalists settled in this part of Canada. We are very sorry the author did not make an index of the genealogies. Judge Savary deserves great credit for the manner in which he has edited the work.

The Stiles Family in America. Genealogies of the Connecticut family descendants of John of Windsor, and Francis of Windsor and Stratford, Conn., 1635-1894 ; the Connecticut-New Jersey families, 1720-1894 ; also, Southern (Burmuda-Georgia family, 1635-1894, with contributions to the genealogies of some New York and Penn. families, with an appendix containing information concerning the English families of the name, by Henry Reed Stiles, A.M., M.D., box 1810 New York City. Royal 8 vo. p.p. xii. + 782, price $5.00. This excellent work is by a well-known historical writer. Dr. Stiles is eminently able to edit superior works like this. His contributions to history and genealogy are models of excellence.

Clarke's Kindred Genealogies. A Genealogical History of Certain Descendants of Joseph Clarke, Dorchester, 1630 ; Denice Darling, Braintree, 1662 ; Edward Gray, Plymouth, 1643 ; William Horne, Dover, 1659 ; and sketches of the Orne, Pynchon, and Downing families, by Augustus Peck Clarke, A.M., M,D., 825 Massachusetts Avenue, Cambridge, Mass., p.p. xi. + 176, price $2.50. This illustrated volume gives valuable information on the families represented. The style is easily understood, thus making the book a real pleasure to peruse. We regret that the author did not give a complete index of the whole book.

The Bi-Centenial Celebration of the First Congregational Church and Society of Danbury, Conn., May 24-31, 1896, 8vo. p.p. 101. The Ecclesiastical Society received a charter from the Legislature May 14, 1696, but the church history probably reaches further back. Historical addresses were by Rev. Albert S. Pierce, Rev. Dr. Thomas R. Noble and others. Mrs. Susan B. Hill, compiler of Danbury history, gives some " Memories of the Old Church," which is very entertaining.

BOOK NOTICES.

Memorial of the De Forsyths de Fronsac, by Frederick Gregory Forsyth, Viscount de Fronsac. To be obtained of James Bennett Forsyth, 256 Devonshire street, Boston, Mass., price $5.00; p.p. 40 8vo. The Forsyth family in France, Scotland, Ireland, and America is here traced. Several fine engravings enhance the value of work. Views in De Frousac's Domain in Acadia are also added.

Ye Catalog of Epitaphs from Ye Old Burying Ground on Meeting House Hill in Methnen, Mass ; published by the Methnen Historical Society. 12 mo. p.p. 116, price $1.00 small edition. The work is arranged in alphabetical order. The old burying ground was laid out in 1878, and for nearly 50 years was the only one in the town.

Descendants of Constant Southworth (second edition), by George C. S. Southworth, 156 Lincoln Avenue, Salem, Col. Co. Ohio, p.p. 31. Southworths are earnestly requested to communicate further information respecting Edward of London and Leyden, and particularly their own family records to the author.

Sir George Yeardley or Yardly, Governor and Captain-General of Virginia, and Temperance (West), Lady Yeardly, and some of their descendants, by Thomas Teackle Upshur, Nassawaddox, Northampton, Co., Va., reprinted from *American Historical Magazine*, Nashville, Tenn , Oct. 1896, 4 to p.p. 36. Well compiled and shows extensive research.

Notes upon the Ancestry of John Platt, b. 1749, Burlington Co., N. J., and also a list of his descendants p.p. 31.

Notes upon the ancestry of Ebenezer Greenough, b. 1783, Haverhill, Mass., and his wife Abigail Israel, b. 1791, Cristine, Del , p.p. 38. These two uniform works are by Mr. Franklin Platt, 1617 Chestnut street, Philadelphia, Penn. They exhibit the results of careful compilation.

The Roger Williams Calendar by John Osborne Austin, Box 81, Prov., R. I. These extracts are published in order to enlarge the field of acquaintance with the works of Roger Williams. He was one of the grandest figures in the history of the race. The author is to be thanked for this noble attempt. There are 370 p.p. + vi. Each page is devoted to a day throughout the year, and extracts are taken arbitrarily from the works of Mr. Williams, and assigned to different days through one year. Price $5.00.

The Bockèe Family (Boucquet) 1641-1897, by Martha Bockee Flint, 3 Barclay street, Pouzhkeepsie, N. Y., price $5.00, 8vo. p.p. 158 + ix. Miss Flint here gives another fine genealogy to the American public. The work has good index and is clear in style. A Peters Lineage and Early Long Island are two works which Miss Flint has edited. Jerome Bocquet was in New Amsterdam as early as 1647, having come from Middelburg, Holland.

Ancestry of John Davis, governor and United States Senator, and Eliza Bancroft his wife, both of Worcester Mass. Compiled by Horace Davis, San Francisco, Cal., 8vo. p.p. 94. This illustrated volume makes quite an addition to American genealogy. Two charts are given at the beginning. The records are given in full and concisely.

Eldredge Genealogy. A record of some of the descendants of William Eldredge, of Yarmouth, Mass., by Zoeth S. Eldredge, Bohemian Club, San Francisco, Cal. 8 vo. p.p. 35. Printed for private circulation. An excellent compilation.

"Jim and His Old Cornet," is the title under which a little book of poems by Louis E. Thayer of Collinsville, Conn. It is in his usual felicitous style, and contains several poems devoted to nature subjects. Price $1.00, for sale by Belknap and Warfield, Hartford.

The Connecticut Quarterly.

"Leave not your native land behind."—*Thoreau.*

THIRD QUARTER.

VOL. IV.   JULY, AUG., SEPT., 1898.   NO. 3.

WASHINGTON

BY DWIGHT C. KILBOURN.

The town of Washington, Conn., was organized in 1779, and is claimed to be the first town in the colonies named after the Father of his Country. It is a hilly and rugged tract of land at nearly the southern end of the Green Mountain Range, with "Mount Tom" for its northern outpost and the beautiful Pomperaug Valley spread at the foot of its southern hills. These hills are seldom ledgy, and are crowned with well cultivated farms and substantial farm houses, homes of thrifty farmers, who live lives of intelligent comfort and support good churches and schools and whose families move in the most cultivated and refined society. Few localities can produce as many well-read and educated, moral, christian men and women as Judea. Stop and talk with that farmer driving his cows home from pasture and he will converse with you intelligently on art, history, philosophy, science of government, or almost any kindred subject, showing that he is a thinker as well as a worker. The story is told by a gentleman who once drove over these hills that he came across two farmers, bare-footed and bare-headed, whose teams were standing at some distance on either side of the fence on which they were seated. They were talking with great vehemence and using considerable gesticulation. Supposing

DAVIES' HOLLOW.

that there was some trouble between these neighbors, he approached them as a peacemaker. To his surprise they were simply having a discussion over the rank which Emerson should hold as a poet and philosopher.

The art of abandoned farms has not yet reached these rural hills. The boys go out into the world and run its commerce, its laws, its trade and its industries but they cling to the old farm, keep the buildings in repair, the fences trimmed up and return ever and anon to rest their tired brains amid these grand views and quiet scenes; and so it has come to pass that we have a township of city people mingling familiarly with the farmers.

A COUNTRY STORE.

Washington is composed of two divisions, the western, or north-western, called New Preston, and the eastern called Judea. The former has attained a wide reputation from its beautiful lake Waramaug, of which we gave some sketches in this magazine last year. It is of Judea we desire now to speak.

Originally Judea was a part of Woodbury, being the west part of the North purchase, and the first settler was Joseph Hurlbut from Waterbury, who built his log cabin in the southern part of the society about 1734. In a short time Increase Moseley, from Stratford, Nathaniel Durkee, Friend Weeks and Samuel Pitcher, all from Norwich, joined the settlement and became neighbors at a distance of from one to five miles apart, and in 1736 the community was so prosperous that a frame house was erected. They did not, while fighting bears and killing deer or scouting for the Indians, forget their religious duties, for Isaac Baldwin came down from Litchfield and preached to them in a bedroom of Joseph Hurlbut's house, which accommodated the people, " Tho' none staid at home in those times who were able to attend," as Rev. Dr. Porter in his notes, expresses it.

ERASTUS HURLBUT.

From the first settlement until the Act of Incorporation in 1779, the settlers were continually asking the General Assembly for some privilege and pestering "Ancient Woodbury" all the while by these applications. In 1739, be-

RESIDENCE OF F. K. ROSSITER.

cause they were fully eight miles from any meeting-house and their wives and children had to tarry at home from the worship of God for about half of the year, they were allowed to get their own preaching for six months in the winter and not required to pay taxes to build a school house in Woodbury Center. In 1741 a committee was appointed who fixed certain bounds and the General Assembly incorporated this people as the Judean Society. This was upon the petition of twenty-six settlers who the next year appeared and represented that they had "Unamymously and Lovingly Agreed upon A Place for to Set a Meeting House," and were granted a right to build a meeting house which eight of the proprietors proceeded to do that year.

The location thus harmoniously fixed upon was substantially that now occupied by the present meeting-house and is known far and wide as "The Green." Why it was so called is unknown, as it was a mass of ledges which even now, after a century or more of years of efforts to hide, crop

RESIDENCE OF E. H. VAN INGEN.

out. Upon one of them was placed a little plain building called the

RESIDENCE OF R. S. BARNES.

academy, and another spot was leveled big enough to set the meeting-house, and then the boys smoothed up a spot big enough to pitch quoits on. This grew to a cricket ground, then to one for base ball, and now the "Green" shows the conquering power of man and art over nature. From the "Green" roads radiate through the ledges to various sections of the town.

VACATION HOUSE.

The church edifice itself, is the third one erected here, and is the result of evolution. The first one built, in 1742, was a small affair, somewhat larger than Joseph Hurlbut's bed-room, and it lasted till 1751, when a more commodious one was erected for Parson Brinsmade to preach in. But that had no steeple, so in 1786, when Rev. Noah Merwin, who had to leave Torrington because they were too poor to support him, came to assist Mr. Brinsmade, they celebrated the event by putting on a steeple and buying a bell. Then a crazy man took hold of the matter and to celebrate Independence Day at the beginning of the century, he set the building on fire,—but the fire works did not develop well and were put out. In April, 1801, he tried it again with better success, and the Rev. Ebenezer Porter, who, after the death of Rev. Noah Merwin, was ordained over this people, had the pleasure of preaching the next Thanksgiving in the present edifice, which was not, however, entirely finished then. This building had originally a regular standard Presbyterian spire, but as the strong doctrine in later years wavered, so this tall spire weakened, and sound timbers decayed and finally it fell over, and the present beautiful Washingtonian design replaced it. Then an or-

"THE SUMACS"
The Gibson House

INTERIOR IN THE GIBSON HOUSE.

gan room was added in the rear, a porch in front, and this unique combination is the pride and glory of all the country round about.

Fortunate as Judea has been with its churches, it has been more so with its ministers, yet it is difficult to tell whether the superiority was not largely the effect of associating with such a people. One of these divines, the Rev Dr. Ebenezer Porter, was ordained over this people in 1796, and for fifteen years, ministered unto them, when he was called to the theological seminary at Andover, where his labors achieved the highest place in the rank of scholars and he was president of that institution several years. After him Rev. Stephen Mason was the pastor for ten years. Then in 1823 the Rev. Gordon Hayes was installed and remained with the church nearly a quarter of a century. During his labors the great excitement of anti-Masonry and Abolitionism de-

THE GUNNERY.

stroyed the usefulness of church work. It can hardly be conceived by us now, the terrible storms of passion that raged and the bitter life-long enmities that resulted. The Masonic Society went down and Masons were a proscribed class —" Sons of Belial,"—but the Abolitionists conquered. The history of the anti-slavery quarrel reads to-day like the feuds of wild clans of old. About 1837 John Gunn (eldest brother of Frederick W.), Daniel G. Platt, father of Hon. O. H. Platt, and Lewis Canfield, with their

FREDERICK W. GUNN.

EPHRAIM KELLY.

wives, went to Hartford to an anti-slavery meeting, and during their three days' stay, became thoroughly converted. After coming home, they started the anti-slavery movement. Parson Hayes fought them from the pulpit, preaching that the bible sanctioned human slavery. The excitement became intense—and the pro-slavery Calvinists would not speak to the abolitionist infidel. In 1839 Miss Abbie Kelley, a

JUDGE DANIEL N. BRINSMADE.   GEN. DANIEL B. BRINSMADE.

prominent abolitionist lecturer, was introduced into Judea, and the following vote upon the church records is given:

AUGUST 8, 1839.

"At a meeting of the Church convened in consequence of a notice of a meeting of the Anti-Slavery Society, at which it was said a female would lecture

Resolved, That we are opposed to the introduction of female public lecturers into this Society by members of this Church, and to females giving such lectures in it."

And Mr. Hayes preached a personal sermon from Rev. ii. 20-22. The consequence was that many members withdrew from the church and some of them never entered the building again, although within less than twenty-five years Lincoln's proclamation of emancipation was issued.

THE STONE SCHOOL HOUSE.

G. A. Hickox, a distinguished son of Washington, in an article on "Olden Times in Judea,"

ays: "For eighty years the Congregational church, its pastors and its lead
ng men, had governed the Judean Society. For forty years they had gov-

G. H. HOLLISTER.

erned the town of Washington.
Judge Brinsmade having exercised,
through most of that time, a sort
of patriarchial control in secular
matters, while the pastors and
deacons dominated the religious and
educational interests of the community. The first break in this solid
formation of church and state was
indirectly occasioned by the French
Revolution. The Puritan ministry
hated French democracy just as sincerely as they hated French Infi-
delity. Thomas Jefferson was a
believer in the Revolution of 1789.
He was attacked from nearly every
Congregational pulpit in the State
as an enemy of religion and of social
order. The result in Washington,
as elsewhere, was a religious schism.
Earnest democrats began to look
about them for some church where
they could worship God without
having their political principles

lenounced as infamous, their political leaders as infidels. So bitter was the

feeling that, in two recorded cases in the town of Washington, democrats were fined for interrupting preachers of the gospel of Federalism. One of them had risen in meeting and shaken his fist in the minister's face, and the other had brandished a formidable looking jackknife at the pastor."

HON. ORVILLE H. PLATT.

DAVIES' HOLLOW

"I am entirely alone, having no society, and nothing to associate with but Presbyterians and wolves;" wrote the distinguished Mary Powell, wife of John Davies, Jr., to her friends in England, from her lonely cabin in Davies' Hollow, where her husband and his father located their homes more than a century and a half ago. Hills on either side, crowned to their summits with massive oak and chestnut trees, a little clearing on the plain, where, amid the stumps, straggling hills of maize and potatoes grew like forlorn hopes. In the never ending woods the squirrels chatted mockingly at her, the deer roamed fearlessly, and often the stealthy Indian lurked, ready to seize any one of the little children that strayed from the settler's cabin. The murmuring of the brook over the stones, and the sighing of the winds through the pines of the valley, were in harmony with her feelings, and no wonder she longed for the green fields of Hertfordshire, and the comforts of that beautiful home she had left,—but the pioneer's wife was brave and lived to see these hills cultivated and the cheerless wilderness blossom like a rose. Now the hillsides are green with grass and John Davies with all the family sleep in the little cemetery, while many illustrious descendants are scattered over this broad land,—one

CHARLES H. NETTLETON.

especially, Charles Davies, LL. D., long a professor at West Point, and author of the valuable series of mathematical works, has been especially prominent in the thoughts of every student tangled in the jungles of plus and minus.

John Davies, the first, was a pioneer Episcopalian, and used to attend the meetings of his then unpopular sect at Litchfield, ten miles or more distant, and gave a deed of some now valuable land to that society in the form of a lease, for nine hundred and ninety-nine years, for "one pepper corn, to be paid annually if lawfully demanded, at or upon the feast of St. Michael the Archangel." I believe the pepper corns are kept in readiness for delivery when called for. As he became

WILLIAM HAMILTON GIBSON.

older, he tired of going so far to church, and built one near the little cemetery in the Hollow. This by migration now stands on the north-west corner of the green in Judea.

Upon the completion of the Shepang railroad in 1872, the station in Davies' Hollow was called "Romford" in honor of Romulous Ford, who was then owner of the Hollow, and made donations of land to the company.

More than fifty years ago the farmers here marketed their products by means of middle-men who carried them to neighboring cities, generally to New Haven, where they sold them and returned proceeds to shipper, less two cents a pound. It made a good business for the transporters, and a swift and sure market for the grower, and for many years the Litchfield county produce brought an advanced

"THE SHADED ROADWAY."

price in the retail markets. Only one of these dealers, so far as the writer knows, has remained in this field of trade, and in our view of "Farmer's Hall," this veteran, Erastus Hurlbut, is seated in the porch of his large general country store, adjoining immense store houses which were formerly necessary in the prosecution of his business. This transporting was done by horses and heavy wagons, starting at all hours of day and night for the long drive of twenty-five miles to New Haven. Mr. Hurlbut says he carried in one week eighty-five heavy hogs, or about twenty-five thousand pounds of pork to market. The business is now insignificant as the farmers are generally engaged in producing milk for the New York market—and the railroad has taken the freighting business from the teams. There can be no dispute however, but that the material prosperity of Washington farmers was largely a result of these commission men.

THE MITCHELL PLACE.

Within the past thirty years a new era has dawned upon these hills. The building of the Shepaug railroad from Hawleyville to Litchfield has rendered them accessible, and city people have availed themselves of this chance to locate for their summer vacation upon these ridges and knolls, their charming cottages, many of them elegant mansions, while some have come back to their ancestral homes, and enjoy the big chimneys and oaken beams that our forefathers thought necessary to stand the brunt of winter's storms and winds.

About these villas, landscape gardening has done its best work, and every cliff and boulder is used to aid the gardener in his effects.

The residence of E. K. Rossiter of New York, is one of the finest of its class. From its broad verandah you can see the rippling Shepaug winding like a silver thread around the base of Steep Rock whose cragged cliffs rise five hundred feet above it, and the smoky train creeps out of the tunnel across the river, and a hundred other varying scenes shift as the eye turns upon them. The Van Ingen mansion, the Brownie Cottage and Mrs. Gibson's are all of them fine, with elegant, well-kept grounds, and there are many others like them. The summer home for poor shop-girls of the city is another institution, built and maintained by Mrs. Van Ingen; it is seen as one comes on the train, way up on the brow of one of the hills, and is occupied in the summer by overworked and tired girl-clerks of the stores of New York.

ELISHA MITCHELL.

They come here for a short vacation, at a nominal charge for board, and can have a restful time.

Another Van Ingen institution is the quaint stone school-house we show. This was built to take the children from the Green, and is an odd specimen of the "bulwarks of the Nation," in a little lot of its own, down by the babbling brook. The old building removed from the ledge on the Green, became the studio of Mr. Gibson at "The Sumacs."

Probably the most important institution of the present day in Washington is that celebrated school, "The Gunnery." Its founder, Frederick W. Gunn, has been gathered to his fathers, and sleeps in the cemetery behind the church. A visitor once asked Mr. Gunn what he was going to do with all those boys romping about the grounds. "Make men of them," he replied;

EARLE BUCKINGHAM.

that was his single thought and aim, and is now the purpose of the present teachers. Dr. Holland, who for many years made Judea his summer home, in his story of "Arthur Bonnicastle," graphically depicts the Gunnery under the title of the "Bird's Nest." "On the whole, 'The Bird's Nest' would have been a good name for it if a man by another name had presided over it. It had its individual and characteristic beauty, because it had been shaped to a special purpose; but it seemed to have been brought together, at different times, and from wide distances. There was a central old house, and a hexagonal addition, and a tower, and a long piazza that tied everything together. It certainly looked grand, among the humbler

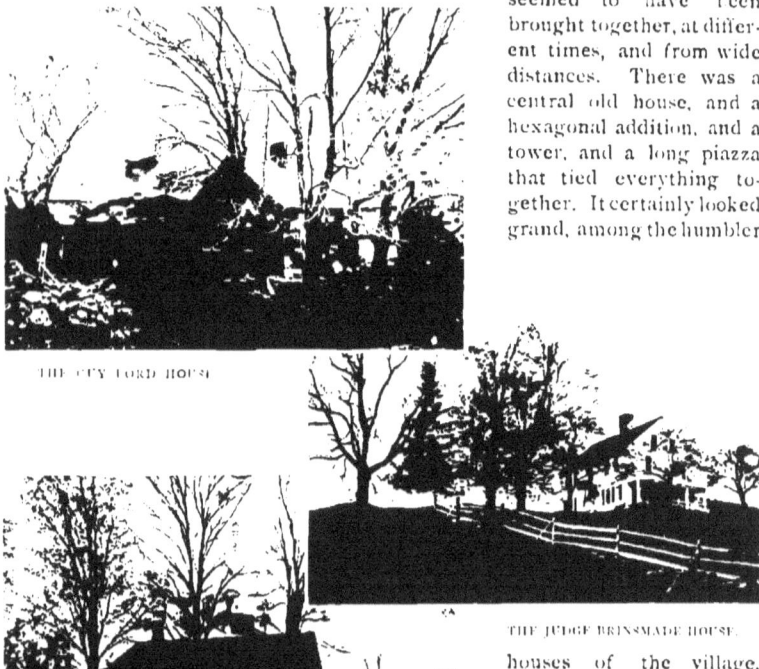

THE CUY FORD HOUSE.

THE JUDGE BRINSMADE HOUSE.

THE SETH S. LOGAN PLACE.

houses of the village, though I presume a professional architect would not have taken the highest pleasure in it. Mr. Bird was a tall, handsome, strongly-built man, a little past middle-life, with a certain fulness of habit that comes of a good health and a happy temperament. His eye was blue, his forehead high, and his whole face bright and beaming with good nature. His companion was a woman above the medium size, with eyes the same color as his own, into whose plainly parted hair the frost had crept, and upon whose honest face and goodly figure hung that ineffable grace which we call 'motherly.'

"Self-direction and self-government, these were the most important of all the lessons learned in the Bird's Nest. Our school was a little community brought together for common objects—the pursuit of useful learning, the acquisition of courteous manners, and the practice of those duties which relate to good citizenship. The only laws of the school were those which were planted in the conscience, reason and sense of propriety of the pupils. The boys were made to feel that the school was their own, and that they were responsible for its good order. Mr. Bird was only the biggest and best boy, and the accepted president of the establishment."

The school is now conducted by John C. Brinsmade, A. M., who is assisted by an able corps of instructors. Mr. Brinsmade married the only daughter of Mr. and Mrs. Gunn, and has been connected with the school nearly thirty years. There is in attendance about sixty boarding scholars.

Another school, for young men preparing for college, is under the direction of Wm. G. Brinsmade, A. M., a brother of the present master of the Gunnery, and occupies a large and elegant mansion on the "Ridge," a knob of land half a mile distant from the Green. The two schools although entirely independent of each other, have between them fine athletic and ball grounds, with tennis court and a series of golf links.

The examinations given are held by a Harvard professor and admit to that university—of which the two Brinsmade brothers are graduates.

There are no manufactories in the town at the present time, and its splendid water-powers are neglected beyond a grist-mill and saw-mill or two. Yet, in former days, many shops and factories existed, and gave promise of great futures. At Woodville, fifty years ago, Chittenden's Iron Works employed an hundred men or more. Down on "Christain Street" lime burning and brick making were carried on. At the falls at New Preston, and all along the Aspetuck, stone saw-mills produced the slabs for monuments, and the marble-quarries at Marbledale, were busy and profitable. At Baldwin's, just north of Goose Hill, a foundry and machine shop turned out large quantities of goods, mostly for farmers' purposes. Captain Center, in the hollow west of the "Green," built and operated a large cotton mill, employing many operatives. Here lived, in his boyhood, Alexander J. Center, the chief engineer of the Panama railroad, which was built largely by his promoting. Now these have disappeared, and many of the dams are gone, while the lone fisherman inveigles the trout amid the ruins.

The modern industries are entirely changed. In the little village at the Depot, two or three small shops are running ; a wagon-shop and a grist-mill. The Echo Farm Company of Litchfield, some years ago, engaged in buying milk here and bottling it, for the New York market. It erected a large building opposite the Depot for this business, which was entirely destroyed by fire a year ago, and has not been rebuilt, but the business is continued in other buildings.

The late Chief Justice Church, in his Centennial address delivered at Litchfield in 1851, on the occasion of the celebration of the one hundredth anniversary of the organization of Litchfield County, dismisses Washington as follows : " Washington has been a nursery of eminent men of whom I cannot now speak without violating my purpose of speaking of the dead and not of the living."

Nearly a half century has passed since then and were the distinguished judge to again address the people his lips would not be sealed, and a host o men would be honored by his eulogy. It is now our glad right to bring forth the virtues and deeds of a few of the many eminent men reared in these borders—while there will be many others equally worthy, whom we cannot have space to mention.

The Brinsmade family has had from the early settlement a positive influence in the building of this society. Daniel Brinsmade, a young parson, just graduated from Yale college, became the spiritual leader of this flock in 1748. He was thirty years old, thoroughly Puritanical and with decided opinions, and for nearly fifty years ministered unto them, in season and out of season. Two causes disturbed his peaceful reign ; one the Revolutionary War with its attendant Patriot and Tory convictions and animosities, and the other the Episcopalian heresy way up in Davies' Hollow. This latter was, however, then in the town of Litchfield. The half-way covenant doctrine also made a ripple of trouble over the calm surface of his religious work. By his marriage with Rhoda Sherman of New Haven, he had two sons, Daniel Nathaniel and Daniel Sherman. He lived on the brow of the hill east of the Green, in a house now torn down, just north of the late residence of Lewis Canfield. He died in 1793.

Hon. Daniel N. Brinsmade, his oldest son, graduated at Yale in 1772, read law with Samuel Canfield, Esq., of Sharon, and pursued his profession in his native town until his death in 1826. He was a Justice of the Quorum, and Assistant Judge of the County Court for sixteen years. He represented his town in the General Assembly at both its May and October sessions for twenty-one years, and was a member of the Convention that adopted the Federal Constitution. He almost believed he held public office by prescription. After the adoption of the new State Constitution of Connecticut in 1818, he was dropped, but the next year he went to Hartford to see what the new order of people could do without him. Taking a spectator's seat in the rear of the hall, he soon became absorbed in the proceedings—and his old experiences revived. Soon a member rose and made a motion. The Judge had been so long accustomed to seconding every motion, whether he favored it or not, just for the sake of having it properly presented for deliberation, that forgetting himself, he immediately exclaimed, "I second the motion." The members turned around astonished to hear it coming from the spectators—when recognizing the form of the veteran legislator of forty-three sessions, they remembered his old habit, and burst into a loud laughter. The old Federalist became now thoroughly disgusted with such " Toleration " legislative proceedings.

He was an active and influential member of the Masonic orders in their different names, representing his home lodge, the Rising Sun, for many years in the Grand Lodge, and held several of the chairs and stations in that body.

Gen. Daniel B. Brinsmade was the only son of Daniel N. and Abigail Farrand Brinsmade, and born in 1782, he lived his life of eighty years in Judea, where his father lived before him. He was one of the leading spirits of his day ; holding the office of town clerk for over forty years, and representing his town, in the General Assembly, several times. He took great interest in military affairs, and was colonel of the Fifth Regiment of Connecticut Cavalry in 1817, and was subsequently made general of the State Cavalry. In 1851 he was honored as the president of the Litchfield County centennial celebration, and exhibited on that occasion the epaulets and scarf worn by General La Fayette during the War of the Revolution, which are heir-looms in the Brinsmade family. He was prominent in Masonic affairs and was Grand Master of the State in 1827 and 1828. One of his four children, Abigail Irene married Frederick W. Gunn, the distinguished teacher, whose only daughter, with her husband, John C. Brinsmade, a grandson of General Brinsmade, now continues the school—thus making a Brinsmade dynasty of a complete one hundred and fifty years.

Near the road from Smoke Hollow to Davies' Hollow, is the depression that marks the home in which Ephraim Kirby was born in 1757. The old farm is now mostly a forest. The Ford family lived a little nearer Mount Tom, in the old house now nearly in ruins, and Davies' Family a half-mile west in the valley. The news that made Putnam leave his plow reached the ears of this boy and he hastened with his flint-lock and powder-horn to Bunker Hill, and for eight years he struggled in Freedom's cause. He was in nineteen battles and skirmishes, and received thirteen wounds, seven of which were sabre cuts at Germantown, where he was left for dead.

At the close of the war he studied law with Reynold Marvin of Litchfield, and also received the degree of M. A. from Yale college. In 1789 he published a volume of reports of the decisions of the courts of his state, being the first volume of reports ever published in this country, and is still a standard authority. He was a member of the Society of Cincinnati, a Free and Accepted Mason, and, held many of the official positions of that order, being the first General Grand High Priest of the General Grand Chapter.

He was honored by his resident town of Litchfield with thirteen semi-annual elections to the General Assembly of Connecticut.

He married Ruth Marvin and had several children, and some of his posterity have been very prominent military men. General Kirby Smith, commanding the last Confederate army that surrendered, was his grandson.

He was appointed by President Jefferson a Judge of the newly organized territory of Orleans, and died while proceeding there to assume the office at Fort Stoddard, on October 2, 1804, aged forty-six years.

One of the most distinguished sons of Judea was the late Gideon H. Hollister, known so well as the historian of Connecticut. He was born in the southeastern corner of the town in the deep valley of the West Sprain Brook, in an old farm-house which was built more than a century and a quarter ago by one of his ancestors, who was an officer in the French and Indian wars. This house has been kept in repair by the Hollister family, who still occupy it and till the ancestral side-hills.

He graduated at Yale in 1840, evincing high scholarship and great literary and forensic talent. Under Judge Seymour's careful training he was admitted to the Litchfield bar in 1842, and soon became and always held the position of a leading attorney in the state until his decease at Litchfield in 1881.

While not holding many high official positions, he had a great political influence. He was sent in 1868 as Minister to Hayti where he remained two years. His obituary in the Connecticut Law Reports, volume 48, is a just tribute of his legal ability. As a lawyer his strength lay in the trials of matters of fact to the jury with which he had few equals. In cross-examination he was wonderfully adroit. The stumbling-block of natural antagonism he avoided with great skill. He often led the witness the way he wished by seeming to desire him to take the opposite direction. When severe, he was terribly severe. His delivery was slow, his manner impressive, his action dignified and effective ; at times he was magnificent, though like all born orators, often disappointing.

He however enjoyed most of all, literary work, and his fame will live long in the published results of his study. The "History of Connecticut" is a rare specimen of good language in historical work. Besides this, he published several works of historical fiction, and was a constant contributor of poetry generally pertaining to historical subjects, to various newspapers and periodicals.

Few men were in such constant demand as he for addresses and orations to be delivered on public celebrations of a memorial or dedicatory nature.

We cannot close this tribute to a warm personal and professional friend without adding extracts from a letter of sympathy received by Mrs. Hollister shortly after his decease. "It was a sudden blow to me as I had not heard of his illness. I cherished for your husband a true friendship, and now only regret that I did not see more of him in these later years. But I looked forward to a closer intimacy as we grew older and had less of life's work and care on our hands. I knew he was always the same friendly and noble man, capable of friendship with whose mind and heart I could ever find a quick sympathy even if I did not see him frequently.

"The long drive we took together last summer when we stopped and dined with Prof. Beers at the lake, will ever be a golden day in my memory.

" We discoursed English literature and the poets. He was in best spirits and I never saw him more full of genial wit, bright criticisms and shrewd observations. His conversation fairly irradiated our circle.

"As we drove all the sunny morning over the hills, he pointed out his favorite views and talked of trees, poetry, men, life and even deeper things still.

" He was peculiar and independent in his tastes. He despised the merely sensational, he had a pure taste. He looked for nature and great and true thoughts expressed with moderative and dramatic force,

> " 'The gift which speaks,
> The deepest things most simply.'

"Something, I feel, has gone out of my own life; and as we grow older our old and heart friends grow fewer.

" Your husband loved Litchfield and every rod of Connecticut soil, he loved his country's great men, but he loved more than all the great souls— the poets that have spoken through all time to all hearts and helped them to think and hope and suffer. * * * Sincerely yours,

J. M. HOPPIN."

One of the farmer boys of Judea now highly honored is Orville H. Platt, who for nearly twenty years has held the office of United States Senator from Connecticut, and for several years has been one of the most influential members of the national council. While one of the busiest men in Washington, he is always ready to greet his Connecticut friends, and never neglects the correspondence of his constituents. He will be seventy-one years old in July, but is strong and vigorous as a young man. Educated in the common schools of his town, he studied law at Litchfield with his townsman G. H. Hollister, and for thirty years was a leading attorney of the state, residing at Meriden. He had a way of stating his views without oratory, so that he was pretty apt to win his cases, and this habit still prevails in his congressional debates. His private life has been such that his opinions were always respected by his fiercest opponents, and his honesty of purpose and integrity of character are, perhaps, the great elements of his success.

Adjoining the Hollister farm on the north was the birth-place of another lawyer, who though not so widely known as Mr. Hollister or Senator Platt, is yet entitled to a niche in the list of Washington's sons. Charles Nettleton, a farmer boy, learned in the wisdom of the old red school-house, studied law with Truman Smith, and enjoyed his starvation period at Naugatuck, when Charles Goodyear was making his interesting and disheartening experiments in hardening caoutchouc—and then removed to New York City, where his business turned into that of conveyancing, which by reason of his careful attention and thorough knowledge of all the necessary details developed into a large practice, employing several clerks. He was a Commissioner of Deeds for every state and territory in the United States. He made a specialty of collecting the statutes and session laws of every state, and of many foreign nations, and had the most complete collection in the country of this particular branch of law. At the time of the Hayes and Tilden election, his whole library was removed to Washington, D. C., for the purposes of reference by the Electoral Commission. He became largely interested in the manufacture and distribution of gas for lighting, and was for some years President of the United Gas Association of the United States. He died in New York city at the age of seventy-two years, on May 5, 1892, and was buried in the cemetery at Washington, by the side of his wife, who preceded him there only six weeks. His only living son, Charles H. Nettleton, is a well-known business man of Derby, Conn., where he holds the management of the gas and electric light industry.

Another whose "Pastoral Days" in summer time were spent amid the "Sumacs" of these rocky spurs was William Hamilton Gibson, the artist-author. He was only in the full prime of manhood when his work ended and he was laid at rest in the cemetery on the hill-side. So much of usefulness seemed to be in store for him that we can but wonder at the edict that summoned him to the last "Home-town." We remember those charming pictures of the birds, the bugs and the beetles, and the "Mysteries of the Flowers," from his deft hand, when this interpreter of nature's enigmas wandered o'er the "Highways and Byways," or saw from his cottage door the sun drinking the morning dew from the shining petals, or lingering over the western hills, as if loath to leave these verdant lawns to the shadows of the night· This "Master of the Pen and Pencil" sleeps near his friend and teacher "The Master of the Gunnery," in that repose that awaits the call that shall welcome them to a land fairer than day.

A student of nature's every phase, with a wonderful power of observation, and philosophical instincts, his writings had a fascinating interest, while his sketches were reproductions of his ideas and his lectures were more than instructive,—and it was not all the result of natural ability, but rather of careful training and untiring industry. He was never idle, his vacations were merely change of location, and meant, he said once, an increase of labor instead of a respite, and it is doubtless true that his death was the result of overwork. He was born in 1850 in Sandy Hook, a part of the town of Newtown—where his mother's people resided, his father being a Boston man with a distinguished ancestry. He learned to love Judea while a student of "The Gunnery," and after establishing his city studio in Brooklyn, he came back each year, and was as fond of her babbling brooks as if to the manor born.

About a mile from "The Green," the shaded roadway between the ledges on the Litchfield road suddenly opens upon a grand panorama of green fields, and miles and miles of peaks beyond, and here stands perched upon a rocky knoll the Mitchell homestead. Near here Elnathan Mitchell built his log house, about 1750. He was a great land holder, and had vast possessions in all the towns round about. For one of his boys, Abner, he built this house in 1792. Abner married Phebe Elliott, and had sons Elisha, Elnathan and Matthew. Elnathan kept this old home, and his grandson Elnathan now occupies it. Here Elisha Mitchell was born in 1793. He loved his books rather than the fields, and became an LL. D., and was a professor of physics in the University of North Carolina. He explored the highest peak of the Blue Ridge, and lost his life in so doing, shortly before the beginning of the Rebellion. The mountain was named Mt. Mitchell in memory of him.

Into this house Earle Buckingham moved with his wife, Helen Mitchell, and here he died. He was a noted school teacher and one of the "old-fashioned singing teachers, who went about the churches in cold winter nights doing good in the scale and clef manœuvering." He was once a member of the state senate.

A mile north of the Mitchell house is an old-fashioned farm-house, where Mrs. Abigail Ford died, three or four years since, at over one hundred years of age. She was born a Logan, and her people lived a mile farther to the northeast, where Matthew Logan took up his share of land more than a century and a half ago. He had a large family of children who have all disappeared from the vicinity, save one family. The old log house in which Seth S. Logan once lived, was built for one of Matthew's sons. Seth Logan was a well-known man, one of the good, big-hearted farmers who had a smile and a cheerful word for everyone and whose hospitality was unbounded. One of the local leaders of his political party, he had high aspirations, and was rewarded by being elected comptroller of his state. At the end of his term of office his health failed and he died soon after, universally lamented. None of his children till the old farm, but his son, Walter S. Logan, a prominent lawyer of New York City, makes this his summer residence.

Such, in brief, is the history of a community that has few parallels among the Puritan towns of our state, and whose light, set under the bushel of religious conservatism, has shown with resplendent lustre all over our broad land, and of whose future under the new conditions of liberal thought and the genesis of modern civilization and development no one can prophesy. It is an interesting problem of modern life, whether the influx of city style, manners and mode of living will destroy the individuality of such rural towns, or whether these influences will themselves be modified, and purified by the pure lives and strong common sense of the country people and thus tend to arrest the strained tension of city hurry and worry, and mould a better sentiment, a truer, higher sense of duty and living, into the realms of commerce and mercantile life. This old society of Judea presents to the student, fond of such matters, a rare field for his investigations, and a summer study in these lofty hills and in this charming society would be a never-to-be-forgotten oasis in life's cares and work.

THE TORIES OF CONNECTICUT.

BY JAMES SHEPARD.

[Concluded from last number]

The bitter feeling against the Tories was more intense during the early stages of the war than at any other time. Those who did the least thing supposed to be favorable to the side of England were stigmatized as public enemies. On the first page of the *Connecticut Courant* was a list of "Persons held up to Public view as Enemies to the Country." It included names from other states as well as our own. Stephen Sears of Sharon and Lieut. Ebenezer Orvis of Farmington were so published. Sears made a confession before the committee of inspection which was accepted. In March, 1776, the Committee of Farmington voted, that Lieut. Ebenezer Orvis, Mrs. Lydia Orvis and Hannah Andruss be "advertised in ye Public Gazette as Enemies to their Country." They had persisted in using the prohibited and detested tea. Later Mr. Orvis made a confession which was voted satisfactory.

At a meeting held in Farmington on December 12, 1774, the town voted to approve the doings of the Continental Congress with only two dissenting voices, those of Nehemiah Royce and Matthias Leaming. They were immediately voted to be open enemies, and all intercourse with them was ordered to be withdrawn until they retracted. It was even attempted to prevent Royce from sending his children to school; but this was voted down. In March, 1775, the committee voted "That Matthias Leaming be advertised in the Public Gazette for a contumacious violation of ye whole Association of ye Continental Congress," and that the evidence against Royce was not sufficient to justify such publication. In May, 1777, however, we find Mr. Royce in the Hartford jail as an inimical person.

Mr. Julius Gay's paper on "Farmington in the Revolution" gives us the story of this Matthias Leaming. He inadvertently conveyed his real estate to his brother, who absconded and the property was confiscated. This brother, Jeremiah Leaming, D. D., was the Episcopal minister who went off with the British at the burning of Norwalk, and is the man before referred to who left the negro Pomp. At one time a mob took his picture, defaced it, and nailed it to a sign post head downwards. He was put in prison and there contracted a hip disease that made him a cripple for life. Matthias petitioned the General Assembly in 1783 for relief, which was denied. He finally had £80 voted him, payable in 1787, but before it became due the

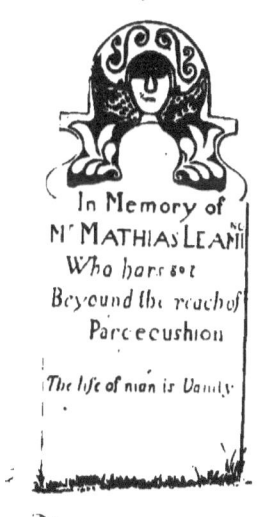

TOMBSTONE TO MATHIAS LEAMING.

treasury was bankrupt. In 1788 the prominent men of Farmington petitioned the General Assembly to assist him in his old age and distress, but no action was taken on said petition, and now, in the old cemetery at Farmington we find a tombstone on which is inscribed, "In memory of Mr. Matthias Leaming Who hars got Beyond the reach of parcecushion, The life of man is vanity."

Judah and David Leaming of Farmington, in their petition for release from jail, said that they were provoked to imprudent utterings by injurious treatment involving "losses of clothing and wages," and the committee who examined them said that their statement was true.

The Rev. John Smalley, of New Britian, was called a Tory because he advised his hearers that they were not bound to keep the Continental Fast. He also spoke reprovingly of fighting against the king, but afterwards he became a firm adherent to the American cause.

An extract from a letter in the *Courant* shows the feeling against the Tories in May, 1776. " By these miscreants the British prisoners are assisted to escape. If these infernal enemies are suffered to proceed in their hellish schemes our ruin is certain, but if they are destroyed the power of Hell and Britain will never prevail against us."

Col. Joseph Barnum, whose son was captured by the British at Fort Washington and literally starved to death, was so exasperated that he took his gun and went in pursuit of Tories to revenge on them the death of his son. He soon saw an innocent Tory at work on his own land, took deliberate aim and shot him, wounding him severely but not fatally.

In July, 1775, a brig owned by Josiah Winslow a well known royalist of Boston, with some 19,000 gallons of molasses on board was forced by a storm into Stonington harbor. The people of Norwich captured it as a prize for the use of the state. It proved a great comfort and luxury to the Continental soldiers and was referred to as "tory molasses."

The Riflemen of New Milford compelled a Tory to walk before them to Litchfield and carry one of his own geese all the way in his hand. At Litchfield they tarred him, made him pluck his goose for his own coat of feathers, and then made him kneel down and thank them for their lenity.

The members of the Church of England had their full share of trouble. The most rabid of the Whigs believed that every Episcopalian was either an open or secret Tory. In 1775, Waterbury voted to have two separate schools, one for Presbyterians and one for the Church of England. In Watertown the windows of the Episcopal church were demolished and the principal members of that church were confined on their farms. In Cheshire they were prevented from building a church. In Woodbury an Episcopal clergyman was fired at from ambush. Later he went to Canada.

Rev. Samuel Seabury, a native of Connecticut and the first Episcopal Bishop in the United States, was taken by about forty armed men at his grammar school at West Chester, New York, and brought to New Haven in November 1775. He was carried in triumph about the city, escorted by a large number of armed men who arranged themselves in front of the house of Capt. Sears and there fired two cannon and made other noisy demonstrations, after which he was placed in confinement. In his petition for release he states that on the day of his arrest some forty armed men went to his house, ordered his wife to open his desk, took his papers and all his money save one English shilling and a few coppers. They insulted one of his daughters by running a bayonet through her cap while on her head and twice through the handkerchief on her neck. They also destroyed a quilt around which his family was at work by cutting it in pieces with their bayonets. He was ordered to be removed by the New York Committee of Safety.

At one period a gloom settled over the prospects of the colonists and the Church party felt almost sure of a speedy triumph, some of the most enthusiastic met together at Waterbury, says Dr. Bronson, and determined in what manner the farms of their opponents should be divided among themselves after the subjugation of the country.

In July, 1776, the Episcopal clergy, whose duty it was to pray for the king and for victory over all his enemies, met in convention and resolved that such prayers " would draw upon themselves inevitable destruction." For a time all public service was suspended and all of their churches closed save those at Newtown and Redding, which were presided over by Rev. John Beach. Mr. Beach declared that "he would pray for the king till the rebels cut out his tongue." Rev. X. A. Welton says of Beach, in the history of Redding, that "a squad of soldiers marched into his church in Newtown and threatened to shoot him if he prayed for the king, but when, regardless of their threats, he went on without so much as a tremor in his voice, to offer the forbidden supplication, they were so struck with admiration for his courage that they stacked arms and remained to listen to the sermon."

A band of soldiers once took him to where an axe and block were prepared for killing him, and one of them said, "Now you old sinner say your last prayer." He knelt down and prayed, "God bless King George, and forgive all his enemies and mine for Christ's sake." They let him go.

He was once shot at when in the pulpit at Redding, and the bullet lodged in the sounding-board about a foot above his head. The congregation sprang to their feet to rush from the church, but he soon quieted them and proceeded with his discourse as if nothing had happened.

The Episcopal churches were not only closed by this order but their ministers after a time were mostly banished and the great majority of their people had removed from the state. When they again began to hold public services they generally omitted the prayer for the king or else omitted the Liturgy entirely. The Rev. Matthew Graves, of New London, refused to omit the prayer for the king and as a consequence he was driven from his church on Sunday before he had time to divest himself of his suplice.

The Rev. Abraham Jarvis, of Middletown, who presided over the Episcopal Convention of 1776, opened his church on Sundays, but an attendant says that he "only read some chapters in the Bible and preached a sermon in his own clothes, not daring to read the church service."

The northwest portion of Bristol and the adjoining portions of the town of Burlington, Harwinton and Plymouth was a stronghold of toryism, and meetings were held there of Tories from all parts of the state.

The Rev. James Nichols began his services in Bristol in 1773. He was the last Episcopal minister that went to England for ordination. He was the "designing church clergyman" before referred to in connection with seventeen prisoners from Farmington, most if not all of whom were of his congregation. It is said that he was shot at several times, also that he was taken from a cellar at East Plymouth, tarred and feathered and then dragged in a brook. By these and other acts he was banished to Litchfield. His records show that between the latter part of 1776 and 1781 he administered baptism in his cure on five different occasions. In 1782 we find him again in charge of the church at Bristol.

In the Burlington ledges, at the southwest part of the town, is a cave known as the Tory den. Stephen Graves and his bride of about nineteen lived in a log cabin in the southeast part of Hawinton, within a mile of this cave. He was drafted, hired a substitute, and while his substitute was still in the service at Grave's expense, he was again drafted. This he considered unjust and freely expressed his opinion, thereby incurring the enmity of Capt. Wilson and his company of Sons of Liberty. Soon after this he went to visit his mother at Saybrook. He was pursued and arrested as a deserter, his captors feasting at the taverns, making him pay all the bills. He came so peacefully that they relaxed their vigilance somewhat and he made his escape. On reaching home he hid himself without making his presence known until after his pursuers had been there and his good wife had assured them that Mr. Graves was in Saybrook on a visit. At one time Graves was tied to a tree and severely whipped. At another time it is said that he was hung to a chestnut tree near his house but let down again before he was severely injured. Many of his neighbors were Tories. For sometime he and several companions were compelled to live at the Tory den, and each night the young Mrs. Graves went through the dark and pathless woods, over rocky ledges, to carry them food. The den was often resorted to for shorter periods of refuge. When at work on their farms a band of Tories worked first one farm and then another, so that they might protect themselves. If working alone, or when an overpowering party of Sons of Liberty approached them, they would flee to the Tory den. Their faithful wives were always on the watch, and would blow a horn or a conch shell as a warning at the sight of any of Capt. Wilsons's men, or other Tory hunters. These horns were a source of great annoyance to Capt. Wilson, and he once presented his pistol to the head of a young girl that lived with Mrs. Graves and threatened to shoot her if she did not tell him where the noisy conch shell was concealed.

A Bristol Tory, by the name of Potter, was hung until nearly dead, and one, Joel Tuttle, was hung to an oak tree on Federal Hill in Bristol, and left alone to die. A Whig by the name of Hungerford cut him down, but the kind-hearted Hungerford dared not render other assistance and left the Tory lying insensible on the ground. During the night he so far recovered as to be able to make his way to the Tory den. Many efforts were made to find this hiding place, but its location was never known to any but the Tories until after the close of the war.

Chauncey Jerome of Bristol, a very energetic and powerful man, was taken by a crowd, his shirt pulled up over his head and then his uplifted shirt and arms, with cords around his wrists, were tied to a limb of a tree, preparatory to whipping his bare back. The rod was raised for the first stroke when by a desperate effort the victim escaped and the blow fell upon the body of the tree. With the shirt still hanging on the tree, the bare-back man was soon in the house of his brother-in-law, Jonathan Pond, who stood at the door with gun in hand forbidding any to enter. Mr. Jerome married the widow of his brother-in-law, Moses Dunbar, (Dunbar's first wife was Jerome's sister), and while driving to Hartford one day they stopped for lunch by the roadside before entering the city. Pointing to the place of execution, Mrs. Jerome remarked, "my former husband lies buried under that tree." They removed to Nova Scotia until after the war.

There seems no room for doubt that one of the greatest obstacles the Patriots of the Revolution had to contend with was the Tory. In nearly if not every battle we find in addition to the British regulars in uniform, one or more companies of Tories in ordinary dress. The Tory, Col. John Butler, of Tryon, New York, was in command of the four hundred Tories and Indians at the horrible massacre of Wyoming, which was then a part of Connecticut.

Tory guides led the British Gen. Tryon at the burning of Danbury. He made his headquarters of the house of the Tory, Joseph Dibble. This Dibble was once taken out of his bed at night, by men in disguise, and ducked until he expected to perish. Large stores of provisions were in the Episcopal church at Danbury, and in Dibble's barn. These goods were taken into the street and burnt so as to spare said buildings. A white cross was marked on the Tory buildings to signify " that the destroying angel would pass them unharmed." The Congregational church and every house save those that had the mystic sign upon them were destroyed. " The women and children fled from the jeers of their comfortable Tory neighbors into lonely lanes, damp pastures and leafless woods." A man by the name of Jarvis was one of these Tory guides. He went to Nova Scotia for a time and returned to Danbury to live, but a crowd soon surrounded his father's house, prepared to tar and feather him. His sister concealed him in an ash oven until he could make his escape, never to again set foot in his native place. Another of the Tory guides was Eli Benedict of Danbury. He attempted to reside there again but was threatened with a ride on a wooden horse and fled. Another of the Danbury guides was Isaac W. Shelton. He joined the British on Long Island, and was at one time confined in Hartford jail. After the war he lived in Bristol and acquired a valuable property.

The Tories continually carried on an illicited trade between Connecticut and Long Island. They carried off Tory recruits for the British, and Tory families with large quantities of provisions that were sadly needed here, and much of this work was done under a British flag of truce.

Rev. Dr. Mather and his four sons, of Stamford, were taken from the parsonage at night by eight Tories and carried to New York. One Sunday a party of British troops, mostly Tories, took 48 prisoners, including Dr. Mather, from the church at Darien, while they were singing the first hymn. They stole the horses belonging to the church-goers, and robbed both men and women of their valuables.

Lieut. Barber, of Croton, while taking a walk was shot through the body, by concealed Tories, and died immediately. As to Benedict Arnold, I need only mention his name.

The British and Tories, under Gen Tryon, burned Norwalk and Fairfield in 1779, and the Episcopal clergyman of Norwalk and many Tories went off with them.

New Haven was plundered under the guidance of William Chandler, a captain of a Tory command, assisted by his brother Thomas. Besides robbery and wanton destruction of property, aged citizens, women and children were shamefully abused. The Rev. Dr. Daggett, president of Yale college, would have been murdered had it not been for the interference of the Tory guide Chandler, who was formerly one of Dr. Daggett's pupils. William and Thomas Chandler were the sons of Joshua Chandler whose property in New Haven, valued at £30,000, was confiscated. In March, 1787, they attempted to cross the Bay of Fundy to meet the Commissioners on Loyalists' Claims at St. Johns, in hopes to obtain compensation for the confiscated property. They were shipwrecked on the way, and William, the guide, was crushed to death between the vessel and the rocks. The father landed but soon perished by a fall from a precipice and others of the party perished from exposure.

The British agents long endeavored to make the United States, rather than Great Britain, indemnify the Tories, but Dr. Franklin intimated that an equivalent would be the British indemnification for ravages by their troops, so the matter was dropped.

The many personal abuses and atrocious acts committed during the war only show what a desperate struggle our people passed through. Families were divided. Joseph Ferris of Stamford, a captain in the British army, was taken prisoner by his brother-in-law. Zerubbabel Jerome of Bristol, and his sons Robert, Thomas and Asahel, all four served in the Continental army, the latter dying in the service. His sons Chauncey and Zerubbabel, Jr., were in the Hartford jail together as Tories in 1777. His son in-law, Moses Dunbar, was executed for high treason. Stephen Graves, the Tory, was another son-in-law, as was also Jonathan Pond, who defended Chauncey Jerome. His fourth son-in-law, Joseph Spencer, cannot be definitely placed on either side.

The father of Moses Dunbar was a firm Patriot and they were bitterly opposed to each other, both in politics and religion. By such divisions many descendants from Tory families are eligible to the Sons of the Revolution.

After the war most of the absconding Tories returned and and mingled with the people as before. An exception to this is found in a son of the Rev. James Scovil of Waterbury. After about sixty years residence in New Brunswick, the grievances of this son were as fresh and sensitive as when first inflicted, and he said that "no temptation that earth could present would ever induce him to set foot on soil where he had received such unprovoked and cruel wrongs."

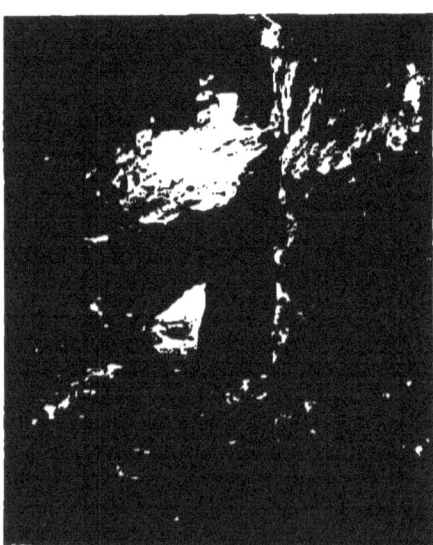

THE TORY DEN.

As a rule however Tories were not so sensitive; they entered into the management of public affairs by voting and holding office, after such privileges had been reluctantly given them. In 1783 the town of New Haven voted to instruct their representatives "to use their influence with the next General Assembly in an especial manner, to prevent the return of these miscreants who have deserted their country's cause and joined the enemies of this and the United States of America during the late contest." But one year after this, Dr. Stiles wrote in his diary, "This day, town meeting voted to readmit the Tories." When the city of New Haven was organized in 1784 there were eight Tories in the common council and about one-third of all the voters in New Haven were Tories. This proportion of Tories may be above the average, but throughout the state, after peace, Patriots and Tories generally dwelt together in harmony, in striking contrast to the Revolutionary times.

Prejudice, passion and social contagion are responsible for much that calm deliberation would not have prompted. We can all pity the Tory, but the purpose of this paper is Tory history with neither condemnation nor approval; still I must say that whatever unwarranted abuses the Tory may have received, those high in authority, the General Assembly, Governor and Council of Safety, were always ready to forgive and "ever willing to exercise lenity and mercy— as far as may be consisent with justice and publick safety." They had large and noble hearts, full of "tenderness and compassion," and thus our state was much more indulgent and charitable to the Tories, than most of our sister states.

WHEN YOUTH IS DONE.

BY ELIZABETH ALDEN CURTIS.

We cannot hope the waning days will pass
    And leave no trace upon the plumed lea,
    Time's foot fall down the years, though light and free,
Still browns the sward, and sears the ripened grass.

So gazing deeply in life's misted glass
    Young charms that, wraith-like, for the nonce we see,
    Fade swiftly, as the early sunsets flee
When night comes down to wrap the still morass.

But there be tender twilights for our years
When we may turn us to abiding cheers.
    Then, sweet my love, reach down your hand to me,
That standing pulse to pulse, and twain in one,
    We fix our perfect joy in memory,
To bless and warm our hearts when youth is done.

LIST OF BURIALS, OR "SEXTON'S LIST," OF THE CENTER CHURCH BURYING GROUND, HARTFORD.

PREPARED FOR PUBLICATION AND ANNOTATED BY MARY K. TALCOTT.

Corrections to be made in Part I—April, May, June Number, '98: 1751, June 23, for Bunes, read Bunce; 1758, Nov. 6, the words "bapt. Jan. 30, 1757," belong with the burial of Nov. 9, "Child of Lieut. Richard Goodman (Hezekiah)."

II.

1765.

May 14 Widow Mabel Bigelow [b. Dec. 13, 1685, dau. of Richard and Elizabeth (Tuthill) Edwards; married Jonathan Bigelow, Dec. 14, 1699].
16 Child of Ezra Andrus.
June 3 Daughter of Samuel Day (Sarah).
12 Son of Aaron Bull.
15 Child of Daniel Olcott.
Child of Mrs. Mary Nevins (Sam'l, infant).
Aug. 30 Wife of Obadiah Spencer (Anna).
Sept. 6 Daniel Edwards, Esq., died at New Haven. [Son of Richard and Mary (Talcott) Edwards, born April 11, 1701].
Oct. 15 Jacob Cadwell Intered at Expence of Pelatiah Pierce.
20 George Lord [son of Richard and Ruth (Wyllys) Lord, born July 8, 1737].
31 Child of James Tilley.
Dec. 2 Child of John Skinner, Jr. (John).

1766.

Jan. 20 Widow Skinner Intered at Expence of Samuel Barnard (The aged widow Elizabeth S.) [Elizabeth, dau. of Deacon Joseph and Elizabeth (Butler) Olmsted), married Joseph Skinner, Jan. 28, 1707-8].
25 Child of Hezekiah Wadsworth (Ezekiel). [Bapt. Nov. 13, 1763].
31 Widow Seymour Intered at Expence of Thomas Seymour, Esq.
Feb. 2 The Wife of Dr. Neal McLean (Hannah). [Dr. Neil McLean and Mrs. Hannah Knowles were mar. May 12, 1757.]
Mar. 27 The Wife of Joseph Bunce.
31 The Wife of Simon Clarke (Sarah).
April 5 The Wife of Silas Andrus (Sarah).
11 Child of Zebulon Seymour [Mary Ann, bapt. in New Hartford, Jan. 21, 1760-61].

April 8 Child of Silas Andrus (Sarah, infant).
26 Mr. Richards. A Frenchman Father of Anson Richards.
26 Sarah Daughter of Widow Anne Humphrey (widow of Dositheus). [Dau. of Dositheus and Anne (Griswold) Humphrey, b. Feb. 26, 1747-8.]
27 Child of Timothy Shepard.
30 Hezekiah Wadsworth [bapt. April 11, 1725, son of Ichabod and Sarah (Smith) Wadsworth].
May 9 Mary Church.
10 The Wife of Samuel Olcott (Mary). Aged 35. [Dau. of John Michael and Margaret (Beauchamp) Chenevard.]
11 The wife of Alexander Chalker (Mary) [dau. of Capt. John and Rachel (Olcott) Knowles, bapt. April 1, 1739].
13 Amy Gilbert.
14 The mother of Susannah Butler (Mrs. Mary).
24 John Knowles [blown up in the school-house. John, son of Capt. John and Rachel(Olcott)Knowles, bapt. April 12, 1752].
24 Levi Jones [blown up in the school-house].
24 Richard Lord, blown up in the school-house, [son of John Hayes and Rachel (Knowles) Lord, bapt. June 14, 1752].
June 2 Dr. Nathaniel Ledyard, blown up in the school-house [son of John and Deborah (Youngs) Ledyard, bapt. Dec. 21, 1740].
4 Two children of Valentine Vawhan.
8 Elizabeth, wife of Valentine Vangu died.
9 William Gardiner, [son of Dr. Syl

CENTER CHURCH BURYING GROUND, HARTFORD. 265

vester Gardiner, of Boston, born March, 1742]. [Buried by Roger Viets).

June 11 Ruth Howard.
12 Elisha Burnham is charged the digging of grave for Richard, blown up in the school-house. [Born March 6, 1748].
29 Ebenezer Catlin. [Son of Samuel and Elizabeth (Norton) Catlin, born July 25, 1724].

July 17 The wife of John Walker (Martha) buried by Rev. Rogers Viets.
25 The wife of Isaac Oakes (Rebecca).

Aug. 9 Child of Lieut. John Cole.
23 Samuel Knowles. [Son of Capt. John and Rachel (Olcott) Knowles, bapt. Oct. 1, 1732].
28 Child of Gideon Bunce.

Sept. 2 Child of Daniel Olcott (Clarissa).
19 Child of Joseph Wheeler.
20 Child of Capt. Daniel Butler (Sarah).
28 Child of Samuel Watrous.

Oct. 9 Child of Ezra Hyde.
9 Child of William Gove (William).
13 Child of William Gove (James).
14 Cyprian Powell is charged the burial of a sister's child.
18 Child of Elijah Clapp.
20 Widow Elizabeth Eggleston, interred at Exp. of the Town.
22 Child of widow Hepzibah Ledyard.

Dec. 16 Mrs. Mary Langrell, died at New Haven. [Mary Hyde of Norwich, born Sept. 22, 1729, dau of William and Anne (Basset) Hyde, mar. March 26, 1754, Thomas Langrell.]

1767.

Jan. 14 Capt. John Cook. Aged 70.
26 The Mother of Daniel Spencer (Widow Ruth). Aged 98.
30 Child of William Hall (Tabitha infant).

Feb. 23 Daughter of William Barnot.
Mar. 2 A grandchild of Capt. Daniel Bull.
16 Child of Moses Hopkins (Ashbel).
17 William Dickinson (son of Moses) killed by discharge of gun.
22 Thomas Seymour Esq., aged 62, [son of Capt. Thomas and Ruth (Norton) Seymour, born July 29, 1705].
28 Child of John Brace.

April 17 Child of John McLean.
May 7 Samuel Watrous.

June 15 Daughter of John Larkum (Sarah) killed by lightning.
17 Two children of Elijah Barret.
19 The wife of Elijah Barret.
30 Child of William Adams Esq. (infant).

July 7 The wife of Moses Hopkins (Elizabeth). [Moses Hopkins and Elizabeth Deming were mar. April 7, 1763.]
8 Child of Ashbel Steele.
8 Child of Robert Sloane (Samuel drowned).
30 Abijah Bunce [son of Joseph and Ann (Sandford) Bunce, bapt. Feb. 10, 1709-10].

Aug. 16 Child of Cable Church (James).
18 Capt. Daniel Butler.

Oct. 3 Child of Elisha Hopkins (James Buckingham).
6 Thomas Bigelow [son of Jonathan and Tabitha Bigelow, in his 31st year].

Nov. 3 Child of Thomas Green.
7 Child of William Stanley.
14 Child of Zebulon Mygatt.

Dec. 7 Child of Phineas Cole (infant).
26 The wife of Isaac Bunce (Anna).

1768.

Jan. 26 Child of widow Sarah Watrous.
Mar. 1 The wife of John Potwine, [Eunice Seymour, dau. of Thomas and Hepsibah (Ledyard) Seymour, born May 6, 1732].
11 Hezekiah Collyer [son of Capt. Hezekiah and Hepsibah, bapt. Dec. 26, 1731].

April 22 Child of Sylvanus Andrus (Rebecca).

May 2 Wife of Ezra Andrus [Anna Bushnell, mar. May 9, 1754].
10 Child of Samuel Marsh (Catherine).

June 26 Thomas Clapp [son of Thomas and Mary (King) Clapp, born in Northampton, March 6, 1712].

July 4 Child of John Burkett (Hannah).
12 Child of Lieut. John Cole.
21 Grove Collyer [son of Capt. Hezekiah and Hepsibah Collyer, aged 29 years].
23 John White [son of John and Mary White, born Feb, 8, 1691].
24 Child of John Dodd (Henry).

Sept. 6 The aged Mr. Hezekiah Goodwin, the father of John Pantry Goodwin, (d. Sept. 5). [Son of Nathaniel and Mehitable (Porter) Good-

LIST OF BURIALS,

win, bapt. March 20, 1692].
Sept. 29 Widow Rebecca Marsh.
Nov. 25 Child of John Barnard, Jr.
    26 William Day "the aged." [Son of John and Sarah Maynard) Day, bapt. April 24, 1692].

1769.
Jan. 13 The wife of Caleb Turner.
    6 Dorothy Woodbridge (The aged Mrs). [Bapt. June 8, 1679, dau. of Joshua Lamb of Roxbury; widow, successively, of Rev. Dudley Woodbridge, and of Rev. Timothy Woodbridge, of Simsbury].
    15 A grandchild of Caleb Turner. (Pelatiah, son of Pelatiah).
    17 Mary Bunce.
    20 Wife of Deacon John Edwards. (The aged Mrs. Christian) [Christian Williamson.]
Feb. 6 Son of Sylvanus Andrus (Lemuel).
    12 Widow Sarah Hollister.
Mar. 10 The mother of Caleb Bull. [Caleb Bull, Sr., mar. widow Elizabeth Bunce, probably widow of Thos., and dau. of Joseph Easton].
    24 Mrs. Sarah Flagg, [wife of Samuel, and dau. of Jonathan and Sarah (Sandford) Bunce].
April 19 A daughter of widow Meriba Nichols.
    26 Elizabeth Hastings.
May 2 Child of James Thompson (infant dau).
    13 Son of Rev. William Patten.
    17 Deacon John Edwards. [Son of Richard and Mary (Talcott) Edwards, born Feb. 27, 1694].
June 16 Child of John Burket (Joseph, inft).
    24 Samuel Williams, drowned, intered at exp. of Dr. Smith (a stranger accidentally drowned).
    30 Child of Daniel Olcott (Daniel).
July 24 Child of Benj. Bigelow, (Roderick).
    27 Child of Capt. Joseph Bunce.
Aug. 23 Infant son of Charles Kelsey, Jr.
Sept. 21 Daniel Seymour. [Born Oct. 20, 1698, son of John and Elizabeth (Webster) Seymour].
    28 Child of Jonathan Gross.
Oct. 7 Child of Joseph Akins.
    9 Two children of Joseph Knox.
Nov. 1 Capt. John Coleman.
Dec. 1 The wife of Isaac Dickinson.
1770.
Jan. 5 Deacon Joseph Holtom. [Born in

Lyme, in 1693, son of John and Sarah Holtom].
Jan. 8 Joseph Olcott. [Bapt. March 23, 1707, son of Thomas and Hannah (Barnard) Olcott].
Feb. 11 Mrs. Hannah Bull.
April 6 Child of Nicholas Brown.
    12 The wife of Ebenezer Watson. [Elizabeth Seymour, born March 18, 1743, dau. of Richard and Elizabeth (Wadsworth)Seymour].
May 7 Richard Edwards. [Son of John and Christian (Williamson) Edwards, born Oct. 26, 1727].
    8 Child of Thomas Sanford, Jr. (Ezekiel).
    9 Son of Zebulon Seymour.
    10 Child of Jared Bunce (George).
    18 Child of Thomas Ensign (infant).
June 6 A sister of Samuel Farnsworth.
    17 The wife of Hezekiah Marsh. [Christian, dau. of Deacon John and Christian (Williamson) Edwards, bapt. Sept. 25, 1720].
    30 Child of Samuel Farnsworth.
July 7 Benjamin Flagg.
    29 Elisha Burnham. [Son of Richard and Abigail (Easton) Burnham, born June 22, 1717].
Aug. 3 Sarah Burnham. [Dau. of Elisha and Sarah (Olmsted) Burnham, born Sept. 27, 1745].
    5 Abigail Burnham. [Dau. of Elisha and Sarah (Olmsted) Burnham, born Oct. 25, 1757].
    17 Widow Meriba Nichols. Aged 67.
    21 Ephraim Burnham. [Son of Elisha and Sarah (Olmsted) Burnham, born May 21, 1751].
    27 Child of Barzillai Hudson.
    20 Wife of Timothy Church (Susanna).
Sept. 5 Wife of Capt. Joseph Barret.
    12 Minor Chalker
    30 William Floyd.
Oct. 27 Anne Eggleston.
Nov. 6 Merion Nevins.
    12 Miss Mary Fielding. Intered at Exp. of Eleazer Pomeroy.
    12 Joseph Wheeler.
    22 Widow Hepsibah Collyer. [Widow of Capt. Hezekiah, born Sept. 13, 1712; dau. of Sergt. Jonathan and Hepsibah (Marsh) Wadsworth].
    25 Child of Dr. Thompson [James, son of Mary].
Dec. 1 Ebenezer Benton. [Son of An-

CENTER CHURCH BURYING GROUND, HARTFORD. 267

drew Benton, bapt. Oct. 18, 1696].
Dec. 24 David Seymour. [Born Oct. 13, 1733, son of Hon. Thomas and Hepsibah (Merrill) Seymour; "He was a very noted Sea Commander"].
16 Child of Robert Branpe [Robert, son of Rob't Bethwright or Branthwait].

1771.
Jan. 4 Child of Ezra Hyde (Ezra).
11 Anna Hopkins, dau. of Thos. Hopkins.
Feb. 11 John Barnard.
Mar. 15 Child of John Skinner (infant dau).
22 Child of Charles Seymour.
Daughter of John Lord (died April 11).
May 1 Child of Isaac Oakes (Thomas, infant).
31 Child or Nathaniel Goodwin (Anne).
30 William Wadsworth (obt. May 29th in the 49th year of his age; born March, 1723). [Son of Joseph and Joanna (Hovey) Wadsworth].
June 5 John Talcott (Capt) [Born Feb. 27, 1699, son of Governor Joseph and Abigail (Clark) Talcott).
July 17 Child of John Burket.
26 Child of Jacob Byington.
Aug. 7 Child of William Hooker, Jr.
10 Child of Consider Burt.
15 Wife of John Skinner. [Mary, dau. of Ephraim and Mary (Nichols) Turner; bapt. Dec. 31, 1704].
19 Child of Tim Shepard, Jr.
Sept. 1 Wife of Eli Shepard.
5 John Ledyard, Esq. a native of England, came to this country when young, Aged 71.
Oct. 15 Widow Mary Nichols. [Widow of Capt. William Nichols].
18 Child of Benjamin Morrison.
25 Child of William Hall.
Nov. 6 Child of Jared Bunce.
9 A Frenchman Intered at Exp. of Thomas Brown.
17 A child of Samuel Filley.
17 Child of Ebenezer Watson.
20 Joshua Carter.
Dec. 23 Wife of Abijah Clark.
26 Child of Jesse Marsh.

1772.
Jan. 3 Wife of William Jepson. [Susanna, dau. of Daniel Collyer, mar. Dec. 21, 1756].
8 Child of Daniel Goodwin.

Jan. 30 Child of John Indicott.
Feb. 5 Mother of Elijah Clapp.
Mar. 3 Eli Shepard.
27 Child of Nathaniel Goodwin.
April 17 Child of John Brace.
23 Child of Benjamin Bigelow.
30 Child of Eleazer Pomeroy.
May 2 Deborah Cadwell.
13 Child of William Myers.
25 Wife of John Skinner, Jr. [Mary Whiting, born 1730; dau. of John and Jerusha (Lord) Whiting.]
June 10 Widow Amy Pratt. [Widow of William Pratt; born Oct. 6, 1704, Windsor, dau. of Nathaniel and Martha (Thrall) Pinney].
20 Child of Daniel Talcott.
21 Daughter of Ashbel Steele.
25 Child of William Hall.
Aug. 2 Child of Ebenezer Adams.
7 Child of Neal McLean, Jr.
10 The father of Simeon Graham. [Samuel Graham].
19 Daughter of William Cadwell, Jr.
23 Capt. Daniel Sheldon. [Son of Deacon Isaac and Elizabeth (Pratt) Sheldon; bapt. June 12, 1726].
27 Child of Ashbel Barnard.
28 James Taylor.
28 Child of Nehemiah Cadwell.
Sept. 14 Widow Lucretia Sheldon. [Lucretia, dau. of Jonah and Susannah (Howard) Gross; born Aug. 21, 1724].
Oct. 20 Joseph Ensign
22 Rev. Edward Dorr. [Born in Lyme, Conn., Nov. 2, 1722; son of Edmund Dorr].
Nov. 2 Child of Joseph Hosmer.
9 Child of Daniel Olcott.
23 Jacob Seymour.
23 Widow Day. Intered at exp. of Sam'l Day. [Elizabeth Andrus, widow of William Day, married April 18, 1717].

1773.
Feb. 20 Child of Zebulon Seymour.
25 A sister of John Wadsworth.
27 William Cadwell, Jr.
Mar. 3 Child of Thomas Hinsdale, Jr.
5 Child of William Ellery.
7 The wife of William Ellery. Experience, dau. of John Ledyard, Esq. [Bapt. April 5, 1747].
8 Chloe Flagg.
May 10 Charles Kelsey, Jr.

3

LIST OF BURIALS,

24 Child of Moses Kellogg.
28 David Shepard.
June 21 Ebenezer Ensign.
Mrs Abigail Wadsworth. [Widow of Rev. Daniel; born April 13, 1707, dau. of Governor Joseph and Eunice (Howell) Talcott].
Aug. 10 Child of William Barnard.
14 Child of Pelatiah Pierce.
15 John Skinner. [Born July 1, 1697, son of John and Rachel (Pratt) Skinner].
27 Thomas Gross. [Son of Freeman and Susanna (Bunce) [Deming] Gross].
28 The wife of William Burr.
Sept. 10 Child of Ashbel Barnard.
14 Child of Aaron Seymour.
21 The wife of Thomas Filley.
25 The mother of Stephen Turner
Oct. 14 Child of William Adams Esq. (Mary, born June 24, 1770.)
Nov. 14 Child of Samuel Benton.
19 Child of James Pratt.
26 Nathaniel Jones.
28 Mrs. Cole. Intered at Exp. of Daniel Goodwin.

1774
Jan. 14 The wife of Eli Warner.
Feb. 8 The wife of Sylvanus Andrus.
21 Timothy Dodd.
23 Child of Thomas Sloane.
Mar. 9 James Bunce. [Son of Sergt. John and Mary (Barnard) Bunce; bapt. March 12, 1693].
23 John Pantry Jones. [Son of Nathaniel and Rebecca (Pantry) Jones; bapt. Aug 9, 1730].
23 The wife of Jonathan Taylor.
April 5 Moses Taylor.
May 20 William Goodwin. [Son of William and Elizabeth (Shepard) Goodwin; born July 9, 1699].
26 Child of Capt. John Chenevard.
June 6 The wife of Capt. John Chenevard, [Hepsibah, dau. of Capt. Hezekiah and Hepsibah Collier; born July 29, 1733].
July 26 The wife of Ezra Corning.
30 Child of Moses Hopkins.
Aug. 20 Alexander Currie.
Sept. 2 Child of James Marsh.
13 Child of Uriah Burkett (Lois).
14 Daughter of Capt. Daniel Skinner.
15 Child of Nathahiel Skinner.
Oct. 12 Lieut John Cole.
27 Child of John Jeffrey.

Nov. 2 Widow Abigail Bunce. [Widow of John Bunce; dau. of Zachariah Sandford; bapt. Oct. 16, 1692].
9 Child of Timothy Bunce.
11 Wife of Asa Benton.
12 Wife of Col. Wyllys (Geo.); Mary, a. 59; d. 11th. [Dau. of Rev. Timothy and Dorothy (Lamb) Woodbridge of Simsbury; born 1716.]
23 Child of Daniel Talcott.
27 John Lawrence, Jr. [Son of Hon. John and Margaret (Chenevard) Lawrence; born Aug. 20, 1749.]
Dec. 3 Daughter of Josiah Clark.
23 Child of Joseph Coit.

1775.
Jan. 2 Thomas Sanford, aged 80
3 John Wadsworth. [Son of Thos. and Sarah Wadsworth; lived on the present corner of Asylum and Trumbull streets, on the old Wadsworth property; aged 92].
12 Son of John Benton, aged 16.
12 Cyprian Powell's mother, aged 70.
13 Child of John Bigelow, aged 3.
29 James Humphrey. [Son of Dositheus and Anne (Griswold) Humphrey; bapt. Oct. 19, 1746 aged 29].
Feb. 3 John Keith. [A native of Scotland; master of one of the transport vessels which carried the troops of the Colony to the West Indies in 1740. At the time of his death a merchant in Hartford; carried to Middletown for burial, aged 71]
5 Samuel Wescaut, aged 20.
5 Wife of Samuel Talcott. [Mabel, dau. of Hezekiah and Elizabeth (Hobart) Wyllys; born Feb. 13, 1713. Aged 62.
7 Minje Thompson. Intered at exp. of John Skinner. Aged 7.
11 Remember Anna Burkett, buried—(This is supposed to be daughter of Sexton) aged 9.
13 Wife of John Dodd, aged 29.
14 Child of Caleb Bull, Jr., aged 5.
22 Child of Jonathan Wadsworth, aged 10.
24 Child of Bille Hooker, aged 2.
25 Child of Jonathan Wadsworth, aged 8.
26 Geo. Olcott. [Son of George and Sarah (Bunce) Olcott; bapt. Oct

CENTER CHURCH BURYING GROUND, HARTFORD. 269

	30, 1700.] Aged 65.
Mar. 14	Child of William Adams, aged 7.
12	Wife of Capt. Daniel. Bull. [Elizabeth] aged 55.
17	Child of Caleb Church, aged 6.
23	Child of Ashbel Spencer, aged 5.
29	Child of Charles Cadwell, aged 5.
April 1	Child of Ezra Hide, aged 6 mo
6	Infant child of Mr. Basset.
7	Phineas Cole, aged 45.
7	Mary Ann Bidwell, aged 26.
11	Child of John Bunce, aged 1.
13	Child of Jos. Boyngton, aged 3 mo.
16	Child of Joseph Bunce, aged 4.
16	Son of Thomas Steele, aged 6.
22	Wife of John Lawrence Esq. [Margaret, dau. of John Michael and Margaret (Beauchamp) Chenevard] aged 49.
27	Child of Caleb Turner, aged 1.
May 16	Child of widow Lydia Olcott, aged 5
19	Samuel Mallery, aged 34.
20	Wife of Samuel Read, aged 32.
24	Moses Dickinson. [Son of Thomas and Mehitable (Meekins) Dickinson] aged 65.
June 9	Joseph Akins, aged 35.
11	William Cadwell.
11	Jno. Calder. Intered at exp. of Geo, Blanchard, aged 5.
17	John McKnell, a soldier, aged 60.
July 19	The mother of Peter Westerly, aged 68.
25	Elias Taylor, a child intered at the exp. of Susannah Curtiss, aged 3 months.
31	Widow Sarah Edwards. [Dau. of Nathaniel and Mary (Stanley) Hooker; born Nov. 7, 1704, mar. 1728 Hon. Daniel Edwards,] aged 70.
Aug. 5	Daughter of widow Abigail Seymour, aged 16.
24	Wife of Joseph Talcott Esq. [Esther, dau. of John and Hannah (Sandford) Pratt] aged 71.
26	Rev. Joseph Howe. [Born in Killingly, Conn., Jan. 14, 1747, son of Rev. Perley Howe; Yale Coll. 1765; pastor South Church, Boston], aged 29. [In Hartford on a visit to his betrothed, Elizabeth Whitman, dau. of Rev. Elnathan].
25	Child of John Wells, aged 2.
27	Child of Benjamin Paine Esq., aged 2.

Aug. 27	Infant child of Benjamin Morrison.
Sept. 6	Niel's wife. Intered at expense of the Town, aged 37.
6	Mr. Shooter. Intered at the exp. of the Town, aged 75.
11	Infant child of Samuel Mattox.
18	Dau. of Martha Drake, aged 16.
18	Infant child of Mary Goodwin.
19	Child of Patrick Thomas, aged 3 weeks.
27	Wife of Caleb Bull, Jr. [Rebecca, dau. of Jonathan Butler, of Harwinton] aged 27.
29	Wife of John Spencer, aged 52.
30	Child of Isaac Sheldon, aged 2.
Oct. 3	Jonathan Seymour. [Son of John and Elizabeth (Webster) Seymour; born March 16, 1703,] aged 73.
6	Child of Isaac Tucker, aged 2.
7	Son of Caleb Bull, aged 9.
10	Child of Samuel Burr, aged 1½.
	Child of Mr. John Cadwell.
18	Child of Hezekiah Turner, aged 7mo
24	Child of Thomas Steele, aged 1.
27	Wife of Bille Hooker, aged 27.
Nov. 10	Mrs. Dorothy Steele. [Widow of Jonathan, dau. of Joseph and Sarah (Webster) Mygatt; born Jan. 26, 1696] aged 80.
11	Wife of Ebenezer Webster. [Hannah, dau. of Robert and Hannah (Beckley) Webster, born Nov. 7, 1695] aged 80.
17	Wife of Blackledge Wells, aged 44.
Dec. 10	Infant child of Jacob Brown.
13	Abner Porter of Tolland, aged 45.
26	Child of John Griggs, infant.
29	Child of James Marr, aged 16.
1776.	
Jan. 14	Child of James Waterhouse (inft).
18	James Sands, a stranger, intered at Exp. of the Town, aged 58.
27	Deacon Ozias Goodwin. [Son of Nathaniel and Elizabeth (Pratt) Goodwin, born June 26, 1689] aged 88.
Feb. 3	Samuel Barnard, born 1719, aged 57
12	Ebenezer Webster. [Son of John and Sarah (Mygatt) Webster, born 1689] aged 86.
14	Infant child of Benjamin Bigelow.
14	Child of Samuel Turner, aged 5.
26	Wife of Timothy Hale, aged 55.
29	The mother of Pantry Jones. [Rebecca Pantry, bapt. Dec. 25, 1692; dau. of John and Abigail (Mix)

LIST OF BURIALS,

Mar. 16 Pantry] aged 86.
      Wife of Moses Ensign, aged 42.
    8 Child of Daniel Talcott, aged 1 mo.
   15 The mother of Capt. Samuel Olcott. [Sarah, widow of Jonathan Olcott, and dau. of Joseph Collyer] aged 63.
   18 The mother of Zebulon Mygatt. [Dorothy, widow of Zebulon Mygatt; dau. of Thomas and Hannah Waters; born Aug. 28, 1704] aged 80
   23 Child of Mrs. Patten, aged 6.
   25 Jacob Wright, aged 76.
   29 Infant Child of Zebulon Seymour.
May 3 Wife of John Wright, aged 47.
   22 Infant child of Daniel Seymour.
June 18 Widow Susannah Grose [Susannah Bunce, widow of Freeman Grose] aged 72.
   22 Wife of Elisha Wells, aged 44.
   23 Timothy Phelps. [Son of Timothy and Sarah (Brown) Phelps, born Aug. 8, 1725] aged 51.
July 8 Sarah Frasier. Interred at the Exp. of Colony of Connecticut.
   13 Child of Jos. Church, Jr., aged 7 m.
   20 Child of Cherry the Prisoner. (Infant).
   25 Wife of Stephen Turner, aged 58.
Aug. 3 Mercy Williamson. [Dau. of Capt. Caleb and Mary (Cobb) Williamson, bapt. Aug. 13, 1699, at Barnstable, Mass] aged 79.
   25 Son of Barnabas Hinsdale, aged 14.
   28 Child of Travis, the Soldier. [Prisoner,] aged 2.
Sept. 1 Wife of Isaac Tucker.
   1 Hannah Shepard, aged 26.
   3 Child of Cyprian Powell, aged 10
   7 Child of Brasillia Hudson, aged 2.
   8 Abigail Holtom. [Dau. of Deacon Joseph and Abigail (Hastings) Holtom: bapt. Jan. 18, 1718-19] aged 57.
   9 Infant child of Rebecca Bly.
   10 Child of Thomas Sanford, aged 4.
   20 Child of Jonathan Bull, aged 1.
   11 Child of Joseph Read, aged 1.
   12 Austin Ledyard. Son of John and Mary (Austin) (Hooker) Ledyard; born 1751] aged 25.
   13 Hezekiah Turner. Interred at Exp. of Town, aged 29.
   15 Child of Jonathan Bull, aged 9.
   15 Child of Nathaniel Skinner, aged 4.
   16 Child of Ashbel Spencer, aged 2.

Sept. 19 Alice Powell. Intered at Exp. of Elizabeth Lord.
   20 Child of Obadiah Spencer, aged 2.
   21 Child of Bevil Watrous, aged 1.
   21 Child of Nathaniel Goodwin, Jr., aged 1.
   21 Child of Caleb Church, aged 2.
   22 Child of Obadiah Spencer, aged 6.
   24 Child of Nehemiah Cadwell, Jr., aged 3.
   25 Dau of Zebulon Seymour, aged 15.
   30 Samuel Goodwin. [Son of Samuel and Mary (Steele) Goodwin; born Oct. 10, 1710] aged 66.
Oct. 1 Samuel Benton's mother, (Miriam,) aged 60.
   1 Daughter of John Bidwell, aged 18.
   1 Wife of John Bidwell. [Mabel, dau. of Solomon Gilman, of East Hartford; born 1711, aged 65.
   2 Child of Aaron Bradley.
   2 Child of William Adams 2d.
   3 Child of John Barnot, aged 3.
   5 Child of Elisha Lord, aged 2.
   6 Son of widow Sarah Farnsworth, aged 9.
   8 Child of Samuel Benton, aged 3.
   9 Child of Thomas Seymour Esq, (infant).
   9 Child of Ashbel Barnot, aged 5.
   9 Child of James Bunce, aged 2.
   10 Widow Wilson. Intered at the Exp. of the Town, aged 65.
   10 Child of Samuel Clark.
   10 Widow Elizabeth Goodwin. [Elizabeth Collier (widow of William), dau. of John and Elizabeth (Humphreys) Collier, born April 14, 1706] aged 70.
   13 Dau. of Elijah Spencer, aged 16.
   19 Son of Jesse Marsh, aged 10.
Nov. 4 Infant child of John Hill.
   11 Capt. Daniel Bull. [Son of Daniel and Mary (Mygatt) Bull; bapt. Oct. 30, 1709] aged 68.
   28 Violetta Goodwin. [Dau. of William and Elizabeth (Shepard) born Oct. 18, 1696] aged 80.
Dec. 14 Robert Currier, aged 62.
   22 Widow Vaughn, aged 40.
   23 Daughter of Matthew Webster, [Mabel, born 1749] aged 27.
   28 The mother of Daniel Goodwin. [Abigail, dau. of John and Mary (Blackleach Wells) Olcott, widow of Daniel Goodwin, born Feb. 15, 1703-4] aged 73.

CENTER CHURCH BURYING GROUND, HARTFORD. 271

1777.

Jan. 2 Wife of Benjamin Townsend. Died with small-pox, aged 48.
6 Joseph Church. [Son of Joseph Church; Yale College, 1768] aged 29.
14 A brother of John Senter, aged 19.
14 Child of Samuel Winship, aged 1.
16 Infant child of Benjamin Morrison.
17 Mrs. Whaples, the aunt of Joseph Barnet, aged 98.
17 The dau. of widow Abigail Phelps. Died with small-pox, aged 20.
18 Child of Aaron Seymour (Infant).
28 Infant child of Patrick Thomas.

Feb. 7 Jonathan Watson. Died with Small Pox; Intered at Exp. of Town, aged 25.
8 Child of Frederick Basset, aged 2.
9 The mother of Nathaniel Goodwin. [Martha, widow of Ozias Goodwin, dau. of Capt. Caleb and Mary (Cobb) Williamson; born Feb. 13, 1700, Barnstable, Mass., aged 76.]
11 Luther Shepard. Died with small-pox, aged 58.
19 Infant child of Mr. Hunting.
22 John Gurney, aged 78.
26 Timothy Crowley. Intered at Exp. of Wm. Knox, aged 40.

Mar. 7 Rev. Elnathan Whitman. [Son of Rev. Samuel and Sarah (Stoddard) Whitman; born in Farmington, Jan. 12, 1709] aged 68.
19 Moses Dunbar. Was hanged and buried at exp. of State (for high treason) aged 40.
20 Child of Timothy Bunce, aged 2.
22 Jonathan Easton. [Son of Jonathan and Elizabeth (Cadwell) Easton, born 1710] aged 65.
23 Wife of Thomas Hinsdale.
24 Rebecca Taylor (Infant).

April 1 Edward Murphy, the Soldier, died with the Small Pox, and buried at Exp. of State, aged 33.
6 Child of Stephen Hutchinson, aged 8 months.
9 Elisha Hopkins. Died with small-pox. [Son of Thomas and Mary (Beckley) Hopkins; bapt. Oct. 17, 1731] aged 45.

May 1 Joseph Barnot, aged 81.
2 Wife of John Bradley, [Mercy, dau. of Ebenezer French of Guilford] aged 76.

13 Elijah Clapp. [Son of Thomas and Mary (King) Clapp] aged 68.
19 A son of John Barnot. Died with small-pox, aged 16.

June 6 Jacob Morris. Died with Small Pox and buried at Exp. of Jona Bull.
10 Wife of Deacon John Shepard, aged 68.
12 Jonathan Olcott. Died with small-pox. [Son of Jonathan and Sarah (Collyer) Olcott, bapt. Aug. 23, 1735] aged 37.
13 Jonathan Ashley. Died with small-pox. [Son of Jonathan and Elizabeth (Olcott) Ashley; born April 30, 1710] aged 70.
22 Daughter of Benjamin Paine Esq, Died with small-pox, aged 18.
26 Infant child of James Thompson.
29 Joseph Hosmer. [Son of Capt. Thomas and Ann (Prentice) Hosmer; born Nov. 27, 1705] aged 71.

July 1 Charles Kelsey, aged 83.
5 Benjamin Segar's infant.
14 Stephen Turner, aged 59.

Aug. 17 Wife of Elisha Butler, aged 60.
21 Child of Samuel Mattox, aged 8.
22 Child of Consider Burt, aged 18 m.
24 Zacheriah Seymour. [Son of Zachariah and Hannah (Olmsted) Seymour; born Sept. 24, 1712] aged 65.
26 Child of Joseph Olcott, aged 2.

Sept. 18 Ebenezer Watson. [Son of John and Bethiah (Tyler) Watson; born in Bethlehem, Conn., 1744; publisher of the Connecticut Courant] aged 33.
20 Child of William Knox, (infant.)
21 Wife of Josiah Blakely, aged 19.
22 Wife of Elisha Skinner, aged 19.
22 Child of Samuel Kilbourn.
26 Child of Jonathan Flagg, aged 2.
28 Polly Vaughn, aged 6.
30 Child of Captain Jeremiah Wadsworth, aged 1.

Oct. 6 Child of Ashbel Steele, aged 1 m.
10 Infant child of John Hill.
18 Child of Robert Brantwaite, (perhaps Betsey, bapt. at Middletown Sept. 27, 1777, aged 1.
22 Child of Frederick Standley, aged 1.
25 Lydia Bigelow, aged 22.
29 Thomas Burr, aged 55.

[To be continued.]

NEW HAVEN DEFENSES IN THE REVOLUTION AND IN THE WAR OF 1812.

BY M. LOUISE GREENE.

During the Revolution, New Haven was a town of between seven and eight thousand inhabitants. Somewhat less than half of these were scattered within the present limits of the city, while the remainder spread themselves over that part of the town which then included what is now known as East, West and North Haven, Hamden, and parts of Woodbridge and Bethany. The original plat of the town, bounded by the present Meadow, George, York, Grove, Olive and Water streets, together with the small spur of land which extended out to receive the shipping, was the most thickly settled, especially on the water side. The harbor then extended much farther into the land than now. Within these limits, or adjacent to them, there was in 1772, counting every dwelling house, "store or shop with a fireplace in it," 440 houses, and in 1775 there were 370 dwelling houses alone, thus giving for that period a well-populated area.

Further, New Haven was one of the two chief towns of the colony, and in the State House the Fall session of the General Assembly duly convened. Then as now it was both a county and a college town. Over the then unfenced and much rumpled Green looked forth both county jail and college chapel, while at the southeast corner centered the many cart-ruts, shortening the distance from the main roads to the public market located there.

To the northeast and northwest of the center of the town loomed the "Old Sentinels," the "Red Mounts" of the early Dutch sailors, at whose base the debris of earlier ages had formed a rough triangle with its apex between the beetling crags of trap and red sandstone, whereon the early planters had sought a haven on the harbor edge. Already to the townsmen the grey-red parapet of West Rock had proved a friend to freedom by safely sheltering the Regicides from the wrath of Charles II, and the day was fast approaching when the trembling people, fleeing from the anger of George III, would seek safety on its heights.

When the Stamp Act and Boston Port Bill made armed resistance probable, the exposed situation of Connecticut was early apparent to her clear-sighted statesmen. With Long Island Sound forming a highway for the enemy's vessels, and its fine harbor of New London coveted as a base for operations between Canada and Delaware, Connecticut would most probably become the object of a regular invasion or of predatory raids across her borders or along her coast. She invited such attacks the more because she soon came to be known as one of the richest and most patriotic of the colonies.

Preparations for defense were begun as early as 1774, when Roger Sherman was preparing to attend the first Continental Congress. The General Assembly of Connecticut ordered the town to double the required supply of

50 lbs. of good gunpowder and 200 cut bullets, and 300 flints per every sixty soldiers, which they had been required to keep on hand ever since 1745. The town of New Haven immediately commanded the construction of a new powder house of sufficient size, and requested the selectmen to see that the powder be quickly obtained.

In December Governor Trumbull received from his son in New York the following advice:

"It will be expedient to secure a supply of powder as soon as possible, the sooner the better, as it is apprehended that if the Admiral carries his present plan into execution of stationing a small vessel in every harbor, creek and bay along shore, that it will be, by and by, next to impossible to secure such supply."

Another letter, written a little later by a Hartford correspondent, an-

FROM AN OLD PAINTING OF NEW HAVEN GREEN, 1779.
The small building in the rear of the White Church was where prisoners were confined during the British Invasion. The buildings shown are, Colony State House, Yale College Chapel, the Brick Church and White Haven Church.

nounces that, "The deliberations of the Assembly are kept very secret, there is a rumor that there is a great deficiency of powder in the colony's military stores, which the governor has a right to supply, and, in order to do so it is decreeded that 300 lbs. of powder and a corresponding proportion of lead is to be purchased at the publick expense, and a ship is to be sent to Holland for the powder."

Whether this particular ship was ever sent I do not know, but if so, it was one of the many sent out from this time forth to the end of the war in search of powder both for home and general defense. Again and again embargoes were raised and special permits granted for cargoes to sail, which at the West Indies or elsewhere, could be exchanged for the great necessity. This letter further states, "the militia in the whole colony is mustered every week ; in most towns, they have a deserter from His Majesty's Forces by way of Drill-Sergeant. Nothing'but a Spirit of Independence would suffer matters to be carried to such extremities." Near North Haven even the clergyman was drilling, the writer says.

New Haven had her train-band militia, and also her famous Governor's Guards. In 1775, the householders divided themselves into two companies, electing their own officers, who, in turn, were subject to Colonel Fitch, whom the Assembly had appointed to have charge of the town supply of powder. Immediately a town-meeting ordered all the inhabitants, who had failed to enroll themselves, to form a third company in like manner. Failing to do this, they were to appear, together with those Tories who had not left town upon a previous order to do so, to show why they hesitated to boldly enlist themselves in the patriot cause. A company of forty artillerists, to have charge of the carriage guns, was formed at the same time. Captain Thomson's company was granted the special privilege of drawing double the usual rate of one-half pound of powder per man, or thirty pounds. Lest the precious stuff should be wasted, it was voted not to use it in weekly drill, and that "no man was to wantonly discharge his gun for the space of two months" under penalty of fine. The same meeting voted, " That the Committee of Inspection at Lyme send an express to Colonel Fitch of the earliest intelligence of the arrival of any fleet or of any hostile appearance on the Sound, and that Captain Sears was to have ready means for transporting similar intelligence of danger from the direction of New York."

It was also voted to ask the General Assembly for row-galleys, floating batteries, and whatever was proper for the defense of the town ; also for a hundred stand of arms to " be kept in the College Library for the use of a company to be formed there."

But, first of all, this same town-meeting voted, "that a Beacon be forthwith erected on Indian Hill, East Haven, and that Phineas Bradley, Mr. Doolittle and Mr. James Rice be a committee to erect the same, according to their best judgement. Voted that said Committee, as soon as the Beacon is finished, fix on a proper day for firing the Same, and give notice thereof, advertising in the papers, and requesting the ministers in the neighboring Towns and Parishes to Communicate the Same to their people, which notice is recommended to be given on Thanksgiving day: Voted that the Beacon be fired by written order from Col. Fitch, and in his absence from Capt. Thomson, Capt. Brown or Capt. Alling, and by no other order or authority......Voted that the Committee to erect the Beacon do build a Watch-Box near the Same, and that Capt. Thomson order a watch to be kept their Continually."

From the new lighthouse in the open mouth of the harbor the lines of the shore and the great hills beyond, present the same general appearance as in the days of '76. The old lighthouse, built in 1856, replacing an earlier one, built in 1780, or possibly before, stands at Lighthouse or Five Mile Point, and Indian Hill, Beacon Hill, Fort Hill or Fort Wooster Hill (as it has variously been called) rises to the height of two hundred feet at its eastern knoll, the chief break in the low lines of the harbor's contour. This elevation stands half way between the town and the pretty baylet of Morris Cove. Some minor changes in the coast line and in the harbor level have occured. For instance, in 1765 Long Wharf was not over thirty rods in length, but the water at its foot was as deep as in 1811, when it was three-quarters of a mile long. This change was due to the annual accumulations of mud, chiefly on the north and west side, which finally resulted in the total filling in of the old winter harbor in the lee of the west shore. The common tide rose, as it now rises, six feet. The beach or shoal, which almost closed the entrance to the inner harbor, is represented on one of President Stiles' maps as touching the west shore at extreme low tide. This beach projected landward in a northeasterly direction to within about two miles of Long Wharf. Opposite to its northern half and about equally distant from the Wharf and Light House Point, close to the shore, so close as to form at high tide a moated island, lay an "insulated rock of considerable elevation above the water." With but ninety rods between it and the beach, it commanded the only channel by which boats of any considerable size could approach the town.

Capt. Thomson, with a detail of thirty men, was ordered by the General Assembly, in October, 1775, to begin the erection of a battery on this rock. Owing to the disquieting rumors of danger from several British fleets, the force was increased to fifty men and the work pushed with vigor, in order to have this Black Rock battery in readiness to receive its share of the six eighteen pounders and ten twelve-pounders ordered by the Assembly, in November, for New Haven. Before the battery could be completed, severe weather put an end to work. The men were dismissed December 23, Capt. Thomson being allowed "£3 for one and one-half month's work in extra cold weather." The men had undoubtedly worked zealously, spurred on, at first, by friendly rivalry with their fellow patriots on the hill behind them, laboring to finish the beacon at the appointed time ; and, at last, by the report from Cambridge of the approach of a hostile fleet.

We have the following notice from the *Connecticut Journal.* " The town of New Haven, having this day erected a Beacon on Indian Hill, at East Haven, now Beacon Hill, about a mile and a half southeast of the town ; and ordered us, their Committee, to give public notice thereof ; we now inform the public in general and the neighboring towns in particular, that the Beacon will be fired on Monday evening next, the 20th instant, at 6 o'clock ; all persons are then desired to look out for the Beacon and take the bearing of it from their respective places of abode, that they may know where to look for it in case of an alarm, which will be announced by the firing of three cannon. If our enemy should attack us, and we be under the necessity of making use of this method to call in the assistance of our brethren, we request that all persons who come into the town will take care to be well armed, with a good musket, bayonet, and cartridge box, well filled with cartridges, under their proper officers,and repair to the State House, where they will receive orders from Col. Fitch, what post to take to.

The ministers of the several parishes of this and the neighboring towns are requested.to mention to their respective congregations the time when the Beacon will be fired.

    Phineas Bradley,
    Isaac Doolittle,   Commissioners.
    James Rice,

          New Haven, 14th November, 1775."

The beacons were either tall trees, roughly hewn of their branches, or masts or poles, with wooden spikes or pegs driven in by which the watch could quickly climb, with lighted torch, in order to fire the basket of combustibles which hung from a crane near the top. The flames, spurting upwards, soon ignited the barrel of tar which frequently topped the pole. Its light by night or its smoke by day spread the alarm throughout the country side. Talcott Mountain, Beacon Hill and Tuthill Heights, Long Island, thus protected the long line of the Connecticut Coast.

A BEACON.

As soon as the colony's marine could be organized, her armed vessels, the Spy, Defense, and later the Oliver Cromwell, cruised at large. Row galleys, or whale boats, carrying ship-guns and fifty men, viz: the Shark, Crane and Whiting (built at New Haven) rendezvoused at New London, and by three well defined courses patrolled the whole coast. Privateers were let loose to prey upon the enemy and brought in many a rich prize as well as much reliable information. A system of espionage was established by the organization of numbers of small light boats, well designated by their name "spy-boats," whose boatmen gave the governor timely information of the enemy's movements, and were often in correspondence with the larger vessels of the colony. The regulations to prevent smuggling and illicit intercourse with the enemy were so strict that at times the people suffered severely from embargoes, and at times "not even a rowboat or a canoe could leave any port, bay, creek or river in the state without a written permit." All had to be drawn up on shore, secured and ready on demand. All suspected vessels were subject to capture or to search.

In order to carry out these measures as well as defend the town, work was begun on Black Rock Fort early in March, 1776, at first with thirty, the following week with fifty men. Capt. Thomson was given as assistants, a Lieutenant and two Sergeants. The fort was finished in June. Orders were issued to build cheap barracks near by, not to cost over £25. £74 were allowed Capt. Thomson toward building the fort, and £200 for his company, the equivalent of a pound in present currency being three and one-third dollars. The work of the fort was so well done that in August a detail from there was ordered to Milford to assist the people in building a similar fortification in their harbor. In the fall Black Rock barracks were finished, shingled and an outside chimney constructed. Mr. Bishop of New Haven was appointed barrack-master.

It must have grown very cold this winter for the cannon at Black Rock were removed to the town. Immediately there followed such a misuse of flags of truce that the guns were promptly sent back again, and a permanent detail, sufficient for firing them, stationed in the new barracks. January 30, 1777, strict orders were given that, "No Vessel or Boat will for the future be permitted to pass Black Rock Battery without a written Licence from one of the Civil Authority of the Towne. Agreeable to a late Resolve of the General Assembly of the State."

The fort proved its usefulness. For instance, the following March, its guards frightened off a British frigate with two or three tenders, trying to creep in close to the east shore. In June, three small vessels were taken in the Sound, with thirteen abscounding Tories on board, and were sent in to Black Rock. That the gunners' shots were not always effective in quite the way they were intended to be, one Capt. Phipps, hailing from the enemy's direction, could vouch for. A shot sent over his deck as an intimation to heave to, fell short of its mark and tore away the greater part of the Captain's lower jaw as punishment for his foolhardiness. At this time the guard consisted of one Lieutenant, one Sergeant, one Corporal and ten or more privates.

The colony had built the fort, private capital a powdermill, and it was expected that the town would take further necessary measures for its own defense. There were ordered in 1778, "two small works at West Bridge, capable of receiving four small pieces of ordinance with a sufficient number of men to defend and serve them well." The works were thought to require "two days work with good team and about seventy days of other labor."

"The only other pass into Town from the Westward," on the slope of East Rock, was defended by an earthwork capable of receiving two or three field pieces, and costing one-half the labor of the preceding. East Haven and West Haven were given one carriage gun apiece, and were required to enroll their inhabitants in the militia. Later slight earthworks were raised at Oyster Point, on the west side, and on the small bluff at Morris Cove, to which on the day of the invasion two small guns were drawn. In addition a gun was planted near the East Haven ferry, and a field piece in the field, a short distance to one side of the fort. On the fatal Sunday of July 4, 1779, the militia were under command of Lieut. Col. Sabin; the Govenor's Guards, under Capt. Hillhouse, who was in the midst of preparations to recruit another company; the artillery, increased to ninety men, was under Capt. Phineas Bradley, and was divided between the town, East and West Haven, their stations being the townplat, the fort and West Bridge,

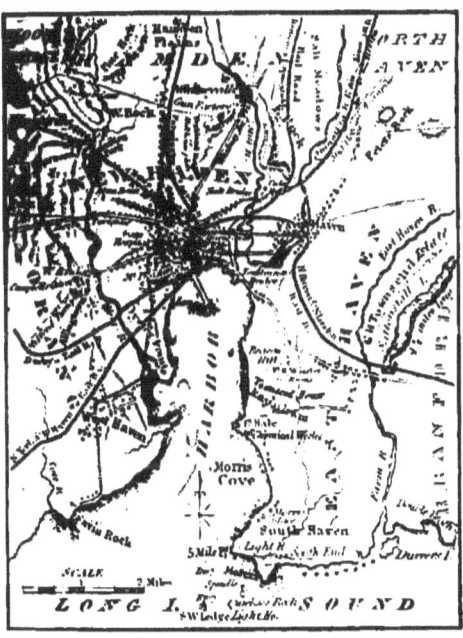

MAP OF NEW HAVEN AND HARBOR.

with guards or pickets thrown out along the coast and the approaches to the town.

The peaceful communion Sabbath ended with the din and confusion of war's alarms, and the intended first public celebration in New Haven of Independence Day was rudely turned from patriotic speeches to patriotic blows in behalf of the liberty they had planned to celebrate ; from precision of military marching with empty guns, to the hurry-scurrying by shortest cut, through woods or across fields, to intercept the enemy, and by whistling bullets from behind fence and tree cut off his approach to the town. Had not the people remained so long unconvinced of danger, success might have crowned their efforts. An express from Westfield (Bridgeport) warned them at 10 P. M., Sunday, that the enemy's fleet was off Stamford Point and headed for New Haven. President Stiles urged the immediate calling in of the militia. But it was not until the watch at Black Rock discovered the advance sails, one mile southwest of the Southwest Ledge (where the new lighthouse stands), and sounded the alarm of three cannon shots, that the town roused to the reality of its danger. Then confusion filled the streets. The bells rang, the drums beat to arms. The Beacon flared the news to the country side. Of the townspeople, a third fled for safety to the Rocks, or further into the country; a third awaited British clemency to Tory friend or lukewarm patriot ; a third rushed to arms. At sunrise the guard at West Haven and President Stiles, stationed with a spyglass in the college tower, saw the enemy prepare to land some fifteen hundred men, under Gen. Garth, commonly called "the Wolf," from the fleet of forty-eight sail, Sir George Collier commanding. The boats went back to land a similar force, under Gen. Tryon, on the east shore.

Gen. Garth's forces, meeting with no opposition, save from the bullets of two retreating guards, who had gone to the shore to report the enemy's movements, marched his men to the West Haven Green, and there rested them, so as to give Gen. Tryon time to land and to join him, about noon, in the town. By the time Gen. Garth was ready to advance, the New Haven people had massed their forces at West Bridge ; the Derby and other militia were pouring in, and Capt. Hillhouse, with many college boys among his volunteers, was near enough to engage the British vanguard and drive it back upon the main. Old President Daggett was in waiting for his own little historic fray, and Bradley's men stood in readiness to remove the planks of the bridge, after Hillhouse's orderly retreat across it, and to cannonade the British descent of Milford hill so warmly as to cause their long detour, of five miles, in the burning sun, to the next ford at Westville, or Hotchkistown. The attempt of the patriots to drag their guns across the fields, and head off the British as they entered from the Derby road, failed for lack of time. The Americans could only fire down upon the enemy as they mounted the steep ascent from Westville, and stubbornly contest every foot of ground to the entrance of the town.

While such were the deeds on the west side, no less brave ones were being enacted on the eastern shore. A small company of East Haven men, with a single cannon, disputed, as long as was reasonable, the approach to the shore, at Lighthouse point, of Tryon's men, who came on in boats, each carrying in the bow a gun. Half a mile from the shore, the line divided, making one landing east of the Point and another in Morris Cove. As the eastern division landed, a British officer fell as Lieut. Campbell had fallen on Milford hill. The patriots retreated along the beach to join their comrades, who had made a stand with two guns at the knoll before mentioned. These, in turn, had to retreat when the British forces joined on the shore of the Cove, and Gen. Tryon, taking possession of the bluff, directed the marines to protect the march of the soldiers, while he signalled to Sir George Collier to move up the fleet in order to silence the guns of the Fort, which were, in his own words, causing him "some little annoyance." As soon as the British had forced their hotly contested march to the point on the highway leading to town, where a side road makes off to the Fort, they halted. Gen. Tryon ordered a party forward to capture the field piece, which Lieut. Pierpont had been serving from the field near the fort, and also to storm the fortifications. The fighting on the road above was resumed, the Americans falling back to Beacon Hill, where they hoped to make a stand, but overpowered by numbers, they had to retreat to the Saltonstall and Branford hills. The enemy took possession of and encamped about Beacon Hill.

Meanwhile, the small garrison of nineteen men at the fort, augmented by a few neighbors, diligently served their guns, under the command of Capt. Moulthrop and Lieut. Bishop. But their scanty ammunition was soon exhausted. They then spiked and dismounted their guns, and retreated along the shore, but were made prisoners by skirmishers before they could come up with their own forces. Silent guns and an empty fort met the storming party, whose occupation of the works was the signal for the men-of-war and transports to move up as quickly as possible, because the tide was falling. Such determined resistance had prevented the meeting of the admiral and the two generals until nearly two o'clock. At that hour the ships lined the whole length of the harbor, and the men-of-war lay on spring cables, with guns run out, waiting the signal to shell the town. The signal was not given. Their reception had been too hot; the chances of foraging or of cattle raiding, the objects of their visit, were not good; the soldiers were plundering and were already so drunk and unmanageable that the marines were forbidden to land for their share of the spoils. The Americans were increasing by hundreds in the outskirts of the town. The British found it impossible to hold the bridge on the east side, and during the next morning Gen. Tryon was forced to yield the stand on Beacon Hill to one thousand Americans under Gen. Ward. These immediately brought field pieces and kept up a constant fire on the anchored ships. The result was that the enemy judged best to quickly embark their troops, and they weighed anchor that evening, after having burnt the public stores and buildings, and seized all the artillery and ammunition they could find. Their last act was to send back a boat to fire the barracks of the Fort which they saw at once reoccupied.

Immediately after the invasion, the state ordered stronger works to be thrown up on Beacon Hill; twelve hundred and fifty men were distributed to the posts between the Connecticut River and Stratford; Branford, Guilford and Saybrook received a special guard, and ninety-four men and officers were ordered to the Fort. In May, 1781, Black Rock was reported as unfit to station men in, but capable at small expense of being made defensible, and "to afford the Necessary Means, which may also have a happy Influence to quiet the fear of the Inhabitants." A request for two brass pieces, together with horses to draw them, to take the place of the old, heavy and unwieldly cannon was concurred in and £100 were forwarded to begin the repairs.

In 1782 the guard at the fort consisted of three officers and nineteen privates. At the close of the war New Haven was required to keep three cannon, mounted and under the care of the commanding officer of the Governor's Guards.

The raid for a few cattle, in 1781, on West Haven, was the only other visit of the enemy to the vicinity.*

From the close of the Revolution, the old fort sank gradually into decay, and in the early years of the century illustrated the Anti-Federal policy, always opposed to the old adage, "In the time of peace prepare for war."

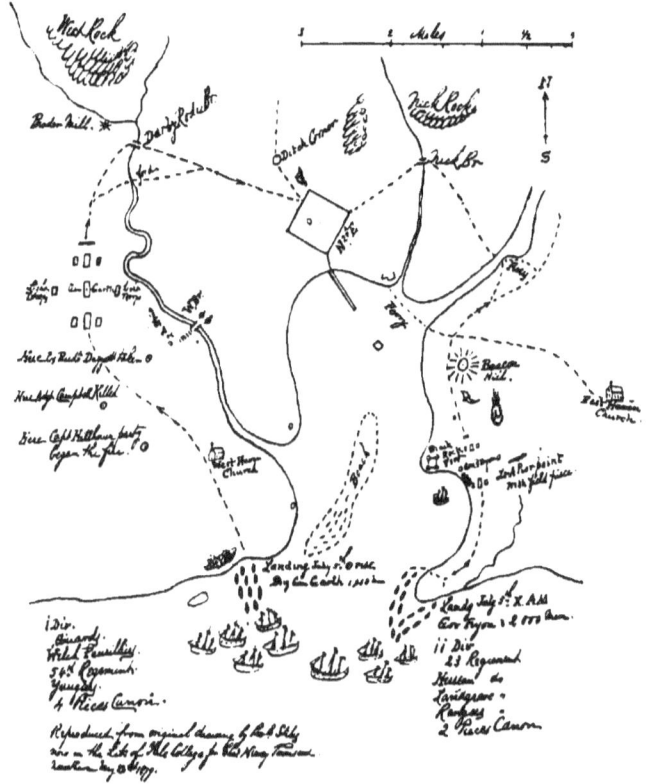

MAP OF BRITISH INVASION.
By permission Capt. C. H. Townsend.

Jeffersonian gunboats, not forts and fortifications, were the order of the day until the war storm of Europe, with its Berlin Decrees, Orders in Council and Milan Decree brought the war clouds to our very door. In 1807 a systematic fortification of the whole Atlantic coast was undertaken. New York and the large southern cities were first considered, later New Haven. An entrance forced either there or at New London would give access to the United States

*No attempt to do more than sketch the invasion is possible here. A very complete account is given in Capt. Charles Hervey Townshend's monograph, "The British Invasion of New Haven." This includes also many personal accounts, letters and extracts from official records.

arsenal at Springfield, as well as to the factories of fire arms and to the powder mills, scattered in the vicinity of both Hartford and New Haven.

The commerce of the latter city was not inconsiderable. Her shipping, reduced by the Revolutionary War to one vessel of thirty tons in 1783, had by the following June increased to thirty vessels engaged in West Indian or foreign trade ; and her seven or eight sloops had increased to fifty-six. In the period, 1804-7, fully one hundred vessels cleared annually for foreign ports. The embargo (December 22, 1807—March 4, 1809) fell with terrific force, and and by July, 1808, seventy-eight out of New Haven's eighty-two vessels were rotting at their wharves. One hundred shipwrights and a host of mechanics and furnishers of ship supplies were out of work. Thirty-two commercial houses watched, with anxious eyes, the bareness of Long Wharf, so recently lengthened to accommodate the expanding trade. The raising of the embargo, notwithstanding the still remaining restriction of the Non-Intercourse Act, directed against the English and French, relieved the town of a poverty, which

NEW HAVEN HARBOR—AFTER AN OLD CUT BY J. W. BARBER.
A, West Rock ; *B*, Long Wharf; *C*, Campbell's Grave; *E*, East Rock; *H*, Fort Hale; *K*, Fort Hale Magazine with Barracks opposite; *W*, Fort Wooster.

had sent about one-ninth of the population to soup kitchens, and driven fully a fifth to subsist on these and other forms of charity. Within a month, thirty vessels had put to sea, and the repeal of the act, May, 1810, brought flourishing times until the embargo of ninety days, which prefaced the outbreak of the War of 1812.

In 1808, "agents were appointed and furnished with funds for the erection of a battery, magazine and barracks for the defense of New Haven harbor." The battery was to be placed on the site of old Black Rock Fort. As the channel had deepened to the eastward, the location was even better than in the days of '79. On April 27, May 3, and May 21, respectively, the United States government bought of Messers Kneeland Townsend, Trueman Colt and Philemon Augur, a tract of land on the east side of New Haven harbor, known by the name of King's Island, with a strip of land for a highway, two rods wide, for $275; a second tract adjoining the harbor, containing one-half acre, for $125; and a third tract of the same size for $30.00.

The battery was to hold six guns, and the barracks to contain forty men, and an appropriation, in accordance with the acts of Congress, of February 11 and June 14, 1809, of $6,295.96 was made for it. The report of December 11, describes it thus: "Fort Hale, situated on the eastern side of the harbor of New Haven, an elliptical enclosed battery of masonry, mounting six heavy guns; a small brick magazine, standing some paces to one side in a field, and brick barracks for fifty men and officers." At the breaking out of the war the guard consisted of seventy-eight artillerists. The magazine held about twenty-five barrels of gun powder. The fort received its name from Captain Nathan Hale, the patriot spy.

At the declaration of war, most of the New Haven merchants called home their ships. About six hundred seamen scattered, some to enlist on board New Haven or other privateers; some to enter the navy, and some to serve on gunboats, which it was soon found necessary to employ in a night patrol of the lower harbor, for almost immediately the Connecticut coast became the swarming ground for privateers and cruisers of both nations. Early in 1813, the British declared a blockade of the whole coast north of the Capes of Delaware, exempting certain blockaded ports for the commerce of neutral nations. Of these New Haven was one. Thus on July 10, 1813, sixteen foreign ships entered and twenty cleared this port. Spanish, Swedish, Norwegian, Portuguese and Russian ships frequented the harbor, with the result that British and American vessels, sailing under false colors, were among them. An attempt to put an end to this sort of thing, by a new embargo bill, failed in the Senate. The British fleet, under Sir Thomas Hardy, began a local blockade in June, and succeeded in shutting up in New London, until the close of the war, the United States frigates Macedonian and Constitution. The temptations to run the blockade were great, for a successful trip was as lucrative as it was hazardous; and from 1812 a regular system of signalling was arranged by which skippers could know when the way was clear to New York, and when likely to be disputed. Still greater were the temptations to the unscrupulous to traffic with the enemy. A rigid enforcement of the rule, that there should be no communication with the foe, except by officers of station under a flag of truce was imperative. For this, the services of the fort, of the Block House, erected at the end of Long Wharf, and garrisoned by native sailors, and of the gunboat patrol were required.

The first alarm, because of special danger to New Haven, came on the night of September 13, 1813, when a British frigate and sloop of war stood close in to the Old Lighthouse. A marauding expedition was feared. The next April a fleet of twenty-five sail destroyed $150,000 worth of property at Saybrook. A week later two of the enemy appeared off New Haven harbor, and as it was known that two frigates, a sloop, a brig and a seventy-four man-of-war were only a few miles off, the people had reason to recall the previous British invasion. In July, sailors, supposed to belong to a British man-of-war, recently seen off Guilford, came ashore at the Lighthouse, on the night of the twentieth, and made searching inquiries concerning the marine guard, the forces in the harbor and the defenses of the town. When, in August, Sir Thomas Hardy made a second attack upon Stonington, the feeling of the town was: " The enemy is hovering on the coast. Where the next blow will be attempted no one can tell. Preparations to repel invasion cannot too speedily be made."

The false alarm of a descent by way of Branford, on September 6th, brought home the fullest sense of peril. Troops were called out ; six hundred men assembled under Col. Sanford. The Horse-Guards were sent to Branford, eight miles away, and patrolled the coast the entire night. The British had landed at Stony Creek and Indian Neck, respectively four and two miles from Branford, and had, while leaving the people unmolested, stolen all their boats. They got away twenty minutes before the arrival of the Branford troops. They had also made a landing at Lighthouse Point in vain search for water.

During the preceding fortnight, a battery of several heavy guns had been erected at the Long Wharf pier. This, though temporary, was capable of re-

WEST HAVEN GREEN.

sisting heavy shot and was thought to be effectual, together with the fort, to protect the shipping against any force which the enemy would adventure into the harbor. But now voluntary subscriptions, in money or in labor, were called for to complete a fort on Prospect or Beacon Hill, " for the common defense of the Harbor, City and Country, and which when finished will afford very great protection to all this part of the coast. Troops," the notice continued, " will be here in a few days to man the works. Persons willing to contribute their services will report to Capt. Boddington or to the Committee. So many have reported that it has become necessary to assign particular days to the different working parties."

Enthusiasm was at a high pitch. The neighboring towns sent parties of a hundred or more men, who came marching in with flags and drums. Several companies had full bands, and were welcomed with military salutes.

4

WEST BRIDGE.

In the North Haven contingent was Doctor Trumbull, the state historian, who though eighty years of age, set an example with his shovel, after recommending their efforts to the favor of Almighty God. The Ring Bolt Guard, comprising the sailors who found themselves ashore, did good service. Societies,

BLUFF AT MORRIS COVE,
From which General Tryon is said to have directed the movements of the British.

like the Mechanics, a literary society, assembled at Tomlinson's Bridge to march for a long day's work on the fortifications. All tolls were remitted to workers coming or going. The first week in October, Captain Northrup's squad of about eighty men from Fort Hale took their turn. By a spontaneous burst of popular favor the new fort received the name of the Revolutionary hero, Gen. Wooster.

NEW HAVEN FROM BEACON HILL.

On September 13, there had arrived two companies of artillery and one company of horse to be stationed near New Haven. Governor Smith recommended to the October Legislature the increase of the artillery, guns for the new fortifications and the granting of a select corps. That body responded by the enlistment of one thousand, three year men for home defense, and a special guard of one hundred men for the fort. Two months later the treaty of Ghent was signed, and early in February the news of peace arrived in America. On February 13th, the cannon of Forts Wooster and Hale thundered the good news to the country round about, and in May, the soldiers enlisted to serve through the war, were discharged.

OLD FORT WOOSTER, BEACON HILL.

The third and last fort on the little rocky isle remains to be described.
In the military report of 1821, the batteries at New Haven were reported
"too small to offer any resistance." In this and the two preceding reports, a
system of fortifications along the entire cost was outlined. It was intended to
have this system developed gradually. The proposed fortifications were listed
in the order of their importance, as of the first, second and third class. It was
proposed to erect new batteries to protect New Haven from depredations of
an enemy, and to make her a port of refuge. Nothing, however, was done
immediately, as New Haven was in the second class. In 1826, the port of
New London had risen to far outrank New Haven, both as a harbor of refuge,
and as a possible
base of operations,
and also as an im-
portant defense for
Long Island Sound
and its commerce.
Hence the military
report that year
suggested the sub-
stitution of a new
work to replace the

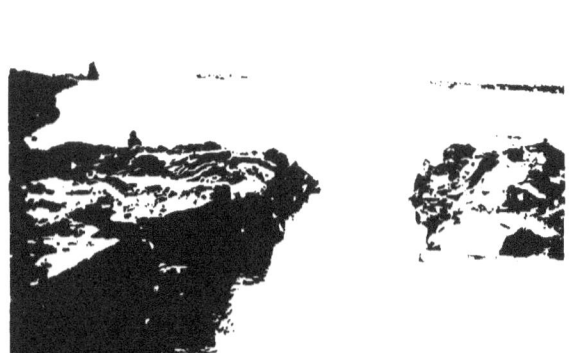

ENTRANCE TO MOAT,
FORT HALE.

slight redoubt at Fort
Wooster, and the en-
largement of Fort Hale,
at a total cost of $59,-
609.18. Little or no
money had been spent on
either fort since the close
of the war. If the new

THE MORRIS COVE BLUFF, FROM FORT HALE.

plan had been carried out, Fort Hale would have cost $31,815.00, and
held twenty-five men in time of peace and two hundred and twenty in
time of war; and Fort Wooster $27,793.00, holding twenty-five men in peace
and one hundred and fifty-five in war. Nothing was done, however. In the
report of 1836, the same recommendation was repeated, with the additional
requirement of new cannon and six barbette guns, thirty-two pounders. By
that time such improvements could not raise either defense above the third
class. Still nothing was done and the fort gradually followed its predecessor
on the road to ruin. Its guard dwindled from the twenty-two men of 1810-11,
and eighty men of 1814. In 1819, a total of fifty men, including one captain,

two lieutenants, three corporals, three sergeants, two musicians, six artificers, and thirty-six matrosses and privates were divided between Forts Trumbull

TABLET MARKING THE SITE OF THE BEACON, BEACON HILL.

(eighteen guns) Griswold (twelve guns) and Hale (six guns). In 1831, the fort was in charge of Capt. Thomas, formerly of the 25th U. S. Infantry, who with his family lived at the barracks.

Late in the history of the Civil War, funds to the amount of $150,000, or over, were appropriated for a modern defense to replace Fort Hale.

During the summer and fall months of 1865, the embankments were built, a parapet on the entire land front and a portion of the water front. A partial rebuilding of the traverses was made necessary because of settling due to the nature of the material used, beach-washed sand. A good clayey soil was obtained about thirty yards from the fort and made excellent material for covering all embankments. No work was done in the winter months, but

RUINED DRAWBRIDGE, FORT HALE.

by the next October, the grading, sodding and grass sowing were completed. A sluice way was cut through the rock at the angle of the ditch and furnished with double gates and an overflow. Five granite plinth blocks were set, a platform laid, six embrasures cut and a drawbridge built, while $10,000 of the appropriation remained unspent. In cutting the sods in the neighboring lots it was found necessary to rope gangs of men to the ploughs as the ground was too light to bear either oxen or horses.

In February, 1867, the public property in tools, etc. was sold at auction, and the fort placed in charge of a keeper. The war was over but for about fifteen years six one hundred pound Dahlgren guns maintained their peaceful watch, until about 1885, when they were removed. The custodian from 1875 to 1893, when the fort was turned over to the New Haven Park Commissioners

DESTROYING OLD FORT HALE, 1795.

as a part of Fort Hale Park, was Capt. Charles H. Townshend. The United States did not renounce its ownership in the Fort Hale property. It is held subject to immediate re-occupation by the government at any time national needs require. The land on which the old magazine stood, King's Island, is considered by military experts a fine location either for defending the city or quelling a riot.

More than thirty years of improvement in the science of attack and defense, and the same number of years of neglect leaves New Haven, a third time, with a ruined fort for her protection.

In the changes and chances of a contest with a foreign power, New Haven may again hear the sound of battle, and the government has made some provision for such a contingency. In such an event the Connecticut men of to-day will prove that they are not one whit less valiant than were their forefathers.

FORT HALE AS IT IS TO-DAY.

BLIND-FOLD.

BY ANNA F. BURNHAM.

I saw a little child with bandaged eyes,
    Put up its hands to feel its mother's face,
She bent, and caught the tender groping palms,
    And pressed them to her lips a little space.

I know a soul made blind by its desires,
    And yet its faith keeps feeling for God's face
Bend down, O Mighty Love, and let that faith
    One little moment touch Thy lips of Grace.

Succory.

By Louise P. Merritt.

The Succory sleeps by the roadside,
A dust-covered, straggling thing,
Unwitting the tender glory
The midsummer sunshine will bring.

The Succory wakes, and upraises
Her daintily-fringed eyes of blue.
No matter how dusty the road-way,
She mirrors the heavenly hue.

Thus, often, we see human nature,
Begrimed by the dust of its place,
Look up; and the heavenly vision
Streams radiant over its face.

A PASTORAL.

A PASTORAL.

Pan rose betimes to guard his flocks;
    In orchards droned the bees;
The warblers came to sing and build,
And, as Pan played, their flute-notes trilled,
    And joy was on the breeze.

Thro' dreamy woodlands babbling streams
    Wound on to meadows fair,
Where crimson amaryllis grew,
And iris, white, and harebells, blue,
    For dryad queens to wear.

So broke the day, the legend says;
    Nymphs wandered in the dew;
The swallows twittered, wheeled, and preened,
The tree-tops laughed, and leaves careened,
    As Pan his syrinx blew.

The day grew langorously sweet
    With dreamings of content;
Soft clouds moved slowly o'er the skies,
While troops of rainbow dragon-flies
    On noonday light besprent.

The shepherds leisurely reclined,
    The fleecy clouds drew near,
As Pan awoke a tender theme,
So sweet, the tree-tops, birds, and stream,
    Enraptured, paused to hear.

The dryads 'mong the lily-bells
    Bad them their swinging cease,
And all the flocks upon the leas
Breathed low beneath the list'ning trees,
    Charmed by the wondrous peace.

At last so slumbrous grew the day,
    (Thus have the sages said)
Poor Pan, aweary, fell asleep;
His pipes no longer charmed the sheep;
    Dark drifted overhead.

And so the leaves and blossoms died,
    And sorrow filled the air;
The nymphs and bees all hid away,
The flocks and birds all went astray,
    While slept their keeper there.

O might we give these storm-swept years,
    And solemn wintry skies,
For summer days, beloved of yore,
And drink their hallowed joys once more!
    But Pan still sleeping lies.

SOME COMMON EVIDENCES OF GLACIAL ACTION IN CONNECTICUT.

BY W. H. C. PYNCHON.

" And feel by turn the bitter change
Of fierce extremes, extremes by change more fierce,
From beds of raging fire to starve in ice
Immovable, infixed, and frozen round,
Periods of time,"   *Paradise Lost.*

GLACIATED SURFACE OF THE TRAP ROCK, TRINITY COLLEGE, HARTFORD, CONN.

That Central Connecticut was once the seat of great volcanic activity is well known. The beds of volcanic ashes which are scattered here and there throughout the valley and more especially the great trap ridges—fragments of what were once great flows of molten lava—bear unerring testimony to this fact. It is readily conceivable that a period of quiet should follow the period of intense action—a period in which things should cool down and return somewhat toward their normal state—but it seems hard to conceive that nature should somewhat later swing to the other extreme and that a period of cold should set in that would suggest a change almost as fierce as that of which Milton speaks. Yet Connecticut passed through an experience like this when the northern half of North America lay buried under the ice and snows of the Glacial Period.

The many people who ask the question, "Where can I see evidences of the Glacial Period?" may be divided into two groups. The former ask for evidence for the Glacial hypothesis, the latter accept the hypothesis and are simply anxious to see the marks of its action which the continental ice sheet left behind it. The discussion which the first question raises is almost wholly outside the scope of this article, and can only be taken up incidentally in answering the second question—the question with which this paper has to deal.

A good while ago geologists observed certain phenomena which seemed to require special explanation. This consisted in the main of large deposits

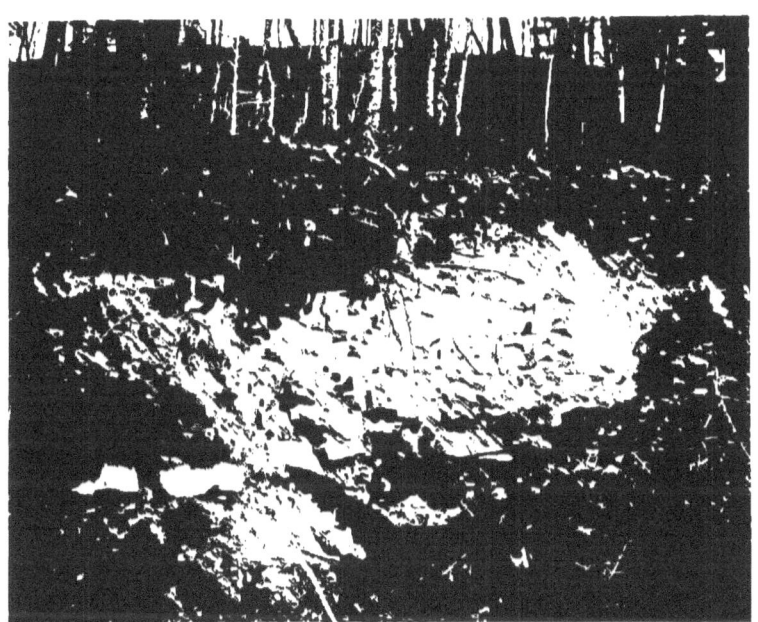

WATER-LAID BED OF SAND AND TRAP FRAGMENTS. CEDAR MOUNTAIN, HARTFORD, CONN.

of gravel and of certain smoothings and groovings of the rocks in certain localities, notably the northern part of the British Isles. These they undertook to explain in various ways, but one theory after another had to be dropped as impossible, until nothing was left but the theory that these phenomena were due to a great sheet of ice covering the region. Later investigation into the "actual workings" of glaciers existing in mountain regions of the present day, and the observation that Greenland is under just such a field of ice, have so strengthened the theory that now it is universally accepted. The question now remains, what are these evidences of glacial action and where can they be seen in Connecticut?

It may be of advantage to pause a moment to consider the nature of a

GLACIAL STRIAE, SUMMIT STREET, HARTFORD, CONN.

modern local glacier, the laws of its motion and the effects which it produces on the region it traverses.

On high ranges of mountains, whose tops are in the region of eternal

DETAIL OF SAND PLAIN, SHOWING THE BEDDING.

cold, the great masses of snow work down the slopes toward the valley that run down the sides of the range. As this mass passes down it becomes condensed by its own weight until it turns into ice, though it is for the most

SEA-ERODED BUTT OF GLACIAL DEBRIS.

STREAM CUTTING AWAY A BANK OF GLACIAL DRIFT, HARTFORD, CONN.

part a white ice. Thus we have a river of frozen water flowing down the valley, and we find that it follows much the same laws as a river of liquid

PERCHED GLACIAL BOWLDER, TAFTVILLE, CONN.

water, for it wears away its banks and carries the waste material thus obtained on with it in its course. The flow of a glacier is necessarily slow—Le Conte places the speed at from one to three feet per day. As the ice stream moves slowly along, fragments of rock roll down upon it from the crumbling cliffs which bound its channel, and the accumulation of these fragments forms a long line of debris on top of the glacier a little way from its edge. These accumulations are known as "lateral moraines." The surface of the glacier is not smooth and unbroken, as might be imagined, but it is very rough and is broken by great rifts called "crevasses." Into the crevasses plunge the streams formed by the melting of the surface ice, and with the water go many of the rock fragments which have been mentioned. The water finds its way through to the bottom and there flows along as a subglacial stream which emerges at the foot of the glacier. The ice as it moves along tears up fragments of rock, and these, together with the fragments which have come down through the crevasses, are ground up and form a mass of debris under the ice known as the "ground moraine."

But the glacier, besides tearing up fragments of rock, does other work. It grinds the rock bed over which it flows to a smooth, undulating surface (for the ice can bend to fit the inequalities of its bed) and on this smoothed surface it cuts, with the aid of imbedded rock fragments, more or less deep grooves. This smoothed surface is called "glaciated surface," and the grooves are called "glacial striae."

Furthermore, it is found that, though the glacier flows steadily down the valley its foot never gets beyond a given point—a point where the temperature is so high that the ice melts away as fast as it comes down from above. But as the ice melts away, it necessarily deposits all the fragments of rock which it has brought with it, and the vast mass of debris which is thus formed is called the "terminal moraine."

Having now considered briefly the workings of a local mountain glacier, let us see if there is a similar action in the case of a great regional ice sheet such as that which covers Greenland. Le Conte estimates the probable thickness of this sheet as from 2,000 to 3,000 feet. It moves steadily seaward breaking up into separate glaciers in the many deep valleys or "fiordes" which indent the coast. These glaciers as they reach the water break up into fragments which float off as the icebergs of the northern seas.

There is good reason to believe that at a certain time in the geological history of the world, known as the Glacial Epoch or Period, a similar ice sheet covered the northern part of North America down to about the 40th parallel of latitude. This regional ice sheet had apparently various stages of advance and retreat, but, when it finally withdrew, it left the surface of the country profoundly modified. It is to call attention to some of these common modifications, especially as seen in Connecticut, that this paper is particularly designed.

Perhaps the first of these evidences of ice action to be taken up is the glaciation of rock areas. Wherever the ice passed over bed rock, it broke off projections and loose fragments and ground down the main mass to a smooth, undulating surface. All the rocks of the state show this action, but it is, perhaps, especially well seen on the trap ridges of central Connecticut. Within the limits of Hartford excellent examples may be found on the ridge where Trinity College stands. Wherever the trap of this ridge comes to the surface the smoothed and almost polished surface can be seen. In some cases actual troughs have been cut in the rock, a fine example having recently been uncovered by the workmen at the city quarry. In other cases the rock shows the finely ruled parallel striae. These are well shown on a small outcrop west of Summit street and just north of the stairs leading down to Zion street. The striae are also clearly defined on the rocks along the New Britain road, a few miles beyond Elmwood.

The interesting question next arises—what has become of the fragments which the glacier tore from the bed rock? This vast amount of broken material or "drift," as it is properly called, is apt to be overlooked on account of its very abundance. The gravelly soil of almost all our cultivated land, the vast

MODIFIED DRIFT, ALLEN PLACE, HARTFORD, CONN.

hills of gravel through which our highways and railroads are cut and of which the latter build their embankments, the steep faced sandy bluffs along our rivers all belong to the vast mantle of drift spread over the land. The portion which rests upon the bed rock and hides it from sight for the most part is usually very firmly compacted of clay and pebbles and is known as "hardpan." This apparently corresponds to the "ground moraine" of the local glaciers.

As the ice moved in general from north to south, it will be seen that the drift is likely to be of the same material as the bed-rock to the north of it. For this reason the drift of central Connecticut is mostly of trap and sandstone or shale, and is usually of a dark red color. Moreover, as these kinds of rock break readily into small pieces, there is a general scarcity of the large rounded fragments commonly known as "bowlders." But when you go into the eastern or western part of the state, regions of tough crystalline rocks containing plenty of light colored components, the aspect of the debris changes. Here the drift becomes very light in color and bowlders of all sizes abound.

Where, along its southern edge, the glacier melted away as rapidly as it advanced, we find the remnants of a vast "terminal moraine." There is a good deal of reason for us believing that Long Island marks the position of this moraine south of Connecticut.

Before speaking more fully of this distribution of the drift, it may be well to note some points in connection with the end of the Ice Age. Without raising any question as to the subdivision of time into which the era may be divided, it may be safely said that gradually conditions so changed that the edge of the ice sheet began to recede toward the north and, as it melted, it of course dropped the drift which it carried. It is due to this that we get the great mass of surface drift which overlies the "hard-pan." It covers hill and dale, and in the regions where bowlders were formed is liberally sprinkled with them. In eastern and western Connecticut it is no unusual thing to find these blocks scattered so thickly over a field that a person may traverse a considerable distance by jumping from one to another. The marked difference between the drift of the central and of the eastern and western portions of the state may be seen in travelling the length of the Valley Division of the New York, New Haven and Hartford Railroad. From Hartford to Middletown the drift is in general of a reddish color and is very free from bowlders. At Middletown the road leaves the Triassic area and passes into the region of the ancient Archaean rocks. The drift at once becomes much lighter in color and bowlders of crystaline rock are seen on every side.

Some of these bowlders are of immense size—one near Mohegan on the Thames River being probably the largest in this country, as far as is known. It is these blocks of the smaller sizes that furnish the material for most of the stone walls. Not infrequently the melting ice left a large bowlder stranded on top of a ledge, where it often forms a "tilting stone" or "rolling rock" of more or less local celebrity. A very beautiful "perched block" of this type may be seen at Taftville, a few miles from Norwich.

But, while the melting glacier deposited the drift in a mixed mass all over the surface of the country, it should be remembered that the flowing water resulting from this very melting re-arranged a large portion of this drift into a distinctly sorted and stratified condition. Such water-assorted drift is generally called "modified drift" or "washed gravel." Sometimes it is arranged in a long, winding embankment or "esker" which probably once partially filled the vaulted channel of some stream running underneath the glacier. "Eskers" are often of such size that they resemble an ancient earthwork or a forgotten railroad embankment. A very fine example may be seen at Compounce Pond near Bristol.

An "esker" usually ends in a more or less level "sand plain," where the subglacial stream, emerging from under the ice, spread the drift out over a considerable area. A section through a "sand plain" shows marked stratification due to water action. These plains frequently occur unassociated with "eskers." The town of Saybrook stands on such a plain, also the town of

Essex. A large part of the city of Norwich is located on a deposit of this kind and the sandy levels lying to the north of New Haven are probably of similar origin. Smaller deposits of "modified drift" may be seen in many places. The gravel which is dug at the head of Allen Place in Hartford is of this nature, and there are similar beds in West Hartford, near Vine Hill. The trolley line from Hartford to New Britain cuts through an interesting deposit of this sort on Newington Avenue, near the north end of Cedar Mountain. Here many layers of fine, white sand rest on a bed of irregular fragments of trap. The structure has unfortunately become much obscured by the action of the elements and the caving of the bank.

Mention should be made of one peculiar form, which deposits of un-modified drift sometimes take. It is that of an elliptical, round-topped hill, with

TYPICAL VIEW OF A REGION COMPOSED ENTIRELY OF GLACIAL DRIFT.

its long axis corresponding to the direction in which the ice was moving. There have been many theories as to just the manner in which these "drumlins" were formed, but none of them are wholly satisfactory. The large hill known as "Buena Vista," lying west of West Hartford, is a good example of this form, and several others of a similar nature are to be seen on the road to Simsbury, about ten miles from the city of Hartford.

These are some of the thoroughly common phenomena which bear witness to the Glacial Period, somewhat after the principle that "a workman is known by his chips." For it should be remembered that these are, in a certain sense, only the chips. The real masterpieces which the ice wrought are far greater. They are the changing of streams and drainage system, the changing of shore lines, the creation of lakes and profound changes in the geographical distribution of flora and fauna. Geologically speaking, the

Glacial Period is a recent event, and the surface of the land has as yet by no means become re-adjusted to the changed condition which followed the invasion of the ice.

Geological phenomena are frequently but the often repeated stages in that recurring circle of events in which Earth's history repeats itself forever. The Preacher spoke truly when he said—" The thing that hath been, it is that which shall be ; and that which is done is that which shall be done ; and there is no new thing under the sun,"—and ages to come may prove that I should have completed the final line of the quotation from Milton, and should not have omitted the words—

" thence hurried back to fire."

TWILIGHT.

BY SALLY PORTER LAW.

When Nature paints the western sky
With pink and blue and red,
And evening shades are drawing nigh,
When Nature paints the western sky
The gentle breezes moan and sigh,
And weep that Day is dead,
When Nature paints the western sky
With pink and blue and red.

"PETER PARLEY"—AS KNOWN TO HIS DAUGHTER.

BY EMILY GOODRICH SMITH.

PART I.

These recollections of my father are rescued from Time's "Omnium Gatherum." They are put upon record, in memory of the children of sixty and seventy years ago, who knew the earliest stories of Peter Parley and studied his lesson books, made so attractive to them ; for the children of those children, who grew up on his school-books, many of whom knew him personally, and for the grandchildren of to-day, who have had their curiosity excited through hearing the odd name of "Peter Parley" mentioned at intervals, and are invading the "query columns" of the newspapers with questions as to his identity.

Every generation or two there is a return wave, which bears upon its crest the name of some prominent character in the past, *quiescent*, though not forgotten. Writers and publishers are quite aware of this fact, and are keenly on the watch for the first sign of a returning wave. Within the last three or four years, the name of the children's friend, Peter Parley, has been upon the lips of those aged readers who learned from his books. Constant mention of him has been made in educational articles in the newspapers, and the magazines have brought him to mind again. Many letters to myself, urging me to write of him and his work, prepared me for the request of the editor of THE CONNECTICUT QUARTERLY to give some reminiscence therein, which I gladly do in a most informal and unpretentious manner. This first part of my story is told entirely from a child's point of view, in language such as a child would employ. Ignoring the royal "we," as unsuited to the subject, I have written simply in the first person, a simple record. In order to avoid repetition, I have not confined myself rigidly to a sequence of dates, but now and then, when speaking of some charactaristic of my father, as, for instance, his love for music, I have grouped together events occuring at wide intervals.

Mr. Goodrich very rarely referred to his family tree. Suffice it to say it was well rooted in English soil, and as early as 1628 there were upon its American branches the names of governors, mayors, senators, diplomats, Revolutionary officers, college presidents, clergymen, and judges. We give a portrait of one of them, an uncle, Elizur Goodrich.

Samuel Griswold Goodrich, Jr., was born in 1793, in Ridgefield, Conn., where his father was pastor for years. Their home was a large rambling house, picturesque in its appearance and surrounded by several acres of very fertile lands, which was carefully farmed and added largely to the comfort of a numerous and growing family. Mr. Goodrich's salary as a clergyman was but four hundred dollars a year. He added to this by taking into his household six or eight young men to fit for college. The old homestead overflowed with life, kindliness and an atmosphere of religion which was never gloomy. In these happy surroundings he grew apace. His mother was Betsy Ely, daughter of Rev. Col. John Ely of Lyme, where she often met our own officers and those of France and Germany. She was a most cultivated woman, but slightly tinged with sadness, caused by the troubles of her country, the disasters which beset her father and by the ingratitude of Congress toward him.

This delightful home was known far and wide in the state for its genial hospitality. Travelers of mark left their servants and equipages at the tavern, but were entertained personally at the parsonage. Here judges and senators, officers of the government and public men of varied opinions often met. Grave discus-

THE FATHER AND MOTHER OF "PETER PARLEY."

sions and learned talk were frequent, and often in their midst would be noticed an eager but modest little lad, listening and sometimes venturing a pertinent question. When on their return that way some of them brought him desired books—others left such behind them for his use. On these he grew and throve and studied and hoped. At five years old he had been sent to a dame school, kept by Aunt Delight Benedict, whose nose and cap ran to the sharpest of points. He started off in high feather, taking his little chair with him. (It had then served several generations, it is one hundred years older to-day.) In this chair Miss Benedict seated him under her wing where she could conveniently tap his head with a huge brass thimble. She called him to read his letters, and with a ruler indicated the one he should name.

"What's 'at? What's that?"

He looked in her face without reply.

At the third question and a prod with the thimble, he said quietly:

"I did not come to tell you the letters, you tell 'em to me."

She looked at him amazed but said no more. At recess she led the culprit home, now and then assisting him by a pull at the ear. His parents were called in solemn conclave and the story told. You could not convince him he had done any wrong. He was willing enough to say he was sorry if he had been rude to "Miss Daylite" but he couldn't see it in that way. "Thammy didn't go to tell Miss Benedict wat's A and wat's B," and there he took his stand. So far school was a failure. Later on he had a few months chance at the "three R's" at "West Lane Academy," and this closed his educational opportunities outside of his home.

Early in his mind blossomed a desire for good literature, fostered to begin with, by a copy of the English "Mother Goose," sent him from London by an uncle. Instead of entertaining him, he was disgusted. The tales were so unmeaning, the poems so silly, the language vulgar. Childlike he at once picked out its most objectionable features and went about repeating some of the undesirable rhymes. In reply to an inquiry from his mother who scarcely recognized her little son in this unusual attitude, he brought her his gift, telling her once for all that he meant to write better books for children ; stories they would love to read, rhymes that would teach something, and facts told in a way that would at first attract, then cling in the mind. Bravely he kept this promise which grew with his growth and developed more and more in his brain the plan for good and entertaining reading for the young, and lesson-books made interesting for the scholar, until Peter Parley had become a well-known and favorite writer for children, and England, America, the Continent and "The Isles of the Sea" knew his works in many languages.

We have not space to tell of the years when he was building his plans, but to his life's end he never forgot what he owed to the advice given him by Miss Lydia Huntley (later Mrs. Sigourney), when, a shy youth of sixteen or seventeen, he was in a book store in Hartford. Through this he studied French, learned to dance, took part in debates, sought the company of refined young ladies, and was one of the fortunate members of her Literary Society, the first of its kind in Connecticut.

Presently, assisted by an uncle, he went abroad for counsel from older and wiser heads. He visited dear, quaint Hannah More at "Berley Wood" and was entertained by her there, coming away greatly encouraged by her sympathy and the gladness with which she welcomed his broad plan for attractive and instructive literature for youth.

He often told me of how carefully he sought a *nom de plume ;* something which would catch and hold the public ear. Many a book has fallen flat on the market because of a faulty title as a send off, which, being withdrawn for a while, renamed and reissued, has floated on to success.

While deliberating on this fact one day, he was declining the verb "*Parler*— to speak," and found what he sought—"Peter the Talker—Peter Parley "—and he adopted it then and there.

His first book was written abroad and published in 1823, "Parley's Tales of the Sea," and had an immense sale. One hundred and sixteen Parley books were his own, and fifty-four compilations, beside "Merry's Museum," published as a monthly for many years; the "Token," a gift book, and "The Cabinet Library." John and Epps Sargent, Royal Robbins, and S. P. Holbrook, Esq., assisted in the larger and more important compilations.

For "Peter Parley's Method of Searching Geography," Mr. Goodrich received $300 and the publisher made a fortune by it. It was translated by our missionaries for use in their foreign schools. Hon. Donald G. Mitchell, in a late work, tells of the recollection of this little book which came over him when he visited the Tower of London.

Of the "Natural History," George Du Maurier says: "Last, but not least of our library, was Peter Parley's 'Natural History,' of which we knew every word by heart."

Mr. Martin, of the "Conversation Corner," in a recent number of the Boston *Congregationalist* writes: "We have no doubt, were it needed, that 1,000 aged people could rise and repeat the widely famous lines, 'The World is round and like a ball, seems swinging in the air.'"

His series of school histories, have been adapted for the blind in raised type, and are still in use in schools. We understand that his "Readers," admirably adapted to interest and improve, are still published in St. Louis.

Charles Sumner found in the depths of a Cornish coal mine a copy of "Tales of the Sea," side by side with one other book—the Bible. In telling my father this, he remarked: "Goodrich, this is fame."

My father was one of those men, who, with a stern profile, had a most winning expression. Every baby stretched out its little arms to him, and children gathered to him like bees, while animals, large and small, regarded him as their friend. In those days when there was no organization for their protection, he was a humane society in himself. He dearly loved his home. He built his place named "Rockland" at Jamaica Plain, near Boston, with careful detail, a house in which he hoped his family would grow and prosper. Every cent of it was paid out of his own honest work. By this time he had become in easy circumstances, enjoying the results of his labors.

The rose garden, built especially for my mother's pleasure, was a perfumed picture and no pains were spared to make it a delight to the eye. Flowering shrubs dotted the brilliant green lawns and loop-holes were cut out to make attractive views. In short, no other gentleman's residence in those days was more perfect or desirable.

A great deal of the time his mind was working to shape some great thought and well we children understood that when we saw him walking up and down on the broad piazza, with his hands behind him, he must not be interrupted. But in the morning, before he went into Boston to business, he always had a frolic or a talk, or a walk with us, and we waited about in the neighborhood for his call to us to brush his coat and see that he was an immaculate gentlemen in every way. Now and then he would have a word to say to the

ELIZUR GOODRICH.
An Uncle of "Peter Parley," connected with Yale College for about 70 years.

gardener or the stable boys as he sauntered down there with us hand in hand. We were never allowed to venture into these regions, but there was a lovely hill rose up just opposite the great barn doors, which, in the early spring, was one carpet of blue violets, with yellow eyes—one could believe a tender cloud had come down upon it like a mantle of beauty.

Here we camped, keeping keen watch for his coming again, and if perchance he was robed in his soft velvet dressing gown, he would have his pockets full of kittens, or an impudent puppy, or some fluffy chickens, just struggling into life; and meanwhile he was filling our small minds with ideas and thoughts of strength and beauty which stayed by us through life. Or, it might be at the "children's hour" before the open grate, when perched on his knees like inquisitive birds, we plied him with questions without stint and listened to stories galore.

How vivid are these scenes. As I "think back" they come before my mind's eye like an old-time daguarreotype scarcely dimmed by age. Among these is a picture of a summer morning, when the family as usual are gathered to see the head of the house "mount and away." He did not care much for a lord, but he dearly loved a fine horse, and always had two or three of them in the stable. Ariel, his riding horse, was standing ready saddled in front of the veranda. She was an exquisite specimen of equine beauty, coal-black, polished like satin, with a white star on her forehead and not another hair upon her save black. She never would tolerate being tied, so a groom stood just in front of her. She obeyed my father with perfect docility but with anyone else she was not reliable and was, to tell the truth, a rather dangerous animal. But this morning she won our fervent gratitude and admiration by an intelligence which seems to me marvelous, at this late day.

My mother, seated on one step of the piazza, had my six months' old brother beside her, holding him by his long dress. All in a flash, no one ever knew how it happened, the baby suddenly rolled over and down beneath the horse's feet. It takes little time to tell, but it seemed hours before we could catch a breath. Then my father said in a scarcely audible whisper, but full of anguish, "Let no one stir." The mare was in evident distress, and understood as well as a human, the terrible danger of the situation. She began an almost inperceptible movement of her small feet, walking slowly, but surely, away from the baby who was calmly looking about him, quite unaware of impending danger.

My parents' faces were white and drawn and my father's lips were set and held between his teeth to keep from groaning aloud. Of course we children could not appreciate the horror that those moments contained, but I never forgot the scene. It was, as it were, seared upon the tablets of my memory.

Meanwhile, our pretty Ariel had moved far enough to one side for mother to grasp and withdraw the child, and then the mare seemed to wilt and a sweat broke out all over her so profuse that great drops fell to the ground.

Later she grew too nervous for everyday use and my father reluctantly sold her. She became a great racer, known as the "Lone Star," and was famous all over the country.

My father early became somewhat of a public man and entered with enthusiasm into politics. As a very young man, when aid to his uncle Gov. Chauncey Goodrich, of Hartford, he had met most of the members of the famous Hartford Convention, and had already made for himself a reputation as a publisher and a man of great literary attainments, beside being an admirable conversationalist and witty speaker and lecturer. My mother, an English woman by birth, was remarkable both as a singer and musician, and between them they drew all that was desirable of surrounding society of talent, culture and charm. Their guests often brought with them foreigners of note, and entertaining ere long became obligatory on account of the position he had attained. At stated intervals father gave large dinner parties to gentlemen, while their wives were enjoying a "dish of tea" in the drawing-rooms, or on the wide veranda at "Rockland." Music was a matter of course, and such "chamber concerts" as were held there were rare treats indeed. Brainard wrote a song for my mother called the "Sea Bird" which she set to an old Welsh air. I heard Daniel Webster ask her for it one evening and she sang it, accompanying herself with the harp. Wild, weird, intense, it seemed to hold something in its measure which seized upon Webster's innermost feelings and he sat where he could watch the singer; as she closed with the last gloomy lines, where the voice mounts higher and higher and then abruptly descends, in a long wail,—he was so motionless that the other listeners noted it,—

> "'Tis the sea-bird, sea-bird, sea-bird,
> Lone witness of despair,
> 'Tis the sea-bird, sea-bird, sea-bird,
> The only witness there."

Then a few liquid notes of the harp and she was the very "mocking-bird "itself. Her trills, echoed through the large rooms and halls —trills I never heard equalled —even Grisi made a fiasco of them. They are unheard now, not only on account of their extreme difficulty, but the present style of musical composition does not lend itself to them.

My father was of an eminently social nature and a delightful entertainer, and he and my mother made their home most attractive. There was always more or less of a house party, and "Afternoon Tea" was known there as an established fact a generation ago.

Of a summer afternoon, elegant equipages from Boston and neighboring towns drove out for a call, or in winter brilliant sleighing parties filled the air with their tuneful bells and not unseldom a delicious seranade would seem to melt in the air.

My brother and I had favorites among these intimate friends. He would draw as near to Webster as he dared, being recognized only by a sudden raising of those great, gloomy eyes and a kindly glance. I was more drawn to Hawthorne, who would sit remote and silent, brooding over the outlines of some of those weird tales which surprised and startled the reading world. His sails were filled out, his ships were going on summer seas, freighted with stories so rare, so fascinating, that they soon reached the "Fortunate Isles." Henceforth he was one of the earliest makers of our literature.

Lothrop Motley, afterward one of the most famous of the great historians of his age, drew us like a magnet.

N. P. Willis, full of life and jokes, bore with us as we drifted up to the two, just for the pleasure of hearing Motley's winning voice or to watch the ripples of laughter running over Willis' speaking face. He was nothing if not roguish and sharp, and at times went beyond the allowances of polite writing and conversation, but with his light curly locks and brilliant eyes, he made a perfect foil to Motley. The latter was a gentleman in every sense of the word, and something in his gracious, quiet manner, presented an example of the best style of an American. In after years he became a giant in literature.

I can remember to-day, though half a century has elapsed, the enjoyment these guests all seemed to feel. In perfect sympathy, drawn together with the high purpose of refining and elevating the world of letters, their faces were instinct with enthusiasm and glowed with the desire to give of their best.

The result of these simple gatherings was world-wide. These sturdy, young Americans went forth to represent the growing literature of a youthful republic. Most, indeed all of them, were for years contributors to the "Token," one of the earliest books edited by Mr. Goodrich, in which the reader will find embalmed some of the choicest gems of poetry and prose. This dainty annual has now become one of the treasured "Americana," found in large city libraries only. It will reward the seeker for "Gems of purest ray serene" are bound between its covers,—a very treasure book. Park Benjamin and Greenwood, Bryant and Doane, Washington Irving, Emerson, Percival, Brainard, and others beside those mentioned above, contributed to make it for seventeen years, a valued and sought for work.

My father's study was a fascinating room into which we ventured, only on distinct permission. Its large square table, covered with green broadcloth, with all the elegant stationery and ornamental paraphernalia so useless to the writer; gifts from many friends of elegant ink-stands, elaborate pen-racks, paper-cutters, erasers, pen-knives and other adjuncts. These were seldom used. I can see now the long black leather portfolio filled with blotted sheets, ink-stained, marred here and there with figures and notes and memoranda thereon. Here he wrote down his thoughts, shaping his sentences as he walked up and down his spacious room, often smiling as a pleasant thought came over him. Now and then casting a loving glance out upon the wide drive-way or down a glorious steep bank where ornamental trees caught the eye. Down this bank in winter we coasted. One sled was built expressly for me with a back and a shelf behind it on which my grand old Newfoundland sat as we flew down the snowy incline, he barking wildly.

CHAIR WHICH "PETER PARLEY" USED IN SCHOOL.

It was always a pleasure, even a rest, for my father to see children at play, and he encouraged the coming of others to join in our happy games. For many years there had been at Jamaica Plain, an important and flourishing boarding school for boys, kept by Mr. Charles Green. There were lads here from the West Indies, the Spanish South, and especially from New England. The Boston contingent was very large. Russell and John Sturgis, Masons, Lowells,

Putnams; young commodores, embryo ambassadors, whose names since those days have gone round the world.

Every other Saturday at Rockland, our lovely home, was a gathering of children. It was an understood fact that the four boys of this school, who had the best all-round record for that term, were invited to join us. This was considered a privilege and much sought after. Thus father secured us desirable boy playmates in a small village, and surrounded himself with the merry faces of youth.

I saw the name of one of these playmates of ours mentioned as an important factor in a recent diplomatic move, within the week, who painted for me such a set of paper dolls, as no modiste's advertisements of to-day can equal.

My father was deeply stirred by martial music, and greatly enjoyed orchestral concerts; but these little home gatherings were his greatest pleasure. His fondness for Scotch songs was remarkable and to gratify his taste my mother took lessons of the famous Dempster. What was an odd feature in this was that father could not catch airs though he recognized them at once. Sometimes when walking up and down thinking out some speech or lecture, we would hear him keeping time to his steps, humming, all on one key,

> "Oh, 'tis my delight of a shiney night
> The season of the year."

That was all, but it seemed to be a great help to him. When we children heard this, we would be "just round a corner" ready to pounce on him, for that remarkable ditty was a signal that he was in a merry mood, and we made the most of such hours. We would dance about him, begging for a walk or a talk, which was our most valued time with him.

He always halted more or less on one knee and kept time to his step with a cane, which had descended to him from Matthew Griswold, and on the broad piazza at Rockland was many an imprint of the brass ferrule. Here we walked with him nearly every day, or down the long drive which was as smooth as marble. He could not mount hills or many steps, as all his life long he suffered from attacks of breathlessness, which were very startling and we never could get used to them. As I write I recall how many a time we waited outside his study door, terror-struck at the attacks which seized him. They would yield after a time of agony, fighting for his breath and leaving his face white and drawn. After it was over, he always had a smile for us, two terrified little mites, his ardent lovers, but he could not speak.

I have wandered far afield from the topic of music and his fondness for it.

The scene changes to the music-room of the Amercian Consul in Paris, where the family, denied of all other guests, were holding their last meeting with John Howard Paine. He was leaving the next day, for Tunis, as Consul. It was far away, remote from kindred and friends; his heart was low and sad, and apprehensive of the outcome; he clung to this home evening and seemed so discouraged and weary that my mother called us to the piano and gently struck the notes of "Home, Sweet Home." Paine buried his face in his hands to hide a few bitter tears. One by one we too broke down, and grasping each by the hand, he hurried from the room. We had one letter from him telling us of the dreary scene of his work, of the Consular rooms stripped of their furniture, their desolate appearance. Then the bitter, bitter news of his sudden death reached us. With no one near who spoke his language, with no friend to close his eyes, he passed away. He, who had thrilled continents with the words of "Home, Sweet Home," was dead, on alien shores, the loneliest man in Christendom.

Many a delightful musicale was held in these pleasant rooms, though not called by such a pretentious name. Ole Bull, Paul Julien, Thalberg and many a genius gave us of his best. My father said he never played upon but one instrument, a whistle made for him by his older brother, "from the old willow which drooped over the mossy home-roof." " 'Twas," said he, "by far the sweetest music of my young life."

Greatly to his delight, as the household grew up to maturity, the two sons developed remarkable musical talent. The younger, the baby of the earlier pages, became not only a most accomplished musician, but a composer as well. By this time we were living in France, and he had the best instructors to be secured. The two brothers had each a "parlor grand" in their apartments, and of a summer eve the brick court of the "Cite Vinde," on the Boulevard de la Madeleine, would be full of listeners to the lovely melodies, and they, with others, played hand pieces with great effect, their little *soirees* being much sought after.

In after years, Chauncey, named for his great uncle, the governor of Connecticut, had become a young man of fourteen, nearly six feet tall and a wonder to his friends. He understood chemistry and mechanism from the letter A. He built a piano of exact proportions and tone. When not wrapped in music, he was absorbed in inventions, the mechanic arts, etc. Thalberg had begged that the lad might remain with him, as a pupil, for two years; he would make him equal to the greatest artist, but father was unwilling. By this time we were on a visit to America, intending to spend a winter in Washington, D. C., and looking forward with delight to the novelty of our Capitol city and its vast interests. Alas for human foresight. But a few days and my father sickened with a dangerous attack of varioloid. He and my mother removed to the rooms occupied by my brothers on an adjacent street, to which we three children went every day and talked to my mother at the window. The anxiety of my parents was of course very great and increased my father's sufferings. After a week or two, Chauncey, who had been passing long hours absorbed in the wonders of the patent office, came home one day, complaining of distressing pains, which, followed by a severe chill, developed into pneumonia. Alone, frightened, and totally unused to illness, I do not know what would have become of us if Miss Dorothea Dix had not at once hurried to our assistance, an angel of mercy. The President sent his physician and offers of sympathy, and help came to us on every hand. Meantime the dread disease worked its will, and one evening his brother and sister watched the sinking breath of the loved one alone. As dawn approached he stirred and whispered, "Tell mother I'm in my boat."

I looked at his watch; it ran down with a sudden whirr. Leaning to glance at the invalid, we saw with a hush of terror that life had passed with the breaking main spring of the watch.

Kind friends took charge of the preparations for the funeral, and my mother was able to come to us then, but poor father bore his anguish alone, without a farewell of the boy in whom he had taken such pride.

Great interest was shown in Washington, for the stalwart, handsome lad was seen by many, and at one or two simple home concerts had improvised melodies which brought tears to the eyes of music lovers. His devotion to the Patent Office had also been noted. It took his life from him.

The inevitable hour came and our rooms at Willard's were filled with sympathizing friends. Fillmore was there, Gen. Marcy stood near the open casket. Clay looked sadly upon the beautiful young face and said to Webster, "We older ones stay and such a lamp of life as this goes out." Both sighed deeply and it was a tearful company that watched the shutting away of so much promise from our eyes. Very many of the friends accompanied us to the Congressional Cemetery on the banks of the Potomac. Here we laid him to rest upon the brow of a hill, where the waters of the river seemed to chant a requiem, and returned heart-broken to our homes.

Our winter plans were blighted, our hopes in our young brother had been stricken down. Mourning, sad and unhappy, we returned to Paris. Thalberg shed tears of regret. The brother closed his piano and seldom played "after Chauncey died." The effect upon my father was lasting. He did not rally from the shock with his usual strength of mind, and long years after we heard him draw a painful sigh as he looked upon the famous artist Cheney's sketch of this bright youth. "'Twas all we had remaining."

At one of the early literary gatherings at Rockland, Cheney was present. He watched Chauncey, who was absorbed in a railroad he was building. The engine was made from a quart cup and ran on a rail of laths, with a great puff of steam, quite down the long hall. Cheney rose and made a request to my father who rung the bell and told the servant who answered it to take Mr. Cheney to the fuel house and see that he found what he wanted.

Child-like, full of curiosity, I followed and saw the artist select three long slim bits of charcoal, rub them to a point on a brick and then return to the reception rooms. Here he took the sketch mentioned above, on the cover of a large paste-board box.

Our home, "Rockland," was one fell day shattered as by a bolt of lightning. My father came out from Boston, silent, white and stern. We had, as usual, run to meet him, but shrank back as he beckoned my mother into his study and closed the door. Later my brother told me that a wicked man had taken all papa's money and we had

SILHOUETTE OF "PETER PARLEY" IN HIS STUDY

not a cent to live on. A friend whom he trusted as he would himself had failed, borrowing from my father such large amounts that it crippled his work, threw him into the debtor's prison and forced him to face the fact that he was a poor man. He passed one night in jail, a short time, indeed, but it seared his heart as with a hot iron.

When this became known, Boston rose to the occasion. He was immediately bailed out. Moneyed men offered him large amounts with which to start again. Harvard College would educate his eldest son. The finest school in Boston opened its doors to the young daughter. But he would accept nothing. He took up his writing again, walking to Roxbury every day, a distance of two and one-half miles. One devoted friend finally persuaded him to accept the loan of a horse and sleigh through the winter, and he began at first principles.

This blow so shattered his home and family that it broke his spirits and shadowed his life for many a day.

In our once happy home men were now seen taking up and carrying away carpets; friends with tears falling fast bore away the rare and beautiful furnishings which came from abroad. We children wandered around like little ghosts, driven from pillar to post in doubt and anxiety untold. Our parents desired to send us to our relatives in Boston; we would not leave them. But I may not prolong the scene. There came a day when there was a great gathering down at the stables, and we children were hidden amidst the blossoms on "Violet Hill." A man was standing on an old chair, pounding the back of it, and, as I thought, saying "Going, going, going, gone!" The horses and carriages went at a private sale. My brother's pretty pony had been driven away. Our pet mooly and her calf trotted lowing down the lane, when Leo, my huge Newfoundland, came dashing up to us, amidst the violets, with a frayed rope about his neck and a dangerous gleam in his usually soft eyes.

William, father's especial valued servant, came running up to me with tears in his eyes, begging me to go with him and help tie the dog under the chaise of a gentleman who had bought him. Sold to a stranger, my dear, dear dog! On whose broad back I had ridden and who had drawn me in my little go-cart all about the place. Never! Spite of poor William Preston's sad word, " Now Miss Meely, he done got to go," I buried my head in the blue blossoms and wailed out, " He's a wicked man to take my dog."

Just then a handsome gentleman came up and said, " What is it, little one? Is he going and you love him?" He shall not leave you. Put this in your little dress pocket and remember that I gave you this, and gave you back your pet because you love him and he loves you and you shall not be separated." I never knew Wm. Preston was pledged not to tell me the name of this good samaritan, who found me faint and sorrowing and poured oil upon my wounds. Not till night,—the last one spent in our beloved home, when I took off my dress did I remember that I had something in my pocket. I thought it was a button. It was a gold piece. A twenty dollar picture!

The good-byes to our people were heartrending. The gardner absolutely refused to go. He planted himself on a sawhorse on the piazza and doggedly sat there. He had neither kith nor kin and was rather uncouth looking, with red hair and those pale blue eyes which are so appealing. One leg was shorter than the other, and when he pushed a wheel-barrow it was a funny sight. But we had been rigidly taught not only politeness, but kindness to all. "A servant," said my father, "is one who serves. He gives us good work in return for good money."

John remained with us. The last straw was when the old nurse and her daughter, our playmate and guardian, came to say good-bye.

The mother was a retainer of the family and had been with us five years, going now to a dear friend in Boston. Mother hastened the adieus,—life was becoming too harrowing. Suddenly the young girl threw her apron or "tier" over her head and wailed out in Scotch, "Oh, my heart is fairly skwinched on me," and ran round the house.

We walked down the drive-way and entered the gardner's lodge, which was to be our refuge. In the next early morning we heard hammering without and went to see what it meant. A fence was being built between us and our early home—we were shut out—"at the gate disconsolate." "Oh, Paradise! Oh, Paradise!" "Going, going, gone!"

(To be Concluded.)

AN OLD DAGUERREOTYPE.

BY ANNA M. TUTTLE.

It has a somewhat bygone look,
This little black, thick-covered book,
Whose velvet welt, whose slender hook,
    Some tarnish shows.
But though elusive to the sight,
Propitious turnings to the light
Will, scarcely dimmed by time's still flight,
    A face disclose.

A stiff, old man, with features dressed
To match his suit of Sunday best;
The high-cut broadcloth, satin vest
    In wrinkled sheen.
The thick stock tied with wifely care
'Neath flapping tabs of linen fair,
The high-brushed peak of thin gray hair,
    All plainly seen.

His look, so solemn and severe,
My childish heart would thrill with fear,
Did I but meet his eye-glance here,
    In days agone.
Yet children loved him well, they say.
And all my awe had fled away,
No doubt, had once those eyes of gray,
    Upon me shone.

My ancestor in direct line,
His blood flows in these veins of mine,
His faults and virtues intertwine
    To tint my own.
I trace him in those I hold dear,
His form and features re-appear,
Wrinkles like his have year by year
    Deepened and grown.

There, close the little faded case,
And lay it in its wonted place,
I like the solemn, shadowy face,
    Let it rest near
The Bible and the huge chapeau
Of training days of long ago,
The sword and cane that yearly grow
    More quaint and queer.

A SOCIAL STRUGGLER.

BY JANE MARLIN.

"Louis Richards called yesterday on his way back to Boston and he has promised to look up my credentials for me at once, so that I can join the 'Daughters of the American Revolution' at their next meeting," said pretty Bessie Bradford across the breakfast table to her young husband, at the same time gracefully brushing a crumb from the spotless table-cloth with her long, aristocratic hand. "I've always intended joining the 'Daughters' you know, and possibly the 'Colonial Dames,' for Mrs. Doane, the State Regent of the Daughters, and a prominent member of the Dames, has been most awfully gracious since I told her that my great-great-grandfather Peck was a major in the Revolution and a personal friend of Washington. Why grandmother says that he so distinguished himself and came home so covered with glory, that the minister stopped preaching the first Sunday he attended church, and said, 'Show Major Peck and his wife to my seat and let every one rise and welcome this brave soldier.' That is a record to be proud of, don't you think? Yes," with a deep sigh, "I am a great stickler for ancestry Dick, and I am going to show these snobs who have cut us because we are poor, that we are entitled, by the right of brains, birth and breeding, to their greatest respect and esteem. Don't laugh, dear, I am most awfully serious and it hurts me to think that you are making fun of me and not giving me your support and sympathy."

"Oh me! oh my! Bessie dear, but I am tired of all this nonsense. What does it amount to any way? We have only a small salary and can't afford to entertain and be entertained by the one hundred and fifty aristocrats that the town boasts of. Why, sweetheart, ten to one of these same Daughters and Dames would be ashamed to have their ancestors come back and pay them a visit, even if they did fight in the Revolution and come over in the Mayflower. I've got you and you've got me, isn't that enough, little wife?"

"O, I suppose so Dick. Of course I am happy with you but I do wish that you cared a little more for the conventionalties and society. Can't you see that our social position isn't as good as the Keiths and they have even a smaller salary? That is because they have established themselves by their pedigree, and blood will tell every time. If you could boast of a major in your family I'll wager that you would be as proud of it as I am and quite as eager to have it known and to join the Sons."

"Indeed, madame! Well, let me tell you that I could easily join the Sons if I cared to do so. I don't say that my great-great-grandfather hob-nobbed with the immortal George, but he served in the war, and that is all that is necessary I believe."

"Yes, that is all that is necessary, but I wouldn't go in on a private. When I parade my ancestors they must be worth parading. What, going? And you were not going to kiss me," and Bessie's eyes filled with tears as she held up her pouting lips.

"Would you kiss her," said Dick, as he led her to the glass and raised her pretty, frowning face, "Yes, I'll kiss away every frown. You are all right lit tle girl even if you have got pedigree on the brain. Look up your old major, God bless him, go ahead and win and no one will be more proud of your social triumphs than I. But it is time that I was at the office, so *au revoir*, madame," and with a light, merry, happy laugh, Dick left the house, mounted his wheel and sped down the hill towards the bank where he was teller.

They had been married not quite two years, and Dick was very fond of his dainty young wife; very proud of her musical ability, for Bessie had a voice like a bird and she was quite the pet of the pastor and parishioners of the old, brick Unitarian church where she sang every Sunday ; and Bessie loved Dick equally well, but she was an ambitious, energetic, little body, full of life and animal spirits, fond of society and its ceaseless round of dinners, dances and teas. This was the one bone of contention between them, society, for which Dick at heart cared so little. Of course he wanted his wife to shine and to establish her as became her beauty and education, but he was poor and plodding, and to be perfectly honest he found it hard to give her the musical instruction that her voice demanded and make both ends meet at the end of the year. Dick had never had much chance to get ahead for his father had died when he was a mere lad, leaving his mother with two younger children and a lot of unpaid bills, and Dick had been forced to give up school and to put his shoulder to the wheel and work for their support. He had loved Bessie secretly for years but it was not until the brother and sister were able to care for themselves, and the mother married again, that he asked her to become his wife and to share his heart and home. He fitted up a pretty little cottage, a few blocks from the bank, and for a year they were as happy as could be ; then Bessie, who had always had a social bee buzzing in her bonnet, discovered that they could never be taken up by the smart set as long as they lived in the unfashionable part of the town. A slave to her every whim, Dick rented a house over on the hill in the right section, and their struggle for social recognition began. The people of the manufacturing town were quite devoid of culture and refinement, two commodities often denied to the *nouveau riche*, so after many months of striving Bessie found herself daily in tears because Mrs. de Snobberleigh or Miss van Ordinaire had cut her. Then aunt Rebecca arrived and told her of her noble ancestor, and her courage and ambition took on renewed force and she resolved to join the Daughters of the Revolution, going in by reason of an ancestor who would, if he were alive, command the respect and recognition of the whole community.

When Dick left she busied herself with her household cares, singing blithley as she thought of the *coup de tonnerre* that awaited the van Ordinaires and de Snobberleighs, both prominent among the Daughters.

Dick, as he worked away at the teller's window, smiled several times to himself, for the morning mail had brought him a large, bulky envelope bearing the government seal. Just before he went out to lunch he opened it, took out the large sheets of paper and as he read them he whistled a little air of the street, with the following refrain : " Dere's No Doubt 'Bout My Bein' High Born." Then he replaced the papers in the envelope and put them away in his desk. Ten days later the postman handed Bessie a letter from the Secretary of the State of Massachusetts, and with trembling fingers she broke the seal, took out the official looking documents, glancing first at the bottom to see if they bore the secretary's name. Yes, there it was in black and white, and beside it a pale green stamp with "*Sigillum Reipublicæ Massachusettensis*," and, at the top, the magic words, " Revolutionary War Service of Nathaniel Peck." As Bessie read down the first page all of the bright, rosy color left her cheeks, the happy light died out of her eyes and her pretty, fresh, face grew pinched and ashen, but she bravely read on to the end, then the papers fell from her nerveless hands and with a great sob of disappointment she buried her face in the cushions of the couch, crying bitterly. There Dick found her when he came home, and to his eager enquiries and demonstrations of love, she pointed to the papers on the floor, then burst into tears again. Dick picked them up and read : " Revolutionary War Service of Nathaniel Peck. Nathaniel Peck appears in a descriptive list of enlisted men belonging to Hampshire County, age nineteen years, statue five feet eleven inches, complexion light, term three months, residence Amherst, vol. 39; p. 217. Appears with rank of private on muster and pay roll of Captain Job Alvord's company, Col. S. Munay's Regt., Hampshire County raised to reinforce the Continental army for three months. Enlisted July 14th, 1780, discharged Oct. 10th, 1780." Poor Bessie, her pride had suffered a terrible fall and she was for a time inconsolable. Dick, good, kind-hearted fellow that he was, picked her up in his arms, and after she was soothed and quieted, and her dampened and ruffled plumage dried and straightened, said : " Don't you mind, Puss, we are all right," and drawing a letter from his pocket he handed it to Bessie and she read, through her tears, of brave, staunch old Colonel Bradford who fought and died for his country and whose great-great-grandson her husband was. What did she do? Well, she just put her arms around his neck, kissed him and told him how proud she was of him, and how she had known from the first that he came of good, old stock.

A few days later Aunt Rebecca came for her annual visit. She had scarcely had time to remove her bonnet when Bessie, vexed and humiliated, brought her the papers which she had received from the Secretary of State with the glorious war record of Nathaniel Peck.

" There, Aunt Rebecca, read about your major, major indeed ! A pretty fool you have led me to make of myself over the old idiot. So the minister stopped his sermon to welcome him, did he? A smart minister, that ! A nineteen-year-old private must have been surprised at such an honor! Men who don't fight and are drafted don't expect such attention from preachers of the gospel. Oh it is disgraceful after I have gone around turning up my nose at dear old Dick, and his family, and they descend from Colonel Bradford who fought so bravely at Bunker Hill. Why I am not fit to wipe their old shoes. I could strangle Nathaniel Peck, yes I could ! " and Bessie, quite out of breath threw herself in a chair. " The worst of it all is the lie I have told Mrs. Doane. What ever will she think of me ? I will never join on such a record, and I told her just before the papers came that I had sent for them and should probably have them ready for the next meeting, which is to-night."

" Wall, Betty, I can't 'zactly see what all this tirade means ; " and the astonished old lady, after reading the papers carefully, took off her spectacles and polished them upon her black silk apron. " I nuver told you that our ancestor 'listed in Massachusetts, dud I ? His wife lived there with her family an' 'twas in Amherst that the minister spoke to him. Your great-great-grandfather was a major in the Revolution, jist as I told you, an' he was a personal friend of Washington. You needn't gone to all this bother 'bout the papers, fer I've gut 'em to hum. I sint for 'em several months ago, thinkin' as how I'd jine the Daughters myself, old as I be ; but I had a little common sense, Betty, and afore I wrote to the Secretary I looked up the gineology and found out that Major Peck 'listed from Connecticut. All you've got to do is to git your papers and then it seems to me that you can hold up your head 'bout as high as anybody I know of."

OLD-TIME MUSIC AND MUSICIANS.

BY N. H. ALLEN.

As outlined in my last article (Vol. III, Page 286), Mr. Flavel Goldthwaite and Mr. Christopher Lyman carried on the work in Hartford, which had been interrupted by the collapse of the Jubal Society, but not until 1827. During the three years, from 1824 to 1827, Mr. Goldthwaite had taught singing schools in the North and South Parishes. From these schools the choirs were recruited by choosing the most efficient singers ; but the larger bodies were known as Singing Societies, and frequently gave concerts. Such a society was also maintained in the Episcopal Parish. An error in the last paragraph of my former article gave the date 1847, when it should have been 1827. The first meeting, held at Major Lynde Olmsted's house, for the purpose of organizing the new Choral Society, was on the 24th of October, and has already been mentioned. Seven gentlemen were present, and later the assistance of five ladies was secured, and the first rehearsal was held. Nov. 8th, in a room under the North Church, where there was a small organ. This room was used by Mr. Salmon Phelps, who had shortly before removed from Hebron to Hartford, as a school-room, and was the stated meeting place of the Society until Jan. 20th, 1828, when it met in the Center Church. No particular night in the week was set apart for rehearsals, and they were as often held on Sunday night as any other. Frequently there would be two rehearsals a week, and again there would be an interval of more than a week.

The following resolution was adopted at the third meeting :

"*Resolved*, That Messrs. Charles Spencer and D. Dutton, Jr., be a committee to call upon Miss Louisa Gillingham, with power to make such arrangement with her, for her assistance in the Society, and for the instruction of the ladies belonging to it, as they shall deem expedient ; provided, however, that they do not obligate the Society for a greater sum than One Hundred Dollars."

This sum Miss Gillingham accepted, and at the fifth rehearsal she was present to assist, and came frequently, but not regularly. Thus Mr. Lyman, the Secretary, records that on the twenty-second of January, 1828, " Miss Gillingham was also present, and sang, most enchantingly, several songs which she expects to sing at the Society's Concert."

The new members who were admitted during the first few months were Dr. John W. Crane, Mr. Anson Colton, Mr. James Bull, Mr. Daniel Townsend, Mr. Aaron Stetson and Mr. Elam Ives, Jr.

This made an active force of eighteen singers, including Mr. Goldthwaite, the leader. Formidable pieces were attempted; how well they were done must be left to conjecture.

The first concert of the Choral Society was given in the Center Church, on Friday evening, January 25th, 1828. On the programme we find choruses from "The Messiah" and "Sampson," by Handel, and the "Hallelujah" from the "Mount of Olives," by Beethoven ; also a full anthem by Kent.

Miss Gillingham contributed generously by singing Handel's "Angels Ever Bright and Fair," Haydn's "With Verdure Clad," and "On Mighty Wings," from the "Creation," and a duett with Miss Lucy Clapp, from Handel's "Judas Maccabeus." It will be seen all through the records of this early society, that a serious purpose actuated the promoters, and very little cheap music appeared on the programs which they brought to a public hearing. It is altogether probable that the performances were far below the standard of to-day ; and it appears from the correspondence of Mr. Goldthwaite and Mr. Lyman (some of which has been given), that they did not even hope to attain ideal results with the material at hand. They just as clearly saw, however, that their labors would be reflected in the work of future societies, and were determined to familiarize the singers under their control—and the public too—with the best choral music obtainable. Acting on this principle, no doubt, the next step was one of seeming rashness, for it was no less than announcing the preparation of the "Messiah," by Handel, for the second concert. Detached choruses from the "Messiah" had been heard in Hartford for more than twenty years. It will be remembered that the Hallelujah Chorus was sung by nearly one hundred voices at the dedication of the present Center Church, December 3d, 1807.

It was the desire of the directors to present the work in its entirety so far as material was available. Four soloists of sufficient culture were not to be had in Hartford. Miss Gillingham was competent to do the work of the soprano, and she did more than that, taking some of the tenor parts, and by transposing some of the alto parts. Mr. Goldthwaite, whose voice apparently was a high baritone, took the bass solos and recitatives, and also some of the tenor numbers; notably " Every Valley Shall Be Exalted." The choruses were sung by nineteen singers, but in this they had a distinguished precedent ; for Handel gave the "Messiah" himself in 1759 with nineteen chorus singers and four soloists. This first performance of Handel's "Messiah" in Connecticut took place in the North Church, Friday evening, April 18th 1828. The accompaniments were played on the organ by Mr. Deodatus Dutton, Jr. Mr. Lyman, as Secretary of the Society, makes this entry in the records:

"The time occupied in the performance was about 2 hours and 20 minutes. Miss Gillingham sung with more than her accustomed excellence, the members of the Society acquitted themselves much to their credit, and the numerous audience retired highly gratified."

The preparations for giving the oratorio were interrupted by a request for the assistance of the society in a cause that was appealing strongly to the humane people of Hartford at that time.

This is set forth in the secretary's record, as follows :

"Sunday evening, March 9th. A suggestion having been made to the officers of the Society that the Ladies of the Committee for collecting contributions for the suffering Greeks, would be glad to have a concert given to assist them in their generous work, a meeting was held this evening at the house of Mr. Charles Spencer to take the subject into consideration. The following resolutions were passed :

"*Resolved*, That a Concert be given by the Choral Society for the benefit of the Greeks.

"*Resolved*, That the avails of the Concert be paid over to the Treasurer of the Greek Committee.
"*Resolved*, That the Concert be given on Friday evening, the 14th instant.
"Major L. Olmsted was appointed a Committee to obtain permission for the use of the Center Church for the occasion.
"Messrs. Goldthwaite and Dutton were appointed a Committee to prepare a bill of music.
                    "Attest.   C. C. LYMAN, Sec'y."

    Rehearsals were held every evening, with full attendance, until the concert was given. Miss Gillingham generously offered her services, and a Mr. Cyrus P. Smith of Brooklyn, "who was fortunately passing through town at the time," was also induced to take part, and sang Handel's "Arm, Arm ye Brave."
    This concert was very well attended, and netted the handsome sum of $153.54, which was added to the Greek fund.
    At a rehearsal held in the North Church, Thursday evening, July 24th, 1828, a communication to the President was read and acted upon. The letter was as follows:

"TO THE PRESIDENT OF THE CHORAL SOCIETY:

    Sir:—I take this method of requesting yourself and the society over which you preside, to confer upon the Senior Class of Washington college a very great favor.
    "It is this: That the Choral Society will sing several pieces of Sacred Music on the approaching Commencement of Washington College. This favor will be received with gratefulness by your petitioners.
                                                  "D. DUTTON, JR.,
"Committee on behalf of the Faculty and Senior Class of Washington College, Hartford, Conn.
    "Thursday, July 24th, 1828."

    This invitation was accepted, and on Thursday, August 7th, Mr. Lyman writes:

    "This day being the Commencement of Washington College, the Society met in the Center Church to assist in the services of the occasion.
    "The following pieces were sung at intervals of the exercises, viz.:

We Praise Thee, O God,	*Jackson.*
Glory Be to God,	*Mozart.*
Then Round About the Starry Throne,	*Handel.*
Achieved Is the Glorious Work,	*Haydn.*
Now the Work of Man's Redemption, } Hallelujah to the Father,	*Beethoven.*

    "Miss Gillingham was also present and sang 'On Mighty Wings,' a song from Haydn's 'Creation.'
    "Mr. James Carter performed the Voluntaries, and Mr. Dutton, *our* Organist, who had also an interesting part in the Collegiate Exercises, played the accompaniments."
                                                  "C. C. LYMAN, Secy."

    Mr. Dutton was a senior in Washington College, which explains the "interesting part" referred to in Mr. Lyman's record. He was then not quite nineteen years of age, and died four years later. He must have been a precocious musician, for he was the first to play the organ placed in the Center Church in 1822.

The midsummer heat seems to have had no depressing effect, for on the 27th of August the society again met for rehearsal, after which the members were entertained by two visiting musicians. "Mr. B. L. Barclay, vocalist and performer of music from England, and Mr. T. T. Dyer, teacher and publisher of music from New York, attended the rehearsal, and after hearing a few choruses performed by the Society, gratified them by the performance of a few favorite airs."

The Society met a part of the time in the North Church and a part in the Center Church until December, 1829, when the meetings began to be held in Dr. J. D. Bull's Hall, corner of State and Front streets. A few orchestral instruments were then brought into use, Mr. Salmon Phelps playing the first violin, and Mr. S. Merrick the second violin, Mr. Lyman the flute, and Mr. Daniel Copeland the double-bass. At this time, too, Miss Caroline Hoadley, Miss Emeline Seymour and Miss Rice joined the chorus. On Sunday evening, February 21st, 1830, the Society met at the South Church to rehearse with the new organ. The last concert mentioned in the records was given April 1st, 1830, in the North Church, and with the notice of a few meetings thereafter the book ceases to give further information.

The name of Miss Louisa Gillingham occurs frequently, and enough to excite curiosity, for she appears to have been educated in a good school, and far in advance of any other singer in Hartford at the time. There were three sisters, all taught by their father, who had been well trained in the pure Italian school of singing and in the English school of oratorio. The sisters were living in New York in 1826, and with Mr. Paddon, gave a concert at the Representative Chamber in Hartford on the evening of August 9th of that year. The program opened with the overture to "The Magic Flute" as a four-hand performance on the piano by Misses A. and L. Gillingham. The rest of the program was made up of vocal solos, duets, trios and one glee for four voices, selected from works by Handel, Haydn, Mozart, Rossini, Bishop and others; a very difficult and exacting list of pieces. I also have the program of a concert which the same company gave in Boston on the 23rd of August, in which many of the same pieces appear.

W. T. BABCOCK.

Miss Louisa Gillingham must have settled in Hartford very soon after this, as the Choral Society procured her services in the autumn of 1827. Miss Emma Gillingham, who also lived in Hartford at the time, became Mrs. Bostwick, and was for many years a favorite singer in this region and in New York.

The program above mentioned is one of a collection of fifty or more, which I have before me, covering the most of the first half of the century, and throwing much light on the musical activity of Hartford and near-by towns. One or two features are striking : the preponderance of vocal music, and the great familiarity with the works of Handel, Haydn, Mozart, and many of the English anthem writers, acquired by our early singers.

Here are several examples of the "List of Tunes" performed by the Euterpian Society in 1817 and 1818 ; quaint sheets, yellow and crumpled, of fine hand-made paper with edges untrimmed. This is quite the fashion now, but it does not seem so sincere. Following these is a very ancient looking sheet with the "order" of a juvenile concert, with the full text of the pieces, and much more cheerful poetry than one would be led to expect. Next comes a "Select Oratorio" by the Psallonian Society, at the Second Baptist Meeting House, West Side, bearing the date May 9th, 1821. This is not a Hartford program, and the name of the town is not given. May it not be Meriden? Tickets were for sale at the stores of Henry Cushing and Oliver Kendall, and the printers were Jones and Wheeler. I would like some assistance in locating this performance. Passing over several concerts by the Jubal Society, we now come to what in these days would be called a song recital. The announcement is made on handsome paper, strikingly printed by P. B. Goodsell. I find the whole document so interesting that I wish to give it entire :—

VOCAL CONCERT.
MR. A. TAYLOR.

At the recommendation of several gentlemen, amateurs of music, and particularly of vocal excellence, has concluded to give another and last concert, at Morgan's Assembly Room, on the evening of FRIDAY, October 10, 1823, for which occasion he has made the following selection of songs, which will be sung by him, accompanied by the Piano-Forte, viz.:—

PART FIRST.

Song. "Alone, retired, beneath some Tree," from the
    opera of "Love in the Desert," composed by . *Braham*
Do., "On this cold, flinty Rock," with the Recitative—
    "Ye gloomy Caves," from the same opera
Do,, "The Thorn," . *Shield*
Do., "Beware of Love," . *Cori*
Do., "Said a Smile to a Tear," . *Braham*
Do., "The death of Abercrombie" *Braham*

PART SECOND.

Song, "Jessie, the Flower of Dumblane," *Smith*
Do., "Scots wha hae wi' wallace bled," written by *Burns*
Do,, "Bonnie Blue," written by Burns *Clark*
Do., "Dulca Domum," *Braham*
Do., "I'll love thee ever dearly," . *T. Cooke*
Do., "The Anchor's weighed, farewell, remember me," *Braham*

In addition to the above Mr. T. will sing (by particular desire) the sacred songs of "Lord remember David," "Fallen is thy throne, O Israel," and "Mary's Tears." Tickets 50 cents, to be had at the bar of Bennett's Hotel, at Morgan's Exchange Coffee House, and at the store of Messrs. Huntington and Hopkins. It is particularly requested that no money be paid at the door. Performance to commence at half-past seven.

A grand concert for the benefit of the Orphan Asylum, in December, 1826, brings our Mr. Taylor before the public again, three years after his "positively last appearance." Other performers were, Mrs. Singleton, Mrs.

Knight, Miss Coates, and Signorina Garcia ; Messrs. Moran, Knight, Gear, Jones, and Weight. Dr. Boyce's duet, "Here Shall Soft Charity Repair" was sung by "Mr. A. Taylor and an amateur." What charitable condescension on Mr. Taylor's part! Who was Signorina Garcia? It is a coincidence that the afterwards great singer Malibran, then known as Signorina Garcia, was in the country at the time, having arrived in New York with her father in the autumn of 1825, and was then seventeen years of age. The rather poor Italian opera company which Garcia brought with him was disbanded in 1826, and he went to Mexico. Marie Garcia had about this time married Eugene Malibran, an elderly and supposedly rich merchant in New York, who very soon after the marriage failed, and became destitute. Madam Malibran remained in this country until September, 1827, working hard to support herself and husband, by singing in public and private concerts. It is hardly supposable that she would be in Hartford to sing at a benefit concert, but she may have been engaged as a special attraction.

An *Oratorio* was given, with Mr. Goldthwaite as leader, by the North Singing Society on Tuesday evening, May 1st, 1827, and was repeated on Thursday evening, May 3rd. An examination shows it to have been made up of parts of Haydn's "Creation," King's "Intercession" and Handel's "Messiah," with a number of single pieces. A note precedes the program, which is as follows: The Society will be assisted in the Oratorio by performers from the different choirs in the city, also by Mrs. Ostinelli, who will preside at the Piano-Forte. She will also sing in several of the pieces.

Miss Pease and *Mr. Newell* vocalists,
Messrs. Ostinelli and *Warren* will perform on the violins.
Mr. Neiber the trumpet, and
Mr. Wetherbee the concert horn.
Mr. A. Copland the violoncello,
Mr. Downes the contra-basso,
Mr. Willoughby the clarionette, and
Mr. Lyman the flute.

From the advertisement of this concert in the *Conn. Mirror* it appears that Mr. and Mrs. Ostinelli, Messrs. Newell, Warren, Neiber and Wetherbee were from Boston. Mr. Paddon, before announced "from New York," found it profitable to remain in Hartford as a teacher. In my collection is the following announcement:

GRAND SACRED CONCERT.

At the Episcopal Church, on Monday next, Sept. 24 (1827) will be performed by Mr. Paddon and his Pupils, a GRAND CONCERT of SACRED MUSIC, consisting of the following sublime Pieces :

PART 1st.

Solo, " Comfort ye my People saith Your God."
Duett, " For the Lord shall comfort Zion."
Solo, " Praise the Lord with cheerful noise."
Duett, " O Lovely Peace with plenty crowned."
Solo, " The Trumpet shall sound and the dead shall be raised."
Solo and Chorus, "Great God, what do I see and hear ?"

PART 2ND.
Duett. " The Lord is a man of war , Lord is His name."
Solo. " Angels ever bright and fair."
Quartette, " Come unto me all ye that labour."
Solo, O had I Jubal's Lyre, or Mirum's trn :ral voice."
Duett. " Turn thee O Lord and deliver my soul."
Solo, " Let the Seraphim in burning Row."

Tickets at 50 cents to be had at H. and T. J. Huntington's Book Store, at Ripley's United, States Hotel and at Bennett's City Hotel.
Hartford, Sept. 27, 1827.

Composers names are not given, but it is easy to detect that, as usual, Handel's name is well in the lead, seven of the twelve pieces being of his composition.

A choral concert was given in Christ Church, Friday evening, May 15, 1829. The names of performers are not given, except that of Miss Louisa Gillingham, who was the soloist.

Mr. B. S. Barclay's concert at Allyn's Hall, August 11, 1829, had a program of sufficient quaintness to be given here entire.

PART I.

Overture—Full Band by Amateurs	*Latour*
Song—MR. BARCLAY, " The Blue Bonnets"	*Braham*
Song—MISS GILLINGHAM, "The Lass O'Gowrie"	
Song—T. S. BARCLAY, "The Maid of Langollen"	*J. Clark*
Glee—Three voices—"The Red Cross Knight"	*Dr. Calcott*
Song—T. S. BARCLAY, "Sound the Horn"	*Alexr. Lee*
Glee—Three Voices—"Dame Durden"	*Nightingale*

PART II.

Overture—Full Band by Amateurs	*Martini*
Song—MR. BARCLAY, "My Bonnie Lass now turn to me," arranged by	*E. Ives*
Song—MISS GILLINGHAM, "I see them on their winding way"	*Haydn-Corri*
Catch—Four voices—"Scotland's Burning"	
Song—T. S. BARCLAY "Said a smile to a tear" accompanied by Mr. Carter.	*Braham*
Catch—Three voices—"Three blind mice"	
"The Hunter's Chorus"—Full vocal and instrumental band	*Von Weber*

On the 8th of October, 1829, Mr. Barclay gave another concert, in the same hall, and, with others, announced the first appearance in Hartford of Miss Pierson, lately from England. From the advent of Dr. Jackson—an English organist trained in the cathedral service who made a brief stay in Hartford in the first years of the century—it will be seen that the taste in vocal music had been formed entirely on English models ; and it was not until the arrival of these educated English soloists, whose names appear in the later programs, that secular music had been given any prominence. The concerts in which they introduced catches, rounds, and glees, with favorite English ballads of the time, led to a demand for chorus music of this sort, which early English composers had bountifully provided. Thus a Glee Club was formed by the most cultured singers in Hartford, and continued several years.

The earliest program I have seen of the Glee Club is dated January 28, 1835. The names of leader and singers do not appear, and probably will not be known, unless the records of the organization should fortunately be discovered. I have reason to believe that the Glee Club was in existence several years, but am now unable to say when it was disbanded. Scattered through this collection of old programs are a few that indicate ambitious performances in neighboring towns. Thus what was called an *Oratorio* was given in Bristol, May 3rd, 1826. It was actually a miscellaneous choral concert, with instrumental overtures at the beginning of each part—the first by "Seignor" Bach—and an oration at the end of the first part. The program does not say who the musicians and the orator were. The concert closed with Handel's Hallelujah Chorus.

Another program is that of a concert of anthems and sacred choruses given on the 14th of March, 1827, in Berlin. A similar concert was probably given in the Presbyterian Church (Worthington Society) Berlin, August 20th, 1828. The program reads: "If fair weather, if not, on the first fair evening." In a former article it was stated that the Worthington Society purchased an organ in Boston, of Leavitt's manufacture, in 1792. This was probably ten years earlier than the first organ appeared in Hartford—that built by Catlin for Christ Church; but it was more than thirty years after Richard Alsop's presentation of an English organ to Christ Church, Middletown.

Mr. E. Ives, Jr, conducted a performance of anthems, hymns and motetts in Wethersfield, April 15th, 1829. This was probably the closing exercise of a term of singing school, when the work was confined to one book, as the page number is given in nearly all cases.

Another out-of-town program is that of a concert given in the Baptist Church, Meriden, May 29th, 1829; and still another, of much later date, given in Bristol, by the Bristol Sacred Music Society, at the Congregational Church, Nov. 8th, 1838.

THOMAS APPLETON.

With a concert given in the Baptist Church, Hartford, Feb. 11, 1835, appears for the first time, the name of a musician, who for many years probably stood at the head of his profession in this city. Mr. Wm. J. Babcock, as organist, accompanist and teacher, did a great deal to shape the course of music in and about Hartford, and tradition has it that some of his accomplishments were very unusual. First, he was a phenomenal sight-reader, and was so well grounded in harmony and counterpoint, as to be able to transpose and play the most difficult oratorio accompaniments in any key desired. It is said that he was not an emotional musician, but in many ways, intellectually, he seems to have been little short of a wonder. No attempt can be made here to give a sketch of his life, as space does not permit. His likeness is presented with this article, but an account of his career must be put off to a later number.

The year 1835 was notable, as in that year the first *three*-manual organ brought to Connecticut, and one of the earliest ever built in America, was set up in the Center Church. An account of the dedication has already been given ; and the case, still in use, although considerably changed about the key desk, is familiar enough to everybody. In the first volume of the *American Magazine of Useful Knowledge*, bearing date of 1835, is a description of this old Thomas Appleton organ, written by the editor, Nathaniel Hawthorne. [It is said that Hawthorne with the aid of his sister, wrote the whole of the first volume of *The American Magazine*, for which, owing to the insolvency of the publishers, they received no pay.]

A part of the description will surely be of interest in this place : " The superb organ, which is represented by the engraving on the opposite page, is just finished at the Manufactory of Mr. Thomas Appleton, for the Congregation worshipping in the Center Church, Hartford. This elegant superstructure, in point of architecture and symmetry of proportion in its exterior, is not surpassed by any Organ extant. Mr. Appleton has comprised in this instrument a greater volume of tone and brilliancy than we have ever witnessed in any Organ of its size. Its dimensions are, 25 feet in height, 14 feet in breadth and 11 feet in depth. It has *three sets of keys*, and 36 register stops, a coupling stop to connect the great organ with the pedals, or both organs with the pedals, and a coupling stop to combine the whole three organs into one.

ORGAN OF CENTER CHURCH, HARTFORD, AS IT ORIGINALLY APPEARED.

"The contents of the above Organ are as follows, viz.: The Great Organ consists of two Open Diapasons, two Stopt Diapasons, one Principal, one Twelfth, one Fifteenth, one Tierce, one Sesquialtera with three ranks, one Cornet with five ranks, one Mixture with three ranks, one Trumpet and one Clarion with seventeen sub-bass pipes, embracing *eight hundred and sixty-seven pipes*.

" The Choir Organ consists of one Open Diapason, one Dulciana, one Stopt Diapason, one Principal, one Flute, one Cremona, and one Basoon, embracing three hundred and forty-eight pipes.

"The Swell Organ consists of one Open Diapason, one Stopt Diapason, one Principal, one Dulciana, one Cornet of three ranks, one Clarionet, and one Hautboy with a Tremlant, embracing three hundred and thirty-three pipes.

"The largest wooden pipe is 20 feet in length, 24 inches deep, and 21 inches in width. The largest metal pipe is 14 feet in length by 9 inches in diameter, and weighs 100 lbs. The whole number of pipes is *fifteen hundred and forty-eight.*

"Other specimens of this experienced artist's workmanship are exemplified in those noble superstructures in Boylston Hall and the Bowdoin Street Church (Boston). We understand that two very first rate and expensive instruments, one for Trinity Church and the other for the Boston Academy of Music, are about being erected in this manufactory, which will doubtless redound equally to the credit of the artist and the honor of our country."

TITLE PAGE OF OLIVER BROWNSON'S "SELECT HARMONY."

Mr. Hawthorne elsewhere writes that organ building may, in the future, be carried farther than this, but he is by no means sure is that it is possible; and yet, when the musician reads the specifications of this primitive work, he will smile, and understand that because it is so hopelessly old-fashioned it is here given as a curiosity. The "superstructure," as Mr. Hawthorne is pleased to call the case, must remain a thing of beauty, however, as long as it endures.

A curiosity of quite another kind is the engraved title page of Oliver Brownson's *Select Harmony*, done by J. Sanford in 1783. It represents the choir standing in the front row of the gallery, around three sides of the church, as was the custom of the time. John Adams, writing from Middletown in 1771, mentions the music he heard there in the meeting house: "The front and side galleries were crowded with rows of lads and lassies, who performed their parts in the utmost perfection. I thought I was wrapped up."

Cheesboro's History of Saybrook mentions the custom of placing the choir as in this picture.

Just above the circle, where the musical notes appear, are the words, "A cannon of four in one," and within the circle are the words, to be sung to the "cannon," as follows:

"Welcome, welcome every guest,
Welcome to our music feast,
Music is our only cheer,
Fills both Soul and ravish'd Ear;

Sacred nine teach us the mood
Sweetest notes be now explor'd,
Softly move the trembling Air,
To compleat our concert fare."

GENEALOGICAL DEPARTMENT.

Querists should write all names of persons and places in such a way that they cannot be misunderstood. Always enclose with queries a self-addressed stamped envelope and at least ten cents for each query. Querists should write only on one side of the paper. Subscribers sending in queries should state that they are subscribers, and preference in insertion will always be given them. Queries are inserted in the order in which they are receized. On account of our limited space, it is impossible that all queries be inserted as soon as querists desire. Always give full name and post office address. Queries and notes must be sent to Wm. A. Eardeley-Thomas, 50th street and Woodland avenue, Philadelphia, Penn. The editor earnestly requests our readers to assist him in answering queries. His duties are onerous enough in other directions, so that only a limited amount of time can be devoted to query researches.

Notes.

Contributed by Rollin U. Tyler, Esq., Deep River.

45 "On a wooden knoll overhanging the Connecticut River, about 100 rods south of Maromas Station of the Conn. Valley R. R., and in the limits of Middletown township is located an ancient burying ground, long since abandoned. It is visible from the R. R. track and only a few rods distant. The grave marks of all kinds indicate that at least 25 or 30 people have been buried there. This is a literatim copy of all the inscriptions that I could find. The original spelling, capitals and alignment are preserved. The inscriptions are all in brown stone, some of which are broken and thrown down. Other grave marks of ordinary native stone."

HERE LIES
INTERR'D THE BODY
OF MR DANIEL
PRIOR WHO DIED
MARCH YE 24 1753
IN YE 89 YEAR OF
HIS AGE

HERE LIES
THE BODY OF MRS
SARAH PRIER LATE
WIFE OF MR. DANIEL
PRIER WHO DEPART
ED THIS LIFE APRIL
YE 11TH 1768 IN YE 57TH
YEAR OF HER AGE

IN MEMORY
OF MRS. MARY PRIOER
FORMERLY THE WIFE OF
MR. JOHN LEUCAS
BUT DIED THE WIFE
OF MR. DANIEL PRIOER
AUGUST YE 8TH 1751 IN
YE 83RD YEAR OF HER AGE

HERE LIES
THE BODY OF
MRS. CHRISTIAN PRIOR
LATE WIFE OF MR.
EBENEZER PRIOR
WHO DIED MARCH YE
25 1761 IN YE 26TH YEAR
OF HER AGE

HERE LIES
INTERR'D THE
BODY OF WIDOW
ABIGAIL LEE WHO
DIED APRIL YE 23RD
1751 AGED 80 YEARS

HERE LIES
THE BODY OF
MRS. MARY LEE
LATE WIFE OF MR.
LEMUEL LEE WHO
DIED JANUARY YE 1,
1752 IN YE 53RD YEAR
OF HER AGE

ANNIE
LEE DAUGHTER
OF MR. LEMUEL AND
MRS. MARY LEE DIED
DECEMBER YE 30
1741 IN THE 23RD
YEAR OF HER AGE

MINDWELL
LEE DAUGHTER OF
MR. LEMUEL AND MRS
MARY LEE DIED
JUNE YE 10 1741
AGED 17 YEARS

HERE
LIES THE
BODY OF MR.
DAVID HOLLISTER JUNER
HE DIED BEING
DROWNED NOVEMBER
THE 26TH 1753 IN THE 31TH
YEAR OF HIS AGE

(ONE FOOT-STONE MARKED
G. W.

(ONE FOOT-STONE MARKED
L. L.

ONE FRAGMENT MARKED
BER YE 14, 174—
YE 2 YEAR OF HER AGE

HEZEKIAH
SON OF MR. HE-
ZEKIAH WHIT-
MORE DIED OCT.
YE 9TH 1750 ONE
YEAR AND 11
MONTHS.

6 COMPLETE EPITAPHS
3 FRAGMENTS

46. Abington, Ct., Cong'l Ch. Deaths

(Continued from page 114.)

1801.

Jan. 17. Mr. Aaron Fay—supposed to

have died in an apopletic Fit, being found dead about half an hour after he was missing—he was in the 56th year of his age.
Feb. 2. Mrs. Lucy, the wife of Mr. John Sharpe, age 72.
Feb 3. Sarah Fraizer.
Feb. 13. Mrs. Edney, the wife of Mr. Nat'l Ayer.
Mar. 4. Mrs. Mary, the wife of Mr. James Trowbridge.
Apr. 12. Mr. Jeduthan Truesdell.
June 5. Mrs Judith, the wife Mr. Edward Paine.
June 29. The widow Ringe.
July 24. Allice Chandler, daughter of Mr. Silas Chandler.
Aug. 19. A child of Mr. Reuben Spalding, age 20 months.
Nov. 24. The wife of Mr. Amariah Storrs.
Dec. 22. Mary, infant child of Amasa Storrs.
1802.
Mar. 6. Mr. Silas Rickard, age between 80 and 90 years.
Mar. 24. A child of Mr. Isaac Rindge.
May 24. Dr. Jared Warner, in the 46th year of his age.
June 10. The wife of Mr. Chester Sharpe.
Oct. 16. A child of Capt. Squire Sessions.
Oct. 16. A child of Mrs. Ford of Hampton.
Nov. 9. Lavinia Goodell, in the 22nd year of her age.
Nov. 20. Mr. Jesse Goodell, in the 26th year of his age.
Nov. 21. A daughter of Obadiah Higginbotham.
Dec. 25. A child of John Bennet.
1803.
Jan. 10. Mrs. Abilene, the wife of Mr. Appleton Osgood, age 41.
Mar. 13. An infant child of Moses Edmunds.
Nathan Chase, son of Mr. Seth Chase, aged 16.
July 26. Mr. Obadiah Higginbotham.
August. Molly Hayward.
Sept. 2. An infant child of Samson Hazard, an Indian residing at Hampton.
Sept. 4. An infant child of } Twins.
Sept. 8. An infant child of } Stephen Utley.
Sept. 13. Oliver Woodworth, aged 6 years, a child of Mr. Woodworth of Norwich, that lived at the house of Mr. Ruben Sharpe and was murdered by Caleb Adams of Brooklyn, who lived at the same place.
Sept. 14. Widow Molly Truesdell, aged 80.
Sept. 16. The wife of Mr. Seth Chase.
Oct 3. Widow Sarah Dean.
Oct. 10 Widow Elizabeth Griggs, in the 87th year of her age.
Dec. 7. Infant child of Dr. David Ingals
Dec. 12. Widow Zerviah Lyon, in the 83rd year of her age.
Dec. 26 Zerviah Goodell, in the 73rd year of her age.
1804.
Jan. 6. Acsah Higginbotnam, aged 24.
Feb. 8. Capt. William Osgood, in the 65th year of his age.
A child of Mr. Sessions, who moved here from Hampton.
April 30. Widow Anne Wheeler, in the 85th year of her age.
June 11. The wife of Mr. Zechariah Osgood, 70th year.
June 20. The wife of Mr. Ebenezer Stoddard, aged 77.
Oct. 6. Mr. Moses Griggs, in the 46th year of his age.
Oct. 8 An infant child of Silas Rickard.
1805.
Jan. 4 Josiah Stowel, aged 21.
Jan. 8. Mr. John Sharpe, aged 78.
Mar. 1. Mr. Nathan Griggs, aged 64.
Mar. 8. Widow Rachel Ashley, aged 70.
April 2. The wife of Aaron Wedge, aged 30.
April 16. Mr. Daniel Goodell, aged 64.
April 20. An infant child of Dr. Joshua Grosvenor.
May 16. Mr. Ephraim Ingals, in the 80th year of his age.
July 23. Mr. Samuel Sumner, in the 79th year of his age.
Aug. 30. The wife of Mr. William Sharpe, aged 66.
Sept. 7. Mr. Ephraim Stowell, aged 72.
Nov. 2. Mr. William Abbott.

(To be continued.)

17. Contributed by George Boughton, Esq, of 47 Division St., Danbury, Ct. Record of marriages by Rev. Samuel Camp, who preached in the Cong'l Ch. in Ridgebury, Fairfield Co., , fromCt

Jan. 18, 1769, to Nov. 21, 1804; he was dismissed in 1804, but lived in Ridgebury until 1813, when he d. act 68-2-20. Ridgebury society is located in a part of both Danbury and Ridgefield. If one party to a marriage lived in the town of Danbury and within the limits of Ridgebury society, and the other lived in Ridgefield and within the limits of Ridgebury society, Mr. Camp describes it accordingly. Upper Salem, Fredericksburgh, Southeast, Philippi, Philipp's Patent, Nine Partners, Cortland's Manor, Poundridge, Little Nine Partners and Duchess Co. are all in N. Y. State.

1769
1—Mar. 6. Peter Castle, junior, of Danbury to Rebecca Osborn of Ridgefield, Ridgebury Parish.
2—Sept. 14. Matthew Northrop to Hannah Abbott, both of Ridgefield, Ridgebury Parish.
3—Nov. 16. Ezekiel Osborn to Sarah Bennett, both of Ridgefield, Ridgebury Parish.
4—Nov. 18. James Lockwood of Noble Town to Mary Street of Ridgefield, Ridgebury Parish.
5—Nov. 29. Samuel Northrup to (Pun?) Riggs.
6—Nov. 29. Abraham Rockwell to Esther Riggs. The two last all of Ridgefield, Ridgebury Parish.

1770.
7—Mar. 22. Daniel Keeler to Abigail Isaacs, both of Ridgefield, Ridgebury Parish.
8—Apr. 26. Jonathan Taylor to Amy Benedict, both of Danbury, Ridgebury Parish.
9—Oct. 8. Aaron Hull to Abigail Whitlock, both of Ridgefield, first society.

1771.
10—April 25. Ephraim Smith of Philippi to the widow Elizabeth Hamblin of Ridgefield, Ridgebury Parish.
11—June 27. Benjamin Jones of Philip's Patent to Elizabeth Rockwell of Ridgefield, Ridgebury Parish.
12—Aug. 14. Thomas Conclin of Salisbury to Anne Keeler of Ridgefield, Ridgebury Parish.
13—Dec. 4. Theophilus Taylor of Danbury to Rachel Northrop of Ridgefield, both of Ridgebury Parish.

1772.
14—Feb. About this time married

Jeremiah Burchard to Phebe Abbott, both of Ridgefield, Ridgebury Parish.
15—June 15. Nehemiah Keeler to Eleanor Rockwell, both of Ridgefield, Ridgebury Parish.
16—Nov. 5. Nathaniel Northrop of Ridgefield to Chloe Baldwin of Danbury, both of Ridgebury Parish.
17—Nov. 19. Timothy Foster to Desire Sears, both of Ridgefield, Ridgebury Parish.
18—Dec. 9, Samuel Baldwin of Danbury to Hannah Northrop of Ridgefield, both of Ridgebury Parish.
19—Dec. Caleb Parmer of Phillippi to Tamer Stevens of Ridgefield, Ridgebury Parish.

1773.
20—Mar. 2 Jeremiah Keeler of Upper Salem to Lydia Keeler of Ridgefield, Ridgebury Parish.
21—Aug. 10. Daniel Tuttle to Naomi Stevens, both of Ridgefield, Ridgebury Parish.
22—Aug. 11. Stephen Sherwood of ---- to Ruth Benedict of Danbury, Ridgebury Parish.
23—Aug. 11. Noah Starr to Sarah Keeler, both of Ridgefield, Ridgebury Parish.
24—Sept. 30. Abijah Rockwell to Lydia Burchard, both of Ridgefield, Ridgebury Parish.
25—Dec. 22. Ezekiel Hodge of the Nine Partners to Massah Foster of Ridgefield, Ridgebury Parish.

(To be continued.)

---

48. Danbury, Conn. Town Records of births, marriages and deaths (copied by Wm. A. Eardeley-Thomas). Vol. I. [Continued from page 115.]

p 358, Joseph Bennet Osborn, son of Jonathan of New Fairfield, m. Aug. 15, 1801, Esther, dau. of Josiah Barnum of Danbury, and had 1, Hiram, Jan. 15, 1802.

Caleb Curtis Gregory, son of John of Danbury, m. Nov. 13, 1796, Desire, dau. of Thomas Sears of Ridgefield, and had 1, John Sears, Oct 3, 1797. 2, Albert, June 7, 1799. 3, Adline, Feb. 21, 1801.

Frederick Jones Whiting, m. May 18, 1783, Rachel, dau. of late Maj. Daniel Starr, and had 1, Henry Starr, Mar 20, 1785. 2, Frederick Augustus, Feb. 24, 1788.

Phineas Lobdell of Ridgefield, m. May

6, 1793, Lucinda. dau. of Thaddeus Bronson of Danbury.
p 359, Ephraim Gregory Stevens, son of the late Thomas Stevens, m. Nov. 20, 1802, Sally, dau. of Joseph Benedict, jr., of Danbury.
Elijah Morris, son of Shadrach, m. Apr. 8, 1798, Olive, dau. of Eliphalet Stevens, and had 1, Jachin, Jan. 12, 1799. 2, John Stevens, Jan. 14, 1801.
Bennet Pepper of Danbury, m. Oct. 19, 1801, Sally, dau. of Luke Gridley of Bristol, and had 1, Gridley, July 22, 1802.
p 360, Eliakim Peck, eldest son of Abijah, b ——, m. Nov. 3, 1786, Polly, 2nd dau. of Caleb Starr, and had 1, Charles, Sept. 4, 1787. 2, Bulah (dau.), Oct. 15, 1789. 3, Sally, Mar. 21, 1792. 4, Starr (son), Apr. 2, 1795. 5, Amarilas (dau.), Nov. 26, 1797. 6, George, Aug 11, 1800.
Peter Benedict, 4th son of Thad'us, Esq., m. Dec 22, 1779, Anne, eldest dau of Abijah Peck, all of Danbury, and had 1, Ezra, Feb. 28, 1781. 2, Betsey, Dec. 16, 1782. 3, Hannah, Dec. 20, 1784. 4, Isaac Hoyt, Dec. 24, 1786, d Dec. 8, 1793 5, Abigail, Jan. 26, 1789. 6, Eli Starr, Sept. 14, 1791. 7, Anne, Jan. 9, 1794. 8, Isaac Hoyt, Dec 12, 1795. 9, Samuel Ward, Mar. 12, 1798. 10, Rachel, Feb. 20, 1801. 11, Deborah, Jan. 23. 1804
p 361, Joseph Taylor, 2nd, b. 1703, d. Nov. 7, 1793.
Richard, a black man, son to Patience, who was a servant for life to Joseph Taylor, b. Dec. 5, 1779, and Richard was married to Isabella, a negro woman, May 1, 1802. Their son, Isaac Sydney, b. Nov. 2, 1803.
Saul, a free black man, married Dosias, b. Mar 11, 1777, a black woman. Their son was born April 18, 1800.

ADDITIONS TO ITEMS on page 115, Jan., Feb., March Number, 8, Danbury Town Records.

James Hodges, *eldest* son of Ezra.
Benedict, *2nd* son of Theophilus.
Thomas Bridgham Benedict.
Lemuel B. Bailey (possibly name should be Samuel), *4th* son of Samuel, m. Abby, *2nd* dau. of Abraham.
Clarissa Stedman, b. *Jan. 23, 1772*.

(To be continued.)

49. Marriages on records of St. John's Protestant Episcopal Church, Stamford and Greenwich, (copied by Wm. A. Eardeley-Thomas). Continued from page 116.
1764.
Feb. 19, Sylvanus Hait and Mary Bets, both of Canaan Parish.
Oct. 21, William Woodward and Amelia Medows of Rye.
Nov. 7, Basil Bartow of Westchester and Clarissa Punderson of Rye.
Dec. 20, James MacDonald of Bedford and Elizabeth Belding of Stamford.
Oct. 29, Zephaniah Hubs and Elizabeth Purdy, both of Rye.
1765.
Jan. 11, William King and Olive Boardman, both of Stamford.
Jan. 13, Jeremiah Anderson of Greenwich and Susanna Willson of Rye.
Feb. 21, James Crawford of Pound Ridge and Rachel Benedict of Ridgefield.
—— John Smith of Bedford and Anne Crawford of Pound Ridge.
Mar. 6, Daniel Heviland and Esther Lawrence, both of Rye.
Mar. 21, William Miller and Mary Haviland, both of Rye.
Mar. 25, Ebenezer Haviland and Thamar Bud, both of Rye.
Mar. 30, Dr. Edward Joyce, N. Y., and Sarah Sacket of Greenwich.
1766.
Jan. 25, Daniel Ghorum and Abigail Waterbury, both of Stamford.
Apr. 1, Nicholas Falch of N. Y. and Sarah Harison of Greenwich.
Apr. 23, Eliot Green and Marcy Seely, both of Stamford.
June 5, John Aspinwall of Flushing and Rebecca Smith of Queen's Village.
1767.
Mar. 19, Jacob Slauson and Kezia Weed, both of Stamford.
1772.
Nov. 10, Silas Hamlin of Amenia Precinct and Polly, dau. of David Lines of Stamford.
1767.
Apr. 23, Nathaniel Munday and Sarah Jarvis, both of Stamford.
June 4, Samuel Whitney of Stamford and Abigail Ferris of Greenwich.
1768.
Jan. 12, Simeon Raymond of Norwalk Sarah P. Sangbon of Stamford.
Sept. 18, Alexander Bishop, jr., and Mary Bates, both of Stamford.
1769.
Jan. 14, Thaddeus Duning of Norwalk

and Mary Goold of Stamford.
Feb. 18, Lewis Marvin of Rye and Sarah Middlebrooks, of Stamford.
Feb. 25, Joseph Smith of Canaan and Mary Waterbury of Stamford.

50. Inscriptions from gravestones in Lieutenant Henry Bennett's Burying Ground in Sherman, Ct., copied and contributed by Wilford C. Platt, Esq., New Fairfield, Ct. [Continued from page 114.]

Ephraim Hubbell, jr, son of Ephraim and Johanna, d. June 6. 1770, aged 27 years.
Kent Wright, who died Oct 27, 1776, aged 37 years.
Daniel Buck, who died Sept. 26, 1802, aged 47 years and 2 months.
Samuel Ackley, only son of David.
Eunice, wife of Benjamin Pickett, died Nov. 6, 1810, aged 76 years.
Judah Morgan, who died April ye 3rd, 1744, in ye 58 year of her age.
Mr. Nathan Hubbell.
Mrs. Mabel Stewart.
Alexander Stewart, Esq.
Copied and contributed by Wilford C. Platt, Esq., Old Leach Burying Ground, in town of Sherman, Conn.
Ichabod Leach, who died May 3. 1813, aged 63 years.
Ruth Leach, wife of Ichabod Leach, who died June 2, 1822, aged 63 years.
Lecty, daughter of Ichabod and Ruth Leach, who died Feb 24, 1789, aged 3 years.
Lecty, daughter of Ichabod and Ruth Leach, who died Jan. 20, 1816, aged 24 years.
David Leach, who died Aug. 28, 1836, aged 57 years.
Lydia, wife of David Leach and daughter of Jonathan Bulkley, who died May 21, 1806, aged 24 years.
Elizabeth Bulkley, daughter to Jonathan and Lydia Bulkley, who died March 19, 1804, aged 22 years.
Lydia, wife of Jonathan Bulkley, who died Aug 31, 1805, aged 52 years.
Jonathan Bulkley, who departed this life Nov. 4, 1815. Born Nov. 15, 1751.
Gideon Congor, son of Joel and Anna Congor, who died April 24, 1800, aged 14 years.
Stephen Davis, who died Dec. 25, 1838, aged 71 years.
Hannah, wife of Stephen Davis, who died Oct. 12, 1829, aged 53 years.
Died March 11, 1801, Electa, daughter of Stephen and Hannah Davis, aged 1 year and 6 months.
Died Oct. 17, 1801, Ruth, daughter of Stephen and Hannah Davis, aged 1 year and 1 month.
Daniel Davis, who died Feb. 5, 1835, aged 38 years.
William Davis, who died June 24, 1839, aged 47 years.

This cemetery is over in the lots, near a swamp, and it is supposed that a great many were buried in what is now the swamp land. There are but few tombstones, a majority of the graves being marked by a common stone, with no inscription placed at their head.

Queries.

153. *White*, Isaac, Sr., of Greenwich, Mass., b. 1720-5, m. Elizabeth ———. Desires his ancestry? I. S. E.

154. (a) *Brown*, Timothy, b. 1742, Enfield, Ct., brother of Col. John and Capt. Jacob, both of Pittsfield. His father was Dan'l Brown, his mother was Mehitable Sanford. Dan'l and family moved from Enfield to Sandisfield, Mass., with "his numerous family" in 1752 and settled the town. Timothy m. "Sarah Paine of Cape Cod"—her parentage wanted. Timothy and Sarah spent many years in Dorset, Vt., and had a large family there, but d. in Troy, N. Y. Think the Paines were a Sandisfield family.

(b) *Collins*, Benjamin, of Lebanon, Conn. He and wife Eliza d. there. I have full records of their children b in Lebanon. Where did Benjamin come from? I think Taunton. I want his ancestry; wife's name and ancestry? They were m. abt 1720. Eight children. H. R. C.

155. *Allen*, Mabel, bapt. July 14, 1754, d. Oct 10, 1799, m. May 20, 1773, Elijah Thompson of New Haven. Can you tell me anything of her ancestry? E. T. F.

156. (a) *Niles*, Ambrose, b. 1740, m. Mary Ransom; d. July 1, 1809; buried in Westchester, New London Co., Conn. Can anyone give the genealogy of his family; also date of birth and marriage?

(b) *Ransom*, Mary, b. 1752, m. Ambrose Niles; d. Aug. 15, 1806. Her family genealogy is desired, especially the name of her father and mother; also the date of her b. and m. K. R. B.

157. (a) *Brace*, Susannah, b. 1714 (Hartford?), d. 1795, Bethlehem, Conn., m. Dea. Samuel, son of Samuel Strong of Northampton. Who were her parents?

(b) *Newell*, Mary, wife of Lieut. John Steele, was dau. of Samuel Newell, prob. of Farmington, Conn. Who was her mother and who Samuel Newell's ancestors?

(c) *Smith*, John, b. Dec. 21, 1710, Hadley, son of John and Elizabeth Hoag Smith; lived in Hatfield; m. Mary ———. Who were her ancestors?
E. S. B.

158. *Chaffee*, William, of Enfield. Ct., was according to tradition of the Forlorn Hope at the storming of Stony Point, and is said to have been the first to plant the American Colors upon the ramparts. Are there any proofs of this?
G. P.

159. (a) *Perry*, Ruhemah (or Amy), b. 1773 in the vicinity of Danbury, Ct., m. as her 2nd husband Obediah Chase. Who was her first husband, by whom she had a dau. Harriet? Was his name Goldsmith?

(b) *Berry*, Richard, in 1647 was living in Boston with Thomas Hawkins. Did Richard m. a dau. of Hawkins? Richard m. Alice ———. Who were her parents? Hawkins had children b. in Boston, 1637 to 1657.

(c) *Perry*, Solomon, b. 1726, m. abt. 1750 Priscilla ———. Who were her parents? He had a bro.-in law Thaddeus Andrews. Solomon had in Ridgefield, Ct., 1, Gilbert. 2, Freeman. 3, Penelope. 4, Anna (m. James Siel). 5, Saunders. 6, David. 7, May Lewis. What became of these children?

(d) *Sherwood*, Jerusha, b. July 11, 1751, Danbury, Conn. (T. R.), m. May 7, 1778, Silas Taylor, b. June 24, 1757. Who were her parents and what their ancestry? Who were his parents and what their ancestry?

(e) *Perry*, Elisha, had b. in Sandwich, Mass., 1, Ruth. 2, James. 3, Elisha. 4, Solomon. 5, John. 6, Maria, b. 1738. In the distribution in 1751 of his estate (Danbury, Ct., Prob. Rec.) mention is made of 3 other children, viz., David, Hannah (m. Thomas Cozier), and Elizabeth (m. Elijah Whitney). When and where these three children born, married and died?
W. A. E. T.

160. *Osborn*, David H., b. 1821 in Weston, Conn. (part now called Easton), was my father. David Osborn, my grandfather, b. 1782 in Fairfield, Conn. (part now called Easton). Ephraim Osborn, my great-grandfather—don't know when or where he was born. Should like to trace the history back.
G. W. O.

161. (a) *Gould*, James, sometime before 1719 with 3 or 5 brothers came from Eng. and settled in Litchfield Co., Conn. He was with John French, Joseph Pigeon, John Cartledge and James Hendrickson at Conestoga, Pa., treating with the Indians, June 28, 1719, and was called captain. Is this the same James Gould, or what relation of a private in the Wyoming Valley Company (raised in Conn.) under Capt. Robert Durkee, Aug. 26, 1776? The private Gould m. Ann Smith, who had lived with Judge Green of New London, Conn. Their children were Peter, Elijah, Samuel and Jacob (b. Jan. 28, 1772, while crossing Wilkesbarre Mts., Pa.)

(b) *Skinner*, Benjamin, of Hartford, Ct., m. Dec. 8, 1791, Abigail Spencer of Hartford. Who were his parents? Later he moved to Winsted, Ct., and took charge of Rockwell's mill. He d. Feb. 8, 1814, aged 48.
L. C. S.

162. (a) *Wildman*, Josiah[4] (Joseph[3], Thomas[2], Thomas[1]), had a daughter Mary, m. Luke Chapin, res. Solon, N. Y., and had 9 sons. Whom did Josiah marry and what children did he have?

(b) *Wildman*, Joseph[5] (Philip[4], Joseph[3], Thomas[2]) had, 1, Abraham[6], m. 2nd Mrs. Sally Nickerson. Who were her parents? What children had Abraham? Who were his other wives (said to have had 3)? 2, Ira[6], m. Alice Ballard. Did he have issue? Who were her parents? 3, Daniel[6], d. unm.

(c) *Wildman*, Uz[5] (Joseph[4], Joseph[3], Thomas[2]) had a son George[6]. Whom did Uz marry? What issue had he? Who was his mother and her parents?
A. W.

DESCENDANTS OF WILLIAM CHASE OF YARMOUTH

BY WILLIAM A. FARDELEY-THOMAS.

[Continued from last number]

38.
235 v. Lot,² Mar. 11. 1716; m. Dec. 27, 1738, Rebecca Wing.
236—vi. "Hanah."³ Sept. 26, 1718. What became of her?
237—vii. Nathaniel,² May —, 1724. What became of him?
238—viii. Mary,³ Jan. 9, 1720-21; m. pub. July 20, 1740, in Y., Nathaniel Covil of Chatham. Did he have children? Who were his parents?
239—ix. Judah,³ Oct. 24, 1726. What became of him?

Isaac and "Charete" had:
240—x. Barnabas,³ April 29, 1731; m., 1749, Lydia Ryder. Who were her parents?
241—xi. Temperance,³ Mar. 4, 1731-2; m. Jan. 23, 1745, Nathaniel Baker.
242—xii. "Charete,"³ July 15, 1736; m., 1757, Sylvanus⁶ Chase 221.
243—xiii. "Mehetable,"³ Aug. 9, 1740; m. pub. Nov. 27. 1755, in H.; m. Jan. 5. 1756, in Y., Isaac Eldridge, Jr., of H. Did he have children? Who were his parents?
244—xiv. "Desier,"³ Mar. 6, 1741-2; m., 1764, Archelus⁶ Chase 862. Did he have children?

39. Samuel⁴ BAKER (Elizabeth³ *Chase*, William², William¹, Daniel *Baker*, Francis¹ Baker) d. Mar. 17, 1775, of "Acky?" Neck m. _____ Patience __ Who were her Parents? She d __ 1750. Samuel⁴ and Patience (_____) Baker had in Y.:

i. Shubal⁵ *Baker*, Mar. 24, 1710; m. —. ————. 1733, Lydia Stuart and had, 1 Silvanus⁶ *Baker*, Mar. 10, 1734-5; m. April 8, 1756, Jane Crowell, and had Silvanus⁷ *Baker*, Dec. 13, 1757; m. Aug. 30, 1780, Phebe⁶ Chase, dau. of Rev. Richard³ (201).
Shubel⁶ *Baker*, had II. Shubel⁷ *Baker*. Nov. 11, 1741; m. 1st Nov. 15, 1764, Rebecca⁶ Chase, dau. of Rev. Richard⁵ (201); m. 2nd July 6, 1787, Elizabeth⁶ Chase, dau. of Abner⁵ (205).
ii. Susannah⁵ *Baker*, June 22, 1711, m. Sept. 18, 1735, Francis⁴ Baker (Samuel³, Nathaniel², Francis¹). Did he have children?
iii. Hezekiah⁵ *Baker*, Aug. 4, 1715; m. Sept. 27, 1744, Mary Stuart.
iv. Tabitha⁵ *Baker*, Mar. 8, 1718; m. Nov. 7, 1748, Joshua Crowell.
v. Desire⁵ *Baker*, Feb. 5, 1720-1; m. Mar. 1, 1743-4, Lot⁴ Baker (John³, John², Francis¹). Did he have issue?
vi. Elizabeth⁵ *Baker*, Sept. 9, 1725. What became of her?
vii. Samual⁵ *Baker*, June 4, 1732; m. Dec. 4, 1755, Rebecca Baker. Did he have issue? Who were her parents?

40. Shubal⁵ and Rebecca⁶ (Chase) Baker had in Y.:
i. Hepzibah⁷ *Baker*, Oct. 15, 1765; m. Feb. 4, 1786, Zenas Chase. Who was his father?
ii. Archelaus *Baker*, Nov. 26, 1767; m. Feb. 5, 1789, Mehitable⁶ Chase, dau. of Abner⁵ (205).
iii. Rebecca⁷ *Baker*, Dec. 19, 1770; m. Apr. 18, 1793, Benjamin Godfrey.
iv. Shubal⁷ *Baker*, July 10, 1772.
v. Ezra⁷ *Baker*, Sept. 5, 1774. ⎫
vi. Michael⁷ *Baker*, Nov. 4, 1776. ⎬ What became of these children?
vii. Ensign⁷ *Baker*, Jan. 3, 1779. ⎪
viii. Temperance⁷ *Baker*, Oct. 15, 1781. ⎭

ix. Abigail³ *Baker*, Nov. 22, 1783; m. Apr. 20, 1807, Edwin Sears. She d. Sept. 18, 1853, in So. Dennis, Mass.
x. Silvanus³ *Baker*, Aug. 24, 1786. What became of him?

41. Elizabeth⁴ *Baker* (Elizabeth³ Chase, Wm.², Wm.¹, Daniel² Baker, Francis¹), b. 1676 in Y; m Nov. 8, 1705 Y., Mass., Nathaniel Baker³; ch,. b. in Yarmouth.
    i. Lydia⁵ *Baker*, Feb. 28, 1705-6; m. June 21, 1737, Joseph White.
    ii. Jacob⁵ *Baker*, Oct. 16, 1707; m. Thankful³ Chase, No. 233, and had Jacob⁶ *Baker*, m. 1764, Rachel Whelden, and had Happy⁶ *Baker*, Sept. 25, 1765; m. Mch. 23 1786, Zenas⁶ Chase, No. 935.
    iii. Phebe⁵ *Baker*, Oct. 11, 1709; m. Sept. 8, 1748, Eleazer O'Kelly.
    iv. Nathaniel⁵ *Baker*, Nov. 20, 1711; m. Temperance² Chase, No. 241, and had Abraham⁶ *Baker*; m. Anna Baxter and had Cornelius³ Baker; m. 1st Polly Chase, (who were her parents?) 2nd Betsey Snow.
    v. Joseph⁵ *Baker*, Mch. 31, 1715; m. July 20, 1738, Elizabeth Berry of Harwich, and had Joseph⁶ *Baker*, Oct 8, 1746; m. Oct. 13, 1765, Priscilla⁶ Chase, No. 874, and had Deborah⁶ *Baker*, Dec. 2, 1767; m, ———, 1786, William⁷ Chase, No. 919.
    vi. Elizabeth⁵ *Baker*, Mch. 31, 1715; m. Apr. 18, 1737, Ephraim Crowell.

44. Tabitha⁴ *Baker* (Elizabeth³ Chase, Wm.², Wm.¹, Daniel² Baker, Francis¹), died ———, 1737; m. Dec. 14, 1717, in Y., Mass., Joseph², son of Jeremiah², David¹ O'Kelly.† Ch. b. in Y., Mass.
    i. Stephen⁴ *O'Kelly*, Sept. 22, 1718; m. pub. Feb. 20, 1742, Thankful⁵ Chase, No. 216.
    ii. Sarah⁴ *O'Kelly*, Feb. 21, 1721-2; m. Jan. 19, 1743-4, Joseph⁵ Chase, No 202.
    iii. Annah⁴ *O'Kelly*, Apr. 28, 1720; m, Aug. 19, 1743, Wm. Smith of Harwich.
    iv. Joseph⁴ *O'Kelly*, Mch. 30, 1728; m. Mch. 8, 1749-50, Elizabeth Chase. Who were her parents?
    v. Jeremiah⁴ *O'Kelly*, May 8, 1730. What became of him?

*Nathaniel² Baker (Francis¹); d. Dec. 1641, Y.; m. ———. She d. Dec., 1641, Y
    i. Samuel³, Oct. 2, 1670; m. July 11, 1702, Elizabeth Berry John² Richard¹.
    ii. Nathaniel³, Jan. 10, 1672; m. Elizabeth⁴ Baker, No 41
    iii. Silas² (probably), m. May 14, 1723, Deliverance³ O'Kelly—Jeremiah² David¹.

†David O'Kelly d. 1696 in Y., Mass.; wife Jane d. Oct. 17, 1711, Y. A tanner in Y., admitted inhabitant 1657 and took the oath of fealty. Records call him David O'Kelly, the Irishman. He signed his will "David O'Keilia." Will dated Feb. 10, 1696, and names wife Jane; sons Jeremiah, David, John, Benjamin and Joseph; daus. Elizabeth and Sarah see Barnstable, Mass. Probate Records.)
    i. Jeremiah²   ; d. Aug. 30, 1721; m.   , Sarah ———————, Who were her parents?
    ii. David²   ; m. Mch. 10, 1692, Anna, daughter. Thomas and Ann (Twining) Bills.
    iii. John²   ; d. Oct. 26, 1691; m Aug. 10, 1674 in Y., Bethia Lewes.
    iv. Benjamin²   ; m. Aug. 2, 1702, Barnstable, Mass., Mercy Lumbert.
    v. Elizabeth²   ; m. May 1, 1717, Silas Sears.
    vi. Sarah², d. July 24, 1715.
    vii. Joseph². What became of him?
    Jeremiah² O'Kelly d. Aug. 30, 1728, in Y.; m.   , Sarah   She d.   , 1717.
    i. Sarah³, Sept. 17, 1680; m. Nov. 1, 1721, Oliver Carpenter.
    ii. Jeremiah³, last of June, 1691; m. Aug. 8, 1710, Charity Pees; he d. 1727, leaving 1, Sarah⁴, Oct. 10, 1715; 2 Jerusha⁴; 3. Elizabeth⁴. Charity m. 2nd 1727, Isaac⁴ Chase, No. 38.
    iii. Joseph³, Apr. 6, 1693; m. Tabitha Baker, No. 44.
    iv. John³, middle of July, 1695; m. Feb. 18, 1719-20, Hannah Eldredge.
    v. Eleazer³, Mch., 1696-7; m.   , Sarah
    vi. Seth³, end of July, 1701; m. Nov. 22, 1720, Mehitable Wing, and had Seth, m. Elizabeth, dau. of Zaccheus Gifford; Zaccheus m. 1st Lydia Dillingham; m. 2nd Sarah Shove.
    vii. Amos³, last day of Mch., 1702-3; m.   , Abigail
    viii. Hannah³, Mch., 1705; m.   , Elnathan Eldredge.
    ix. Deliverance³   ; m May 14, 1723, Silas Baker Nathaniel² Francis¹.

PUBLISHER'S NOTE.

With the next issue of the Quarterly we shall have completed four years. The reception has been so favorable, the demand for historical matter so constant, that we have been seriously handicapped by the infrequency of the issue. We have, found it necessary, in order to meet the growing demand, to publish oftener. We therefore take pleasure in announcing that, beginning January 1899, we shall publish monthly, under the name of "The Connecticut Magazine." This will enable us to give our patrons a much better magazine, more complete in every detail. It will be our aim to keep up the high standard of the Quarterly in every particular, and to improve where we see opportunity. The subscription price will be the same as at present, $1.00 per year. Single numbers 10 cents each. Although each number will not have so many pages as a present number of the Quarterly, the 12 numbers combined will contain more than a hundred pages in excess of what a yearly volume of the Quarterly contains. So for the same price our readers will have the advantage of possessing much additional material.

The Connecticut Magazine will be under the same general editorial management as the Quarterly has been for the last three years, thus insuring a continuance of the same lines in general plan and scope, and also insuring an improvement in many ways indicated by past experience. The business department will be under the supervision of Mr. Edward B. Eaton, who will be associated with the present publisher in the production of the Magazine. We desire to make the coming issues of the Magazine as complete a record of Connecticut history as possible and shall need to represent the towns given in the earlier numbers again in certain praticulars as they were incompletely done at the time. We hope to increase our already large circulation by thoroughly representing the State in the best possible manner and appealing to local pride which all our citizens feel in the interests of our commonwealth, so that every one will want to possess the work from the start for its intrinsic value and merit.

Further particulars will be given in our October number.

HISTORICAL NOTES.

The exercises held at the dedication of the monument in memory of Rodger Ludlow, the founder of Norwalk, held at East Norwalk on June 23, were of a unique character, and were planned by the Norwalk antiquarian, Rev. C. A. Selleck, to whose untiring zeal the monument is due.

The design of the monument is massive and simple. A great block of granite rests on a low stone base, on which is inscribed "Roger Ludlow." At each corner of the block are polished pillars, supporting a capstone, surmounted by a large polished ball of the same granite, set in a carved socket. On the north side is a bronze bass relief executed by a Connecticut artist, representing Ludlow purchasing the land from the Norwalk Indians. On the south side is a bronze tablet which is inscribed as follows:

"This stone, erected December, 1895, commemorates the purchase from the aboriginal inhabitants, made February 26, 1640, by Roger Ludlow, deputy governor of the colony of Connecticut, framer of its first code of laws, and founder of Norwalk, of all the lands, meadows, pastures, trees, whatsoever there is, and grounds between the two rivers, the one called Norwalke an the other Soakaluck, to the middle of sayed rivers from the sea, and a day's walk into the country."

This handsome memorial of Norwalk's founder was erected by Mrs. William K. James on land given for the purpose by J. R. and William Marvin.

The present monument was set in place last autumn, replacing one erected in 1895, which was of unsatisfactory design.

CONSTITUTION OF THE FIRST TEMPERANCE SOCIETY IN WOODBURY.

[Contributed by Edward S. Boyd.]

Woodbury is one of the old towns in Connecticut, being organized in 1670. We give below a copy of the constitution of the first temperance society in the town. The date is probably about 1821 :

CONSTITUTION OF WOODBURY TEMPERANCE SOCIETY.

ART. 1. This Society shall be called "The Woodbury Temperance Society," auxiliary to the temperance society of Litchfield County.

ART. 2. Any person subscribing this constitution shall be a member of this Society.

ART. 3. The members of this Society, believing that the use of intoxicating liquors is, for persons in health, not only unnecessary, but hurtful and that the practice is the cause of forming intemperate appetite and habits; and that while it is continued, the evils of intemperance can never be prevented, do therefore agree that we will abstain from the use of distilled spirit, except as a medicine in case of bodily hurt or sickness; that we will not use it in our families, nor provide it for the entertainment of our friends, or for persons in our employment; and that in all suitable ways we will discountenance the use of it in the community.

ART. 4. The officers of the Society shall be a President, Vice-President, Secretary, and Treasurer, to be chosen at each annual meeting of the Society; and who shall perform the duties customarily assigned to such officers.

ART. 5. The officers of the Society in their associated capacity shall constitute an executive committee to carry into effect all votes and orders of the Society, & to devise and recommend the best means of accomplishing its benevolent designs.

ART. 6. The Society shall meet annually and at such other times as shall be judged necessary by the executive committee.

Members of the Society.
Saml R. Andrew
Grove L. Brownwell
Seth Miner
Elijah Sherman, Jun.
Judson Blackman
Benj. H. Andrew
Reuben H. Hotchkiss
Ira Thomas
Walter Cramer
Gilbert S. Uliner
John Cramer
Truman Hunt
Judah Baldwin
Silas Clark

Members of the Society.
Geo. W. Hurd
Jared Allen
Dr. Fred'k B. Woodward
Saml W. Judson
Gould C. Judson
Wm. B. Hotchkiss
James Cramer
David A. Tuttle

FROM THE SOCIETIES.

STATE CONFERENCE, D. A. R.

The state conference of the Daughters of the American Revolution was held at Norwich on May 26th. In spite of the unpleasant weather a large delegation was present in Slater Memorial Hall at 11 o'clock, the hour of the opening exercises. All the chapters but four were represented.

The meeting was called to order by the State Regent, Mrs. Sara T. Kinney of New Haven, and the prayer of invocation was offered by Mrs. Bulkley of Southport. The Regent of the Faith Trumbull Chapter, Mrs. Bella P. Learned, made the address of welcome, to which the State Regent made a fitting reply.

The first paper was read by Mrs. A. J. J. Perkins, who gave an account of the life of Faith Robinson Trumbull, wife of Governor Jonathan Trumbull —"Brother Jonathan"—after whom the chapter is named. Mr. Jonathan Trumbull, president of the Connecticut S. A. R., and grandson of Gov. Trumbull, was then introduced and spoke a few words in praise of the patriotism of the Connecticut D. A. R. and warmly commended the work they were trying to do at the present time. Miss Root of the Katherine Gaylord Chapter, Bristol, made a report for the committee appointed to investigate the expense of printing a book of biographical sketches of the heroines of the different chapters, and of the real or patent daughters of the State. After her report had been accepted, Miss Ellen Larned of the Elizabeth Porter Putnam Chapter, read a paper entitled "A Few Hints." She made a strong plea for the value of the personal element in the preservation of historical data, this being her own special branch of historical research. She claimed that personal incident is more valuable than anything else in fixing an historical fact in the memory, and told several amusing stories to illustrate her point. But she warned her hearers to be very sure that the incidents they relate as to the achievements of their ancestors are perfectly true and concern their own grandfathers and grandmothers and not the ancestors of some one else.

The singing of the hymn, "Home and Country," written by Miss Ella A. Fanning of Norwich and set to music by Mr. J. Herbert George, also of Norwich, and now adopted as the hymn of the Connecticut D. A. R., closed the exercises of the morning, after which all present adjourned to Breed Hall where luncheon was served.

The first paper of the afternoon session entitled "War and the Prison Ships During the Revolution" was read by Mrs. Virginia Chandler Titcombe of Fort Greene Chapter, Brooklyn, N.Y. Probably many present, even those fairly conversant with Revolutionary history, had very scant knowledge of this subject, and were surprised and shocked to realise how great was the number of American prisoners who died on three ships in the harbor of New York between 1776 and 1783, 11,000 on one of them alone—the Jersey. She gave a most graphic and moving account of the sufferings endured by these prisoners, any one of whom could have purchased his liberty by espousing the British cause. Not one was ever found who was willing to do so. The bones of these martyrs in the cause of liberty, after many years of neglect, were at last collected and interred at Fort Greene, where they now rest. A movement is now on foot now among the patriotic women of Brooklyn to raise funds to erect a monument to the memory of these heroes.

An original poem, "Quo Vadis?" was then read by Mrs. Mary Bolles Branch of the Lucretia Shaw Chapter, of New London. This was followed by a paper on "New England Divines, and Marriage Customs in Colonial and Revolutionary Times," by Mrs. Kate Foote Coe of the Susan Carrington Clark Chapter, of Middletown. The last paper of the session, on "Norwich Town Old Green," was given by Mrs. J. Porter Rudd, of Norwich.

Mrs. Kinney announced the responses she had received to the circular calling on chapters throughout the state for aid for the wounded soldiers and sailors in the present war. Most gratifying success was reported, $1,000 having been pledged as well as other aid. The regent of the Simsbury Chapter had given her check for $2,000 for an ambulance for the Red Cross and had also promised to be responsible for the salary of a nurse. The money pledged by the Connecticut D. A. R. is to be used for the purchase of supplies for the hospital ship Relief.

The Melicent Porter Chapter of Waterbury sends the first nurse to the front, Miss Cherrie Morton French of Waterbury, whose mother is one of the charter members of the chapter. Mrs. Cuthbert Harrison Slocumb of Groton made a strong appeal to the chapters of eastern Connecticut for aid for the soldiers then in camp at Niantic and Fort Griswold, Groton.

The exercises closed with the singing of "America." The literary exercises were interspersed with excellent instrumental and vocal selections by local talent.

Later an informal reception was held at the Norwich club for those who remained in the city until the evening trains.

The Daughters of Litchfield and Washington have organized a chapter and named it the Judea Chapter D. A. R. On June 9th they held a meeting at the home of Mrs. Gunn, in Washington, and elected the following officers :—Regent, Mrs. F. W. Gunn ; Vice-Regent, Mrs. John L. Buel ; Registrar, Miss Fannie P. Brown ; Cor-Sec., Mrs. George C. Woodruff ; Rec-Sec., Mrs. Wm. Brinsmade ; Treas., Mrs. W. J. Ford ; Historian, Miss Frances Hickox ; Board of management, Mrs. H. W. Wessells, Mrs. S. Ford Seeley, Mrs. W. H. Church, Miss Anna Brinsmade and Miss Ruth McNeill.

The memorial of the first English settlement in Connecticut, recently erected by the Abigail Wolcott Ellsworth Chapter of Windsor, marks a spot as interesting and important to the people of our state as any that have been commemorated of late. The boulder, of which we give a picture, is about a mile from Windsor center, on what is known as "The Island."

At the dedication, an historical paper was read, prepared by Deacon Jabez H. Hayden, an address given by Mrs. Kinney, and other appropriate exercises were enjoyed by the large number of people present.

We are glad to note the general response made by the various chapters to the request for aid to the soldiers in the present war and the efforts of the Society in this direction, as well as its interest in preventing the desecration of the Flag, and increasing the teaching of patriotism in our schools by the system of prizes offered for essays by the pupils, are to be heartily commended. They show themselves to be progressive, fully alive to the desirability of doing useful work.

On May 14th, 1898, the ruins of old Fort Decatur were marked by the Belton Allyn Society, C. A. R. of Gales Ferry. This spot, most beautifully situated on Allyn's Mountain, north of Gales Ferry, historic from the fact of Decatur's sojourn there for 21 months while watching his fleet which was blockaded in the Thames by an English fleet in New London harbor in the War of 1812, is important to be commemorated, and Mrs. William Moulthrope, the president of the Society, deserves credit for her successful efforts.

The inscription is on the face of a huge boulder, and reads as follows:
This boulder
was marked by
The Belton Allyn Society, C. A. R.
of Gales Ferry
as being the
north boundary
of Fort Decatur
that was erected
in the
years 1813 and 1814
to protect ·
Decatur's fleet from
the British.

THE CONNECTICUT FORESTRY ASSOCIATION.

Contributed by Miss Mary Winslow, Secretary

"He who plants a tree, plants a hope."

In December, 1895, certain individuals of this state, realizing and deploring the fact that the magnificent forests of our country are being rapidly swept away, and desiring especially that the woods of Connecticut shall be preserved, and its people educated to protect shade and ornamental trees, banded themselves together for this work, drafted and signed a constitution, and thus was founded The Connecticut Forestry Association. It was regularly organized the following year, has now a membership of fifty or over, and holds its annual meetings upon Arbor Day.

The objects of the association as set forth in its constitution, are substantially as follows: To develop public appreciation of the value of forests and of the need for preserving and using them rightly; to forward the establishment of forests, parks and reservations, advocating the introduction of rational forest management in such lands; to disseminate information relating to the science of forestry and the care of trees; to encourage the study of forestry and kindred topics in the schools. The association is not restricted in its efforts, to the state of Connecticut, but its influence will be used also for the advancement of national forestry.

The first president of the association, and one of its founders, was Rev. Horace Winslow of Weatogue (Simsbury), who declined re-election this year on account of ill-health. Mr. Winslow has ever been a friend of trees—planting, guarding, cherishing them. Many years ago, when pastor of a church at Rockville, he planned for that place two parks, securing sites, raising money, grading and setting out a number of trees. So that Rockville owes her now beautiful pleasure grounds, in the heart of the city and full of fine shade trees, as much to his individual efforts as to the gifts of funds from other citizens.

Mr. Winslow's successor as president of the Forestry Association is Major Edward V. Preston of Hartford, also a lover of trees and interested in their preservation. A man in active business, he will undoubtedly accomplish much for the development of the association and the enlargement of its usefulness. The vice-president is Hon. T. S. Gold, long and well-known as state secretary of agriculture. The other officers for 1898 are as follows:

Corresponding secretary, Miss Mary Winslow, Weatogue; recording secretary, Prof. John B. McLean of Simsbury; treasurer, Mr. Alfred Spencer Jr., Hartford; auditor, Mr. Appleton R. Hillyer of Hartford; advisory board, the above named officers and John B. Lewis, M. D., and Ellen R. Carr, D. D. S., both of Hartford.

At the last annual meeting, Mr. Gold read an excellent paper upon "Forestry in Connecticut," which was followed by a general discussion participated in by Judge Loomis of Suffield, Maj. Preston, Mr. McLean, Mr. J. Hale of Glastonbury and others. It was stated that many people are not aware that there is a state law by which trees upon the highways may be preserved from removal, if marked with certain spikes which are furnished by the secretary of agriculture. The spikes are headed with the letter C, denoting that the trees thus marked are henceforth under the protection of the state.

At this meeting the members passed resolutions relating to the death of Dr. Birdsey G. Northrop, the "Father of Arbor Day," in Connecticut. They also instructed the secretary to prepare and transmit to our members of congress, a remonstrance against the passage of the Forest Reserve amendment to the Sundry Civil Bill, then pending in the United States Senate. This was accordingly done and a reply was received from every Connecticut senator and representative, all of them expressing sympathy with the efforts of the association and most of them promising to do their best to prevent the passage of such an unwise measure, which, if enacted into law, would abolish at one stroke, the forest reservations set aside by President Cleveland. It is evident that the country needs arousing to the fact that forests, aside from their commercial value, have almost as great a worth, in that they hold in place the soil of mountain sides, prevent in large degree, destructive floods, conserve moisture for irrigation purposes and stream-flow in dry seasons, purify the atmosphere and modify climatic rigors.

At the last session of the legislature, a member of the association sent in a bill to have all locomotives provided with spark-arresters. Although several of the committee on agriculture, to which it was referred seemed favorable to the passage of this bill, yet it was adversely reported and thus killed for that time. Many citizens apparently do not know that hundreds of acres of woodland in this state are burned over nearly every year, set on fire by sparks from locomotives.

As the dues of the society are moderate, one dollar for annual and fifteen dollars for life membership, it is hoped that the good people of Connecticut may largely identify themselves with this organization, so helping to make our little state already generously prepared by nature, a veritable garden of beauty, and to preserve for *all* the inhabitants of this country, their children and children's children if may be, to remote generations, a fragment at least of those mighty primeval forests, which in all their grandeur once covered great portions of the continent and are still, it is supposed, without a peer on the face of the globe.

"The Grate That Heats."
Jackson Ventilating Grate.
Heats on two floors.

Highest Award, World's Fair, '93.
Thousands now in use.
Our customers are our references.
Do not regard this grate as simply a luxury for Spring and Fall. It will heat two large rooms when the mercury outside is at zero or below, and will thoroughly and constantly ventilate the rooms without an open window or any draught.
Favor yourself and us by proving the luxury, the cheerfulness, the healthfulness and the economy of these grates.
Call and investigate or send for an illustrated catalogue.

Stoughton & Taylor,
38 Ann St.,
Hartford, Conn.

Mantels, fireplace fixtures, tiles, delft, Kenton Vitrea, etc.

Huntsinger's Business College

Is the leading school of Connecticut for business or short-hand training. Day attendance over 200 pupils. Seven skillful, polite and obliging teachers. This school has placed 198 graduates in good-paying positions the past fifty-one weeks.

No term divisions and new pupils enter every week. We do all that can be done to place graduates in situations. Full information for the asking. Visitors welcome.

✤ Where to go for Good Printing and Bookbinding. ✤

The Horton Printing Co.

Have one of the best equipped plants in the state for turning out the highest class of work at lowest prices.

. . SPECIAL ATTENTION . .

Given to Original Designs in Printing and Bookbinding.

We carry a Special Line of . . .

✦ FINE STATIONERY ✦

Which for variety and low prices cannot be equalled.

Steel Plate Engraving and Printing,

IN UP TO DATE STYLES.

OPERA HOUSE BLOCK, MERIDEN, CONN.

PRINTERS OF
THE CONNECTICUT QUARTERLY

Vol. IV.   October, November, December, 1898.   No. 4.

THE CONNECTICUT QUARTERLY

Illustrated Articles
in this Number:

Salisbury,

Hamden,

Peter Parley,

Connecticut Almanacs of the Last Century,

Notes on Forestry in Connecticut,

Etc., Etc.

See Contents on First Page.

$1.00 a Year.   HARTFORD, CONN.   25 cts. a Copy.

THE CLEF MALE QUARTET

HIGH GRADE CONCERT, SOCIAL AND FUNERAL WORK.
Solos furnished also if desired
"Of EXQUISITE Tone Color and Musical Interpretation."
For Terms and Dates, address
WILLIAM RICHARD GRIFFITH, Business Manager,
COURANT BUILDING, HARTFORD, CONN.

You can save money by traveling via the

Philadelphia, Reading and New England Railroad.

If you have made up your mind to go to any point in the West let us save you money on your ticket and give you the very best route and train service.

Only one change of cars between Hartford and way stations and Chicago.

Train leaving Hartford at 12.40 P. M. connects at Campbell Hall with the fast Chicago express made up of Pullman Sleepers and Elegant Reclining Chair Cars via O. & W. and Wabash roads, through to Chicago without change (chairs free to through passengers) arriving at 9 P. M. Only one night on the road and three dollars saved.

For information apply to W. W. JACOBS & CO., Main Street, H. R. GRIDLEY, 18 State Street, Hartford, E. S. BATCHELDER, Springfield, Mass., or local agents.

W. J. MARTIN, Genl. Pass. Agt.,

HARTFORD, CONN.

The Connecticut Quarterly

AN ILLUSTRATED MAGAZINE

Devoted to the Literature, History, and Picturesque Features
of Connecticut

PUBLISHED QUARTERLY
BY THE CONNECTICUT QUARTERLY COMPANY

66 STATE STREET, COURANT BUILDING

GEORGE C. ATWELL, EDITOR.   HARTFORD, CONN.

CONTENTS.

Vol. IV   October, November, December, 1898.   No. 4

Mount Carmel—The Sleeping Giant.		*Frontispiece.*
Salisbury. Illustrated.	*Ellen Strong Bartlett,*	345
Forestry in Connecticut.	*T. S. Gold,*	372
Hamden. Illustrated.	*J. H. Dickerman,*	376
Judge Not. Poem.	*Louis E. Thayer,*	390
The Deciphering of Ancient Manuscripts,	*Edwin Stanley Welles,*	391
Youth and Nature. Poem.	*Nellie Wooster Cooley,*	393
The Row of Maples. A Story.	*Albert L. Thayer,*	394
Peter Parley—As Known to His Daughter. Illus.	*Emily Goodrich Smith,*	399
Connecticut Almanacs of Last Century. Illustrated.	*Albert C. Bates,*	409
Not Forgotten. Poem.	*Susan Benedict Hill,*	416
List of Burials, Center Church Burying Ground, Hartford.		417
Copied and annotated by *Mary K. Talcott*		
Departments.—GENEALOGICAL DEPARTMENT.		421
HISTORICAL NOTES.		423
PUBLISHER'S NOTES.		424
INDEX FOR THE YEAR 1898, GENEALOGICAL DEPARTMENT.		426

Copyright, 1898, by GEO. C. ATWELL (*All rights reserved*).
Entered at the Post Office at Hartford, Conn., as mail matter of the second class

Profitable Investments

$10 a month for 120 months, paid on the Shares of The Connecticut Building and Loan Association, of Hartford, Conn., will produce $2,000. If death occurs in the meantime the Shareholder's heirs, or his estate, will receive the $2,000, and, besides, the book value of his shares.

Income producing city and village real estate, and a paid-in-cash guarantee (Reserve) Fund of $100,000.00 form together the security offered to Shareholders. Assets over $500,000.00. Accredited agents throughout Connecticut and in other States. Correspondence solicited.

E. C. LINN, Secretary,
252 Asylum St.,
Hartford, Conn.

JUST ISSUED

Edition limited to 300 Numbered Copies, with rubricated title page, printed on heavy linen paper of Antique finish.

Births, Marriages and Deaths, returned from Hartford, Windsor and Fairfield, 1631-1691, and entered in

The Early Land Records of the Colony of Connecticut, Volumes I and II, of Land Records, and No. D of Colonial Deeds.

The Religious Herald.

336 Asylum Street,
Hartford, Conn.

Congregational Weekly of Connecticut.

Single Subscriptions and Renewals, $1.00
New Subscribers (in clubs of five),   500

REUBEN H. SMITH,

Editor and Proprietor.

TRANSCRIBED AND EDITED
BY
EDWIN STANLEY WELLES,
Member of the Connecticut Historical Society.

These records now for the first time printed, should be possessed by genealogists and historical libraries.

Price, $1.50.

Address EDWIN STANLEY WELLES,
NEWINGTON, CONN.

❦ The Connecticut Quarterly. ❦

$1.00 a Year.   25 Cents a Copy.
Payable in Advance.

All subscriptions taken with the understanding that they expire after four numbers have been sent. Unless renewed we discontinue sending.

When change of address is desired give both old and new address and we should receive notice at least two weeks before the first of the first month of the quarter.

Vol. I and Nos. 3 and 4 of Vol. II out of Print. We have a few of Nos I and 2 of Vol. II. Price, 25 cents a copy.

HENRY S. HOUSE, Mgr. Subscription Department.

... THE ...

CONNECTICUT QUARTERLY,

AN ILLUSTRATED MAGAZINE,

DEVOTED TO THE

Literature, History, and Picturesque Features

OF

CONNECTICUT.

Vol. IV.

JANUARY TO DECEMBER, 1898.

HARTFORD, CONN.

Copyright, 1898 by GEORGE C. ATWELL.

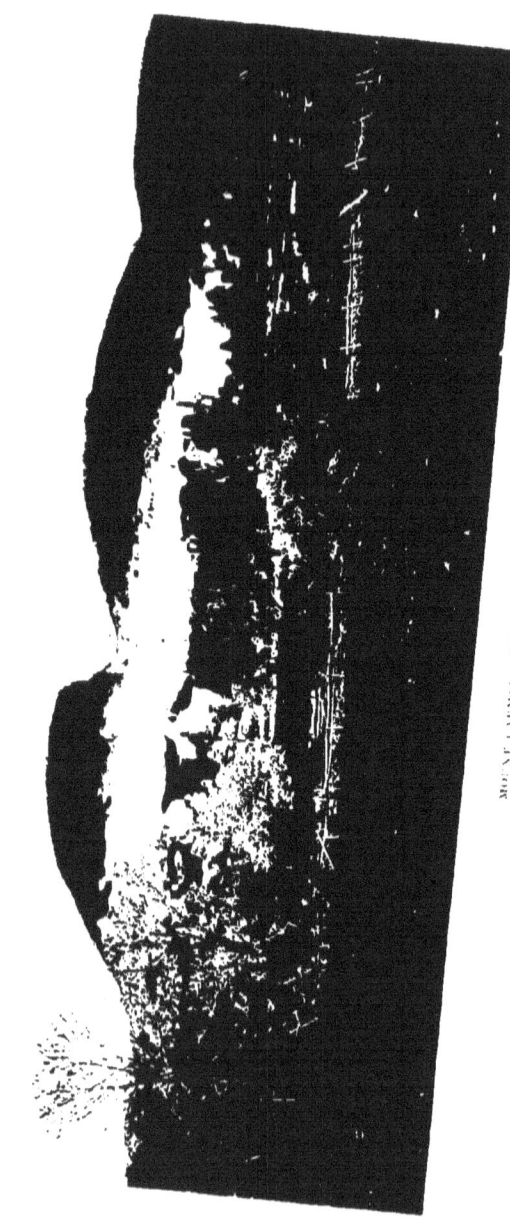

MOUNT CARMEL—"THE SLEEPING GIANT"

The Connecticut Quarterly.

"Leave not your native land behind." *Thoreau.*

FOURTH QUARTER.

VOL. IV.   · OCT., NOV., DEC., 1898.   NO. 4.

※

SALISBURY

"A Puritan Arcadia among the Hills." —*Dr. Bushnell.*

BY ELLEN STRONG BARTLETT.

SOLDIERS' MONUMENT.

SALISBURY is tucked away in the northwestern corner of the state, among the rocks and hills, as if her beauties were to be screened from the gaze of careless eyes, and to be reserved for the enjoyment of those who seek them with a fixed purpose.

We speak of "old Salisbury;" the adjective is applicable to the hills and streams that have smiled to the heavens for centuries, but it scarcely belongs to the town, on the scale of Connecticut history. In fact, it might be called "young Salisbury;" for when the impulse for discovery and colonization had spent itself in the southern and middle portions of the state, and the trials and discomforts of founding a commonwealth had passed into the steady strain of established social relations, that impulse did not die; but gaining new force by former success, drove men forth from their peaceful homes, on the ceaseless westward quest which must find its end in another age than ours.

These "Western Lands" were a wilderness in the eyes of the Hartford and New Haven colonists. The secrets of the sylvan retreat were rudely disclosed during the last days of King Philip's war, when a band of savages, defeated by the white men, fled through the pathless woods, to join the Mohawks near Albany. Major Talcott, of Hartford, pursued them hotly, and, matching the Indian wiliness, surprised them at a ford on the west bank of the Housatonic river. There, in the grey light of early dawn, the paleface and the redskin met in a fierce conflict; and the paleface triumphed, killing or capturing fifty of the foe. No poet was there to sing the wild struggle in the midst of Nature's choicest scenes, and yet the

STREET AT THE "CENTRE."

wild, selected beauty of the land must have made its impression on those Hartford men.

Full of apprehensions before the dreaded arrival of Sir Edmund Andros, the Colonial Assembly granted to Hartford and Windsor so much of that region "as lay east of the Housatonic;" but after fear was dispelled, there was sad quibbling in the effort to ignore the grant. A compromise was effected, and an appointment was made to the claimants, soon after 1688. The land which was afterwards Salisbury and other neighboring towns, remained the property of the Colony. Six hundred and twenty-eight acres of land in the town were given to Yale College in her early days, and are still her property, leases being given by her for nine hundred and ninety-nine years.

BY THE WOHOOASTCOOK.

In 1720, men from Livingston

STREET WEST OF THE WOLHOUSE BROOK

Manor, in New York, purchased of the Indians land on the west bank of the Housatonic, and began a settlement in what was called Weatogue, later. Not the glitter of gold, but the more prosaic attraction of rich stores of iron drew the first Connecticut settlers hither. In 1731, the Colonial Assembly granted to Daniel Bissell, of Windsor, the one hundred acres of the "ore-bed in Salisbury." Samuel and Elisha Forbes, of Canaan, were also well-known proprietors of ore-beds; and Thomas Lamb, who, for the settlers, bought land of the Indians for "eighty pounds and divers victuals and clothes," and who built the first forge at Lime Rock, was an early owner of what was known as Hendrick's ore-bed. The struggle with Nature must have tested the powers of those pioneers, push-

ALEXANDER HAMILTON HOLLEY.

ing their way through the wilderness, for the climate was severe, and the hills which concealed their grand but forbidden rocks with dense forests were the fastnesses of bears, wolves, and other unfriendly beasts. Connecticut pluck triumphed, however, and the settlement quickly assumed form and secured recognition from the Colonial authorities. In 1732, Salisbury township was surveyed and divided into twenty-five "rights," which proved to be a tempting investment, in Hartford chiefly, being sold there by the Governor and Company in 1737. Of these rights, one was reserved for the first minister who might be settled there ; one for the support of the ministry ; and one for the school ; provision being made thus in advance for religion and education in the town, which received its charter in October, 1741.

THE SWIFT HOUSE—OFTEN CALLED "THE MONTGOMERY HOUSE."
From an old print in possession of Judge Donald J. Warner.

Thomas Lamb, who seems to have been a daring speculator, bought all the water power in town, and according to Mr. Crossman's historical sermon of 1803, was not ignorant of modern methods of self-aggrandizement. For some years the ground was burned every autumn, to insure fertile crops the next year, and Thomas Lamb took the opportunity of the bleak appearance caused thereby to assure the Commissioners sent from the General Court that the land was hardly worth public attention, and that there ought to be only a few "rights." His practices do not appear to have brought prosperity to him, for he left town about 1746, and went to sea.

True to the traditions of the fathers, the church was the center of the plan of the founders,—literally the central part here, for the General Court ordered that the meeting-house should be so placed that its "sill inclose the stake driven into the exact center of the town." There was some lack of accuracy in measuring the geographical center, but from an ecclesiastical and political point of view, there was no failure in carrying out the directions of the General Court. The land on which the old church stood, about opposite the present parsonage, was given by Colonel Robert Walker, of Stratford. Nothing could be more unassuming than the first meeting-house in Salisbury,—a log-house thirty feet by twenty-five, which was divided into two parts ; one, to serve as a church, the other, as a dwelling-house for the minister. This useful building was outgrown after a few years, but the first minister was ordained within its walls, and it was an improvement on his

THE DR. JOSHUA PORTER HOUSE.

first abode in one end of a blacksmith's shop, where stools served for chairs, and slabs for tables.

The man who was then made the head of the infant community was one to leave a lasting impression on his people, for he was a natural leader.

Some time before, Jonathan Lee, a Coventry lad, born July 10, 1718, had gone to Yale to study. He was graduated in 1742, and must have had his share of social as well as collegiate honors ; for it appears that he had entrance to President Clap's family. He came to the notice of the settlers in Salisbury, and, being of fine figure and pleasing manners, and in the bloom of his twenty-fifth year, he seemed to them a very desirable addition to their colony. So, in January, 1742, they asked him to be their minister. He must have been coy or extraordinarily cautious, for he considered the matter for seven months. As with most deliberate people, his pondering resulted in an unchangeable decision ; for he remained with the church in Salisbury until the day of his death, in 1788. But perhaps the seven months were not wholly occupied in prayerful consideration of the needs of the Salisbury church, and perhaps the answer depended on the reply of some one else, for, two weeks after accepting the other of the Salisbury people, he carried away his trophy from New Haven in the shape of Elizabeth Metcalf, the step-daughter of President Clap. She probably made her bridal entry to town on horseback, as it was summer, and neither snow-shoes nor ox-sleds would be necessary; and as all the luxury that she could bring would be what could be squeezed into her share of the compound meeting-house, it follows that she must have left the flesh-pots of Egypt behind her. But what a lasting luxury of glorious air and scenery was hers! We wish that Elizabeth Lee had kept a diary, as did her illustrious step-father; very entertaining would it be now. Probably the cares of housekeeping in the church-parsonage left no opportunity for literary pursuits; or, perhaps, she was too wise to trust her thoughts and observations to paper. She could have described the cheerful suggestions lurking in the portholes and towers of

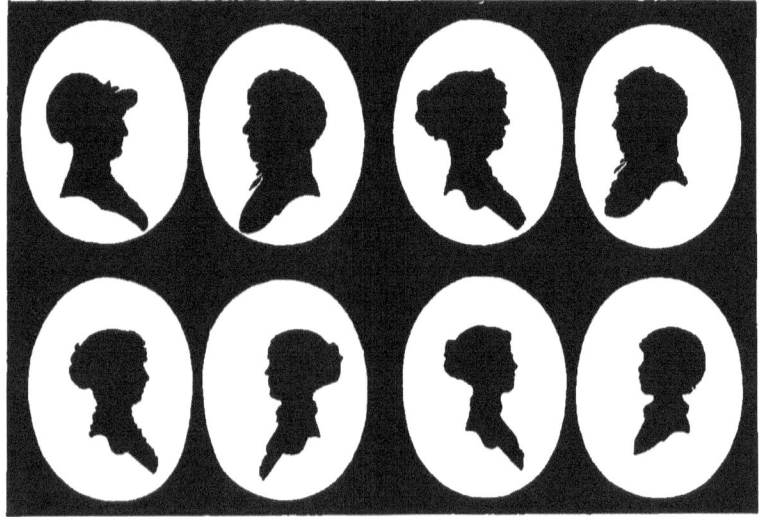

THE BALL FAMILY.

From old silhouettes originally in the Ball house . . . Lois (Camp) Ball . . Thomas Ball (parents); Maria, Roberts, Sally . . . Emily . . Caroline . . James (children). From the original in possession of Judge Donald J. Warner.

her dwelling, and the four forts in the settlement, a forethought for the war-whoop and the night attack of Indian neighbors; she could have said that the salary of forty pounds made it necessary for her husband's dignified back to bend beneath the load of his own wheat, carried to the mill to be ground; she could have described the prowling bears and wolves, the "Christopher canoe place," probably Christopher Dutcher's ferry, and the Burrall's bridge, built in 1744, the next not until 1760. She could have said that the school of the town began in 1743, and that in that year, two school houses were within its limits, one at Lime Rock, the other at Salisbury; and that the course embraced reading, writing, arithmetic, and the Assembly's Catechism.

If only our conscientious foremothers had neglected their duty a little, and had scribbled a few diverting notes by the way for our benefit!

THE CONGREGATIONAL CHURCH

The settlers were not long satisfied with their cramped Sabbath quarters, and in 1749, they decided to build a larger and better church. For that purpose, a committee was appointed: Captain Samuel Beebe, Thomas Chipman, and Ensign Samuel Bellows. The festivities usually attendant on a "raising"

CORNER OF OLD CEMETERY AND LOCK-UP.

ST. JOHN'S EPISCOPAL CHURCH.

were not omitted, for Mr. Bellows was directed to procure "16 gals. of rhum and half one hundred weight of shuger and two pounds of allspice for raising the meeting house." Besides that, Sergeant Samuel Moore was told to buy "eight bushels of wheat" to be made into cake to be used on the same occasion. The cooks had to begin at the foundation in those days. With all this, the building was raised, November 24 and 25, 1749. The "rhum" and cake, and the sturdy hearts and hands of the workers helped to make a building that was used for a half a century, and which still exists as a framework for the Town Hall, opposite the present church. The sermons of the handsome young Mr. Lee were not heard from that pulpit alone; for he held services on each Sabbath at three separate places: Lakeville, then called "Furnace Village;" Lime Rock, then known as the "Hollow," and Salisbury proper. Perhaps the open air exercises required for all this Sunday labor strengthened the sermon-making brain for activity so constant as that. Stray rays of light are thrown on the life of the settlements, by the pages of the first

THE BUSHNELL TAVERN.

volume of church records, bound in pigskin, where we find that every domestic beast had a kind of Greek cross branded by the "brander" and that hogs were allowed, by formal resolution to run on the common. A strong hint of terrors of the time is found in the bounty of three pounds (a large sum for the time and place) offered for each wolf that should be killed, and also that of a shilling for the death of each rattlesnake. Far from being the resort of fashion, the "solitary places" were then the cause of anxiety and fear. As Mr. Crossman naively remarks, "the burning, with the ponds, mountains, and cliffs of rocks, made the face of nature appear forbidding to those who were not appraised of the fertility of the soil.

JUDGE DONALD WARNER.

But iron, which lured the settlers from the rich meadows of the Connecticut and the Farmington, gave the chief occupation of the first years. At first the ore was carried in leather bags on the backs of horses by the "Ore Path" from Ore Hill to the iron works at Great Barrington. Very near the present railroad in Lakeville is the well which was "Ethan Allen's Well." It is recorded that a forge existed at the "Hollow," now Lime Rock, in 1734; and from that day to this, one has not ceased to be in operation there. There was also an iron furnace at "Furnace Village," now Lakeville. Here the Salisbury men, John Hazleton and Ethan Allen, (later of Ticonderoga renown) and Samuel Forbes, of Canaan, built and used a furnace in 1762. But, wherever the center, the signs of activity in the manufacture of the useful metal appeared on all sides. Ore beds were opened at various places, the rude machinery of those days was taxed to the utmost to make the earth give up its treasures, and many furnaces sent forth their fiery blasts to transmute the rough ore into saleable iron. Of

MAPLE SHADE HOTEL.

these ore-beds, "Old Ore Hill" is the oldest in the state, and the most notable. There a hundred acres had been granted to Ephraim Williams. In fact, "Town Hill," in spite of the fierceness of the winter winds' attack, was the spot originally meant for the town, and a wide street led from that straight to the "Old Ore Bed." The imposing buildings of the Hotchkiss School stand on the place set apart for a public square. Let no one say that the strict men of those days did not have an eye for the beauties of Nature.

Iron became a sort of circulating medium, and promissory notes were more frequently made payable in iron than in money. The iron obtained here was superior to all other iron in toughness and durability ; and therein was Salisbury's destinctive claim to Revolutionary glory.

SCOVILLE MEMORIAL LIBRARY.

We all know how faithfully the little state of Connecticut and her grand old governor, Jonathan Trumbull, were Aaron and Hur to Washington during the distressful days of lack of all commissary supplies; how almost everything, from food and clothes to horses and wagons was provided for the Continental army by their heroic efforts ; but that would not have sufficed if Connecticut earth and Connecticut ingenuity and skill had not produced the cannon to give in thundering tones, on sea and land, the message from Freedom's hills. No sooner had the "shot heard round the world" given the signal than the Salisbury furnaces were summoned to do their best. Secure among the hills, they were never interrupted by fear of attack or capture, and proudly did they do their work.

Before the war, Richard Smith, an Englishman, bought the furnace at

"Furnace Village," then the only foundry in Connecticut. He wisely returned to the mother country, when he found that he could not sympathize with the rebellious feelings of his neighbors; and he abandoned his estate here, so that the state took possession, making Dr. Joshua Porter its agent. To this furnace came frequent orders for shot, shell, cannon, and chains, from the Governor and Council, for the use of the army and the navy. Whether Richard Smith objected to having his guns turned on him, so to speak, history does not report.

Hither came the statesmen of the time, Jay and Morris, and Trumbull, and Hamilton, to look with anxious eyes on those furnace fires, perhaps to wonder whether the Salisbury iron would still be true to its reputation. One

READING ROOM, SCOVILLE MEMORIAL LIBRARY.

flaw in a cannon might decide the fate of a battle and so turn the course of empire. Bostwick Hill, between Salisbury Center and Lakeville, was the target against which the cannon were tried. Many cannon balls of the ancient kind were found imbedded in the earth when it was cultivated as a farm, and Mr. Milton Robbins has one of those balls in his possession. The old ore-beds did honor to the state in which they lay, and sent forth cannon that did their stern work on many a Revolutionary field.

Here, at Lakeville, were made the armaments whose volleys began the long list of our naval honors. From this spot were trundled out the cannon which served Commodore Truxton, on the Constellation, in those desperate conflicts which resulted in the defeat and capture of the French frigates, L'Insurgent and La Vengeance, in 1789, thus averting the danger of war after Jay's treaty;

and in 1798, when the Constitution went to sea, she carried forth Salisbury cannon for her historic career.

For generations, the iron industry has been continuous here, where have been made cannon and anchors for the government, and rifle iron for the arsenals at Springfield and Harper's Ferry. By the Bessemer steel process, good steel can be made from inferior grades of iron, and modern methods of manufacture and transportation have taken away all chance of monopoly from the Salisbury ore-beds, but the superiority of its iron is still undisputed, and the remains of the ancient hoisting machinery and furnaces, and the wan spaces of the ore-beds themselves are features of the landscape that remind us of what has been.

ON THE ROAD UP MOUNT RIGA.

But the "loud-mouthed dogs of war," and the emblematic anchors were not the only things which Salisbury contributed to the Revolutionary war. Men, of the best blood and staunchest hearts, went out from the mountain town. Patriotism was in the very air the citizens breathed. It was to the neighboring town of Litchfield that the statue of George III. hurled from its pedestal in New York, was brought to be cast into bullets to be fired at his Majesty's soldiers. Some time before, the Rev. Jonathan Lee had seized the august opportunity of an election sermon before the Governor and the General Court, to utter the suggestive words: " Dominion or right to rule, is founded neither on nature or grace, but in compact and confederation." Some Salisbury men had gone to the French war, making a part of the five thousand men whom Connecticut, in a few days, raised and sent to the field, in addition

LOTUS LAKE, MT. RIGA.

to those forces she had already sent. As early as 1756, the soldier's spirit had been shown in the organization of two military companies in the town ; and prompt response was made to the call for troops in 1775. During the Revolutionary war, twenty-one officers and more than one hundred non-commissioned officers and privates served in the army.

Among the officers were Colonel Blagden, Major Luther Stoddard, and Dr. Joshua Porter, who, with Dr. Solomon Williams, had migrated from Lebanon, Conn. Dr. Porter, as Colonel of Militia, was present at Burgoyne's surrender ; and besides that, was of notable service as Continental agent for cannon, shot, and

SUMMER COTTAGE OF DONALD T. WARNER, ESQ., MT. RIGA.

so forth. Colonel Ethan Allen, who makes so piquant a figure on the Revolutionary scene, and who wrote a narrative of his experiences as a British captive, was a dweller here for some years, and, as has been said, was one of the proprietors of the old furnace. From Salisbury went out the first efficient cavalry that joined the Continental army, Colonel Elisha Sheldon's troop of horse, which did most valuable service. Throughout the war, the gallant town gave even more than the required support to the army; it exceeded the quotas of men and supplies; it paid bounties in addition to those offered by the state, and, often when even the undaunted Governor Trumbull was on the verge of despair, did his appeal for help in an emergency bring forth new recruits, and fresh stores of food, clothing, and ammunition from this remote corner of the state.

SAGE'S RAVINE.

Of Burgoyne's surrendered army, several regiments were quartered in Lakeville and Salisbury, on their way to Hartford. One of the Hessian soldiers, John Lotz, was so well pleased by his surroundings, that he deserted from his regiment, and became a miller here. The tents of the captives stretched out for a mile or more, and the officers made merry in the midst of their misfortune, by giving a ball in the house of Lieutenant Ashbel Beebe, on Beebe's Hill. A portable wine chest left by them, is still treasured as a memento of their stay.

REMAINS OF FORGE WHERE ANCHOR OF "THE CONSTITUTION" WAS CAST.

In the words of Judge Church: "We may say, boastingly, that our mines furnished the material, our streams the power, and our citizens the labor, by which much efficiency was given to the great cause of American independence."

The associations of the famous war were strengthened by the presence of three citizens who dwelt in the town after the army was disbanded : Archibald Campbell, Joseph Hollister, originally from Glastonbury, who was with Putnam, and commanded a guard on the Hudson which captured a British soldier bearing messages from Burgoyne to Clinton ; and John Russell, Sergeant of Artillery in the New York line, who was in the military family of Washington.

Of distinguished men in professions other than that of war, the town has seen a great number. The Rev. Jonathan Lee moved among his people as a strong power for good until the frontier hamlet had grown to be a place of importance commensurate with the dignity of its pastor. He was his own law in certain matters, evidently, if we may trust specimens of his church records: as the following, copied *verbatim et literatim* from the baptismal register. He was fond of Latin, and the page begins with a Latin sentence and then goes on—"—for Ephraim Ketcham viz. Sarah & one & onemore name forgot and Hannah 65 " (*that is 1765*) —" for Joshua Porter's wife Joshua ; 60 & Abigail ; 62 & Eunice & peterBuell 73 & Augustus " ! *non memor temporis*, Sept."!

It is pleasant to see his " 44 years in the service of Christ " commemorated on the church walls by a tablet raised one hundred years after his death by Mr. Jonathan Scoville. Mr. Lee is buried in the old burying ground back of the Town Hall.

We catch a glimpse of another holy man, the Rev. Mr. Crossman, who was here from 1796 to 1812, whose untiring ministrations to the sick in an epidemic of typhoid fever ended in his own death. Blessings on his memory!

There was another long pastorate among this people, that of the Rev. Adam Reid, D. D., who, coming hither from the Scotch Highlands, made a home for forty years in this other land of loch and glen and ben. He was a master in theology, a forcible teacher, a noble man, revered by his people. He ceased not to write sermons even to the day of his death. Said one of his hearers, " When Dr. Ried stops preaching, I feel as if I had dropped from a height." His success as a " fisher of men " was perhaps promoted by the ardor with which he accepted the gifts of Providence in this fisherman's paradise. It is said that many jolly days were spent by him in the company of Henry Ward Beecher, while scouring the countryside in pursuit of this favorite sport. Like Mr. Lee, Dr. Reid was here during a war, the civil war with all its intensity of feeling.

Dr. Reid died September 23, 1877.

From that congregation have gone forth eighteen ministers, two of them missionaries : four governors, Jonas Galusha, for several years a popular governor of Vermont ; Thomas Chittenden, governor of Vermont, with the exception of one year, for eighteen years, from 1778 to 1797 ; Martin Chittenden, his brother, also a governor of Vermont ; and our own honored governor, Alexander Hamilton Holley : Three State Chief-Justices, Nathaniel Chipman, an officer in the Continental army, who became Chief Justice of Vermont, his brother Daniel Chipman, being also a prominent Vermont lawyer ; Chief-

Justice Spencer, of New York; and Samuel Church, Chief-Justice of Connecticut, a man who won and deserved the highest esteem as a lawyer, a scholar, and a public-spirited citizen: three United States Senators, eight members of Congress, two lieutenant-governors, and military and naval officers galore. Judge Church was a classmate of Calhoun, at Yale. He was an authority on local history, and gathered his knowledge together in some notable addresses on anniversary occasions.

The first lawyer in the town was Jabez Swift, of Kent. In 1773, he built the stately stone house on Town Hill, often called the "Montgomery House." He planned more lavishly than his means seemed to warrant, so that the ball-room was not finished before his death, which occurred while he was with the army near Boston; but the beautiful house, with its spacious rooms, its rich cornices and ceilings, its daintily ornamented walls, its fine hall, and its imposing entrance, stood among its gardens, as a landmark in the country, for many years. Mrs. Swift was connected with the Livingstones, who owned large tracts of land in the vicinity. In 1774, the house was sold to Heman Swift, who sold it in 1776 to Robert Livingstone. His cousin, Janet Livingston, who married General Montgomery, is said to have been a visitor here at times; and on account of the retired situation, to have been residing here when the sad news of her husband's death at Quebec reached her, although she went to the Hudson to receive his body when it was brought thither. The saddle and accoutrement of the lost hero were brought to his widow at this house. As the years passed, the house was used as an inn, and then was inhabited by some one who did not know the actual or the historic value of the mansion; so that at last, for lack of repairs, trifling at first, it fell into a state of decay before the day came when the hand of a Daughter of the Revolution or a Colonial Dame could be reached out to save it. Its exquisite mantels and other wood-work were taken by those who chose to buy them, and some of them now adorn fine houses in Sharon, Conn. At last it became unsafe, and its walls were partly torn down, to reappear in the buildings of the Hotchkiss School. The sight of the pathetic ruin must bring regret to every lover of colonial homesteads and of our historic mementos.

Another lawyer of genius and eccentricity was Colonel Adonijah Strong, a pupil of Swift. Stories still linger of his rather boisterous wit. His successor in his profession and ability was his son, the Hon. Martin Strong, whose son, the Hon. Theron Strong, continued the family reputation in the state of New York. Another pupil of Colonel Strong, was Joseph Canfield, an able lawyer, and a noted contemporary of the latter was General Elisha Sterling. All of these men filled various positions of trust in state affairs many times and were truly well-tried "public servants."

The medical profession was not left behind in the list of noted men. The first one to take his rounds over the hills with his saddle-bags was Dr. Solomon Williams, who probably emigrated from Labanon, Conn. Little is known of him except that he died in 1757, to be succeeded by another Lebanon man, a Yale graduate (1754) Dr. Joshua Porter, whose highly successful labors in his profession and in public life made his career a long succession of benefits to his fellow-citizens. What ceaseless energy was his! For half a century, one of the best physicians of his time; during the war, a colonel of militia and an efficient agent for the Continental Congress; for thirteen years, an Associate Judge of the County Court; for sixteen years, a Chief Justice of the County Court; for twenty years a Selectman; for thirty-five years a Justice of the Peace; thirty-seven years, Judge of Probate for the district of Sharon; for fifty-one sessions, from 1764, a member of the Assembly,—he yet found time to live ninety-five years, and to be loved and honored throughout that long period. If anyone did, he must have deserved a "well done" when he went up higher. Verily, there were giants in those days.

He is buried in the old cemetery. His house is still standing in Lakeville, the chimney bearing the date of its erection, 1774. The tall sycamore which rears its unswerving trunk in front, is one of two trees planted by the doctor himself. His son, Peter B. Porter, was, with De Witt Clinton, of great in-

AT TWIN LAKES.

fluence in promoting the Erie Canal. His services in the field, in the war of 1812, won for him thanks and medals from Congress, and he was asked by the President to be commander-in-chief of the army. He was Secretary of War under President John Quincy Adams.

Another interesting figure in the medical annals of the town was Dr. Samuel Cowdray, who lived near "Camp's Forge," now Chapinville. He became a naval surgeon, and was on board the fated "Philadelphia" when she fell into the hands of the Barbary pirates in those days when their atrocities paralyzed the powers of Europe. The weary months spent in Tripoli as a slave were perhaps cheered by the company of another Salisbury man, who was a captive in Tripoli, and was inspired to describe his sufferings in verse, under the name of "The Horrors of Slavery."

Three brothers, Caleb, Luther, and Benajah Ticknor, all became doctors of high repute. The first was interested in the beginnings of a library in the town, was the author of several medical works, and had a large practice in New York. Dr. Luther Ticknor remained here, being at one time president of the State Medical Society, while the third, the oldest of eight children had a romantic career. A struggle with poverty and with various conditions antagonistic to the pursuit of knowledge seems to enhance the magnificent results that he achieved. His extensive travels as a naval surgeon made him conversant with men and things, and persistent study made him proficient in eight languages. He is said to have conversed in Latin with a Hindoo Brahmin. Neither adversity nor success seemed to diminish his greatest charms, a benevolent heart and courteous manner.

It was of such times and such people that Dr. Bushnell spoke when he looked backward from the days of 1851. "If our sons and daughters should assemble, a hundred years hence, they will scarcely be able to imagine the Arcadian pictures now so fresh in the memory of many of us, though to the younger part already matters of hearsay more than of personal knowledge or remembrance. The spinning wheels of wool and flax that used to buzz so familiarly in the childish ears of some of us, will be heard no more forever, seen no more, in fact, save in the halls of Antiquarian Societies, where the delicate daughters will be asking, what these strange machines are, and how they were made to go? The huge, hewn-timber looms, that used to occupy a room by themselves, in the farmhouses, will be gone, cut up for cord wood, and their heavy thwack, beating up the woof, will be heard no more by the passer-by, not even the Antiquarian Halls will find room to harbor a specimen. The long strips of linen, bleaching on the grass, and tended by a sturdy maiden, sprinkling them each hour, from her water-can, under a broiling sun, thus to prepare the Sunday linen for her brothers and her own outfit, will have disappeared, save as they return to fill a picture in some novel or ballad of the old time. The heavy Sunday coats, that grew on sheep individually remembered, more comfortably carried in warm weather on the arm, and the specially fine-striped, blue and white pantaloons, of linen just from the loom, will no longer be conspicuous in the processions of footmen going to meeting, but will have given place to showy carriages, filled with gentlemen in broadcloth, festooned with chains of California gold, and delicate ladies holding perfumed sun-shades. The churches, too, that used to be simple brown meeting-houses, covered with rived clapboards of oak, will have come down, mostly, from the bleak hill tops into the close villages and populous towns, that crowd the waterfalls and the railroads ; and the old burial places, where the fathers sleep, will be left to their lonely altitude, token, shall be say, of an age that lived as much nearer to heaven and as much less under the world. Would that we might raise some worthy monument to a state which is then to be so far passed by, so worthy in all future time to be held in the dearest reverence."

Dr. Bushnell's prophecies seem a little archaic, but his experience enabled him to give a sunnier picture of New England life than we see in the heavy shadows of Miss Wilkins.

And then the Holleys, "shall they be forgot:
Who shall be named, if they're remembered not:
The vigorous offshoots from a sturdy stem,
Where will you find a brotherhood like them?
Strong as the iron wherein their townsmen deal,
Ay, and as true and springy as the steel.*

Seldom has one family so many able men : Luther Holley, one of the best specimens of the self-made man, one, too, who could repeat "Paradise Lost" from memory ; John M., the surveyor ; Rev. Horace Holley, D. D., one of the most brilliant pulpit orators of Boston, and afterwards the president of Transylvania University ; Orville, distinguished as a lawyer and editor ; Myron, lawyer and reformer, of whom it is said that without his great executive ability, the Erie Canal would have been a failure, and whose work as a pioneer in the Anti-Slavery work is commemorated by a fine monument at Mount Hope, Rochester, paid for by one cent contributions of the Liberty Party ; Governor Alexander Hamilton Holley, who was a landmark in the town and state for many years ; his son, Alexander Lyman Holley, the metallurgist and engineer, who introduced to this country the Bessemer process of making steel, and whose brilliant achievements as a writer, orator, and scientific man made him famous on two continents.

Salisbury has given us men of note in the educational field, too ; Caleb Bingham, the compiler of the famous old school reader, "The National Preceptor;" the Rev. Chauncey Lee, Professor Church, the mathematician, of West Point ; Professor Chester Averill, the chemist, of Union College, and many others. One of the early inhabitants was Sergeant Samuel Moore. His eldest son and namesake was a famous mathematician in his day, and has the honor of having written the first American work on surveying, a work long used and highly esteemed. It was his renown as an instructor in surveying that brought hither Alexander Hamilton for a brief time of study.

Perhaps, all unconscious of the brilliant career before him, the precocious youth, who was to win the friendship of that great man who had looked into surveying, too, in his youth, then gathered some strength from Nature's calmness before the plunge into the whirl of his life. He lived in a small house, opposite the present house of Mr. Silas Moore, and in the second story front room, he studied, taking his meals across the street, in a larger house where Mr. Moore's house stands now, the old house being at present a yellow barn in the rear. He was to young and undeveloped then for people to think of laying away wine-glasses and plates as soon as he had touched them as was already happening with Washington : but these facts are scrupulously remembered.

Salisbury has had its share of the strange and marvelous. Ghosts have enjoyed the moonlight here with great freedom. The "moving rocks" on the banks of Washining Lake can probably be explained ; but for the mystery of the famous stone throwing, no solution has ever been found. On November 8, 1802, suddenly, in the midst of bright days and calm nights, three houses in Sage's Ravine suffered a bombardment of pieces of mortar, and of stones of a kind not known in that region, continuing several days and nights, fifty panes of glass being broken. The direction and violence of the missiles

*Pierpont.

was such as to forbid the supposition that they had been dropped from the roof of the house, and although vigilant watch was established, no possible human agency could be discovered for the attack which seemed to come from the sunlit air itself with the force of demoniacal possession ; and yet, the stones stopping unaccountably within the limits of the window sills, appeared to be held in control by the same magic. There was a fine text for the lovers of blood-curdling imaginary tales, and amply was it "improved."

When the Western Reserve became a subject of popular interest, the men of Salisbury were especially aroused; in fact the track was surveyed by Augustus Porter, a son of Dr. Joshua Porter, one of his assistants being John M. Holley. The map of Ohio still gives Salisbury reminiscences in the names of the towns of Canfield and Johnston, in Trumbull county. The Everts family was prominent there, too.

The name of the town, in spite of a clinging, absurd tradition that it has given honor to a transient inhabitant, of little importance beyond being convicted of murder, seems to be another instance of the fondness of the New England people for the sweet names of the mother-country. Of all the villages within the town limits,—Lakeville, Lime Rock, Chapinville, Hammertown, Ore Hill,—few seem to have had Indian names. On the west bank of the Housatonic is Weatogue, a repetition of the Weatogue which is a part of Simsbury, on the banks of the Farmington. This is sometimes explained by the flight of Indians friendly to the English, from the center of the state during King Philip's war, and by their transference of the old name to the new home ; and sometimes, by an exchange of lands between the settlers.

Salisbury street in not adorned by stately colonial houses, and yet it has a self-possessed air, with not a trace of neglect or thriftlessness about its comfortable abodes. The arching canopy of trees, that surest mark of a true New England village, and the well-kept paths make the loiterer quite indifferent to summer sun or shower. It does not command the far reaching prospect of meadows and blue hills, or the glint of a parallel-rolling river, but at one end it is crossed by the generous, sparkling Wochocastigook, gem of woodland streams, with its airy bridge, and at the other, the Cobble, a rocky knoll, a hundred feet high, lures you with its easy nearness, and the imposing front of Barack Matiff towers over you, bearing aloft its curious cross-shaped tree, and recalling by its name the fact that there was a large proportion of Dutch families among the early inhabitants. A little upward stroll in the sunset-time will bring you to lovely harmonies of hill and dale each step disclosing new beauties. The Ball house, the oldest inhabited one in town, is just in sight, but is two or three miles away from the street. The house was built by Deacon Luke Camp, a pioneer of the town, and a man prominent in church and town affairs. Lois Camp was born, was married, and always lived in the house, where she died when very old. Thomas Ball died in 1812, of a fever which was epidemic then.

The Vandusens, one of the Dutch families that migrated from New York in 1720 to Weatogue, and other families, were attached to the Church of England ; and after various efforts, their descendants built the tasteful St. John's Church, in 1824 This "red church," (in village parlance,) and the "white church," built in 1800, with its harmonious combination of gables, point across the street to the tiny lock-up, about large enough for a doll's house, but quite sufficient for the incarceration of transgressors in Salisbury, as the visible token of the restraining influence of their work ; and a little farther on, the grey, granite walls of the Scoville Memorial Library, make a picture in a green frame.

Did I say that the shaded street was a trait of a New England village? Truly, it is the token of the careful forethought of former generations. The tasteful modern library might almost as surely be called a hall-mark of a Connecticut or Massachusetts town, and it tells of the loving remembrance of the men of to-day.

This library has a history which runs far back of the attractive modern building. The Englishman, Richard Smith, who was the owner of the ore-bed before the Revolution, was evidently a man of advanced ideas. He was not wholly absorbed in mining and money-making ; for he had at least two hundred books sent from England for the beginning of a library ; and he so interested his neighbors that a Library Association was formed, November 18, 1771. Thirty-four persons subscribed sums varying from £1 to £5 each. The book which contains the original agreement and subscriptions of the founders has been preserved. The diction may seem as old-fashioned as the paper, but the standard of good citizenship, which led men, within thirty years of their first struggles with bears and wolves, to contribute money for a public library can bear comparison with that of the inhabitants of flourishing cities at the present day.

The preamble is as follows : " Whereas, we the subscribers looking upon it consistent with our duty to promote and encourage every rational Plan that may be proposed for the Encouragement of true religion ; for the Promoting of Virtue, Education and Learning : for the Discouragement of Vice and Immorality ; and whereas the fitting up of a Library of Books upon true Piety, Divinity, &c., hath been proposed by a Number of Gentlemen in this town ; Taking the above mentioned Plan into Consideration and maturely considering of the same judge that a Library of Books on Divinity, Philosophy, and History, &c., may be condusive to bring to pass the above laudable design, we therefore do, for the obtaining and procuring the said Library, mutually covenant and agree with each other to pay the several sums," etc.

"Signed : Joshua Porter, Nathaniel Evarts, Lot Norton, Samuel Moore, Jun.," etc.

A generation passed, and a native of Salisbury, the Caleb Bingham before mentioned, once the owner of the farm between the lakes which was afterwards the home of Mr. Frederick Miles, removed to Boston, and from his new home, in January, 1803, he sent back a token of interest in the form of one hundred and fifty books, which formed the "Bingham Library for Youth." Thus Mr. Bingham has the honor of being the first man in this country to give a library, especially devoted to the interests of the young. The next addition was the "Church Library," the gift of Miss Harriet Church, the daughter of Mr. Frederick Church, and the niece of Judge Church. After some years, these beginnings were gathered together, with additional purchases, and the Town Hall became the shelter of the collection.

Then came the happy thought of another man of Salisbury birth, Mr. Jonathan Scoville, of Buffalo, who bequeathed a sum for a library building. Members of the family of Mr. Nathaniel Church Scoville took up the cause with zeal, gave more money, and have since borne the running expenses of the Library, and have contributed large numbers of books. The work of building was completed in 1894. The cool grey granite of which it is made was given by the owner of a home quarry, within three-quarters of a mile, for Salisbury is rich in marble and other building stone. Taste and liberality have made it beautiful without and within. Chimes ring out the hours from the tower, and the books go forth every day to bless all who live or even sojourn in the town. Many objects of local and historical interest have been in the cases of the reading-room ; dainty pieces of old china, silver, and needlework, old books, old newspapers, etc. Over the fireplace is a small bit of carved stone from the cathedral in Salisbury, in old England. It was given by the Dean and Chapter of Salisbury, at the request of the Rev. John Calvin Goddard, of Salisbury, Conn. Over the slab is an inscription : " A Gift from the Cathedral of Salisbury, England, carved in the XV Century." Probably the panel was once a part of the Hungerford Chapel, as it has the chained raven of the Hungerford family, and the coat-of-arms, a lion rampant amid three fleurs-de-lis, which belonged to a family that intermarried with the Hungerfords.

The building includes an attractive hall, with a piano, and a small stage suitably equipped for private theatricals, and, below stairs, a kitchen, and pantries ; all forming a central and convenient place for various festive, literary, and musical occasions.

When you explore the yellow pages of the original book of records of the "Smith Literary Association," you find curious entries. The language, spelling, and punctuation, are careful and scholarly, and the regulations show that the books were regarded as treasures to be cherished. Number 11 says that "No Partner shall take out of the Library at one time more than three Books; and if any Person shall be uneasy about a Book, he shall have it for one Copper more, and so on to the highest bidder." It is not only in the days of "Trilby" and "Quo Vadis" that there has been competition for a desired book. Two or more inspectors were appointed, who were to "carefully examine all books returned and assess damages." That their duties were scrupulously performed is made evident by the closely written pages of reported injuries and subsequent fines. The utmost accuracy was observed in setting down the date, the number of the book, the character of the damage inflicted, and the page which had suffered ; as, "1773. Jan. 18, 173,22,99, Jared Everett, greas'd P. 28,—£o, s. o, d. 9. 1774, May 14, Samuel Moore, Jr.,—Leaves doubled down, £o, s. o, d. 2.

Some men, probably the inveterate readers, seem to have wasted their substance grievously in book-fines, being frequent transgressors. The necessity of holding a candle in the hand, near the page, probably explains the numerous cases of "greasing," and the occasional "drops of tallow." There is a hint of driving over rough roads to return the books when the monthly opening of the library occured, in "muddying several leaves, 2s." Some people were evidently really careless, for we see "dirtying and tearing, 2s ;" "leaves cut and doubled, 6d ;" "nastying with ink ;" "tearing civers and outside leaf ;" (cover is invariably spelled with an 'i.') And so the list runs on. The heaviest fine is 5s. for "tearing the civers and dirtying." It must have been an aggravated offence. Undoubtedly much heartburning and many hot disputes arose from this exact inspection ; but it taught the proper care of books, and people always value most that which is not too easily secured.

The books were quite worth the care which was given them, and the selection shows great taste and discrimination. With few exceptions, the list reads like one prepared now for a course in literary classics, and the two hundred volumes comprise history, travels, poetry, essays, philosophy, religion, biography, mythology, and,—two novels: "Pamela," (spelled Parmelia) and "Sir Charles Grandison." It is no wonder that Salisbury produced so many intellectual men, when the circumstances of their youth were such as to make them carefully read such books as "Paradise Lost," "Paradise Regained," "Pope's Homer," Dryden's Virgil," the "Spectator," and "Tatler," the letters of Chesterfield, the works of Smollett, Montesquieu, Goldsmith, (and Whiston's Theory !) and translations of Josephus, Seneca, Cato, Fenelon. One book is comprehensive in subject, "The World;" and great liberality in religious taste is shown. The Koran is in friendly companionship with a Dictionary of the Bible, a Dictionary of Arts and Sciences, and an "Impartial History of the Church of Christ."

One of the oldest books is "A Collection of Articles, Injunctions, etc., London, Printed for Robert Paulet, at the Bible, Chancery Land, near Fleet-street, 1675." The frontispiece is the "Seales of the Armes of the Bishops of England," and among them is that of "Sarum," afterwards to be made famous by Reform Bills and Macauley. The book is partly in English and partly in Latin. "Echard's Ecclesiastical History, 1718," "Neal's History of the Puritans, London, 1754," in two large volumes, and "Hutchinson's History of Massachusetts Bay " show traces of much reading. You almost hear the voice of Jonathan Edwards coming across the mountain, when you pick up the first edition of "The Freedom of the Will" ending "Your obliged Friend and Brother, J. Edwards, Stockbridge, July 25, 1757." Here is also his "Original Sin," "re-printed in London in 1766."

The books in the "Bingham Library for Youth" were read with great avidity. Some of them are in existence now. "Plutarch's Lives," "Chivalry of the Crusades," "The Barbary States," "George Washington," are sobered by eminently proper work like "Address to a Young Lady," and "Human Prudence," which would be sure to be well preserved in almost any library.

Ideas do go "marching on;" and when you look about the attractive reading-room, with its rugs and window seats and pictures, you feel that the idea which animated Richard Smith and those who followed him, found an expression fuller than would have been possible for them in those days, in the beautiful gift and fostering care of the Scoville family; and you feel sure that the resulting pleasure and benefit which are evident already will not find their bounds of time and place here, but in those far reaching circles of influence which we contemplate in imagination.

Among the features of Salisbury Street are the Soldiers Monument, the old Stiles house (1770), and another old house with the double piazzas that are often seen in this part of the country, which was once the "Bushnell tavern," and the watering place for horses, known as "The Kettle." This is one of the large iron kettles once made on Mt. Riga for use in farmers' establishments, in boiling large quantities of vegetables, etc., for stock. The water which pours into the kettle is from pure mountain springs, and the saying is that if you drink of it, you will certainly return to Salisbury. Lakeville and Salisbury Center really form one continuous street of more than two miles, and the variety of trim lawns, groves of forest trees, and picturesque reaches of water is very pleasing. Near the banks of Lake Wonoscopomuc are the shaded grounds of Holleywood, the residence of the late Governor Holley, and near by is the "old Holley place" with its stately columns of the old style. Other places of modern elegance are on the banks of the lake, which mirrors the groves around it and the creamy masses of the Hotchkiss school which stands like a Temple of Fame on a very Hill of Science. Lakeville demands a separate account.

In Salisbury, Nature asserts herself royally. The little state that has given to the world the cotton gin, the telegraph, and anaesthesia was not neglected in the distribution of romantic scenery, and in this northwestern corner is a treasure of wild beauty. The town that holds the highest land in the state, Bear Mountain, two thousand, three hundred and fifty feet high, the greatest number of lakes, its share of the most copious waterfall, in the state, besides thirty-three kinds of ferns, and mines and quarries galore, has attractions for every lover of Nature. Here it was that Beecher wrote a great part of his delightful "Star Papers," and thereby introduced the general public to the charms of this region. Between the clasping fingers of the Taconic range are dells and ravines of choicest beauty. Votaries of Nature turn to Sage's Ravine as to one of her inmost shrines. Folded between Mt. Riga and Mt. Everett, the northern bank of its dashing waters forms a part of the boundary line between Connecticut and Massachusetts. Moss-grown rocks are piled in confusion, while from far above come tumbling and foaming the pure and sparkling waters of woodland springs, leaping from side to side in that ecstasy of perpetual motion that is the charm of a waterfall, or lingering in dusky, transparent pools, beloved of dainty trout. Adventurous trees climb up, taking root and gaining nourishment in ways inscrutable to us. And in their shade a perpetual coolness reigns, the glossy mountain laurel and the dainty wood-flowers drink the refreshing spray. Of this charming bit of wildness, it has been said that it was the mate of Bash-Bish Falls, on the reverse side of the mountain. The Housatonic forms the boundary line between Canaan and Salisbury, and the two towns divide the honor of the fall of the Housatonic. The height is seventy feet, and the graceful turn, the wooded slopes above, and the abundant stream churned into foam are always a delight to the eye.

The hilltops which command far reaching views are more than can be climbed in many a pilgrimage. Lion's Head, a bold, rock-faced spur and Clark's Cobble, and Barack Matiff guard Salisbury street; the dwellers on Welles Hill, or Rose Hill, as it used to be called from the wealth of roses cultivated there, have the near and distant hills and the lakes in charming combination; from Bald Peak and Bear Mountain extended, comprehensive views are gained, and the delight of an outlook from Prospect Hill on a clear day, who shall fitly describe? Woodlands, hills, meadows, villages, the winding Housatonic, the lakes in pleasant companionship and the blue Catskills beyond, are all combined as by an artist's hand.

The really unique thing in the town of Salisbury is Mount Riga. The village street is six hundred and ninety feet above the sea level, but Mount Riga rises its long ridge more than eleven hundred feet higher than that. For four miles the road ascends in the midst of over-arching trees, of vast banks of ferns with all their harmony of curves, of thickets of blackberry vines, of mountain laurel, of flowers that love the shade. Here and there a turn and an opening give a chance for an outlook towards Lion's Head with its mass of foliage, and sometimes a woodman's path leads off through dusky, suggestive vistas. By your side, for the whole distance rushes and sparkles the Wochocastigook, gurgling in dark coverts, or flashing over mossy rocks in the light of a curious sunbeam, which strives to penetrate the secrets of the place. You feel that nymphs and dryads are lurking in these depths of shade, that here Titania's court still holds its revels, and that all the creatures of the land of myth and of enchantment dwell here, having held undisturbed possession since primeval days ; you think that you hear the rush of a Bacchic dance, you almost catch the glimmer of a goddess of the woods ; and—suddenly, you come on an abandoned furnace, a dam, two or three grey houses, and a wild, lonely lake upon the mountain top. Are you in a dream ? Is this the land of the Sleeping Beauty ?

No: this is what is left of the village of Mount Riga, once a very hive of industry. Long ago, perhaps early in this century, this was the center of activity in Salisbury. The iron ore which was laboriously dug from the ore-beds was still more laboriously dragged up the mountain to be smelted in the furnaces which blazed for half a mile along the stream. The deep lakes are on the summit of the mountain ; the forest was everywhere ; so charcoal and water power, two necessary adjuncts of iron manufacture, were here in great abundance. Dragging the ore uphill to be converted into iron and then dragging it down again for sale was not so foolish as it seemed, for there were no railroads then, and the route to the Hudson River, on which boats could carry the heavy loads to market, was over this very mountain ; so that really the furnaces were at a half-way house. The name is said to have been corrupted from "Mt. Righi," given by Swiss workmen.

Mr. Joseph Pettee, who married Joanna Everett, a cousin of Edward Everett, came hither from Boston, and in company with Mr. John C. Coffing and Mr. John M. Holley, the father of Governor Holley, established extensive iron works; so that the stillness of the lakeside on the mountain-top was turned into the roar of business. Mr. Pettee lived in the large house by the first lake. The house has handsomely wainscoted rooms and staircase, and is still used in the summer as a clubhouse for fishermen. Houses for workmen sprang up in great numbers, and soon the busiest traffic of the town was in the village on Mount Riga. The Salisbury woman who wish to buy a silk dress in the town must go up to Mount Riga, for there was the largest and best equipped "department store," employing four clerks. The number of inhabitants may be inferred from the school which counted seventy or eighty. Sufficient grass was found for supporting cows, and flax was raised in quantities large enough to feed the looms which made the homespun linen for the use of the inhabitants, but vegetables and fruits were brought from below. The business of this thriving iron foundry was conducted by means of a mail once a week, when a man brought the accumulated letters and newspapers, certainly a happy contrast to "extras" once an hour. It is said that the first temperance association in Litchfield county was formed among the workmen on Mount Riga, and that in the excitement following a temperance meeting, all the liquor in the store was brought forth and poured into the rushing waters of the stream. On Sundays, those who could, drove to the " to church ; and for those who staid behind services were held in the schoolhouse or in the grove. Those were red letter days for the villagers when some great work was accomplished, notably that day when the great anchor for the Constitution was finished, and amid ringing of bells, and cheering of men, was dragged off to the Hudson by six yoke of oxen. The official inspection of the anchors took place annually in the late autumn or early winter, and was one of the greatest events of the year on Mount Riga. The testing was done by means of high tripod-like frames, from which the anchors were dropped to the ground. If they bore the blow without injury, they were pronounced worthy to hold a struggling ship in storms at sea. The presence of naval officers who were sent by the government to perform the duty of inspection gave occasion for all kinds of festivities ; and the pretty girls looked back on the balls given then on the mountain top as the culmination of the gayeties of the season. Hither came Katherine Sedgwick, one of the first American women to achieve a name by her pen ; here she got the inspiration for her story, "The Boy of Mount Righi." Hither she brought Fanny Kemble, from Stockbridge by the way of Salisbury, who delighted to drive four-in-hand, at the head of a merry party of girls. Profound was the impression that she made, cracking her long whip, or breaking eggs with her teeth when they had a wayside lunch; and especially striking was the effect of independence of the trammels of society produced by her short skirt, and that very mannish thing, a broad-brimmed Leghorn hat tied under her chin with a ribbon !

Years passed : and a workman in England sealed the fate of the village on Mount Riga ; for when railroads came, the iron horse could carry all the iron over long distances on level ground for a less price than that for which oxen could drag it up hill and down. So about 1847, the work stopped, the furnace fires went out, and in the valley below, the transferred labor found another and more convenient scene. The men took their families with them ; their frail houses, built on stilts, without cellars, quickly fell into ruins, and became fuel for the last lingering inhabitants, and it was not long before the nymphs of mountain and lake could claim their own again. All is silent now, save for the song of forest birds, the plash of water, and the movements of the hunter and the fisherman, who delight to camp here in summer. Somewhere in the woods, there is a graveyard, and two or three houses remain on the road that leads to Millerton. One is the last schoolhouse which was built there, and another in an old grey house, with a glowing flower garden in front ; within are two old people. One of the rooms, is almost filled by the ponderous loom beside which the weavers used to keep up their weary tread. The lakes are mirrors of solitude, and the forest whispers to itself that the episode of man's invasion is ended, and that Nature is free once more. An ideal deer-park, a spot for a hermitage it might be, but never again will a manufacturing village be seen amid the fastnesses of Mount Riga.

This is not a proof of decay in New England, as is sometimes inferred by outsiders when they see a house abandoned for something better, perhaps : to prove the contrary, you have simply to remember that in 1880, thirty-eight thousand tons of iron were produced in the town, to look at the evidences of prosperity in Lakeville, and to know that the Barnum and Richardson Company has recently purchased all the important iron mines in the town, and is continuing with success the business which has not known cessation.

In the winter 1897-8, occured a remarkable ice-storm; for two weeks Mount

Riga was an ice palace indeed. Many a merry party made the ascent of the mountain by unfrequented ways, in order to see the fascinating scene. Every bough pendant with its weight of ice, and every twig flashed in the sunlight as if encrusted with diamonds. When the crystal arches broke, great was the destruction of trees. One twig was weighed with its two-inch coat of ice. It weighed more than three pounds. When the ice melted, the twig weighed one ounce!

Among all the charms that Nature has lavished on the town, the lakes are preëminent. They are six in number. Near the Wononpakok, is charming Interlachen and the Wononscopomuc, which renders the scenery around Lakeville fascinating. Its name means "clear water," and it is fed entirely by springs. On its eastern side was the Indian council ground, long marked by a tall elm. Near it an old Indian burial place. In the southwest corner of the town, at the western end of Indian Mountain, and near Indian Lake, the Moravians had a mission, a "monastery" for the Indians, and there the missionary is buried. In the northern part of the town, are the well-known "Twin Lakes," the choicest morsel in the feast of scenery. They are often called "Washining" and "Washinee." J. Hammond Trumbull, the unquestioned authority on Indian lore, says, in his "Indian Names of Connecticut," that the original Indian names were "Panaheconnok," meaning a "place or lake not inclosed;" and "Hokonkannok," the "other lake." On the west side of Panaheconnok is an old burying ground which must be an Indian one, as none for whites has existed since the place was settled. The "between the lakes" drive is a favorite one, and is full of charm. On the bosom of Hokonkannok is a beautiful wooded island, with cottages hidden in the trees, and on its shore, are "camping grounds" known to many a party of pleasure-seekers. An old fisherman boasts of having fished here with men from all over the United States. Near the north base of Tom's Hill, is an old red house built before the Revolution. Its extraordinarily heavy beams were designed for a protection against Indian attacks. The cottagers on the the wooded high ground on the east side of the lake have spread before them a prospect of rare beauty,—the lake and island, the rolling, overlapping Taconic hills, Bear Mountain, holding up the monument which Robbins Battell placed on its summit as a token of its sovereignty over all Connecticut hills, the graceful outlines of Mount Everett, its mate just over the Massachusetts line; while, in the shadowy cleft between, Sage's Ravine betrays itself sometimes by foam, as does the cascade on Bald Rock. This is the place for wonderful sunsets with crimson hues on sky and lake, and purple depths of mountain shadows.

Babes Hill and Tory's Hill commemorate by their names, traditions of the region. From the rocky outposts of Tom's Hill, so much more poetically called Mount Eschol by the early settlers, on account of the abundant grapes there, you can look down on the fields of Sheffield, in Massachusetts, and far over the undulating blue of the Berkshires. Bryant's Monument Mountain majestically faces you, and you feel in this enchanted region you have verified the poet's promise:

> "Thou shalt look
> Upon the green and rolling forest tops
> And down into the secrets of the glens,
> And streams that with their bordering thickets strive
> To hide their windings."

NOTES ON FORESTRY IN CONNECTICUT.

BY T. S. GOLD.

Natural conditions of soil and climate favor forest growth in New England. Witness the almost unbroken forest that covered the whole country, with trees centuries old, yet vigorous and sound.

To confine our remarks to Connecticut, in the early part of the present century large tracts of this primeval forest were still standing, and the surveyor could trace lines of the original surveys by trees blazed in the original "layout" of land to the "proprietors." Some of these old landmarks still remain, the only living things that connect us with our ancestors, living witnesses of their toils and hopes.

While these original forests have yielded to the progress of civilization, its demands for timber and fuel, yet a changed condition within the last half century—the use of coal for fuel and the resort to the forests of Canada, Oregon or Georgia for lumber—has turned the tide, and nature reasserting her claims, is clothing again with trees all waste land encroaching upon the borders of cultivated fields, to a degree, so that viewed from our highest hill-tops a wood growth seems to cover the whole country, and as nature rarely works in an economic way, according to our ideas, we find the forest holding a low place in the estimation of our farmers, as something that may be endured, but not to be encouraged.

Occasionally white pine and hemlock reproduce from seed a thick forest growth, even taking possession of the neglected pastures, yet more often the present scattered growth of these timber trees with limbs and knots has so little present or prospective value in the public eye that the whole thing is pronounced a failure. Chestnut and some other deciduous trees sprout from the stump, and grow rapidly to market value.

The scattered trees of all kinds that spring up in hedge rows and neglected places, are largely of valueless varieties, as choke cherries, seeded by birds, and well adapted to feed and shelter them, are only a nuisance agriculturally, and from this start we do not know where to draw the line, till we reach some oak or ash or hickory left to itself in some neglected corner, that may become a stately tree, the most beautiful thing of life we can leave to those who shall come after us, as a testimonial of our regard for them, that they may find enjoyment in some material object we have nurtured for them. It must be admitted that we have too much of this useless growth; hedge-rows are a damage to field culture—they harbor worms that destroy our fruit and fungi that, checked in our orchards, find here convenient homes in wild trees of allied species; but encourage nature and the result is comfort and beauty —an indiscriminate fight will be a losing one—ten white birches or wild cherries will spring up where we destroy one. Should we not rather use them for nurse trees for better kinds of forest growth, that when they have lived their short lives they may give place to something of value, that the world will need and prize? This is only one suggestion that comes up in viewing the question of forestry.

The planting of seeds of pine among such small and scattered growth of shrubs and trees, that furnish just shade and shelter enough to protect the young seedlings and later yield to their overpowering growth, or removal by the ax before the young pines become weak and spindling, would not be a costly experiment, and if successful would prove a good investment.

We have much land in Connecticut that has been cleared and cultivated that should have been allowed to remain in forest. Hillsides too steep for profitable culture, as rains wash away all fertility from uncovered soil—or even the soil itself—and rocky land, where the good pasture grasses have yielded to the more hardy and persistent weeds, promise a good return in timber if planted with black walnut or chestnut, both rapid growers, and valuable for timber or lumber.

The white ash would do better in the moist and rich intervals. It grows rapidly and will always be in demand for agricultural implements and machinery.

A knowledge of the times of gathering the seeds, how and when and where to plant them, of the various forest trees, the maple, the ash, the black walnut, the chestnut, the hickory, the larch, the pine and the hemlock, and the willow, would enable the farmer to wage a more pleasant and profitable warfare with the worthless bushes of small growth, as hardhack (Potentilla fruticosa), white bush (Andromeda), sweet fern (Comptonia asplenifotia), red raspberry, blackberry, as well as those of larger size as the alder and the white birch, than is now attempted with the bush scythe in the dull muggy days of July and August—where the hired man takes his vacation, and is equally with his employer disgusted with the results of his labor. Enough has been done in this line already to prove its feasibility, and nature herself, in her happy moods, when seed has fallen on good ground, has shown us by example the possibilities in this kind of work.

Orchards of nut bearing trees, the improved varieties of chestnut and hickory nut, promise well to be a source of profit to the cultivator in the near future, while the grafting of the native seedling trees, so that they may produce chestnuts as large as small apples, in favorite nooks and corners, should add to the attractiveness of a country place so as to double its value as a summer residence.

I can see one drawback to this happy result. The question of *meum* and *tuum*, of ownership may arise. The small boy will have his share—as we have all been boys or girls, we can pardon this—but the Sabbath-day ranger, who takes a bagful for his family or for market, we detest him more in our prospective nut culture than in our peach orchards.

CLIMATIC EFFECTS OF FORESTS.

Besides the value of timber in forests and the increased beauty of the country from roadside tree planting, there are other economic questions of greater importance that demand consideration.

The effect of forests upon the conservation of water supply, both of rain and snow, of modifying destructive winds, is better shown where reforesting has produced favorable results. The baleful effects are more sudden from forest ruin than the happy ones from forest restoration.

It is an admitted fact that the destruction of the forests about the head waters of our rivers has resulted in failure of the even flow of water, in both extreme low water and disastrous freshets.

The forest cover develops and preserves the forest mat of moss and leaves that acts as a sponge to absorb and hold water from rainfalls and melting snow, gradually feeding springs and streams.

The lumberman by his slashing, leaves an inviting field for fire, the careless hunter furnishes the spark, or the thriftless squatter sets the fire to clear up pasture for his cow, and thousands of acres of this priceless absorbent, accumulated by nature through past centuries, all the time doing its silent work, goes up in smoke, leaving the hillsides, the water sheds of the country, as bare as barn roofs, bare not only of all organic material as soil, but also deprived of all young forest growth and seeds that would otherwise, by nature's provision speedily reclothe these mountains with their natural forest cover. This fearful waste of these bounties of Providence is followed by inevitable consequences.

Devastating freshets from sudden melting of snow by rain, while the ground is frozen and the rivers blocked with ice, succeeded by the drying up of springs, and of the fountain streams that feed our rivers, these are facts that cannot be disputed. Abundant evidence exists of their sad reality.

This is an old story but no less pitiful in its frequent repetition, but it must be repeated by the press and from the platform discussed everywhere by lumbermen and sanitarians, become a part of education from the district school to the university, to counteract the national disregard for forests, the result of generations engaged in their destruction.

Civilized man takes possession of a country covered with primeval forests and by wanton waste unsettles the balance of waterfall and its safe delivery to the ocean. Mountain torrents scour and scar the lands about the head waters of rivers and deposit silt and gravel lower down and about the mouth, obstructing navigation with sand bars and choking harbors.

Individuals, towns or even states can do little to control this matter; a few thousand acres of denuded forest near the headwaters of the Connecticut in

Vermont or New Hampshire can have but little effect on the flow of this river in Connecticut. But anyone who visits that region, who has any knowledge of rural affairs or will take the trouble to carefully investigate the conditions, will see how the even flow at the mouth is dependent upon an even supply at the source. While some of the springs on our hillsides appear to be as permanent as the hills themselves, yet all observant farmers notice the failure of springs and the diminished flow of brooks from the clearing of forest lands, even where fire does not follow to complete the devastation. In a forest the snow lies level and melts slowly, often from beneath, the forest bed absorbing the moisture. In open ground it thaws rapidly by sun and rain, and the frozen ground prevents the water from soaking in, and it flows in destructive torrents. Again the forests have much influence in restraining the violence of winds—a wind blowing over a forest is checked in its velocity and modified in its temperature. Clumps of trees on the mountain side or even in the narrow valleys often delay currents of air or divert them from their course, so that the growth of all kinds, but especially evergreens, materially modifies the local climate, an influence extending to unexpected places.

In connection with this, notice the effect of clumps or rows of evergreens as shelter for orchards, gardens, and farm buildings. This may be carried much farther for other uses, and clumps of evergreens forming windbreaks will serve a good purpose in protecting highways and railroads from snow drifts. Not only good judgment from appearances but familiarity with the locality is needed in effectively placing these windbreaks. Currents of air sweep through hollows as well as over hilltops, and they may be obstructed or diverted often at quite a distance from where they produce trouble.

In view of these facts, the United States government should do much more than they have yet done in protecting the national domain from spoilation and waste, enforcing laws for the protection of timber lands, not only for the timber itself but for those other purposes of national prosperity which they furnish.

The state of New York is setting a noble example by her reserves in the Adirondack Forests. Connecticut in her laws acknowledges these truths but has little power to control matters. We must use our influence with the general government to do for the whole country what is necessary and proper, and by a general diffusion of knowledge on these subjects prevent these great outrages upon posterity.

The sanitary effects of a pine forest around a residence is well known, but little regarded. Memorial Trees, or those that become such, having been planted by some ancestor or some noted person in past time, and now alone remain as testimonials of their kind foresight, are worthy of our care and study. May the memory of the tree planters be ever green with us, who enjoy the fruits of their labors. May the aroma of their good deeds perfume our souls, as our senses are refreshed by the odor of bursting bud and blossom and waving foliage, and as we recline in their shade in summer and seek their shelter in winter and recall with affection the planters and remember them with gratitude, let us also remember God the Creator of all things good, and who has made it our privilege, as well as duty to be co-workers with him in adorning our heritage.

"Be aye sticking in a tree Jock. It'll be growing while ye're sleeping."

HAMDEN.

BY J. H. DICKERMAN.

Whitney Avenue, leading north from New Haven, is adorned with elegant residences throughout the two mile limit to the Hamden line. Thence it continues in unbroken characteristic elegance of country homes, due north the entire length of the town. The New Haven Street Railway Company have lately extended their road eight miles through this thoroughfare and now the electric car, with "Whitney Avenue" gilded on its crest, is making its frequent run to Mt. Carmel.

Historically, Hamden obtained its charter in 1786, previous to that date being a portion of New Haven. The parish of Mt. Carmel received a colonial charter in 1757, and became the earliest settled portion of the town. The area of the township is about twenty-two square miles with a population of four thousand. Manufacturing gives employment to a large portion of the inhabitants. In the belt bordering New Haven, market gardening is a large interest of recent years so that land now valued at several hundred dollars an acre, would a few years ago not have brought ten dollars an acre.

The first settlers, who had the pick of selection, must have chosen high ground, rendered dry and salubrious, and offering artistic views of rare beauty. We find such entrancing scenes overlooking valleys now filled by smoke stacks of factories and the nearby houses of the operatives.

A little research may reveal the belongings of a former homestead. A decayed apple tree putting forth a few blooms, a lilac bush or a pear tree, per-

THE MOUNT CARMEL CHURCH

haps the cellar is not all obliterated—certainly the stone walls remain, showing where once were highways, often on exact compass lines due north by south or east by west, with fields well defined. Here is woodland and forest growth of value, a soil generous and fertile and often not much encumbered by stone, highways all laid out with enduring fence, and fields ready to clear and cultivate.

Formerly two chartered turnpike roads and one canal entered New Haven through the town of Hamden. At the present time three lines of electric roads and two steam roads have their terminals in this town or pass through it in reaching the city.

The Cheshire turnpike company received a charter in 1800. Much dissatisfaction was afterward expressed by the residents who were forced to pay a

THE OLDEST HOUSE IN HAMDEN.

toll for what before had been a free road. The toll-gate was placed a short distance north of the Mt. Carmel church and south of what was then known as "The Steps," the latter being a stair-like formation in the trap rock, which the building of the turnpike and later, the canal, obliterated.

In 1822 the Farmington Canal Company was chartered and work commenced in 1825. The site of the canal in the town of Hamden was in close proximity to the turnpike road. The former was abandoned in 1849 by substituting a steam road contiguous to the tow-path. The turnpike company became disintegrated by the building of the railroad, which for several miles in Hamden occupied a portion of the traveled road. So much danger was incurred to passing teams that the town took action with the railroad company to

SITE OF FORMER CANAL AND STEAM ROAD BEDS, SHOWING FORMER HIGHWAY AND ELECTRIC ROAD.

have the steam road-bed removed to the west far from all public highways, with no grade crossings. By a singular coincidence the same ground once occupied by the steam road-bed and abandoned for that purpose during a period of twelve years has now become the road-bed of the electric tramway. Thus we have in close proximity, the remains of the former canal, steam railroad, the electric road and the highway; also at "The Steps," Mill River defiles through a narrow gorge of trap rock at the base of Carmel, in close contact with these different lines of travel. The turnpike companies released their charters in favor of the town about 1855, leaving the roads free for public travel. The townsmen have availed themselves of the statute providing state aid in stone road building, and there are now several miles of macadam roads in the town. In the southwest section of the town, known as Hamden Plains, Robert Dickerman and a few others gave three thousand dollars to build a macadam pavement on Circular Avenue for the benefit of the farmers and gardeners in that section. Wherever such a highway is well made an immediate increase in land value is apparent.

Foremost among those who have added to the welfare of the town of Hamden, Eli Whitney, the inventor of the cotton-gin will ever be remembered. He purchased in 1798, the site of Todd's grist mill, two miles from New Haven and established there the first factory in America for the making of fire-arms, thus founding Whitneyville. The first dam was built here by the town of New Haven before 1686. The present one was erected by the New Haven Water Company in 1860 and now stands thirty-four feet and eleven inches high, forming a reservoir that affords a daily amount the year round of 120,000,000 gallons. This was the first of what is now a series of reservoirs built on different streams, that supplies New Haven with water. By the erection of the dam at Whitneyville by the Water Company three mill sites above it were submerged.

HAMDEN.

The second dam in Hamden appears to have been erected on the same stream in Mt. Carmel and used for a grist mill. Not far below this site a dam was built to run a mill for fulling cloth, which passed from existence more than seventy years ago. No record appears when these dams were erected. The first site is now utilized by the Mt. Carmel Axle Works. Between this dam and the one at Whitneyville is a dam running the silk factory of Hermon Clarke; the next south runs the brass and iron foundry of Walter Woodruff & Sons, the next dam works the Beers Grist Mill and below this a dam furnishes water power for the New Haven Web Company in Centerville. One more dam at Augerville gives power for the manufacture of augers and bits. Each of these manufacturing sites gives employment for operatives whose homes form a continuous village through nearly the entire length of the town. The largest number of employees in any one establishment is at the Web Company in Centerville.

Much of the wealth created by the manufactures in Hamden has gone out from the place to its non-resident proprietors. The Mt. Carmel Axle works is a notable example of this, which commenced business here in 1842 under the control of Henry Ives, who later became a resident of New Haven, where his successors in the business still live. The Candee Rubber Company, one of the first, if not the first concern in the country to make rubber goods, was first established in Centerville, this town, where the very large profits made in a few years, enabled the company to build the extensive factories in New Haven where the business is still conducted. Very little money by way of permanent investment made by the Rubber Company remained in Hamden. The New Haven Web Company, which now occupies the original site of the Candee Rubber Company, have in its manager and superintendent, residents of the town, who have built handsome residences in Centerville. Some portions

ROMAN CATHOLIC CHURCH AND STREET VIEW—MOUNT CARMEL.

TOWN HALL AND CHURCH AT CENTERVILLE

of the profits remain in the way of extensive factories and numerous homes for the employees. Electric street lights and half a mile of excellent macadam road in Centerville are some of the features of improvement emanating from the Web Company.

The town hall at Centerville is a creditable structure of brick and stone designed by Prof. William P. Blake of Hamden, and was erected by the town in 1888.

Prominent in Centerville, in the decade previous to 1860, was the famous

STREET VIEW, CENTERVILLE

"Rectory School," organized and conducted by the Rev. C. N. Everest, being one of the first institutions of learning to adopt military training in the educational system. The school often numbered eighty cadets and was well known and popular throughout the United States. A school is still continued in the same buildings by William C. Raymond.

James Ives was a notable example of a successful inventor and manufacturer, who spent his fortune as accumulated, in his native parish of Mt. Carmel.

His works still remain in evidence of his executive ability and are of permanent utility in Mt. Carmel. The institution known as the Mt. Carmel Childrens' Home, for the care of Protestant children of this state, is beautiful in its situation and surroundings. It remains as at the decease of Mr. Ives, which previous to that was his family residence. The building before being

FACTORY OF NEW HAVEN WEB CO., CENTERVILLE.

converted into a residence by Mr. Ives was built and christened "The Young Ladies' Female seminary," under the care of Miss Elizabeth Dickerman and her sisters. A few boys were admitted and I well remember the gifted teacher in my first introduction there into the higher branches of English literature. The "Principal" with her two sisters figure as the heroines in the book of "The Sisters," by Rev. J. P. Warren, D. D., at one time pastor of the Mt. Carmel church.

The oldest house now standing, and still one of the best preserved, in the town of Hamden, is situated next the Mt. Carmel church. It was built by the Rev. Nathaniel Sherman, during his pastorate, which extended from 1769 to 1772. Tradition has it that he was the whole three years in building it, and had to leave it almost as soon as finished. It was quite a mansion for those days and the lumber, brick, nails, etc., were all brought from Boston.

MT. CARMEL CHILDREN'S HOME.

"The old homestead, formerly the home of Deacon Ezra Dickerman, is still standing where now hourly pass the trolley cars with their numerous throngs of seekers for business or pleasure. From there have gone out a family, many of whom have become conspicious in their various spheres in the world's work. Among these were the "sisters" before referred to; the Rev. George Sherwood Dickerman, D. D., an eminent divine of New Haven; Edward Dwight Dickerman, also of New Haven, who has compiled after many years research, and published at his own expense, the genealogical history of the Dickerman family; Watson Bradley Dickerman, who became president of the New York Stock Exchange and was a successful business man of New York; and Capt. Ezra Day Dickerman who served his country in the civil war and died from wounds there incurred.

Sterling Bradley, a life-long resident of Hamden, became the sole proprietor of the Cheshire turnpike during the latter part of the time when toll was collected. His stalwart form was a familiar figure, usually accompanied by a team of unusually fine oxen. At one period his home became the country tavern that furnished refreshment to the throngs of people that traveled over his road. The distance of thirteen miles from New Haven to Cheshire was traveled by the mail and passenger coaches in those days in one relay of horses, and this section then enjoyed the reputation it has since

JAMES IVES

maintained, of being the best and pleasantest drive for the entire distance of any road in the whole country. The fine Bradley farm still remains an heirloom in the family, and such was the permanent character of his work that fence walls of stone and cast iron posts with chestnut rails remain as he built them, fifty years ago.

No man in a community becomes a sharer with the people in their joys and sorrows like the village doctor, and Hamden has been fortunate in having the uninterrupted service of almost fifty years of Dr. Edwin D. Swift. He was born in Sharon, this state, in 1825, passed his boyhood in Cornwall, graduated at the New York University in March, 1849, and settled in Hamden in May of the same year. I well remember an early call of introduction he made to my father's family, where his practice has been a continued success in relieving pain and distress. May he still have many years in which to extend relief to suffering humanity.

THE EZRA DICKERMAN HOMESTEAD.

Charles Brockett, whose brick mansion still stands as he built it, was the earliest in the manufacture of steel carriage springs. His father's old homestead still stands on the opposite corner of the original turnpike highway, where he vigorously conducted the cooperage business in making casks for the West India trade. Charles Brockett early acquired a competence from the excellence of his

REV. GEO. SHERWOOD DICKERMAN

DR. EDWIN D. SWIFT.

carriage springs, which always bore the highest certificate of quality. As early as 1858 the town sought his guidance as manager of town business, which position he held through four terms of continued service during the troublous time of the civil war. He skillfully avoided litigation in the extremely difficult adjustment of new road construction when the New Haven Water Company appropriated much of the town's highways in, and adjacent to, Whitneyville. James J. Webb and the writer were members of the board of selectmen during the two years of Charles Brockett's administration, and well do I remember the different phases of public life that often occurred in dealing with contractors and the management of public and private interests.

The highway in its changed situation now stands a perpetual reminder of the great benefit to travel, which formerly passed where is now the bed of the lake, and which in its old layout was much of the course on swampy land, and often perilous with deep mud.

CONGREGATIONAL CHURCH, WHITNEYVILLE.

The Rev. Austin Putnam was pastor of the church in Whitneyville during fifty consecutive years and endeared himself in the hearts of his people. The following extracts are taken from his Historical Discourse preached July 9, 1876, and published more fully in the History of Hamden. "The present pastor was installed on the 31st day of October, 1838. The church at that time was small and feeble. It consisted of about seventy-five members. The growth of the church during the last forty-eight years has not been rapid, but it has been steady and healthy. We have given to other churches many more than they have given to us. Where, for instance, are the Fords and the Gilberts and the Bassetts, once so numerous and so strong among us? They are nearly all gone. In their removal from the world the church sustained a great, and as it seemed at the time, an irreparable loss. But God, who is ever mind-

REV. AUSTIN PUTNAM.   REV. JOSEPH BREWSTER.

ful of his people has been pleased to raise up others to take their places. . . . . And we shall die but the church will live. For the source of life is not in man but in God. During this period of our history our house of worship was rebuilt at an expense of about ten thousand dollars. We have a commodious, pleasant and attractive house of worship, and we owe no man anything but love. Our expenses have been comparatively small but they have always been promptly met. The pastor has always been satisfied with his salary, and whenever his people have changed it as they have done several times, they have always made it more instead of less, and this they have done entirely of their own free will without any solicitation or suggestion from him. And he has never had to ask or wait for his money."

Rev. Joseph Brewster, for nearly thirty years rector of Christ Church New Haven, began his residence in Hamden in 1865. "Edge

RESIDENCE OF J. H. DICKERMAN.

THE WEBB PLACE.

Hill" as he named his little farm is beautifully situated on the hills to the east of the old "Ives Station" where is now the Mt. Carmel post-office. Mr. Brewster was never so happy as when planning to increase the beauty of his grounds. Before a tree was planted he would view the place from every side, and again after considering the effect from every point of view, he would cut a tree here or trim a branch there, and open up some unexpected vista. In this beatiful spot he sought respite from his parish work. Resigning the rectorship of Christ Church in 1881, he was rector of Grace Church in Centerville for two years, and again in 1892-4 he had charge of this little church.

Mr. Brewster was not identified with Hamden so closely as his long residence would warrant, as his duties took him away and he had many interests elsewhere. He died in Brooklyn Nov. 20, 1895, where he was then rector of St. Michael's Church.

All of Mr. Brewster's four sons graduated at Yale College. Subsequently one of them became a member of the bar while three followed their father's

J. H. DICKERMAN.

JAMES J. WEBB.

footsteps in entering the Episcopal ministry, Right Rev. Chauncey B. Brewster present Bishop-Coadjuter of Connecticut, Rev. Benjamin Brewster of Colorado Springs and Rev. William J. Brewster of Northford, Conn.

Pre-eminent among the many elegant homes which adorn Whitney Avenue in Hamden is the home of James H. Webb descended to him from his father, James J. Webb, who distinguished himself by his untiring zeal to promote and improve the agriculture of his native state. Born in Litchfield county, he spent many years in life "on the plains" and in New Mexico. His anecdotes of personal travel there while engaged in the mercantile business in Santa Fe would fill a volume of very interesting

"EDGE HILL." — THE BREWSTER PLACE, MT. CARMEL.

RESIDENCE OF ROBERT DICKERMAN, HAMDEN PLAINS.

narrative. Having amassed a considerable fortune by his indomitable perseverance, he bought the present Webb farm which had formerly been owned by planters of the West Indies, who made this their summer home. I

"IVY NOOK"—FORMERLY THE RESIDENCE OF ELI WHITNEY, JR.

well remember the place as the home of the families of the Van den Heuvel's and the Walters, who were the owners of rich sugar estates and sent their sweets to the New Haven market, in return shipping horses, mules, casks, hoops and staves. The hickory poles of Hamden formerly found an excellent market in supplying the planters' demand. Kiln-dried corn meal was also a large product exported from a mill at Mt. Carmel.

Under Mr. Webb's efficient management the farm became a garden in

CHURCH AT HAMDEN PLAINS.

productiveness. Becoming interested in all means to increase fertility, commercial fertilizers were brought into use, and to insure uniform quality and to protect farmers from fraud in their purchases, he saw the great benefit science might give and became the prime mover in promoting the Agricultural Experiment Station at New Haven. Mr. Webb's zeal and labor in this effort were untiring and overcame many difficulties, and after the station under its efficient Director and assistants became a potent factor, the venders of inferior fertilizers disappeared from the market Mr. Webb as president of the New Haven County Agricultural Society, president of the New Haven Farmer's Club and member of the State Board of Agriculture, also as State Senator, became well known near by and abroad, and left as an enduring monument to his labor, the mansion and extensive barns and large farm, which extends both sides of Whitney Avenue to Mill River on the west and the Ridge Road on the east. The place may be known as the Webb farm for many generations.

SUMMIT MOUNTAIN COTTAGE.

Prof. William P. Blake, editor of the "History of the Town of Hamden,

Conn.," published after
the centennary of the
incorporation of the
town, has a residence at
Mill Rock, a rugged and
picturesque spur of East
Rock, which site affords
most extensive and delightful views of New

Haven Harbor, Long Island
Sound and the surrounding
country. He is well known
throughout the country as an
expert mining engineer, having traveled over a great portion of the world in scientific
researches.

In ante-bellum days
when the "darky" raised the
cotton and the scion of the

SUMMER RESIDENTS ON THE MOUNTAIN.

slave oligarchy thronged college halls, I often witnessed a long line of
carriages at the foot of Carmel in waiting for their occupants, who were regaling themselves with the splendid view from the Giant's brow. To those
students from the low lying cotton belt,
such a view must have been entrancing
and well worth the high fees of carriage
hire which brought them to the spot.
The only record I know of a party passing a night on the brow, or head of the
"Giant," was related to me last year by
one of the party, who is now the president of the University of Arizona.
In the early days of the discovery of
gold in California, a party of three,
to inure themselves to camp life as
they expected to find it, previous to
their start for the gold fields, carried
on their backs provisions and blankets,
including a ten gallon keg of water, to
the top of the "Giant" and there passed
the night. I remember the light as it
glowed in the night air, seen from my
father's farm house.

ELEPHANT'S HEAD, ON MT. CARMEL.

William Haskwell, a swiss surveyor in the employ of the government, drew a camp wagon to the top of the eastern part of the mountain and passed three weeks there with his party about 1832. Mrs. Chapman made a record of being one of a picnic party who visited the mountain on the eighth of January, 1847, and again visited the scene in August, 1897, walking from the foot to the summit in company with her daughters and grand-daughters. A club-house, owned by ten young men, was built on the summit in 1897, also in the same year Robert C. Bell of Granby, Mass, erected a house for a summer residence.

Future generations will crowd our valleys and busy hands fill our mills. The cities now on every side will expand. Boroughs of to-day will be cities in the coming generation. The electric car will whir along our hillsides and bring to them the workers in the valleys for pure air and salubrious homes. Then will lights gleam from the mountain tops as from there we now see them border the Sound, the city streets and the low-lying coast line. The town of Hamden has too much artistic beauty in its hills to be always passed by and ignored by the busy crowd who throng about one of the oldest universities in the land.

JUDGE NOT.

LOUIS F. THAYER.

I deem it sin to mark or judge a man
By grade of birth or any social clan :
To tender to him favors, other than

His just deserts. For wherefore is the sense
In catering to a mask of dim pretense,
And losing sight of self emoluments ?

The storm beat reed can only show the stress
Of outward force—its drenched leaves express,
Only a mute, dumb nothingness.

How can we hope to so judge circumstance,
That we may see the sad flood of mischance,
And read a soul by guilt that may enhance ?

What moisture lingers in that cold cliff, so
The moss can cling there, feed—and feeding grow ?
We mortals guess and guessing cannot know.

Could we but see the brighter self within
The form we loathe as being one of sin—
Could we but know where that dark soul had been!

"Here in the mire rolled that soul," we say,
Throwing a curse upon our brother clay—
Unknowing what pure deed was done that way.

We read of One, whom we have never seen,
Touching and healing the low and mean,
Deem we, their presence made His self less clean?

Look in the mire where you have said "he rolled,"
Perchance the very prints it still may hold
Of one who knelt and prayed there in the cold.

Sure as a man contain a germ of soul,
His deeds will, to the sceptic world, unroll
A broken life that might have been made whole.

THE DECIPHERING OF ANCIENT MANUSCRIPTS.

BY EDWIN STANLEY WELLES.

The greatest danger attending genealogical investigations is that of inaccuracy. For some it would be astonishing to know how many errors exist in many of the printed historical and genealogical works.

One is apt to think he is on pretty safe ground when he cites a statement from some well-known authority, but even such an authority may sometimes be quickly confuted by comparing his dates with those of some ancient manuscript.

Written records are undoubtedly the basis of sound genealogical work. And whenever they are to be had, they should be closely scanned. While in some instances such manuscripts are not allowed to be examined, because of their fragile condition, as a general rule, public manuscript records are open to the public for their inspection.

But oftentimes these records, particularly the most ancient, are a "sealed book" to the investigator. For example, let us glance a moment or two at the first page of the "Hartford Town Votes," with the heading, "Hartforde 1635." A fac-simile of this page which was undoubtedly written a few years later than its date, is given in the latest published volume of the Connecticut Historical Society's Collections, and illustrates some of the nice questions which perplex the student of records. For some persons, indeed, a page of Xenophon's Anabasis would be much easier reading. Not only is the spelling diverse, and as arbitrary as the ingenuity of men can devise who follow no established rules of orthography, but the capitalization and punctuation are quite as unsettled.

In fact, one who makes it a business to examine ancient documents finds himself sometimes actually hesitating as to the spelling of some simple and familiar word. He catches himself writing some archaic form that would make him an object of ridicule at a modern grammar school. But he has weightier difficulties yet to surmount. Many of the ancient characters and abbreviations are strangely peculiar and have long been obsolete. Among the first votes of the little settlement at Hartford, here is this wise regulation: "Itis ordrd that euery howse shall haue a Ladder or tre at Most wch shall reach [   ] Two ffoote of the Topp of his howse," etc. The word "that" looks as much like "qat" as anything else. A combination somewhat resembling the letter "q" stands for, or is a hurried "th," while "h" in these earliest records is written very generally with the loop under instead of above the line. So the article "the" in places appears with this combination character and "e." Later it simplified into a "y," and "the" is ordinarily "y^e" though it was pronounced "the" as we pronounce it, and not "ye" as many people fancy.

"V" was frequently written as "u," and "u" as "v." "J" as a small letter was often identical with "i." Some of the ancient "e's" at first are puzzling. They look to one acquainted with the Greek alphabet very much like secondary form of small theta (☉) while "c" as a capital resembles a large theta (⊖), and as a small letter, little tau (τ). "S" as an intermediate letter was often written with a loop under the line, and "f" was as often double "f." Yet it should not be forgotten that even these forms were more or less variant in the oldest records. Mr. Edward Hopkins, first Secretary of the Connecticut Colony (1639-40), writing about the time the earliest Hartford votes were entered, makes no abbreviation of "the" and "that" nor does his successor in office, Mr. Thomas Welles (1640-48) in the fac-simile specimens of their handwriting, as shown in the first volume of the Colonial Records of Connecticut. Moreover, many of these archaic forms, to a large extent disappeared in a generation or so.

A few of the more common abbreviations should be indicated. "Y^e" as already mentioned, stood for "the" "y^t" for "that;" "w^{ch}" for "which" "wth" for "with" and "s^d" for said. "P^r" was a contraction for syllable, like "per," and used as a word or a part of a word. A mark over a letter designated some contraction; frequently the omission of the following, which was often the final consonant of a word, or the substitution of a single for a double consonant. Thus "fr$\bar{o}$" means "from." and "su$\bar{m}$er," "summer." Sometimes, it is amusing to find this mark employed to designate the contraction of a double consonant, when in correct spelling but one consonant as written, should be used. In the perusal of these antiquated records, many have been perplexed by apparently irreconcilable dates. Some dates as written are, indeed, irreconcilable, but much confusion will be obviated by understanding the old style calendar.

Approximately correct as the calender arranged by Julius Cæsar was, its error in reckoning had amounted to about ten days in the time of Pope Gregory XIII.

That prelate distinguished his career by issuing in 1582 a decree amending the Julian Calendar so as to make it conform to our modern calendar. He ordered the 5th of October, 1582, to be called October 15.

This sensible as well as scientific improvement but slowly won acceptance in Protestant England.

For several centuries the new year in England began on the 25th of March, commonly called Lady Day, which was the feast of the Annunciation to the Virgin Mary.

But in 1751, Parliament passed an act known as the statue of the 24 George II, ch. 23, which made the requisite changes.

It recited that, "Whereas the legal supputation of the year of our Lord in that part of Great Britain called England, according to which the year beginneth on the twenty-fifth day of March, hath been found by experience to be attended with divers inconveniencies, not only as it differs from the usage of neighboring nations, but also from the legal method of computation in that part of Great Britain called Scotland, and from the common usage throughout the whole kingdom, and thereby frequent mistakes are occasioned in the dates of deeds and other writings and disputes arise therefrom" . . . . "Be it enacted, . . . that in and throughout all his Majesty's dominions and countries in Europe, Asia, Africa, and America, belonging or subject to the crown of Great Britain, the said supputation according to which the year of our Lord beginneth on the twenty-fifth day of March, shall not be made use of from and after the last day of December one thousand seven hundred and fifty-one ; and that the first day of January next following the said last day of December shall be reckoned, taken, deemed and accounted to be the first of the year of our Lord one thousand seven hundred and fifty two." This statute further enacted that Sept. 3, 1752 should be reckoned as Sept. 14, thus cancelling the eleven days difference between the new and old styles. These facts must be constantly borne in mind when examining the more ancient records.

Thus January 1710 would be nine months later than April 1710.

Yet a date would often be so explained, as for instance, " January 1710-11," that the intelligent reader is in no danger of error. Aside from the genealogical information to be gathered from these old time documents, they possess a value of far wider scope. As John Fiske observes in the Bibliographical Note to his " Beginnings of New England,"—"Town histories, though seldom written in a philosophical spirit and apt to be quite amorphous in structure, are a mine of wealth for the philosophic student of history." And the time-stained records of town and church, rude as they often appear to us and quaint with the manners of generations ago, are unquestionably the warp and woof of our early New England town histories.

YOUTH AND NATURE.

NELLIE WOOSTER COOLEY.

When life is in the bud, God Pan's a friend,
   Quick to his reedy tune young hearts respond,
Each stone's a symbol and deep meanings blend
   With river, meadow and the blue beyond.

Far-off horizon in rare sunset glory,
   To Youth's outreaching soul placeth no bound.
Fantastic cloud forms tell to him a story
   Of castles, where both friends and fame are found.

Nor does the dreamer ever cease the dreaming,
   Nor does God Pan grow weary of his pipe.
The world of youth enchanted with its seeming,
   For Youth alone the fruits of life are ripe.

O calm, clear-visioned Age, how strange the pact
To pay life's alchemy for barren fact !

THE ROW OF MAPLES.

BY ALBERT L. THAYER.

On the old Litchfield turnpike, Canton, Connecticut, stands a country seat, which, though old, is in a good state of preservation. Hands that could not abide the uncouth and rough ways of finishing house exteriors in the early days of our forefathers have some time in recent years rudely torn away the old style blackened and mossy clapboards and replaced them with more modern ones of narrower width, yet the dignity of the old country house still asserts itself, and a refined aristocratic air of an almost forgotten past seems lingering over the dwelling, appealing to you as you pass it by and pleading for at least a glimpse of recognition.

For twenty years or more previous to 1890 the old house had been for a large part of the time uninhabited, but occasionally tenanted for a season; its doors stood invitingly open to the summer breezes, and the sun glinted its rays at hide and seek through the dense foliage of the maples that stood by the door-yard fence, and children's voices occasionally fell pleasantly upon the ear, and for the time the passing neighbor would perhaps forget the story of the past and the memories which haunted this almost forsaken spot.

At such times of re-inhabitation the old place looked warm and even cheerful, but when the cold winter winds drove in whirling gusts across the level lots at its rear, sides and front, with not a ray of light from the windows in the darkest nights or the sight of a human being near, nor the sound of a voice or even the bark of a dog to denote the slightest approach to occupancy, the old habitation looked dreary enough, and the lonely traveler quickened his pace as he passed, and seemed to see around it forms that were no more of this life, and to hear voices long since silenced on earth.

A few more years of neglect would have allowed the mosses and lichens again to clothe its sides, and some future generations might perchance gaze upon its exterior and view it much as it appeared to me thirty years or more ago, but at this date the old place has passed into new hands and has lost its sombreness, and exhibits the care and attention of its new owner who, perhaps, may here read and learn for the first time the early history of his home.

When my attention was first called to the dwelling and its surroundings I was but a young lad, and would have passed it by with a casual glance, perhaps, but for good old Dr. F———, with whom I was riding.

Stopping his horse directly in front of the house and pointing at it with his whip he said, "Look that place all over carefully, note the beautiful maples set so symmetrically on a true line and equi-distant one from another; take it all in and come over to my house to-night, and unless called away I will tell you a story about this once happy home and those who lived here many years ago that I think will interest you.

I was about fifteen years old then and a favorite with the doctor, who was our family physician, and I often went with him on his drives over the Canton and Simsbury hills; he was a good companion for a real live boy, and although he was then sixty to seventy years of age, he could adapt himself with equal facility to the young or old, wise or unlearned, and I still retain in my mind many a tale that he told which he had received direct from his father, who in colonial times had a blacksmith shop on the turnpike, and who had more than once set shoes for the horses of both Continentals and Redcoats during the trying times of the Boston siege.

Well, of course I was on hand at the doctor's house early that evening—really before he was ready to see me; he was finishing his supper as I entered, and a quizzical look came over his face as he noted my earnestness and eagerness; a few powders must be put up for old Deacon Mahew, a little white and red mixture for the boy who sat on the woodbox in the corner to take to his father, and when at last the good doctor was ready I was running over with impatience.

"Let's see," he said, "I was about ten years old, and that would make it 1806—yes it was that year the trees I showed you this morning were set out. The house sheltered as happy a family as it has ever been my lot to meet; the father was a true gentleman with a touch of gentle refined dignity in his manner; a man of fine feelings, a good neighbor and a Christian. The mother was a nice white-haired lady whose pleasant face was always lighted with a smile, and her soft blue eyes beamed kindly on us boys when we visited her son Edward, which we often did, though he was several years our senior. This youth had been away to school—in Albany, I believe—and had returned after a year's absence to gladden again the old home. As trips of such magnitude were uncommon to our people he was looked upon as a great traveler, and of course he was talked about and criticised a great deal; but he came home to work, his year of study had not spoiled him, and his hammer and axe rang out from morning to night as he repaired fences and gates and made the waste places glad. Many were the bushes grubbed out of the pastures by his willing hands, many gaps in the walls and rail fences were deftly repaired ; he found plenty to do, and after a day of laborious toil he would trudge across lots to the pastures on the distant mountain side and drive home the cows, enlivening the way with his merry whistle or cheerful song.

"It was at this time that we began to hear considerable about psychology or animal magnetism, as some of the people called it, and it became rumored about that Edward was an adept at the science, and many were the impossible and weird stories told about him in father's shop by the neighbors who came in to chat over their morning or afternoon pipe ; but as no one could ever find any real foundation for these yarns the topic gradually lost its interest, though many of the people regarded the young man with suspicion, and some did not hesitate to call him "a child of Satan." If Edward ever heard any of this talk he made no sign, and went on about his work calmly as ever, but he was of too restless a disposition to long remain quietly at home, and soon made arrangements to go to Texas, there to branch out as a physician, his study in Albany having been that of medicine. And now he declared his intention to set out a row of maples on the highway the whole length of his father's front line, 'something for the people to remember me by if I never come back,' he said—prophetic words—how often those trees call him to remembrance you can imagine when I have finished my story. All of us boys were greatly interested in the project, and day after day we followed Edward back and forth from the mountain where he procured the trees to the home where he transplanted them, so true to the line he had stretched three feet from the old wall and fence ; as he worked we would help him by holding the trees while he packed them nicely with soil, adjusting the fibrous roots to their natural positions, even digging little trenches for them to run in, 'so they won't know they've been moved,' he said ; 'they wouldn't feel at home in any new position ; it would be like you boys lying in bed with your feet on the pillows should I change them from the ways they so long have known.' And he would talk to the trees, he loved them so, and would tell us beautiful stories about them. I remember he blazed the north side of each tree with his axe before taking it out of the ground, and set the same with regard to points of compass, because, as he said, it stood to reason that *that* side must be able to stand the cold northern blast better because it had always faced it. Often he would sing to us, such strange wild songs some of them were, too, and when he roared out right lustily, 'My name was Captain Kidd, when I sailed ! when I sailed !' our ecstacy knew no bounds ; delicious cold tremors crept up our backs, and if this song was chosen as a parting ode at eventide, we hurried home closely together imagining that every shadow was the shade of the departed pirate, and the boy who was left alone at the cross-roads to reach home as best he could planned not the order of his departure, but legged it nimbly over field and fen, not delaying on account of the briers, which flourished so luxuriantly in the pastures.

"The last tree was at length set in place, and the October days had drawn to a close, a cold November had come in with leaden-hued skies, and the trees shivered in the chilling breezes.

"With regret we learned that our friend was to start for Texas at once, and feeling it our duty to see him off, had early on a clear, crisp morning met at the cross-roads to go in a body and bid him farewell.

"We arrived at his home in good season ; young Edward was standing on the doorstep with his father, his face was sad, and his mother had one corner of her apron pressed to her eyes ; a small horse-hide trunk stood on end, strapped ready for the journey. We heard the horn of old Valentine, the stage driver, at Canton street, a half mile away ; the father started as the shrill notes reached his ears ; he raised his hands reverently ; Edward removed his cap, and the tremulous parental palm was laid on his head, a low 'God bless and ever keep you, my boy,' and then the father stepped hurriedly into the house while the mother, throwing herself on Edward's neck, sobbed out her anguish in a pitiful way. We looked on in sadness ; such sights were new to us ; we were filled with wonder and awe. The wheels sounded on the hard roadbed, the hoofs pounded quickly the frozen earth, a blare of the horn and 'Val' drew up his leaders so suddenly that they fairly sat on their haunches. A quick tossing up of the trunk and strapping of the boot, a hasty hand shaking with every boy, another kiss for mother, a shout in the door 'good-bye father,' a jump to the driver's seat, a snap of the whip and the noblest young man I ever knew was gone—had left us forever.

"Letters came from him regularly to his parents, and as he often sent some message to the boys we heard his letters read ; he seemed to be doing well and he apparently liked the locality, although he sometimes wrote of much lawlessness around him—there seemed to be little of the New England law and order he was used to—but he had secured a good practice and was now a full fledged M. D. At last, however, came a letter that broke his parents' hearts ; a letter which they were not prepared to read ; a letter that shattered their hopes and proved the means of carrying them to their graves. I have it here if you care to read it," and he took from his secretary drawer a paper yellow with age. I grasped it eagerly, and while I read the old doctor tipped back his chair and clasped both hands behind his head. This is a copy of the letter just as it was written :   "TEXAS,

MAY 20, 1809.
"DEAR FATHER AND MOTHER :

"After much deliberating I have concluded to write you. *Once* there would have been no need to deliberate over the question of writing a letter to the parents I love so well, but *now* when the old hearts may break under the blow I am about to deal them you cannot wonder that I hesitated and for a time deemed it best to die and make no sign, and thus gradually drift out of your lives and without your ever really knowing but that I was still alive and well, though for some reason you could not divine had for a time thought best to keep silent; and then I thought you might learn of my fate, and knowing nothing further would think your boy had died to expiate some crime. O father! mother! by this time you have thought the worst; by the time you read this letter the hand which penned it will be cold in death. I look at myself, so young and strong, perfect in health and all that makes life enjoyable and ask God how He can let such a life go out in such a way, but I know it must be right or He would not allow it, even now I *hope* though I feel there is no hope for a continuance of earthly life for me. I will briefly give you the particulars of the event which has reduced me to such straits. Only two evenings ago I was in the company of young people about my age and the talk drifted into the subject of animal magnetism. O fatal topic ; none of those present had ever seen a display of the force and foolishly desirious of distinguishing myself I boasted of my powers in this direction and offered to apply the test to any one or all. Only one, the beautiful daughter of a high official consented to the experiment and I soon placed her under the control of my will when she suddenly gasped, her head fell forward and I saw at once that something serious had happened. I sprang to her side, passed my hands before her face and applied the usual restoratives, but in vain—she was dead. Her father was hastily summoned and he entered with his officers. I was at once placed in the charge of soldiers and the body of the unfortunate girl was carried to her home where I too was taken. I was given forty-eight hours in which to restore her to life. I have wept and prayed, but she is dead and no earthly power can bring her to life again. I have had no trial but am condemned to die, and my watch tells me that in one short half hour more I shall be led out to execution. As God knows my heart, I am no criminal. You will think well of your boy and never believe anything contrary to what is written, for with the shadow of death before me and the hope of a speedy resurrection in our Saviour I certify to its truth.

"Good-bye my father, and farewell my mother ; live to a good old age and do not let this blow crush you completely. I wish I could save you from this sorrow but I cannot.

"The officer is here, he says I must go *now*. I have tied up my effects and marked them for you and I trust they will reach home safely. It is not my lot to rest near my home, my grave will be unknown save to a few soldiers and to Him with whom all things are open as a book. But I must go, the officer is impatient to quench the life that still hopes and reaches out to you, my father and my mother.

"God bless you both and bring us together again at last.

Your loving son,
EDWARD."

I found myself crying when I finished the letter, the old doctor looked a me and nodded as if in approval of my course, and taking up the story where the letter left off he said, "The bundle came with his watch and other effects all right but nothing more was ever heard of this manly young fellow and no doubt his sentence was carried out, and now when I pass the house and see it going to wreck and ruin, and note how tall the maples have grown which he brought from the hill yonder when they were about the size of whip stocks, I think and think of the changes and happenings of life, how they go contrary to all rule or reason of our own, and yet we know they are wisely ordered, but I don't know, I don't know," he mused, "over there," and he pointed toward the Canton church yard, "lie the father and mother; heart-broken, they did not long survive their son, and I am sure I hope they are all now happy together in the country beyond."

The good doctor bowed his head and poked the fire idly with the tongs, the flames darted lightly up the chimney and lighted his good old strong face over which the shadows of sad memories seemed to be playing and quietly I raised the door latch and went silently out so as not to disturb him in his retrospect.

"PETER PARLEY" AS KNOWN TO HIS DAUGHTER

BY EMILY GOODRICH SMITH.

PART II.

Since writing the first part a friend tells me that a disastrous fire had a great deal to do with father's failure, and that some borrowed money had not been returned, so he started in the old road again and worked like a beaver in Boston all day, and at night sat behind a heavy screen while my patient mother wrote to his dictation, on the other side.

He had a haunting fear of blindness and had twice crossed the ocean to consult European experts for this trouble of the eyes. A bright light was always kept burning in an adjacent room. Once through the neglect of a servant it was not trimmed and went out, and at midnight he wakened and an agonized cry rang out in the startled house, "Mary, Mary, I am blind! I am blind!" Thus he prepared four lectures: the most daring and successful of which was "Ireland and the Irish." There had been for a long time a growing feeling against the Irish, superinduced by some unsavory reports regarding a convent at Charlestown near Boston. Nor was this feeling entirely in the lower element but had permeated the upper classes also. A mob had risen and destroyed much property belonging to the Roman Catholic Church, besides burning a large business block, ruining the houses of the laboring poor and annihilating the small and pitiful holdings of recent emigrants. It was in the cause of these latter that my father pleaded.

He had traveled in the old, old land, had noted her grand castles, talked with her sages, looked deep into her rich language and had determined to make a plea for her people, whom we had ourselves called to us with open arms and cheerful voice and make their home.

But he was startled, almost dismayed when he beheld the audience gathered to hear him in Tremont Temple—an audience Daniel Webster would have valued. As he took his seat in the rostrum beside the Rev. Dr. Channing, he saw my mother, who was in one of the front pews, put her hand twice to her head. He still retained his high hat.

The moment had arrived. He rose to the introduction of the most Reverend Doctor, raising his hat as he did so. "Ladies and gentlemen," he said, "I am so unaccustomed to public speaking that I do not know enough to remove my hat in your presence. Pardon my awkwardness and hear me for my cause." This brought him at once in touch with his audience who were pleased with his quick wit. He carried them with him holding their interest throughout, and as he closed repeating one verse of that sad poem,

> "The harp that once through Tara's halls,
> The soul of music shed,
> Now hangs as mute on Tara's walls,
> As though that soul were dead."

They gave him generous applause and the papers next day commended his lecture highly. He delivered it forty times.

I went with him once to some stately old town, riding in style in an elegant carriage sent for him. Over the pulpit of the old church in which he spoke, hung what looked like a very heavy cover, and as I watched it I was sure it swayed; I was alone in my glory in a little corner pew, in full view. I was about to cry out to warn him that he would be crushed, when a lady near put her hand upon me as father rose in safety and as everyone applauded vigorously. I took a hand in and so got rid of my nervousness.

We stayed with President Someone that night and the next morning the gentleman took me to an immense toy factory and gave me my choice of its contents. I froze at once to a miniature cooking stove with elaborate paraphanalia, but he persuaded me to choose a very costly wax doll. She was taller than I and a queen—fastened to a pedestal and her crown screwed on! When we reached home I begged for it to be removed. Henceforth if she were especially good she had a night cap for a change. Her name was Amelia.

Just as we started away from our pleasant visit at President Blank's in the carriage, the doll toppled over and gazed out of the window. Father was convulsed with laughter and a jolly crowd who had gathered to see us off, gave round after round of cheers. Many years after as father and I were walking on the Rue de Rivole, Paris, Queen Amelia passed us bowing from her carriage. Memory gave us a second hearty laugh.

I have said that Mr. Goodrich entered into politics, but after all it was rather against his will. He disliked the fighting spirit it seemed to engender between the hitherto best of friends. Daniel Webster rebuked him kindly but firmly for his stand-offish attitude, and bade him use the great rights and privileges of a rising young American, for until now father had never voted.

MEDALLION PRESENTED MR. GOODRICH AT PARIS.

This command of the great Daniel brought him to a decision and he was put to work in the Whig ranks. He was appointed delegate to the Whig convention to nominate someone to represent the ninth district in congress. On the first ballot, he was to his surprise, the highest candidate but one- of course he withdrew. Alexander Everett who had been a conspicious Whig came out for Jackson. This of course injured his cause, his own publisher, Bowen, being against him. Father defeated him, without any desire of his own, and Everett, who had been very friendly toward him became very bitter. Benjamin F. Hallett, one of his supporters and editor of an influential paper in Boston, attacked father as "Peter Parley," most harshly accusing him of ungentlemanly and dishonorable conduct. Mr. Goodrich was justly indignant and, strong in his sense of right, hastened to Mr. Hallett's home and angrily rang the bell. A lovely young girl of ten or twelve with startled look answered the summons. "Is Mr. Hallett in?" asked my father. "Mother," said the girl in a soft voice, "has father come in?" "No, dear," replied a gentle lady-like woman who came at her call, "Will you not step in, sir?" A curly headed urchin clung to her skirt and as usual with children, was fascinated by my father's face, stern though it was. He put out a tiny hand to shake that of the visitor, and with that touch every atom of rancor faded from my father's's heart. "So," he said to himself, "this man who seemed to me to be full of hatred and cruelty has a beautiful home, a loving, tender wife and children. He cannot be so evil as I deemed him. I will wait," and so saying he left the house, a wiser and much happier man. Some months later mutual friends brought them together thinking it a pity two such bright spirits should work at cross purposes. Mr. Goodrich related the incident to Mr. Hallett who was much touched, and, with explanations they became good friends.

Most appropriately come in here another typical "Peter Parley" anecdote. We are in the English Channel on our way to London from Paris. My mother's relatives, who had ostracised her for years because she married an "impecunious Yankee" had made the *Amende honorable* and invited them to come and make acquaintance. Father who was always for peace, consistent with conscience, was a mind to accept. The letter urging this said: "Bring the children," so my brother and I were with them. It was a fine day but a sharp wind had raised a choppy sea, one which thumped you on one side and then on the other, and not leave you a moment of repose between jerks. The worst kind of a sea to endure. Father who was always a martyr to nausea, without obtaining relief, was prone upon a mattress laid in a shaded corner of the deck. Seeing how pale and suffering he looked, I wanted to try a remedy, and taking a big book of illustrations with me I sat down beside him. He could no more resist pictures than any child. Soon my brother prowling in search of me came into the group and a few wandering children joined us. We were quite absorbed over the views for a while and then suddenly I said: "Father tell us a story, a *true* story." There was a traveling vehicle of the most stylish appearance, on a small deck appropriated to such, with three men servants, a governess, two saddle horses, and a couple of rakish ponies. The parents, seasoned travelers, chatted complacently together, taking no notice of two wan and discouraged little men of six and nine years who did not know what ailed them, but the motion of the carriage added to that of the boat was harrowing indeed. They had been watching us for some time and I purposely raised by voice as I asked for a story. "Ma can't we go and hear it?" said the smallest boy. She shook her head. Father said, "Emily, go and invite them to join us," and I, nothing loath, started away, and because I had never been taught that riches or rank made anyone any better than a simple little Yankee girl, I went up to the carriage and held out my hand, but withdrawing it at once I said, "I forgot that you English people do not shake hands unless you are introduced." I heard my father's amused laugh, and that of the travelers was not far behind. The boys did not wait for the supercilious servant to help them down, but clambered out, took my hands and running, were soon seated by the mattress, while above it was an older audience of which "Peter Parley" was quite unaware. He began, "Once upon a time," and with a settling down to listen and a long breath of satisfaction we were ready with an eager look in our eyes which was his inspiration. "Once upon a time, there was a famous snow storm, famous because there had never been such an one before and there has never been such an one since, though in those days they were remarkable for length and depth of fall. You little English lads have no idea of a snow storm, a few big flakes at most and a fog eats them up. But it had been storming more and more rapidly for three days when I started out to carry food to a starving family. They were without any the day before. I jumped on my pony Bob and with a basket slung about my shoulders I was off. I knew every path, every tree, almost every branch, but by this time the whole world was a dazzling white though it was so dark beneath the

THE SOUTHBURY HOME.

heavily laden trees that I had at times to feel along the great trunks to find the deep cuts or "blazes" made by an axe to guide travelers. The snow was already two feet deep and the cart path quite obliterated "—." Wot is 'bliterated?'" asked the smallest boy. "Right you are, my lad. It is your privilege to ask questions and there is one who will never refuse to answer them and he is your friend P. P. It means 'rubbed out,' nothing left of it.

"I kept steadily on with no thought that I might turn back, tho' at times the lonely little traveler was almost buried by the white masses which the wind tossed from the overhanging branches, and it was growing piercingly cold. Suddenly there was a rush, a roar, a blinding, whirling mass enveloped us that knocked me from Bob, but I clung to the basket still. Gasping, trembling, we struggled up to find we had wandered from the path and our way was blocked all about by an avalanche fallen from above. I was in despair. Never before had I known what helplessness, loneliness and desolation meant. But I was trained to quick thought and set about getting out of our snow prison, though the wind piled the drift higher and higher, faster and faster and we made no headway.

"Just then a strong hand grasped Bob's bridle and the collar of my coat, and with a wrench and a twist we were freed by 'Old Witch Sarah,' the weird hermitess of the mountain. Now my children there is no such thing as a witch. A name is fastened on some poor creature whose face is marred, whose reason is broken by sorrow. Let us beware how we fix upon anyone so harsh and cruel a name.

"Sarah, by main effort dragged us into a sheltered spot, and while I was trying to get back my breath, she fed Bob a loaf of bread, bathed his forehead and lips with snow water until he was some what restored from his exhaustion.

"'Go back, boy,' she said, 'to your sheltered home and thank God you are not without one; also that Witch Sarah has saved you from a snowy grave. Hasten for you can go no further. Turn about while you may. In an hour disaster and death will be abroad in the forest.'

"The pony picked up his courage and his feet together and in three laborious hours—as the wind was now with us—we reached home, where they were beginning to be greatly alarmed, and this is the tale of the historic storm of 1807." As he closed the parents of the boys at once introduced themselves and urged father to use their carriage to our hotel. He did not accept this most generous offer but did enjoy a glass of most excellent port wine from their elaborate medicine chest which was built under the front and back seats of the carriage. This was divided into compartments with silver boxes and crests and cut glass bottles with monograms and every drug useful or otherwise known to man.

"Yours is elegant but I think ours is more convenient," I said, "show it to them please, father." He laughed and touched a strap across his shoulder holding a morocco wallet of about a foot long and three inches high inside of which was a tin box with a cover on hinges. There were five parts within. In one, gum camphor, in a second, rhubarb, third guaicum, fourth sol-volatile and fifth laudanum. These were balanced by a traveling flask of brandy. "And with these," said by father, "I can circumnavigate the globe."

A rare evening was arranged for us in Florence, Italy, when Mr. Goodrich and his family was passing a winter there. It was planned by Charles Lever, the clever Irish author at Casa Guidi. Mr. Browning brought his invalid wife into the drawing room and placed her in her own peculiar chair. There were gathered there the Storys, Gibson and Powers the sculptors, both Tennysons—and I liked Frederic best, who has just died,—James Russell Lowell, Lamertine, Longfellow and Buchanan Read and family, Trollope and others. Father was seated on a hassock with two ranges of children about him—and many of a larger growth around the room. He was to tell them stories, and they wanted to know particularly about himself. So he told these people—many of them English -of his going to fight when Tryon burned Danbury and had appeared with his fleet off New Haven during the revolution. How one night he was sentinel and a movement in the thick brush near him caused him to challenge. No answer. '"Who goes there? Advance and give the countersign, or I fire,' and I did. Great excitement. We heard calvary retreating it was a disgusted cow with her calf galloping down the road."

He told them how hard he had worked to reach his present position in letters as the veritable and only Peter Parley and a sanctimonious fraud, an Englishman by name of "Old Mogridge" was writing unwholesome books for children under his name, making thousands of illegal dollars thereby to the detriment of father's purse. We closed with an hour of social enjoyment and left early as Mrs. Browning was an invalid. This evening was long talked of in Florence.

After our return to our summer home at Courbevoir, near Paris, a shattered man enfeebled by grief came to our door. It was the poet-painter, Buchanan Read, who had left his tiny wife and child in a cholera grave at Rome. We took him in and comforted him.

BURIAL LOT AT SOUTHBURY.

We were in America and heard her sing, when Jenny Lind made her debut at Castle Garden. Never had I seen my father so disappointed. He told Barnum that he did not consider her a prima donna; that she had little presence, not much magnetism and her appearance was anything but striking. Barnum winked and said, "So?"

A sad event occurred when we were spending a few days at Fire Island. There came a night when there was a fearful storm and a ship in dire distress was firing signals. The next morning it was learned that Margaret Fuller Ossoli and her husband and child had sunk to a watery grave.

"It was awful, sir," said one of the wrecked sailors talking to my father the next day, "awful indeed. They could all have been saved if Mme. Ossoli would have cast off her heavy garments, but she did not and so carried the young and loyal husband down with her, and between them they carried that pretty bairn."

At the beginning of the second year of Mr. Fillmore's incumbency we were in Paris and Mr. Goodrich consul. Never was there a more acceptable one. He had keen foresight, sagacity, quick wit, suavity, authority when needed and a most friendly and sympathetic soul. All these talents he used for the benefit of his countrymen and when he was superceded, great was the regret.

A medallion of himself by Adam Salomon, a famous sculptor, was presented him, of the size of a large dinner plate of silver triple gilt and elegantly framed. A petition to retain him signed by two hundred and fifty French and American merchants was sent to the United States in vain. During his consulate, Henry Shelton Sanford, who was United States attache at Paris, found my father a staying power. Sanford was stiff, unyielding and his countrymen feared to ask favors of him. He was born in the "Hollow" in ancient Woodbury, in a little house where was manufactured the tinware for all the neighboring towns and here were found the supplies for the calithumpian serenades for half the county.

During all our years abroad my parents had many young people under their fostering care. I mention but two of them. Elsie Henslee the *protegee* of many Boston gentlemen, who studied music at the Paris "Conservatoire," became a prima donna, and married the then King of Portugal, and is now, if I mistake not, the Countess Elda, much beloved and admired at Lisbon, where she is now one of the court favorites. The second was Rosalie Benedict, only daughter of Mr. and Mrs. Abner Benedict of New York. They brought her over and placed her in school, where after they left, my mother found the girl ill with nostalgia. She at once brought her to our home. I shared my pretty room with her and we were a happy pair, until one fall day, when the news came of the awful disaster to the "Artic," in which her parents had sailed. It became my painful lot to break to her the tidings of her double loss. Some fiend had sent her a package of newspaper cuttings in which it was told that the last seen of her parents, they were on their knees on a raft and the sharks clambering over the sides. I held her close to my heart for three days and thus saved her from insanity, but among the many sore hurts of my life, this one stands preeminent.

Our family returned to the United States when the first break in the household began. The children scattered to different homes. Then my father decided to give up the New York house and bought a quaint old brick mansion at Southbury, Conn., which he improved and beautified to his heart's content.

At this time his mind was full of a great work he was preparing, a natural history in two large volumes, in which the engravings alone cost thousands of dollars. He rode on his bay mare through woods and over streams for two summers, studying every animal or insect with which he came in contact. He was called "the old gentleman" for twenty miles around and at every lane and by-way he was known and loved. Women brought him cookies and milk, and he enjoyed them in the shade by their doors, and the children hunted bugs and birds for him to study, to which he was giving up the last years of his life. This work was a most arduous one and he overtaxed his strength bringing back the old distressed turns of his early manhood. The book was dedicated to Agassiz, who himself commended it as a most rare and exhaustive work—the best work of a great man.

The quiet people of the little village of Southbury had rather dreaded the coming of a city family to their midst, but they had learned one and all to value him as a neighbor and friend, and when one day in May, 1860, the stage driver came up the street calling out "Mr. Goodrich is dead, Mr. Goodrich is dead in New York," there was mourning indeed; but it was only too true. He had gone down to the city Monday on business and on Wednesday had passed away while quietly talking with my brother in his home. Most of the family were at Southbury.

Stern as was heaven's decree in thus calling him from us, we did not repine.

He had died in his full vigor of mind, all in a moment as he had often wished. With that sad Civil War coming on he would have been heartbroken, for he dearly loved the Union, and was himself greatly beloved in the South, where his books were in general use.

His remains were borne to St. Bartholomew's Church in the city where services were held, and he lay for twenty-four hours while sad crowds passed about him. General Dix, the publishers Appleton, Derby, Goupil, and many friends were his pall bearers. The "Marble Cemetery" offered us a lot, but he had elected to lie in "God's Acre" where the sun shines and where the rain falls upon the grassy mound. Mr. Hoey, president of Adams Express Company had the body reverently and tenderly borne to his Southbury home free of charge and on Sunday the 13th of May, we laid him at rest. Crowds had been gathering, churches were closed for twenty miles away—on the sloping hill-sides in front of the house were waiting masses who had come to pay their last tribute to a great man, known the world over as the "Children's Teacher and Friend." After short services at the house, friendly farmers and neighbors took up the casket. Everyone had taken a last sad look at that clear cut face with the color still in the cheeks and the lips as though ready to speak. Children led the way to the adjacent village cemetery, strewing flowers and singing as they moved. For the last time I took my brother's arm, the brother who has been with me through every page. Oh ye, who are blessed with this relationship, cherish it in your heart. There is none more generous, more lasting, more true.

The season was advanced and the "blossom wind" was shedding the petals from the apple orchard 'neath which we passed—the casket was covered with the rose colored down fall. In a lot above the side hill in full view of the main street, all the mortal remains of the Hon. Samuel Griswold Goodrich were laid. Sunrise and sunset alike glow over the mound. Stately robins seem watching there. Wild vines and blossoms trail across the lot, and he is surrounded by nature's freedom, which he loved. And there we bade him adieu.

His faithful wife, Mary Boott Goodrich, of London, England, was buried near him in 1868.

A simple slab of Italian marble marks his resting place, name and date, without eulogy, but a dog-eared book is a speaking emblem of his life work.

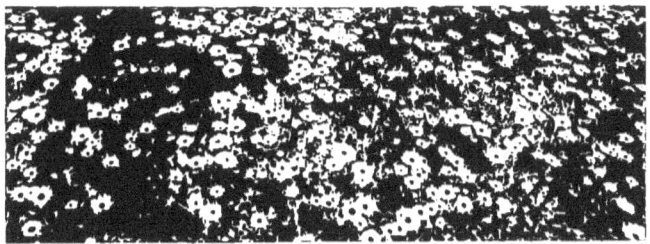

CONNECTICUT ALMANACS OF LAST CENTURY.

BY ALBERT C. BATES.

About a half century ago the old fashioned almanac, such as was known to our ancestors, was largely pushed aside by the more ambitious advertising almanac whose reason for being was to make known the unrivaled virtues of somebody's bitters or pills. This in turn has been superceded by the ever present calendar which now greets the eye with the unrivaled advantages of some life or fire insurance company.

In former times the almanac occupied an important and conspicuous position in the household economy. Hanging in its accustomed place beside the great fireplace the margins of its pages were most convenient for jotting down miscellaneous notes and memoranda, and with such they are often filled. Household receipts, the text of Sunday's sermon, when the sheep were turned into the mountain pasture, the death of a neighbor, an unusually severe storm, the appointment of fast day—all were noted in the almanac. Sometimes they were interleaved with blank pages on which more extended notes were entered, forming often a daily journal of important happenings and notes on the weather.

The weather predictions of the old almanacs are often startling, and the usual arrangement of printing by which one prediction was made to extend over several days gave an increased opportunity for it to prove correct. A few of the more curious are here given.

The weather grows more unsettled.
The clouds denote wind and rain.
Pleasant sun.
Looks likely for rain but there will probably be none.
It may thunder in some places.
Perhaps smoky air.
Now comes rain.
A pretty warm day (February 15).
Unusual weather.
It may gather up for a storm.

These little pamphlets usually of from 16 to 24 pages and about $3\frac{1}{2}$ by inches in size contain much that is of interest. First comes the usual data, such as the sun's and moon's rising and setting, the movements of the planets tides, eclipses, and church days. Then information of the dates of the freemen's meetings, the times and places of the setting of the courts, interest tables, the principal roads with the distances from town to town, and sometimes the names of the innkeepers in the different towns. And last come sketches, anecdotes, and items of information, interest, and amusement, some of which would hardly find a place in publications of the present day. There is usually a poem, stilted in style, with full rounded periods, and more or less solemn in subject. One commences thus:

Begin the year with serious thought,
How many the last to the grave were brought,
Thy turn may come thou knowest not when,
Be sure thou art prepared then.

In England almanacs have been known since before the invention of printing. The first printing press within what is now the United States was set up in Boston in 1639, and an almanac was printed the same year.

The first Connecticut man to compile an almanac was John Tulley, who lived at Saybrook Point He was born in England in 1638, was for many years town clerk of Saybrook, and was a man of superior education. He tried his hand at almanac making as early as 1677, a manuscript almanac by him for that year being still preserved.* In 1687 his first printed almanac appeared, and the series was continued until 1702, when he "dyed as he was finishing this Almanack; and so leaves it as his last Legacy to his Country-men." "This almanac for 1687 was the first New England almanac in which the holidays of the Episcopal church were entered in the calendar, and the first

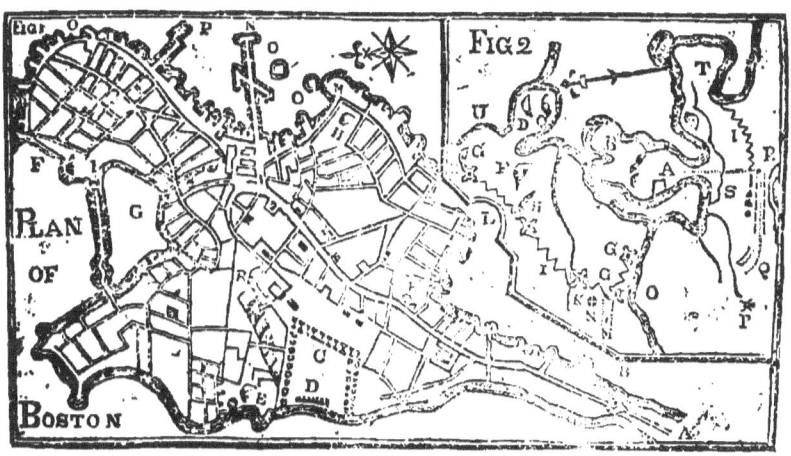

MAP OF BOSTON,
From Bickerstaff's Almanac for 1770.

Figure 1. A, The Neck; B, Fortification; C, Commons; D, Battery; E, Magazine; F, Charleston Ferry; G, Mill Pond; H, Fort Hill; I, Corpse Hill; K, Liberty Tree; L, Windmill Point; M, South Battery; N, Long Wharf; OO, Island Wharfs; P, Hancock's Wharf; Q, North Battery; R, Beacon Hill.
Figure 2. A, Boston; B, Corpse Hill; C, Charleston; D, Bunker's Hill; E, Winter Hill; F, Cobble Hill; GGG, Forts; H, Prospect Hill and Upper Fort; II, Provincial Lines; K, Lower Fort; M, Main Guard; N, Cambridge College; O, Charles River; P, Pierpoint's Mill; Q, Fasciene Battery; R, Roxbury Hill Lines; S, Ministerial Army's Lines; T, Dorchester Hill and Point; U, Mystic River.

that began the year with the month of January. Opposite to Jan 30, is the entry, 'King Charles murdered.'" At this time there were two recognized methods of reckoning time, the hisorical which commenced as now on the first

*Statement of Mr. James Terry of New Haven.

day of January, and the ecclesiastical year which commenced on the twenty-fifth of March. In all the earlier seventeenth century almanacs March appears first in the arrangement of the months, while January and February follow December. There being no printing press in Connecticut all of Tulley's almanacs were printed in Massachusetts, either in Boston or Cambridge.

Thomas Short, in 1709, removed from Boston to New London and established the first printing press in Connecticut An almanac by Daniel Travis appeared that year with the imprint New London. In spite of the imprint the almanac was doubtless printed by William Bradford in New York, where he printed an almanac the same year with the imprint, "Printed and sold by N. Boon, Boston."

In 1713, Short having previously died, Timothy Green of Boston, whose father and grandfather had been printers before him, removed to New London and set up a press. There he printed Moss' almanac for 1720, perhaps the first almanac printed in the state. Rev. Joseph Moss, the author of the almanac, was a graduate of Harvard in 1699 and received the degree of M. A. from Yale in 1702 From his graduation until 1706 he was Rector of the Hopkins Grammar School in New Haven, and from that time until 1731 was the settled pastor over the church in Derby.

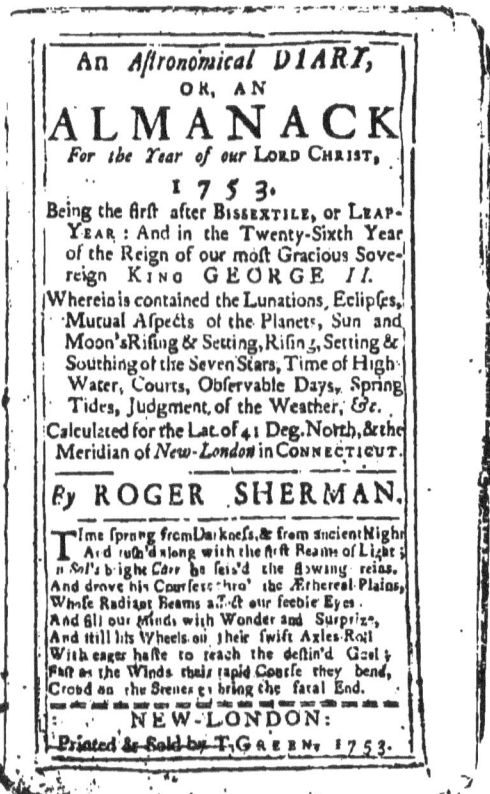

Robert Treat of Milford, grandson of the governor of the same name, a graduate of Yale in 1718 and tutor in the college in 1724 and 1725, was the author of an Almanack of Celestial Motions for the years 1723, 1725, 1727, and perhaps for the intervening years. These were printed by Green at New London.

Roger Sherman of New Milford, the well known statesman and signer of the Declaration of Independence, appears in 1750 in the role of almanac maker.

His almanacs were continued until 1761, with the possible exceptions of 1757 and 1759. They were printed in New York, Boston, New London, and New Haven, sometimes simultaniously in more than one place. In 1753 and 1754 they were printed in New London by Green, and in 1756 and 1758 in New Haven by James Parker. Mr. Sherman's almanac makes this remarkable prediction for Dec. 2, 1754: "Freezing cold weather, after which comes storm of snow, but how long after I don't say." Boutell in his life of Sherman gives the following anecdote. He had been holding court in the forenoon of a very fair day. When the court adjourned for dinner, some of the young lawyers reminded him that his almanac predicted a heavy rain for that day. He said nothing but came into court after dinner with his cloak. Before the adjournment at night a severe storm came up, in which all the company at the Court House were drenched, except Mr. Sherman, who was protected by his cloak.

Miss Caulkins says that beginning with 1751 an almanac was annually printed at New London, the issue for the first few years being by James Davis. This is apparently an error as his almanac for 1755 printed by T. and J. Green at New London says that "This is the First Off-Spring of a Young Parent."

In 1726 Nathaniel Ames of Bridgewater, Mass., issued the first of the series of almanacs which was continued by his son of the same name until 1774, and became the most popular almanac in New England. They were originally printed in Boston, but their popularity caused them to be reprinted in many places. The earliest Connecticut reprint was at New

Haven commencing in 1755 and continuing until 1774, printed first by J. Parker and later by Benjamin Mecom and by T. & S. Green; next at New London by T. Green, from 1758 to 1774; next at Hartford by T. Green commencing in 1765 and continued from 1771 by Ebenezer Watson. After Ames' death in 1774 the publication was continued as "Watson's Register and Connecticut Almanack," the calculations being by Nehemiah Strong of Yale College. Watson dying in 1777 the series was continued as the Connecticut Almanack until 1782 when Strong began to issue them under his own name.

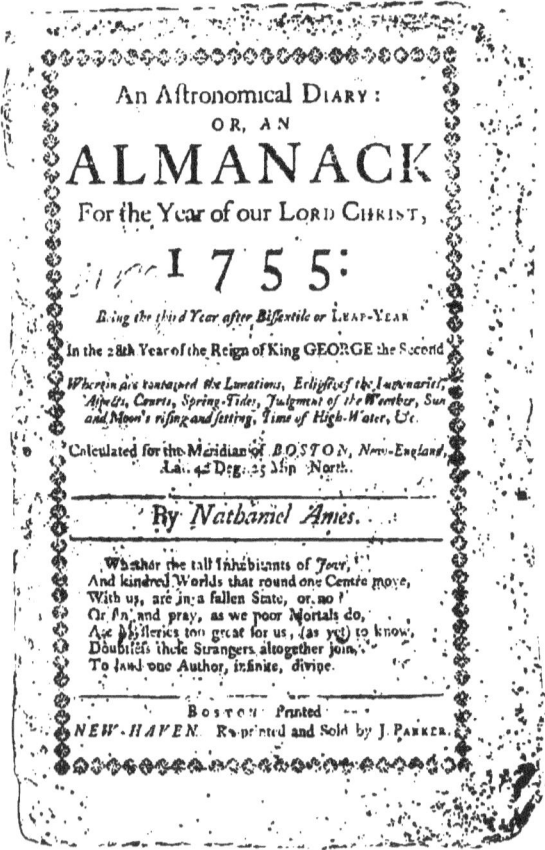

An "American Almanack" described as by "N. Ames, Esq., Professor in the College of Berlin," was published by T. Collier in Litchfield for 1790, 1791, and possibly for a few years earlier. The N. Ames Esq., was probably Nehemiah Strong, in whose name Collier printed an "Astronomical Diary Calendar or Almanack" for 1792 and 1793, and "The Connecticut, Massachusetts, New York and Vermont Almanack" for 1795. After serving as a tutor at the College, then as the settled minister at Turkey Hills, Mr. Strong returned to Yale and was elected to the Professorship of Mathematics and Natural Philosophy, which position he retained from 1770 to 1781. Later he resided successively at Newtown, New Milford, and Stratford, where he died in 1807. After having tried his hand upon the calculations for Watson's Register Prof. Strong in 1782 began the publication in Hartford of a series of almanacs under his own name, which he continued until his death; printed until 1770 by Hudson and Goodwin and later by N. Patten, and also beginning with 1787 by Elisha Babcock. Commencing with 1800 he also published at

Hartford a diminutive "Connecticut Pocket Almanac." Another series described as by "Isaac Bickerstaff," beginning also in 1782, and continuing through the century was printed at Hartford sometimes by Nathaniel Patten and sometimes by Elisha Babcock. It is believed that Strong was responsible for at least a portion of this series.* Still another series of which he was probably the author appeared in New Haven as by "Hosea Stafford," commencing in 1776 and continuing into this century.

The pseudonym "Isaac Bickerstaff" had been used as early as 1768 on a series of almanacs compiled by Benjamin West and printed in Providence, R. I. It was also used on a series printed in Norwich by John Trumbull from 1776 to 1798; but whether the Norwich "Isaac" was West, Strong or some other compiler it is impossible now to determine. In the number for 1777 Bickerstaff says in an address "to the reader:" "The general approbation you have been pleased to favour me with, has excited the envy of some, and drawn upon me the malice of others. They say that there is no such man as I am; and have spread this notion so thoroughly in the country, that I have been frequently told it to my face by those that do not know me. Therefore to vindicate my own honor, I make this public declaration, which I desire may 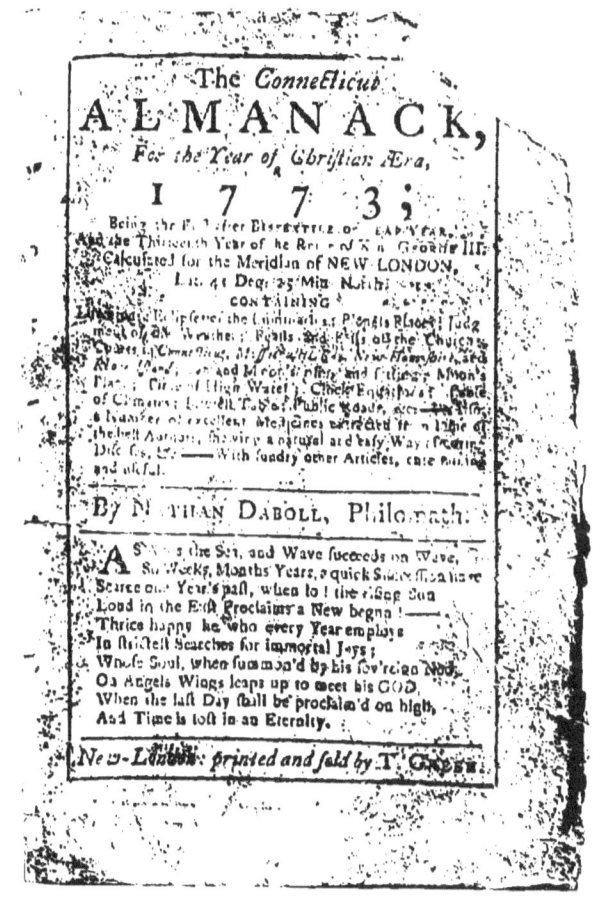 be believed viz.: That what I have written heretofore, and do now write, neither was or is written by any other man or men, person or persons whatsoever."

*Note by the late J. Hammond Trumbull.

"The public have been greatly imposed upon by some late pretenders to this art"—almanac making—says Joseph Prindle of New Milford in the introduction to his issue for 1760, which was printed by Parker at New Haven; and Prindle appears to believe that all previous errors have been corrected in his work. The "College Almanack" for 1761 and 1762, printed at New Haven, was "by a student at Yale College" who has succeeded well in concealing his identity. "Poor Roger's American Country Almanack" for 1763, was printed at New Haven. It is said to have been the work of one Moore, and the name is evidently an imitation of the "Poor Richard" almanacs issued at an earlier date by Benjamin Franklin. Samuel Ellsworth of Simsbury issued an "Astronomical Diary" for four years commencing with 1765. They were printed at Hartford by T. Green.

"Navigation, surveying, gauging, dialing and other mathematics" were taught, as he announces, by Clark Elliot of New London, who beginning in 1767 was the compiler of "The Connecticut Almanack." Green the printer in announcing this almanac says that "it is hoped that all persons who are well wishers to the government will discountenance the bringing of other almanacs into it for the future; especially so long as they can be supplied on as easy terms with those of our own production." Nevertheless in the same announcement he proposes to reprint "a sufficient number" of Ames' almanacs "to supply all our customers who will not be contented without them." The issue was continued until 1770 with Elliot's name, when it is said that he made an error in his calculations and afterwards refused to allow his name to appear upon the title; and the issue was continued by him, commencing in 1772, under the pseudonym of Edmund Freebetter.

Nathan Daboll of Groton commenced in 1773 the most popular series of almanacs ever issued in this state, the publication of which has been continued by his son and grandson successively to the present day. His name is found on the issues for 1773 and 1775, and then disappears until 1793, which is the beginning of an unbroken series with the Daboll name.

Elliott and Daboll both appear to have had an interest in the series of "Edmund Freebetter" almanacs which were issued at New London from 1772 ts 1792, with the possible exception of 1775. The earlier years were doubtless the work of Elliot, the issue for 1774 being announced as by one "whose calculations, under a different signature, have for several years been greatly approved of throughout New England." The calculations for the 1779 issue "are the performance of the most approved astronomer in this state." The later years of the series are known to have been the work of Daboll; but when he superceded Elliot it is impossible to determine. Possibly Daboll was a pupil of Elliott, that each had a pecuniary interest in the publication, and that they worked together—the pupil learning and gradually assuming the labor of the compilations which had first been made by the older man. A Freebetter almanac was also printed at Hartford for 1777, and at Norwich for 1778, 1785, 1786, and perhaps other years.

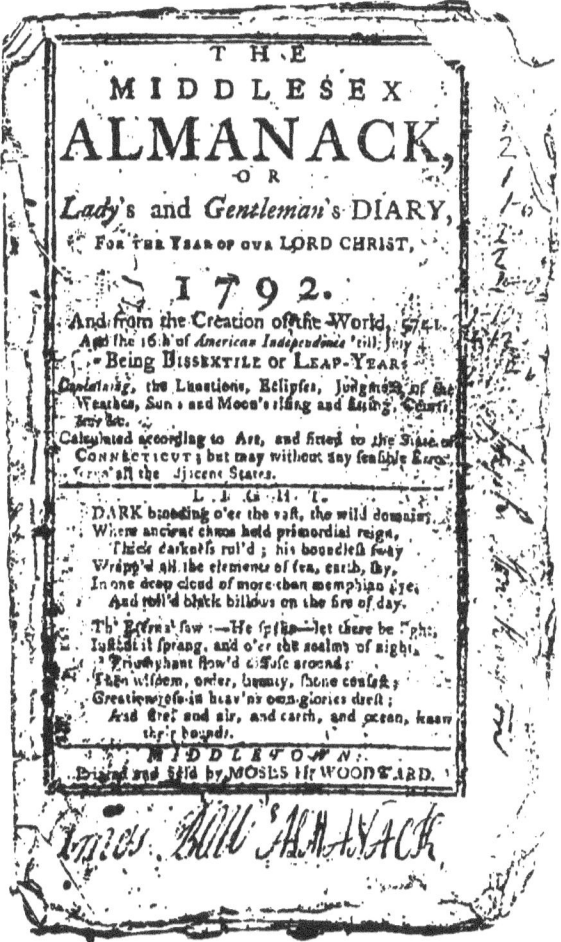

Next comes an almanac by Nathaniel Low calculated for the meridian of Boston, which was reprinted at Hartford by Watson for the years 1772, 1773, 1774. Joseph Perry of New Haven issued an "Astronomical Diary" as early as 1773 and as late as 1784; but it is uncertain whether or not it was issued for all the intervening years. An almanac for 1775 by Lemuel Warren was calculated not only for the meridian of Norwich but "also for the meridian of mirth and jolity, and may, without any sensible error, be adopted to the pericraniums of all those who understand an Ape from an Apple, or a B from a Battledore." This was Warren's first and last attempt at almanac making. Another, of which but a single issue is known, is "The New England Almanack" by F. B. for 1778, printed at Hartford by N. Patten. The United States Almanack for 1783 by Andrew Beers, and a series of "Beers' Almanac and Ephemeris" commencing in 1790 were printed at Hartford, and commencing with 1797 they were also printed at Danbury. Eben W. Judd of Waterbury, "student of mathematics under Dr. Joseph Perry," published an almanac from 1785 to 1790; the first being printed at Hartford and the following years at Litchfield. Under the author's pseudonym of "Nathan Ben Salomon X. Y. Z." Meigs, Bowen and Dana of New Haven printed an almanac for 1785 and 1786. Woodward and Green, publishers of the Middlesex Gazette at Middletown, issued the "Middlesex Almanac" for 1787, 1788, and probably other years. "Father Abraham's Almanack" for 1782, printed at Hartford, and the "Farmer's Almanack by J. Weatherwise" for 1799 and 1800 printed at Norwich, are imitations if not reprints of "Father Abraham's Almanack, by Abraham Weatherwise" which was printed at Philadelphia as early as 1772.

The Connecticut State Register, issued for 1785, 1786, 1789 and annually thereafter was published "with an almanac by Nathan Daboll."

This completes the list of the more important and possibly of all the series of Connecticut almanacs of last century; although it probably does not mention all the years in which some of the series were printed, as no copies for some can now be found. It is hoped that the sketch will prove of some interest both to the general reader and to the more exacting bibliographer.

[NOTE. The illustrations are from almanacs in the Connecticut Historical Society, excepting the Daboll and Bickerstaff, which are in the Watkinson Library, Hartford.]

NOT FORGOTTEN.

(ROBERT LOUIS STEVENSON.)

SUSAN BENEDICT HILL.

Home and at rest ; oh, trees that guard his sleep,
    Watch well the sacred treasure which you keep,
And starry sky with all your golden eyes,
    Shine soft upon the summit where he lies
In slumber sweet--never to wake again
    To all life's weariness and bitter pain.
We stand beneath the shadow of his tomb ;
    He dwells where flowers of thought immortal bloom.
Through spaces wide his happy spirit strays,
    And finds new wonders all the heavenly days.

LIST OF BURIALS, OR "SEXTON'S LIST," OF THE CENTER CHURCH BURYING GROUND, HARTFORD.

PREPARED FOR PUBLICATION AND ANNOTATED BY MARY K. TALCOTT.

III.

1777.
Nov. 5 Cannon, the prisoner. Interment Charg'd William Hosmer, aged 32
14 Jonathan Thorn, aged 53.
20 Child of John Caldwell, aged 1½.
26 Child of Frederick Basset, [Willimytje] aged 12.
Dec. 8 Infant child of Allan McLean.
23 Daughter of Simeon Judd, aged 23.

1778.
Jan. 5 Two children of William Olcott, aged 3 years, and 3 months.
14 Infant child of Capt. John Chenevard.
18 Bush, the prisoner. Intered at Exp. of Barsillia Hudson, aged 37.
20 Infant child of Elijah Hubbard.
21 John Bradley. [Born in Guilford. Nov. 7, 1700; son of Stephen and Sarah (Ward) Bradley] aged 77.
32 Child of Gurdon Wadsworth, aged 5 mos.
Mar. 1 Widow Lydia Goodwin, aged 87.
14 Infant child of John Caldwell.
25 Infant child of Consider Burt.
April 12 Wife of Deacon Daniel Hinsdale, aged 68.
13 Child of Capt. Samuel Matox, aged 11.
16 The mother of Frederick Bassett, [Else, wife of John,] aged 79.
23 The wife of Capt. Thomas Hopkins. [Alice, dau. of Samuel and Alice (Hooker) Howard] aged 38.
May 5 Ichabod Wadsworth. [Son of Capt. Joseph and Elizabeth (Barnard) Wadsworth] aged 90.
15 Infant child of William Collyer.
17 Child of Ebenezer Neland, aged 5 m.
21 Child of Oliver Ellsworth, Esq., aged 1½.
25 Wife of Stephen Wilson, aged 28.
29 Child of Samuel Winship, aged 6 m.
June 30 Peter Westerley, aged 44.
July 2 A Prisoner. Intered at Exp. of Barsillia Hudson.
9 Child of James Seymour, aged 5 m.

13 Child of Cotton Murry, aged 1.
17 Child of William Stanley, aged 5.
Aug. 15 Child of Benjamin Watrous, aged 1.
25 Joseph Wadsworth. [Son of Capt. Joseph and Elizabeth (Barnard) Wadsworth; born 1682, died Aug. 24, 1778] aged 96.
26 Child of Frederick Bull, aged 1.
Sept 16 William Olvord, aged 37.
16 Child of Daniel Spencer, aged 1.
18 Benjamin Dodd, aged 57.
20 Child of Daniel Cotton, aged 1
25 Child of Daniel Pierce, aged 1
29 Infant Child of John Wilson.
Oct. 2 Infant Child of John Jeffrey.
3 Infant Child of Allen McLean.
5 Child of Isaac Seymour, aged 23.
7 Child of Moses Kellogg, aged 4.
9 Daughter of Moses Kellogg, aged 4.
9 Infant Child of Robert Branfurt.
10 Child of Samuel Talcott, aged 1.
25 Child of Samuel Burr, aged 2.
27 Child of Samuel Coon, aged 3.
29 Infant Child of Daniel Hinsdale.
Nov. 3 Child of Amos Weslin.
3 Two Soldiers and One Child; no names or ages.

David Farnsworth } Executed as spies on Rocky Hill, having been condemned by a Court Martial at Danbury.
John Blair.

9 Child of James Marsh, aged 4.
Wife of Charles Merrill, (Christian) aged 23.
A Negro Soldier; no age or name.
24 Infant Child of Roswell Stanley.
Infant Child of Enos Doolittle.
Dec. 6 Samuel Day [son of William and Elizabeth (Andrus) Day, bapt. March 13, 1719-20] aged 59.
7 Elizabeth Day, aged 57.
9 Infant Child of Charles Merrill.
19 Widow Abigail Seymour, aged 55.
30 Infant Child of Caleb Bull, Jr.

LIST OF BURIALS.

1779.
- Jan. 13 Daughter of John Watson aged 19.
- 17 Infant Child of Capt. John Barnot.
- 25 Jonathan Bigelow [son of Jonathan and Mabel (Edwards) Bigelow, bapt. June 27, 1714] aged 65.
- 31 Daughter of Samuel Filley, aged 14.
- Feb. 4 Child of Benjamin Segar, aged 6 months.
- 15 Wife of William Olcott, [Abigail Cowles of East Hartford.] aged 24.
- 22 Infant Child of John Spencer Jr.
- Mar. 3 Child of Mrs Lawrence, aged 6 months.
- 7 Daughter of John Watson, aged 25.
- April 2 Son of Aaron Seymour, aged 10.
- 23 Ralph Pomeroy's Infant Child.
- May 2 Infant Child of Asher Church.
- 28 Infant Child of Frederick Bull.
- June 6 Child of Joel Boyington, aged 1.
- 8 Widow Ashley (Mary) [Mary Barnard, widow of Joseph Ashley], aged 92.
- 17 Infant Child of John Bidwell Jr.
- 27 Samuel Chipman, aged 20.
- 30 Infant Child of Thomas Stone.
- July 22 Wife of Daniel Wells (Lydia), aged 64.
- 29 Child of Hezekiah Olcott [Infant].
- Aug. 12 Child of Jeremiah Wadsworth.
- 15 A Prisoner Interred at Exp. of William Barnot, aged 40.
- 15 Child of Thomas Sloan, aged 5.
- 18 Elisha Wells, aged 50.
- 20 Infant Child of Hezekiah Olcott.
- 31 Daughter of Capt. Samuel Olcott (Sally).
- Sept. 5 Child of John Cable, aged 1.
- 9 Child of John Cowdry, aged 8 months
- 15 Child of Roswell Wattels, aged 1.
- 20 Infant Child of Zebulon Seymour.
- 18 Child of John Brace, aged 4.
- 20 Child of Gurdon Wadsworth, aged 1.
- 21 Child of John Bunce Jr., aged 1.
- 24 Child of Joseph Bull, aged 1.
- 26 Child of Prudence Carroll, aged 1.
- 29 Child of Reuben Hadlock [Infant].
- Oct. 6 Daniel Butler, aged 43.
- 31 Infant Child of Joseph Bigelow.
- Nov. 7 Infant Child of Peletiah Pierce.
- 10 Infant Child of Elisha Shepard, aged 1.
- Dec. 30 Wife of Isaac Oakes, aged 36.

1780.
- Jan. 31 Infant Child of Elisha Lord.
- Feb. 9 Wife of Ashbel Spencer, aged 38.
- Mar. 2 Infant Child of Josiah Blakely.
- 18 John Bordwell.
- 25 Wife of John Bunce, Jr. [Susannah, dau. of Capt. Nathaniel and Abigail (Jones) Kilbourn, bapt. July 4, 1756] aged 24.
- April 4 Infant Child of John Coon.
- Infant Child of Frederick Bunce.
- 22 Wife of Samuel Bunce, aged 26.
- 24 Daughter of Roswell Wattles, aged 9.
- 27 Elisha Butler, aged 65.
- May 14 Child of Peg Glines, aged 1.
- 16 Infant Child of Isaac Seymour.
- 27 Wife of Aaron Seymour [Abigail], aged 32.
- 31 Daniel Spencer, aged 75.
- June 16 Widow Elizabeth Butler, aged 94.
- 31 Infant Child of John Spencer, Jr.
- 21 Child of Caleb Turner, Jr. aged 1.
- 26 John Bigelow [son of Lieut. Timothy and Abigail (Olcott) Bigelow born Nov. 20, 1730] aged 38.
- July 16 Deborah, Wife of Epaphras Bull, daughter of John Coleman, Esq. [and Deborah Ledyard, his wife], aged 26.
- 23 Son of Moses Hopkins, aged 16.
- 30 Child of Benjamin Bigelow, [Infant].
- Aug. 14 Child of Daniel Curtis, aged 9 months
- 20 Child of Cotton Murray, aged 8 months.
- 26 Wife of Ebenezer Barnard, (Thankful) [daughter of Cyprian and Mary (Spencer) Nichols, bapt. July 22, 1722], aged 57.
- 28 Infant Child of James Hosmer.
- Sept. 1 George Blanchard, aged 40.
- 9 Infant Child of Samuel Benton.
- 30 Wife of Nathaniel Skinner [Rebecca], aged 31.
- Oct. 12 Infant Child of John Phillips.
- 18 Infant Child of Hezekiah Olcott.
- Dec. 1 Joseph Talcott, Esq. [no age given].
- 17 Infant Child of Jonathan Flagg.
- 22 The mother of Elijah Barret, aged 78
- 23 Daniel Butler, aged 77.

1781.

Feb. 4 Richard Williamson, aged 74
Mar. 1 Capt. William Tiley [he had been master of a sloop, and kept the tavern formerly Ebenezer Williamson's, one of the original members of Christ Church. Annals of Ch. Ch., by C. J. Hoadly] aged 60.
12 Benjamin Smith, A Soldier.
April 1 Infant Child of Barnabas Hinsdale.
14 Edward Dodd, [son of Edward and Lydia (Flower) Dodd, bapt. July 18, 1714], aged 66.
20 Child of Haswell (the printer to George Goodwin), aged 2.
27 Jared Seymour [son of Hon. Thomas and Hepsibah (Merrill) Seymour born Jan. 13, 1731], aged 51.
May 6 The wife of Amos Hinsdale [Experience] aged 60.
16 Daughter of John Spencer, aged 32.
20 Thomas Warren, aged 65.
20 Pegga Agnes, daughter of William Bull, aged 20, [Mrs. Margaret Aggnis.]
June - Son of John Shepard, aged 5.
18 Wife of John Bunce, aged 54.
25 Capt. John Olcott [son of Jonathan and Sarah (Collyer)Olcott, bapt. Oct. 6, 1728] aged 53.
July 10 Wife of Thomas Sloane.
Aug. 2 Isaac Seymour, [son of Isaac and Agnes (Humphreys) Seymour, born 1747] aged 34.
20 Infant Child of Mrs. Hunting.
24 Infant Child of Eleazur Wales.
25 Infant Child of Capt. John Chenevard.
- Daughter of John Sheldon, aged 30.
28 Daughter of William Ellery [Mary, born June 15,1762], aged 19.
30 Infant Child of Eliazur Wales.
Sept. 4 Infant Child of Elisha Lord.
10 Infant Child of Elijah Barrett.
13 Deacon Daniel Hinsdale [son of Barnabas and Martha (Smith) Hinsdale, born May 15, 1708], aged 73.
21 Child of Peter Vandevert, aged 3 mos.
Oct. 7 Child of John Morgan. [Infant]. Sister of Benjamin Bigelow, [daughter of Benjamin and Levinah (Thomas) Bigelow, aged 19.
Nov. 6 Child of George Burnham, aged 1.
7 The Wife of Daniel Bigelow, [Elizabeth Butler, married Feb. 19, 1701] aged 43.
29 Infant Child of Nehemiah Hubbard.
Dec. 1 The Wife of Nehemiah Hubbard, aged 28.
3 Tim" Phelps [son of Timothy and Abigail (Edwards) Phelps, born Oct. 15, 1755], aged 23.
15 Sister of John Pantry Jones [Jerusha, dau. of John Pantry Jones, bapt. April 1, 1759, gr. dau of Nathaniel and Rebecca (Pantry) Jones], aged 23.
16 Infant Child of Daniel Olcott.

1782

Jan. 1 Son of Widow Abigail Chadwick, aged 20.
11 James Seymour [Son of Richard and Elizabeth (Wadsworth) Seymour, born Oct. 3, 1751], aged 30.
15 Infant Child of Levi Kelsey.
22 Wife of William Stanley, [Ruth Seymour, born Feb. 7, 1740, dau. of Hon. Thomas and Hepsibah (Merrill) Seymour], aged 42.
25 Benjamin Paine, Esq. aged 54.
Feb. 5 Child of Theodorus Barnard, died with Small Pox, aged 1
12 Daughter of Josiah Brunson, aged 23.
17 Infant Child of Moses Morse.
21 Wife of Stephen Hutchinson, aged 27.
22 Nathaniel Goodwin [son of Daniel and Dorothy (Cole) Goodwin, bapt. Nov. 13, 1743], aged 38.
25 Child of Samuel Williams of Saybrook, aged 5 months.
27 Child of John Bolles, aged 2.
Mar. 14 Mary Ann, wife of Thomas Y. Seymour, [daughter of Col. William Ledyard and Anne Williams his wife, born in Groton Feb. 16, 1763], aged 19.
17 Child of John Cadwell, aged 3.
April 5 Elihu Wadsworth [son of Elihu, and grandson of Ichabod and Sarah (Smith) Wadsworth] aged 25.
May 1 The Mother of Elisha Warren, aged 65.

LIST OF BURIALS.

	4	Daughter of Timothy Spencer, aged 7.
June	24	Wife of Col. Gibon, the Frenchman, aged 40.
July	10	Daughter of Jonathan Huntington (Silence), aged 14.
	15	Daughter of John Bunce, aged 29.

1782.

July	27	Infant Child of John White, Jr.
	28	Two Children of Joseph Ferry.
Aug.	22	Neal McLean, aged 70, (probably "Niel McLean, the old soldier," to whom the selectmen of Hartford were directed to give a small piece of land, and a house on the bank of the Little River, "for his use as long as he lives."
Sept.	8	Infant Child of Mary Andrus.
	20	Child of Capt. William Bull, aged 1.
Oct.	7	Infant Child of Consider Bowen.
	15	The wife of Consider Bowen, aged 26.
	18	The wife of Barnabas Hinsdale [Magdalen Seymour, daughter of Capt. Jonathan and Mary (Bull) Seymour,] aged 42.
	28	The Wife of James Tilley (Phebe), aged 42.
	28	Infant Child of a Waggoner.
	30	Joseph Barret, aged 63.
Dec.	4	Son of Widow Lydia Olford, aged 9.

1783.

Jan.	7	Daughter of John Roberts, aged 6.
	18	Obadiah Spencer, aged 31.
	31	Zebulon Spencer, aged 77.
Feb.	24	Child of Roderick Bunce (Infant).
	26	Mrs. Bunce (Elizabeth Barnard), wife of Robert King, 2d wife of James Bunce; burial ch'd Moses Burr; aged 85.
	27	Doctor Gibbon, aged 55.
Mar.	4	Child of William Wodsworth, aged 2.
	4	Child of Consider Burt, aged 1.
	27	The Mother of John White [Sarah Carter, widow of John White, married Dec. 2, 1714], aged 91.
April	5	Infant Child of Geo. Nichols.
	6	Geo. Bunce, aged 32.
	10	John Burket, aged 55.
	14	Elizabeth Bunce, aged 67.
May	3	Infant Child of William Collyer.
	4	Son of John Lawrence, Esq. (Roderic), aged 36.
	21	Dr. William Jepson [an apothecary from Boston, settled in Hartford about 1757, kept a store at the sign of the Unicorn and Mortar; one of the original members of Christ Church. Annals of Christ Church, by C. J. Hoadly], aged 50.
	25	Caleb Turner, aged 76.
	27	Daughter of Mrs. Lodema Goodwin, aged 14.
June	1	Tim⁰ Pratt, aged 32.
	17	Child of Prudence Carrole, aged 2.
	17	Infant Child of William Pratt.
	17	Child of Peter Vandervert, aged 1 mo.
	16	Infant Child of William Pratt.
	23	Child of Aaron Cook, aged 1.
	25	Child of William Andrus, aged 5.
	25	Nathaniel Goodwin [son of Ozias and Martha (Williamson) Goodwin, born Dec. 26, 1731], aged 51.
	28	The Wife of Capt. James Nichols (Mary Wadsworth), married Jan. 12, 1737-8, aged 70.
	28	Infant Child of Stephen Skinner.
Aug.	2	Infant Child of John P. Wyllys.
	5	Abijah Clark, aged 53.
	10	The Wife of John P. Wyllys, [Jerusha, dau. of Col. Samuel and Mabel (Wyllys) Talcott, bapt. April 11, 1756, aged 27.
	16	Infant Child of Joseph Bull.
	21	Samuel Howard [son of Samuel and Alice (Hooker) Howard], aged 52.
Sept.	3	Ephraim P. Bicknell, burial charged Daniel Goodwin, aged 14.
	10	A Man Drowned. Intered at Exp. of Town, aged 27.
	14	Child of John Bolles, aged 5 mos.
	26	Wife of Joseph Bull (Esther), aged 41.
Oct.	10	Infant Child of Caleb Bull, Jr.
Nov.	14	Child of Obadiah Spencer, aged 1.

1784.

Jan.	5	Infant Child of Thomas Stone.
	9	Child of William Barnot, aged 2.
	13	Mrs. Keith, Intered at Exp. Jno. Lawrence, Esq. (widow of Capt. John Keith, and mother of John Lawrence, Esq.) [Marian, dau. of Capt. John and Margaret Beauchamp], aged 88.
	17	Doctor Neal McLean [he practiced medicine in Hartford and had a country seat near the line between Bloomfield and Hartford], aged 82.

GENEALOGICAL DEPARTMENT

Querists should write all names of persons and places in such a way that they cannot be misunderstood. Always enclose with queries a self addressed stamped envelope and at least ten cents for each query. Querists should write only on one side of the paper. Subscribers sending in queries should state that they are subscribers, and preference in insertion will always be given them. Queiries are inserted in the order in which they are received. On account of our limited space, it is impossible that all queries be inserted as soon as querists desire. Always give full name and post-office address. Queries and notes must be sent to Wm. A. Eardeley-Thomas, 50th street and Woodland avenue, Philadelphia, Penn. In future it will be optional with queriest to have name and address, or only initials published.

163. *Cruttenden*, Abraham, m. Jan., 1741, Sarah Parmelee (or Barnaby); he was born in Durham, Conn., and was prob. living there when he married. The records of Durham, Middletown and Wallingford have been searched. A reward of $2.00 will be given for the marriage with proofs. Mrs. H. E. Fowler, box 373, Guilford, Conn.

164. *Fellows*, Ephraim, William and Thomas were among those granted land in 1738 in Canaan at its first settlement. Did they move there from Plainfield or Stonington, Conn.? Both places have been named. Did Ephraim have a son Ephraim? S. F. T.

165. *Gridley*, Elnathan (m. Sarah ———), desires his line back to Thomas of Windsor, who m Mary Seymour.

(*b*) *Roberts*, Jonathan, of East Hartford. m. Ruth Judson, b. Apr. 23, 1766 Desired ancestry of Jonathan and Ruth. G. H. T.

166. *(a) Briggs*, Edward, m. abt. 1776 Anna Chase; moved from Dartmouth, Mass., to Quaker Hill, N. Y. Who were ancestors of Edward and Anna?

(*b*) *Leach*, Amos and wife Mercy lived in New Fairfield, Conn. What was her maiden name? Who were their parents? They were born about 1710.

(*c*) *Osborn*, Stephen, b. 1748 in Danvers, Mass., m. 1775 Sarah Bourn. Who were their ancestors?

(*d*) *Wanzer*, Abraham, moved from Long Island 1736 to New Fairfield, Conn. What Long Island town did he come from?

(*e*) *Whaley*, Hezekiah, b. about 1760 is said to have come from near New London. Who were his parents? W. C. P.

167. *Taylor*, Job, b. July 24, 1750, m. Anna Ross, b. July 24, 1751, and had Phebe, b. July 24, 1784, Groton, Conn., m. Solomon Spencer of East Hartford. Job kept a tavern at Groton and in some skirmish the dead were brought there and laid on the floor. The family went to Marshfield, Vt., where he d. about 1841, and his two wives d. there. Who were the parents of Job Taylor and Anna Ross? J. S. F.

168. *(a) Perry*, Eleazer m. int. March 14, 1740-41 in Dartmouth, Mass. T. R. Mercy Hix, who were their parents? issue were 1, Joseph, Sept. 20, 1741. 2, Mary, Dec. 25, 1742. 3, Sarah, June 29, 1746. 4, Eliphal, May 13, 1748. Whom did these marry? A Joseph and Mary Perry had Freeman b. Dec. 22, 1761.

(*b Balmer*, Joseph had a son, Thomas B———— b., about 1846, m. 1st———— and had Annie; m. 2d, abt. 1871 Susan (b. abt. 1849) dau. of James and Mary (St. Arnold) Holliday; Thomas B. and Susan had 1, Wm. Henry, Sept. 12, 1873. 2, Thomas Albert, Sept. 3, 1875, L'Anse, Mich. 3, James Walter. 4, Mary. 5, Veronica. 6, John Edward. Who were parents of Joseph Balmer? Who were parents of Mary St. Arnold? Her father was a Frenchman and her mother a full blooded Chippewa Indian. T. A. B.

169. *Cooke*, Sarah b. May 12, 1753 (or 1754), m. 1st, ——— Preston, (first name uncertain, may have been Aaron.) He was robbed and mortally wounded by the British at the Brandywine Battle, Sept. 11, 1777. Starting for home he died and was buried in New Haven. Sarah Cooke is supposed (though not proven) to have been dau. of Joseph, of Torrington, Conn., and descended from Capt. Aaron Cooke, of Windsor, Conn. Information desired regarding her ancestry and clues to Preston's family connections. E. H. T.

170. *Stone*, John of Danbury, Conn., m. Elizabeth, dau. of Mathew Crofoot, of Danbury. He died at Danbury, abt. 1791, leaving a widow and six children. Who was the father and where did the family originate? The widow moved to Litchfield, Conn., m. a Palmer and d. aged almost 100, in Warren, Conn.
R. S. H.

171. *Watson*, John and wife Dinah of Spencer, Mass., had 1, John, March 6, 1762. 2, Jacob, Jan. 1, 1765. 3, Enoch, Aug. 30, 1767. Lydia, Oct 1, 1769. 5, Leonard, Jan. 13, 1772. 6, Henry, Oct. 29, 1774. 7, David, Oct. 2, 1776. 8, Sally, Dec. 8, 1779. Mr. Watson d. Nov. 20, 1802. The son, Jacob, m. 1st, Mary Adams of Brookfield; m. 2nd, Olive Knight; m. 3rd, Mary Parmenter, of Oakham, Mass. I wish to trace them out. [Ed. Querist gave no name and no address; postmarked from Spencer, Mass., and only the initials.]
A. J. W.

172. *Young*, Wm., one of the original proprietors of Nottingham and Barrington, N. H., in 1721 m. Hannah Healy, of Cambridge. Where was William born and what were the names of his parents? Sir John Young was one of the three original grantees of the land from Boston northward. He came over in 1628, and his three sons followed in 1630. The youngest son, it is thought, was Samuel. What were the names of the other two sons and where did they settle? S. Y. G.

173. *Mosher*, Stephen of Lyme, Conn., was a soldier in the Revolution. What was his ancestry? L. E. M.

174. (a) *Wildman*, Ezra of Danbury, sold for $53.00, land at Maple Swamp, on Feb. 25, 1814 to Robert Perry and Anna, his wife, of Stockbridge, Mass.; Joseph B. Osborn, and Esther, his wife, of Great Barrington, Mass.; James Abbot, and Rebecca, his wife, of Danbury; Elind Barber, and Anna, his wife, of Southwick (Danbury Land Records). Anna Perry was dau. of Joseph Barnum. Who were parents of Ezra and Robert? Was there any relationship between these parties?
(b) *Chace*, Abigail wife of Newburn, buried Jan. 8, 1753.
Chaise, Benjamin son of Newbold, buried Aug. 20, 1750.
Chase, Thomas son of Thomas and Mary, buried July 12, 1721.
Chase, Mary wife of Thomas, buried June 26, 1732.
Chase, Thomas buried Aug. 27, 1734. These are from the records of Christ Church, Philadelphia. Who were parents of Newbold, Newburn, Thomas and Mary? C. P. B.

175. *Kimball*, Lucy m. Sept. 14, 1755, Asher Flint, of Windham, Conn., died Oct. 20, 1800, in Tolland County. Who were her parents?
Miss M. B. Flint, 281 Mill St., Poughkeepsie, N. Y.

176. *White*, Isaac of Greenwich, Mass., b. 1725-30, had two children, b. there; Sarah, 1748, and Isaac, Jr., 1752. What was his ancestry? B. S. E.

177. *Chase*, William, was in Yarmouth, Mass., as early as 1639. The birth, marriage and death of all his descendants desired to complete the Genealogy.
Editor.

178. *Perry*, Milla b. 1763 (?), dau. of Elisha and Hannah Perry. Whom did she marry and where settle? S. E. P.

179. (a) *Holmes*, Joseph b. 1758, m. 1778, Lydia Curtis. Who was his father? The mother of Joseph is said to have been Phebe ———. Who were her parents? She m. 2d Chileab Smith. This Holmes family is supposed to have lived in Nine Partners, Duchess Co., N. Y. There are and have been many residents there of this name, but there seems to be no relation with our Joseph.
(b) *Holmes*, Francis of Stamford, Conn., wife Ann, had a son John Holmes m. Rachel Waterbury, and had a son David Holmes b. abt. 1672, m. ——— and had Jonathan, b. abt. 1700, m. Dorothy ——— and had Jonathan b. abt. 1725, m. abt. 1744 ——— and had two dau. Martha and Mary. Who were parents of Ann and Dorothy? Who was mother of Martha and Mary? Whom did David and Jonathan Holmes marry? R. E. H.

HISTORICAL NOTES.

TWO HUNDRED DOLLARS REWARD.

[Contributed by James F. Savage.]

[Advertisment in "Columbian Centinel and Massachusetts Federalist," Boston, Mass., Saturday Oct. 22, 1803.]

ABSENTED herself last night from the service of MR. RUTLEDGE a negro woman, who is his property, named PHILLIS. She is 35 years old, about 5 feet 8 inches high, of a yellowish complexion (between that of a negro and mulatto) thin, has lost her front teeth, has thick lips and a scar, from having been burnt when a child upon her breast, near the right shoulder about half the size of a dollar. Phillis wears gold bobs in her ears, and a black straw bonnet. She carried with her petticoats of blue cloth, dimorthy, black calimanco red home spun; a dark calico gown with yellow spots, one of black and white, one of white checked muslin; she also took with her eight yards of dark calico with bright yellow spots, two cheched aprons not made up, new red and white cotton handkerchiefs, with many other articles of dress. *Phillis* was a good cook, washer-woman and cake baker.

A black fellow named PETER, also absented himself from the service of *Mr Rutledge*, some weeks past when he was at *Boston*. *Peter* is not quite 6 feet high, much pock-marked, had red eyes, and his upper front teeth wide apart. He is an excellent coachman, a tolerably good cook, plays the tamborine, and is very fond of dancing. *Peter* is a little bald, wears his wool in a short queue, and occasionally wears ear-rings. He took with him a variety of clothing. Whoever will apprehend and deliver these slaves to the subscriber, or secure them in any goal in New England so that he may get to them, shall receive the above reward of 200 dollars, or 100 for either of them.

CHESTER CLARK.

Weathersfield, Conn., Oct. 15, 1803.

A SKETCH

Contributed by Mrs. W. L. Horne.

Closely identified with the early history of Connecticut was a man of whom it seems fit that I, a lineal descendant should here give a brief sketch.

Rev. Henry Smith settled at Wethersfield, Conn, about 1636, and with the early and troublesome history of that period, was a strong and important factor over the first regularly organized church at that place. He was installed in 1641, first pastor, a position he filled until his death in 1648.

Historians have done him honor, and of him it is written: "Not only a patriarch of one of the best sustained and most accomplished families in New England, but a gentleman of uncommon culture.

Brought from England by him, and now in the possession of Mr. Gilbert Smith of Sharon, Conn. (a great grandson of Gov. John Cotton Smith, a lineal descendant of Rev. Henry) is a silver tankard with the family coat of arms, with the motto, "*Carpe Diem*," beautifully engraved thereon. This valuable piece of silver is still in excellent state of preservation.

His last will and testament is to be found among the Colonial records at Hartford and is a unique document.

Of interest to a few may be this brief mention of the first pastor, of the first church to be organized on the banks of the Connecticut River.

[Contributed by William Wallace Lee.]

[The following is of interest as a forerunner of the Declaration of Independence at Philadelphia, having occurred ten days earlier.]

At a meeting of the inhabitants of King's District in the County of Albany, legally warned by the committee of said County at the house of

169. *Cooke*, Sarah b. May 12, 1753 (or 1754), m. 1st, ———— Preston, (first name uncertain, may have been Aaron.) He was robbed and mortally wounded by the British at the Brandywine Battle, Sept. 11, 1777. Starting for home he died and was buried in New Haven. Sarah Cooke is supposed though not proven) to have been dau. of Joseph, of Torrington, Conn., and descended from Capt. Aaron Cooke, of Windsor, Conn. Information desired regarding her ancestry and clues to Preston's family connections.   E. H. T.

170. *Stone*, John of Danbury, Conn., m. Elizabeth, dau. of Mathew Crofoot, of Danbury. He died at Danbury, abt. 1791, leaving a widow and six children. Who was the father and where did the family originate? The widow moved to Litchfield, Conn., m. a Palmer and d. aged almost 100, in Warren, Conn.   R. S. H.

171. *Watson*, John and wife Dinah of Spencer, Mass., had 1, John, March 6, 1762. 2, Jacob, Jan. 1, 1765. 3, Enoch, Aug. 30, 1767. Lydia, Oct 1, 1769. 5, Leonard, Jan. 13, 1772. 6, Henry, Oct 29, 1774. 7, David, Oct. 2, 1776. 8, Sally, Dec. 8, 1779. Mr. Watson d. Nov. 20, 1802. The son, Jacob, m. 1st, Mary Adams of Brookfield; m. 2nd, Olive Knight; m. 3rd, Mary Parmenter, of Oakham, Mass. I wish to trace them out. [Ed. Querist gave no name and no address; postmarked from Spencer, Mass., and only the initials.]   A. J. W.

172. *Young*, Wm, one of the original proprietors of Nottingham and Barrington, N. H., in 1721 m. Hannah Healy, of Cambridge. Where was William born and what were the names of his parents? Sir John Young was one of the three original grantees of the land from Boston northward. He came over in 1628. and his three sons followed in 1630. The youngest son, it is thought, was Samuel. What were the names of the other two sons and where did they settle?   S. Y. G.

173. *Mosher*, Stephen of Lyme. Conn., was a soldier in the Revolution. What was his ancestry?   L. E. M.

174. (*a*) *Wildman*, Ezra of Danbury, sold for $53 00, land at Maple Swamp, on Feb. 25, 1814, to Robert Perry and Anna, his wife, of Stockbridge, Mass; Joseph B. Osborn, and Esther, his wife, of Great Barrington, Mass.; James Abbot, and Rebecca, his wife, of Danbury; Elind Barber, and Anna, his wife, of Southwick (Danbury Land Records). Anna Perry was dau. of Joseph Barnum. Who were parents of Ezra and Robert? Was there any relationship between these parties?

(*b*) *Chace*, Abigail wife of Newburn, buried Jan. 8, 1753.

Chatse, Benjamin son of Newbold, buried Aug. 20, 1750.

Chase, Thomas son of Thomas and Mary, buried July 12, 1721.

Chase, Mary wife of Thomas, buried June 26, 1732.

Chase, Thomas buried Aug. 27, 1734. These are from the records of Christ Church, Philadelphia. Who were parents of Newbold, Newburn, Thomas and Mary?   C. P. B.

175. *Kimball*, Lucy m. Sept. 14, 1755, Asher Flint, of Windham, Conn., died Oct. 20, 1800, in Tolland County. Who were her parents?
     Miss M. B. Flint, 281 Mill St.,
     Poughkeepsie, N. Y.

176. *White*, Isaac of Greenwich, Mass., b. 1725-30, had two children, b. there; Sarah, 1748, and Isaac, Jr., 1752. What was his ancestry?   B. S. E.

177. *Chase*, William, was in Yarmouth, Mass., as early as 1639. The birth, marriage and death of all his descendants desired to complete the Genealogy.
     Editor.

178. *Perry*, Milla b. 1763 (?), dau. of Elisha and Hannah Perry. Whom did she marry and where settle?   S. E. P.

179. (*a*) *Holmes*, Joseph b. 1758, m. 1778, Lydia Curtis. Who was his father? The mother of Joseph is said to have been Phebe ————. Who were her parents? She m. 2d Chileab Smith. This Holmes family is supposed to have lived in Nine Partners, Duchess Co., N. Y. There are and have been many residents there of this name, but there seems to be no relation with our Joseph.

(*b*) *Holmes*, Francis of Stamford, Conn., wife Ann, had a son John Holmes m. Rachel Waterbury, and had a son David Holmes b. abt. 1672, m. ————— and had Jonathan, b. abt. 1700, m. Dorothy ————— and had Jonathan b. abt. 1725, m. abt. 1744 ————— and had two dau. Martha and Mary. Who were parents of Ann and Dorothy? Who was mother of Martha and Mary? Whom did David and Jonathan Holmes marry?   R. E. H.

HISTORICAL NOTES.

TWO HUNDRED DOLLARS REWARD.

[Contributed by James F. Savage.]

[Advertisment in "Columbian Centinel and Massachusetts Federalist," Boston, Mass., Saturday Oct. 22, 1803.]

ABSENTED herself last night from the service of MR. RUTLEDGE a negro woman, who is his property, named PHILLIS. She is 35 years old, about 5 feet 8 inches high, of a yellowish complexion (between that of a negro and mulatto) thin, has lost her front teeth, has thick lips and a scar, from having been burnt when a child upon her breast, near the right shoulder about half the size of a dollar. Phillis wears gold bobs in her ears, and a black straw bonnet. She carried with her petticoats of blue cloth, dimorthy, black calimanco red home spun; a dark calico gown with yellow spots, one of black and white, one of white checked muslin; she also took with her eight yards of dark calico with bright yellow spots, two cheched aprons not made up, new red and white cotton handkerchiefs, with many other articles of dress. *Phillis* was a good cook, washer-woman and cake baker.

A black fellow named PETER, also absented himself from the service of *Mr Rutledge*, some weeks past when he was at *Boston*. *Peter* is not quite 6 feet high, much pock-marked, had red eyes, and his upper front teeth wide apart. He is an excellent coachman, a tolerably good cook, plays the tamborine, and is very fond of dancing. *Peter* is a little bald, wears his wool in a short queue, and occasionally wears ear-rings. He took with him a variety of clothing. Whoever will apprehend and deliver these slaves to the subscriber, or secure them in any goal in New England so that he may get to them, shall receive the above reward of 200 dollars, or 100 for either of them.

CHESTER CLARK.

Weathersfield, Conn., Oct. 15, 1803.

A SKETCH.

[Contributed by Mrs. W. L. Horne.]

Closely identified with the early history of Connecticut was a man of whom it seems fit that I, a lineal descendant should here give a brief sketch.

Rev. Henry Smith settled at Wethersfield, Conn, about 1636, and with the early and troublesome history of that period, was a strong and important factor over the first regularly organized church at that place. He was installed in 1641, first pastor, a position he filled until his death in 1648.

Historians have done him honor, and of him it is written: "Not only a patriarch of one of the best sustained and most accomplished families in New England, but a gentleman of uncommon culture.

Brought from England by him, and now in the possession of Mr. Gilbert Smith of Sharon, Conn. (a great grandson of Gov. John Cotton Smith, a lineal descendant of Rev. Henry) is a silver tankard with the family coat of arms, with the motto, "*Carpe Diem*," beautifully engraved thereon. This valuable piece of silver is still in excellent state of preservation.

His last will and testament is to be found among the Colonial records at Hartford and is a unique document.

Of interest to a few may be this brief mention of the first pastor, of the first church to be organized on the banks of the Connecticut River.

[Contributed by William Wallace Lee.]

[The following is of interest as a forerunner of the Declaration of Independence at Philadelphia, having occurred ten days earlier.]

At a meeting of the inhabitants of King's District in the County of Albany, legally warned by the committee of said County at the house of

William Warner, inn-keeper in said dictrict, on Monday the 24th day of June, 1776, for the purpose of electing twelve delegates to represent said County in the Provincial Congress be voted : First, that Daniel Buck be moderator of this meeting. Second, that the present Committee's Clerk, be clerk of this meeting. Third, that the District books be delivered to the care of sd Committee's Clerk, until the next district meeting. Fourthly, voted that a committee be chosen by this meeting for the purpose of drawing up instructions for a new form of government to be introduced by sd delegates. The question being put whether the said district chooses to have the United Americal Colonies independent of Great Britain. Voted unanimously in the affirmative. Sixthly, voted, that Messrs William B. Whitney, Asa Waterman, Philip Frisbe, Martin Beebe, Elisha Pratt, Capt. Baldwin, Daniel Buck, Elijah Bostwick, Gidion King, Jarvis Mudge, Samuel Johnson, John Gillit, Lieut. Herrick, Joseph Wood, John Wadsworth, Samuel Baley, be a committee for to draw up instructions for the purpose aforesaid.

Can anyone give us information in regard to the authorship and publication of the following verses?

THE AMERICAN TAXATION.

Whilst I relate my story, Americans give ear,
Of Britains fading glory, you presently shall hear ;
It is a true relation, attend to what I say,
Concerning the taxation in North America.

The cruel lords of Britain, who glory in their shame,
The project they triton, they joyfully proclaim :
'Tis what they're seeking after, our rights to take away.
And rob us of our charter, in North America.

They searched the gloomy regions of their infernal pitt,
To find amongst those legions, one who excel'd in wit ;
To ask of him assistance, and tell them how they may.
Subdue with resistance, this North America.

Old Satan the arch traitor, resolved a voyage to make,
Who rules sole navigator, on the infernal lake ;
Into the British Ocean, he launched far away,
To land he had no notion, in North America.

PUBLISHER'S NOTES.

As announced in our last number we are obliged, on account of the growing demand for more frequent issues of THE QUARTERLY, to change it to a monthly publication. On next to the last page we show a reduced facsimile of the new cover design for the monthly. As will be readily seen, the idea in producing this, has been to make improvements and bring it to our requirements at the same time preserving the identity of THE QUARTERLY cover, so as to be readily recognized as the same magazine.

THE CONNECTICUT MAGAZINE will in the future pay especial attention and devote a large amount of space to illustrated articles of the historic towns of the state. In the publication of the magazine as a monthly it will be possible for us to give representation to a larger number of the towns each year than would be possible were it to continue as a quarterly.

It is also intended to publish illustrated biographical sketches of those men who in years past have helped to make the history of Connecticut what it is to-day.

But while the magazine devotes itself so largely to historical and descriptive matter, it never loses sight of the fact that fiction claims a share of its attention. It will be of interest to many to know that a serial story by Mrs. William E. Simonds, will appear, commencing with our first issue, entitled "Fifteen Love," a sequel to "In Satan's Kingdom."

To people who are interested in

PUBLISHER'S NOTES.

traceing ancestral lines the Genealogical Department will be of more than passing interest and will be conducted on improved lines in reference to Connecticut genealogy.

The other departments will also be unusually attractive.

In all respects, we shall exert ourselves to make THE CONNECTICUT MAGAZINE the best and most complete periodical of like nature devoted to a local field. Let others speak a few words for us, as to what we have done: —

"THE QUARTERLY keeps up to a high standard and occupies a hitherto unexplored field. The departments, Genealogical, Historical and Social are a feature of this meritorious local publication.—*Hartford Courant.*

"This excellent magazine, devoted chiefly to Connecticut subjects, and exquisitely illustrated, continues to grow in public favor. It justifies the publisher's characterization of the general scope and character of the magazine as a publication devoted to the "literature, history and picturesque features of Connecticut."—*Hartford Times.*

"The letter press in this magazine is always a joy and the illustrations are the finest of any of the monthlies. In a literary sense it deserves the highest praise, for it is more and more evident that a high order of merit is insisted upon as well as interest in the articles."—*New London Telegraph.*

"It is the best local publication produced in this country and should have the hearty support of all."—*Winsted Herald.*

"As usual it is generously and artistically illustrated, and its varied articles are well and entertainingly written. This valuable magazine is constantly growing in popularity and it is gratifying to note that it is winning its way on its merits."—*Bristol Herald.*

"The above sketch and verses are taken from THE CONNECTICUT QUARTERLY, Hartford's superb magazine. Every reader who invests twenty-five cents for a number of THE QUARTERLY gets big dividends in return."—*Bristol Press.*

"That excellent magazine, THE CONNECTICUT QUARTERLY, is doing much to awaken citizens of this good old state to the manifold beauties of its scenery, and acquaint them with its early history. . . . One lays down the magazine with the resolve to visit the quaint old towns of which he has just

read and to see at close range the attractive places described therein."—*Manchester Herald.*

"Gives a great deal of modern information as well as the best historical facts. It is profusely and beautifully illustrated.—*New Milford Gazette.*

". . . . . These, with many other sketches, stories and poems make up the contents of this issue, a number that does great credit to THE QUARTERLY, the foremost periodical of the state."—*New Britain Herald.*

"This publication is worthy of the hearty support of the people of Connecticut, as it serves as a medium for the interchange of opinions and facts upon our state history, which is one to be proud of, and offers a suitable repository on all historic, genealogical, and antiquarian lore that is or ever will be of interest to the inhabitants of Connecticut."—*Bridgeport Standard.*

The foregoing favorable and representative notices are but a very few of those we have received of like nature, and we shall certainly aim to keep our present high standard and make from time to time such improvements as we see opportunity to.

Although a continuation of THE QUARTERLY, THE CONNECTICUT MAGAZINE will be in itself as complete a representation of the state as we can possibly make it, the towns that were in the early numbers of THE QUARTERLY needing further notice at some future time, so we would wish all to begin with the first of the year and thus insure having a complete file of the Magazine.

The subscription price of THE CONNECTICUT MAGAZINE will be $1.00 a year, and the twelve numbers will make a much larger volume than the four numbers of THE QUARTERLY. As stated in our last number the Magazine will be under the same general editorial management as THE QUARTERLY has been and the business department will be under the supervision of Mr. Edward B. Eaton.

We hope to be favored with the continued support of the people of the state which they have so generously given us in the past and assure them that we shall do our best to deserve it.

GENEALOGICAL DEPARTMENT.

INDEX NOTES AND QUERIES.

Abbott Hannah 331
   James 422
   Phebe 331
   William 330
Abernathy Elizabeth 224
Ackley David 333
   Samuel 114, 333
Adams Caleb 330
   James 116
   John 116
   Mary 422
   Nathaniel 117
   Richard, 116, 223
   William 116
Akin Elisha 115
   Josiah 115
   Margaret 115
   Patience 115
Allen Mary 115
   Philip 115
   Samuel 116
Alling Asa 116
   Caleb 116
   Hannah 116
   Keziah 116
   Mabel 333
   Roger 116
   Ruth 116
Amsdell Mr. ——— 113
Anderson Adnah 223
   George 222
   Jeremiah 332
   Lemuel 222
   Stephen 222
   Thomas 222
   William 222
Andrews Thaddeus 334
Ashley Clarissa 116
   Enoch 116
   Rachel 330
Aspinwall John 332
Austin Alvin 117
   Andrew C 117
   Anthony 117
   Daniel 117
   Linus 117
   Nathaniel 117
Ayer Edney 330
   Nathaniel 330
Babbit Zephaniah 221

Badger Enoch 223
   Giles 223
   John 223
   Nathaniel 223
Bailey Caroline 115
   Hannah L 115
   Lemuel B 115, 332
   Samuel 115, 332
Baker Charety 221
Baldwin Chloe 331
   John 225
   Samuel 331
Ballard Alice 334
Balmer Annie 421
   James W 421
   John E 421
   Joseph 421
   Thomas A 421
   Thomas B 421
   Veronica 421
   Wm Henry 421
Banks Samuel 219
Barber Eliud 422
   John 219
Barlow Peleg 219
Barnaby Sarah 421
Barnum Amy 220
   David 220
   Ebenezer 220
   Esther 331
   Evaline 220
   F. Jane 220
   Ira 220
   John 220
   Joseph 422
   Josiah 331
   Matthew 115
   Oliver 220
   Orva L 220
   Polly 115
   Thaddeus 220
Bartow Basil 332
Bates Mary 332
Beaman Gamaliel 225
   Mary 225
Beecher Sarah 116
Bekell Thomas 115
Belding Elizabeth 332
Benedict Aaron 115

Benedict Abigail 332
   Amos 115
   Amy 331
   Anne 332
   Annis 115
   Betsey 332
   Deborah 332
   Eleazer 115
   Eli S 332
   Ezra 332
   Hannah 332
   Isaac H 332
   Jonas 115
   Joseph 332
   Nancy 115
   Peter 332
   Rachel 332
   Ruth 331
   Sally 332
   Samuel W 332
   Sarah 115
   Thaddeus 332
   Theophilus 115, 332
   Thomas B 115, 332
Benham Cornelia 220
Benjamin Hannah 117
Bennet (t) Benjamin 114
   Henry 114, 333
   John 113, 330
   Joseph 116, 219
   Mary 114
   Sarah 331
Berry Alice 334
   Richard 334
Betts (tts) Anne 221
   Elizabeth 116
   Mary 332
Bigelow Patience 223
Birchard Hannah 225
Burchard Jeremiah 331
   Lydia 331
   Thomas 225
Birdsall Nathan 115
Bishop Alexander 332
   James 224
   Rebecca 224
   Silvanus 116
Blackwell Samuel 210
Blague Elizabeth 225
   Henry 225
   Joseph 225

Blague Martha 225
  Nathaniel 225
  Philip 225
  Rebecca 225
Blake Mary 222
Boardman Olive 332
Booth Alice, 224-5
  Charles 224
  Elisha 224
  Hannah 224
  Henry 224-5
  John 224
  Jonathan 224
  Thomas 224-5
  William 224
Borden Amly 118
  John 118
  Mary 223
Boughton George 330
Bourne John 219
  Sarah 421
  William 219
Bouton Deborah 117
  Mary 117
Bowing Samuel 113
Brace Susannah 334
Bradley Betsey 220
Brewster Anne 225
  Nathan 225
  William 223
Briggs Asa 220
  Daniel 222
  Edward 421
  Hannah 225
  William 225
Brockway Wolston 225
Bronson Lucinda 332
  Thaddeus 332
Brown Abigail 222
  Bezaleel 115
  Daniel 333
  Elizabeth 115
  Hannah 117
  Jacob 333
  John 333
  Stephen 222
  Timothy 333
Buck Daniel 333
Bud Thamar 332
Bulkley Elizabeth 333
  Jonathan 333
  Lydia 333
Bull Isaac 115
  John 115
Bullard Abigail 224
Bunce Joseph 224
  Martha 224
  Mary 224
Burcnard see Birchard
Burr Sarah 221
Burt Mary 118
Burton Emily 221
  Maria 221
  Mary S 221
  Patrick 221

Burton Selden M 221
Button see Bouton
Camp Samuel 330
Carpenter Ebenezer 224
  Samuel 114
Cartledge John 334
Case John 224
Castle Peter 331
Chace see Chase
Chaffee William 334
Chaise see Chase
Chandler Mrs ———— 114
  Alice 330
  Silas 114, 330
Channibg Polly 117
Chapin Luke 334
Chase Abigail 422
  Abraham 115
  Anna 439
  Benjamin 118, 422
  Bethiah 118
  Constant 224
  Daniel 115
  Desire 115
  Elizabeth 118
  Ezekiel 118
  Henry 115
  Holder 223
  Jacob 118
  John 118
  Joseph 118
  Mary 118, 422
  Naomi 118
  Nathan 330
  Nathaniel 118
  Newbold 422
  Newburn 422
  Obadiah 334
  Philip (pe) 118
  Samuel 118
  Sarah 118
  Seth 330
  T[heodore] R 118
  Thomas 422
  William 118, 422
Clark Adam S 114
  Hannah 225
  John 225
  Sally B 114
Clason Stephen 219
Cleveland Rachel 117
Cogswtll Edward 117
Cole Lucy 116
  Sarah 222
Collins Benjamin 333
Colored (people) Dosias 332
  Isabella 332
  Isaac S 332
  Patience 332
  Richard 332
  Saul 332
Comstock James 116
Conclin Thomas 331
Congor Gideon 333
  Joel 333

Cooke Aaron 422
  Francis 222
  Joseph 422
  Sarah 422
Cooper Rebecca 224
  Samuel 224
  Sarah 224
  Triphena 224
Copp John 218
Corbin Elizabeth 221
Cornell Nicholas 118
Cornwall William 117
Cory Keziah 115
Cowdrey John 114
  Katherine 114
Cozier Thomas 334
Crafts Joseph 113
Cramner Elieabeth 116
Crawford Anne 332
  James 332
Crofut Benjamin 115
(Crofoot) Elizabeth 422
  Matthew 422
  Rachel 115
Cruttenden Abraham 421
Cunningham Peter 113
Curtis Daniel 117
  Lydia 422
  Thomrs 117
Dakin Timothy 115
Davis Daniel 333
  E'ecta 333
  Hannah 333
  Martha 225
  Mary 118
  Ruth 333
  Stephen 333
  William 333
Day Levi 113
Dean Sarah 330
Dennison Thomas 113
Dibble Mary 111
Dibblee Fyler 116
Dimmock Mabel 117
Disbrow Dimon 220
  Lydia A 220
Dodge William 116
Doty Elijah 115
Dunham Hannah 118
  Joseph 118
  Stephen 118
Duning Charlotte 225
(Dunnig) Ebenezer 225
  Thaddeus 332
Durkee Lydia 223-4
  Robert 334
Easton William M 221
Edmunds Moses 330
Ellis Gideon 219
  Philip 219
Elwell Hannah 220
  John 220
  Sally B 220

GENEALOGICAL INDEX.

Fairfield James 224
Falch Nicholas 332
Farnham Isaac 114
　Sarah 118
Fay Aaron 329
Fellows Ephraim 421
　Thomas 421
　William 421
Ferris (s) Abigail 332
　Benjamin 115
　Joseph 115
　Reed 115
　Zebulon 115
Fettie Amy 221
Field Zachariah 117
Fish Mersey 115
Fitzhubert Nicholas 224-5
Flint Asher 422
　M[artha] B 422
Flowers Joseph 221
　Rhoda 221
　Wealthy 221
Ford Mrs ——— 330
　Rachel 224
Foster Job 219
　Joseph 219
　Massah 331
　Timothy 331
Fountain Aaron 218
　Ann M 320-21
　Anthony 220-21
　Antone 220-21
　Belichy 220
　Charles 221
　Cornelius 221
　Garrett 221
　Gideon 221
　Hannah 220
　Jacob 221
　James 221
　James H 218
　John 221
　Joseph 219
　Maragrietye 221
　Margaret 221
　Matthew 218-19
　Moses 218-19
　Phebe B 220-21
　Samuel 219
　Vincent 220-21
Fowler H——— E 421
　Hannah 115
　Mary 116
　Stephen 115
　Susanna 116
Fraizer Svrah 330
Freeman Elizabeth 219
　Mercy 220
French John 334
　Sarah 117
　Thomas 117
Fry Tarnasin 222
Fuller Jonathan 219
Garrison Hannah 220
(Gerretson) John 221
Ghorum see Gorham

Gibbs Abigail 118
　Robert 118
　Samuel 219
Gifford Jesse 219
Gilbert James 224
Goldsmith Mr ——— 334
　Harriet 334
Goodell Amasa 113-14
　Jerusha 113
　Daniel 330
　Jesse 330
　Lavinia 330
　Lucinda 114
　Marcia 113
　Oliver 113
　Zachariah 114
　Zerviah 330
Goold Elijah 334
(Gould) Jacob 334
　James 334
　Mary 333
　Peter 334
　Samuel 334
Gorham Daniel 332
　Isaac 223
　Jabez 223
　John 223
　Phebe 115
Green Eliot 332
　Judge 334
Gregory Abby 115
　Abraham 115
　Adline 331
　Albert 331
　Caleb C 331
　Elizabeth 218
　John 331
　John S 331
Gridley Elnathan 421
　Luke 332
　Sally 332
　Shomas 421
Griggs Mrs ——— 114
　Elizabeth 113, 330
　Hannah 113
　Hezekiah 113
　Moses 330
　Nathan 330
　Polly 113
　Sally 113
　Samuel 113
Grinnell Benjamin 118
　Daniel 118
Griswold Elias 221
Grosvenor Amos 114
　Esther 113
　Joshua 113-14, 330
　Walter 113
Hait Elizabeth 219
(Hoyt) Lucy 115
　Sylvanus 332
Hall Mary 118
Hamblin Abigail 221
(Hamlin) Elizabeth 331
　Joel 117
　Oliver 117

Hamlin Silas 332
Hamilton Daniel E 115
　Ezra 115
　Hozea 223
　Joseph 115
Hancox Abigail 116
　William 116
Harding William A 221
Harison Sarah 332
Harper Stephen 219
Hatch Moses 219
Hathaway Benjamin 118
　Betty 118
　Clothier 223
　Deborah 118
　Guilford 118
　Hannah 118
　Isaac 118
　Jacob 118
　Joel 118
　John 118
　Joseph 118
　Melatiah 118
　Nicholas 118
　Philip 118
　Sarah 223
Haviland Daniel 332
(Heviland) Ebenezer 332
　Isaac 115
　Mary 332
Hawkins Claraina 225
　Thomas 334
Hayward Molly 330
Hazard Samson 330
Hazen Elizabeth 116
H aly Hannah 422
Hendrickson James 334
Hickling Caty 114
　John 114
　Thomas M 114
Hicks Benjamin 113
Higginbotham Acsah 330
　Obadiah 330
Hilliard Joseph 221
Hills Amos 222
Hoag Abner 115
　Benjamin 115
　David 115
　Elizabeth 334
　Jane 220
　John 115
　Moses 115
　Stephen 115
Hodge Ezekiel 331
　Keziah 220
Hodges Ezra 115, 332
　James 115, 332
Holliday James 421
　Susan 421
Hollister David 329
Holly John 115
　Selleck 116
Holmes David 422
　Francis 422

Holmes John 422
  Jonathan 422
  Joseph 422
  Martha 422
  Mary 422
  Reuben 219
Hopkins Elizabeth 222
Horton Jeremy 224
Hoskins Anna 118
  Ebenezer 222
  Samuel 222
Hotchkiss Ruth 224
How(e) Epinetus 126
  George 224
  John 224
Howland Desire 223
  Prince 115
Hoy John 115
Hoyt see Hait
Hubbard Anna 223
  Elizabeth 115
  Thomas 223
Hubbell Dennis 114
  Ephraim 114, 333
  Johannah 114, 333
  Levi 114
  Nathan 114, 333
  Richard 222
Hubs Zephaniah 332
Hugford Elizabeth 116
Hull Aaron 331
Hunt James 115
  William 116
Hyde Humphrey 222
Ingals Benjamin 114
  Daniel 113
  David 114, 330
  Ephraim 330
Isaacs Abigail 331
James Sarah 116
Jarvis Polly 116
  Srsah 332
Jeans William 222
Jenney Hicks 219
Jennings Alice 221
  Eli 220
  Jeremiah 222
  John 222
  Joshua 222
  Lyman 220
  Matthew 222
  Orpha 220
Jessup Nathaniel 116
Johnson Benjamin 225
  Eliza 225
  Ephraim 225
  Henry 116
  Mary 225
  Nathan 225
  Stephen 225
  Sylvester 225
  William 218
Jones Benjamin 331
Journeay Catherine 221

Joyce Edward 332
Judson Ruth 421
June Deborah 219
  Hannah 219
  James 218-19
  Joshua 218-19
  Mary 218 19
  Nathaniel 219
  Peter 219
  Ruth 219
  Sarah 219
  Thomas 219
Keeler Anne 331
  Daniel 331
  Jeremiah 331
  Lydia 331
  Nehemiah 331
  Sarah 331
Kelley Wing 115
Kelsey Jane 117
  Sarah 117
Kent Deborah 118
Ketchum John 115
  Joseph 218
Kilburn Adna 225
  Dexter 225
  Elmira 225
  Emily 225
  Fernanda 225
  George 225
  Manda 225
  Mary 225
  Samuel 225
  Susan 225
  Uri 225
Kimball Lucy 422
King Elizabeth 115
  James 115
  Sarah 118
  Silas 117
  William 332
Kingsley Uriah 113
Knap(p) Elizabeth 223
  Israel 116
  Nathaniel 218
Knight Olive 422
Kruzer Cornelius 221
L——— 329
Ladd Jonathan 117
Lamphear Mary 223
Lawrence Esther 332
  Samuel 223
  Zeruah 223
Leach Amos 421
  David 421
  Ichabod 333
  Lecty 333
  Lydia 333
  Ruth 333
Lee Abigail 329
  Annie 329
  Lemuel 329
  Mary 329
  Mindwell 329
  Solomon 225
Leucas John 329

Lewis Joseph 224
  Rachel 222
Lines David 332
  Polly 332
Lobdell Phineas 331
Lockwood Deborah 116
  James 331
  Sarah 115
  Silas 116
Loder John 115
Lord William 223
  Wyllis 118
  Zelotis 118
Lupton Rebecca 223
Lyon Betsey 113
  Hannah 113
  Pelatiah 113
  Zerviah 330
MacDonald James 332
  (McDonold) Lewis 218
McKenbey James 115
Madison Mary 224
Makepeace Thomas 118
Maltby Timothy 117
Marley David 117
Marvin Lewis 333
Mason John 222
May Prudence 223
Mead Jamima 116
  Rachel 115
Medows Amelia 332
Meigs Concurrence 222
  Elizabeth 222
  John 222
  Mary 222
  Tryal 222
Mercer ——— 221
Merritt Nehemiah 115
Meyer Mary 221
Middlebrocks Sarah 333
Middleton William 116
Miles Hannah 223
Miller William 332
Mills Zebadiah 218
Money Samuel 219
Moore Mr ——— 224
Morgan Judah 333
Morris Elijah 332
  Jachin 332
  John S 332
  Shadrach 332
Morse John 113
Mosher Stephen 422
Moss John 223
Munday Nathaniel 332
Nash Betsey 220
Newell Mary 334
  Samuel 334
Newman Elizabeth 222
Newton Ella 116
  Louise H 220

Nichols Aaron J 221
  Daniel 218
  Isaac 221
  Isaac A 221
Nickerson Sally 334
Niles Ambrose 333
Noble Daniel 114
Northrop David 114
  Hannah 331
  Matthew 331
  Nathaniel 331
  Rachel 331
  Rebekah 114
  Samuel 331
Norton Lydia 115
Nye Mary 219
Oakley Phebe 223
Olding Sarah 118
Olmstead Hezekiah 221
  Sarah M 221

Osborn Aaron 114
  David 334
  David H 334
  Ephraim 334
  Ezekiel 331
  Hiram 331
  Jonathan 331
  Joseph B 331, 422
  Massa 114
  Phebe 114
  Rebbecca 331
  Stephen 421
Osgood Abilene 330
  Appleton 113, 330
  William 330
  Zechariah 330
Owen Phoebe 116
Paine Edward 330
(Payne) Joseph 116
  Judith 330
  Nathan 114
  Sarah 333
  William 116
Palmer Mr ———— 422
(Parmer) Caleb 331
  John 219
  Love 117
Pangbon Hannah 116
  Sarah 332
Parkinson Christopher 221
Parmelee Asahel 118
  Gilbert 117
  Jeremiah 118
  Lemuel 117
  Nathaniel 117
  Rhoda 118
  Sarah 421
  Stephen 118
Parmenter Mary 422
Parmer see Palmer
Parsons Tabitha 117
Partridge Hannah 225
Payne see Paine
Pearce Alphonso 220
  Alvah S 220

Pearce Ambrose B 220
  Amzi H 220
  David 220
  David A 220
  David B 220
  Edward H 220
  Ethel M 220
  Evaline 220
  George N 220
  Harriet A 220
  Ira B 220
  Nathaniel S 220
  Philo S 220
  Thaddeus B 220
Peaslee Ebenezer 115
Peck Abijah 115, 332
  Amarilas 332
  Amer 116
  Anne 332
  Bulah 332
  Charles 332
  Edwin 115
  Eliakim 332
  Frederick 115
  George 332
  Henry 115
  James S 115
  Sally 332
  Sophia 115
  Starr 332
Pepper Bennet 332
  Gridley 332
Perine Joseph 221
  Margaret A 221
Perry Ann 219
  Anna 219, 334, 422
  Amy 334
  Celia 219
  Charles 219
  David 334
  Deborah 219
  Deliverance 219
  Eleazer 219, 421
  Eliphal 219, 421
  Elisha 334, 422
  Elizabeth 219, 334
  Ezra 219
  Freeman 334, 421
  Gilbert 334
  Hannah 219, 334
  James 334
  Joanna 219
  John 219, 21, 334
  Joseph 421
  Lydia 219
  Maria 334
  Martha 219
  Mary 421
  May Lewis 334
  Meribah 219
  Milla 422
  Patience 219
  Penelope 334
  Rebecca 219
  Robert 422
  Reuben 219
  Ruhemah 334
  Ruth 219, 334
  Sarah 220, 421
  Saunders 334

Perry Seth 220
  Solomon 334
Peters John S 118
  John T 118
Phillips Anne 115
Picket Benjamin 333
  Eunice 333
Pigeon Joseph 334
Platt Stephen 116
  Wilford C 114, 333
Preston Mr ———— 422
  Aaron 422
Prioer Christian 329
(Prier) Daniel 329
(Prior) Ebenezer 329
  Mary 329
  Sarah 329
Punderson Clarissa 332
Purdy Elizabeth 332
Ramsdell Jane 220
Ransom Mary 333
Raymond Ebenezer 219
  Lemuel 115
  Simeon 332
  William 219
Reade John 118
Rickard Silas 114, 330
Riggs Esther 331
  Pun 331
Rindge Mrs ———— 330
(Ringe) Isaac 330
Roberts Jonathan 421
Rockwell Abijah 331
  Mr ———— 344
  Abraham 331
  Eleanor 331
  Elizabeth 331

Rogers Jane 116
Ross Anna 421
Rugg Abigail 222
Russell William 115
St Arnold Mary 421
Sackett(t) Jonathan 222
  Nathaniel 115
  Sarah 224, 332
Sanders Hannah 219
Sanford Mehitable 333
Scofield Elizabeth 116
  Elnathan 222
  Jonas 219
Scott Emily 221
Sears Desire 331
  Thomas 331
Seely Abijah 115
  Ezekiel 115
  Lydia 115
  Mercy 332
  Nathaniel 116
Sessions Squire 330
Seward Samuel 115
Seymour Mary 421

GENEALOGICAL INDEX.

Sharpe Chester 330
  John 330
  Lucy 330
  Reuben 330
  William 330
Shepard Amos 117
  Anne 117
  Jonathrn 117
  Joshua 117
  Love 117
  Nathaniel 117
  Oliver 117
  Prudence 117
  Rosswell 117
  Simeon 117
Sherman Abigail 118
  Elizabeth 118
  Hannah 118
  Henry 118
  John 118
  Peleg 118
  Philip 118
  Samson 118
  Samuel 118
  Sarah 118
Sherwood Abel 220
  Hannah 115
  Jerusha 334
  John 218
  Rebecca 220
  Stephen 331
Siel James 334
Sill Elijah 114
  Mary 114
Simmons Lydia 118
  Martha 118
  Meribah 118
  Rebecca 118
Skinner Benjamin 334
  Richard 117
Slade Henry 118
Slauson Jacob 332
Smielan Franklin 221
  Henry J 221
  John 221
Smith Abraham 218
  Ann 334
  Asa 223
  Chileab 440
  Ephraim 331
  Jeremiah 223
  John 332-4
  Jonathan 223
  Joseph 333
  Nathan 116
  Rebecca 332
Soule George 115
Spalding Ephraim 224
  Reuben 330
Spencer Abigail 334
  Solomon 439
Spooner Sarah 118
Stanley Mary 117
Starr Caleb 332

Starr Daniel 331
  Noah 331
  Polly 332
  Rachel 331
Stedman Clarissa 115, 332
  Thomas 115
Steele John 334
Sterling William 219
Stevens Abigail 220
  Eliphalet 332
  Ephraim G 332
  Naomi 331
  Nathan 220
  Olive 332
  Phebe 220
  Tamer 331
  Thomas 332
Stewart Alexander 114, 333
  [see also
  Stuart] Mabel 114, 333
Stille John 221
  Phebe 221
Stoddard Ebenezer 330
Stone John 440
Storrs Amariah 330
  Amasa 330
  Mary 330
Stowsl Mrs ———— 113
  Ephraim 330
  Josiah 330
Strange Alice 178
  Lot 118
Street Mary 331
Strong Samuel 334
Stuart Abigail 219
  [see also
  Stewart] John 219
Sturtevant Seth 220
Sumner Nancy 113
  Samuel 114, 330
Sutton Sands 116
Swift Jabez 219
  Mary 219
Tait (Tart) Elizabeth 222
Talcott Gaius 115
Taylor Job 439
  Jonathan 331
  Joseph 332
  Phebe 439
  Silas 334
  Theophilus 331
Terry George 118
Thomas Abraham 115
Thompson Anthony 224
  Elijah 333
  Eunice 224
  James 224
  Samuel 224
  William 116
Tobey Ellis 219
Townsend Platt 115
Tripp Isabel 118
  Martha 118

Trowbridge James 330
  Mary 330
  Nelson 114
  William 114
Truesdell Jeduthan 330
  Molly 330
Tryon Oliver 115
Tuller Amos 224
  Elisha 224
  John 224
  Joseph 224
Tupper Abigail 219
  Elizabeth 219
Tusten Elinor 225
Tuttle Daniel 331
Twichell Benjamin 225
Tyler Rollin U 329
Underwood Polly 117
Utley Stephen 113, 330
Vandeventer Elizabeth 221
Vassall ———— 116
W———— G———— 329
Wagner Maria 221
  Tobias 221
Wakeman John 222
  Sarah 222
Wanzer Abraham 421
Ward Andrew 117
  Esther 117
  John 117
Warrer Daniel 223
  Jared 113, 330
  William 223
Warren Rebecca 118
Warriner Abner 223
  James 223
  Moses 223
  William 223
Waterbury Abigail 116, 332
  Mary 333
  Rachel 422
Watson David 422
  Enoch 422
  Henry 422
  Jacob 422
  John 422
  Leonard 422
  Lydia 422
  Sally 422
Way William 222
Weaver Abraham 221
Wedge Aaron 330
Weed Asa 115
  Kezia 332
  Levi 115
Welch Catherine 115
  Hannah 115
Whaley Hezekiah 421
Wheeler Anne 330
  David 117
  Dobson 115
  Experience 225
  Hannah 117
  John 113

GENEALOGICAL INDEX.

Whelpley Miss ——— 218
White Isaac 333, 422
  Nathaniol 225
  Sarah 440
Whitford Foster 224
Whiting Elijah 334
  Frederick A 331
  Frederick J 331
  Henry S 331
Whitlock Abigail 331
Whitmore Hezekiah 329
Whitney Nathan 221
  Samuel 332
Wildman Abraham 334
  Daniel 334
  Ezra 422
  George 334
  Ira 334
  Joseph 334
  Josiah 334
  Mary 334

Wildman Philip 334
  Thomas 334
  Uz 334
Williams Martha 223
  Mary 222
  Thomas 222
  William 117
  Zipporah 117
Willson Susanna 332
Wilmot Alexander 224
  Hannah 224
Wing Edward 115
  Jedidiah 115
  John 115
Winslow Hepzibah 116
  John 115
Witter Hannah 223
  William 223
Wood James 225
  John 225

Wood Joseph 225
  Julia 225
Woodin Charles 220
  Harriet 220
Woodmansee, Hannah 115
  Thomas 118
Woodruff Benjamin 225
  Joseph 225
  Matthew 225
Woodward William 332
Woodworth Oliver 330
Woolman Margery 115
Wright Elizabeth 223
  Kent 333
Wyman Ashley 116
  Solomon 116
Young John 422
  Samuel 422
  William 422

CORRECTION.

Page 115, line 4, first column, "Gaius" Talcott, not Gains.
  " 330, last line, second column, "Ct." (meaning Connecticut), should be after "co" and before "from."
  " 331, first column, No. 5, "Pun" should be "Preive."
        second column, Caleb C Gregory m Desire, dau. of " Knoles " Sears says my copy (W. A. E. T.).

Page 332, first column, " p 360 Eliakim Peck m Nov" 8 not 3rd, and his dau's name should be Amarillus.

Page 334, first column, 159 (c) No. 7 " May Lewis" should be Maj(or) Lewis.

Vol. V.   JANUARY, 1899.   No. 1

$1.00 a Year.   HARTFORD, CONN.   10 Cts. a Copy.

Fac-simile of cover of THE CONNECTICUT MAGAZINE, three-quarter size
(See Publishers' Notes   p. i)

$1.00 PER YEAR Still $1.00 PER YEAR

SUBSCRIBE EARLY

FOR THE

Connecticut Magazine
(FORMERLY CONNECTICUT QUARTERLY.)

With the New Year this popular publication will adopt the name of the **Connecticut Magazine,** preserving the high standard of its reading matter and illustrations.
It will deal with

Connecticut Historical Matters,
    Authors and Public Men,
        Picturesque Features,
           Literature, Science and Art,
                Genealogy,
                    Industries.

NOTICE: There is no increase in

Subscription Price, $1.00 per year.

Send in early that the publishers may gauge the Edition.

THE DEPARTMENTS:

GEO. C. ATWELL, Editor.   EDWARD B. EATON, Business Mgr.
    ELLIOTT J. PERKINS, Advertising Manager.
H. PHELPS ARMS, Art Dept.   HENRY S. HOUSE, Subscriptions.

66 State Street, Hartford, Conn.

DID YOU KNOW

that.....

Is the Leading Business=Training School of Connecticut? . . . .

DID YOU KNOW that our teachers instruct from 8 in the morning until 4 in the afternoon?

DID YOU KNOW that visitors are astonished at the "air of business" that prevades every part of our course?

DID YOU KNOW that our efforts are directed to making business people out of our pupils?

DID YOU KNOW that we placed 238 graduates in good paying situations the past fifteen months?

DID YOU KNOW that we are always glad to aid graduates in securing employment?

Why not begin a business or shorthand course now?

New pupils enter every week. Catalogue and Journal free.

C. M. Huntsinger

30 Asylum St., Hartford.

✽ Where to go for Good Printing and Bookbinding. ✽

The Horton Printing Co.

Have one of the best equipped plants in the state for turning out the highest class of work at lowest prices.

. . SPECIAL ATTENTION . .
Given to Original Designs in Printing and Bookbinding.

We carry a Special Line of . . .

✽ FINE STATIONERY ✽
Which for variety and low prices cannot be equalled.

Steel Plate Engraving and Printing,
IN UP TO DATE STYLES.

OPERA HOUSE BLOCK,   MERIDEN, CONN.

PRINTERS OF
THE CONNECTICUT QUARTERLY

www.ingramcontent.com/pod-product-compliance
Lightning Source LLC
Chambersburg PA
CBHW031955300426
44117CB00008B/765